Family Interaction

STEPHEN J. BAHR

Brigham Young University

Family Interaction

MACMILLAN PUBLISHING COMPANY
NEW YORK

Copyright © 1989 by Macmillan Publishing Company,
a division of Macmillan, Inc.

Printed in the United States of America

Macmillan Publishing Company
866 Third Avenue, New York, New York 10022

Collier Macmillan Canada, Inc.

Library of Congress Cataloging-in-Publication Data

Bahr, Stephen J.
    Family interaction / Stephen J. Bahr.
        p.   cm.
    Includes index.
    ISBN 0–02–305181–7
    1. Family   2. Family—United States.   I. Title.
HQ518.B25 1989   88–18672
306.8′5—dc19   CIP

Printing: 1 2 3 4 5 6 7   Year: 9 0 1 2 3 4 5

To Carol
and
our children
Matt, Ben, Scott, Mike, Carmen, and Susan

Preface

This book is designed for an introductory sociology of the family course taught in departments of sociology and family studies. My purpose is to help students gain an understanding of the processes involved in family interaction.

The sociological study of the family has sometimes been seen as impractical and not relevant to the real problems that individuals face in family life. In this text I show how family research can be useful to both professionals and family members. For example, the data reviewed in Chapter 10 on the interface between families and work will be profitable for managers as well as family members. In Chapter 11 I discuss how parental involvement in their children's schooling is often different for working-class and middle-class parents. This information will be useful for prospective teachers, administrators, and parents. In Chapter 16 the process of divorce and the consequences for adults and children are explored. This knowledge will help students who have experienced or will experience a divorce in their family and may enable students who become attorneys to be more sensitive than most of today's lawyers to the needs of children.

These are only three examples of how the research reviewed in this text may be applied to real situations. Many different types of people, including teachers, managers, attorneys, government administrators, nurses, and doctors, will find the information in this work useful.

I begin the book by defining what a family is and what functions families perform. Families in different cultures, subcultures, and social classes are described to gain an understanding of the diversity of family life across the globe. I also discuss how families in general have changed during the past century and how individual families change as they pass through the life course. Key family processes are examined, including mate selection, marital adjustment, conflict management, and socialization of children. I explore the interface between family interaction and five societal institutions and discuss contemporary family issues. The book concludes with a chapter on how family life alters as the members age.

There are several unique features of the text. First, it is based on the review of relevant, current research on each topic. If studies were sometimes contradictory or inconsistent with popular beliefs, I still included them, and every effort was made to be objective and balanced. For example, I identify both the negative and positive functions of family conflict. In the chapter on divorce I review how divorce may improve one's life situation as well as how it may be stressful.

Second, a number of important topics are included—work, education, government, health, and religion—that are usually not part of a text about the family. In each case I show the interface between the family and the institution.

Third, the family is a legal institution, and laws are an important part of our culture. Throughout the text I identify and explore the legal implications of sexual behavior, marriage, child socialization, family violence, and other family processes.

Fourth, chapters are included on four particularly important societal issues: violence, divorce, alternative family forms, and gender roles. Family violence is a current issue that is on the pages of newspapers almost daily. Separation and divorce have become very common and are faced by millions of Americans. There are a number of different family forms, including unmarried couples, childless couples, single-parent families, and remarried families, and it is important to identify the diversity that exists in family life. Finally, perhaps no social issue has been more controversial or touches all of us more directly than gender roles.

Fifth, I have used true case histories in almost every chapter to illustrate concepts and show how the research applies to real-life situations. I have modified details slightly, however, to protect the privacy of the families and individuals involved.

Finally, although this text has a number of distinctive features, it will fit well into most courses that focus on the family. Major theoretical frameworks are identified and used. I have organized the book around family development over the life course as a way of structuring the material and showing how families change over time. The standard major topics are covered, including premarital sex, mate selection, marital adjustment, conflict and power, child socialization, and aging, and historical and cross-cultural materials form a vital part of the book.

Acknowledgments

I am grateful to the many individuals who contributed to the completion of this book. First and foremost I thank my wife, Carol, and my children for their love and support. Norene Petersen and Kimberly Hansen supplied superb clerical assistance. Christine Cardone, acquisitions editor; Linda Greenberg, production supervisor; and the staff of Macmillan Publishing Company were patient and encouraging, and provided needed technical support to move the book to publication. The Family and Demographic Research Institute and the Department of Sociology at Brigham Young University furnished institutional support. The following reviewers gave a number of useful suggestions: Rocco Corporale, St. John's University; Lucy Rose Fischer, St. Olaf College; J. Jack Melhorn, Emporia State University; Harry Perlstadt, Michigan State University; and Jill Quadagno, University of Kansas. Finally, I thank my many students and friends whose real family experiences were used in the cases presented in this text.

Contents

PART I

Families in Time and Space

CHAPTER 1

Introduction

"Do you, Lorraine, agree of your own free will and choice, to take Michael as your husband and stand by him in sickness and in health, for better or for worse?"

"I do."

"Do you, Michael, agree of your own free will and choice, to take Lorraine as your wife and stand by her in sickness and in health, for better or for worse?"

"I do."

"I now pronounce you husband and wife."

Lorraine and Mike kiss and march down the aisle. They are now officially married and will begin their marital career. They have become a family.

The family is one of our most important social institutions. Anthropologist George P. Murdock (1949) studied 192 different societies and concluded that the nuclear family is a necessary institution, existing in all known human societies. Although the nature of the nuclear family varies in different cultures and time periods, most individuals grow up in some type of nuclear family (Goode 1982; Reiss 1976).

This book is about interaction within families and has four major parts. First, we examine the diversity in family interaction across different cultures and time periods. Second, we analyze how interaction within families changes throughout the life course. For example, a newly married couple interacts differently than a middle-aged or retired couple. Third, exchanges between the family and other social institutions are explored. Institutions such as schools, churches, and governments all influence families in a variety of ways. Finally, several contemporary family issues are discussed.

In this chapter we define what a family is and how it is formed. Then major functions of families are identified, followed by an exploration of family roles. The final sections discuss family research and theory, provide an introduction to major theoretical perspectives used in family research, and summarize the major points in the chapter.

What Is a Family?

A **nuclear family** is a kinship group of two or more persons who live in the same household and are related by marriage, blood, or adoption. A childless

This American family from the early 20th century reminds us of the many different types of families that exist in the world.   *Photo courtesy St. Mary's Romanian Orthodox Church, Cleveland, Ohio.*

couple, a couple with two children, and a mother and her child are all different types of families. A couple with children is probably the most popular conception of the family, although other family types are common. The number of single-parent families in America has increased substantially in recent years.

Most individuals belong to at least two different family systems during their lives. The **family of orientation** is the family in which one was born and raised. The **family of procreation** is the system created by a couple who marry.

The **extended family** is a combination of two or more nuclear families across generations. For example, a grandmother living with her married son, his wife, and their children would be described as an extended family.

The most common form of marriage is **monogamy,** which is one female married to one male. However, polygamous marriages have existed throughout history. **Polygamy** is the practice of having two or more mates at the same time. There are three types of polygamy: (1) **Polygyny** is the marriage of one male to two or more females. (2) **Polyandry** is the marriage of one female to two or more males. (3) **Group marriage** is the marriage of two or more males to two or more females. Societies that practice polyandry or group marriage are rare. Throughout American history monogamy has been the accepted form of marriage, although polygamy has been tried by several different groups.

Family Formation

In most societies families are created by a public marriage ceremony. To have a legal marriage in the United States, a marriage license must be obtained and a formal marriage ceremony must be performed by an authorized individual. The marriage certificate is then filed with the state so that the marriage is officially recorded and becomes part of the public record.

Many familylike relationships exist that do not begin with a legal marriage ceremony. For example, some couples cohabit without legally marrying. They live together in an intimate relationship and share resources. A division of labor with rights and responsibilities is established and some bear and raise children.

Although formal marriage remains the normatively preferred status, cohabitation has become an accepted type of relationship. Two recent court cases in the United States illustrate how cohabitation is becoming a social and legal relationship much like marriage.

First, let us examine the famous case of Lee and Michelle Marvin (**Marvin v. Marvin,** 18 Cal.3d 660). They lived together for seven years without being married. After they separated, Michelle filed suit against Lee for one half of the $3.6 million he earned during the time they lived together and for support payments. Michelle said they had made an oral agreement that included the following: (1) While they lived together they would combine their efforts and earnings and would share equally any and all property accumulated as a result of their efforts, whether individually or combined. (2) They would present themselves to the general public as husband and wife. (3) Her contribution would be companion, homemaker, housekeeper, and cook. Shortly after they began living together, she gave up a career to devote all her time to being a companion and homemaker. She maintained that he agreed, in return, to provide for all of her financial support and needs for the rest of her life.

Lee Marvin filed a motion to dismiss the suit on the grounds that the contract was primarily payment for sexual services. Such contracts violate public policy and are unenforceable. The trial court ruled in favor of Lee Marvin and dismissed the suit.

Michelle Marvin appealed the decision and the California Supreme Court ruled that the trial court erred in dismissing the suit. In their written opinion of the case they made three major points: (1) The mores of society have changed and cohabitation without marriage is common and accepted by many as a legitimate type of relationship. (2) A man and woman who live together without marriage should not be denied access to the courts. Cohabitation does not in itself invalidate agreements relating to earnings, property, or expenses. Agreements will be enforced unless they are based on unlawful payment for sexual services. (3) If no formal agreement exists, behavior of the parties may be used as evidence of an implied contract or some tacit understanding.

The California Supreme Court sent the case back to the lower court for trial. At the trial Michelle Marvin was awarded $104,000 for rehabilitation as a career woman. However, Lee Marvin appealed the ruling, arguing that Michelle Marvin did not leave a bona fide singing career to cohabit with him. Prior to cohabitation she had been only temporarily employed as a singer at a nightclub.

Lee Marvin won the final appeal and was not required to pay Michelle Marvin anything.

The *Marvin* case illustrates that cohabitation without marriage is a valid relationship with legal rights and responsibilities. When disagreements arise, the courts can enforce those obligations just as they do in divorce actions. In this sense, a cohabiting couple is a family both socially and legally. Cohabitation fulfills many of the same functions as formal marriage, and it is increasingly accepted as a legitimate marriagelike relationship. Many other state courts in the United States have made decisions that treat cohabitors and married couples similarly (Crutchfield 1981).

On the other hand, the *Marvin* case shows that cohabitation does not enjoy the social and legal acceptance that formal marriage does. If Michelle and Lee Marvin had been legally married, she would have been entitled by California law to one half of the $3.6 million he earned during their seven-year relationship. If she had left a bona fide singing career to cohabit, she would have received $104,000. But Michelle Marvin received nothing.

In the following case, the U.S. Supreme Court ruled that in nonmarital relationships fathers have custody rights similar to married individuals (*Stanley v. Illinois*, 405 U.S. 645, 1972). Joan and Peter Stanley lived together intermittently for eighteen years and had three children during that time. When Joan Stanley died, the state of Illinois declared the children wards of the state and placed them with court-appointed guardians. Peter Stanley was an unwed father and had no parental rights under Illinois law. The legal definition of *parent* in Illinois was the father or mother of a legitimate child, the natural mother of an illegitimate child, or any adoptive parent. Peter Stanley had never been shown to be an unfit parent but was presumed to be unfit because he had never married Joan Stanley. He filed a suit claiming that he had been denied the equal protection of the laws guaranteed him by the Fourteenth Amendment, because married fathers and unmarried mothers could not be deprived of their children without evidence of unfitness. The lower courts ruled in favor of the state of Illinois. On appeal, the U.S. Supreme Court said that the right to conceive and raise one's children is a basic civil right and that the law recognizes family relationships not legitimized by a marriage ceremony. They ruled, therefore, that the Illinois law denied Peter Stanley equal protection and was unconstitutional.

Stanley v. Illinois shows that parent-child relationships are legally recognized whether or not a formal marriage ceremony has taken place. Marriage may be preferred but unwed parents are entitled to all the legal protections of married parents. Other court cases have established that illegitimate children have the same legal status as legitimate children, including the right to receive an inheritance, survivors' annuities, public assistance, disability benefits, and workers' compensation benefits (Stenger 1981).

Earlier we defined the family as a kinship group of two or more persons who live in the same household. The way the majority of people decide to form a family is through a formal marriage ceremony. However, many relationships that do not conform to the marriage laws are accepted and given legal recognition.

This trend toward a broader definition of the family is not unique to the United States. In Trinidad, Rodman (1971) found that formal marriage is preferred but nonlegal unions are common and accepted. In many other cultures (including Europe and South America) nonmarital unions also occur frequently and are socially acceptable.

Family Functions

The family is an important social institution because of the **family functions** it fulfills. Murdock (1949) made an extensive study of family functioning in many different societies. He concluded that the nuclear family has four universal functions: (1) economic cooperation, (2) sexual relations, (3) reproduction, and (4) socialization of children (Murdock 1949). Although Reiss (1976) discovered some societies in which the nuclear family did not perform all of these functions, he did find that in all known societies the nuclear family provided nurturant socialization of the young. Despite the exceptions noted by Reiss, the nuclear family provides the four functions identified by Murdock in most cultures and in a vast majority of the world's population.

The major family functions may be grouped into three categories: (1) affection, (2) economic cooperation, and (3) socialization of children. Although the family does not have a monopoly on these three functions, it is an institution whose major purpose is to fulfill these tasks for society. Let us look at the role of the family in performing each of these functions.

First and foremost, the family is an affectional unit. Mate selection is generally based on love between a man and a woman. Sexual relations between husband and wife are expected in marriage and the absence of sexual contact is grounds for annulment or dissolution in American and English law.

The sexual relationship between husband and wife is only part of the affectional role the family plays in society. Parent-child and sibling bonds are also often strong and loving. The family is one of the few groups in which membership is based on who you are rather than on what you can do. It is an intimate, personal group where one is accepted, nurtured, and loved simply because he or she is a member of the family.

Several early sociologists observed that intimate, informal primary group associations were becoming less common, and formal, contractual relationships more common as society became more urban (Durkheim 1966; Maine 1888; Tonnies 1957). This trend toward formal secondary groups left the family as the major group of intimacy and affection. William F. Ogburn (1933) studied family change during the first third of the twentieth century and maintained that the affectional function of the family had maintained its importance while other family functions had declined. He identified seven major family functions: (1) economic, (2) protective, (3) recreational, (4) educational, (5) religious, (6) status placement, and (7) affectional. Ogburn argued that all except affectional were increasingly being performed by other institutions.

More recently, Lasch (1977) has described the modern family as a haven in a heartless world. His work affirms the importance of the family as an affectional unit in an achievement-oriented society in which relationships tend to be formal.

The second major function of the families is economic cooperation. Legally and socially, marriage is an economic partnership. Married couples are expected to pool their resources, share a household, and divide their labor. Much economic consumption occurs by family units. For example, houses and food are usually purchased by families and jointly shared. Money and property acquired during marriage are generally considered to be jointly owned and must be equitably distributed if divorce occurs. Unwillingness to contribute to the economic support of one's spouse is grounds for divorce in many jurisdictions. In divorce actions one spouse is often ordered by the court to give the other spouse money and property, which shows that marriage is defined by law as an economic partnership.

Although bearing and raising children are two separate tasks, they tend to go together and are the third major function of families. The vast majority of children are raised by at least one of their biological parents. In this book, therefore, reproduction and socialization are combined into one general function called socialization. Because of the intimate, permanent nature of the family, it appears to be better suited than any other institution or group to socialize children.

In summary, although there are many types of families that function in different ways and at varying levels of competence, most families in most societies fulfill three major functions: (1) affection, (2) economic cooperation, and (3) socialization of children. Other groups and institutions contribute to these tasks in various ways, but according to law and custom these are the three essential functions of the family.

Family Roles

In families, as in any group, essential tasks need to be identified and work needs to be divided up. Various tasks tend to be grouped together into packages in a process called **role differentiation.** Family members are assigned to perform certain roles and this is called **role allocation** (Turner 1970). Within each culture there are expectations concerning what tasks go together and who should perform them. These norms about family life provide a social structure that shapes and limits behavior. For example, cooking meals and washing clothes are usually part of the housekeeper role, even though there is no necessary connection between the two tasks.

Nye (1976) has identified eight major family roles, each with a set of normatively defined tasks with rights and responsibilities. The provider, housekeeper, child care, child socialization, recreational, kinship, sexual, and therapeutic roles will each be described here briefly.

The primary task of the provider role is to earn money for necessary goods and services. Traditionally this role was assigned to the husband. In recent years more wives have been sharing the provider role, but many couples still consider it an optional role for wives and a prescribed role for husbands. Husbands are still legally required to support their families.

The housekeeper role includes purchase and preparation of food, housecleaning, and care of clothing. This role has traditionally been assigned to the wife although involvement of the husband may be increasing.

The tasks of the child care role are to protect and provide adequate physical

Recreation is an important part in family interaction, as shown by this brother and sister playing the piano together.   *Ulrike Welsch.*

care for the children. Child socialization involves the training of children in social skills and values that they need to function in society.

The recreational role consists of planning and organizing leisure activities, and the sexual role includes expectations regarding physical intimacy. The kinship role involves the frequency and nature of interaction with relatives. Finally, norms regarding interpersonal help and problem solving are called the therapeutic role. Listening, being sympathetic, and helping with problems are all part of this role.

Although there are cultural expectations regarding each of the eight roles, there is also some latitude in how they are assigned and performed. Each family establishes its own system of roles based on individual preferences, talents, and situations. One family member may take primary responsibility for a role, but often the various roles are shared. For example, the provider and child socialization roles tend to be shared in American society.

In summary, various family activities become clustered into roles and assigned to various family members. Roles may be culturally prescribed (**normative roles**) or may emerge out of ongoing family interaction (**emergent roles**). Once the system of family roles is established, normal interaction will break down if individuals do not play their roles (Turner 1970).

Family Research and Theory

Before embarking on our journey into family life, it is useful to discuss how social scientists go about studying and explaining issues related to family interaction. Most studies begin with some questions and some possible answers to the questions. The answers are hypotheses that need to be tested to determine if they are correct. Taken together the hypotheses form an explanation of the phenomenon being studied.

Explanations of various family behaviors are called theories. For example, a theory of marital dissolution would explain why some couples divorce and others remain married. Theories are maps that help us organize and understand our social world. They are tools of understanding and are never complete. As new information is obtained theories must be revised or discarded. Our social world is constantly changing and so our theories must be updated frequently.

We all use theories in our everyday life. Suppose you believe in the statement "spare the rod and spoil the child." This would be part of your own individual theory about how children learn. It is a belief that children who are not physically disciplined will become spoiled. It may have been reinforced by the ideas of others and by observing unruly, demanding children who were never or seldom spanked. This set of observations is your own personal research in which you tested and confirmed your belief that children who are "spared the rod" will be spoiled.

All of us test our ideas informally through personal experience and observation. For example, Bill may suspect that Tom does not like him. If he notices that Tom does not wave when he drives by, Bill's suspicion has been confirmed by his observation. In actuality, Tom may not dislike Bill, but Bill's personal conclusion is that he does.

In studying family life, social scientists do a similar type of thing, except they attempt to be more explicit in formulating and testing their ideas. For example, the statement "Spare the rod and spoil the child" is not sufficiently precise for testing. Spoiling the child could refer to many different types of behavior, including aggressiveness, compliance with parental requests, social competence, or internalization of certain values. Similarly, sparing the rod may refer to lack of physical punishment or to permissiveness in general.

To become an answerable question the statement needs to be reformulated. Sparing the rod could be defined as "amount of physical punishment" and "aggressiveness" as one type of spoiling. The research question would then become: Are children who receive physical punishment less aggressive than children who receive little or no physical punishment? This could be tested by comparing the aggressiveness of children who come from homes with different amounts of physical punishment.

If children who are spanked regularly are found to be less aggressive than those who are not spanked, the research would confirm the hypothesis. If the research did not confirm it, confidence in the hypothesis would be diminished.

Family scholars attempt to define their terms precisely and formulate their ideas into answerable research questions. Research results are organized into a set of ideas that become a theory about a particular aspect of family life.

The building blocks of these theories are variables and propositions. A **variable** is the name of a concept and must have two or more values. Aggressiveness is a variable and may vary from low to high. Spanking is a variable and could vary from none, to a small amount, to a large amount. Gender is a dichotomous variable with two values, male and female.

A **proposition** is a statement about the relationship between two or more variables. "Spare the rod and spoil the child" is a proposition. The first variable is the amount of rod and the second is the amount of spoiling. Two other examples of propositions are: (1) The greater the income level, the higher the marital satisfaction, and (2) The greater the amount of physical punishment, the lower the level of aggressiveness in children. The variables are income level, marital satisfaction, physical punishment, and aggressiveness.

A **hypothesis** is a proposition that is designed for empirical testing. Propositions are often stated in general terms whereas hypotheses are phrased more concretely so that the variables can be measured directly.

In a proposition (and a hypothesis) the variable that precedes and causes the other is called the **independent variable.** The variable that is caused or affected by the other is labeled the **dependent variable.** In the preceding examples, (1) amount of income was the independent variable while marital satisfaction was the dependent variable, and (2) amount of physical punishment was the independent variable while amount of aggressiveness was the dependent variable.

If both variables in a proposition move in the same direction, it is called a **positive relationship.** For example, in the following proposition the relationship between income and marital satisfaction is positive: The greater the income level, the higher the marital satisfaction.

When two variables move in opposite directions, it is called a **negative relationship.** For example, the following relationship between physical punishment and aggressiveness is negative: The greater the amount of physical punishment, the less the level of aggressiveness in children.

Sometimes variables have a **curvilinear relationship,** as shown in Figure 1·1.

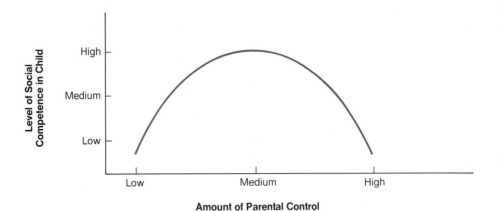

FIGURE 1·1

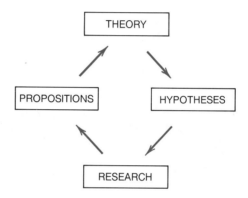

FIGURE 1·2

As parental control increases from low to medium, the competence of a child increases. As control increases from a medium to high level, the competence of a child decreases.

Research is systematic observation to determine the amount of support for a hypothesis or set of hypotheses. Hypotheses are usually derived from propositions that are more general than the hypotheses.

A **theory** is a set of two or more interrelated propositions that explains a phenomenon. Some theories are relatively simple and explain a specific type of behavior, such as a theory of marital dissolution. Other theories are general and are designed to explain many different types of family behavior. Several general family theories are introduced in the next section.

There is a constant interplay between theory and research as shown in Figure 1·2. Theory generates hypotheses that are tested in research. The results are used to revise propositions that are used to build and modify theories.

Major Family Theories

Many different theories are used in the study of family life. In this section six commonly used theories will be identified and described: (1) Symbolic

Interaction Theory; (2) Family Development Theory; (3) Social Exchange Theory; (4) Systems Theory; (5) Conflict Theory; and (6) Feminist Theory. The purpose is to introduce you to these six theories and not to provide a detailed examination or evaluation of each. Although other theories exist, these six were chosen because they are general, well known, and have stimulated a considerable amount of research. Each of the theories has its own perspective but they are not mutually exclusive, as some use similar concepts and propositions.

Symbolic Interaction Theory

One of the most widely used theories in the study of families is the **symbolic interaction theory.** A basic assumption of symbolic interaction theory is that humans live in a symbolic environment and use complex symbols. It is not sufficient to look objectively at behavior, because understanding comes only by studying perceptions and interpretations. Another assumption is that humans are introspective and develop a definition of self. The development of self-concept is ongoing and is influenced by the roles one plays. Finally, in this theory humans are viewed as actors who do not simply react to external social forces.

Symbolic interactionists often conceive of the family as a group of interacting personalities on a stage. Just like in a theatrical production, each person is assigned a role with definite expectations. Nevertheless, people are creative and play their roles differently than others would play them. How roles are played depends on personal definitions of situations, self-concepts, and the reactions of others.

Because of this conception of the family as a system of actors playing roles, symbolic interaction theory is sometimes referred to as **role theory** (Burr et al. 1979). Role differentiation and role allocation are processes that are often studied by role theorists (Turner 1970).

The key concepts of symbolic interaction theory focus on perceptions and enactment of roles within the family. Several important concepts are the following: definition of the situation, role taking, role making, role enactment, role expectations, role strain, and marital satisfaction.

Definition of the situation is how you perceive a particular event or situation. *Role taking* is the ability to mentally put yourself in the role of the other, and imagine how things look from the other's point of view. *Role making* is how roles are formed in the process of interaction. *Role enactment* is the perception of how you perform a particular role or set of tasks. For example, a wife has a perception of how well she and her husband perform in providing income, managing their income, and socializing children.

Role expectations are specific ways of behaving that are anticipated and desired. For example, a husband may expect that his wife helps earn the family income, and a wife may expect that her husband spends time with her and listens to her problems. *Role strain* is perceived stress, worry, and anxiety about a particular role. *Marital satisfaction* is the extent to which expectations and desires are met.

Examples of propositions from symbolic interaction theory are (1) The greater the quality of spouse role enactment, the greater the marital satisfaction, (2) the greater the consensus on role expectations, the greater the marital satisfaction, and (3) the greater the role strain, the lower the quality of role enactment.

Symbolic interaction theory has generated research on many aspects of family life, including sexual permissiveness, mate selection, marital quality, parent-child relations, and family violence. For a thorough examination of the theory and its propositions, see Burr et al. (1979).

Family Development Theory

Family development theory espouses many of the same assumptions and concepts as symbolic interaction theory. The differentiating characteristic of the theory is its focus on family change over time. Family development theory was formulated explicitly to deal with family transitions as families pass through the life course. It views the family as a semiclosed system of interacting personalities. A major assumption is that family life cannot be understood

As one observes family members interacting together, one realizes that family interaction is complex and can be studied from a number of different perspectives. *David S. Stricker/The Picture Cube.*

apart from human development (Mattessich and Hill 1987).

The key concepts of family development theory reflect the emphasis on family time: family career, family life cycle, developmental task, and role sequence. **Family career** is the developmental path of a given family. **Family life cycle** is a set of stages that a typical family passes through during the life course. A *developmental task* is what a family needs to complete to maintain functioning at a particular stage. *Role sequence* is how roles change over time. These concepts will be described more fully in Chapter 2.

Family development theory has generated research on marital satisfaction, division of labor, marital power, parental satisfaction, and employment outside the home. There have been numerous studies on how marital satisfaction changes across the stages of the life cycle. Examples of propositions are (1) There is a curvilinear relationship between stage of family life cycle and marital satisfaction. From early marriage until the launching of children marital satisfaction tends to decrease; after the launching stage marital satisfaction tends to increase. (2) There is a curvilinear relationship between stage of family life cycle and the employment of women. The employment of women is high during early marriage, decreases during childbearing and child-rearing stages, and increases during the launching and empty nest stages of the family life cycle. Mattessich and Hill (1987) provide a review of family development theory.

Social Exchange Theory

The basic tenet of **social exchange theory** is that humans make choices based on perceived rewards and costs. It is assumed that humans are rational beings who attempt to minimize costs and maximize rewards. Individuals and groups will repeat behavior that is rewarded. If all perceived alternatives are costly, they will choose the least costly alternative.

Some key concepts in exchange theory are rewards, costs, profit, comparison level, comparison level of alternatives, and reciprocity. A *reward* is defined as anything that is pleasurable or satisfying, whereast *costs* are things that are disliked or unsatisfying, including rewards forgone as well as punishments. *Profit* is rewards minus costs. *Comparison level* is a standard one uses to evaluate the perceived profit from a given relationship or course of action. For example, a relationship that is perceived to be more rewarding than costly would be above one's comparison level. *Comparison level of alternatives* is the comparison of a relationship or course of action with perceived alternatives. One might be unsatisfied with a marriage but continue it because one perceives it is better than perceived alternatives; the marriage would be below the comparison level but above the comparison level of alternatives. *Reciprocity* is the mutual exchange of behaviors, such as when a husband compliments his wife after she compliments him.

Nye (1979) has identified some general sources of rewards and costs. One of the most common rewards is money and other physical resources. Prestige and social approval are rewarding to most people, as well as autonomy, equality, and security.

Social exchange theory draws concepts from psychology and economics. Behavioristic psychologists analyze behavior in terms of costs and rewards, and economic explanations also assume that humans are rational and that choices are based on perceived utility.

Nye (1979) has shown how exchange theory can help explain many types of family behavior, including marital timing, sexual behavior, marital stability, and family violence. Examples of propositions Nye has derived from exchange theory are (1) Married men are more likely to engage in extramarital sexual intercourse than are married women. (2) Child abuse is more frequent in single-parent than in two-parent families. (3) When men provide higher-than-average material rewards to a family, marital dissolution rates will be lower than average. For a thorough discussion of exchange theory and the family see Nye (1979).

Systems Theory

In recent years a number of family scholars have used general **systems theory** in their study of families. Proponents claim it is a new scientific theory that enhances our understanding of family dynamics. Others view it as an orienting perspective rather than a theory.

The point of departure in family systems theory is to view the family as a system that is more than the sum of the individual characteristics of each family member. No matter how intimately we know the personalities, goals, values, and backgrounds of family members, we will not understand their family system unless we examine them *as they interact.*

A useful analogy is the chemical combination of two parts hydrogen and one part oxygen. That interaction creates water, which has characteristics completely different from hydrogen or oxygen. We will never gain an understanding of water by studying oxygen and hydrogen separately. Similarly, systems theorists maintain that no matter how much we know about the individual members of a family, we will have an incomplete and inaccurate picture of that family unless we examine them operating as a system. The interaction of the members creates an entity that is more than just the sum of the individual personalities.

Key concepts in systems theory are boundary, permeability, input, output, family rules, morphogenesis, and morphostasis. A *boundary* is the definition of who is included in the family. Some families have very definite boundaries whereas in others the boundary between the family and the outside world may be ambiguous. *Permeability* is the extent to which the boundaries are open or closed. Some families are very open whereas others have closed boundaries that are difficult to penetrate.

Input is a stimulus from the environment, for example, the loss of a job. *Output* is a family's response to a particular input. Research has shown that families respond very differently to external crises such as unemployment.

The way a family responds to various inputs depends on the *family rules* for processing information. Broderick and Smith (1979) state that the central concern of systems theory is how families process inputs.

In all systems there is a need for order and constancy and there is some attempt to maintain the status quo. This is called **morphostasis.** At the same time, change is often required to meet the demands of new situations and to grow. This pressure to innovate, grow, and change is often called **morphogenesis.**

Systems theory has frequently been used to analyze family communication and how inputs from the larger society affect family communication and interaction (Hill 1972; Kantor and Lehr 1975; Watzlawick, Beavin, and Jackson 1967). Although systems theory has promise for understanding family interaction, it is an orienting perspective rather than a theory with a set of interrelated propositions. Its concepts sensitize us to view the family a certain way and ask certain questions, but a systematic set of propositions that apply to the family has not yet been developed. However, the concepts are very useful for describing family interaction.

Broderick and Smith (1979) maintain that we need descriptive data on family interaction before systems theory develops further. We know relatively little about how boundaries are established and maintained, how inputs are related to outputs, or about the processes of decision making and control. Broderick and Smith (1979) provide a good overview of systems theory as applied to the family.

Conflict Theory

The basic premise of **conflict theory** is that conflict is endemic to families and society. Conflict is not something negative that is to be avoided, but is a natural part of everyday life and is necessary for growth and change.

Sprey (1979) has identified the basic assumptions of conflict theory. First, humans are self-oriented and will pursue their own interests at the expense of others. Second, there is a scarcity of most resources, which leads to competition for those resources. Third, it is assumed that inequality always exists among family members and among individuals and groups in society. Fourth, confrontation within and between groups is continuous and is needed for change and growth. The self-orientation, scarcity, and inequality result in continuous competition and conflict.

Some of the major concepts used by conflict theorists are competition, conflict, consensus, power, and aggression (Sprey 1979). *Competition* is negative interdependence resulting from scarce resources. Gains for one person or group often result in losses for another person or group. Sprey (1979) defines *conflict* as a confrontation over scarce resources or incompatible goals. *Consensus* is the degree of agreement over an issue or use of a resource. *Power* is an attribute of a relationship and is the potential to influence another in the face of differences. An intentional attack or violent confrontation is defined as *aggression*. Threats, promises, bargaining, and negotiation are also important concepts in analyzing family conflict.

Conflict theorists have tended to avoid identifying explicit propositions, although many propositions are implicit in their analyses of conflict. Examples of propositions suggested by Sprey (1979) are (1) Relationship conflicts are more threatening to the quality and stability of marriages than instrumental conflicts. Relationship conflicts concern autonomy and authority. Instrumental conflicts concern decisions about specific tasks or activities such as what movie to go to or where to go on a vacation. (2) The greater the expectation of consensus on important issues, the greater the frequency and level of conflict in a marriage. (3) The greater the motivation to remain together, the greater the quality of conflict management skills. (4) The greater the communication skills, the greater the quality of the conflict management skills. (5) The greater the behavioral and attitudinal flexibility, the greater the level of trust in a relationship. For a discussion of how conflict theory helps understand family life see Sprey (1979).

Feminist Theory

Feminist theory is a type of conflict theory in which the focus is on patriarchy and sexism. Society is viewed as a two-class system, men and women. Traditionally men had the power in society and within the family. They made the laws, controlled the property and money, and were viewed as the head of the household. Women did much of the work in the home but were not recognized or adequately paid for their services. In short, women were the victims of male domination.

Ferree and Hess (1987) have identified some of the specific assumptions of feminist theory. First, there is a rejection of value-free theory and research. "Objectivity" is seen as a myth that is used to support male biases. Intuition, empathy, and passion are important female characteristics that have been ignored in male-dominated science and it is argued that these qualities should be part of theorizing and research. Second, feminists reject the positivistic division between theory and practice, and between the researcher and those who are researched. They contend that the researcher is part of the research and that empathy is important in studying society and family. Third, attention is focused on conflict, inconsistency, ambivalence, and guilt. According to feminists, social structures have contradictory impulses and personal experience should be brought into research and theorizing.

Some of the major concepts of feminist theory are *conflict, struggle, resistance, ambivalence,* and *gender.* Research has focused on sex differences, sex roles, sexuality, and gender stratification.

This theoretical perspective has not explicitly identified sets of propositions. It is an orienting framework that aims to approach the study of gender and family life from a different perspective. It questions the general scientific paradigm that has been used to study the family, asks many new questions, and focuses on gender roles in society. The traditional family is viewed as a male-dominated institution that has exploited women. Hess and Ferree (1987) provide a thorough analysis of theory and research from a feminist perspective.

As mentioned earlier, this introduction to six theoretical perspectives is necessarily brief and only identifies the perspective of each theory along with a few key assumptions and concepts. Each theory may be viewed as a different set of lenses. When individuals view family life from one theory they focus on somewhat different issues and ask different questions than when they use another theory.

Conclusion

Sometimes people say that theory is impractical and does not relate to real life. "It's good in theory but it doesn't work in practice" is a common complaint. Such statements show a lack of understanding of theorizing, for there is nothing more practical than good theories. They are indispensable as tools in organizing and understanding the social world about us. All of us use a type of theory building and testing of these theories in our own lives. Our common experiences and observations are the research, and our beliefs about the world are our theories. Thus, the dichotomy between theory and practice is a false one.

As we have seen, one can study families from many different perspectives. Each theory has strengths and weaknesses and no single theory adequately explains the many aspects of family life. Thus the approach in this text is eclectic, and a number of different theoretical perspectives are used to help you understand and explain various aspects of family interaction.

Many people are concerned about modern family life. With a high divorce rate and escalating violence, the American family is often portrayed as being under pressure, in trouble, unstable, and even dying. Although there have been profound changes in family life, there may be more stability and continuity than meets the eye. Some of the recent changes have vastly improved the quality of family life. Despite its problems, the vast majority of Americans continues to marry and derive some of its greatest satisfaction from family relationships.

Studying family life is a challenging and fascinating experience. It takes effort and skill to understand the complex situations, and it is often painful to view the difficult problems many families encounter. Yet much wisdom can be gained if one observes carefully.

Summary

1. Many consider the family to be the basic social unit of society. A nuclear family may be defined as a group of two or more persons who live in the same household and are related by marriage, blood, or adoption. It usually consists of a couple with or without children, or one parent with at least one child. There are a variety of relationships that are called families.

2. In most cultures a family is formed by a public ritual called a marriage ceremony. However, many family relationships are formed without a formal ceremony. Cohabitation and the birth of a child often create a family without a formal marriage.

3. Families play an important role in fulfilling a variety of human needs. Three of the major functions that most families in most societies fulfill are affection, economic cooperation, and socialization of children.

4. Some family roles are determined by cultural norms whereas others emerge from ongoing interaction. The provider, housekeeper, child care, child socialization, kinship, recreational, sexual, and therapeutic roles are the eight major areas of activity in the family.

5. Families are small groups that may be studied using the scientific method. Theories are ideas or sets of propositions guiding the research process. A proposition is a statement about the relationship between two or more variables. A hypothesis is a proposition that is specific enough to be tested in actual research. Theoretical ideas are used to formulate specific questions (hypotheses) for testing in actual research. The research usually consists of observation and/or interviewing of some type, and the results are used to refine propositions and theoretical ideas.

6. Six commonly used theories in family study are symbolic interaction, family development, social exchange, systems, conflict, and feminist.

Important Terms

- conflict theory
- curvilinear relationship
- dependent variable
- emergent roles
- extended family
- family career
- family development theory
- family functions
- family life cycle
- family of orientation
- family of procreation
- feminist theory
- group marriage
- hypothesis
- independent variable
- *Marvin v. Marvin*
- monogamy
- morphogenesis

- morphostasis
- negative relationship
- normative roles
- nuclear family
- polyandry
- polygamy
- polygyny
- positive relationship
- proposition
- research
- role allocation
- role differentiation
- role theory
- social exchange theory
- symbolic interaction theory
- systems theory
- theory
- variable

Questions for Discussion

1. What is the marriage law in your state? What types of relationships are prohibited by law? What happens to individuals if they violate these laws?
2. How have marital customs changed in the past fifty years? What do you feel are the consequences of these changes?
3. To what extent are nonmarital relationships given legal recognition and protection today?
4. What are the three major family functions? Can you think of marriages in which these three functions are not fulfilled? What are those marriages like in structure and interaction?
5. What does it mean to say, "The whole is more than the sum of the parts"? Give two examples to illustrate your answer.
6. Identify the eight family roles identified in the chapter and give an example of each.
7. Take the eight family roles you identified in question 6 and identify societal expectations for males and females in each role. Be specific and identify what types of behaviors are (a) prohibited, (b) required, (c) preferred, and (d) optional.
8. How do you think males and females differ in their marital role expectations?
9. What are your personal expectations in these eight roles, and how do they differ from societal expectations?

10. Identify two roles in your family of orientation or procreation that are not normative but have emerged out of family interaction.
11. Identify what you feel are the major stages or transition points of average American families as they go through the life course.
12. Give a concrete example of the following terms:
    proposition
    hypothesis
    variable
    independent variable
    dependent variable
    negative relationship
    positive relationship
13. What do the *Marvin* and *Stanley* cases tell us about the marital norms in the United States?
14. Which of the six theoretical perspectives do you like the best? Why? Which do you like the least? Why?
15. Identify some strengths and weaknesses of each of the six theoretical perspectives. What do you think is the unique contribution of each theory?

Recommended Reading

LEE, G. R. 1977. *Family structure and interaction: A comparative analysis.* Philadelphia: Lippincott. Chapters 3–5 provide a good discussion of the origins and universality of the family and variations in family forms.

References

BRODERICK, C., and J. SMITH. 1979. The general systems approach to the family. In *Contemporary theories about the family,* vol. 2, ed. W. R. Burr, R. Hill, F. I. Nye, and I. L. Reiss, 112–129. New York: Free Press.

BURR, W. R., G. K. LEIGH, R. D. DAY, and J. CONSTANTINE. 1979. Symbolic interaction and the family. In *Contemporary theories about the family,* vol. 2, ed. W. R. Burr, R. Hill, F. I. Nye, and I. L. Reiss, 42–111. New York: Free Press.

CRUTCHFIELD, C. F. 1981. Nonmarital relationships and their impact on the institution of marriage and the traditional family structure. *Journal of Family Law* 19:247–261.

DURKHEIM, E. 1966. *The division of labor in society.* Translated from the French by George Simpson. Glencoe, IL: Free Press.

FERREE, M. M., and B. B. HESS. 1987. Introduction. In *Analyzing gender: A handbook of social science research,* ed. B. B. Hess and M. M. Ferree, 9–30. Newbury Park, CA: Sage.

GOODE, W. J. 1982. *The family.* 2d ed. Englewood Cliffs, NJ: Prentice-Hall.

HESS, B. B., and M. M. FERREE. 1987. *Analyzing gender: A handbook of social science research.* Newbury Park, CA: Sage.

HILL, R. 1972. Modern systems theory and the family: A confrontation. *Social Science Information* 10:7–26.

KANTOR, E., and W. LEHR. 1975. *Inside the family.* San Francisco: Jossey-Bass.

LASCH, C. 1977. *Haven in a heartless world: The family besieged.* New York: Basic.

MAINE, H. S. 1888. *Ancient law.* 3d American—From 5th London ed. New York: Henry Holt.

MATTESSICH, P., and R. HILL. 1987. Life cycle and family development. In *Handbook of marriage and the family*, ed. M. B. Sussman and S. K. Steinmetz, 437–469. New York: Plenum.

MURDOCK, G. P. 1949. *Social structure*. New York: Free Press.

NYE, F. I. 1976. *Role structure and analysis of the family*. Beverly Hills, CA: Sage.

NYE, F. I. 1979. Choice, exchange, and the family. In *Contemporary theories about the family*, vol. 2, ed. W. R. Burr, R. Hill, F. I. Nye, and I. L. Reiss, 1–41. New York: Free Press.

OGBURN, W. F. 1933. The family and its functions. In *Recent social trends in the United States*, 661–708. New York: McGraw-Hill.

REISS, I. L. 1976. *Family systems in America*. 2d ed. Hinsdale, IL: Dryden.

RODMAN, H. 1971. *Lower-class families: The culture of poverty in Negro Trinidad*. New York: Oxford University Press.

SPREY, J. 1979. Conflict theory and the study of marriage and the family. In *Contemporary theories about the family*, vol. 2, ed. W. R. Burr, R. Hill, F. I. Nye, and I. L. Reiss, 130–159. New York: Free Press.

STENGER, R. L. 1981. Expanding constitutional rights of illegitimate children, 1968–80. *Journal of Family Law* 19:407–444.

TONNIES, F. 1957. *Community and society* (Gemeinschaft and Gesellschaft). Translated and edited by Charles P. Loomis. East Lansing, MI: Michigan State University Press.

TURNER, R. 1970. *Family interaction*. New York: Wiley.

WATZLAWICK, P., J. BEAVIN, and D. JACKSON. 1967. *Pragmatics of human communication*. New York: Norton.

CHAPTER 2

Family Development over the Life Course

Introduction

Helen and Don Ferrell met at college and married during the Great Depression. He was 22; she was 21. Don finished his degree soon after they were married and took a job in Idaho with the U.S. Forest Service. Over the next seven years they had four children, three boys and one girl. Helen was 22 when she had her first child and was 28 when she had her last.

Helen did not work while the children were preschoolers, but began working part-time at age 34, when her daughter began first grade. At age 36 she began working full-time as a medical stenographer.

Their second child, a boy, was born with crippled arms and legs. They had the difficult task of raising a handicapped child and seeing him go through numerous operations, but they have lived to see him obtain a master's degree in social work, marry, and have children.

When Helen was age 40, her oldest child left home to attend college in Colorado. When she was 46, her daughter, the youngest child, left home to attend college.

All of the Ferrell children married and had children of their own. Helen and Don saw their children as often as they could, but all of them lived in other states.

Helen and Don continued working until Don reached age 60. Don decided that the extra time he could work would not improve his retirement significantly, so he took an early retirement. Helen retired at the same time, and they sold their home and moved to Colorado where they had grown up.

After retiring, Helen and Don spent time traveling, pursuing hobbies, and seeing their siblings, children, and grandchildren. They traveled extensively in the United States and visited Russia, Great Britain, and Mexico. They were active in their church and in an organization for federal retirees.

Two years ago, at age 70, Don had a serious heart attack and died. This was a very difficult transition for Helen, because Don and she had been so close. Since Don's death Helen has lived alone. One son lives in the same town and

The composition and needs of families change as they pass through the family life
cycle.   *Antonio Mendoza/The Picture Cube.*

her daughter and another son live within two hundred miles. Her other son
lives in California. She regularly sees the three children who live close by and
sees her son who lives in California about twice a year. She has ten grandchildren and enjoys visiting them. Helen loves to quilt and had made a quilt
for each of her grandchildren. She is in relatively good health and remains
active in her church.

The Ferrell family can be used to illustrate the concepts of family life cycle
and family career. **Family life cycle** refers to a set of stages that the typical or
average family passes through over the life course (Glick 1977). The stages
that most families pass through are marrying, bearing and raising children,
launching children, living again as a couple, and the death of one spouse. The
term **family career** is used to describe the temporal sequence of stages of one
particular family. Each family has a unique developmental path or career that
is different from any other family.

In this chapter, we examine family development over the life course using the concepts of family life cycle and family career. Then major developmental tasks of families over the life course are identified and described. Finally, using the family life cycle, we compare family change in the United States and Japan.

Family Life Cycle

There are a variety of ways to delineate life cycle stages depending on what is considered to be a critical transition point. Early formulations identified four stages, which were (1) married couple, (2) couple with one or more children, (3) couple with one or more adult self-supporting children, and (4) couple becoming old (Loomis 1934; Rowntree 1906; Sorokin et al. 1931). Other categorizations of the life cycle have focused on children and their place in school. Reference is made to the preschool period, the elementary school period, the high school period, the college span, and the all-adult family (Bigelow 1936; Kirkpatrick et al. 1934). The most detailed classification has been the twenty-four stages by Rodgers (1964, 1965).

One of the most useful categorizations of the family life cycle has been the six stages identified by Glick (1947, 1955, 1977). His stages are (1) first marriage, (2) birth of first child, (3) birth of last child, (4) marriage of first child, (5) marriage of last child, (6) death of one spouse. Glick's conception is particularly useful for analyzing families over time and comparing families in different cultures.

The most widely used set of family life cycle categories is Duvall and Hill's (1948) eight stages, which are as follows (Duvall and Miller 1985): (1) married couples (without children); (2) childbearing families (oldest child, birth to 30 months); (3) families with preschool children (oldest child $2\frac{1}{2}$ years to 6 years); (4) families with school children (oldest child 6 to 13 years); (5) families with teenagers (oldest child 13 to 20 years); (6) families launching young adults (first child to last child leaving home); (7) middle-aged parents (empty nest to retirement); (8) aging family members (retirement to death of both spouses).

The beginning of each stage is a critical transition that requires a change in roles and tasks. Thus, marriage is a union between two individuals and requires their adjustment to each other. At the birth of the first child, a variety of parental tasks are suddenly required that were not necessary during early marriage. The development of the oldest child is assumed to include important changes in family tasks, as shown by stages 3 through 5. For example, when the oldest child enters school, family patterns change dramatically. Family members must now plan their day around the school schedule. When children begin leaving home, the size of the family decreases and the nature of parental responsibilities changes. The departure of the last child produces additional changes in parental roles and requires that the couple adjust again to living as a pair. Retirement is a symbol of aging and results in further changes in family roles.

The basic criterion for the demarcation of one stage from the next is the amount of transition that is required (Rowe 1966). Transitions required by

For many couples the family career begins with a formal marriage ceremony and wedding celebration, as shown by this young couple cutting their wedding cake. *Ulrike Welsch.*

illness, occupational mobility, employment of the wife, separation, and divorce are important but have been excluded from life cycle categorizations because they are not necessarily part of the normal development of typical families.

One of the frequent criticisms of family life cycle as a concept is that it does not include some important family transitions (Mattessich and Hill 1982, 1987). For example, divorce and remarriage have become common transitions in the United States, yet are not included in the stages of the family life cycle. This problem is compounded in countries where extended families are common because there may not be a distinct period of family contraction among extended families.

Although the concept of family life cycle does not capture all important family transitions, it is a useful concept to describe and understand family change. The general pattern of family development appears to be universal. Getting married, having children, raising them, launching them, and living as aging parents are all typical transitions in most cultures. The number of stages can be modified for a particular situation or culture.

Family Career

The concept of family career may be more usable than the concept of family life cycle because it is not restricted to a particular sequence of stages. Therefore, it can be applied more readily to individual families and atypical transitions (Aldous 1978; Rodgers 1973; White 1987).

A career is a course of action of a person through life and is usually described as a temporal sequence of events (Stein 1984; White 1987). The concept of career is usually applied to occupations, but is relevant to families also.

Each family career is unique because each family faces situations and events that no other family does. For example, the second Ferrell child was born with crippled arms and legs. This changed the entire family system. There were many difficulties in raising a handicapped child and transitions to school, dating, and marriage were different. Families may face serious illnesses or the death of a family member. Some children are mentally handicapped and require special attention. Others get involved in using illicit drugs or other delinquent behavior.

Each family is embedded in a larger social system and culture, and its career is influenced by cultural expectations and societal laws. In most societies, for example, parents are expected to send their children to school. Each family is greatly affected by the nature of the school environment and its schedule. Parents who do not send their children to school may receive social and legal sanctions, and may have their children removed from them if appropriate education is not given. Governments may also remove children from the home if neglect or abuse occurs.

A family is influenced by both internal and external forces. External events include such things as unemployment, depressions, and wars. For example, Helen and Don married during the Great Depression, which had a great impact on their lives. It modified their outlook on work and money and made them more frugal than they might have been otherwise. Jobs were very difficult to obtain at that time, and when Don was offered a job with the U.S. Forest Service, he accepted it rather than continue with his education. He would have preferred to finish his master's degree, but could not pass up a good job.

Internal forces are events that happen within the family, such as the birth of a handicapped child. Such a crisis alters plans, outlook, and child-rearing attitudes. Alcoholism, divorce, and delinquency are other internal family situations that can greatly alter a family career.

During a family career, change may be continuous or discontinuous. **Continuous change** is gradual, such as the physical and mental development of children. Parents do not treat their children as minors one day and as adults the next day, but rather gradually let them assume various adult roles as they grow and learn appropriate social and emotional skills.

On the other hand, some change occurs abruptly at **critical transition** points. These changes precipitate major reorganization of roles within the family as they enter a new stage. For example, the birth of a child is an abrupt transition. One day there is no child, the next day there is feeding, dirty diapers, and a multitude of other tasks required to care for the child. Similarly, the transition to school is abrupt. Parents must suddenly make sure that their child gets to school and back home safely, and must help with school assignments. Births, entering school, marriage, and death are all critical transitions that represent **discontinuous change.**

Family Developmental Tasks

As families pass through their careers there are at least five major **family developmental tasks** that are important in all cultures (Mattessich and Hill 1982). The first is **physical maintenance.** Families need to obtain food, clothing, housing, and adequate medical care. Children must be protected from physical harm. A minimal standard of cleanliness must be maintained, and the health of family members must be attended to.

Earlier we identified eight family roles. The provider, housekeeper, and child care roles are all involved with physical maintenance. The provider role has to do with obtaining adequate money to purchase family supplies. The housekeeper role has to do with maintaining the household, including cleaning the house, washing the clothes, and preparing the food. The child care role includes tasks necessary to feed, clothe, and protect children.

The second major developmental task is to socialize family members for roles inside and outside of the family. **Socialization** is training family members to perform necessary roles, including roles outside the family such as taking a job. It also includes teaching family members to get along with each other and to meet family expectations, such as helping to prepare food and clean the house.

A third developmental task is the **maintenance of morale.** Family roles will be performed efficiently only if members receive emotional support and understanding. If family members become too discouraged, needed tasks will not get done. Family functioning will deteriorate if some family members refuse to cooperate or don't care what happens to the others. Attending to personal problems and feelings is an important aspect of family morale.

The therapeutic role, the kinship role, the recreational role, and the sexual role all deal with some aspects of family morale. The therapeutic role is particularly important because it deals with interpersonal problems. If family members are criticized or don't feel like they are important, motivation may drop.

A fourth developmental task of families is **social control.** All families have rules, rewards for compliance, and penalties for violation of rules. For example, children may be denied television privileges if they do not make their beds, and a wife may refuse a husband's sexual advances because he got drunk. Family members may receive money, candy, or praise if they comply with certain rules. Methods of social control will vary as the family passes through its career. Spanking may be used to discipline a three year old, and denying the use of the family car may be the sanction for a seventeen year old.

The fifth developmental task is the **acquisition of family members** by birth or adoption. One of the universal tasks of family life is reproduction. The family is the primary agent for bringing children into the world and raising them. In all cultures the birth of a child is an important event, and bearing children is seen as one of the purposes of marriage.

These five developmental tasks are important in all cultures, but vary as families pass through their careers (Mattessich and Hill 1982). The nature of physical maintenance and socialization is different for teenagers than pre-schoolers. Similarly, maintenance of morale and methods of social control differ by age of family members and family size. The task of acquiring new members is completed when childbearing ends.

Developmental tasks are similar to the three family functions identified earlier, although there are two important differences. First, morale and social control are not listed as family functions. Second, change over time is the emphasis in developmental tasks. The question is how tasks change as families pass through the life cycle.

Family Change in the United States and Japan

The work of Glick (1947, 1955, 1977), Norton (1983), and Kumagai (1984) shows the usefulness of the family life cycle model for understanding family change. Glick (1977) examined the median age at first marriage, birth of first child, birth of last child, marriage of last child, and death of one spouse for women born in different cohorts between 1880 and 1960. A **cohort** is a group of people born during a given period, such as during a given year or decade.

He found that from 1930 to 1950 there was a decrease in the average age at first marriage. Those married in the thirties had an average age at first marriage of 21.4 years, compared to those married in the fifties who had an average age at first marriage of 20 years. Age at marriage increased during the sixties and seventies to 21.2 years.

The average age of women at the birth of their first child did not change dramatically over this eighty-year period, although it was somewhat lower for those who married in the fifties and sixties than those who married earlier or later.

There was a decrease in the age of women at the birth of the last child. For women married between 1900 and 1910, the average age at birth of the last child was 32.9, compared to 29.6 among women married in the seventies. This was caused by a decrease in fertility among women born in later years.

The most dramatic change has been an increase in the age at which one spouse dies. Among women married between 1900 and 1910, the average age when their husbands died was 57. Among women who married in the seventies, the average age at which their husbands will die is projected to be 65.

These changes have resulted in a contraction of the child-rearing period and

Family roles expand during the childrearing stage when children must be watched, cared for, and trained.   *Janice Fullman/The Picture Cube.*

an expansion of the empty nest period of the family life cycle. For example, for women married between 1900 and 1910, their childbearing occurred over ten years and their husbands lived about a year and a half after the marriage of the last child. Among those married in the seventies, the period of child-bearing was only seven years and their husbands lived an average of thirteen years after the marriage of the last child.

A recent analysis by Norton (1983) extends the work of Glick and shows how divorce affects these family life cycle transitions. Norton (1983) found a decrease in age of first marriage, a drop in the age at which the birth of the first child occurred, and a large decrease in the age of women at the birth of their last child. For example, among women married once and never divorced, the 1910 to 1919 cohort had their last child at age 32. Comparable women born between 1950 and 1959 had their last child at age 23. A similar trend occurred among women married once and currently divorced, and among women married twice and currently married.

Kumagai (1984) compared the family life cycle of families in Japan and the United States. It was found that in Japan age at marriage and age of the mother at birth of first child has increased. Total fertility rates of Japanese women have been decreasing over the last sixty years. This has resulted in a large decrease in the period of childbearing among Japanese women. For example, the time period between marriage and the birth of the last child was fifteen years for women married in the 1930s, and only three years among women married in the 1970s. Today it is roughtly two years. Japanese women marry at about age 25, have their first child at about 26, and their last child by age 28.

The overall family career of Japanese women closely resembles that of American women. In both countries fertility has dropped dramatically and people are living longer. This has extended postparental married life to one third of the total married years.

Summary

1. The succession of critical stages through which the typical family passes during its lifespan is the *family life cycle.*
2. The two most common categorizations of the family life cycle are those by Glick (1947, 1977) and Duvall and Hill (1948). Glick's stages are (1) first marriage, (2) birth of first child, (3) birth of last child, (4) marriage of first child, (5) marriage of last child, (6) death of one spouse. The stages of Duvall and Hill are (1) married couples, (2) childbearing families, (3) preschool families, (4) school families, (5) teenage families, (6) launching families, (7) middle-aged families, and (8) aging families.

3. The term *family career* may be used to describe the temporal sequence of stages of a particular nuclear family.
4. Families are embedded in a larger social system and are influenced by their culture. They are also influenced by external forces such as wars, depressions, and unemployment, and by internal events such as delinquency, divorce, alcoholism, and disease. Family change may be continuous, such as the development of children, or abrupt, such as the birth of a child.
5. The timing of family events, the content of family roles, and societal expectations differ culturally and historically. However, the general shape of family development appears to be universal.
6. There are at least five major developmental tasks that are important in all cultures as follows: (1) physical maintenance, (2) socialization of family members, (3) maintenance of family morale, (4) social control, and (5) acquisition of family members.
7. The family life cycle in the United States and Japan has changed considerably during the past eighty years. There has been a contraction of the childbearing and child-rearing stages and an expansion of the empty nest and aging family stages.

Important Terms

- acquisition of family members
- cohort
- continuous change
- critical transitions
- discontinuous change
- family career
- family developmental tasks
- family life cycle
- maintenance of morale
- physical maintenance
- social control
- socialization

Questions for Discussion

1. What is the family life cycle?
2. What are the strengths and limitations of the concept of family life cycle?
3. How does the Ferrell family fit into the normal categories of the family life cycle? In what ways is it similar to and different from the typical U.S. family?
4. What is a family career?
5. How is the family career concept useful?
6. What is the difference between the terms "family career" and "family life cycle"?
7. Take the family of orientation of (a) your mother, (b) your father, and (c) yourself. Trace the family career of each of these families.
8. Compare the families of orientation of your mother, father, and yourself on age at first marriage, age at first birth, age at last birth, marriage of first child, marriage of last child, and death of one spouse. Compare to the results of Glick (1977) and Norton (1983).
9. Describe some of the external and internal influences on your family of orientation. Identify the major continuous and abrupt (discontinuous) changes.
10. How were the major family developmental tasks met in your family of orientation, and how did they change over the family career?
11. What are the major changes that have occurred in the life cycle of American and Japanese families over the past century?

Recommended Reading

KUMAGAI, F. 1984. The life cycle of the Japanese family. *Journal of Marriage and the Family* 46:191–204.
NORTON, A. J. Family life cycle: 1980. *Journal of Marriage and the Family* 45:267–275

References

ALDOUS, J. 1978. *Family careers.* New York: Wiley.
BIGELOW, H. F. 1936. *Family finance.* Philadelphia: Lippincott.
DUVALL, E. M., and R. L. HILL. 1948. *Report of the committee on the dynamics of family interaction.* Washington, DC: National Conference on Family Life.
DUVALL, E. M., and B. C. MILLER. 1985. *Marriage and family development.* 6th ed. New York: Harper & Row.
GLICK, P. C. 1947. The family cycle. *American Sociological Review* 12:164–174.
GLICK, P. C. 1955. The life cycle of the family. *Marriage and Family Living* 17:3–9.
GLICK, P. C. 1977. Updating the life cycle of the family. *Journal of Marriage and the Family* 39:5–13.
KIRKPATRICK, E. L., M. COWLES, and R. TOUGH. 1934. *The life cycle of the farm family.* Research Bulletin No. 121. Madison, WI: Agricultural Experiment Station, University of Wisconsin.

KUMAGAI, F. 1984. The life cycle of the Japanese family. *Journal of Marriage and the Family* 46:191–204.

LOOMIS, C. P. 1934. *The growth of the farm family in relation to its activities.* Raleigh, NC: Agricultural Experiment Station, North Carolina State College.

MATTESSICH, P., and R. HILL. 1982. *Family development and life cycle research and theory revisited.* Minneapolis: Minnesota Family Studies Center, University of Minnesota.

MATTESSICH, P., and R. HILL. 1987. Life cycle and family development. In *Handbook of marriage and the family,* ed. M. B. Sussman and S. K. Steinmetz, 437–469. New York: Plenum.

NORTON, A. J. 1983. Family life cycle: 1980. *Journal of Marriage and the Family* 45:267–275.

RODGERS, R. H. 1964. Toward a theory of family development. *Journal of Marriage and the Family* 26:262–270.

RODGERS, R. H. 1973. *Family interaction and transaction: The developmental approach.* Englewood Cliffs, NJ: Prentice-Hall.

ROWE, G. P. 1966. The developmental conceptual framework to the study of the family. In *Emerging conceptual frameworks in family analysis,* ed. F. I. Nye and F. M. Berardo, 198–222. New York: Macmillan.

ROWNTREE, B. S. 1906. *Poverty: A study of town life.* London: Macmillan.

SOROKIN, P. A., C. C. ZIMMERMAN, and C. J. GALPIN. 1931. *A systematic sourcebook in rural sociology,* vol. 2. Minneapolis: University of Minnesota Press.

STEIN, J., ed. 1984. *The Random House college dictionary.* Rev. ed. New York: Random House.

WHITE, J. M. 1987. Researching developmental careers: The career conformity scale. *Journal of Family Issues* 8:306–318.

CHAPTER 3

Family Variation and Change

Introduction

Ching and Ta Sao are a young married couple in Shanghai, China. They were introduced to each other by a friend. Although they made the decision themselves to marry, they sought and received permission from their parents. Had their parents opposed the marriage, they would not have gone against their wishes. Their wedding was simpler than traditional Chinese weddings. In the cities there has been a trend away from the elaborate, expensive weddings that used to be common in China (Engel 1984).

At the time of their marriage, Ta Sao was 24 and Ching was 22, and they began their marriage living with Ta Sao's parents. Although they would have preferred to have their own place, housing is scarce in China and they had not been able to save enough money to build a new house. Ta Sao hopes to build a new wing on to his parent's house sometime. Ching and Ta Sao both are employed, which is common in China today.

About a year after their marriage they had a baby girl who is now four years old. They would like to have another child and wish they could have a son. However, there is social and economic pressure from the government to limit Chinese families to one child. Children with no siblings are given priority for medical treatment and for admittance into kindergarten. Women who become pregnant a second time are asked to obtain an abortion and if they do not, a fine of about 30 percent of the couple's joint wages is levied until the child is seven years old (Fraser 1983).

There are several benefits to living with Ta Sao's parents. First, his mother helps with the household chores. Second, she is able to watch their child while they are at work. There is limited day care for preschool children and they prefer to have their daughter cared for by her grandmother. Third, Ta Sao and Ching are able to take care of Ta Sao's parents as they age. Being responsible for aging parents is an important obligation in Chinese society and the current law affirms that obligation. Ta Sao's father is 62 and is not in good health.

His mother is 57 and is in relatively good health, but cannot do as much as she used to.

Ching and Ta Sao are a typical Chinese couple. They have some characteristics of traditional Chinese couples yet their lives reflect social changes that have occurred in modern China.

In this chapter, family life in three different countries (China, Japan, and the Soviet Union) and in three ethnic groups (American blacks, Hispanics, and Jews) are described briefly to gain an understanding of some of the similarities and differences in families throughout the world. The purpose is not to provide a detailed description of family life in other cultures, but to illustrate selectively the variation in family life and how it has changed recently.

China was chosen because it is the most populous country in the world and has had extensive changes in family life during the past fifty years. Japan has a family heritage somewhat similar to China but is more industrialized and has a different political system. The Soviet Union was included because it is a world power that has experienced dramatic political and social changes in this century. American blacks are the largest minority in the United States and their family life provides a contrast between the real and ideal. Hispanics were added because they are the second largest minority in the United States and have a history quite different from American blacks and whites. American Jews were included because they are a prominent ethnic and religious group in the United States with a strong family heritage.

The extent and quality of family research varies among countries and ethnic groups and it was not possible to get information that was strictly comparable from all of the six family types. Therefore, the descriptions of family life in this chapter are necessarily incomplete. Nevertheless, similarities and differences among the six types are identified for several important family characteristics.

General characteristics of families within each of the six cultures are identified. Although the characterizations provide a general overview of what families are like within each culture, it must be remembered that family life is not homogeneous in any of these societies or ethnic groups. There is often variation by region, generation, and social status (de Valdez and Gallegos 1982). Before describing these six family types, let us examine how families are influenced by the larger culture.

Cultural Influences on Families

One important aspect of culture is the **economy.** Families must adapt to the existing economy in order to survive. For example, during the Depression in the thirties, families had to change their consumption patterns and alter the division of labor. Women and children were forced to seek employment and birthrates decreased. In some cases family decision making was altered.

Another important part of the culture that affects families is **technology.** During the past fifty years there has been a technological revolution that has had profound effects on families. Improvements in health care and nutrition have decreased mortality rates at all ages and extended the lifespan. The result has been that families spend more years in the empty nest stage and as aging families. Technology has also produced improved contraception which, along with other social and demographic factors, has decreased birthrates. Small numbers of children per family have eased the burden of child socialization and enabled large numbers of women to enter the labor force. The need for children to acquire new technological knowledge has resulted in extended schooling, which has increased the period of adolescence. Communication and transportation developments have allowed families to be more mobile and changed family recreation.

Governments make laws that impact on family life in a variety of ways. Laws passed in the Soviet Union after the revolution appeared to lessen family responsibility. China passed a law designed to stop rapid population growth, and the government is attempting to limit families to one child, which goes strongly against Chinese tradition. In the United States legalized abortion has decreased family size and limited the number of babies available for adoption. A thorough examination of how governments impact on family life is given in Chapter 12. Now we turn to an examination of family life in these three countries and three subcultures.

The Chinese Family

For centuries the family was the core of Chinese life. The purpose of the family was to have children and continue the family line. The traditional **Chinese family** was important for religious worship, socialization of children, and economic sustenance. It was a strong and stable unit in which roles were defined by age and sex, the old had more status than the young, and men were superior to women. Sons were valued more than daughters because they carried the family name and continued to live with the family after marriage whereas daughters would leave and join the family of their husbands. Marriages were arranged by parents or their representatives, and the needs and interests of the extended family were the determining factors rather than the wishes of the couple. Young people did not choose who they would marry and sometimes did not see their spouse until the wedding day (Engel 1982). After the marriage was arranged, the groom's family would pay a bride price, which consisted of gifts and money to the bride's family.

The wedding was a ritualistic transfer of the bride from her family of orientation to her husband's family. On the wedding day there was often a large feast and an unveiling of the bride. Virginity of the bride but not the groom was an implied condition of the marriage contract. Failure to provide proof of virginity could result in divorce or reclamation of the bride price (Engel 1982). Divorce was rare in traditional China but could occur by mutual consent of the family heads. It was not a decision of the couple.

After the revolution in 1949, the People's Republic of China passed a new marriage law that mandated voluntary mate selection and sexual equality, and prohibited bride price, child marriage, concubines, and plural marriage. The minimum age for marriage was set at 20 for men and 18 for women. In 1980 the marriage law was modified and the marriage age was raised to 22 for men and 20 for women. The new law also encouraged simple wedding ceremonies.

The Chinese government has attempted to limit population growth by pro-

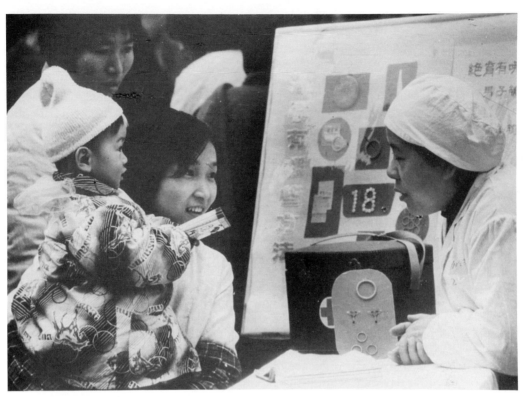

In an attempt to limit their burgeoning population, the People's Republic of
China has established programs to help couples limit their families to one child.
Here a doctor offers advice and free contraceptives in an open-air medical booth in
downtown Beijing. *Courtesy China Reconstructs.*

viding incentives for late marriage and one child families. For example, couples
get extra leave from work if they marry at least three years after the legal age.
If a woman bears her child after age 24 she is entitled to one hundred days of
paid maternity leave. Couples with only one child receive cash subsidies, free
hospitalization, and priority in housing and job assignments. As noted earlier,
couples are assessed a substantial fine for having a second child (Fraser 1983;
Palmer 1986).

A variety of social changes have accompanied the new marriage law. There
has been a large population increase accompanied by crowding and limited
housing, which limits spatial mobility. A trend toward more individualistic
attitudes is also evident.

These changes have modified the Chinese family significantly. Age at marriage increased from an average of 18.9 years in 1950 to 22.7 in 1982 (Banister
1984). The number of children born per family decreased from 5.25 in 1940
to 2.63 in 1981. In urban areas it was only 1.39 in 1981 (Chen 1985).

The reduction in family size has lessened the burden of child rearing and
household chores and enabled many Chinese women to enter the labor force.
Among women age 20 to 49, 91 percent are employed outside the home (Engel
1982). Forty percent of the Chinese labor force are women (Hare-Mustin and
Hare 1986).

Marrying and having children continue to be key aspects of Chinese life, and marriage is nearly universal for women. By age 29, 99 percent of all women have married. Men marry later than women and more men never marry. By age 29, 87 percent of men have married (Banister 1984). Children are highly valued and many Chinese view American voluntary childlessness as strange (Hare-Mustin and Hare 1986). Divorce is infrequent but has increased in recent years (Banister 1984; Liao 1987). Life expectancy has increased dramatically from 40.3 in 1953 to 64.7 by 1982 (Banister 1984).

There are fewer extended families than in the past. However, the housing shortage and lack of finances require some new couples to live with one of their parents (Chen 1985). Young couples earn comparatively low salaries when they marry and many have a child just when they are beginning their careers. They often prefer that their parents care for their child while they are at work. Although the power of the extended family has decreased, it continues to be an important ceremonial and ritualistic unit. Families are still expected to care for their sick and aged (Palmer 1985).

Although there is an official commitment to equality for women, women still have the major responsibility for children in China. Women are defined more by the mother role than wife role. The family is seen as the mainstay in China and the mother is the core of the family.

In summary, the Chinese family has decreased in size while the life span has increased. Both the trend toward individualism and the new marriage law have decreased the influence of kinship. However, housing shortages and the need for day care require that many married couples live with one of their parents. These changes have occurred more slowly in rural areas than in the cities.

The Japanese Family

The traditional **Japanese family** was similar in many respects to its Chinese counterpart. There was great respect for the aged, it was important to continue the family line by bearing sons, and the oldest son stayed in the household when he married. The other children left the household when the oldest male married, or even before he married (Sorensen 1984).

After World War II, women were granted legal equality with men and were able to own property and have free choice in mate selection. Social and legal changes along with urbanization gradually weakened the patriarchal extended family and placed more emphasis on the nuclear family. Marriage continues to be almost universal in modern Japan. By age 40 more than 95 percent of Japanese women and men marry (Kumagai 1984).

The timing of marital events has changed substantially. Age at first marriage has been getting older, partly because of increased emphasis on educational attainment. Today the average age at marriage for women is 25. Childbearing begins soon after marriage but only one or two children are born. In 1930 Japanese women had their first child at age 23, whereas in 1980 average age at first birth had increased to age 26. The average woman is age 28 when her last child is born.

A decline in fertility has decreased average household size from 5 in 1940

Japanese women usually have one or two children, born when the mother is between the ages of 25 and 30. Here a young Japanese mother helps her son on a
railway platform in Japan. *Ken Kobre/Picture Group.*

to 3.11 in 1985 (Kumagai 1984). The total span from marriage to birth of the
last child was 15 years in 1930. This decreased to 3 years in 1970, and to 1.7
years in 1980 (Kumagai 1984).

There is an increasing preference of Japanese couples to live separate from
their parents after marriage (Campbell and Brody 1985). Kumagai (1984) reports
that 60 percent of all Japanese households are nuclear families. However, there
is still a strong tradition for children to care for their aging parents. Adult
children and parents often move into the same household when parents become
widowed or ill. Seventy-four percent of the elderly live with relatives, and two
thirds of the impaired elderly are cared for by their families (Campbell and
Brody 1985).

The prevalence of households shared by married couples and their parents
has actually increased since 1975. This trend is due partly to the growing
number of women entering the labor force. Parents who live with their children
can care for their grandchildren while their children work (Campbell and Brody
1985).

Women in Japan tend to favor egalitarian gender roles. For example, 86 percent of Japanese mothers feel that husbands should share in the housework when wives are employed (Bankart and Bankart 1985). However, American women agree more consistently with egalitarian ideals than Japanese women (Campbell and Brody 1985), and most Japanese women still adhere to a rather traditional division of labor by gender (Kumagai 1984).

A comparison of child rearing in Japan and the United States was recently done by Durrett et al. (1986). They compared thirty caucasians and fifty-two Japanese mothers who had healthy firstborn infants who were three to four months old. Through interviews and observation they obtained an assessment of mother-child interaction and of mother's perception of emotional support received from her husband.

Husbands were perceived to be more supportive, sensitive, cooperative, accepting, and respectful in America than in Japan. Among both Japanese and American mothers, the perception of support from their husbands influenced interaction with the infants. In both cultures, the more the mother perceived support from her husband, the more she was involved with her infant. Compared to the American mothers, the Japanese mothers emphasized responsibility more and were more likely to use personal appeals to teach principles to their children.

In summary, the Japanese family comes from a tradition somewhat similar to the Chinese family, and both have become smaller and more nuclear in recent years. Major changes have been later age at marriage, a decrease in the birthrate, a large increase in life expectancy, and a increase in paid employment among women. Gender roles have become more egalitarian but women continue to do most child care and housekeeping tasks. There is still a strong family orientation and the expectation that married children will care for their aging parents.

The Soviet Family

Before the revolution, the **Soviet family** tended to be large, stable, and supported by religion and extended kin. After the revolution in 1917, the new Soviet government radically changed marriage and divorce laws in an attempt to alter the power of existing groups. The church lost its power to solemnize marriages and men and women were declared equal. Abortion was legalized and laws against adultery, bigamy, and incest were eliminated. Divorce became easy to obtain and the legal obligations between parent and child were minimized. The traditional family was seen as an institution that enslaved women and perpetuated the power of existing religious and political groups. The new laws were not designed to eliminate the family but rather to remove the inequities associated with it (Glass and Stolee 1987).

The decreased legal responsibility for children and spouses added to the social crisis that occurred after the revolution. In the years that followed, abortion, divorce, and delinquency increased dramatically while birthrates declined.

To counteract these problems, a new code of family law was enacted between 1934 and 1936. Its purpose was to stabilize the family by forcing people to assume more responsibility for family members, especially children, the sick, and the aged. Marriage and childbearing were encouraged, nontherapeutic abortions were banned, and divorce was made more difficult and costly. Parents were considered responsible for their children's acts and penalties for divorced fathers who did not pay child support were increased. Parenthood was extolled as a patriotic duty (Glass and Stolee 1987). Following these changes, rates of juvenile delinquency and divorce decreased.

Recent changes in family life in the Soviet Union are similar to those that have occurred in China and Japan. Perevedentsev (1983) has observed four recent trends in family life in the Soviet Union. First, there is movement away from the patriarchal type of family to more equality between husband and

In the Soviet Union, dating and mate selection have become more detached from the family. Mate selection is based on mutual attraction and young people usually meet in leisure activities such as dances.   *R. Koch/Contrasto/Picture Group.*

wife. Second, families have become more nuclear. Less often do several generations live together in the same household. Third, the division of labor has changed as the proportion of employed women has increased. Finally, a decrease in the birthrate has reduced average family size substantially.

There have been a number of other changes in the Soviet family system. Dating and mate selection have become more detached from the family of orientation. Mate selection is now based on mutual attraction and young people usually meet during some leisure activity. Parents are informed of the marriage, but their permission is not sought (Perevedentsev 1983).

There has been a substantial change in premarital sexual activity. Perevedentsev (1983) reports that in the past the overwhelming majority of newlyweds had no premarital sexual experience. Today satisfying sexual needs has become separated from family life and a substantial number of young people have premarital sexual experience.

Contrary to trends in China and Japan, age at marriage in the Soviet Union has become younger in recent years. Similar to Japan, childbearing tends to occur soon after marriage and only a small percentage of couples have more than two children. A major reason for the decrease in fertility is the high rate of female employment, which is encouraged in the Soviet Union (Von Frank 1979). Almost all Soviet women are employed and they make up half of the Soviet labor force (Perevedentsev 1983). The demands of employment and children conflict, because child care and household tasks are still primarily the women's responsibility.

As with many developed countries in the world, there has been an increase in divorce in the Soviet Union (Tiit 1982). Perevedentsev (1983) speculates that the increase is a result of a reduction in the wives' economic dependence on their husbands as well as a decrease in their responsibility for children.

In summary, the major changes in the Soviet family are similar to those in many other industrialized countries. Mate selection has become freer, family size has decreased, female employment has increased, divorce has increased, and the length of life has expanded considerably.

The American Black Family

Blacks are the largest minority in the United States and make up about 12 percent of the population (U.S. Bureau of the Census 1986). The following section on the **American black family** relies heavily on the work of Robert Staples (1984), an authority on the black family in America.

Blacks are traditional in their values regarding family, work, and religion. They believe in the family as an institution, and it is their greatest source of life satisfaction. Among both men and women, those who are married are happier than those who never married, or who are divorced or separated (Broman 1988; Zollar and Williams 1987). Most blacks marry and want to structure family roles in a traditional way (Staples 1984).

There is some evidence that blacks are less permissive sexually than whites. Blacks are more likely than whites to require affection as a basis for sexual relations, and among sexually active teenagers white women have had more sexual partners than black women (Staples 1984).

Children are very important in black families. Almost all fertile black women bear children, and the role of mother is more important that any other role, including that of wife (Glick 1981; Staples 1984). Children come first in the lives of most black mothers and there is a fierce loyalty between mothers and their children (Ball 1983). Among whites, having children is associated with a decrease in satisfaction, whereas among blacks having children is not associated with lower satisfaction (Ball 1983; Broman 1988; Glen and McLanahan 1982).

The traditional nature of black family norms is also shown in their attitudes toward abortion and the feminist movement. Blacks are more negative toward abortion than whites, and black women are underrepresented in the feminist movement. They tend to define the roles of men and women in the family rather traditionally. The man is viewed primarily as the provider while the woman is the one who cares for the children and household.

Nobles (1981) identified three important aspects of black family life. First, blacks have strong family ties. Parents show unconditional love for their children and there is strong mutual respect between parent and child. Second, family roles are flexible, allowing family boundaries to stretch to accommodate specific conditions and individual preferences. Finally, blacks have strong kin-

A striking feature of American black families is the relatively high proportion of single-parent homes—44 percent of black families are headed by women. Here a young single mother enjoys an activity with her three children.   *Bob Daemmrich.*

ship networks. Relatives provide concrete aid and help the family solve its problems. Kin are a buffer and provide needed support.

Although attitudes of blacks toward family life are traditional, actual family behavior is unconventional in some ways. One of the distinguishing features of current black families is the relatively high proportion of single-parent homes. The most significant change in the black family during the past thirty years has been the large increase in female-headed households. In 1960, 21 percent of black families were headed by women, compared to 44 percent in 1985 (U.S. Bureau of the Census 1980, 1986). Only 40 percent of black children under 18 live with both parents compared to 80 percent of white children (U.S. Bureau of the Census 1986).

The primary reason for the large proportion of single-parent families is the high rate of marital disruption among blacks. Among ever-married persons age 25 to 54, 32 percent of blacks are separated or divorced compared to only 15 percent of whites (U.S. Bureau of the Census 1986). Staples (1984) estimates that about one in two white marriages will eventually end in divorce compared to two of three black marriages. Furthermore, black women are less likely to remarry than white women (Glick 1981).

Unmarried cohabitation is more common among blacks. Unmarried couples represent about 2 percent of the households in the general population, compared to 3.5 percent of all black households (Glick 1981).

Blacks tend to have more children than other groups in the United States, although there has been some convergence in recent years. The annual fertility rate (births per 1,000 women age 15–44) is 82 among blacks compared to 63 among whites (National Center for Health Statistics 1987).

Childbearing before age 20 and outside of marriage is common among blacks. Over 40 percent of black women bear a child before age 20 compared to only 20 percent among whites (Staples 1984). Among blacks, 60 percent of live births are to unmarried women, compared to 14 percent among whites (National Center for Health Statistics 1987).

Why do so many blacks not follow the traditional family patterns that they believe in? According to Staples (1984), a primary reason is that many black men are unable to adequately perform their role as economic provider due to poverty and the effects of **institutional racism,** which is cultural discrimination based on existing norms and social structures. This creates stress among those that marry and reduces single black women's interest in marriage.

It is well documented that unemployment and financial problems create stress that increases the risk of marital dissolution. Black men with serious employment problems have marital disruption rates three times higher than the average family (Staples 1984). Other social characteristics of blacks create strain and increase their risk of marital disruption, such as their tendency to live in urban areas, the independence of women, early age at marriage, early childbearing, and higher levels of education of women relative to their husbands. Black women are more likely than white women to marry a man with less education than they have. Sixty percent of black wives are employed compared to only 49 percent of white wives (Glick 1981).

The shortage of black men at marriageable ages also decreases the opportunity of some black women to marry and have a traditional family (Glick 1981). Among blacks between the ages of 20 and 29, there are only 91 men for every 100 women. The comparable **sex ratio** among whites is 102 men for every 100 women. Among blacks ages 35 to 39, there are only 84 men for every 100 women (U.S. Bureau of the Census 1986). Staples (1981) estimates that among single college-educated blacks the ratio of men to women is only one to two. However, the central factor in the gap between black ideology and black family structure is the inability of black males to meet the normatively prescribed responsibilities of husband and father.

One way to cope with economic stress and marital disruption is to incorporate relatives into the household. About 14 percent of black families do this compared to only 7 percent of white families (Glick 1981). This allows resources to be pooled, provides emotional and economic support, and is an effective coping mechanism, as evidenced by the low welfare rate among black extended families. In contrast, white extended families had higher-than-average welfare rates (Osmond and Martin 1983).

Support from kin also helps adults and children adjust psychologically. Dressler (1985) found that blacks who receive support from extended kin have fewer symptoms of depression. Kellam, Ensminger, and Turner (1977) studied the psychological and social adjustment of children from poor black families in Chicago. They found that children from mother-grandmother families had social and psychological adjustment comparable to children from two-parent homes, whereas children living in one-adult or remarried homes had significantly lower social and psychological adjustment.

Another way to cope with economic problems is to receive public assistance. Osmond and Martin (1983) found black women with dependents had a higher work rate and lower welfare rate than comparable white women, which is evidence of the strong work ethic among black families.

In summary, black families strongly value marriage, having children, raising those children, working hard, and teaching their children to achieve. They tend to be religious and supportive of their kin. Often this traditional family ideal is not realized fully because of the inability of black males to fulfill the traditional role of provider, due to poverty and institutional racism. The strains in the black family have produced a high rate of marital dissolution. The extended family and flexible family roles are used to help cope with economic stress and marital dissolution. Families in which relatives are incorporated are common among blacks and provide monetary and emotional support.

The American Hispanic Family

Individuals of Hispanic descent are the second largest minority group in the United States comprising about 7 percent of the population (U.S. Bureau of the Census 1986). Over 80 percent live in urban areas where they have migrated to seek employment. Many have difficulty finding employment because of limited education and job skills. Less than half of Hispanics over age 25 have completed high school and over half live in urban poverty (de Valdez and Gallegos 1982).

Hispanics include persons whose ancestors came from Mexico, Puerto Rico, Cuba, and other countries in Central and South America. They are sometimes called Mexican Americans because Mexico borders the United States and many

American Hispanics came from there. However, Hispanic is a more appropriate term because many come from countries other than Mexico. The term **Spanish origin** is also used occasionally to refer to Hispanics.

The **American Hispanic family** has a strong family orientation. Rothman, Gant, and Hnat (1985) maintain that the family is more important for one's identity among Hispanics than among blacks or whites. Family cohesion is valued and it is felt that individual interests should not take precedence over family interests. Affection and harmony are emphasized rather than individualism and materialism. When individuals need help they turn to their families and kin first. There is also a norm that families should take care of their aged members (de Valdez and Gallegos 1982; Rothman et al. 1985). Religion is important for identification and internal support; the marjority of Hispanics are Catholics.

There is more marital **exogamy** (marrying outside one's ethnic group) than in the past, and women appear more likely to do so than men. Occupation is important in explaining exogamy among Hispanics. The chances of a Hispanic woman marrying a non-Hispanic are higher if the man has higher economic status than the woman or her family (Mittelbach and Moore 1968).

Among Hispanics the husband-father is seen as the head of the family and is expected to support and protect his wife and children. Although he shows affection for and plays with his children, the father is to be respected and obeyed. The wife is perceived as warm and affectionate, and is expected to care for the house and children. She is sometimes portrayed as an obedient servant who must acknowledge the authority of her husband (Staton 1972). Zapata and Jaramillo (1981) suggest that this is a stereotype and that Hispanics tend to perceive husband and wife relations as more egalitarian than patriarchal. Family roles in Hispanic-American families may be less rigid than is often assumed (Zapata and Jaramillo 1981).

Children are important to Hispanics and they tend to have children quickly after marriage. Their fertility is 42 percent higher than in non-Hispanic marriages. The annual fertility rate (births per 1,000 women ages 15 to 44) is 94 among Hispanics compared to 82 among blacks and 63 among whites (Ventura 1987, 1988). Hispanics have more nonmarital births than whites but fewer than blacks. Thirty percent of all Hispanic births are to unmarried women compared to 12 percent among whites and 61 percent among blacks (Ventura 1987).

Marital disruption is less common among Hispanics than among blacks or whites, even though Hispanics tend to marry early and have relatively low socioeconomic status. Frisbie et al. (1985) found that they have rates of separation and divorce 8 to 12 percent below those of whites.

Hispanics have fewer single-parent families than blacks but more than whites. Two thirds of Hispanic children live with both parents, compared to 80 percent of white children and only 40 percent of black children (U.S. Bureau of the Census 1986).

According to Zapata and Jaramillo (1981), Hispanics have child-rearing attitudes similar to whites and blacks. Educational achievement is emphasized as much as it is in white families, and aspirations for boys and girls are similar. Academic achievement is related to the support for education given in the family. The higher the father's education, the greater the emphasis on educational achievement and the greater the autonomy granted to children (Anderson and Evans 1976).

Obedience to parents is an important value taught to Hispanic children. In a comparison of perceptions of Hispanic and white children, it was found that Hispanics perceive less autonomy and that their parents are less willing to explain reasons for punishment (Anderson and Evans 1976). They were also less confident than white children that their efforts at school would make a difference and that they could manipulate their physical and social world.

In summary, Hispanics emphasize family cohesion, kinship ties, and religion. Affection and harmony are more important than individualism and material goods. They have relatively high fertility and low divorce rates. Births among unmarried women are higher than among whites but lower than among blacks. Similarly, Hispanics have more single-parent families than whites but fewer than blacks. Children are important and are taught to respect and obey their parents. Although there is a tradition of male authority, recent research shows a trend toward egalitarian relations between husband and wife and toward equal treatment of female and male children. Child-rearing attitudes appear to be similar to those of blacks and whites in the United States.

The American Jewish Family

Jews are an ethnic or cultural category as well as a religious one. The family has always played a central role in Jewish life as a source of nurturance and to promote group survival (Brodbar-Nemzer 1988). In the **American Jewish family** marriage is meant to be a lifelong partnership, although Jewish tradition permits divorce.

The importance of the family among Jews was demonstrated in a study done by Brodbar-Nemzer (1986). He examined how marital status, support, and stress affected the self-esteem of Jews, Protestants, and Catholics. He found that the self-esteem of Jews was affected more by these family relationship variables than the self-esteem of the Protestants or Catholics.

One of the distinctive features of Jews is their high rate of marriage. Estimates are that 98 percent eventually marry (Brodbar-Nemzer 1988). By comparison, about 94 percent of the American population marry at least once (Bahr 1986). Jews also tend to marry other Jews. Although exogamy has been increasing among Jews, it is much less likely for them than for Catholics or Protestants (Glenn 1982). Age at marriage tends to be older among Jews than among other ethnic or religious groups in the United States (Brodbar-Nemzer 1988).

Although marriage is central to Jewish life, fertility has been low for many years. Jewish fertility has been at about the replacement level for most of this century and remains close to that level (Brodbar-Nemzer 1988). The **replacement level** is a completed **fertility rate** of 2.1 children per woman. Although the fertility rates of other ethnic groups have decreased in recent decades, Jewish fertility is considerbly lower than the fertility of American black and Hispanic families (U.S. Bureau of the Census 1986).

In the United States education tends to have a negative influence on fertility; women with more education tend to have fewer children. Among Jews the opposite is true; women with the highest levels of education tend to have more children than less educated women (Brodbar-Nemzer 1988).

The divorce rate among Jews is low compared to the rates among blacks, Hispanics, Catholics, and Protestants. Although the divorce rate among Jews has increased during the past twenty-five years, it remains considerably lower than the divorce rate among these other groups (Brodbar-Nemzer 1988).

Attitudes about family issues tend to be more liberal among Jews than among Catholics and Protestants. Education among women is encouraged and attitudes about family roles tend to be egalitarian (Brodbar-Nemzer 1986; Chi and Houseknecht 1985).

In summary, marriage is central to Jewish life for nurturance and support, and almost all Jews eventually marry. They tend to marry late, have few children, and hold egalitarian attitudes toward family roles. Although exogamy has increased in recent years, they tend to marry other Jews and have a relatively low divorce rate for American society.

Conclusion

In this chapter we have briefly examined six types of families. There are many other ethnic groups and countries that could have been included. The purpose in this chapter was not a comprehensive review of family life across the globe, but a selective examination of family life in three countries outside the United States and three ethnic groups within it. It is hoped that this introduction will stimulate you to examine families in these and other cultures in more detail.

Although the extent and nature of family change varies by culture and subculture, there appear to have been a number of changes that have affected families in many countries of the world. These include an increase in age at marriage, employment of women, egalitarian attitudes, divorce, and life expectancy, and a decrease in fertility.

Summary

1. The economy, technology, and government are three aspects of culture that influence families. Families are economic units and are greatly affected by depressions and unemployment. Technology changes have altered many aspects of family life, including birthrates, schooling, communication, and life span. Laws that have altered fertility rates are one example of how government policies may affect families.

2. In the traditional Chinese family, sons married and lived in the household of their parents. Status was based on age and sex. The young deferred to the old and females deferred to males.

3. The modern Chinese family has become more nuclear and egalitarian. Family size has decreased, life expectancy has increased, and there is less emphasis on kinship. However, because of housing shortages and the need for day care, many young couples live with their parents. The changes are less pronounced in rural than urban areas.

4. The traditional Japanese family was similar to its Chinese counterpart, and in recent decades it too has become smaller, more nuclear, and more egalitarian. Japanese marry late, have few children, and live a long time. Most women are employed and they are expected to care for their aged parents.

5. After the revolution in 1917 the laws and social conditions altered the Soviet family significantly. Birthrates decreased while abortion, divorce, and delinquency increased. In an effort to counteract these social problems, marriage, fertility, parental responsibility, and family stability were encouraged.

6. The modern Soviet family has become more egalitarian, more nuclear, and smaller. Female employment has increased, mate selection is based on free choice, and the divorce rate has risen.

7. American black families have a traditional orientation but are unconventional because of the inability of the black male to fulfill the provider role adequately, due to poverty and institutional racism. Blacks have higher-than-average fertility and divorce, which has resulted in a higher-than-average proportion of single-parent families. Roles within the black family tend to be flexible and ties to kin are strong. Blacks have a strong work ethic and low rates of public assistance when compared to whites similarly situated.

8. Hispanics in America tend to have strong family ties and emphasize cohesion and harmony. Fertility is relatively high and the incidence of divorce is less than among American whites and blacks. Births to unmarried women and the number of single-parent families are higher than among whites but lower than among blacks. Traditionally, the role of the husband was to protect and support his wife and children, while the wife's role was to be affectionate and care for the household and children. Recent evidence suggests that Hispanics have become more egalitarian in husband-wife roles and in child-rearing practices.

9. The family is central to Jews as a source of identity, nurturance, and support. Almost all Jews marry and have children, although they tend to marry late and usually limit the number of children to two. Divorce is discouraged and divorce rates are relatively low, although they have increased in recent years. Their attitudes about family roles tend to be egalitarian.

10. In many countries of the world similar changes have occurred. Age at marriage, employment of women, egalitarian attitudes, marital disruption, and life expectancy have increased while fertility has decreased. The smaller family size and increased life span have decreased the family burdens of women and given them many productive years without the traditional responsibilities of child care.

Important Terms

- American black family
- American Hispanic family
- American Jewish family
- Chinese family
- economy
- exogamy

endogamy

- fertility rate
- global family changes
- government
- institutional racism
- Japanese family

- replacement level
- sex ratio
- Soviet family
- Spanish origin
- technology

Questions for Discussion

1. Describe the traditional Chinese family.
2. How has the Chinese family changed in recent years?
3. What are some reasons why the Chinese family has changed?
4. Describe the traditional Japanese family.
5. How has the Japanese family changed in recent years?
6. What are some reasons why the Japanese family has changed?
7. How has the Soviet family changed in recent years and why?
8. What are the major changes in the American black family in recent years and why have they occurred?
9. What is the difference between the ideal and actual black family and why does this difference exist?
10. Describe the American Hispanic family and how it has changed in recent years.
11. Describe the American Jewish family and some of its recent changes.
12. Compare the Chinese, Japanese, Soviet, American black, American Hispanic, and American Jewish families. In what ways are they similar and in what ways are they different?
13. What are some of the inaccurate stereotypes commonly held about the six types of families?
14. What are some of the family changes that have occurred across the globe?
15. Is family life becoming more similar in different countries around the world? Which aspects are converging and which are not?

Recommended Reading

ENGEL, J. W. 1984. Marriage in the People's Republic of China: Analysis of a new law. *Journal of Marriage and the Family* 46:955–961.

ROTHMAN, J., L. M. GANT, and S. A. HNAT. 1985. Mexican-American family culture. *Social Service Review* 59:197–215.

References

ANDERSON, J. G., and F. B. EVANS. 1976. Family socialization and educational achievement in two cultures: Mexican-American and Anglo-American. *Sociometry* 39 (3):209–222.

BAHR, S. J. 1986. Family formation. In *Utah in demographic perspective*, ed. T. K. Martin, T. B. Heaton, and S. J. Bahr, 71–79. Salt Lake City: Signature Books.

BALL, R. E. 1983. Marital status, household structure, and life satisfaction of black women. *Social Problems* 30:400–409.

BANISTER, J. 1984. An analysis of recent data on the population of China. *Population and Development Review* 10:241–271.

BANKART, C. P., and B. M. BANKART. 1985. Japanese children's perceptions of their parents. *Sex Roles* 13:679–690.

BRODBAR-NEMZER, J. Y. 1986. Marital relationships and self-esteem: How Jewish families are different. *Journal of Marriage and the Family* 48:89–98.

BRODBAR-NEMZER, J. Y. 1988. The contemporary American Jewish family. In *The religion and family connection: Social science perspectives*, ed. D. L. Thomas, 66–87. Salt Lake City: Bookcraft.

BROMAN, C. L. 1988. Satisfaction among blacks: The significance of marriage and parenthood. *Journal of Marriage and the Family* 50:45–51.

CAMPBELL, R., and E. M. BRODY. 1985. Women's changing roles and help to the elderly: Attitudes of women in the United States and Japan. *Gerontologist* 25:584–592.

CHEN, X. 1985. The one-child population policy, modernization, and the extended Chinese family. *Journal of Marriage and the Family* 47:193–202.

CHI, S. K., and S. K. HOUSEKNECHT. 1985. Protestant fundamentalism and marital success: A comparative approach. *Sociology and Social Research* 69:351–375.

DE VALDEZ, T. A., and J. GALLEGOS. 1982. The Chicano familia in social work. In *Cultural awareness in the human services*, ed. J. W. Green, 184–208. Englewood Cliffs, NJ: Prentice-Hall.

DRESSLER, W. W. 1985. Extended family relationships, social support, and mental health in a southern black community. *Journal of Health and Social Behavior* 26:39–48.

DURRETT, M. E., P. RICHARDS, M. OTAKI, J. W. PENNEBAKER, and L. NIQUIST. 1986. Mother's involvement with infant and her perception of spousal support, Japan and America. *Journal of Marriage and the Family* 48:187–194.

ENGEL, J. W. 1982. *Changes in male-female relationships and family life in the People's Republic of China*. Research Series 014, Hawaii Institute of Tropical Agriculture and Human Resources, College of Tropical Agriculture and Human Resources, University of Hawaii at Manoa.

ENGEL, J. W. 1984. Marriage in the People's Republic of China: Analysis of a new law. *Journal of Marriage and the Family* 46:955–961.

FRASER, S. E. 1983. China: Family size and current population policies. *Journal of Family Welfare* 30:40–48.

FRISBIE, W. P., W. OPITZ, and W. R. KELLY. 1985. Marital instability trends among Mexican Americans as compared to blacks and anglos: New evidence. *Social Science Quarterly* 66 (3):587–601.

GLASS, B. L., and M. K. STOLEE. 1987. Family law in Soviet Russia, 1917–1945. *Journal of Marriage and the Family* 49:893–902.

GLENN, N. D. 1982. Interreligious marriage in the United States: Patterns and recent trends. *Journal of Marriage and the Family* 44:555–566.

GLENN, N. D., and S. McLANAHAN. 1982. Children and marital happiness: a further specification of the relationship. *Journal of Marriage and the Family* 44:63–72.

GLICK, P. C. 1981. A demographic picture of black families. In *Black families*, ed. H. P. McAdoo, 106–126. Beverly Hills, CA: Sage.

HARE-MUSTIN, R. T., and S. E. HARE. 1986. Family change and the concept of motherhood in China. *Journal of Family Issues* 7:67–82.

KELLAM, S. G., M. E. ENSMINGER, and K. J. TURNER. 1977. Family structure and the mental health of children. *Archives of General Psychiatry* 34:1012–1022.

KUMAGAI, F. 1984. The life cycle of the Japanese family. *Journal of Marriage and the Family* 46:191–204.

Liao, C. 1987. *Marriage and divorce in traditional and modern Chinese society.* Seminar paper, Department of Sociology, Brigham Young University, Provo, UT.

Mittelbach, F. G., and J. W. Moore. 1968. Ethnic endogamy—the case of Mexican Americans. *American Journal of Sociology* 74 (1):50–62.

National Center for Health Statistics. 1987. *Advance report of final natality statistics, 1985.* Monthly Vital Statistics Report, vol. 36, no. 4, Supplement. DHHS Pub. No. (PHS) 87–1120, July 17. Hyattsville, MD: Public Health Service.

Nobles, W. W. 1981. African-American family life. In *Black families,* ed. H. P. McAdoo, 77–86. Beverly Hills, CA: Sage.

Osmond, M. W., and P. Y. Martin. 1983. Women, work, and welfare: A comparison of black and white female heads of households. *International Journal of Sociology of the Family* 13:37–56.

Palmer, M. 1986. The People's Republic of China: Some general observations on family law. *Journal of Family Law* 25:41–69.

Perevedentsev, V. I. 1983. The Soviet family today. *Sociology and Social Research* 67:245–259.

Rothman, J., L. M. Gant, and S. A. Hnat. 1985. Mexican-American family culture. *Social Service Review* 59 (2):197–215.

Sorensen, C. 1984. Farm labor and family cycle in traditional Korea and Japan. *Journal of Anthropological Research* 40:306–323.

Staples, R. 1981. Race and marital status: An overview. In *Black families,* ed. H. P. McAdoo, 173–175. Beverly Hills, CA: Sage.

Staples, R. 1984. *Changes in black family structure: The conflict between family ideology and structural conditions.* Paper presented at Black Family Conference, Brigham Young University, Provo, UT.

Staton, R. D. 1972. A comparison of Mexican and Mexican-American families. *The Family Coordinator* 21:325–330.

Tiit, E. 1982. Risk factors leading to marital dissolution in the Estonian SSR. *Journal of Divorce* 5:61–73.

U.S. Bureau of the Census. 1980. *Statistical abstract of the United States: 1980.* Washington, DC: U.S. Government Printing Office.

U.S. Bureau of the Census. 1986. *Statistical abstract of the United States: 1987.* Washington, DC: U.S. Government Printing Office.

Ventura, S. J. 1987. *Births of Hispanic parentage, 1983 and 1984.* Monthly Vital Statistics Report, vol. 36, no. 4, Supplement (2), DHHS Pub. No. (PHS) 87–1120, July 24. Hyattsville, MD: Public Health Service.

Von Frank, A. A. 1979. *Family policy in the USSR since 1944.* Palo Alto, CA: R & E Research Associates.

Zapata, J. T., and P. T. Jaramillo. 1981. Research on the Mexican-American family. *Journal of Individual Psychology* 37:72–85.

Zollar, A. C., and J. S. Williams. 1987. The contribution of marriage to the life satisfaction of black adults. *Journal of Marriage and the Family* 49:87–92.

PART II

Establishing and Maintaining Family Life

CHAPTER 4

Premarital Sexual Standards and Behavior

Introduction

Lorraine and Michael met while they were students at the University of Minnesota. Michael was beginning his senior year and Lorraine was a sophomore. Michael's roommate was dating Lorraine's sister, and they got Lorraine and Michael to agree to a blind date. At the time Lorraine was dating another man regularly and was not particularly interested in dating Michael. However, to please her sister, she consented to go out with Michael once. Michael was not expecting much from a blind date but decided to accept the invitation.

Lorraine and Michael were pleasantly surprised on their date. To her surprise, Lorraine found Michael to be interesting and attractive and she was glad she had consented to go on the date. Michael thought Lorraine was warm, pleasant, and nice looking. It was the only blind date that he had ever enjoyed.

Michael decided to ask Lorraine out again, and because she had enjoyed their first date, she accepted his invitation. Their second date was as enjoyable as the first and Michael asked her for another. They became strongly attracted to each other and began to date regularly and have sexual relations occasionally.

Both Michael and Lorraine had had sexual relations with other persons previously. Lorraine had gone with a boy regularly in high school and had had sexual relations with him a few times. Many of her high school and college friends were sexually active, which was considered approporiate if you really liked someone. Michael also had had sexual relations with a girl he had previously dated. Both Lorraine and Michael felt that premarital sex was acceptable in today's world among people who are strongly attracted to each other. They felt, however, that contraception must be used to avoid premarital pregnancies.

Michael and Lorraine have sexual standards similar to most young Americans. Premarital sexual relationships are acceptable if there is affection between the partners, but promiscuity is viewed negatively.

In this chapter sexual standards and behavior among the unmarried are examined. We begin with a discussion of sexual socialization, followed by a look at premarital standards and behavior and how they have changed in America. Then we identify characteristics associated with premarital sexual behavior. Finally, we look at contraception, pregnancy, abortion, and births among the unmarried.

Sexual Socialization

Although sexual behavior has a biological base, sexual desires and behavior are influenced strongly by **sexual socialization.** The research of Harlow and Harlow (1962) suggests that learning may have a stronger influence on sexual behavior than is often assumed. The Harlows removed infant monkeys from their mothers and raised them in cages without physical contact with other monkeys. Although these monkeys were provided with good food and had normal physical development, they did not have normal sex drives as adults and would not mate. The Harlows' research suggests that sexual desire is not simply a biological drive which develops instinctually. Sexual attitudes and desires are a product of socialization and are learned gradually.

Early in life one develops an identity as a male or female, and one gradually becomes aware of the heterosexual nature of marital and romantic relationships. Later, knowledge about sexual functioning is obtained along with a self-perception of attractiveness to others.

During adolescence one's peer group becomes influential in sexual socialization. As young people become concerned about their attractiveness and popularity, feedback from peers becomes increasingly important. Information from parents about sexuality is often limited, and adolescents turn to their peers for information. The high degree of age segregation in our society facilitates peer influence (DeLamater 1981).

Premarital sexual activity is viewed somewhat ambiguously in many groups. Most societies do not openly encourage premarital sexual activity but many are very accepting of it. However, most societies disapprove of childbirth outside the marital relationship (Goode 1982). Even in cultures where premarital sex is encouragged, it is usually expected that marriage will occur before the birth of a child. Goode (1982) notes that every society has some rules against bearing children casually.

Sexual Standards

Each individual develops a sexual standard about the acceptability of various sexual activities. Reiss (1960, 1967) has identified four different premarital sexual standards: (1) abstinence, (2) double standard, (3) permissiveness with affection, and (4) permissiveness without affection. **Abstinence** is the belief that there should not be sexual activity before marriage.

According to the **double standard,** premarital sexual activity is acceptable for men but not for women. For example, in traditional Chinese society it was important for women to be virgins at marriage although there was no such expectation for men. In 1967 Reiss found that 24 percent of the females and 30 percent of the males in the United States believed in the double standard. Research in the eighties indicated that the double standard may have disappeared, although women who participate in casual sex are evaluated more negatively than males who participate in casual sex (DeLamater 1981; Sprecher, McKinney, and Orbuch 1987).

Permissiveness with affection was the standard held by Lorraine and Michael and is the most prevalent standard in American society today (Reiss 1980). According to this standard, premarital sexual intercourse is acceptable if there is strong affection between the partners.

According to the standard of **permissiveness without affection,** sexual activity is appropriate even if there is no emotional relationship between the man and woman. The purpose of sexual activity is physical pleasure, and one may have sex with any other person who is willing.

Sexual standards appear to be influenced by four major variables. First, adolescents tend to have more permissive standards if their peers engage frequently in premarital sexual activity. Second, adolescents have more permissive standards when their parents' standards are more permissive. Third, those who attend religious services are less likely to have permissive premarital standards. Finally, sexual experience has an effect on sexual standards. Young persons with restrictive standards tend to become more permissive after they have had sexual experience. This suggests that premarital standards are not static but evolve over time and that there is a tendency to resolve inconsistencies between behavior and standards (DeLamater 1981; DeLamater and Mac-Corquodale 1979; Thornton and Camburn 1987).

Premarital Sexual Behavior

How active sexually are individuals who have never been married? A large majority of individuals participate in premarital sexual activity. A summary of the sexual activity of never-married American women is shown in Table 4·1. Almost one in five has had sexual intercourse by age 15. This increases to two in five by age 17 and surpasses 50 percent by age 18. By age 19 two thirds of never-married American women have had sexual intercourse (U.S. Bureau of the Census 1986).

A survey of never-married American women between the ages of 20 and 29

TABLE 4·1 Percentage of Never-Married Women Who Have Had Sexual Intercourse

Age	Total	White	Black
Total	61	58	80
15–19 years	43	40	58
15 years	18	17	28
16 years	29	27	41
17 years	40	36	55
18 years	54	50	76
19 years	66	63	81
20–24 years	73	70	91
25–44 years	82	80	96

SOURCE: U.S. Bureau of the Census 1986:66.

revealed that 82 percent have had sexual intercourse (Tanfer and Horn 1985). About half of those women were currently sexually active.

Among young married couples between the ages of 18 and 24, Hunt (1974) found that 95 percent of the men and 81 percent of the women reported having had premarital sexual intercourse. Taken together, these data suggest that in America at least eight of ten women and nine of ten men have sexual intercourse before they marry.

It appears that premarital sexual activity has been increasing in recent years. In a survey of college students, Robinson and Jedlicka (1982) found that the proportion of men who had premarital intercourse increased from 65 percent in 1965 to 77 percent in 1980. The comparable figures for college women were 29 percent and 64 percent, respectively (see Table 4·2). Heavy petting was reported by 85 percent of the males in 1980, an increase from 71 percent in 1965. Among females heavy petting increased from 34 percent in 1965 to 73 percent in 1980.

Three major conclusions can be drawn from these findings. First, among both men and women there has been an increase in premarital sexual activity. Second, more men than women participate in premarital petting and intercourse. Third, increases in premarital sexual activity have been greater among women than among men, which has reduced gender differences.

Recent research suggests that there is a contradiction between behavior and standards of young college students in the United States. Robinson and Jedlicka (1982) observed a **new double standard** that is characterized by greater restrictions on the sexual behavior of others than on self. Although the percentage of college students with premarital coital experience has increased, there also has been an increase in the proportion of college students who consider premarital coitus immoral and sinful.

A similar finding was reported in a study of unmarried college students conducted by Jacoby and Williams (1985). Regardless of their own sexual experience, respondents had a preference for virgins as dating and marriage partners. There was no evidence of the traditional double standard but also no evidence of an egalitarian standard, which is the tendency to choose someone with about the same sexual experience as oneself. Rather, they found a single standard for both males and females that was similar to the old double standard

TABLE 4·2   Percentage of College Students Having Premarital Intercourse (1965–1980)

Year	Males		Females	
	%	N	%	N
1965	65.1	129	28.7	115
1970	65.0	136	37.3	158
1975	73.9	115	57.1	275
1980	77.4	168	63.5	230

SOURCE: Robinson, I. E., and D. Jedlicka. 1982. Change in sexual attitudes and behavior of college students from 1965 to 1980: A research note. *Journal of Marriage and the Family* 44:238, Table 1. Copyrighted 1982 by the National Council on Family Relations, 1910 West County Road B, Suite 147, St. Paul, Minnesota 55113. Reprinted by permission.

held by males. That is, there was a consistent preference for dating and marrying someone who had no more than moderate sexual experience (up to light petting), regardless of the respondent's past sexual behavior. Even men and women who had much sexual experience showed a preference for dating and marrying partners with less experience than they themselves had. Jacoby and Williams refer to this as the "selfish standard."

Correlates of Premarital Sexual Behavior

What are the characteristics that differentiate adolescents according to premarital sexual behavior? Age, gender, race, emotional involvement, religiosity, sexual standards, peer attitudes and behavior, parental sexual attitudes, premarital sexual behavior of parents, and sex education are some of the major correlates of premarital sexual behavior.

Age

The proportion of never-married persons who participate in various types of premarital sexual activity increases with age, as shown earlier in Table 4·1. As one gets older the opportunities for sexual involvement generally increase.

Gender

As mentioned earlier, men are more likely than women to participate in premarital sexual activity, although gender differences have decreased somewhat in recent years. However, Roche (1986) found no differences between females and males at more advanced stages of dating. In fact, among those involved in serious romantic relationships (being engaged or being in love with only one person), more women than men engaged in heavy petting and sexual intercourse, as shown in Table 4·3. Thus, it is only at the early stages of dating that men are more permissive than women.

TABLE 4·3   Percentage Reporting Premarital Sexual Behavior by Dating Stage and Gender

Dating Stage	Light Petting		Heavy Petting		Sexual Intercourse	
	Females	*Males*	*Females*	*Males*	*Females*	*Males*
1. Dating with no particular affection	8	25	6	18	4	15
2. Dating with affection but not love	26	50	19	33	11	18
3. Dating and being in love	59	81	42	68	32	49
4. Dating one person only and being in love	88	92	82	81	68	63
5. Engaged	94	94	93	88	81	74

SOURCE: Adapted from Roche, J. P. 1986. Premarital sex: Attitude and behavior by dating stage. *Adolescence* 21:110, Table 1. Reprinted by permission.

Race

Premarital sexual intercourse is somewhat more frequent among blacks than whites. Among women between the ages of 15 and 19, about 65 percent of blacks have had premarital sexual intercourse compared to 39 percent of the whites (Shah and Zelnik 1981). The percentage of never-married American women ages 20 to 29 who have had premarital sexual intercourse is 90 among blacks and 80 among whites (Tanfer and Horn 1985). Blacks are also more likely than whites to be currently sexually active (Bachrach and Mosher 1984). However, among those who participate in premarital sex, whites are more promiscuous than blacks in that they have more partners and a greater frequency of intercourse (Zelnik, Kantner, and Ford 1981).

Emotional Involvement

Extent of emotional involvement with another person is positively associated with premarital sexual intercourse. At the early stages of dating, heavy petting and intercourse are relatively infrequent, although a large percentage of young people who are in love or engaged are involved sexually, as shown in Table 4·3 (Roche 1986). Even among those with restrictive sexual standards, premarital sexual intercourse tends to increase as emotional intimacy increases (DeLamater and MacCorquodale 1979).

Religiosity

Those who attend church regularly are less likely to have had premarital coitus (Christensen and Johnson 1978; Clayton 1972; DeLamater 1981; Hong 1983; Miller and Simon 1974; Thornton and Camburn 1987; Zelnik et al. 1981). Among women ages 15 to 19, those who were rated as low on religiosity were more than twice as likely to have had premarital sexual intercourse as those rated high on religiosity (Zelnik et al. 1981). In a study of never-married women ages 20 to 29, Tanfer and Horn (1985) found that only 67 percent of the very religious have had premarital coitus, compared to 85 percent of those who are somewhat religious, and 91 percent of those who are not at all religious.

Sexual Standards

The effects of sexual standards on sexual experience are shown in a national survey of women ages 15 to 19 by Shah and Zelnik (1981). Respondents were divided into three categories according to their sexual standards. The first standard was "sexual intercourse is okay, even if the couple has no plans to marry." The second standard was "sexual intercourse is okay, but only if the couple is planning to marry." The third standard was "sexual intercourse is never okay before marriage." Those who felt that premarital sexual intercourse is never acceptable had a much lower rate of premarital sexual intercourse, as shown in Table 4·4. For example, among whites who said premarital sex was never acceptable, only 7 percent had premarital sexual experience, compared to 74 percent among those who accepted premarital sexual intercourse. People may change their standards based on experience, but standards appear to be a fairly strong deterrent of premarital sexual behavior.

TABLE 4·4 Percentage of 15–19-Year-Old Women With Premarital Sexual Experience, by Respondent's Opinion on Premarital Sex, by Race

Respondent's Opinion on Premarital Sex	Black		White	
	Percentage	N	Percentage	N
Acceptable	84.1	345	73.5	310
Acceptable if engaged	61.7	193	52.4	580
Never acceptable	23.9	155	7.2	585

SOURCE: Shah, F., and M. Zelnick. 1981. Parent and peer influence on sexual behavior, contraceptive use, and pregnancy experience of young women. *Journal of Marriage and the Family* 43:342, Table 3. Copyrighted 1981 by the National Council on Family Relations, 1910 West County Road B, Suite 147, St. Paul, Minnesota 55113. Reprinted by permission.

Peer Attitudes and Behavior

The sexual attitudes and behaviors of close friends are associated with premarital sexual activity (Clayton 1972; DeLamater and MacCorquodale 1979; Schultz et al. 1977). Billy and Udry (1985) suggest that peer influence might be greater among females than males, and among whites than nonwhites. Not

Sexual attitudes and behaviors of adolescents are influenced by the attitudes and behaviors they observe in their peers. *Stephen Shames/Visions.*

only are people influenced by their friends, but they choose friends who have values similar to their own.

Parental Sexual Attitudes

Sexual attitudes and behavior tend to be influenced by the attitudes of parents. Mothers with more permissive attitudes tend to have children with more permissive attitudes, and children who are more sexually active (Thornton and Camburn 1987).

Parental Premarital Sexual Behavior

Research indicates that parental premarital sexual behavior may be associated with their children's premarital sexual behavior. Newcomer and Udry (1984) found that the sexual behavior of the mother when she was an adolescent was related to the current sexual behavior of her child. Those with premaritally experienced mothers were more likely to have had sexual intercourse than adolescents of mothers who had not been active premaritally. They hypothesize that biological as well as social factors influence this intergenerational transmission.

Thornton and Camburn (1987) found that adolescents had a higher probability of premarital sexual activity if their mothers had been pregnant premaritally. They suggest that mothers' premarital sexual behavior is related to mothers' attitudes, which in turn affect adolescent attitudes and behavior.

Sex Education

Data regarding the effects of **sex education** are inconclusive. In a national sample of adolescents between the ages of 15 and 16, Furstenberg, Moore, and Peterson (1985) found that the prevalence of sexual intercourse was 50 percent higher among those who had *not* had a course on sex education. Only 17 percent of those who had a sex education course reported sexual activity compared to 26 percent of those who had not had a sex education course (Furstenberg et al. 1985). On the other hand, Marsiglio and Mott (1986) found that adolescents ages 15 and 16 who took a sex education course had a slightly higher rate of sexual activity than adolescents who had not taken a sex education course. Marsiglio and Mott also found that adolescents who had received sex education were more likely to use **contraceptives** effectively, the net result being that sex education had little effect on pregnancy. Dawson (1986) reported that formal sex education had no effect on teenage sexual activity or on the risk of pregnancy among sexually active teenagers. Similarly, Hanson, Meyers, and Ginsburg (1987) found that sex education and birth control knowledge do not increase or decrease the chances of out-of-wedlock childbearing. All of the four studies described here used national probability samples. The conclusion is that sex education has no consistent effect on premarital sexual activity or fertility.

Most teenagers use no contraception when they begin having sexual intercourse. Sex education courses have been designed to inform teenagers about methods of contraception and encourage their use. *Dan Ford Connolly/Picture Group.*

Communication with Parents About Sex

Furstenberg et al. (1985) reported that adolescents who talked to their parents about sex tended to have lower levels of premarital sexual activity. Youths ages 15 to 16 who had neither talked to their parents about sex nor had a sex education course had the highest prevalence of sexual intercourse, 31 percent. Adolescents who had both talked to their parents about sex and had completed a sex education course had the lowest rate of premarital intercourse, 16 percent. Adolescents who either talked to their parents about sex or had a sex education course reported intermediate levels of sexual activity. It would appear that for adolescents who do not get sex education from their parents or from a sex education course, the risk of premarital sexual activity tends to be higher.

The findings of Furstenberg et al. (1985) suggest that communication with parents may help explain the contradictory results regarding the effects of sex education on premarital sexual behavior. Differences between youth who did and did not receive sex education were modest among those who talked to their parents about sex. However, among youth who did not talk to their parents, sexual activity was almost twice as high among those who did not receive sex education compared to those who did. Thus, in other research the effects of sex education on premarital sexual behavior may have not been evident because communication with parents about sex was not taken into account. It appears that sex education decreases premarital sexual activity among teenagers who do not talk to their parents about sex.

Other Factors

Unmarried women are less likely to be sexually active if they live with both natural parents, go to school, have high educational aspirations, and are employed (Newcomer and Udry 1987; Tanfer and Horn 1985; Zelnik et al. 1981). Premarital sex is more common among those who marry than among the never married (Zelnik et al. 1981). This is so partly because the anticipation of marriage acts to facilitate sexual activity, and partly because pregnancy may sometimes trigger a marriage.

Theories of Premarital Sexual Behavior

A large amount of research has been conducted on premarital sex, and it is difficult to integrate the many variables that may affect sexual attitudes and behavior. The influences of peers, parents, and religion suggest that interactional theory may be useful in understanding and explaining premarital sex. Sexual attitudes appear to be learned in the process of communication and interaction within small groups.

Gilbert, Bauman, and Udry (1986) use exchange theory to explain adolescent sexual behavior. They hypothesize that sexual behavior will increase as perceived rewards increase and perceived costs decrease. Some perceived rewards may be excitement, good physical feeling, making partner feel good, feeling more loved, and liking partner more. Perceived costs could be losing respect for self, worrying about pregnancy, losing respect of friends, parents finding out, and health risks. They examined how perceived rewards and costs were related to subsequent sexual behavior of adolescents. They found that perceived profit (rewards minus costs) was significantly related to subsequent premarital sexual behavior. Their research demonstrated that exchange theory is useful in organizing research findings and explaining premarital sexual behavior.

Contraception

One of the risks of premarital sexual activity is pregnancy. Almost all societies disapprove of childbirth outside of marriage, even those that permit premarital sexual activity (Goode 1982). There are three ways to avoid births outside of marriage. First, premarital sexual activity may be avoided. Second, contraception may be used. Third, abortion may be used to terminate any pregnancies that happen inadvertently. Some unmarried adolescents choose none of these alternatives and bear a child outside of marriage. In this section we will review the extent of contraceptive use among unmarried adolescents.

As premarital sexual activity has increased in America, greater numbers of teenagers have been exposed to the risk of premarital pregnancy. However, the increased pregnancy risk has been moderated to some extent by higher proportions of teenagers using contraception effectively and consistently (Ventura 1984). However, most never-married persons begin sexual intercourse long before they begin contraception. Sixty percent of young women use no contraception the first time they have sexual intercourse (Zelnik et al. 1981). In fact, the average time span between first intercourse and first contraceptive

Teenagers who become pregnant seldom think about the consequences for their lives, such as how caring for a young child may interfere with school, work, and other activities. Here a young single mother attempts to attend class and watch her son at the same time. *Ulrike Welsch.*

use is eight months, even though 80 percent have intercourse again within three months (Tanfer and Horn 1985).

The use of contraception varies according to age. Among women under age 14 at their first intercourse, less than 20 percent use any contraception at their first intercourse. However, among women who are 18 or 19 at first intercourse, more than 50 percent use a contraceptive device at their first intercourse (Zelnik et al. 1981).

The younger a woman at first intercourse, the longer it takes her to begin using contraceptives. It takes an average of two years for women who had their first intercourse at age 14, but only three months for women who had their first intercourse at age 18. One in five never-married women do not begin using contraceptives until after they experience a pregnancy (Tanfer and Horn 1985).

Almost half of the never-married women in the United States are currently exposed to the risk of pregnancy (currently sexually active and not sterile or pregnant). Among women ages 15 to 19, about one in three is exposed to the risk of pregnancy (Bachrach and Mosher 1984).

Among never-married women who are currently exposed to the risk of pregnancy, about one fourth are using no contraception. This percentage is greater among younger women. About one in three sexually active teenagers uses no contraception (Bachrach and Mosher 1984).

The most common method of contraception is the pill, followed by the condom and diaphragm. Among women ages 15 to 19, 62 percent use the pill,

22 percent the condom, and 6 percent the diaphragm (Bachrach and Mosher 1984). Relatively small percentages use the various other types of contraceptives. Younger women are more likely to use the pill or condom whereas older women are more likely to use sterilization, the diaphragm, or an intrauterine device (IUD). The condom is the most frequently used method at first intercourse, but its use decreases with time (Tanfer and Horn 1985).

Blacks are somewhat less likely than whites to use contraception, but are more likely than whites to use more effective birth control methods such as the pill (Tanfer and Horn 1985; Zelnik et al. 1981). Among never-married women ages 20 to 29, 40 percent of the blacks but only 23 percent of the whites used the pill at first intercourse (Tanfer and Horn 1985).

What are some characteristics associated with contraceptive use among the unmarried? Contraceptive use increases as women become older, and those who have experienced a pregnancy are more likely than others to begin using a contraceptive device (Zelnik et al. 1981). Family stability (living with both natural parents) and socioeconomic status are positively related to contraceptive use among teenagers. Polit-O'Hara and Kahn (1985) observed that unmarried adolescent couples with good communication patterns are more likely to practice effective contraception. Being religious, employed, and in school also are associated with contraceptive use among never-married women (Tanfer and Horn 1985).

Premarital Pregnancy

About one third of sexually active teenage women have a premarital pregnancy (Robbins, Kaplan, and Martin 1985; Tanfer and Horn 1985; Zelnik et al. 1981). What are characteristics associated with premarital pregnancy? One of the most important variables is age at first intercourse. The younger the age at first intercourse, the greater the length of exposure to the risk of pregnancy, which is positively correlated with the prevalence of premarital pregnancy (Tanfer and Horn 1985; Zelnik et al. 1981). Other variables that are associated with the risk of premarital pregnancy are family stress, father absence, low socioeconomic status (SES), and school difficulties (Robbins et al. 1985; Tanfer and Horn 1985).

Abortion

Once a pregnancy occurs, a woman must choose between abortion and childbirth. If the latter is chosen, she may put the child up for adoption or choose to rear the child herself. Both of these decisions may be affected by desires and opportunities for marriage.

Abortion has become a common choice among women who become pregnant. Excluding miscarriages and stillbirths, about 36 percent of all pregnancies are voluntarily terminated by abortion (Powell-Griner 1987).

Before 1973, abortions were illegal, except in cases where the pregnancy was a threat to the physical health of the mother or was the result of rape. In 1973, laws prohibiting abortion were declared unconstitutional by the U.S. Supreme Court in **Roe v. Wade** (410 U.S. 110). The court ruled that a woman's right to privacy guaranteed by the constitution includes her decision to terminate a pregnancy. *Roe v. Wade* made abortion legal and limited the degree to which states could regulate abortion. Later Supreme Court decisions established that a woman has a right to an abortion even if her parents or husband are opposed to it.

There has been much public debate about abortion since the *Roe v. Wade* decision. The attitude of the general public toward abortion is mixed. In a recent Gallup poll respondents were asked the following question: "The U.S. Supreme Court has ruled that a woman may go to a doctor to end pregnancy at any time during the first three months of pregnancy. Do you favor or oppose this ruling?" Forty-five percent favored the ruling, 45 percent opposed the ruling, and 10 percent had no opinion (*Gallup Report* 1986). The responses tended to be somewhat more favorable among the young, those with college degrees, and blacks.

More than 80 percent of Americans think women should be able to obtain a legal abortion if the woman's health is seriously endangered, if she became pregnant as a result of rape, or if there is a strong chance of a serious defect in the baby. However, those types of cases account for only a small minority of abortions in America. Less than half of Americans favor abortion if an unmarried woman becomes pregnant, if a married woman does not want the child, or if the family cannot afford the child (Granberg and Granberg 1980; Sackett 1985). The debate over abortion will undoubtedly continue, but abortion is here to stay. Recent Supreme Court decisions have affirmed that the abortion decision is a woman's private right that states may not interfere with (Ford 1983).

Following *Roe v. Wade*, the frequency of abortions in the United States rose dramatically. In 1972 there were about half a million legal abortions, and this increased to 1 million in 1975 and 1.5 million in 1980. Since 1980 the number of abortions has increased only slightly to 1.6 million (Powell-Griner and Trent 1987; U.S. Bureau of the Census 1986).

In 1972 there were less than two abortions for every ten live births. By 1975 there were more than three abortions for every ten births, and by 1980 there were about four abortions for every ten births. The ratio of abortions to live births has changed only slightly since 1980 (Powell-Griner 1987; U.S. Bureau of the Census 1986).

Women who obtain abortions tend to be unmarried and young, as shown in Table 4·5. Almost 80 percent of abortions are performed on unmarried women, and 60 percent are performed on women below age 25. More than one fourth are among women who are teenagers (Powell-Griner 1987; U.S. Bureau of the Census 1986).

Among unmarried women there are eleven abortions for every ten live births, compared to less than one abortion for every ten live births among the married. There is a curvilinear relationship between age and the **abortion ratio,** as shown in Table 4·5. The abortion ratio decreases with age up to age 35 and then after that point it increases with age. Women age 15 to 19 have seven abortions per ten live births, compared to two among women age 30 to 34 and seven among women over age 40.

Whites have almost three abortions for every ten births whereas blacks have about seven abortions for every ten births. For white women, abortion ratios

TABLE 4·5   Legal Abortions by Selected Characteristics

	Percentage Distribution	Abortions per 1,000 Live Births
Total	100.0	364
Age of Women:		
Less than 14	0.2	1947
14	0.8	1501
15–19	24.5	729
20–24	34.7	414
25–29	21.2	242
30–34	11.4	226
35–39	5.5	358
40 or more	1.5	692
Race:		
White	70.0	307
Black	30.0	646
Marital Status of Women:		
Married	21.9	68
Unmarried	78.1	1102

SOURCE: Powell-Griner 1987:2,4,11,12.

are lowest among women with college degrees. Among black women, abortion ratios tend to be lowest among women who have not completed high school (Powell-Griner 1987).

Among both blacks and whites, the unmarried have much higher abortion rates than the married. Among the married, blacks have an abortion ratio almost three times greater than whites. However, among the unmarried, the abortion ratio is three times greater among whites than blacks, as shown in Table 4·6. Unmarried whites have about sixteen abortions for every ten births, whereas unmarried blacks have only five abortions for every ten births.

About 60 percent of women who receive abortions have had no previous abortions or births. **Suction curettage** is the procedure used in 95 percent of abortions and complications are reported for less than 1 percent of all cases. **Saline instillation** is used in less than 2 percent of all abortions and accounts for 25 percent of all complications. Nine of ten abortions are performed in the first trimester of pregnancy and almost half are performed in the first eight weeks (Powell-Griner 1987).

Powell-Griner and Trent (1987) suggest that exchange theory is useful in explaining abortion decisions. They observed that women who tend to have abortions are those who find childbearing most costly. For example, unmarried

TABLE 4·6   Abortions Per 1,000 Live Births by Race and Marital Status

	Married	Unmarried	All
White	58	1625	243
Black	161	537	383
All	68	1102	263

SOURCE: Powell-Griner 1987:4.

women have much higher abortion rates than married women, and the costs of having a child are much greater for them. There are strong norms against nonmarital births, and being a parent is more difficult and expensive for a single than a married woman.

Another variable related to abortion is age, with abortion ratios being higher among those in their teens and those above age 35 than among those in their late twenties and early thirties (see Table 4·6). Teenagers may find pregnancies more costly than older women because their pregnancies are often unplanned and outside of marriage. Woman over age 35 are likely to find childbearing more costly than younger women because they probably have reached or surpassed their intended family size, and they have a greater risk of having complications or a defective fetus. Similarly, Powell-Griner and Trent (1987) used costs to explain differences in abortion ratios.

Premarital Births

Following pregnancy, some unmarried women do not choose abortion, but decide to have the child. Some marry before the birth of their child, but increasing numbers are having their children outside of marriage. In the United States, births to unmarried women have become a public concern. On December 9, 1985, the cover story of *Time* magazine was on teen pregnancy in America. The article noted the increasing incidence of sexual activity and pregnancy among teenagers, some reasons for the increase, and the social and economic costs associated with teenage pregnancy.

What are the facts regarding births to unmarried women in the United States? A summary of birthrates among all women and unmarried women is shown in Table 4·7. The following seven conclusions can be drawn from the data in the table:

1. Among both the married and unmarried, blacks have higher birthrates than whites.
2. Birthrates are much lower among unmarried than among married women.
3. Among blacks and whites, birthrates have decreased dramatically during the past twenty-five years. However, there has been a substantial increase in nonmarital births during the same time period.
4. Birthrates are much lower among teenagers than among women over age 20.
5. Among the unmarried, black fertility has been decreasing while white fertility has been increasing. This has led to a convergence of black and white unwed birthrates. In 1960 the birthrate of unmarried black women was more than ten times greater than the birthrate of unmarried white women. By 1984 unmarried births were less than four times greater among blacks than whites. Thus, the overall increase in births outside marriage during the past twenty-five years has been due to the white population.
6. There has been a steady increase in births to unmarried women between the ages of 15 and 19, from fifteen per thousand in 1960 to thirty per thousand in 1984.
7. Among unmarried women ages 20 to 24, the birthrate decreased from 1965 to 1975 but has increased since then.

TABLE 4·7   Birthrates by Race and Age for All Women and for Unmarried Women

	1960	1965	1970	1975	1980	1983
Births per 1,000 Women:						
All	118	97	88	66	68	65
Whites	113	91	84	63	65	62
Blacks	154	133	115	88	88	81
Ages:						
15–19 years	89	71	68	56	53	51
20–24 years	258	195	168	113	115	107
25–29 years	197	162	145	108	113	108
30–34 years	113	94	73	52	62	67
Births per 1,000 Unmarried Women:						
All	22	24	26	25	29	31
Whites	9	12	14	12	18	20
Blacks	98	98	96	84	81	77
Ages:						
15–19 years	15	17	22	24	28	30
20–24 years	40	40	38	31	41	43
25–29 years	45	49	37	28	34	37
30–34 years	28	38	27	18	21	23

SOURCE: U.S. Bureau of the Census 1986:59,61.

The decrease in marital fertility along with the increase in white nonmarital fertility has produced a large increase in the ratio of nonmarital to marital births. As shown in Table 4·8, births to unmarried women were only 5 percent of all births in 1960. By 1980 they had increased to 18 percent of all births, and in 1985 they were 22 percent of all births.

Table 4·9 shows first births by time period, age, and marital status of mother. Among young teenagers (ages 15 to 17) the proportion of first births that were premarital increased from 22 percent to 57 percent over a thirty-year period. Among teenagers between the ages of 18 and 19, the comparable percentages were 14 percent and 40 percent. These figures show the dramatic increase in nonmarital births among the unmarried.

What are some of the characteristics associated with nonmarital births? Hanson et al. (1987) found that steady dating had a stronger association with premarital childbearing than any other variable. They reported that sex ed-

TABLE 4·8   Births to Unmarried Women as Percentage of All Births by Race and Year

	1960	1965	1970	1975	1980	1985
Total	5	8	11	14	18	22
White	2	4	6	7	11	14
Black	NA	NA	38	49	55	60
Hispanic	NA	NA	NA	NA	NA	30

SOURCE: U.S. Bureau of the Census 1986:61; National Center for Health Statistics 1987:31; Ventura 1988:9.

TABLE 4·9   Percentage Distribution of All First Births by Period, Age, and
Marital Status of Mother

		Period of First Birth						
		1947–1952	1952–1956	1957–1964	1965–1966	1967–1971	1972–1976	1977–1982
Age:								
15–17	Premarital births	22	26	31	34	46	53	57
	Premarital conceptions	20	25	24	28	32	27	24
	Postmarital conceptions	58	49	45	38	22	20	18
18–19	Premarital births	14	12	14	16	21	32	40
	Premarital conceptions	12	15	21	27	30	27	24
	Postmarital conceptions	74	74	65	57	50	41	36
20–24	Premarital births	5	5	6	8	10	13	16
	Premarital conceptions	6	7	8	10	12	10	10
	Postmarital conceptions	89	87	86	82	78	77	74
25–29	Premarital births	3	3	4	6	4	4	4
	Premarital conceptions	4	2	4	4	4	3	5
	Postmarital conceptions	93	95	92	90	92	93	91

NOTE: Some of the percentages do not total 100 because of rounding error.
SOURCE: U.S. Bureau of the Census 1985:63.

ucation and knowledge of contraception were not related to the chances of
having a child outside of marriage. However, when adolescents and parents held
values that stressed responsibility, teenage childbearing was significantly lower.
Hanson et al. (1987) also noted that young women were less likely to have a
child outside of marriage if they had high educational expectations and had
parents who were concerned about and monitored their activities.

In their study of women between ages 15 and 19, Zelnik et al. (1981) observed
that women were much more likely to have an illegitimate child if they were
in the lowest rather than highest socioeconomic status level. Teenagers who
lived with both natural parents were less likely to have a child before marriage
than teenagers who lived in single-parent homes. Conversely, Zelnik et al.
(1981) found that girls from stable, upper-class families were more likely to
marry if they became pregnant. Furthermore, pregnant women in their later
teens were more likely to marry than those in their younger teens, and whites
were more likely to marry than blacks.

Of all unmarried teenage women who are pregnant, about one in three
marries before her child is born. Thirty years ago the comparable percentage
was about one in two (O'Connell and Rogers 1984). The decrease in proportion
of pregnant women who marry has been particularly dramatic among blacks.
In 1950 about 26 percent of pregnant, unmarried black women married before
the birth of their first child, compared to only 9 percent in 1980. Comparable
percentages for whites are 60 percent and 51 percent (O'Connell and Rogers
1984).

The negative consequences of out-of-wedlock births have been well documented (Moore et al. 1979; Nye 1976; O'Connell and Rogers 1984; Simkins
1984; Ventura 1984). Women who do not marry face the difficult task of raising

and supporting a child alone. They often discontinue their education, which reduces their employability and income prospects. Those who marry have relatively high rates of marital disruption; almost 30 percent have separated from their husbands within five years of the marriage. By comparison, only 18 percent of women who are not pregnant at marriage separate within five years of their marriage (O'Connell and Rogers 1984). Women who have a child before marriage tend to have relatively low family incomes, particularly if their marriage fails (O'Connell and Rogers 1984).

Factors that lessen the welfare dependence of unmarried mothers are (1) support from the family of origin (2) education, and (3) increased career motivation (Burden and Klerman 1984). Thompson (1986) examined how various social supports influence the stress associated with mothering and general psychological well-being among teenage mothers. She found that whites had significantly more stress than blacks and speculated that this may be due to better family and community support mechanisms within black culture. White families may not have developed coping strategies for the complex life changes that accompany teenage childbearing as blacks have. Thompson also found that psychological well-being was higher among those who had completed high school and among those who received support from a male companion. Education may increase the opportunities and coping responses of a young woman, and the support from a male may help fulfill needs of attachment and security as well as economic needs. These data suggest that alleviating the negative consequences of early childbearing will require support from community, family, and friends.

Summary

1. Gender identity and sexual behavior are influenced strongly by socialization, especially from family and peers.
2. There are four premarital sexual standards in America: (a) abstinence, (b) the double standard, (c) permissiveness with affection, and (d) permissiveness without affection. Permissiveness with affection is the most popular standard in America today among the unmarried. Sexual standards are influenced by parents, religion, peers, and sexual behavior.
3. At least eight out of ten women and nine out of ten men have sexual intercourse before marriage. More men than women participate in premarital sex but recent increases have been greater among women than men. This has reduced male and female differences.
4. There is some evidence of a new double standard in which dating and marriage preference is for someone with little sexual experience, even though one has had premarital sexual experience.
5. The prevalence of premarital sex increases with age. Males participate in premarital sex more than females, although gender differences have decreased in recent years.
6. Blacks participate in premarital sex more than whites, although among the sexually active, whites are more promiscuous than blacks.
7. The more one is emotionally involved, the more likely that premarital sexual activity will occur.

8. Those who attend religious services regularly and have standards against premarital sex are less likely to have had premarital sexual intercourse.

9. One's sexual behavior is related to the attitudes and sexual behavior of one's friends.

10. Adolescents whose parents accept premarital sex are more likely to participate in premarital sex than adolescents whose parents do not accept premarital sex. Adolescents whose parents had premarital sex are more likely to participate in premarital sex than adolescents whose parents did not have premarital sex. Communication with parents about sex and having a sex education course tend to decrease premarital sexual activity.

11. Most adolescents do not use contraception at the time they first have premarital sexual intercourse. The average length of time between first intercourse and use of contraception is eight months.

12. Blacks are less likely to use contraception than whites, but blacks who use contraception are more likely to use effective methods.

13. The most common form of contraception is the pill, followed by the condom.

14. About one third of sexually active adolescents experience at least one pregnancy. Pregnancy is more likely to occur among women with early first intercourse, low socioeconomic status, absent father, school difficulties, and high family stress.

15. Abortion became legal after the U.S. Supreme Court ruled in *Roe v. Wade* that a woman's right to privacy includes the right to terminate her pregnancy. Less than one half of Americans favor the Supreme Court decision in *Roe v. Wade*.

16. After *Roe v. Wade* there was a dramatic increase in the number of abortions in the United States. There are presently more than 1.5 million abortions per year. Eighty percent of abortions are performed on unmarried women and 25 percent on teenage women.

17. The ratio of abortions to live births was two to ten in 1972, while today it is almost four to ten. Among the unmarried, there are about eleven abortions per ten live births, whereas among the married there is less than one abortion per ten live births. Abortions are more frequent among blacks, but unmarried whites have more abortions than unmarried blacks.

18. Birthrates are substantially lower among the unmarried than married, and among teenagers than those over age 20. Among the married and unmarried, birthrates are higher among blacks than whites.

19. There has been a large *decrease* in the marital birthrate and a substantial *increase* in the nonmarital birthrate.

20. Births have been decreasing among unmarried blacks and increasing among unmarried whites. Thus, the increase in unwed births in the United States has been due largely to increases in nonmarital fertility among whites.

21. Births among the unmarried were 5 percent of all births in 1960, whereas in 1985 they were 22 percent of all births.

22. Nonmarital births are more common among those who date steadily, do not live with both parents, and are in the lowest socioeconomic group. When parents care about and monitor their daughter's activities and emphasize responsibility, the chances of their daughter having a child out-of-wedlock are decreased. High educational expectations are also associated with lower rates of nonmarital childbearing.

23. Some of the major negative consequences of nonmarital births are interruption of education of the mother, low family income, and divorce.

Important Terms

- abortion ratio
- abstinence
- contraception
- double standard
- new double standard
- permissiveness with affection
- permissiveness without affection
- *Roe v. Wade*
- sex education
- sexual socialization
- suction curettage

Questions for Discussion

1. What are the major institutions that influence sexual standards and behavior? How strong is their influence?
2. How have premarital sexual standards changed in recent years?
3. How might sexual behavior have an influence on one's premarital standards?
4. In America about how many men and women have sex before they are married?
5. What is the new double standard in America?
6. In recent years whose behavior (men or women) has changed the most? How?
7. Identify how each of the following variables are related to premarital sexual behavior: age, gender, race, emotional involvement, religion, sexual standards, peers, parents, communication with parents about sex, sex education, and family structure.
8. About how long, after first intercourse, do unmarried persons begin using contraceptives?
9. Why do so many couples have premarital intercourse without using some form of contraception?
10. What are some social characteristics that are related to higher use of contraceptives?
11. What are the differences between blacks and whites in contraceptive use?
12. What are the most common methods of contraception?
13. About what percentage of women become pregnant before marriage in the United States?
14. What are some of the social characteristics that are associated with probability of premarital pregnancy?
15. About how many abortions occur out of every ten pregnancies?
16. Summarize the major finding in *Roe v. Wade*.
17. What is the attitude of people in the United States toward *Roe v. Wade*?
18. How have abortion rates changed since *Roe v. Wade*?
19. What is the ratio of abortions to live births in the United States? How has this changed during the past twenty-five years?

20. What is the ratio of abortions to births among the unmarried and among the married?
21. About what proportion of abortions are performed on unmarried women?
22. What is the most common method of abortion?
23. Summarize what you know about birthrates among the married, unmarried, blacks, and whites.
24. With increased use of contraception and abortion, one would expect that the rate of pregnancies among the unmarried would have decreased. Why has the rate of pregnancy increased?
25. What are some of the major negative consequences of unwed births?
26. What evidence do you have that sexual drives are socially rather than biologically determined?
27. How have sexual standards in America changed in recent years?
28. What are the differences between whites and blacks in births to unmarried women? How have these rates changed in recent years?
29. What might be done to decrease the rate of premarital pregnancy and out-of-wedlock births?
30. What might be done to lessen the negative economic consequences of nonmarital births?

Recommended Reading

HANSON, S. L., D. E. MEYERS, and A. L. GINSBURG. 1987. The role of responsibility and knowledge in reducing teenage out-of-wedlock childbearing. *Journal of Marriage and the Family* 49:241–256.

POLIT-O'HARA, D., and J. R. KAHN. 1985. Communication and contraceptive practices in adolescent couples. *Adolescence* 20:33–43.

References

BACHRACH, C. A., and W. P. MOSHER. 1984. *Use of contraception in the United States, 1982.* Advance Data from Vital and Health Statistics, no. 102, DHHS Publication No. (CPHS) 85–1250. Hyattsville, MD: Public Health Service.

BILLY, J. O. G., and J. R. UDRY. 1985. The influence of male and female best friends on adolescent sexual behavior. *Adolescence* 77:21–32.

BURDEN, D. S., and L. V. KLERMAN. 1984. Teenage parenthood: Factors that lessen economic dependence. *Social Work* 29 (1):11–16.

CHRISTENSEN, H. T., and L. B. JOHNSON. 1978. Premarital coitus and the southern black: A comparative review. *Journal of Marriage and the Family* 40:721–732.

CLAYTON, R. R. 1972. Premarital sexual intercourse: A substantive test of the contingency consistency model. *Journal of Marriage and the Family* 34:273–281.

DAWSON, D. A. 1986. The effects of sex education on adolescent behavior. *Family Planning Perspectives* 18:162–170.

DELAMATER, J. 1981. The social control of sexuality. *Annual Review of Sociology* 7:263–290.

DELAMATER, J., and P. MACCORQUODALE. 1979. *Premarital sexuality: Attitudes, relationships, behavior.* Madison: University of Wisconsin Press.

FORD, N. 1983. The evolution of a constitutional right to an abortion. *The Journal of Legal Medicine* 4 (3):271–322.

FURSTENBERG, F. F., JR., K. A. MOORE, and J. L. PETERSON. 1985. Sex education and sexual experience among adolescents. *American Journal of Public Health* 75:1331–1332.

GALLUP REPORT. 1986. *Public remains divided on 1972 abortion ruling.* Gallup Report nos. 244–245 (January–February):17–18.

GILBERT, M. A., K. E. BAUMAN, and J. R. UDRY. 1986. A panel study of subjective expected utility for adolescent sexual behavior. *Journal of Applied Social Psychology* 16:745–756.

GOODE, W. J. 1982. *The family.* (2d ed.). Englewood Cliffs, NJ: Prentice-Hall.

GRANBERG, D., and B. W. GRANBERG. 1980. Abortion attitudes, 1965–1980: Trends and determinants. *Family Planning Perspectives* 12 (5):250–260.

HANSON, S. L., D. E. MEYERS, and A. L. GINSBURG. 1987. The role of responsibility and knowledge in reducing teenage out-of-wedlock childbearing. *Journal of Marriage and the Family* 49:241–256.

HARLOW, H. F. and M. K. HARLOW. 1962. Social deprivation in monkeys. *Scientific American* 207:137–147.

HONG, S. 1983. Gender, religion, and sexual permissiveness: Some recent Australian data. *The Journal of Psychology* 115:17–22.

HUNT, M. 1974. *Sexual behavior in the 1970s.* Chicago: Playboy Press.

JACOBY, A. P., and J. D. WILLIAMS. 1985. Effects of premarital sexual standards and behavior on dating and marriage desirability. *Journal of Marriage and the Family* 47:1059–1065.

MARSIGLIO, W., and F. L. MOTT. 1986. The impact of sex education on sexual activity, contraceptive use and premarital pregnancy among American teenagers. *Family Planning Perspectives* 18:151–162.

MILLER, P. Y., and W. SIMON. 1974. Adolescent sexual behavior: Context and change. *Social Problems* 22:58–76.

MOORE, K. A., S. L. HOFFERTH, S. B. CALDWELL, and L. J. WAITE. 1979. *Teenage motherhood: Social and economic consequences.* Washington, DC: The Urban Institute.

NATIONAL CENTER FOR HEALTH STATISTICS. 1987. *Advance report of final natality statistics, 1985.* Monthly Vital Statistics Report, vol. 36, no. 4, Supp., July 17. DHHS Pub. No. (PHS) 87–1120. Hyattsville, MD: Public Health Service.

NEWCOMER, S. F., and J. R. UDRY. 1984. Mothers' influence on the sexual behavior of their teenage children. *Journal of Marriage and the Family* 46:477–485.

NEWCOMER, S. F., and J. R. UDRY. 1987. Parental marital status effects on adolescent sexual behavior. *Journal of Marriage and the Family* 49:235–240.

NYE, F. I. 1976. *School-age parenthood: Consequences for babies, mothers, fathers, grandparents, and others.* Extension Bulletin 667. Cooperative Extension Service, Washington State University, Pullman, WA.

O'CONNELL, M., and C. C. ROGERS. 1984. Out-of-wedlock births, premarital pregnancies and their effect on family formation and dissolution. *Family Planning Perspectives* 16(4):157–162.

POLIT-O'HARA, D., and J. R. KAHN. 1985. Communication and contraceptive practices in adolescent couples. *Adolescence* 20(77):33–43.

POWELL-GRINER, E. 1987. *Induced terminations of pregnancy: Reporting states, 1984.* Monthly Vital Statistics Report, vol. 36, no. 5, Supp. (2). DHHS Pub. No. 87–1120. Hyattsville, MD: Public Health Service.

POWELL-GRINER, E., and K. TRENT. 1987. Sociodemographic determinants of abortion in the United States. *Demography* 24:553–561.

REISS, I. L. 1960. *Premarital sexual standards in America.* New York: Free Press.

REISS, I. L. 1967. *The social context of premarital sexual permissiveness.* New York: Holt.

REISS, I. L. 1980. *Family systems in America.* 3d ed. New York: Holt.

ROBBINS, C., H. B. KAPLAN, and S. S. MARTIN. 1985. Antecedents of pregnancy among unmarried adolescents. *Journal of Marriage and the Family* 47:567–583.

ROBINSON, I. E., and D. JEDLICKA. 1982. Change in sexual attitudes and behavior of college students from 1965 to 1980: A research note. *Journal of Marriage and the Family* 44:237–240.

ROCHE, J. P. 1986. Premarital sex: Attitude and behavior by dating stage. *Adolescence* 21:107–121.

SACKETT, V. 1985. Split verdict: What Americans think about abortion. *Policy Review* 32:18–19.

SCHULTZ, B., G. BOHRNSTEDT, E. BORGATTA, and R. EVANS. 1977. Explaining premarital sexual intercourse among college students: A causal model. *Social Forces* 56:148–165.

SHAH, F., and M. ZELNIK. 1981. Parent and peer influence on sexual behavior, contraceptive use, and pregnancy experience of young women. *Journal of Marriage and the Family* 43:339–348.

SIMKINS, L. 1984. Consequences of teenage pregnancy and motherhood. *Adolescence* 19(73):39–54.

SPRECHER, S., K. McKINNEY, and T. L. ORBUCH. 1987. Has the double standard disappeared?: An experimental test. *Social Psychology Quarterly* 50:24–31.

TANFER, K., and M. C. HORN. 1985. Contraceptive use, pregnancy and fertility patterns among single American women in their 20's. *Family Planning Perspectives* 17(1):10–19.

THOMPSON, M. S. 1986. The influence of supportive relations on the psychological well-being of teenage mothers. *Social Forces* 64:1006–1024.

THORNTON, A., and D. CAMBURN. 1987. The influence of the family on premarital sexual attitudes and behavior. *Demography* 24:323–340.

U.S. BUREAU OF THE CENSUS. 1985. *Statistical abstract of the United States: 1986.* Washington, DC: U.S. Government Printing Office.

U.S. BUREAU OF THE CENSUS. 1986. *Statistical abstract of the United States: 1987.* Washington, DC: U.S. Government Printing Office.

VENTURA, S. J. 1984. *Trends in teenage childbearing, United States, 1970–81.* Vital and Health Statistics. Series 21, no. 41. DHHS Pub. No. (PITS) 84–1919. Washington, DC: Public Health Service, U.S. Government Printing Office.

VENTURA, S. J. 1988. *Births of Hispanic Parentage, 1985.* Monthly Vital Statistics Report, vol. 36, no. 11, Supp. DHHS Pub. No. (PHS) 88–1120, February 26. Hyattsville, MD: Public Health Service.

ZELNIK, M., J. F. KANTNER, and K. FORD. 1981. *Sex and pregnancy in adolescence.* Beverly Hills, CA: Sage.

CHAPTER 5

Dating and Mate Selection

Introduction

On their first date, Lorraine and Michael enjoyed each other's company and discovered that they had similar likes and dislikes. This made it easy to talk to each other and soon they began to share intimate aspects of their lives. As they got to know each other better, they found that their values were similar and that they had compatible goals. As their relationship developed they began to see themselves as a couple and to be viewed by others as a pair.

Michael and Lorraine dated all during the school year and Michael went home to meet Lorraine's parents during spring vacation. Michael proposed to Lorraine just before his graduation in May and they set their wedding date for August.

In almost all cultures marriage is considered to be the most normal and desirable status for adults. About 95 percent of all persons in the United States eventually marry and if the marriage fails most marry again (Bahr 1986; U.S. Bureau of the Census 1986).

The process of mate selection varies across cultures. In some cultures marriages are arranged by the parents and romantic love has little influence on the outcome. Occupational skills and family status usually are important criteria in arranging marriages and dating plays little or no part in the mate selection process.

In other cultures, including the United States, mate selection is considered to be the choice of the individuals who marry. In these societies **dating** is important as a means for young people to meet, interact, and choose someone to marry. The U.S. Supreme Court has ruled that the right of individuals to marry whoever they choose is guaranteed by the Constitution (**Loving v. Virginia** 388 U.S. 1, 1967). Even when mate choice is considered to be free, there are a variety of direct and indirect ways in which family, friends, and the larger culture influence mate selection.

In this chapter we examine the process of mate selection. We begin with a brief discussion of how mate selection is influenced by the broader culture. Then we examine the purpose and nature of dating. This is followed by a review of theories of mate selection and a discussion of the nature of love and how it develops. We conclude with an examination of cohabitation as a stage in the mate selection process.

Cultural Influences on Mate Selection

The type of family system in a culture is related to the extent to which mate selection is free. In societies with complex extended families, such as ancient China, mate selection tended to be arranged. In societies with nuclear families, free choice of mate tends to be the norm.

This issue was examined in detail by Lee and Stone (1980). They compared **family complexity** and mate selection in 117 different societies. They found that romantic love and free mate selection usually went together and were less common among cultures with extended families than among those with nuclear families. Free mate selection was also more common among cultures with neolocal residence customs. Neolocal residence means that couples establish their own residence apart from both families of orientation.

Upon reflection, it is understandable why arranged marriages are more common in cultures with extended family systems. In such societies a marriage adds a new member to the existing family, and the other family members will have to live in the same household as the new couple. On the other hand, in a nuclear family system new couples establish separate households and kin therefore do not have as much to lose if the mate choice is poor.

In all cultures and subcultures, norms define a field of eligibles who are considered acceptable marriage partners, and there tends to be a preference for marrying someone similar to oneself in social class, race, and ethnic group. Even when mate selection is "free" there is social pressure to date and marry someone similar to oneself, and social activities tend to be structured by social status and ethnic group. For example, a woman from an upper-class family may be discouraged from dating men from the lower class. She is likely to live in an upper-class neighborhood and attend a prestigious college, and therefore, most of the men she associates with are likely to come from a social background similar to hers. Lower-class men may have social characteristics that she finds unattractive, and may not be able to achieve occupationally what she would prefer. Resesarch continues to show that people tend to marry others who are similar to themselves in race, social status, and religion (Glenn 1982; Goode 1982).

Dating

In recent years there has been a trend in many cultures toward more autonomy in mate selection (Murstein 1980). For example, in Japan and China mate selection is changing from an arranged to a free choice system as the nuclear family becomes more common (Lee and Stone 1980). When mate selection becomes more autonomous, dating becomes more important in the process of selecting a spouse.

In cultures with free mate selection, dating has at least three purposes. First, dating is an important aspect of adolescent socialization. It provides opportunities to interact with the opposite sex and learn how to relate to them. Second, dating is recreational and is enjoyable in its own right. Third, dating allows young people to meet and evaluate potential mates. It enables them to get to know attractive people and see if they would make a suitable spouse.

In some groups, dating partners are rated according to their prestige and ability to provide a thrill rather than on characteristics of more meaningful relationships. To be highly rated as a date a man must be well dressed and prominent in activities, have money and a nice car, dance well, and be a "smooth" talker. A highly rated woman must be good looking and popular, and have nice clothes, a smooth line, and the ability to dance well.

Because this type of dating is oriented toward thrills and exploitation rather than mate selection, Willard Waller (1937) called it the **rating dating complex.** Although exploitive dating undoubtedly continues in many places, Gordon (1981) thinks that it was more common during the 1920s than it is today. Prestige, good looks, popularity, and smoothness are still important, but Gordon did not find dating to be as exploitive as described by Waller.

Choosing a Mate

In recent years mate selection has become more autonomous in many countries of the world. Increasingly young people have freedom to choose their mate without direct influence from their parents. Social conditions in many countries in Asia and Africa are changing to allow greater choice in mate selection (Murstein 1980). For example, in the Soviet Union a large majority of marriages are love matches (Perevedentsev 1983). In China and Japan the number of arranged marriages is diminishing, particularly in urban areas (Engel 1984).

In a system of free mate selection, what are the characteristics that influence the choice of mate? Why are two people attracted to each other and how does their relationship develop? Why do some relationships continue while others are terminated? These are age-old questions that are difficult to answer. Nevertheless, romantic attraction is influenced by identifiable social characteristics. There are stages of progression that characterize the development of intimacy in many couples. In this section we will review what is known about the development of romantic relationships.

Homogamy Theory

Perhaps the most common explanation for romantic attraction is the **homogamy theory** or "birds of a feather flock together." According to this theory we tend to be attracted to someone who is like ourselves.

A substantial amount of research is consistent with the theory of homogamy. Hill, Rubin, and Peplau (1979) studied 220 couples in the Northeast, 103 who had broken up and 117 who had stayed together. They found dating partners who were similar in age, educational plans, and intelligence were more likely to stay together. Differences in interests, backgrounds, sexual attitudes, and ideas about marriage were common reasons given for breakups.

People tend to marry others who are similar with regard to age, race, IQ, education, socioeconomic status, and religion (Murstein 1980). There is also evidence that marriage partners tend to have similar interests, values, and personalities. Sternberg (1986) found that similarity is an important ingredient in the development of love relationships. People are more likely to develop

People tend to date others who are like themselves, as shown by these college couples in sports cars and similar attire. *Read D. Brugger/The Picture Cube.*

relationships with and marry people who are similar to themselves, and they tend to be happier in those relationships than couples who are less similar.

Chambers, Christiansen, and Kunz (1983) found that similarity of physical features may also affect mate selection. They took pictures of both partners of newly married and engaged couples. Judges were asked to try to match couples and to consider facial features as well as general body build and coloring of hair, skin, and eyes. The judges were able to match couples much more frequently than would be expected by chance. Chambers et al. concluded that similar physical appearance is one factor in the formation of interpersonal relationships.

There are several possible ways that individuals may become similar physically to their spouses. It may be the result of a narcissistic tendency to marry someone like yourself. Perhaps people feel attracted to and choose someone who resembles a parent. Whatever the mechanism, their findings suggest that homogamy theory works not only for values and personality traits, but also for physical features.

Complementary Need Theory

Another explanation of mate choice is Winch's (1958) **complementary need theory.** Although Winch acknowledged that sociocultural characteristics may determine a field of eligibles, he maintained that complementary personality traits are a major determinant of romantic attraction. For example, Winch hypothesized that a person who is nurturant will be attracted to a person who needs to be nurtured. Similarly, a strong, dominant personality may be attracted to one who is more submissive. The basic idea of Winch's theory is that two people will be more compatible and develop romantic attraction if they have complementary personality traits. Some have labeled this the opposites attract theory, because the matching traits are on opposite ends of a continuum, that is, dominance and submissiveness.

Winch (1967) found some support for three different types of complementariness: (1) nurturance-receptiveness; (2) dominance-submissiveness; and (3) achievement-vicariousness. Kerckhoff and Davis (1962) found some evidence that complementary needs operated after initial homogamous filtering. However, in a number of other studies no support was found for complementary needs as a basis for mate selection (Murstein 1980; Winch 1967). Overall, there is little support for the idea that people are attracted to and marry someone with a complementary personality. In fact, the evidence suggests just the opposite, that we tend to be attracted to someone with personality characteristics similar to our own.

However, there is some evidence that individuals with feelings of personal inadequacy are more likely to be attracted to someone with complementary traits. For example, individuals high in self-acceptance tend to be similar to their spousees in personality, whereas individuals with low self-acceptance tend to be less similar to their spouse (Murstein 1980). This suggests that some people may seek a mate who compensates for their deficiencies.

Filter Theory

Theories of homogamy and complementary needs are too simplistic, in that they do not adequately deal with the development of a relationship over time. Kerckhoff and Davis (1962) attempted to capture the dynamic nature of mate selection by combining homogamy and complementary needs into a two-stage process called the **filter theory.** They hypothesized that social similarity and value consensus are important early on, but that complementary needs are important later in the development of a relationship. According to their theory, homogamy acts as an initial filter and couples who do not have similar social characteristics and values will tend to break up.

Dating partners with simiilar values will move to the second filter, which is complementary needs. If they do not have complementary needs they will tend to break up, even if they have similar values. Thus, according to Kerckhoff and Davis, both value consensus and complementary needs are important for the development of a relationship.

The filter theory of Kerckhoff and Davis was important because it integrated homogamy and complementary need theories, and it viewed mate selection as an ongoing process. However, research has not supported the complementary need aspect of Kerckhoff and Davis' theory (Murstein 1980; Winch 1967).

Stimulus-Value-Role Theory

Murstein (1970, 1971, 1980) developed a process theory of mate selection called the **stimulus-value-role theory.** He maintains that attraction depends on the exchange of assets and liabilities that each persons brings to the relationship.

In his theory three types of variables influence the relationship. In the *stimulus* stage, attraction is based on good looks, social skills, reputation, and mental abilities. Individuals are drawn to each other based on an equitable exchange of these characteristics. In the *value* stage couples assess their attitudes and values regarding marriage, sex, and life to determine if they are compatible.

The third stage is an assessment of *role compatibility.* It is an examination of how self and partner will perform in various marital roles, including provider, housekeeper, sexual partner, and child trainer. Each person has expectations regarding the various roles in marriage, and in this stage there is an assessment of how well they anticipate that their expectations will be met.

Research supports many aspects of the stimulus-value-role theory. Murstein (1980) found some support for thirty-three of thirty-nine hypotheses relevant to his theory. Partners who passed through the stimulus and value stages tended to be similar in physical attractiveness and values. Degree of perceived similarity was related to self-acceptance; those with high self-acceptance were more likely to perceive that their partner was like themselves. Individuals who

Couples who date and marry tend to have similar social characteristics, and often are similar in physical features. *Jeff Dunn/The Picture Cube.*

successfully passed through all three stages were likely to cohabit or marry. Physical attractiveness, value similarity, role compatibility, self-acceptance, and sex drive were all found to be related to mate choice.

There was evidence of a bargaining process in which personal assets and liabilities are assessed and equity is sought. Murstein (1980) found that the degree of choice in mate selection depends on the number of personal assets and liabilities. Real choice occurs only among those with many interpersonal assets and few liabilities. In the bargaining, individuals with limited assets or many liabilities often *settle* for each other rather than really choosing each other.

There is some question about the exact sequence of the stages in the stimulus-value-role theory. Murstein (1980) acknowledged that the three sets of variables may all operate during the courtship process, although he maintained that each set of variables operated primarily at one stage.

Lewis' Theory of Premarital Dyadic Formation

Lewis (1972) reviewed existing literature on mate selection and identified six pair processes that he hypothesized operate in a fixed developmental sequence (called the theory of **premarital dyadic formation**). The first stage is the process of perceiving similarities. According to Lewis, **perceived similarities** is a necessary condition for further development of a relationship. When couples perceive that they are similar they tend to feel positive about each other and are likely to become more involved. If they perceive that they are dissimilar in values, interests, or personality, they will probably discontinue the relationship. Thus, perceived similarity is important as a selection-rejection mechanism at the early stages of dating relationships.

The second stage of relationship development is the process of achieving **pair rapport.** In this stage there is an attempt to communicate and develop rapport with the other person. Unless people feel that they can talk to their dating partner, the relationship will tend to be unsatisfying and will probably be dissolved. Ease of communication appears necessary for early dating relationships to continue.

The third process, according to Lewis, is the development of **self-disclosure.** After couples perceive that they are similar and develop some rapport, they tend to become more open and disclose themselves to each other. Self-disclosure tends to be reciprocal in that as one person discloses the other is more likely to disclose.

The fourth stage is the development of role taking. When people disclose themselves, others are able to understand their perspective and role take more accurately. Research has confirmed that **role-taking accuracy** is correlated with the stage of involvement in a relationship. Lewis suggests that role-taking accuracy operates as a selection-rejection mechanism at later stages of dyadic involvement. If one is not able to role take accurately or empathize with the other person, happiness will decrease and misunderstanding will result. On the other hand, if one feels that the other is able to empathize and see things from his or her point of view, the relationship is more likely to continue and and develop.

The fifth stage in the process is achieving **interpersonal role fit.** This is a process of fitting two personalities together. It includes identifying personality similarities and differences and the extent to which the two people will be able to work together. Adequate role fit depends on achieving some consensus on the division of roles. Perceiving how you and your potential partner will fit together in earning the money, making decisions about spending money, having and raising children, and caring for the house are all important role decisions. As a couple achieves a reasonable consensus on who performs various role tasks, they are more likely to stay together. Other research has shown that conflicts between role expectations and actual role performance influence marital satisfaction (Bahr, Chappell, and Leigh 1983; Burr et al. 1979; Rollins and Galligan 1978).

The final stage in relationship development is the process of achieving **dyadic crystallization.** During this stage the two partners form an identity as a couple, establish boundaries with the outside world, and increase their commitment and involvement. They begin to function as a dyad and view things more in terms of *we* rather than *me.*

Lewis hypothesized that these six stages are sequential and that development of one stage does not occur until the previous stage is completed. That is, usually couple rapport will not be developed until the partners perceive that they are similar, and self-disclosure tends to occur only after they develop some rapport. Self-disclosure is necessary before role taking will be accurate, and role-taking ability is needed to determine role fit. Only after two people perceive that they have role compatibility will they gain an identity as a couple.

Lewis' theory is consistent with much existing research and appears logical. Lewis (1973) tested his theory on ninety-one dating couples over a period of two years. The data supported the theory, particularly for the middle stages of the model. Pair rapport affected development of self-disclosure, which influenced role-taking accuracy, which was significantly related to later development of role fit. Although similarity of perception was not strongly related to pair rapport and role fit did not have a strong influence on dyadic crystallization, there was some support for both processes. Overall, Lewis found support for twenty-nine of thirty-five hypotheses derived from his theory.

The research of Shea and Adams (1984) supports Lewis' theory in that they found a positive relationship between self-disclosure and the development of romantic love. Hill et al. (1979) found that dating couples that did not break up tended to have similar values and role compatibility, findings that are consistent with the theories of both Lewis and Murstein.

Lewis' theory of premarital dyadic formation could be used in a variety of ways. His six stages might be useful in evaluating dating relationships. For example, one could determine the degree to which a given couple has completed the six processes. One would predict that dating couples who do not complete each process are more likely to break up than couples who do. One might counsel others not to become engaged or marry unless they have obtained a reasonable degree of self-disclosure, role-taking accuracy, and role fit.

Examining these six processes might provide clues as to why a given relationship is not progressing or dissolves. Lack of development at one stage may explain why many dating couples break up, even though they may be compatible in many ways. Lewis' theory suggests that feelings of attraction depend on intimacy as well as on practical concerns such as division of labor and role fit. A pair may be very similar in social characteristics, but if they are not able to self-disclose, the relationship is likely to break up or be unhappy. Even if they have high self-disclosure and high role-taking accuracy, they are likely to run into difficulties if they do not have adequate role fit. Furthermore, psychological problems or inappropriate social skills may preclude adequate development at a given stage and lead to the breakup of a dating relationship. For example, a fear of intimacy or the inability to express individual feelings would inhibit the development of self-disclosure and role-taking accuracy.

The theory would predict that couples who have short courtships and do not establish all of these processes would have less happiness and a greater chance of divorce. Finally, the theory could be used to examine the marital dissolution process. It is possible that couples go through these six stages in reverse order during the process of alienation that precedes divorce. The extent to which alienation is a deterioration of these six processes needs to be explored.

Other Characteristics

There are a variety of variables which may influence choice of mate that are not explicitly included in existing theories. **Fear of intimacy** and parental approval are two variables that appear to influence the mate selection process.

FEAR OF INTIMACY.   Some people have a fear of close relationships, which blocks the development of intimacy. In a study of 107 women between the ages of 18 and 36, Lutwak (1985) found that about one third had a strong fear of intimacy. The women feared getting hurt in an emotional relationship and therefore would not let themselves become too involved emotionally. They tended to resist risk taking and had a strong need for safety and security.

When one loves another person there is always the possibility of disappointment, misunderstanding, and hurt. Intimacy opens one's inner self to another, which makes each person vulnerable. Intimate relationships always have some problems and pain. Fitting two people's lives together creates some mutual dependency.

The women who feared intimacy were afraid of dependency and felt the possibility of hurt was not worth the risk of trying. They would not let themselves become involved in an intimate relationship because it would make them vulnerable to hurt, including a possible loss of identity.

People with a strong fear of intimacy will have difficulty disclosing themselves and forming the bonds needed for a close, emotional relationship. This will inhibit role taking and good communication. Thus, even if two people are reasonably well matched in terms of background, values, and personality, they will not be able to develop good self-disclosure, role-taking ability, and role fit if they have a strong fear of intimacy.

We do not know how prevalent fear of intimacy is in the general population. In Lutwak's (1985) college sample, about one third of the women had a strong fear of intimacy. Research in the general population is needed to determine the extent to which individuals fear intimacy and the effect of this on the development of relationships.

PARENTAL INVOLVEMENT.   In the study by Hill et al. (1979), pressure from parents was the reason given by some for terminating their dating relationships.

Leslie, Huston, and Johnson (1986) studied this issue more closely using 159 college students over a four-month period. They found that parents usually supported their children in their dating, particularly if their children were highly involved. However, parental support did not have a significant influence on relationship development.

Johnson and Malardo (1984) studied the extent to which parents, siblings, relatives, and friends interfered with dating relationships. They found that there was little interference at the early or later stages of dating. However, negative interference by parents or relatives sometimes occurred at the intermediate stages of involvement, which is when a couple begins dating regularly but before any formal commitments are made. Interference at this stage may reflect anxiety of friends and parents as existing relationships are altered and the possibility of a commitment is approached.

Comparison of Murstein's and Lewis' Theories

The major difference between Murstein's and Lewis' theories is that Murstein's is derived from a more general theory of social exchange and Lewis' is an interaction theory. According to Murstein, mate selection is a bargaining process in which characteristics are evaluated and exchanged. First there is an assessment of personal characteristics, then an examination of attitudes and values, followed by an evaluation of role compatibility. Throughout these three stages, Murstein emphasizes that attraction is based on an exchange of personal assets and liabilities. Lewis' theory, on the other hand, focuses more on perceptions, communication, and role taking than on exchange.

In both theories the initial attraction appears to be based on social simi-

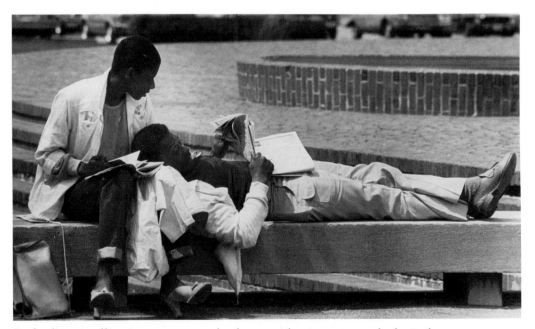

As dyadic crystallization occurs, couples form an identity as a couple, begin functioning as a unit, and develop boundaries.   *Ellis Herwig/The Picture Cube.*

larities, although Murstein emphasizes the exchange value of personal characteristics rather than similarity. It appears that exchange value is usually higher when characteristics are similar.

The last stage of Murstein's theory is similar to Lewis' fifth stage. Murstein calls it an *assessment of role compatibility* whereas Lewis uses the term *role fit*. Both seem to refer to the degree to which various marital roles are compatible. Again, Murstein focuses more explicitly on bargaining to achieve role fit.

Lewis' emphasis on communication is shown in stages 2 through 4, with the development of rapport, self-disclosure, and role taking. These processes are not explicit in Murstein's stages, although they might be important in the bargaining process.

In both Murstein's and Lewis' theories, fear of intimacy and parental involvement could affect relationship development. Fear of intimacy may interfere with bargaining and cause one to perceive that a potential exchange is too costly. Similarly, fear of intimacy may inhibit self-disclosure that is needed for relationship development. Strong parental disapproval could affect relationship bargaining as well as limit communication and the perception of role fit.

Love

The development of love is an important aspect of the mate selection process. In societies with free mate choice one of the primary criteria for marriage is love. Most young people would not think of marrying someone they do not love.

What is love? Although it is considered to be the basis for marriage, it is difficult to define. According to Sternberg (1986) love is composed of three elements: (1) intimacy, (2) passion, and (3) commitment.

The intimacy component refers to feelings of closeness, bondedness, and connectedness. **Intimacy** includes sharing feelings, giving emotional support, being understood, and having high personal regard for the other. Intimacy is the most important element of love, according to Sternberg.

A second aspect of love is **passion,** which is a state of intense longing for association with another. Sexual desires are an important part of passion, although it also includes needs of self-esteem, nurturance, and affiliation.

The third aspect of love in Sternberg's theory is the **commitment** component. This consists of the decision to love and a commitment to the love.

Using these three components, Sternberg has identified a taxonomy of eight different **types of love,** as shown in Table 5·1. *Nonlove* is when there is no intimacy, passion, or commitment. *Liking* is feeling warmth and closeness without passion or commitment. *Infatuated love* is an intense attraction without intimacy or commitment. In *empty love* there is commitment but nothing else. *Romantic love* has intimacy and passion but no long-term commitment. *Companionate love* includes personal intimacy and commitment but no passion. The term *fatuous* means mindless or silly, and *fatuous love* is based on passion and commitment but does not have intimacy. Finally, *consummate love* has all three elements and is the type of love many people strive for.

TABLE 5·1   Taxonomy of Kinds of Love

Kinds of love	Intimacy	Passion	Commitment
Nonlove	−	−	−
Liking	+	−	−
Infatuated love	−	+	−
Empty love	−	−	+
Romantic love	+	+	−
Companionate love	+	−	+
Fatuous love	−	+	+
Consummate love	+	+	+

NOTE: + = component present; − = component absent.
SOURCE: Sternberg, R. G. 1986. A triangular theory of love. *Psychological Review* 93:123. Copyright 1986 by the American Psychological Association. Reprinted by permission of the author.

Attaining consummate love, however, is no guarantee that it will continue.

Sternberg did not suggest any developmental ordering of his types of love. In some romantic relationships intimacy develops before passion, such as the friendship that later turns into a romance. In others, passion occurs before intimacy, such as an intense infatuation or "love at first sight," which develops into romantic love as intimacy develops.

The theories of Murstein and Lewis imply that passion tends to precede intimacy. For example, passion is probably one major component of the stimulus stage in Murstein's theory. Similarly, in Lewis' theory the development of intimacy (i.e., rapport, self-disclosure, and role taking) tends to occur after an initial attraction that is based partly on passion.

The theories of Murstein and Lewis also suggest that intimacy tends to precede commitment. In Murstein's theory, commitment comes in the final stage of relationship development, whereas in Lewis's formulation, dyadic crystallization includes a decision to operate as a pair and a commitment to that decision.

Thus, there may be a pattern or developmental sequence in Sternberg's types of love that could be predicted from the theories of Murstein and Lewis. It could be hypothesized that infatuated love would tend to precede romantic love which would tend to precede consummate love. With time, consummate love may evolve into companionate love for some couples. If intimacy decreases with time, companionate love might turn into empty love. There is no prediction for liking, because the theories suggest that passion tends to precede intimacy. Because intimacy appears to precede commitment, it is predicted that there would be relatively few couples with fatuous love and that they would have a higher-than-average dissolution rate because of the lack of intimacy. Research is needed to determine the frequency of these different types of love and how they change in the mate selection process.

The feelings of love toward another depend not only on feelings of self for other, but also on perceived feelings of other for self (Sternberg 1986). This finding suggests that **reciprocity** is important in the development of love and that love develops incrementally as there is mutual self-disclosure.

Although the development of love relationships is a gradual process, Berg and McQuinn (1986) have observed that differences between dating relationships that continue and those that terminate are apparent early in a relationship. They interviewed thirty-eight heterosexual couples who had recently begun dating and reinterviewed both partners four months later. At both interviews they obtained extensive information about the relationship, including amount of self-disclosure and feelings of satisfaction, love, and closeness. They found that couples who were still dating after four months had experienced more self-disclosure and feelings of love at the initial interview than couples who had broken up. The differences between the couples intensified over time. Berg and McQuinn concluded that the stability of a dating relationship can be predicted fairly accurately early in the relationship. Their research suggests that intimacy is a critical element in relationships and that infatuated and fatuous relationships will tend to be unstable because of their lack of intimacy.

Cohabitation

There has been a large increase in premarital cohabitation in the United States during the past fifteen years. In 1985 the number of cohabiting couples was almost four times greater than the number in 1970 (U.S. Bureau of the Census 1986). In a national survey of never-married women between age 20 and 29, Tanfer (1987) found that 30 percent had cohabited at some time in their lives, and 12 percent were currently cohabiting. In a study of marriage license applications in Oregon, Gwartney-Gibbs (1986) found that 53 percent were cohabiting in 1980.

Cohabitation is defined as two unrelated adults of the opposite sex who share the same household. In 1985 there were approximately two million unmarried couples in the United States, and they comprised about 4 percent of all couples (Spanier 1983; U.S. Bureau of the Census 1986). Most of the increase in unmarried cohabitation has occurred among relatively young adults. About half of all cohabiting persons have been previously married, and three in ten unmarried couples have one or more children present in the household (Spanier 1983).

Tanfer (1987) examined some of the characteristics that differentiate cohabitors from noncohabitors. Women with less than a high school education were three times more likely to cohabit than women with a college degree. Cohabitors were more likely to come from a single-parent family and tended to start their sexual careers earlier than women who had not cohabited. There was no difference between black and white women in the proportion that had cohabited or were cohabiting. Women with no religious preference were almost twice as likely to have cohabited as women with a religion (Tanfer 1987). Compared to couples who do not cohabit, couples who cohabit tend to be less homogamous in terms of age, previous marital status, and race (Gwartney-Gibbs 1986; Skolnick 1981).

There appears to be very little difference between cohabitors and noncohabitors on a variety of issues, including self-esteem and sex role attitudes (Tanfer 1987). Couples that cohabit appear no less likely to marry or break up than noncohabiting couples (Hill et al. 1979; Risman et al. 1981). However, cohabitors seem to experience more intimacy and self-disclosure than noncohabiting couples, but less commitment to the relationship than married couples (Risman et al. 1981; Skolnick 1981).

Cohabitation tends to be viewed as a step in the courtship process rather than as an alternative to marriage (Tanfer 1987). It is an intermediate stage or trial marriage, which has less commitment than marriage but more commitment than steady dating. Cohabitors tend to accept marriage as the ideal and a large majority want to marry and think they will marry (Gwartney-Gibbs 1986; Lewin 1982; Risman et al. 1981; Skolnick 1981; Tanfer 1987). Thus, the wedding has become a rite of transition rather than a rite of confirmation.

In summary, cohabitation has become part of the courtship process for a significant number of Americans. It is not viewed as an alternative to marriage but as a stage in the transition to marriage. The decision to cohabit is usually made without any parental involvement, and often without even informing the parents. Parental involvement in courtship has decreased during the past century and cohabitation seems to reduce that involvement even further.

Summary

1. Romantic love and free mate selection tend to go together and are less common in societies with extended family systems.
2. Dating has at least three purposes. It is enjoyable, it helps adolescents learn to interact with the opposite sex, and it provides a way for young people to choose a mate.
3. The rating dating complex is a situation where dating is oriented toward exploitation and thrills rather than toward the development of lasting relationships.
4. Dating and mate selection have become more autonomous in many countries of the world.
5. According to homogamy theory, we are attracted to people similar to ourselves in social and personality characteristics. Research is consistent with homogamy theory in that people tend to choose spouses who are similar to themselves in age, race, religion, education, socioeconomic status, values, personality, and physical features.
6. Complementary need theory asserts that we are attracted to individuals with personality characteristics opposite from ourselves. Much research is not consistent with complementary need theory, except that individuals low in self-acceptance tend to marry someone with traits different from themselves.
7. The filter theory of Kerckhoff and Davis hypothesized that matching on social characteristics and values is the first stage in the mate selection process, and matching on complementary needs is the second stage.
8. According to stimulus-value-role theory, mate selection is an exchange process that has three stages. First, attraction is based on personal characteristics such as good looks, personality, social skills, and reputation. Second, there is a matching of attitudes and values. The third stage is an examination of how well two people fit in terms of role expectations.
9. There are six sequential processes in Lewis' theory of premarital dyadic formation: (1) perceive similarities, (2) achieve pair rapport, (3) develop

        self-disclosure, (4) learn to role take accurately, (5) achieve interpersonal role fit, and (6) crystallize as a dyad.

10. Some individuals have difficulty developing close relationships because fear of intimacy interferes with the development of self-disclosure and the establishment of interdependency.

11. Dating and mate selection tend not to be influenced directly by parental desires and involvement.

12. Love is a combination of intimacy, passion, and commitment. The theories of Murstein and Lewis suggest that passion tends to precede intimacy which tends to precede commitment.

13. Feelings of love depend on reciprocity; that is, they depend on feelings of other for self as well as on feelings of self for other.

14. The amount of love and self-disclosure exhibited early in a dating relationship is predictive of the stability of that relationship.

15. There has been a fourfold increase in the number of couples living together without marriage. Unmarried couples comprise about 4 percent of all couples in the United States.

16. Cohabitation is a stage in the courtship process between steady dating and marriage. Most cohabitors accept the ideal of marriage, intend to marry, and say children should be raised in a legal marriage.

Important Terms

- cohabitation
- commitment
- complementary need theory
- dating
- dyadic crystallization
- family complexity
- fear of intimacy
- filter theory
- homogamy theory
- interpersonal role fit
- intimacy

- *Loving v. Virginia*
- pair rapport
- passion
- perceived similarities
- premarital dyadic formation
- rating dating complex
- reciprocity
- role-taking accuracy
- self-disclosure
- stimulus-value-role theory
- types of love

Questions for Discussion

1. How is family structure related to the type of mate selection in a society?
2. What are three functions of dating? Are there other purposes of dating that were not mentioned in the chapter?
3. Describe the rating dating complex.
4. To what extent does the rating dating complex exist among your reference group? Give evidence to support your answer.
5. Identify as much evidence as you can that supports homogamy theory. Identify as much evidence as you can that is not consistent with homogamy theory.
6. Do opposites attract? If so, in what ways?

7. How is dating and mate selection a bargaining process?
8. Do couples go through a series of stages in courtship, as suggested by Murstein and Lewis?
9. How might Murstein's theory be used to evaluate a dating relationship?
10. How might Lewis' theory be used to evaluate a dating relationship?
11. Identify some personality characteristics that might retard the development of intimacy.
12. To what extent and in what ways do parents and friends influence dating and mate selection?
13. Give a specific example of each of the eight types of love identified by Sternberg.
14. How is reciprocity related to the development of love?
15. Does love take time to develop or does it develop very quickly? Explain.
16. Are the findings of Berg and McQuinn consistent with Lewis' theory? In what ways?
17. What are some motivations for cohabitation?
18. How are cohabiting and noncohabiting couples similar, and how are they different?
19. Is cohabitation a stage in the mate selection process or is it a variant family form? Explain.
20. How has cohabitation affected mate selection in the United States?

Recommended Reading

BERG, J. H., and R. D. McQUINN. 1986. Attraction and exchange in continuing and noncontinuing dating relationships. *Journal of Personality and Social Psychology* 50:942–952.

STERNBERG, R. J. 1986. A triangular theory of love. *Psychological Review* 93:119–135.

References

BAHR, S. J. 1986. Family formation. In *Utah in demographic perspective,* ed. T. K. Martin, T. B. Heaton, and S. J. Bahr, 71–89. Salt Lake City: Signature Books.

BAHR, S. J., C. B. CHAPPELL, and G. K. LEIGH. 1983. Age at marriage, role enactment, role consensus, and marital satisfaction. *Journal of Marriage and the Family* 45:795–803.

BERG, J. H., and R. D. McQUINN. 1986. Attraction and exchange in continuing and noncontinuing dating relationships. *Journal of Personality and Social Psychology* 50:942–952.

BURR, W. R., G. K. LEIGH, R. D. DAY, and J. CONSTANTINE. 1979. Symbolic interaction and the family. In *Contemporary theories about the family,* vol. 2, ed. W. R. Burr, R. Hill, F. I. Nye, and I. Reiss, 42–111. New York: Free Press.

CHAMBERS, V. J., J. R. CHRISTIANSEN, and P. R. KUNZ. 1983. Physiognomic homogamy: A test of physical similarity as a factor in the mate selection process. *Social Biology* 30:151–157.

ENGEL, J. W. 1984. Marriage in the People's Republic of China: Analysis of a new law. *Journal of Marriage and the Family* 46:955–961.

GLENN, N. D. 1982. Interreligious marriage in the United States: Patterns and recent trends. *Journal of Marriage and the Family* 44:555–566.

GOODE, W. J. 1982. *The family.* 2d ed. Englewood Cliffs, NJ: Prentice-Hall.

GORDON, M. 1981. Was Waller ever right? The rating and dating complex reconsidered. *Journal of Marriage and the Family* 43:67–76.

GWARTNEY-GIBBS, P. A. 1986. The institutionalization of premarital cohabitation: Estimates from marriage license applications, 1970 and 1980. *Journal of Marriage and the Family* 48:423–434.

HILL, C. T., Z. RUBIN, and L. A. PEPLAU. 1979. Breakups before marriage: The end of 103 affairs. In *Divorce and separation*, ed. G. Levinger and O. Moles, 64–82. New York: Basic.

JOHNSON, M. P., and R. M. MALARDO. 1984. Network interference in pair relationships: A social psychological recasting of Slater's theory of social regression. *Journal of Marriage and the Family* 46:893–899.

KERCKHOFF, A. C., and K. E. DAVIS. 1962. Value consensus and need complementarity in mate selection. *American Sociological Review* 27:295–303.

LEE, G. R., and L. H. STONE. 1980. Mate-selection systems and criteria: Variation according to family structure. *Journal of Marriage and the Family* 42:319–326.

LESLIE, L. A., T. L. HUSTON, and M. P. JOHNSON. 1986. Parental reactions to dating relationships: Do they make a difference? *Journal of Marriage and the Family* 48:57–66.

LEWIN, B. 1982. Unmarried cohabitation: A marriage form in a changing society. *Journal of Marriage and the Family* 44:763–773.

LEWIS, R. A. 1972. A developmental framework for the analysis of premarital dyadic formation. *Family Process* 11:17–48.

LEWIS, R. A. 1973. A longitudinal test of a developmental framework for premarital dyadic formation. *Journal of Marriage and the Family* 35:16–25.

LUTWAK, N. 1985. Fear of intimacy among college women. *Adolescence* 20:15–20.

MURSTEIN, B. I. 1970. Stimulus-value-role: A theory of marital choice. *Journal of Marriage and the Family* 32:465–481.

MURSTEIN, B. I. 1971. A theory of marital choice and its applicability to marriage adjustment. In *Theories of attraction and love*, ed. B. I. Murstein, 100–151. New York: Springer.

MURSTEIN, B. I. 1980. Mate selection in the 1970s. *Journal of Marriage and the Family* 42:777–792.

PEREVEDENTSEV, V. I. 1983. The Soviet family today. *Sociology and Social Research* 67:245–259.

RISMAN, B. J., C. T. HILL, Z. RUBIN, and L. A. PEPLAU. 1981. Living together in college: Implications for courtship. *Journal of Marriage and the Family* 43:77–83.

ROLLINS, B. C., and R. J. GALLIGAN. 1978. The developing child and marital satisfaction of parents. In *Child influences on marital and family interaction*, ed. R. M. Lerner and G. B. Spanier, 71–105. New York: Academic.

SHEA, J. A. and G. R. ADAMS. 1984. Correlates of romantic attachment: A path analysis study. *Journal of Youth and Adolescence* 13:27–44.

SKOLNICK, A. 1981. The social contexts of cohabitation. *Journal of Comparative Law* 29:339–358.

SPANIER, G. B. 1983. Married and unmarried cohabitation in the United States: 1980. *Journal of Marriage and the Family* 45:277–288.

STERNBERG, R. J. 1986. A triangular theory of love. *Psychological Review* 93:119–135.

TANFER, K. 1987. Patterns of premarital cohabitation among never-married women in the United States. *Journal of Marriage and the Family* 49:483–497.

U.S. BUREAU OF THE CENSUS. 1986. *Statistical abstract of the United States: 1987.* Washington, DC: U.S. Government Printing Office.

WALLER, W. 1937. The rating and dating complex. *American Sociological Review* 2:727–734.

WINCH, R. F. 1958. *Mate-selection: A study of complementary needs.* New York: Harper.

WINCH, R. F. 1967. Another look at the theory of complementary needs in mate selection. *Journal of Marriage and the Family* 29:756–762.

CHAPTER 6

Adjusting to Marriage

Introduction

Lorraine and Michael were married in a Protestant church in Chicago. Members of both families were at the wedding along with some close friends from high school and college. Michael is 23, recently completed his college degree in computer science, and has just begun a job with a firm in Chicago. Lorraine is 21, has completed two years of college, and plans to continue her education in Chicago. They want to have one or two children but plan to wait a year or two before beginning their family. Lorraine and Michael love each other and are looking forward to living together and raising a family.

Michael and Lorraine discover that living intimately with another person requires accommodation and compromise. They now see each other in many new situations, including when the other is unkempt and tired. Each has personal habits that are annoying to the other. For example, Michael is very neat and always places his clothes in the laundry basket when he undresses. Lorraine, however, has always dropped her clothes on the floor when she undresses. This bothers Michael because he doesn't like his place to be cluttered. Lorraine feels like it is no big deal, because it doesn't really dirty the place and she usually picks things up the next day. On the other hand, Michael doesn't rinse the sink out carefully when he shaves and this leaves a residue. This seems rather thoughtless to Lorraine who likes her bathroom fixtures to be clean.

Another adjustment for Michael and Lorraine is learning to fit their different recreational interests together. He loves to play tennis and has several friends that he frequently plays with. She gets irritated at the amount of time he plays tennis, particularly if he doesn't consult her before he makes his plans.

They also must decide on a reasonable division of labor within and outside the household, and learn to jointly manage their resources. They are used to making purchases without consulting anyone, and now they must take into account the other's wishes.

No matter how well two people are matched or how much they are in love, differences will emerge that require adjustment. Some couples are able to adjust to each other and find marriage to be fulfilling and satisfying. Others find that many of their marital expectations are not met and become disappointed and unsatisfied with their marriage.

In this chapter we look at how individuals adjust to being married and identify variables that influence marital quality. We begin by examining how marriage may affect one's health. Then we explore gender differences in marital roles and how they are related to stress and mental health. Next is an analysis of marital communication followed by a review of correlates of marital satisfaction.

Marriage and Health

Compared to unmarried persons, married individuals are happier, healthier, and less prone to premature death (Gove 1972; Haring-Hidore et al. 1985; Veenhoven 1983). This is true among women as well as men, and research among Mexican Americans and Europeans has produced similar results (Markides and Farrell 1985; Veenhoven 1983; Verbrugge and Madans 1985). Gove, Hughes, and Styles (1983) found that marital status was a better overall predictor of mental health than education, income, age, race, or childhood background.

What is there about marriage that promotes health and happiness? There

Married individuals tend to be happier and healthier than unmarried persons because the intimacy of marriage helps them withstand various stresses. *Ulrike Welsch.*

are two possible explanations. First, those who are healthier and happier may be more likely to marry. Healthy, well-adjusted persons make better spouses and will be more attractive to potential mates. Individuals with serious physical or mental problems may have difficulty getting married. If they get married, perhaps they are at greater risk of divorce. The net result is that those with better mental and physical health have a greater chance of marrying and staying married.

The second explanation is that marriage may buffer or shield individuals from stresses that produce physical and mental illness. The intimacy of marriage may insulate one from the effects of various stresses and thereby lead to better health.

There is considerable evidence that marriage does insulate individuals from the effects of various stresses. Pearlin and Johnson (1977) found that married persons were significantly less depressed than formerly or never-married persons. The relationship between marital status and depression persisted even after the effects of sex, age, and race were accounted for. There was a large difference between the widowed and married in depression, a difference that would not appear to be accounted for by selection. A summary of the research is shown in Table 6·1.

Pearlin and Johnson studied the effects of three specific strains: economic stress, social isolation, and parental responsibilities. To measure **economic stress** they asked respondents how often they do not have enough money to afford adequate food, medical care, and clothing. Regardless of marital status, depression was more common among those with severe economic stress, and a greater proportion of unmarried than married faced such a crisis. However, Pearlin and Johnson also observed that the unmarried had greater vulnerability to depression under conditions of severe economic stress. For example, for those experiencing economic hardship only 26 percent of the married were very depressed compared to 50 percent of the unmarried. The difference between depressed marrieds and unmarrieds increased as economic stress became more severe, as shown in Table 6.2. The same patterns occurred when married persons were compared with the never married, widowed, or divorced and separated.

Another strain examined by Pearlin and Johnson was **social isolation.** Respondents were asked (1) how many really good friends they had, (2) how long they had lived in the neighborhood, and (3) about voluntary associations. These

TABLE 6·1   Marital Status and Depression (Percentages)

Depression	Married	Never Married	Formerly Married	Types of Formerly Married		
				Widowed	Divorced	Separated
High 1	12	20	27	22	27	32
2	14	18	20	22	14	25
3	18	23	17	15	16	23
4	29	24	18	21	22	10
Low 5	27	16	18	20	21	10
N =	(1589)	(288)	(415)	(172)	(141)	(102)
	Gamma = .26					

SOURCE: Pearlin and Johnson 1979: 707, Table 1. Reprinted by permission.

TABLE 6·2 Economic Strains, Marital Status, and Depression (Percentages)

Depression	Severe Strain		Moderate Strain		No Strain	
	Married	Unmarried	Married	Unmarried	Married	Unmarried
High 1	26	50	19	29	9	15
2	17	15	22	21	12	18
3	8	12	16	27	19	17
4	26	16	27	13	30	26
Low 5	23	7	16	10	30	24
N =	(73)	(92)	(335)	(220)	(1175)	(383)
	Gamma = .43		Gamma = .24		Gamma = .17	

SOURCE: Pearlin and Johnson 1977: 708, Table 2. Reprinted by permission.

items were pooled to form an index of isolation from extrafamilial relations. Compared to the married, the unmarried were more likely to be depressed by a given amount of isolation. For example, among those with considerable isolation, 28 percent of the unmarrieds were highly depressed compared to only 13 percent of the marrieds. The difference between unmarrieds and marrieds in depression was greater under conditions of high isolation, as shown in Table 6·3.

Economic stress can have an adverse effect on marriages. This family has just learned that they have lost their farm. *Stephen Shames/Visions.*

TABLE 6·3   Social Isolation, Marital Status, and Depression (Percentages)

	Considerably Isolated		Fairly Isolated		Not Isolated	
Depression	Married	Unmarried	Married	Unmarried	Married	Unmarried
High 1	13	28	11	24	11	21
2	15	19	13	15	14	16
3	18	19	18	20	19	22
4	28	21	30	21	29	20
Low 5	26	13	28	20	27	21
N =	(270)	(200)	(315)	(135)	(957)	(343)
	Gamma = .32		Gamma = .35		Gamma = .20	

SOURCE: Pearlin and Johnson 1977: 710, Table 3. Reprinted by permission.

The third type of strain examined by Pearlin and Johnson was amount of parental responsibility, which was measured by the number of children at home. Only among the unmarried was there an association between parental responsibility and depression. Among the unmarried the percentage of highly depressed persons increased from 20 percent among those with no children, to 26 percent among those with one or two children, to 34 percent among those with three or more children. The rate of depression among persons who were married did not vary by number of children (see Table 6·4).

Pearlin and Johnson concluded that married persons withstand various stresses better than single persons. Married persons had less depression even when there were no strains, but differences between married and single persons in depression were greatest when circumstances were the most difficult.

Research by Kessler and Essex (1982) is consistent with Pearlin and Johnson's findings. They examined economic strain, housework strain, and parental strain. Married people were exposed to the strains as frequently as the non-marrieds, but had significantly less depression. Kessler and Essex concluded that married people are emotionally less damaged by stressful experiences than unmarried people. Overall, the data suggest that marriage helps individuals withstand various stresses (Gove et al. 1983).

What is there about marriage that helps people withstand stress? It seems to be the quality of the marital relationship rather than marital status per se that affects mental health. For example, Gove et al. (1983) found that individuals

TABLE 6·4   Number of Children at Home, Marital Status, and Depression (Percentages)

	Number of Children					
	Three or More		One or Two		None	
Depression	Married	Unmarried	Married	Unmarried	Married	Unmarried
High 1	12	34	12	26	11	20
2	12	18	14	20	17	19
3	16	17	19	24	20	19
4	31	16	28	18	27	23
Low 5	29	15	27	12	25	19
N =	(458)	(89)	(715)	(179)	(416)	(435)
	Gamma = .42		Gamma = .36		Gamma = .19	

SOURCE: Pearlin and Johnson 1977: 711, Table 4. Reprinted by permission.

in unhappy marriages had poorer mental health than individuals who were not married. Similarly, Kessler and Essex (1982) observed that intimacy was an important resource that accounted for some of the differences between the mental health of marrieds and unmarrieds. Russell et al. (1984) found that emotional loneliness was the best predictor of depression, and that individuals with romantic friendships had much less emotional loneliness.

A spouse is a companion, someone who cares, listens, and supports the other partner in times of trouble. On the other hand, individuals in unhappy marriages will not feel intimacy and support, and the result is that they are no different from single people in rates of mental illness.

Women, Marriage, and Stress

Some researchers have suggested that being married is more stressful for women than men, and causes married women to have poorer mental health than married men (Bernard 1972; Gove 1972). They have argued that for women marital roles are confining, stressful, and limit their opportunities. In short, they maintain that marriage may be beneficial for men but performing traditional marital roles makes women sick.

There are three ways in which marriage might create stress for women. First, the career development of women is often restricted when they marry. Their primary role is wife and mother, and career development is subordinated to family demands. This often results in delaying or terminating educational and occupational desires while the husband pursues his occupational goals. Second, women are assigned the child care and housekeeping roles that do not provide intellectual stimulation, prestige, power, or money. Third, married women who work still perform most of the household chores (Coverman and Sheley 1986). Thus, women are in a double bind. If they don't work they sacrifice career development; if they do work they have the dual burden of employment and household chores.

Although marriage may create stress for women, all available data show that married women have better mental and physical health than single women. Either married women have less stress than single women, or the intimacy of marriage insulates married women from the effects of the stresses. The research of Pearlin and Johnson (1977) and Kessler and Essex (1982) suggests that the intimacy of marriage reduces the negative effects of stresses among married women, particularly under conditions of high stress. Having a good marriage was associated with good mental health among women and men according to Gove et al. (1983).

Even though married women have better mental health than single women, marriage still may be more stressful for women than men. Cleary and Mechanic (1983) studied this issue among a sample of one thousand people in a midwestern community. They found little difference between men and women in role satisfaction, support, or amount of stress. Nevertheless, women had more depression than men when faced with similar strains. They concluded that it is important to distinguish between the presence and the impact of the strain.

Cleary and Mechanic found that the combination of being a parent and working contributes to depression in women but not in men. Employed married women had slightly less depression than housewives, but employed women with children at home had more depression than housewives with children at home. Apparently, the dual demands of being employed and being a mother were stressful for women because they tended to do a majority of the child care and household chores when they were employed (Coverman and Sheley 1986).

A study in Los Angeles produced similar conclusions (Aneshensel, Frerichs, and Clark 1981). Men were less depressed than women, and married persons were less depressed than unmarried persons. The largest sex differences in depression existed when children were in the household, again suggesting that parenthood is more stressful for women than men.

Verbrugge (1986) has studied how male and female roles are associated with physical health. She found that poor physical health is associated with few roles or excessive role demands. Women more often than men had very low or very high demands, which affected their health. This difference in roles may account for some of the difference in the mental health of married men and women.

In a cross-national comparison, D'Arcy and Siddique (1985) found a difference between married men and women in distress. Although both married men and women had better psychological health than single men and women, married women had more anxiety and depression than married men. Role overload, social isolation, poor quality of family life, and economic dependency were some of the variables that appeared to contribute to depression in married women. Men, on the other hand, were much more likely than women to be dependent on alcohol. This suggests that men and women may have different coping mechanisms for distress. In women anxiety and depression are more common whereas men are more prone to alcohol dependency and conduct disorders.

Overall, the evidence consistently shows that married women have better physical and mental health than unmarried women, but married women have poorer mental health than married men. This gender difference may be attributed to stressful roles required of women in marriage. Poor marital communication may be another factor that contributes to stress among married women.

Marital Communication

Establishing and maintaining **positive communication** patterns is undoubtedly one of the most important tasks in a marriage. Unless messages can be sent and understood, there will be misunderstanding, dissatisfaction, and loneliness. Feelings of emotional closeness and intimacy are dependent on being able to communicate attitudes and feelings. Poor communication is the most frequent reason given by couples for entering marital therapy (*Marriage and Divorce Today* 1986).

Once communication patterns are established they are difficult to change and they have long-lasting effects on a relationship. For example, Markman (1981) evaluated the communication of couples planning marriage. He found that the more positively that premarital couples rated their communication, the more satisfied they were with their relationship five years latter.

Comparisons of satisfied and unsatisfied couples reveal significant differences in their communications patterns. Levenson and Gottman (1983) found that compared to satisfied couples, unsatisfied couples showed less positive affect, more negative affect, and more reciprocity of negative affect. Negative reciprocity is responding to a negative comment with another negative comment. These patterns were especially evident during discussion of problems. Other research has found that satisfied couples show more humor, laughter, and support, and less defensiveness than unsatisfied couples (Mischler and Waxler 1968; Riskin and Faunce 1970).

Margolin and Wampold (1981) studied thirty-nine couples intensively over a five-week period. The twenty-two distressed couples who were seeking marital therapy were rated as high in distress by their therapist, and scored below average on two marital adjustment scales. The seventeen nondistressed couples were not seeking therapy and scored above average on two marital adjustment scales.

The nondistressed couples showed more verbal positive behavior (agreeing, approval, humor), more nonverbal positive behavior (assenting, smiling), more problem-solving behavior (accepting responsibility, compromising, problem solving), more neutral behavior, and less negative behavior (complaining, criticizing, denying responsibility, excusing, putting the other down). And the distressed couples were more likely to show negative reciprocity.

Ting-Toomey (1983) studied intimate communication among thirty-four married couples. She categorized their communication into three types: integrative behavior, disintegrative behavior, and descriptive behavior. **Integrative behavior** includes confirming (acceptance of feelings and ideas); coaxing (flattery, gentle appeals, humor); compromising; and agreement. **Disintegrative behavior** includes confronting (attacks, criticisms); complaining; defending; and disagreement. **Descriptive behavior** includes acts that facilitate information flow, such as descriptions, explanations, and questions.

Ting-Toomey observed that low-adjustment couples had two characteristics that differentiated them from high-adjustment couples. First, their communication was more structured and predictable than high-adjusted couples. Second, the low-adjusted couples engaged in more negative reciprocals such as confront-confront, confront-defend, complain-defend, and defend-complain. Jacobson, Waldron, and Moore (1980) also observed that distressed couples reacted much more to negative stimuli than nondistressed couples.

Rusbult, Johnson, and Morrow (1986) found a similar phenomenon among dating couples. The way in which partners responded to destructive behaviors was the best predictor of relationship health. Couples in nondistressed relationships were more likely than couples in distressed relationships to respond to negative messages with positive communication, such as discussing problems, suggesting solutions, compromising, and supporting the partner in the face of criticism.

Positive communication skills include sending clear and congruent messages, empathy, supportive statements, and effective problem solving. Criticism, complaining, disagreement, ignoring the other, refusing to talk, and double messages are examples of negative communication. Olson, Russell, and

Sprenkle (1983) and Anderson (1986) have found that family cohesion and adaptability are related to positive communication skills.

Cohesion is the amount of attachment, closeness, and emotional bonding among family members. Families with very low cohesion have such low attachment that there is almost no group. Such a family may be labeled *disengaged*. Families with very high cohesion have such strong attachment that there is little individuality. They may be described as *enmeshed*. Families with moderately low cohesion are called *separated*, and families with moderately high cohesion are considered *connected*.

Adaptability is the ability of a family to change in response to stress. Families with very low adaptability change so little that they are called *rigid*. On the other side of the scale are families with so little structure that they are called *chaotic*. *Structured* families are moderately low in adaptability, and *flexible* families have moderately high adaptability.

Olson et al. (1983) have placed cohesion and adaptability in a two-dimensional matrix that they call the **circumplex model.** It is a useful framework

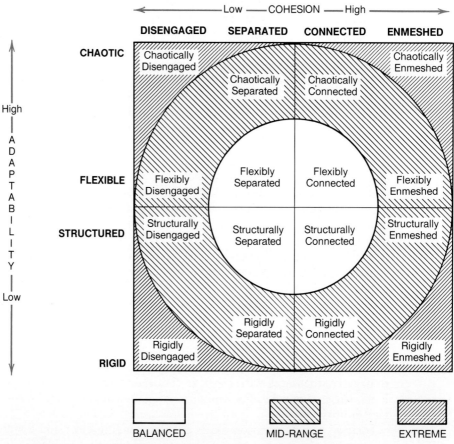

FIGURE 6·1   Circumplex Model: Sixteen Types of Marital and Family Systems

SOURCE: Olson, Russell, and Sprenkle. 1983. Reprinted from *Family Process* Vol. 22 #1, March 1983 with permission of the copyright owner.

for studying families and can be used by therapists in diagnosing family problems and designing treatments. A diagram of their model is shown in Figure 6·1. Sixteen family types, grouped in three more general categories, can be identified using this matrix. Families with very low or very high values on both dimensions are labeled **extreme.** Those very high or very low on either cohesion or adaptability are called **mid-range.** The term **balanced** is used by Olson et al. to describe families with moderate values on both cohesion and flexibility.

There are three major conclusions that can be drawn from the circumplex model. First, balanced families tend to have more positive communication skills than extreme families (Anderson 1986). Second, positive communication skills will enable balanced families to change their cohhesion and adaptability more easily than extreme families. Third, balanced families have a larger repertoire of behaviors than extreme families. The result is greater satisfaction and more adequate functioning among balanced families than among mid-range or extreme families.

In summary, research on couple communication shows that compared to unsatisfied couples, satisfied couples have more positive and varied communication, are more balanced in cohesion and adaptability, and are less reactive to negative messages. When their spouse sends a negative message, individuals in satisfied marriages are less likely to simply respond with another negative message.

Marital Satisfaction

Most people enter marriage with the expectation that it will be very satisfying. Some married couples are very satisfied, some are very unsatisfied, and many are somewhere in between. One of the most frequently asked questions is what are the characteristics of satisfying marriages? In this section we will review some of the major variables that have been found to be predictive of marital satisfaction.

Marital satisfaction is a subjective evaluation of the overall quality of marriage. It is the degree to which needs, expectations, and desires are met in marriage. Some persons may have a very stable and healthy marriage by some objective standard and yet feel dissatisfied. Others may feel very satisfied even though a therapist or objective observer might rate the quality of their marriage as much below average.

Marriage is complex and is influenced by many factors. No matter how well matched two people are, there is no guarantee that they will be satisfied. Some couples who appear to have everything going for them end up miserable. Others with characteristics that usually produce dissatisfaction end up very satisfied.

Although it is difficult to predict marital satisfaction, there are a number of characteristics that tend to be associated with it. Exchange theory is a useful framework in explaining how these characteristics influence marital satisfaction. In general, individuals who are competent and provide rewards for their spouse are going to have a spouse who is satisfied and, consequently, are more likely to receive rewards from their spouse. The following is a brief overview of some of the specific variables found to be predictive of marital satisfaction.

Role Consensus

In Chapter 1 we identified the (1) provider, (2) housekeeper, (3) child care, (4) child socialization, (5) therapeutic, (6) sexual, (7) recreational, and (8) kinship roles. The amount of **role consensus** partners have on each of these eight major family roles has been found to be strongly related to marital satisfaction (Bahr, Chappell, and Leigh 1983; Burr et al. 1979). Couples with much disagreement on these roles tend to have low marital satisfaction. Those with agreement on who should do what and how it should be done tend to be more satisfied in their marriages. The role consensus enables them to have high role fit and function effectively as a couple.

Spouse Role Competence

A second important predictor of marital satisfaction is spouse **role competence.** People who enact their family roles competently will make their spouses happy (Bahr et al. 1983; Burr et al. 1979; Rollins and Galligan 1978).

What types of role competencies are particularly important for marital satisfaction? Nye and McLaughlin (1982) found that performance of the therapeutic role was most important. Those who enact the therapeutic role competently are available to talk to their partners about their problems. They listen, offer suggestions, and generally provide sympathetic understanding.

Performance in child socialization and child care roles is also important for the satisfaction of both spouses. Husbands who are good fathers and help care for and teach the children tend to have happier wives. Conversely, wives who perform well in these two roles have husbands who are more satisfied. However, the husband's enactment of the child care role affects the wife's satisfaction more than the wife's enactment affects the husband's satisfaction. Perhaps this is because the child care role has tended to be assigned to women in our society. Women's performance of child care tasks is expected whereas the husband's involvement may be viewed as a special service for his wife.

The wife's competence in housekeeping and recreational roles has only a small effect on the husband's marital satisfaction, and the husband's performance in housekeeping and provider roles also has only a small influence on the wife's marital satisfaction (Bahr et al. 1983; Nye and McLaughlin 1982). This suggests that it is interpersonal skills rather than occupational success that are most crucial for marital satisfaction.

Equity in role performance is also important. Yogev and Brett (1983) observed that perceiving that their spouse does his or her share of the family work was the factor that differentiated satisfied from unsatisfied couples. This included child care as well as housework.

Companionship

Couples who participate in frequent activities together have significantly higher marital satisfaction. Miller (1976) found that companionship was the best predictor of satisfaction among seven different variables he examined. Companionship was defined as participating in joint activities together, such as visiting friends, going to a movie or other entertainment, spending time together talking, entertaining friends at home, taking a drive or walk, and eating at a restaurant. Other researchers have found that doing activities together, particularly if they require communication, are related to satisfaction in marriage (Barnett and Nietzel 1979; Fowers and Olson 1986; Jacobson et al. 1980; Orthner 1975).

On other hand, a lack of companionship is one of the distinguishing characteristics of unhappy couples. Hayes, Stinnett, and Defrain (1980) studied 138 men and women who experienced divorce in their middle years. They found that through the years the number of activities shared by these couples had decreased. Other things took precedence, such as work, children's activities, and individual interests. When asked what they did together, many of these couples could not think of anything. Some mentioned a trip or activity that occurred years ago. They did not participate in enjoyable activities together and had no reservoir of happy memories.

Positive Communication

A large body of research shows that positive communication skills are important for the development of satisfying marriages. As mentioned earlier, positive communication skills include such things as sending clear and congruent messages, listening, showing empathy, expressing support, and being able to negotiate. Positive communication skills are necessary for competent performance of the therapeutic role.

The research cited earlier shows that satisfied couples are much more likely than unsatisfied couples to possess positive communication skills (Fowers and Olson 1986; Levenson and Gottman 1983; Margolin and Wampold 1981; Olson et al. 1983; Rusbult et al. 1986; Ting-Toomey 1983. In satisfied couples there is more acceptance, less criticism, and less reaction to negative messages (Jacobson et al. 1980). Satisfied couples express more affection and provide more support and encouragement than unsatisfied couples (Fiore and Swensen 1977). Unsatisfied couples participate in less self-disclosure, and what disclosing they do tends to reveal more negative feelings (Levinger and Senn 1967). Bell, Daly, and Gonzales (1987) have shown that the following skills are critical in maintaining marital satisfaction: honesty, listening, openness, physical and verbal affection, confirmation, sensitivity, and supportiveness.

The study of unhappy couples by Hayes et al. (1980) illustrates how lack of positive communication skills can contribute to marital problems. These respondents mentioned how their mates frequently criticized them and made derogatory remarks, and three fourths felt that their partners had not been easy to talk to. They complained that their partner was unable or unwilling to talk, especially to share feelings, and was too judgmental. Many of the couples had a pattern of not communicating about their differences and spent little time in communication.

One of the critical communication skills is the ability to negotiate and solve problems. All couples have differences, and the inability to negotiate those differences may block future communication. Menaghan (1982) studied marital coping strategies and found couples who ignored problems increased their immediate distress and did nothing to solve the problem. Couples who negotiated did not immediately have less stress but had fewer problems later on.

Noller (1981) found that individuals in unsatisfying marriages were not able to decode messages from their spouse as well as individuals in satisfying relationships. However, they were able to decode messages from opposite-sex strangers as well as persons from satisfying marriages did. This suggests that the communication problem of the unhappy couples is not due to lack of skill, but instead may be a consequence of the unhappy relationship rather than the cause of it.

Self-Disclosure

Self-disclosure is revealing personal information about oneself to another person, including feelings, needs, and attitudes. As suggested earlier, self-disclosure may be considered to be a positive communication skill, however, it depends on more than one's ability of expression. It also relies on several personal and relationship characteristics, including self-esteem, acceptance, trust, affection, and reciprocity. It is discussed separately here because it has been found to be a particularly important determinant of marital satisfaction.

Self-disclosure is necessary for the development of intimacy, and a number of scholars have found a positive relationship between self-disclosure and marital satisfaction (Bell et al. 1987; Burke, Weir, and Harrison 1976; Gilbert 1976; Grinker 1967; Hansen and Schuldt 1984; Jorgensen and Gaudy 1980; Waring and Chelune 1983). When individuals self-disclose, it improves their own marital satisfaction as well as that of their spouse (Hansen and Schuldt 1984).

Research has identified two major differences in the self-disclosure of satisfied and unsatisfied couples. First, satisfied couples have more self-disclosure than unsatisfied couples. The act of sharing one's feelings apparently increases understanding and relationship satisfaction. Second, dissatisfied couples share more negative feelings (Levinger and Senn 1967). Thus, unsatisfied couples not only have less self-disclosure but the disclosure they do have tends to be negative. Any positive feelings are left unsaid. The combination of low quantity and low quality self-disclosure is detrimental for marital satisfaction (Schumm et al. 1986).

The conclusion to be drawn from the research is that both the quantity and quality of self-disclosure are important for the development of marital intimacy. Quantity is important but is not enough by itself. If self-disclosure is primarily sharing of critical, bitter feelings, it is not likely to enhance marital satisfaction.

This finding suggests that simply increasing self-disclosure will not automatically improve marital satisfaction. If increased self-disclosure results in more criticism, it is unlikely that the quality of the marriage will be improved. Teaching couples how to disclose positive feelings may be one way to improve marital relationships (Schumm et al. 1986).

Most researchers have found a positive relationship between self-disclosure and marital satisfaction: the more the self-disclosure, the greater the marital satisfaction. However, Gilbert (1976) hypothesized that the relationship was curvilinear: Self-disclosure improves satisfaction up to a certain point, beyond which it hurts marital satisfaction. This issue has not been fully resolved in research. At present all we know is that couples who disclose little will have low marital quality. It is possible that too much self-disclosure may have negative consequences. However, it appears that for most couples, the problem is too little rather than too much self-disclosure. In general, higher levels of self-disclosing behavior have been found to increase several dimensions of marital intimacy, and greater marital intimacy is associated with better emotional health as well as higher levels of marital satisfaction (Hames and Waring 1980; Waring and Chelune 1983; Waring and Russell 1980).

Reciprocity

Reciprocity has also been found to be an important determinant of marital quality. For example, if a husband thinks his wife has strong affection for him, he will tend to have strong affection for her. If she thinks he has high regard for her, she will tend to have high regard for him. Dissatisfaction occurs if feelings of affection and commitment are not reciprocated (Schafer and Keith 1984). According to Sternberg (1986), feelings of affection for another actually will diminish if it is perceived that those feelings are not reciprocated.

Equity

Feeling that one is getting out of the marriage what one put in is also related to marital satisfaction. The greater the perceived inequity, the lower the marital satisfaction. Those who feel underbenefited have less satisfaction than those who feel overbenefited, but those who perceive equity have the highest satisfaction (Davidson 1984). Men are more likely to feel anger at inequity, and women are somewhat more likely to feel sadness and depression as a result of marital inequities (Sprecher 1986).

Self-Esteem

Several researchers have found a correlation between self-esteem and marital adjustment (Barnett and Nietzel 1979; Bell et al. 1987; Chesser et al. 1979). Individuals with high self-esteem may have higher levels of self-disclosure than individuals with low self-esteem, resulting in better communication and higher marital satisfaction. Furthermore, Schafer and Keith (1984) found that self-concept is a predictor of marital role performance, which is related to marital satisfaction (Bahr et al. 1983). Thus, self-esteem appears to be an important predictor of marital satisfaction, but its effect operates primarily through other variables, such as self-disclosure and role performance.

Money

There is no evidence that money is positively associated with marital satisfaction. Neither income, occupational prestige, nor performance in the provider role have been found to have a significant impact on marital satisfaction (Bahr et al. 1983; Brinkerhoff and White 1978; Nye and McLaughlin 1982; Jorgensen 1979).

However, economic hardship does affect marital satisfaction. Brinkerhoff and White (1978) studied both families that were marginal economically as well as stable working-class families. The former were families whose incomes were close to the poverty level—the amount established by the government to meet basic necessities. They found that subjective economic satisfaction was an important determinant of marital satisfaction among the marginal families but not among the stable working-class families.

The results suggest that level of income may negatively affect marital satisfaction among couples with incomes near the poverty level. Raising one's income above the poverty level may decrease stress and improve marital satisfaction. However, additional income increases are not likely to improve marital satisfaction further. This is what Brinkerhoff and White refer to as a *threshold effect*. Within a certain low-income range, marital satisfaction will increase as income increases. Beyond that range, income is not an important factor.

Liker and Elder (1983) studied how severe economic loss during the Depression affected marital relationships. They found that heavy income loss affected marital satisfaction through two intervening variables, financial disputes and personal instability. First, income loss increased financial disputes, which tended to decrease marital satisfaction. Second, income loss increased the personal instability of men, which weakened marital satisfaction.

However, these effects were strongest among marriages and husbands that

Wise money management and joint financial decision-making tend to be associated with high levels of marital satisfaction. Here a young couple shop for home appliances together.   *Read D. Brugger/The Picture Cube.*

were weak before the income loss. For example, income loss was more likely to decrease marital satisfaction if marital quality was poor before the income reduction. Similarly, husbands with unstable dispositions prior to the economic loss were more likely to become worrisome and explosive after the income loss. The income loss appeared to aggravate existing problems.

These data suggest that severe economic hardship may create stress on any marriage, but particularly among those without personal and marital coping resources. On the other hand, many couples with a strong marital bond are able to adapt even in the face of severe economic stress.

There is some evidence that money management influences marital satisfaction. Schaninger and Buss (1986) found that couples with less husband dominance and greater wife involvement in monetary decisions tended to have higher marital satisfaction. There also appeared to be a different spending pattern among happy than unhappy couples. Happily married couples spent more purchasing their home, household appliances, and recreational vehicles, whereas unhappy couples tended to spend more on stereos, televisions, and living room furniture (Schaninger and Buss 1986).

In summary, marital happiness does not necessarily increase as income increases, but severe economic hardship may strain marital relations. Couples with incomes near the subsistence level and couples who face sharp income decreases tend to have low levels of marital satisfaction. More money does not make one happier, but having an adequate income and managing it as a couple are associated with greater marital satisfaction.

Religiosity

Religiosity has been found to be a significant predictor of marital satisfaction (Albrecht 1979; Filsinger and Wilson 1984; Fowers and Olson 1986; Heaton 1984; Wilson and Filsinger 1986). Regardless of denomination, individuals who attend religious services regularly have higher marital satisfaction than non-attenders. Similarly, those who score high on measures of religious belief tend to rate their marriages as happier than persons who say they are unreligious (Heaton 1984; Wilson and Filsinger 1986).

Emotional Maturity

It is logical that a person who is emotionally mature will make a better spouse. Mature individuals are likely to be able to perform marital roles adequately and adjust to the needs and expectations of their spouses. Cole, Cole, and Dean (1978) found that both self-rated and spouse-rated emotional maturity were related to marital satisfaction. For example, the wife's assessment of her husband's emotional maturity was correlated with her marital satisfaction and with his marital satisfaction. Similarly, his assessment of her emotional maturity was related to his and her marital satisfaction.

Gender Roles

Gender role behavior is related to marital satisfaction too. Antill (1983) found that couples in which both husband and wife were rated high on *femininity* were much happier than couples in which only one partner rated high. Femininity was defined as being cheerful, affectionate, sympathetic, sensitive, understanding, warm, tender, gentle, and yielding (Antill 1983). Similarly, Kalin and Lloyd (1985) suggested that the characteristics labeled feminine in our society are conducive to satisfying personal relationships. These characteristics appear essential for adequate performance of the therapeutic role.

Others have noted that individuals high on both femininity and *masculinity* tend to have higher marital satisfaction than sex-typed individuals (Fowers and Olson 1986; Kalin and Lloyd 1985; Murstein and Williams 1983). Masculinity refers to such things as being assertive, ambitious, decisive, aggressive, dominant, and willing to take risks.

Wilson (1982) analyzed sex role attitudes and found that both women who were highly traditional or highly feminist tended to have low marital satisfaction. The highly traditional women used emotional manipulation to influence their husbands, and this strategy may have interfered with positive communication. The feminist women tended to use confrontation rather than accommodation and this may have accounted for their marital difficulties.

According to Li and Caldwell (1987), the direction of husband-wife differences in sex role attitudes are related to marital satisfaction. They examined marital satisfaction among four types of couples: (1) traditional husband/traditional wife; (2) traditional husband/egalitarian wife; (3) egalitarian husband/traditional wife; (4) egalitarian husband/egalitarian wife. They found that marital satisfaction was the lowest when the husband's sex role attitudes were traditional and the wife's were egalitarian. On the other hand, the highest level of satisfaction was among couples with an egalitarian husband and traditional wife. Li and Caldwell suggest that this may be due to a greater willingness to compromise in couples composed of this combination. For example, an egalitarian husband may be willing to accommodate because he feels he should relinquish some of the control traditionally given to men. On the other hand, a traditional husband may not feel it is appropriate for a man to give up some of the control traditionally given to men, while his egalitarian wife may not be willing to tolerate his expectation of male control.

Stage of Family Life Cycle

Several scholars have found that marital satisfaction varies according to stage of family life cycle. Marital satisfaction tends to decline from the beginning of marriage until children are launched. Then marital satisfaction increases as couples move through the postparental period and into retirement (Lupri and Frideres 1981; Rollins and Cannon 1974; Rollins and Feldman 1970). However, the magnitude of the change is not large. Over 90 percent of the variation in marital satisfaction is not due to life cycle stage (Rollins and Cannon 1974; White 1987).

Parenthood

It is widely believed that children have a negative effect on marital satisfaction. The research cited earlier (Lupri and Frideres 1981; Rollins and Cannon 1974; Rollins and Feldman 1970) shows that marital satisfaction decreases when children enter the household and increases when children leave. A number of others have found lower levels of marital satisfaction among couples with children (Figley 1973; Glenn and McLanahan 1982; Renne 1970).

In a recent longitudinal survey, however, White and Booth (1985) found no relationship between presence of children and marital satisfaction. They interviewed 220 couples in 1980 and in 1983. All were childless in 1980 and 113 were still childless in 1983. Although there was a general deterioration of marital quality over the three-year period, there was no difference between couples with and without children. The transition to parenthood did not affect marital satisfaction, frequency of disagreements, or number of marital problems. White and Booth concluded that having a child does not produce a decrease in marital quality.

Premarital Cohabitation

In Chapter 5 it was noted that cohabitation has become a stage in the mate selection process for some couples. Living together prior to marriage may provide additional time to test the relationship and insure that one is compatible with one's partner. Although this hypothesis appears logical, two recent studies are not consistent with it.

DeMaris and Leslie (1984) examined the relationship between cohabitation and subsequent marital quality among 309 recently married couples. Having cohabited premaritally was associated with lower marital satisfaction for both spouses, even after controlling for sex-role traditionalism, attendance at religious services, education, and presence of children. In a similar study Watson (1983) also observed that noncohabitors had higher marital satisfaction scores than cohabitors.

Why are cohabitors less satisfied than couples who do not cohabit prior to marriage? DeMaris and Leslie (1984) suggest that rather than acting as a filter that screens out less compatible couples, cohabitation may select couples who have characteristics associated with lower marital satisfaction. For example, cohabitors may expect more from marriage or may not adapt as well to the role expectations of traditional marriage. Whatever the mechanism, DeMaris and Leslie think the difference is not due to the experience of cohabitation itself but to differences in the kinds of people who do and do not cohabit.

Conclusion

Almost all adults eventually marry and seek a warm, satisfying marital relationship. Yet many who marry are disappointed and find marriage unsatisfying. In this chapter we have identified some of the characteristics that have been found to be related to marital satisfaction. Some of the most important couple characteristics are role consensus and positive communication skills. Personal characteristics such as self-esteem, role competence, and emotional maturity influence the degree of marital satisfaction.

Social exchange theory helps us understand how these characteristics may affect marital satisfaction. For example, rewards received in a marriage are likely to be higher when role consensus is high. Similarly, one who performs marital roles competently will be rewarding to his or her spouse. Overall, it appears that couple and personal characteristics with high interpersonal exchange value are going to be positively related to marital satisfaction. The more one's characteristics are rewarding to another, the higher the level of satisfaction. However, as noted earlier, equity is important in the exchange. Those who feel overbenefited are less satisfied than individuals who feel equity in their marital exchanges.

Summary

1. Among both women and men, married persons are healthier and happier than unmarried persons.
2. Economic strain, social isolation, and parental burdens have less effect on married than single persons.
3. The difference between married and single persons in amount of depression tends to be greatest when life circumstances are the most difficult. This suggests that marriage insulates people against the negative effects of certain stresses.
4. It is the quality of the marriage rather than marital status per se that affects mental health. Individuals in unhappy marriages tend to have poorer mental health than unmarried persons.
5. Women tend to have poorer mental health than men, and this is because women are more likely to have either too few or excessive role demands.
6. Being a parent tends to be more stressful for women than men because women do most of the child care.
7. Being an employed parent is more stressful for women than men because women tend to do the majority of child care and household chores even when they are employed.
8. Compared to unsatisfied couples, satisfied couples have more positive verbal and nonverbal communication, show more variety in their communication patterns, are more balanced in cohesion and adaptability, and are less reactive to negative messages.
9. Emotional maturity, high self-esteem, and moderate sex role attitudes are associated with higher marital satisfaction. Maturity and self-esteem help one adjust to marriage and communicate adequately. Those with extreme sex role attitudes (strongly traditional or highly feminist) appear to have more difficulty communicating in marriage.
10. Role consensus, role competence, companionship, equity, and religiosity have a positive association with marital satisfaction. Consensus on marital roles facilitates communication, and competence in enacting marital roles enhances feelings of satisfaction. Enactment of therapeutic, child care, and child socialization roles appears particularly important.
11. Positive communication skills are related to marital satisfaction. These skills include sending clear and congruent messages, listening, showing empathy, expressing support, the ability to disclose feelings, and the ability to negotiate.
12. Money does not bring marital happiness but economic hardship can be stressful. The ability to manage money adequately as a couple is related to marital satisfaction.

13. Parenthood does not appear to be related to marital quality, although there tends to be a slight reduction in marital satisfaction during the child-rearing years.
14. Couples who cohabit before marriage have slightly less satisfaction in their marriages than couples who do not cohabit before marriage.

Important Terms

- adaptability
- balanced
- circumplex model
- cohesion
- descriptive behavior
- disintegrative behavior
- economic stress
- equity
- extreme

- integrative behavior
- mid-range
- positive communication
- reciprocity
- role competence
- role consensus
- self-disclosure
- social isolation

Questions for Discussion

1. How is marital status related to health and why?
2. In what ways are marital roles more stressful for women than men? In what ways are they more stressful for men than women?
3. What are positive communication skills?
4. How stable are marital communication patterns?
5. How do distressed and nondistressed couples compare on communication patterns?
6. What is the circumplex model? Give a description of what each of the four types of extreme couples would be like. Describe the characteristics of each of the four types of couples in the balanced range.
7. How is family communication related to cohesion and adaptability?
8. In what ways do family communication, cohesion, and adaptability change as a family passes through the family life cycle?
9. How is self-disclosure related to marital satisfaction?
10. How is reciprocity related to communication and marital satisfaction?
11. How is self-esteem related to marital communication and marital satisfaction?
12. What is equity and how is it related to marital satisfaction?
13. How are sex role attitudes related to marital satisfaction?
14. Why do people who score high on femininity (as defined in the chapter) tend to have higher-than-average satisfaction?
15. What have we learned from the existing research about the relationship between economic variables and marital satisfaction?
16. How does money management differ between satisfied and unsatisfied couples?
17. How is religiosity related to marital satisfaction and why?

18. How is the family life cycle related to marital satisfaction and why? How strong is the relationship between the family life cycle and marital satisfaction?
19. How do children affect marital satisfaction?
20. Why do couples who cohabit before marriage tend to have lower marital satisfaction than couples who have not cohabited before marriage?
21. What is marital satisfaction? Why is it important?
22. Suppose you have been asked to give a talk to a group of young engaged couples about marriage. Based on what you have read in this chapter, what would you tell them?
23. Suppose you have a friend who is having marital difficulties. Based on what you have read in this chapter, what would you tell her or him?

Recommended Reading

FOWERS, B. J., and D. H. OLSON. 1986. Predicting marital success with PREPARE: A predictive validity study. *Journal of Marital and Family Therapy* 12:403–413.

MENAGHAN, E. 1982. Measuring coping effectiveness: A panel analysis of marital problems and coping efforts. *Journal of Health and Social Behavior* 23:220–234.

TING-TOOMEY, S. 1983. An analysis of verbal communication patterns in high and low marital adjustment groups. *Human Communication Research* 9:306–319.

References

ALBRECHT, S. L. 1979. Correlates of marital happiness among the remarried. *Journal of Marriage and the Family* 41:857–867.

ANDERSON, S. A. 1986. Cohesion, adaptability and communication: A test of an Olson circumplex model hypothesis. *Family Relations* 35:289–293.

ANESHENSEL, C. S., R. R. FRERICHS, and V. A. CLARK, 1981. Family roles and sex differences in depression. *Journal of Health and Social Behavior* 22:379–393.

ANTILL, J. K. 1983. Sex role complementarity versus similarity in married couples. *Journal of Personality and Social Psychology* 45:145–155.

BAHR, S. J., C. B. CHAPPELL, and G. K. LEIGH. 1983. Age at marriage, role enactment, role consensus, and marital satisfaction. *Journal of Marriage and the Family* 45:795–803.

BARNETT, L., and M. NIETZEL. 1979. Relationship of instrumental and affectional behaviors and self-esteem to marital satisfaction in distressed and nondistressed couples. *Journal of Consulting and Clinical Psychology* 47:946-958.

BELL, R. A., J. A. DALY, and M. C. GONZALES. 1987. Affinity-maintenance in marriage and its relationship to women's marital satisfaction. *Journal of Marriage and the Family* 49:445–454.

BERNARD, J. 1972. *The future of marriage.* New York: Bantam.

BRINKERHOFF, D. B., and L. K. WHITE. 1978. Marital satisfaction in an economically marginal population. *Journal of Marriage and the Family* 40:259–267.

BURKE, R., T. WEIR, and D. HARRISON. 1976. Disclosure of problems and tensions experienced by marital partners. *Psychological Reports* 38:521–542.

BURR, W. R., G. K. LEIGH, R. D. DAY, and J. CONSTANTINE. 1979. Symbolic interaction and the family. In *Contemporary theories about the family,* vol. 2, ed. W. R. Burr, R. Hill, F. I. Nye, and I. Reiss, 42–111. New York: Free Press.

CHESSER, B., A. PARKHURST, and D. SCHAFFER. 1979. Marital adjustment: Controlling the tendency to distort evaluations. *Home Economics Research Journal* 8:27–36.

CLEARY, P. D., and D. MECHANIC. 1983. Sex differences in psychological distress among married people. *Journal of Health and Social Behavior* 24:111–121.

COLE, C. L., A. L. COLE, and D. G. DEAN. 1978. *Emotional maturity and marital adjustment: A decade replication.* Paper presented in the Research and Theory Section at the National Council on Family Relations Annual Meetings, Philadelphia, PA October 19–22.

COVERMAN, S., and J. F. SHELEY. 1986. Change in men's housework and child-care time, 1965–1975. *Journal of Marriage and the Family* 48:413–422.

D'ARCY, C., and C. M. SIDDIQUE. 1985. Marital status and psychological well-being: A cross-national comparative analysis. *International Journal of Comparative Sociology* 26:149–166.

DAVIDSON, B. 1984. A test of equity theory for marital adjustment. *Social Psychology Quarterly* 47:36–42.

DeMARIS, A., and G. R. LESLIE. 1984. Cohabitation with the future spouse: Its influence upon marital satisfaction and communication. *Journal of Marriage and the Family* 46:77–84.

FIGLEY, C. R. 1973. Child density and the marital relationship. *Journal of Marriage and the Family* 35:272–282.

FILSINGER, E. E., and M. R. WILSON. 1984. Religiosity, socioeconomic rewards, and family development: Predictors of marital adjustment. *Journal of Marriage and the Family* 46:663–670.

FIORE, A., and C. H. SWENSEN. 1977. Analysis of love relationships in functional and dysfunctional marriage. *Psychological Reports* 40:707–714.

FOWERS, B. J., and D. H. OLSON. 1986. Predicting marital success with PREPARE: A predictive validity study. *Journal of Marital and Family Therapy* 12:403–413.

GILBERT, S. J. 1976. Self-disclosure, intimacy, and communication in families. *The Family Coordinator* 25:221–231.

GLENN, N. D., and S. McLANAHAN. 1982. Children and marital happiness: A further specification of the relationship. *Journal of Marriage and the Family* 44:63–72.

GOVE, W. R. 1972. The relationship between sex roles, marital status, and mental illness. *Social Forces* 51:34–44.

GOVE, W. R., M. HUGHES, and C. B. STYLE. 1983. Does marriage have positive effects on the psychological well-being of the individual? *Journal of Health and Social Behavior* 24:122–131.

GRINKER, R. R. 1967. *Toward a unified theory of human behavior.* 2d ed. New York: Basic.

HAMES, J., and E. M. WARING. 1980. Marital intimacy and nonpsychotic emotional illness. *Psychiatric Forum* 9:13–19.

HANSEN, J. E., and W. J. SCHULDT. 1984. Marital self-disclosure and marital satisfaction. *Journal of Marriage and the Family* 46:923–926.

HARING-HIDORE, M., W. A. STOCK, M. A. OKUN, and R. A. WITTER. 1985. Marital status and subjective well-being: A research synthesis. *Journal of Marriage and the Family* 47:947-953.

HAYES, M. P., N. STINNETT, and J. DeFRAIN. 1980. Learning about marriage from the divorced. *Journal of Divorce* 4:23–29.

HEATON, T. B. 1984. Religious homogamy and marital satisfaction reconsidered. *Journal of Marriage and the Family* 46:729–733.

JACOBSON, N. S., H. WALDRON, and D. MOORE. 1980. Toward a behavioral profile of marital distress. *Journal of Consulting and Clinical Psychology,* 48:696–703.

JORGENSEN, S. R. 1979. Socioeconomic rewards and perceived marital quality: A reexamination. *Journal of Marriage and the Family* 41:825–835.

JORGENSEN, S. R., and J. C. GAUDY. 1980. Self-disclosure and satisfaction in marriage: The relationship examined. *Family Relations: Journal of Applied Family and Child Studies* 29:281–287.

KALIN, R., and C. A. LLOYD. 1985. Sex-role identity, sex-role ideology and marital adjustment. *International Journal of Women's Studies* 8:32–39.

KESSLER, R. C., and M. ESSEX. 1982. Marital status and depression: The importance of coping resources. *Social Forces* 61:484–507.

LEVENSON, R. W., and J. M. GOTTMAN. 1983. Marital interaction: Physiological linkage and affective exchange. *Journal of Personality and Social Psychology* 45:587–597.

LEVINGER, G., and D. J. SENN. 1967. Disclosure of feelings in marriage. *Merrill-Palmer Quarterly* 13:237–249.

LI, J. T., and R. A. CALDWELL. 1987. Magnitude and directional effects of marital sex-role incongruence on marital adjustment. *Journal of Family Issues* 8:97–110.

LIKER, J. K., and G. H. ELDER, JR. 1983. Economic hardship and marital relations in the 1930s. *American Sociological Review* 48:343–359.

LUPRI, E., and J. FRIDERES. 1981. The quality of marriage and the passage of time: Marital satisfaction over the family life cycle. *Canadian Journal of Sociology* 6:283–305.

MARGOLIN, G., and B. E. WAMPOLD. 1981. Sequential analysis of conflict and accord in distressed and nondistressed marital partners. *Journal of Consulting and Clinical Psychology* 49:554–567.

MARKIDES, K. S., and J. FARRELL. 1985. Marital status and depression among Mexican Americans. *Social Psychiatry* 20:86–91.

MARKMAN, H. J. 1981. Prediction of marital distress: A 5-year follow-up. *Journal of Consulting and Clinical Psychology* 49:760–762.

MARRIAGE AND DIVORCE TODAY. 1986. *MDT survey: Poor communication key marital problem of clients entering therapy.* Vol. 2, no. 52, July 28.

MENAGHAN, E. 1982. Measuring coping effectiveness: A panel analysis of marital problems and coping efforts. *Journal of Health and Social Behavior* 23:220–234.

MILLER, B. C. 1976. A multivariate developmental model of marital satisfaction. *Journal of Marriage and the Family* 38:643–657.

MISCHLER, E. G., and N. E. WAXLER. 1968. *Interaction in families: An experimental study of family processes in schizophrenia.* New York: Wiley.

MURSTEIN, B. I., and P. D. WILLIAMS. 1983. Sex roles and marriage adjustment. *Small Group Behavior* 14:77–94.

NOLLER, P. 1981. Gender and marital adjustment level differences in decoding messages from spouses and strangers. *Journal of Personality and Social Psychology* 41:272–278.

NYE, F. I., and S. McLAUGHLIN. 1982. Role competence and marital satisfaction. In *Family relationships: Rewards and costs,* ed. F. I. Nye, 67–79. Beverly Hills, CA: Sage.

OLSON, D. H., C. S. RUSSELL, and D. H. SPRENKLE. 1983. Circumplex model of marital and family systems: VI. Theoretical update. *Family Process* 22:69–83.

ORTHNER, D. K. 1975. Leisure activity patterns and marital satisfaction over the marital career. *Journal of Marriage and the Family* 37:91–101.

PEARLIN, L. I., and J. S. JOHNSON. 1977. Marital status, life-strains and depression. *American Sociological Review* 42:704–715.

RENNE, K. S. 1970. A multivariate developmental model of marital satisfaction. *Journal of Marriage and the Family* 38:643–657.

RISKIN, J., and E. E. FAUNCE. 1970. Family interaction scales: III. Discussion of methodology and substantive findings. *Archives of General Psychiatry* 22:527–537.

ROLLINS, B. C., and K. L. CANNON. 1974. Marital satisfaction over the family life cycle: A reevaluation. *Journal of Marriage and the Family* 36(2):271–272.

ROLLINS, B. C., and H. FELDMAN. 1970. Marital satisfaction over the family life cycle. *Journal of Marriage and the Family* 32:20–28.

ROLLINS, B. C., and R. GALLIGAN. 1978. The developing child and marital satisfaction of parents. In *Child influences on marital and family interaction*, ed. R. M. Lerner and G. B. Spanier, 71–105. New York: Academic.

RUSBULT, C. E., D. J. JOHNSON, and G. D. MORROW. 1986. Impact of couple patterns of problem solving on distress and nondistress in dating relationships. *Journal of Personality and Social Psychology* 50:744–753.

RUSSELL, D., C. E. CUTRONA, J. ROSE, and K. YURKO. 1984. Social and emotional loneliness: An examination of Weiss's typology of loneliness. *Journal of Personality and Social Psychology* 46:1313–1321.

SCHAFER, R. B., and P. M. KEITH. 1984. A causal analysis of the relationship between the self-concept and marital quality. *Journal of Marriage and the Family* 46:909–914.

SCHANINGER, C. M., and W. C. BUSS. 1986. A longitudinal comparison of consumption and finance handling between happily married and divorced couples. *Journal of Marriage and the Family* 48:129–136.

SCHUMM, W. R., H. L. BARNES, S. R. BOLLMAN, A. P. JURICH, and M. A. BUGAIGHIS. 1986. Self-disclosure and marital satisfaction revisited. *Family Relations* 35:241–247.

SPRECHER, S. 1986. The relation between inequity and emotions in close relationships. *Social Psychology Quarterly* 49:309–321.

STERNBERG, R. J. 1986. A triangular theory of love. *Psychological Review* 93:119–135.

TING-TOOMEY, S. 1983. An analysis of verbal communication patterns in high and low marital adjustment groups. *Human Communication Research* 9:306–319.

VEENHOVEN, R. 1983. The growing impact of marriage. *Social Indicators Research* 12:49–63.

VERBRUGGE, L. M. 1986. Role burdens and physical health of women and men. *Women and Health* 11:47–77.

VERBRUGGE, L. M., and J. H. MADANS. 1985. Social roles and health trends of American women. *Health and Society* 63:691–735.

WARING, E. M., and G. J. CHELUNE. 1983. Marital intimacy and self-disclosure. *Journal of Clinical Psychology* 39:183–189.

WARING, E. M., and L. RUSSELL. 1980. Family structure, marital adjustment, and intimacy in patients referred to a consultation-liaison service. *General Hospital Psychiatry* 3:198–203.

WATSON, R. E. L. 1983. Premarital cohabitation vs. traditional courtship: Their effects on subsequent marital adjustment. *Family Relations* 32:139–147.

WHITE, J. M. 1987. Marital perceived agreement and actual agreement over the family life cycle. *Journal of Comparative Family Studies* 18:47–59.

WHITE, L. K., and A. BOOTH. 1985. The transition to parenthood and marital quality. *Journal of Family Issues* 6:435–449.

WILSON, G. D. 1982. Feminism and marital dissatisfaction. *Personality and Individual Differences* 3:345–347.

WILSON, M. R., and E. E. FILSINGER. 1986. Religiosity and marital adjustment: Multidimensional interrelationships. *Journal of Marriage and the Family* 48:147–151.

YOGEV, S., and J. BRETT. 1983. *Perceptions of the division of housework and child care and marital satisfaction.* Evanston, IL: Center for Urban Affairs and Policy Research, Northwestern University.

CHAPTER 7

Conflict and Power

Introduction

As Lorraine and Michael are adjusting to being married, conflicts arise in several areas. Michael works long hours and leaves almost all of the household chores to Lorraine. She resents this because she is going to school and doesn't feel it is fair for her to do all of the housework. They sometimes have arguments over this and Michael has agreed to help more, but still he does not always do what he said he would do.

Their conflicts over housework are the result of differing role expectations. Lorraine expects Michael to do more housework than he thinks he should do. Although Michael feels he should help some, he thinks Lorraine should do the majority of housework because he is providing the income for the family.

Another area of disagreement is money. Michael is a very organized person and likes to plan everything. He does not like to buy anything unless they can pay cash for it. Lorraine thinks that type of thinking is unrealistic. She would like to purchase a second car and does not want to delay the purchase until they have saved enough money for it. Furthermore, Lorraine does not feel that she should consult with Michael over every purchase that she makes. She wants some financial autonomy and feels like his monetary desires are too constraining.

Whenever two people live in close contact, conflicts occur. In this chapter we begin with a discussion of the nature of conflict and identify common areas of marital conflict. Then we explore conflict management and how it relates to marital satisfaction. Finally, we review power and control in interpersonal relationships and discuss how they are related to marital satisfaction.

What is Conflict?

Conflict is contending or fighting that occurs when the behavior of one partner blocks the goals of the other. One seeks to achieve a desired outcome that the other resists because it appears costly. For example, Lorraine feels she is spending too much time on housework because Michael is not doing his share of the work. His behavior reduces the time she has available for other things. Similarly, Michael desires to use their money somewhat differently than Lor-

Conflict is a normal part of married life, and can have both negative and positive
consequences. The critical question is the nature of the conflicts and how they
are managed. *Jean Boughton/The Picture Cube.*

raine does. Money is a scarce commodity and both cannot have their desires
met. Scarce resources, such as limited amounts of money, are often at the
heart of conflicts.

Felstiner, Abel, and Sarat (1981) have identified four characteristics of conflict.
First, it is *subjective* in that it is not necessarily linked to objective, observable
behavior. Conflict begins when there is a perception of interference or wrong-
doing. That perception is not necessarily shared by all family members and
may result simply from changes in feelings. Second, because feelings are unstable and may change repeatedly, conflicts tend to be *unstable.* Therefore, the
conflict process is difficult to predict and may change unexpectedly. Third,
conflicts tend to be *reactive.* One responds to another in an iterative manner;
that is, one makes a charge, the other defends and makes a countercharge, the
first responds to the countercharge, and so on. Finally, conflict is a *complicated*
process. It is complicated because of the subjective and unstable nature of
feelings and perceptions. It involves ambiguous behavior, faulty recall, and
unclear rules (Felstiner et al. 1981).

Functions of Conflict

Sometimes individuals assume that conflict hurts marriages and that it should be kept to a minimum. However, some very satisfied couples have conflicts regularly, whereas some very unsatisfied couples rarely have open conflict. One recent study of divorced couples indicated that almost one half seldom had a quarrel (Hayes, Stinnett, and Defrain 1981).

Family conflict has several positive functions. First, conflicts may stimulate interaction and emotion. People who clash are not bored and so conflict may add spice to one's life. Second, conflicts may increase the likelihood of effective problem solving by stimulating discussion, guarding against premature closure of an issue, and preventing a family from uncritically accepting information, opinions, and suggestions. Third, conflict often clarifies rules and positions. After a conflict you usually know where individuals stand on an issue and know what the rules and expectations of group members are. Fourth, conflict may be cathartic in that it enables family members to express themselves and get their feelings out in the open. Thus, family conflict is not just something to be avoided. It is an important part of family interaction and has several beneficial consequences.

However, conflict can hurt family cohesion and the ability of families to function effectively. Conflicts sometimes increase tension and hostility, which interfere with effective communication and problem solving. The hostility generated can decrease morale and result in feelings of rejection. As a result, some may withdraw from the family or react in aggressive and violent ways. Sometimes a spiral of hostility is created in which conflicts become increasingly severe and violent. Thus, one of the major risks of conflict is the possibility of escalation.

Areas and Types of Conflict

People have conflicts over many different issues and their responses vary widely. In this section we identify common areas of marital conflict and their manifestations.

Nye (1976) has examined conflict and control within each of eight family roles (see Table 7·1). The role of greatest conflict is socialization of children. Nye did not ask the respondents specifically about money, but other research has found that couples frequently have this type of conflict. For example, Blood and Wolfe (1960) found that money and children were the two most frequent areas of conflict. Madden and Janoff-Bulman (1981) observed that spending money and relations with relatives were the two most frequent areas of conflict, followed closely by conflicts over the children. Division of household chores, child care, and communication were also common areas of conflict.

No matter what the area of conflict, it may take many different forms. **Overt conflict** is open conflict that both parties are aware of and face directly. **Covert conflict** is hidden or concealed conflict. For example, in a covert conflict Michael might say, "No, I'm not angry that you spent some money without consulting

TABLE 7·1   Frequency of Conflict in Family Roles by Sex of Respondent (in percentages)

Role	Very Frequent or Frequent	Sometimes	Seldom	Never	Total
Socialization					
Wives' Reports	7	47	47	9	100
Husbands' Reports	6	34	48	11	99
Child Care					
Wives' Reports	0	15	51	33	99
Husbands' Reports	4	20	54	22	100
Provider					
(Husband's Occupation)					
Wives' Reports	1	10	32	58	101
Husbands' Reports	5	10	38	47	100
Provider					
(Wife's Occupation)					
Wives' Reports	1	12	20	67	100
Husbands' Reports	4	7	29	60	100
Housekeeper					
Wives' Reports	2	16	41	40	99
Husbands' Reports	3	20	45	31	99
Kinship					
Wives' Reports	5	18	51	26	100
Husbands' Reports	3	21	50	26	100
Recreation					
Wives' Reports	1	24	47	28	100
Husbands' Reports	2	20	50	28	100

SOURCE: Nye 1976:170, Table 9.8. Reprinted by permission.

me," and then purposely not do his share of the housework to get back at his wife. Lorraine may openly agree to Michael's desire not to buy a car, but may get back at him by purposely overspending on other things. Although covert conflict is not admitted openly, it is still conflict and may be very vicious.

Conflict may also be divided into physical and nonphysical. **Physical conflict** is an actual attack or threat of attack on another with physical force. It includes shoving, slapping, hitting, kicking, or throwing things. **Nonphysical conflict** is the use of words and other means to gain control of the other person. For example, in a recent conflict Lorraine said to Michael, "If you don't start cleaning up after yourself, I am going down and get the second car that I want." Michael responded, "Will you stop being so childish! That will just delay even longer our buying a car." Nonphysical conflict usually includes name calling and put-downs, but may also include things such as ignoring the other, spending money, not doing the chores, or making a mess. It includes any attempt other than physical force to defeat the other or get even.

Conflict may also be instrumental or expressive. **Instrumental conflict** includes actions with a specific purpose. For example, instrumental conflict would be Lorraine's purposely not cleaning up after Michael in an effort to get him to realize his neglectfulness and change his ways. Similarly, a parent may spank a child with the intent of teaching him an important lesson.

Expressive conflicts are emotional outbursts that are based more on feelings than rational consequences. They usually do not have a specific purpose other than the expression of emotions, such as anger, frustration, and hurt. For example, violently attacking a spouse is usually an expressive conflict. Another example is a husband who fought bitterly to obtain custody of his children when his wife filed for divorce. The court battle was devastating to himself emotionally and monetarily and hurt his children deeply. His actions were an expression of anger and an attempt to hurt his wife rather than a rationally thought-out action.

There are societal norms regarding acceptable forms of conflict. For example, it is acceptable to spank a child on the buttocks but not to hit him or her with the same force on the head. Yelling at a child may be more acceptable than yelling at a spouse. Instrumental conflict appears to be more acceptable than expressive conflict. Families often establish rules about what is acceptable and unacceptable when conflicts arise.

Physical conflict rarely occurs in the absence of verbal (nonphysical) conflict. Straus (1974) found that as verbal aggression increases, the level of physical aggression increases. However, many verbal conflicts do not lead to physical conflict.

A conflict that is primarily instrumental often becomes expressive as individuals contend with each other. Most conflicts have both instrumental and expressive elements to them. For example, a father who is punishing his son to teach him a lesson may expressively lash out at him after his son calls him a "stupid jerk."

Overt conflicts sometimes occur because of covert conflicts. For example, a father who yells at his son over a minor infraction (overt, nonphysical, and expressive conflict) may simply be reacting to a covert conflict he has had with his wife. Although she has said she is not angry, she has covertly withheld affection until he starts helping more around the house (covert, nonphysical, instrumental conflict).

Sometimes individuals do not recognize or admit their covert conflicts. One couple was having many conflicts over intimacy, money, child rearing, and division of labor. She was a poor money manager and repeatedly would write checks when they had nothing in the bank. Over a period of time her behavior brought the family near bankruptcy, even though they had a sizable income. She would excuse her behavior by saying that a family member needed or wanted the thing she purchased. However, an analysis of the timing and nature of her purchases showed that they came directly after conflicts with her husband. She did not seem to be spending for physical necessities, but rather to hurt her husband. Although she never admitted this to her husband or even to herself, her spending was to get even with him for perceived grievances. It was her way of asserting herself, hurting him, and showing that she did not have to comply.

Family members often have mixed motives in their conflicts. For example, Lorraine wants to get Michael to help more around the house but wants to maintain a positive relationship. Michael wants Lorraine to spend less money but wants her to have nice clothes and feel positive toward him. Although they may lash out in anger and try to hurt the other, they still love each other and want to cooperate.

Managing Conflicts

All families have conflicts and the critical issue is how to manage them. Broderick (1977) has identified three major ways people attempt to manage conflicts. He labels these (1) power confrontations, (2) rules, and (3) principles.

Power Confrontations

Broderick refers to his first mode of conflict management as hedonistic zero-sum **power confrontations.** This strategy is an attempt to unilaterally impose one's will on the other. It is based on self-interest and is called zero-sum because whatever one wins the other loses. There is a direct confrontation and the one with the greater power defeats the other.

Power confrontations are frequently used in conflicts. A father who threatens his children with a beating if they do not go to bed is one example of a power confrontation. Because of his superior physical power his children obey rather than risk a beating, even though they do not want to go. He wins and they lose.

These power confrontations need not be based on physical force. For example, suppose a father tells his teenage son that he cannot use the car unless he does the dishes. Even though the boy does not want to do the dishes, he complies because his father controls the car. As far as the dishes go, the father wins and the son loses.

Broderick (1977) maintains that there are only two circumstances under which families can survive if zero-sum power confrontations are the primary method of conflict management. First, the parties must be evenly matched so that their wins and losses are about equal. Individuals who continually lose and have no hope of ever winning are likely to try to gain additional resources or leave the family.

A second situation where power confrontation may be the primary method of family conflict management is when the weaker person perceives no alternatives. For example, Gelles (1976) found that some abused wives stayed in their marriages because they felt they had no realistic alternatives.

Rules

Another method of managing conflicts is to use preestablished **rules.** For this procedure to work, family members must accept the rules and feel some responsibility to follow them. The specific rules may be explicitly negotiated, may emerge out of previous situations, or may be adopted unwittingly from societal norms. There are three major types of rules, according to Broderick (1977): (1) rules about distribution of resources, (2) rules about allocation of authority, and (3) rules about negotiation.

DISTRIBUTION. **Rules about distribution of resources** govern the direct allocation of family resources. A mealtime dispute in the Martin family illustrates how rules may be used to manage conflict. In addition to the mother and father, there are three boys in the Martin family. Matt is 8, Ben is 7, and Scott is 5. As they get ready for dinner, Ben sits down without washing his hands. Mrs. Martin asks him to go wash his hands. While he is gone Scott sits in the place where Ben had been sitting. When Ben returns he yells, "That is my place! Get out of there, I was there first!" Scott responds, "You left, so now it is my place." Ben yells back, "That is my place and you know it. Get off or I'll knock you off!" "No way," Scott says. Ben then shoves Scott off the chair and claims the chair. Scott gets up and tries to push Ben off the chair, but Ben is bigger and stronger and just punches Scott and knocks him to the floor. Scott begins crying loudly. At this point Matt is irritated at their yelling and says, "Ben and Scott, stop acting like babies or I'll pound you both!" Ben says, "Go ahead and try. I'm not afraid of you." At this point Mr. and Mrs. Martin intervene.

After dinner when things have calmed down, Mr. and Mrs. Martin sit their children down to talk about the problem. They explain that meals have become very unpleasant because of all the yelling, hitting, and fighting over who sits where. They ask the boys if they enjoy the fighting. All three boys express dislike for the fights and wish things were more pleasant. After some discussion, Mrs. Martin suggests that they have assigned seats. Then everyone will know where his seat is, and they won't have to fight over who sits where. The children agree and seats are assigned.

Next evening Ben sits in Scott's assigned seat. Scott yells at Ben to get out of his seat. Ben is about to hit Scott when Mrs. Martin says, "Ben, this is Scott's seat. Remember, you agreed to sit over in this other chair." Ben remembers the new family rule and reluctantly moves to his assigned place. The rule has been used to manage the conflict over seats.

Rules can be made about how to distribute any valued resource, including money, use of the family car, or seats at the dinner table. The rules reduce power confrontations by giving presolutions to potential problems. In our example, a power confrontation over seats is avoided by the rule about seat allocation.

AUTHORITY. **Rules about allocation of authority** specify who has the legitimate right to make decisions in a certain area. For example, Michael and Lorraine have agreed that he has the final say regarding what type of car to purchase, and she has the final say regarding what furniture to put in the house. Michael decided to purchase a Honda Accord, and Lorraine agreed even though she wanted a different car. Similarly, Michael let Lorraine chose the couch even though he did not particularly like the style or color.

The Martins also illustrate how rules about authority may be used to manage family conflicts. They have a rule that each person has authority over his or her belongings. Each of the boys has his own bicycle. Scott's bike has a flat tire and he is too small to fix it himself. Mr. Martin has not had time yet to fix it. Scott wants to go bike riding and asks Ben if he can use Ben's bike. Ben says no. Scott goes to Mr. Martin, hoping that he will overrule Ben. Mr. Martin talks to Ben and asks Ben to let Scott ride his bike. Mr. Martin says Scott will not hurt it and that Ben is not using it. It is not Scott's fault he has a flat tire. Ben still firmly says no. With some impatience and anger, Mr. Martin tells Ben he is being selfish and that he ought to let Scott use his bike. At this point Ben responds, "Dad, you have said that we each have control over our own things. That is my bike and I do not want Scott to ride it." Mr. Martin remembers the rule, and complies with it. He then tells Scott that he is sorry that there is no bike to ride, that he wishes Ben would share his bike, but that it is Ben's bike and Ben is in charge of it.

Mr. Martin or Scott could have had a power confrontation with Ben. However, because of the rule that each family member controls his own property, Mr. Martin and Scott deferred to Ben even though they strongly disagreed with him.

NEGOTIATION.   **Rules about negotiation** specify how conflicts may be negotiated. In all types of conflicts there are rules about what is fair. In conflicts between nations it is usually more acceptable to shoot guns than to use biological warfare. In football it is fair to tackle the quarterback as long as he has the ball, but illegal to tackle him after the ball has left his hand. In families it is acceptable to spank a young child but not your spouse.

All families set up rules about what are acceptable tactics when conflicts occur. In the Martin family there are two major rules for negotiating conflicts. First, it is unfair to physically hit another. You may confront, yell, cry, express hurt, or withdraw, but it is not fair to hit. Second, it is unfair to attack the personal integrity of another. You may say you are angered by a particular act, but it is inappropriate to generalize that to a person's self. For example, if Scott takes Ben's bike without permission, it would be unfair for Ben to hit Scott or to say, "You good-for-nothing slimy piece of snot!" Rules about negotiation are particularly important in regulating conflict and keeping it from escalating beyond tolerable limits.

It is important to distinguish between rule making and rule enforcement. A family may be democratic in the formation of rules but assign one person the responsibility to enforce a rule.

The critical aspect of rules is that they be mutually agreed upon. Only when individuals agree with a rule can compliance be expected. Rules will not eliminate conflicts over an issue, but will help regulate conflict if the family members generally agree with the rule.

Principles

The final method of resolving conflicts is to use a few general principles. **Principles** are rules but are more general. To have a specific rule to manage every different type of conflict would result in a large number of rules, although conflicts could be managed with only a few general principles if they are internalized and applied by family members.

For example, if the Martin children had internalized a general concern for each other, there would not have been a need to assign seats at the table. When Scott returned from washing his hands he would tell Ben he was there first and ask him to move to another seat. Ben, out of concern for Scott, probably, would comply with Scott's request and move. If Ben didn't want to move,

Scott, out of concern for Ben, would not scream or hit but would take another place.

There would not be a need for a variety of rules about where to sit, when to be home, or about not using other people's things. Because they all had a concern for others, they would not do things to knowlingly hurt or inconvenience others.

The use of principles requires a certain level of empathy and maturity among family members. The principles will work only if family members have internalized them and can apply them to specific situations. Young children generally do not have the maturity to use principles, and it is rare for families to operate primarily at this level.

Family conflict is complex and most families operate at all three levels, depending on the nature of the conflict. For example, Lorraine and Michael use principles with regard to physical intimacy. There is no need to establish specific rules because both are sensitive and conflicts are resolved because of concern and empathy. With regard to household chores, however, they have established some specific rules to help resolve conflicts that arise. Lorraine has authority over conflicts within the house (food, furniture, etc.), while Michael has the right to make final decisions for things outside the house (yard, automobiles, etc.). They do occasionally have a power play over household chores and over kinship relations.

Conflict and Marital Satisfaction

Marital satisfaction is influenced by the way conflicts are perceived and handled, as well as by the type of marital control. In this section we review the research on conflict and marital satisfaction.

One relevant variable is perception of **control** over conflicts. People who feel that they have some control over their conflicts tend to have higher marital satisfaction than people who feel they have no control (Madden and Janoff-Bulman 1981). Feeling that one has some control apparently leads to the perception that the conflict is manageable.

Covert conflict management strategies such as denial, displacement, and disengagement tend to lower marital satisfaction (Galvin and Brommel 1986). In **denial** a person verbally denies the conflict but nonverbal signals indicate otherwise. For example, Michael might say, "That didn't bother me," when in fact he is extremely angry and upset. **Displacement** occurs when anger toward one person is displaced on to another. To illustrate, Mr. Martin may scream at Scott for doing some little thing, when Mr. Martin is really upset at Mrs. Martin. **Disengagement** is avoiding the other person and expressing hostility through lack of interaction. Denial, displacement, and disengagement tend to decrease marital satisfaction because conflicts are not dealt with directly until they build to a very high level and explode into a serious overt conflict.

Gunnysacking is a common overt strategy that tends to decrease marital satisfaction (Galvin and Brommel 1986). Grievances are stored covertly until they reach an intolerable level, and then one grievance becomes a last straw and all of the stored-up grievances are dumped on the other person. The dumping of a large number of grievances all at once tends to increase negative feelings and usually results in counterattacks. Most important, the various grievances cannot be dealt with constructively, simply because there are too many problems to deal with simultaneously.

Negative reciprocity is a common response in conflicts. When one receives a complaint, one gives a countercomplaint rather than trying to understand the complaint. High levels of negative reciprocity have been shown to decrease the level of marital satisfaction (Krokoff 1987).

What are some of the conflict management strategies that tend to improve marital satisfaction? One of the most important factors is to listen for understanding rather than for judgment. Another is neutral communication that expresses understanding and tends to decrease the competitive nature of the interaction (Galvin and Brommel 1986; Mandersheid et al. 1982). Unless there is flexibility and a willingness to compromise, the conflict is more likely to escalate.

The ability to manage conflict also depends on the trust and security in a relationship. Rands, Levinger, and Mellinger (1981) found that when there was trust and security, openly confronting conflict tended to improve marital satisfaction. However, among couples low in trust and security, confrontation could escalate the conflict and cause deterioration of the relationship.

In summary, with appropriate conflict management, marital satisfaction tends to increase rather than decrease following a conflict (Hagen and Burch 1985). Management techniques that tend to be associated with higher satisfaction are high levels of empathy, flexibility, and compromise and low levels of blaming, attacking, and negative reciprocity. Having a certain level of trust and security also is a critical element in being able to manage conflict.

Power and Control

Power is at the heart of conflict management. One of Broderick's methods of conflict resolution is the power play in which one attempts to coerce another into compliance. Whether or not a power play is attempted may depend on perceived power. For example, Scott may not attempt to overpower Ben, simply because Ben is larger and stronger and Scott knows he will lose. Therefore, Scott may negotiate and attempt to establish rules. Or Scott may seek a coalition with another sibling to overpower Ben. If a power play is attempted, the more powerful will win.

People often talk about power, but what is it? **Power** generally refers to the ability of one person to modify the behavior of another. It is potential and does not necessarily imply the exercise of that potential. Lorraine might have great power over Michael and may choose not to use it.

There are two other concepts that are often confused with power. First, there are attempts by one person to change the behavior of another. This is called a **control attempt** (Rollins and Bahr 1976). A control attempt may be a single gesture or a series of gestures. For example, if Lorraine says to Michael, "I have lots of homework tonight, so you do the dishes, " this is a control attempt.

Second, there is the actual outcome of a control attempt, which is called **control.** This is a behavioral outcome, the actual modification of the behavior of one by another. The amount of control of one person over another depends on compliance with control attempts, and may vary from low to high. For example, if Michael complies with almost all of Lorraine's control attempts, her control over him would be very high. If Michael rejects almost all of Lorraine's control attempts, her control over him would be very low.

Power is not an individual attribute but is relational. That is, power makes sense only in relation to others. To say that Lorraine is powerful makes little sense unless the relationship is specified. She may be powerful relative to Michael and weak relative to her mother.

Furthermore, power is a meaningful concept only when a conflict exists between two or more persons or groups. The power of one person as a basis for control over the behavior of another person is meaningless if the other

Money is one of the most frequent areas of marital conflict. Here a husband and wife openly discuss their financial differences and negotiate a financial plan that they both can accept. *Frank Siteman/The Picture Cube.*

person would have behaved in the same manner if the power was absent. For example, if Michael plans on doing the dishes and Lorraine says, "Do the dishes," it is questionable that her power was a basis for control. He would have done the dishes even if she had said nothing.

Power and control are specific to situations or roles. For example, Michael may have more power in the provider role while Lorraine may have greater power in the housekeeper role. They might have an overall balance of power even though each is more powerful in specific roles or situations.

Marital control is the degree to which one partner complies with the control attempts of the other. When Lorraine makes a control attempt, Michael may reject or comply with the attempt. For a given situation or time sequence, the amount of control of Lorraine over Michael would be the ratio of his compliance to the total control attempts of Lorraine. Similarly, the amount of control of Michael over Lorraine would be the ratio of her compliance to his total control attempts. It is possible for both to have a large amount or a small amount of control over the other. If they both rejected a high proportion of each other's control attempts, they would each have a low level of marital control. **Relative control** would be the ratio of Lorraine's control to Michael's control.

Resources and authority have been identified as two major bases of marital power and control (Rollins and Bahr 1976). **Resources** are anything that one may give to another to satisfy needs or attain goals. Possible resources include good looks, sexual prowess, communication skills, information, prestige, and money. An important aspect of a resource is that it may be given or withheld.

Authority refers to norms about who "ought to" control different situations in marriage. It is what is considered proper for a man or woman.

Five major concepts have been identified: authority, resources, power, control attempts, and control. These five concepts will now be used to explain how marital control is achieved. As we use these concepts to analyze marriages, four things should be emphasized. First, these five concepts are relational, in that their meaning depends on the level of the wife relative to the husband. For example, we are interested in the relative control between husband and wife. Second, relative authority, relative resources, and relative power do not exist independently of the perceptions of the marriage partners. Their perceptions are real to them and the basis for their actions. Third, power and control are relevant only when conflict exists between the marriage partners. Fourth, relative power and relative control may vary from one area of marriage to another.

The five concepts have been integrated into a simplified model of marital power (see Figure 7·1). The model states that resources can accrue because of the norms (Proposition 1). When norms give one spouse the right to exercise power, this tends to increase opportunities for resource acquisition. For example, a husband may become more competent at monetary decision making if the norms state that he should make those decisions. Over time he will acquire skills that a wife may not have the opportunity to develop.

Propositions 2 and 3 state that the perception of power depends on resources and authority. The more resources Michael has that are valuable to Lorraine, the more she will perceive that he has power. Similarly, the more the societal and family norms recognize Michael as the legitimate authority of the marriage, the more perceived power he will hold.

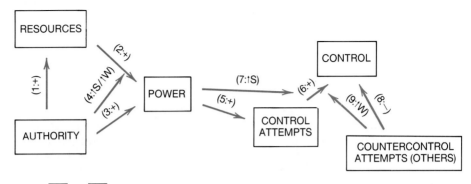

FIGURE 7·1   A Simplified Model of Social Power

SOURCE: Rollins, B. C., and S. J. Bahr. 1976. A theory of power relationships in marriage. *Journal of Marriage and the Family* 38:622. Copyrighted 1976 by the National Council on Family Relations, 1910 West County Road B, Suite 147, St. Paul, Minnesota 55113. Reprinted by permission.

Authority influences the effect of resources on perceived power (Proposition 4). To illustrate, suppose that according to the norms Michael should have the final say regarding monetary decisions. Michael and Lorraine may both recognize that he "should" have more say regarding monetary decisions. Furthermore, suppose that Lorraine has greater skill than Michael in making monetary decisions. Even with her greater competence, Lorraine is likely to defer to Michael in the face of a monetary conflict because the norms say that is the way it "should" be. The effect of her resource (monetary competence) on her power will be lessened because of the norms. Thus, norms that specify one spouse or the other as the authority will have the effect of reducing the impact of resources on power. Under conditions of equalitarian norms, the effect of resources on power will be greater than when norms are not egalitarian, because egalitarian norms do not condition or interfere with the impact of resources on power.

The greater the perceived power, the more likely one will make a control attempt (Proposition 5). If Michael feels like he has power over Lorraine, he will likely make control attempts. If he feels he has little power over Lorraine and that she will not listen to him, he will probably not attempt, for example, to influence her decision to buy a couch.

The model shows that the control of one partner over the other depends on the number of control attempts (Proposition 6). That is, the more control attempts Michael makes, the more control he will exercise over Lorraine.

The effect of Michael's control attempts are conditioned by Lorraine's perception of Michael's power (Proposition 7). The more power she attributes to Michael, the more likely she will comply to a control attempt.

The amount of control of one partner over another also depends on the number of countercontrol attempts (Proposition 8). **Countercontrol attempts** are control attempts by other persons that conflict with the control attempts of a spouse. An example would be Lorraine's friends suggesting that she buy a new couch although Michael tells her not to do so.

Countercontrol attempts not only affect control directly but they condition the effect of control attempts on control (Proposition 9). To illustrate, the countercontrol attempts of Lorraine's friends to buy a couch are going to lessen the effect of Michael's directives not to buy a couch.

The model in Figure 7·1 shows how authority, resources, power, and control attempts affect control. However, the model does not show the relative nature of marital power and control. A wife's control over her husband depends on her control attempts toward him, her perception of relative power, her perception of relative authority, and her perception of relative resources. Similarly, his control over his wife depends on his control attempts toward his wife and his perceptions of relative authority, resources, and power.

For a variety of reasons, two partners' perceptions of relative authority, resources, and power are likely to be different. Each partner has had different background experiences, is a different gender, and performs somewhat different roles in a marriage.

In order to take these differences into account, the theory in Figure 7·1 has been expanded (see Figure 7·2). Although the complexity of Figure 7·2 may be difficult to follow, the concepts are the same as those shown in Figure 7·1. Figure 7·2 simply shows how relative marital control depends on the control attempts and perceptions of both partners.

An important aspect of control is the way a control attempt is made. If Michael warmly says to Lorraine, "Please, let's try to follow the budget we agreed upon," he is likely to get a very different response than if he yells, "Stop spending money so carelessly!"

Control attempts can be divided into three types: (1) induction, (2) coercion, and (3) manipulation. **Induction** is a persuasive attempt to try to get the other to comply. For example, Mr. Martin might say, "It is late, I am tired, and you children have school tomorrow. Don't you think you should go to bed?" An example of a coercive control attempt would be Mr. Martin saying, "It is time for bed. Get into bed or I will spank your bottoms!" **Coercion** is using force or a force threat to obtain compliance (Rollins and Thomas 1979). **Manipulation** is a covert control attempt in which the other is not aware of the control attempt. One tries to obtain compliance from the other without the other being aware of it. For example, if Mr. Martin has Scott sit on the bed while he reads the child a story, Scott may fall asleep, which was Mr. Martin's purpose all along even though Scott was unaware of his intentions. The *covert* nature of manipulation is its defining characteristic.

Coercion is very effective in obtaining immediate compliance but increases

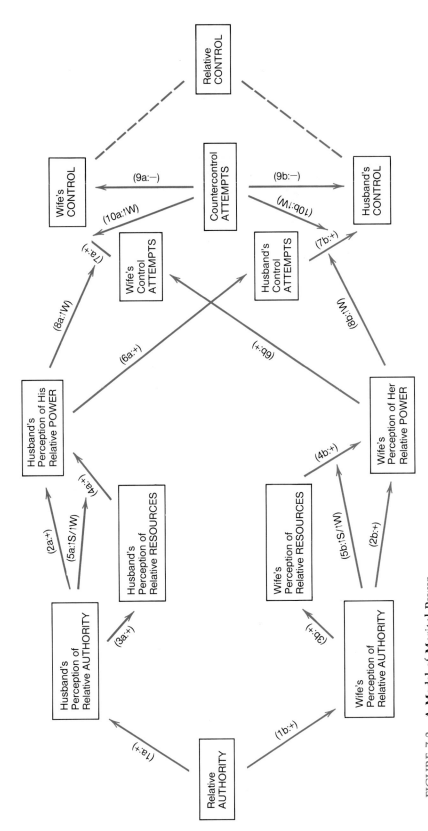

FIGURE 7-2 A Model of Marital Power

SOURCE: Rollins, B. C., and S. J. Bahr. 1976. A theory of power relationships in marriage. *Journal of Marriage and the Family* 38:624. Copyrighted 1976 by the National Council on Family Relations, 1910 West County Road B, Suite 147, St. Paul, Minnesota 55113. Reprinted by permission.

negative feelings and may increase resistance to future control attempts. Induction tends to be associated with control but does not result in resentment and future resistance. Manipulation may be effective when other types of control attempts do not work, but has the risk of being discovered, which may result in resentment and resistance to future control attempts (Mooney 1984; Rollins and Thomas 1979).

Who Has the Power and Control?

One of the questions frequently asked about marriage is, "Who has the power?" This is difficult to answer because of the complexity of marital interaction. Studies have shown that marital partners themselves cannot identify reliably who has the final say in conflict situations. Broderick's (1977) typology shows why. Michael may win some conflicts by power play but many other conflicts may be resolved by rules or principles. Therefore, it may be inaccurate to describe Michael or Lorraine as the more powerful. Furthermore, control is often exchanged. Lorraine may give in to Michael in one situation if she can get her way in another situation. If we were to look only at the one situation it may appear that Michael has the power, when in reality they are egalitarian.

Another complicating factor is manipulation. Norms may prescribe the man as the more powerful, but a woman may exercise control through manipulation.

Although they are difficult to measure, conflict, power, and control are important aspects of marital relations. The questions of what married couples fight over and who has control still remain, and many scholars have attempted to respond to them. Although their answers must be considered tentative because of the complexity of conflict and power, it is interesting to explore their findings.

Studies of who has the control in marriage have not been entirely consistent. Employment of the wife tends to increase her control over financial matters but decrease her control over household decisions (Bahr 1974a). A summary of perceived control within each of the eight family roles is shown in Table 7·2. The husbands tended to win more conflicts than wives regarding socialization, their occupation, and recreation. The wives were more likely to win conflicts over child care, housekeeping, and their occupation. Conflicts over kinship tended to be managed in a more egalitarian way.

Some of the differences in husbands' and wives' perceptions of conflict resolution are interesting. Husbands were more likely than wives to perceive that there is conflict in the child care role and more likely to perceive that the conflict is resolved according to their wishes. The wives were more likely than the husbands to feel that the husband wins more conflicts in recreational issues than the wife. Overall, the wives perceived that there was less conflict than the husbands.

Katz (1983) did a comparative analysis of marital control in Belgium, Canada, France, Greece, Israel, Japan, and the United States. She found that in all seven countries there is a tendency toward marital equality even though the countries vary in cultural background and in level of modernization. Katz concludes that among modern urban families there is no longer male dominance but an equal balance of power and control.

TABLE 7·2 Resolution of Conflict by Role and Sex of Respondent (in percentages)

Role	Conflict Resolved in Favor of						
	Husband Always	Husband More	Equal	Wife More	Wife Always	No Conflict	Total
Socialization							
Wives' Reports	12	38	27	17	0	6	100
Husbands' Reports	9	35	30	18	2	6	100
Child Care							
Wives' Reports	6	15	24	26	1	27	99
Husbands' Reports	5	24	31	24	3	12	99
Provider							
(Husband's Occupation)							
Wives' Reports	36	16	4	1	0	43	100
Husbands' Reports	36	23	8	1	1	31	100
Provider							
(Wife's Occupation)							
Wives' Reports	9	8	8	14	9	52	100
Husbands' Reports	6	8	10	22	13	42	101
Housekeeper							
Wives' Reports	2	4	7	45	7	34	99
Husbands' Reports	1	8	8	45	15	22	99
Kinship							
(Your Kin)							
Wives' Reports	5	8	43	14	2	28	100
Husbands' Reports	8	31	36	5	1	20	101
Recreation							
Wives' Reports	7	34	27	9	0	24	101
Husbands' Reports	6	26	38	14	0	17	101

SOURCE: Nye 1976: 173, Table 9.9. Reprinted by permission.

Control and Marital Satisfaction

Research has shown that married couples who are egalitarian in relative control are more satisfied than couples in which control is unequal (Mashal 1985). It appears to be difficult to maintain close, interpersonal relationships when there is an imbalance in power and control (Kipnis 1972). Martin and Osmond (1975) found that power asymmetry leads to mutual distrust and interpersonal exploitation, whereas symmetry is associated with higher satisfaction.

If marriage is conceived as a social exchange, then it follows that *the greater the control of each partner over the other, the greater the marital satisfaction of each partner.* The essence of this hypothesis is that when marital partners give in to each other relatively frequently, the relationship is enhanced. Responding positively to a spouse's request when one would prefer not to may ease tensions and be interpreted as an expression of love. For example, at his wife's request a husband may willingly change his child's diaper even though he detests the task. He may honor many such unpleasant requests because he values the relationship with his wife and loves her. Viewed in a social exchange perspective one might say his wife has power over him because she has resources to fulfill his needs. Frequent rejection of one's requests (control attempts) by his partner would tend to produce the opposite effect. It would be frustrating, reduce goal attainment, produce conflict, and decrease marital satisfaction.

This hypothesis distinguishes **amount of control** from relative control (who has more control). In an egalitarian relationship each might have little or much control over the other. A husband may have more control than his wife and yet have little control over her. And it is possible for a husband in an egalitarian relationship to have more actual control than a husband in a husband-dominant relationship. In the latter case, the husband may have little control over his wife, even though he has more control than she has. The important consideration is that the *relative* control of husband and wife does not indicate the degree to which one controls the other, but only that one has more, the same, or less control than the other.

This hypothesis requires one important qualification. The positive relationship between control and satisfaction would only hold up to a certain level of control, beyond which satisfaction would tend to decrease because the relationship would become stifling. Thus, when control of one over the other becomes excessive, the relationship may become overly restrictive and individuality will be lost.

The relationship between control and satisfaction is a reciprocal process within the family system rather than a simple cause-and-effect relationship. Although control has been identified as the independent variable, changes in satisfaction may produce changes in control. For example, if a relationship becomes unsatisfactory to the wife for some reason, this is likely to produce a reduction in her responsiveness to her husband. If satisfaction increases for some reason, responsiveness to the other would tend to increase.

Because the control of the husband is independent of the control of the wife (as shown in Figure 7·2), the control of one spouse could be high while that of the other is low. Thus, four types of marital control are possible if the level of husband and wife control is dichotomized: (1) In the **syncratic** type both husband and wife have a high degree of control over each other. (2) The wife is high on control and the husband low on control in the **wife-dominant** type. (3) The **husband-dominant** type includes those couples with high husband control and low wife control. (4) Both husband and wife possess a small amount of control in the **autonomic** type.

TABLE 7·3   Marital Satisfaction by Type of Marital Control (in percentages)

Would marry same person again**	Husbands' Perceptions				Wives' Perceptions			
	*Syncratic	Hus. dom.	Wife dom.	*Autonomic	*Syncratic	Hus. dom.	Wife dom.	*Autonomic
Certainly	76	68	39	57	85	56	44	26
Probably	16	25	39	30	12	20	33	44
Undecided or no	8	8	23	13	4	25	22	31
	100%	101%	101%	100%	101%	101%	99%	101%
N	106	40	13	47	104	61	9	39

* *Syncratic:* husband and wife were both high on level of control; *autonomic:* husband and wife were both low on level of control.
** Based on the question "If you were to marry again, would you want to marry the same person"
SOURCE: Bahr 1974b:26, Table 1. Reprinted by permission.

Satisfaction with Communication About Personal Problems by Type of Marital Control (in percentages)

Satisfaction with communi- cation**	Husbands' Perceptions				Wives' Perceptions			
	*Syn- cratic	Hus. dom.	Wife dom.	*Auto- nomic	*Syn- cratic	Hus. dom.	Wife dom.	*Auto- nomic
Satisfied	62	78	25	48	62	38	44	47
Unsatisfied	38	22	75	52	38	62	56	53
	100%	100%	100%	100%	100%	100%	100%	100%
N	100	36	12	44	100	61	9	38

* *Syncratic:* husband and wife were both high on level of control; *autonomic:* husband and wife were both low on level of control.
* Based on the question "Do you wish you could talk more to your wife (husband) about your problems than you do?" Respondents were asked to reply yes or no and explain their answer.
SOURCE: Bahr 1974b:27, Table 2. Reprinted by permission.

As noted earlier, couples with an imbalance of control tend to be less satisfied than couples that are more egalitarian (Marshal 1985). Furthermore, Bahr (1974b) found that egalitarian couples with high levels of control (syncratic) tend to be more satisfied than egalitarian couples with low levels of control (autonomic), as shown in Table 7·3. For both men and women the highest levels of satisfaction occur in the syncratic type. The men have the lowest satisfaction when they are low in control and their wife is high in control (wife-dominant). Women tend to be low in satisfaction when they have little control and their husband is high in control (husband-dominant), although they are lowest in satisfaction when both spouses are low in control (autonomic).

Table 7·4 shows satisfaction with marital communication by type of marital control. The data show that satisfaction was higher among syncratic than autonomic types and that inequality was related to unhappiness, especially for the partner with less control. Wives were very unsatisfied with communication when their husband was dominant, and similarly men were very dissatisfied when their wife was dominant. However, men were generally satisfied with communication when they were dominant, whereas women tended not to be satisfied when they were dominant. This is probably related to the norms in our society, which are much more accepting of male than female dominance.

Conclusion

Conflict is a pervasive, necessary aspect of family life and may have constructive and destructive consequences, depending on the nature of the conflict and how it is managed. Absence of conflict is not an indication of marital satisfaction or stability.

The way conflicts are managed influences marital satisfaction. Avoiding conflict tends to be associated with lower levels of satisfaction. Confronting conflict tends to increase marital satisfaction if there is trust, flexibility, and empathy and not too much blaming and negative reciprocity.

The nature of conflict management depends on the control structure of families. Control is an exchange process in which there is a constant negotiation based on resources and norms within and outside the family.

Inequality in power and control impedes marital communication and is associated with low marital satisfaction. This may be explained by social exchange theory, because inequality impedes exchange. Equality leads to higher satisfaction because it is more rewarding than being dominated or dominating. Similarly, high compliance with control attempts by both partners is an indication of mutually rewarding exchanges.

Summary

1. Conflict is disagreement in which one blocks the desires of another. It tends to be subjective, unstable, reactive, and complicated.
2. Conflict exists in all groups and is a normal, recurrent characteristic of family life.
3. Conflict may stimulate interaction, aid in problem solving, clarify rules, and be cathartic. It may also decrease cohesion, increase tension, interfere with communication, and lead to aggression and violence.
4. The most common areas of marital conflict are money, children, and relatives.
5. Conflict may be overt or covert, physical or nonphysical, and instrumental or expressive.
6. Power confrontations, rules, and principles are three ways to manage conflicts. There are rules about (1) distribution of resources, (2) allocation of authority, and (3) negotiation.
7. Denial, displacement, disengagement, gunnysacking, blaming, attacking, and negative reciprocity are conflict tactics that tend to decrease marital satisfaction. Nonjudgmental listening, empathy, flexibility, and willingness to compromise are conflict tactics that tend to increase marital satisfaction.
8. When trust and security are high, confrontation tends to increase marital satisfaction. When trust and security are low, confrontation tends to decrease marital satisfaction.
9. Control is a behavioral outcome of a control attempt, which is a specific attempt to obtain compliance in the face of conflict. Power is the perceived ability to influence another. Control is influenced by control attempts, countercontrol attempts, and perceived power. Control attempts are affected by perceived power, which in turn is influenced by resources and authority.
10. Control attempts may be inductive, coercive, or manipulative.
11. Perceived marital control tends to be egalitarian. Wives tend to have more control than husbands with regard to child care, housekeeping, and their own occupation. Husbands tend to have more control than wives in the areas of child socialization, recreation, and their own occupation.
12. An imbalance of power and control is associated with relatively low marital satisfaction, particularly for the partner with less control.
13. Couples with equality of control and higher-than-average control over each other (syncratic) tend to have higher satisfaction than couples with equality of control and below-average control over each other (autonomic).

Important Terms

- amount of control
- authority
- autonomic
- coercion
- conflict
- control
- control attempt
- countercontrol attempt
- X covert conflict
- denial
- disengagement
- displacement
- expressive conflict
- X gunnysacking
- husband dominant
- induction

- X instrumental conflict
- manipulation
- nonphysical conflict
- X overt conflict
- physical conflict
- X power
- power confrontations
- principles
- X relative control
- resources
- rules
- rules about allocation of authority
- rules about distribution of resources
- rules about negotiation
- syncratic
- wife dominant

Questions for Discussion

1. Give some examples of common marital conflicts.
2. In what ways can conflict benefit families?
3. In what ways can conflict hurt families?
4. Give examples of overt and covert conflict, physical and nonphysical conflict, and instrumental and expressive conflict.
5. Give an example of a power confrontation, a conflict being resolved through rules, and a conflict resolved through principles.
6. Give an example of how conflicts may be resolved through rules about distribution of resources, rules about allocation of authority, and rules about negotiation.
7. Discuss the difference between power and control.
8. Discuss how marital control is related to marital satisfaction.
9. What types of communication styles are likely to help resolve conflicts?
10. Why is imbalance of power likely to result in low marital satisfaction?
11. Distinguish between absolute control and relative control. More specifically, how are syncratic couples different from autonomic couples as explained in the chapter?
12. Observe a couple interacting and record the number of control attempts made by each and the outcome of the control attempts. Also record the topic of each control attempt. Then discuss what type of control structure the couple has and what you learned from the observation.
13. How might the power and control structure of a married couple be changed?
14. Under what conditions is confrontation likely to hurt marital satisfaction, and when is it likely to help marital satisfaction?
15. Is openness always a good thing? Is compromise always a good thing? Explain.

Recommended Reading

Krokoff, L. J. 1987. The correlates of negative affect in marriage. *Journal of Family Issues* 8:111–135.

Rands, M., G. Levinger, and G. D. Mellinger. 1981. Patterns of conflict resolution and marital satisfaction. *Journal of Family Issues* 2:297–321.

References

Bahr, S. J. 1974a. Effects on power and division of labor in the family. In *Working mothers*, ed. L. W. Hoffman and F. I. Nye, 167–185. San Francisco: Jossey-Bass.

Bahr, S. J. 1974b. Conjugal power and marital satisfaction. *Family Perspective* 8:19–29.

Blood, R. O., Jr., and D. M. Wolfe. 1960. *Husbands and wives—the dynamics of married living.* New York: Free Press.

Broderick, C. B. 1977. Power in the governance of families. In *Power in families,* ed. R. F. Cromwell and D. H. Olson, 117–128. Beverly Hill, CA: Halsted.

Felstiner, W. L. F., R. L. Abel, and A. Sarat. 1981. The emergence and transformation of disputes: Naming, blaming, claiming . . ." *Law and Society Review* 15:631–910.

Galvin, K. M., and B. J. Brommel. 1986. *Family communication—cohesion and change.* 2d ed. Glenview, IL: Scott, Foresman.

Gelles, R. J. 1976. Abused wives: Why do they stay? *Journal of Marriage and the Family* 38:659–668.

Hagen, B. J., and G. Burch. 1985. The relationship of group process and group task accomplishment to group member satisfaction. *Small Group Behavior* 16:211–233.

Hayes, M. P., N. Stinnett, and J. Defrain. 1981. Learning about marriage from the divorced. *Journal of Divorce* 4:23–29.

Katz, R. 1983. Conjugal power: A comparative analysis. *International Journal of Sociology of the Family* 13:79–101.

Kipnis, D. 1972. Does power corrupt? *Journal of Personality and Social Psychology* 24:33–41.

Krokoff, L. J. 1987. The correlates of negative affect in marriage. *Journal of Family Issues* 8:111–135.

Madden, M. E., and R. Janoff-Bulman. 1981. Blame, control, and marital satisfaction: Wives' attributions for conflict in marriage. *Journal of Marriage and the Family* 43:663–673.

Mandersheid, R. W., D. S. Rae, A. K. McCarrick, and S. Silbergeld. 1982. A stochastic model of relational control in dyadic interaction. *American Sociological Review* 47:62–75.

Martin, P. Y., and M. Withers Osmond. 1975. Structural asymmetry and social exchange—a sex-role simulation. *Simulation and Games* 6:339–365.

Mashal, M. M. S. 1985. Marital power, role expectations and marital satisfaction. *International Journal of Women's Studies* 8:40–46.

Mooney, L. 1984. The social psychology of power. *Sociological Spectrum* 4:31–51.

Nye, F. I. 1976. Family roles in comparative perspective. In *Role structure and analysis of the family,* ed. F. I. Nye, 149–174. Beverly Hills, CA: Sage.

Rands, M., G. Levinger, and G. D. Mellinger. 1981. Patterns of conflict resolution and marital satisfaction. *Journal of Family Issues* 2:297–321.

Rollins, B. C., and S. J. Bahr. 1976. A theory of power relationships in marriage. *Journal of Marriage and the Family* 38:619–627.

ROLLINS, B. C., and D. L. THOMAS. 1979. Parental support, power, and control techniques in the socialization of children. In *Contemporary theories about the family*, ed. W. R. Burr, R. Hill, F. I. Nye, and R. L. Reiss, 317–364. New York: Free Press.

STRAUS, M. A. 1974. Leveling, civility, and violence in the family. *Journal of Marriage and the Family* 36 (1):13–30.

CHAPTER 8

Sex and Fertility

Introduction

One of the major adjustments in marriage is the development and maintenance of physical intimacy. When two people marry it is expected that they will have sexual intercourse. A marriage that is not consummated may be annulled, and permanent refusal to have sexual intercourse is grounds for divorce. In most societies sexual intercourse with anyone but your spouse is proscribed.

With sex and marriage come decisions about whether or not to have children, and how soon. One of the purposes of marriage is the bearing and raising of children.

Michael and Lorraine have adjusted relatively well sexually. They love each other and enjoy sex, although they have had some doubts and misunderstandings over sexual behavior. Sometimes Michael initiates sexual activity when Lorraine would prefer not to participate. This has been difficult to talk about and has resulted in some misunderstandings and conflicts. Both Lorraine and Michael feel strongly that they should not have sexual intercourse with anyone else. Yet, as the regularity of marriage sets in and pressures of work and school are present, sex is not always as exciting as they had anticipated. Although both feel that they should not have sex outside of marriage, both wonder if the other has had sex with someone else or would like to.

Both Lorraine and Michael would like to have children, but they have decided to wait until Lorraine finishes her college degree. This will enable them to become more prepared for the responsibilities of parenthood.

In this chapter we review recent research on the sexual role within marriage. This includes a discussion of norms, behavior, sexual satisfaction, and extra-marital sex. Then we examine trends in world population and variables that affect fertility decisions.

Sexual Role in Marriage

Sexual Norms

Traditionally men are viewed as the initiators of sexual activity. Recent research indicates that men continue to feel more comfortable than women in initiating sexual behavior (Grauerholz and Serpe 1985).

Carlson (1976) found differences between husbands and wives in their feelings about who should initiate sexual behavior. Almost half of the men felt that husbands and wives should have equal responsibility for initiating sex, although 44 percent felt that husbands should have the primary responsibility for initiating sex. Women, on the other hand, were more likely than the men to say that the husband should be the initiator. Only a quarter of the women said husbands and wives had equal responsibility for initiating sex, and about half of the women felt that men should have the primary responsibility for initiating sexual activity.

In Carlson's (1976) study he asked couples how they felt if a husband or wife rarely consented to have sexual intercourse. The results are shown in Table 8·1. More than 90 percent of the men and 80 percent of the women disapproved of spouses who rarely consent to sexual activities, which is evidence of an expectation of sex within marriage. Men tended to feel more strongly about it than women, as a higher proportion of men than women strongly disapproved of spouses who rarely consent to intercourse.

TABLE 8·1   Sanctions Against Spouse Who Rarely Consents to Have Sexual Intercourse (in percentages)

Attitude	Husband's Report		Wife's Report	
	Husband Who Refuses	Wife Who Refuses	Husband Who Refuses	Wive Who Refuses
Strongly Disapprove	81.3	78.9	65.5	67.3
Mildly Disapprove	9.1	12.2	16.8	16.8
No Feeling One Way or the Other	9.6	8.7	16.8	15.4
Approve	—	0.5	1.1	0.5
Total	100.0	100.3	100.2	100.0
Total (N)	198	208	191	202

SOURCE: Carlson 1976:104, Table 6·1. Reprinted by permission.

There is strong disapproval of extramarital sexual behavior (Carlson 1976; Klemmack and Roff 1980; Thompson 1984a). Carlson (1976) reported that over 80 percent of husbands and 85 percent of wives disapproved of extramarital sex under any circumstances. Even people who were themselves involved in extramarital relationships tended to believe that such involvements are wrong and detract from a marriage (Thompson 1984a).

Sexual Behavior and Satisfaction

Research on actual behavior indicates that husbands initiate sex much more than wives do. In Carlson's (1976) study, 80 percent of both spouses said that the husband initiates sexual behavior more than the wife. This is consistent with the wives' expectation that the husband should initiate sex, but inconsistent with the husbands' preference for shared initiation of sex.

Sometimes one spouse desires sex at a time when the other would prefer not to have it. Carlson (1976) found that in most cases individuals participate when their spouse desires sex, even though they may not desire sex at the time. However, wives are less likely to participate in sex when desired by husbands, than are husbands when desired by wives, as shown in Table 8·2.

The data suggest that wives are less interested in sexual activity than husbands. They desire sex less, are less likely to initiate sex, and more likely to refuse sex than husbands. In the study by Carlson (1976) more than 70 percent of the respondents reported that husbands desire sex more than wives, whereas less than 10 percent said that wives desire sex more than husbands (see Table 8·3).

Most couples enjoy sexual activity most of the time. Among Carlson's (1976) sample over 90 percent of husbands and wives said they usually or always enjoyed sex. However, a greater percentage of husbands than wives reported that they always enjoy sex. Other researchers have also found similar differences between husbands and wives. For example, Schenk, Pfrang, and Rausche (1983) observed that sexuality was less important and satisfying for women than for men. Denney, Field, and Quadagno (1984) found that the somewhat lower sexual satisfaction among women may be due to a desire for more foreplay and afterplay.

The couple's satisfaction with marital sexualilty appears to be dependent on their overall satisfaction with the relationship. For example, Schenk et al. (1983) found that satisfying sexual relationships existed only in happy marriages. Furthermore, they found that sexual satisfaction was not related to

TABLE 8·2 Behavior of Spouse Who Does Not Desire Sex When Other Spouse Desires Sex (by sex of respondent; in percentages)

Action Of Spouse Not Desiring Sex	Husband's Report		Wife's Report	
	Wife Desires Sex When Husband Does Not	Husband Desires Sex When Wife Does Not	Wife Desires Sex When Husband Does Not	Husband Desires Sex When Wife Does Not
Never Participates	1.5	2.0	1.5	2.0
Occasionally Participates	9.8	27.5	6.9	10.3
Usually Participates	42.4	53.9	37.9	65.0
Always Participates	22.0	10.3	28.1	19.2
This Never Happens	24.4	6.4	25.6	3.5
Total	100.1	100.1	100.0	100.0
Total (N)	205	204	203	203

SOURCE: Carlson 1976:106, Table 6·2. Reprinted by permission.

TABLE 8·3   Spouse Who Desires Sex More Frequently (by sex of respondent; in percentages)

Desire	Husband's Report	Wife's Report
Husband Much More Frequently	37.2	34.6
Husband Somewhat More Frequently	41.6	38.1
Husband and Wife the Same	13.0	20.0
Wife Somewhat More Frequently	6.8	6.3
Wife Much More Frequently	1.5	1.0
Total	100.1	100.0
Total (N)	207	205

SOURCE: Carlson 1976:108, Table 6·3. Reprinted by permission.

personality traits. The quality of the relationship appears to be the strongest correlate of sexual satisfaction.

Extramarital Sex

Although there is a strong norm against **extramarital sex,** many married persons participate in extramarital sexual relationships sometime during their marriages. Surveys indicate that almost 50 percent of married women and more than 50 percent of married men engage in extramarital sex at some time (Bell, Turner, and Bosen 1975; Buunk 1980; Hite 1981; Hunt 1974; Pietropinto and Simenauer 1977; Thompson 1983).

Extramarital involvements may be emotional, sexual, or both. Thompson (1984a) studied extramarital involvements of almost four hundred subjects in Western Australia. Almost half (44 percent) of his respondents said they had had some form of intimate involvement outside of their marriage or cohabiting relationships. Men were slightly more likely to be involved than women, 46 percent to 42 percent, respectively. A summary of the responses is shown in Table 8·4. A number of other researchers have found that men are more likely than women to be involved in extramarital sex (Buunk 1980; Hunt 1974; Johnson 1970; Thompson 1983).

Women were somewhat more likely than men to be in love extramaritally

TABLE 8·4   Percentage with Extradyadic Involvement by Type and Sex

	Females	Males
Emotional Only (in love)	21	13
Sexual Only (intercourse)	16	31
Emotional and Sexual	18	21
Total (Percentage with any extradyadic involvement)	42	46
N	(206)	(142)

SOURCE: Thompson, A. P. 1984a. Emotional and sexual components of extramarital relations. *Journal of Marriage and the Family* 46:38. Copyrighted 1984 by the National Council on Family Relations, 1910 West County Road B, Suite 147, St. Paul, Minnesota 55113. Reprinted by permission.

without having sexual intercourse, whereas men were more likely than women to be involved sexually but not emotionally. There were about equal proportions of men and women who were involved both emotionally and sexually. When the overall incidence of extramarital involvement was tabulated (emotional, sexual, and emotional and sexual), female rates were similar to males (Thompson 1984a).

There is widespread belief that extramarital relationships are wrong and hurt marriages (Thompson 1984b). Although those involved extramaritally have more accepting attitudes than those not involved, even those who are involved tend to perceive that extramarital sex is wrong and detracts from the marriage (Thompson 1984a). Relationships that are both emotional and sexual are rated as more wrong than relationships that are sexual but not emotional, and sexual nonemotional relationships are rated more wrong than emotional nonsexual relationships (Thompson 1984a).

Most people say that it is unlikely that they would pursue an extramarital relationship (Thompson 1984a). Given this perception, why do so many actually become involved in extramarital sex? Research has found two major correlates of extramarital involvement. First, the lower the quality of the marriage, the greater the probability of extramarital involvements. This has been termed the **deficit model** of extramarital sex. Individuals are induced into extramarital involvements because their marriage is unhappy. Various rationalizations for their behavior are developed based on their marital deficits. Thompson (1983) estimates that the qualitative characteristics of the marriage account for about 25 percent of the variance in extramarital sexual behavior. A number of researchers have found that extramarital sexual behavior is more likely when marital satisfaction is low (Bell et al. 1975; Edwards 1973; Edwards and Booth 1976; Johnson 1970).

Although there is a strong norm against extramarital sex, about half of all married men and women engage in extramarital sex sometime during their marriages.
Dances, parties, and work activities provide many opportunities to meet potential extramarital sexual partners. *Ellis Herwig/The Picture Cube.*

Second, personal readiness is related to extramarital sex. **Personal readiness** involves a socialization process in which extramarital sex is portrayed as desirable and acceptable. This usually involves knowing and talking to others who engage in it. It also may include changes in one's personal value system, the development of justifications for involvement, perceived opportunity for involvement, and a sense of isolation or alienation (Thompson 1983). Some researchers suggest that marital and coital dissatisfaction will lead to extramarital sex only when combined with a sense of personal alienation (Maykovich 1976).

Other personal characteristics found to be associated with the likelihood of extramarital sex are the need for intimacy, emotional independence, and sex role egalitarianism (Buunk 1980). Social background characteristics have been found to have relatively small correlations with extramarital sexual behavior (Thompson 1983).

Given that extramarital sex is proscribed in our society, it is not surprising that it produces emotional turmoil. It tends to be associated with internal conflict and guilt for the one engaging in extramarital sex, and it is often infuriating and shattering to the partner if it is discovered (Thompson 1983). Extramarital involvements often signify limited honesty and openness in communication and may deflate a partner's feelings of esteem and attractiveness.

In trying to understand and deal with extramarital sex, people often use the deficit model. That is, extramarital sex is viewed as the result of marital problems and dissatisfactions. Another view is the **personal growth model,** which suggests that extramarital sex arose out of a desire for new experiences and wider intimacy.

Extramarital sex is still viewed as a serious marital violation, and there is a tendency to consider divorce upon discovery of it (Thompson 1984b). However, many are ambivalent about separation and divorce, and hesitate to take action (Thompson 1984b).

There are no data on the duration and quality of marriages following an extramarital crisis. However, evidence suggests that many of those involved in extramarital sex do not easily or quickly terminate those relationships (Thompson 1984b).

Fertility

With sexual activity and marriage come decisions about contraception and childbearing. One of the important decisions of married couples is if and when to have children. Decisions about bearing children are influenced by a variety of personal, family, and cultural forces. Before discussing fertility decisions on an individual level, it is useful to review some of the major rates and trends in **fertility** and population growth in the world and United States. This provides a needed perspective when reviewing decisions about childbearing.

World Population

At the end of 1988 there were 5 billion people on the earth, and the world population is projected to increase to 6.2 billion by the year 2000 (Population Reference Bureau 1987; Yanagishita 1988). About 75 percent of the world lives in less developed countries, with more than 20 percent of the world's population in China. Birth and death rates vary greatly among the different countries. The life expectancy in developed countries is about 73 years and women have an average of 1.9 births in their lifetimes. In less developed countries life expectancy is about 58 years and women average 4.5 births (Bouvier 1984).

NORTH AMERICA.   In 1986 the United States was the fourth most populous country with 241 million people (Population Reference Bureau 1986a). Only China, India, and the Soviet Union have more people. The United States has about 4.8 percent of the world's population.

The **total fertility rate** is the average lifetime births per woman that would occur if current age-specific fertility rates continue. A graph of total fertility in the United States from 1920 to 1985 is shown in Figure 8·1. Fertility decreased almost to two children per woman during the Depression and then increased dramatically after World War II. Since 1960 there has been a large decrease in fertility, and average lifetime births per woman has been below two since 1973. In 1985 the total fertility rate in the United States was 1.8 births per woman (National Center for Health Statistics 1987). There also has been a shift toward later childbearing (U.S. Bureau of the Census 1985).

In Canada the pattern of a childbearing has been similar to the United States. There was a large number of children born after World War II and a large decrease during the past two decades. Births per woman was 3.9 after the war and decreased to 1.7 in 1986. There were about 26 million persons in Canada in 1986 (Population Reference Bureau 1986a).

WESTERN EUROPE.   The number of people in Western Europe was about 350 million in 1986, or about 7 percent of the world's population (Population Reference Bureau 1986a). In recent years birthrates throughout Europe have been below the **replacement level,** which is the number of births required to replace

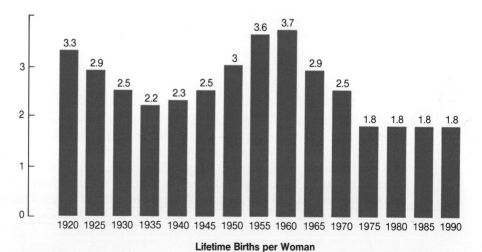

Lifetime Births per Woman

FIGURE 8·1   Total Births per Woman Implied by Age-Specific Fertility Rates: United States 1920–1990

SOURCES: U.S. Bureau of the Census 1985:8, 1986:58; National Center for Health Statistics 1987:16

the number of deaths. In modern society the replacement level is about 2.1 births per woman. The total fertility in Europe was 1.8 in 1986, and West Germany had the lowest fertility with only 1.3 births per woman (Population Reference Bureau 1986b).

SOVIET UNION AND EASTERN EUROPE.   The Soviet Union and countries in Eastern Europe had increases in fertility following World War II, but they were smaller and briefer than those in the United States. In recent years they have had low birthrates, which has induced some of the countries to initiate policies to encourage childbearing, including family allowances, paid maternity leave, and limiting access to abortion. In 1986 there were about 280 million people in the Soviet Union. They continue to have low fertility rates that are below the replacement level (Population Reference Bureau 1986a).

ASIA AND PACIFIC.   The Asian region contains over half of the world's population. In 1986 it had 2.7 billion people and six of the ten most populous countries in the world (Population Reference Bureau 1986a). After World War II death rates declined in Asia while birthrates continued at high levels, re-

The Asian region contains over half of the world's population, and China's 1.1 billion people comprise about 21 percent of the world's population. In this picture children line up for public transportation in Shanghai, China.   *A. Bradshaw/Sipa Press from Picture Group.*

sulting in rapid population growth. The Asian countries have developed at different rates, and population is still growing rapidly in many of the countries. Fertility continues to be high in India, Pakistan, and Bangladesh and their populations are expected to grow rapidly during the next two decades. Women average 5.3 births in these three countries. China instituted a one child policy that has reduced its growth substantially (Tien, 1988). Countries in Southeast Asia have also reduced their population growth considerably. Japan reduced its birthrate during the fifties and more recently South Korea, Singapore, Thailand, Malaysia, and Indonesia have experienced rapid decreases in fertility. For example, South Korea reached a total fertility rate of 2.1 children per woman in 1986, and Singapore's rate dropped to 1.7 (Population Reference Bureau 1986a).

MIDDLE EAST AND NORTH AFRICA.   People in the Middle East tend to marry early and have large families. Cultural attitudes encourage childbearing and contraceptive methods are not widely used. Although fertility continues to be high in the Middle East, death rates have been declining because of improved public health practices. The result has been rapid population growth and relatively young populations.

The Middle East had about 286 million people in 1986, which was approximately 6 percent of the world's population (Population Reference Bureau 1986a). The average lifetime births per woman is about six. If current rates continue, the population in the Middle East will double in about twenty-five years (Population Reference Bureau 1986a).

SUB-SAHARAN AFRICA.   About 9 percent of the world's people live in sub-Saharan Africa. The total population was 452 million in 1986. They are a diverse group that live in forty-six different countries and have more than eight hundred ethnic groups. Fertility is higher in this region than any other region in the world. In Western Africa the average number of children born per woman was about 6.9 in 1984. Poverty is a serious problem and death rates are also very high. The population is very young with over 40 percent of the population under age 15 (Population Reference Bureau 1986a).

LATIN AMERICA AND THE CARIBBEAN.   During the fifties and sixties there was rapid population growth in Latin America due to a decline in the death rate. Before 1965 the average number of births per woman was more than six. Since 1965 fertility has decreased considerably because of greater availability of contraception along with educational and occupational opportunities for women. In 1986 women in Latin America averaged about four births during their childbearing years. The total population of 417 million in the region was just over 8 percent of the world's population (Population Reference Bureau 1986a).

Explaining Fertility

Birthrates vary greatly among different couples and different areas of the world. In the United States the average completed fertility is less than two children per woman whereas in West Africa it is seven. Why do birthrates vary so much and what factors influence an individual couple's decision to have children? In this section we will review what we know about fertility decisions.

One of the major factors influencing fertility is the cultural norms about childbearing. For example, in the Middle East, a family's prestige is affected by the number of children a woman has. In such areas sex roles tend to be traditional, and a woman's major role is to bear and raise children and care for husband and children. In such countries there is strong cultural pressure to have many children. On the other hand, in countries like the United States, womanhood and family prestige are not connected to number of children.

Economic factors also influence fertility decisions. In agricultural areas children may be an economic asset because they are needed to work on family farms and tend livestock. In more developed areas children are often an economic liability. They do not produce family income yet consume a sizable proportion of the family resources. In addition, they require extensive schooling to become productive citizens. Espenshade (1984) estimates that in the United States a family with one child can expect to commit about 30 percent of its total expenditures per child. In families with three children nearly 50 percent of the total family spending is for the children.

A number of researchers have studied how various economic, cultural, and attitudinal variables affect childbearing. Defronzo (1976) found that states with higher median male incomes had higher fertility rates, which supports the idea that couples in better economic situations tend to have more children. Bahr, Chadwick, and Stauss (1975) observed that fertility was related to relative economic status, which was the degree to which one's income was higher or lower than persons of similar age, education, and occupation. They reported that within lower birth orders (0 to 2 children) **relative income** had a positive association with fertility—those who earned higher-than-average incomes, given their education and occupation, tended to have more children. However, among those with three children, relative income did not effect the decision to have an additional child.

Birthrates during the Depression decreased as shown in Figure 8·1, which further supports the hypothesis that economic factors affect fertility decisions. Raising children is expensive in developed societies, and those with higher incomes are somewhat more likely to have children.

Research has consistently shown that female education, employment, and income are negatively related to fertility. Ewer and Crimmins-Gardner (1978) found that the income variable that most consistently related to fertility was the wife's income. The less the wife earned, the more children she had. One of the reasons for low fertility rates in the Soviet Union is the high rate of female labor force participation (Pankhurst 1982). The decline in Iranian fertility between 1952 and 1976 was due primarily to increases in female education (Nassirpour 1985).

There are reciprocal influences between female employment and fertility. Women who are employed tend to have fewer children and having children may constrain employment (Ewer and Crimmins-Gardner 1978). Research by Powers and Salvo (1982) has shown how desire for employment is associated with lower fertility. Woman who are not in the labor force but desire employment have significantly fewer children than women who are not in the labor force and do not desire employment (Powers and Salvo 1982).

Because of high birthrates, countries in sub-Saharan Africa have very young populations. Forty percent of the population is under age 15, poverty is a serious problem, and death rates are high. *Cynthia Ryan/Visions.*

Attitudes regarding sex roles have been shown to have a powerful influence on fertility decisions. Women who are more egalitarian and less traditional in their conception of sex roles tend to have fewer children (Bagozzi and Van Loo 1980; Beckman et al. 1983; Callan 1985; De Vos 1980). Part of the effect of education on fertility is attitudinal. Those with more education tend to have more egalitarian attitudes, which may inhibit childbearing. Religion is also related to egalitarian attitudes and to fertility. Those who are affiliated with a religion tend to have more children than those with no religious affiliation, and childlessness is more common among those without a religion (Mosher and Bachrach 1982; Mosher and Hendershot 1984).

Although there is a trend toward more egalitarian sex role attitudes in the United States, there is still a strong commitment to parenthood. Being childless is considered to be a disadvantaged status and voluntary childnessness is rare. Only 2 percent of ever-married women in their childbearing years are voluntarily childless (Blake 1979; Mosher and Bachrach 1982; Straits 1985).

Those who choose not to have children tend to marry later than average, be well educated, have high status occupations, have high incomes, and be nonreligious (Bloom and Trussell 1984; Mosher and Bachrach 1982). Similarly, Kenkel (1985) found that low-income high school women who desired to remain childless had higher social mobility aspirations, were less willing to accept the position of "housewife only," and expected to marry at later ages than comparable high school women who wanted children.

The data on childlessness suggest a conflict for many women and men. Parenthood is highly valued, yet having children is costly financially and socially. Education and employment are also highly valued and are needed to support children, yet employment may interfere with child care and children may constrain one's occupational opportunities. Furthermore, an occupation is important for achieving social recognition and for fulfilling desires for personal growth, and children may retard one's success and fulfillment occupationally.

The solution to this dilemma is to delay childbearing and limit the number of children one has. This enables women to complete their education and become employed as well as becoming mothers. In the United States there has been a trend toward delaying the first birth. About one third of first births in the United States are now to women age 25 or older (U.S. Bureau of the Census 1985; Wilkie 1981). Many of the women who have delayed having children do want to have children later but they want to fulfill their own needs and obtain some economic security first. Education is one of the major influences on delayed childbearing (Bloom and Trussell 1984).

To this point we have considered cultural, economic, and social influences on fertility. Cohort also influences fertility decisions. As noted in Chapter 2, a **cohort** usually is defined as a group of people that were born during a given period. It is well known that people in different age cohorts have different levels of fertility. For example, people who married during the Depression had lower fertility rates than cohorts who married before or after that period. Similarly, the Vietnam War and associated economic uncertainty appeared to affect individuals' childbearing decisions (Rindfuss, Morgan, and Swicegood 1984).

One important consideration when studying the fertility of any culture is its use of contraception. In developed societies contraception is more widely available and its use is considered more acceptable than in undeveloped societies. Education tends to increase knowledge of contraception and attitudes favoring its use.

Childlessness

As mentioned earlier, voluntary childlessness is rare among married people. Fertility rates have declined dramatically in the developed world but most who marry still desire and have at least one child. Two very strong norms in American society are that married couples should have and should want to have a child (Miall 1985).

Poston and Trent (1982) have observed that there is a curvilinear relationship between childlessness and development. Among **developing countries** the rate of childlessness will decrease as development increases. Apparently improved medical care decreases involuntary childlessness as a country becomes more modern. On the other hand, they found a positive relationship between development and childlessness among **developed countries;** that is, the greater the development, the higher the childlessness. This may be because more choose childlessness in developed countries as educational and occupational opportunities for women increase. As mentioned earlier, those who voluntarily choose childlessness tend to be well-educated persons who are very successful occupationally and nonreligious. Ramu (1985) observed that career success of the wife was a key factor differentiating voluntarily childless couples from couples with children.

Summary

1. Men are more likely than women to feel that husbands and wives should have equal responsibility for initiating sexual activity.
2. Most married persons strongly disapprove of spouses who rarely consent to sexual activity.
3. A large majority of married men and women strongly disapprove of extramarital sexual activity.
4. Husbands tend to desire sex more frequently than wives do.
5. Wives are less likely to initiate sex and more likely to refuse a sexual initiation than husbands.
6. Most individuals participate when their spouse desires sexual activity, even if they do not desire sex at the moment.
7. Most married individuals enjoy sexual activity most of the time.
8. Sexual satisfaction depends on overall marital satisfaction.
9. Almost half of the women and over half of the men engage in extramarital sexual sex sometime during their married lives.
10. Extramarital involvements may be sexual, emotional, or both. Men are more likely than women to have sexual involvement without emotional involvement, whereas women are more likely to have emotional involvement with no sexual involvement.
11. Although men are more likely than women to participate in extramarital sexual behavior, when both emotional and sexual involvements are considered, the proportion of men and women involved extramaritally is about equal.
12. The two major reasons for extramarital sexual involvement are an unsatisfying marriage and personal readiness. The latter involves a socialization process in which one develops justifications and attitudes conducive to extramarital involvement.
13. Most people, even those who participate in extramarital sex, believe that extramarital sex is wrong and damages the marital relationship.
14. Fertility rates vary across the various regions of the world. North America, Europe, and the Soviet Union have total fertility rates of about 1.8 births per woman. Latin America has fertility rates about 4 births per woman, while Asian fertility varies greatly; there are about 5.3 births per woman in countries like India but only about 2 births per woman in countries such as Japan and South Korea. The Middle East has high fertility rates, averaging about 6 births per woman, while in some African regions the average woman has 7 births during her lifetime.
15. Fertility is affected by cultural norms about childbearing, economic constraints, and the availability and use of contraceptive devices.

16. Women tend to have fewer children as they become more educated, have less traditional sex role attitudes, become employed in the marketplace, attain higher status occupations, and earn more money.

17. Although fertility rates have decreased substantially in recent decades, there is still a strong commitment to parenthood in most countries. Being childless is considered to be a disadvantaged status and in the United States voluntary childlessness is rare. Only 2 percent of ever-married women in their childbearing years are voluntarily childless.

18. Those who choose to be voluntarily childless tend to marry late and be well educated, nonreligious, and have high status occupations and high incomes.

19. Among developing countries, the amount of childlessness tends to decrease as development increases. Among developed countries, the amount of childlessness tends to increase as development increases.

20. The conflict between being a parent and achieving educationally and occupationally is diminished by marrying later and having fewer children than in the past.

Important Terms

- cohort
- deficit model
- developed country
- developing country
- extramarital sex
- fertility

- personal growth model
- personal readiness
- relative income
- replacement level
- total fertility rate

Questions for Discussion

1. What are the differences between men and women in their feelings about who should initiate sex? What effects could this difference have on sexual satisfaction?

2. Why are women less likely to initiate sex and more likely to refuse sex in marriage?

3. Are women really less interested in sex than men? Why or why not?

4. Use exchange theory to explain the differences between men and women in sexual attitudes and behavior. Then use role theory and biological theory to explain the same thing. How do the three theories differ in their view of sexuality?

5. To what degree is sexual satisfaction in marriage dependent on overall marital satisfaction? To what degree is overall marital satisfaction dependent on sexual satisfaction? What implications do your answers have for marital counseling and sex education?

6. Why are men more involved than women in extramarital sexual behavior and women more involved than men in extramarital emotional behavior? What implications does your answer have for improving marital satisfaction?

7. Why do so many individuals become involved extramaritally although they feel it is wrong and will hurt their marriage?
8. Summarize fertility rates and trends in the major regions of the world. How do you expect fertility will change within each region during the next decade?
9. Why do fertility rates vary so much among the different regions? Do you think fertility rates in the various regions are going to converge during the next twenty-five years? Why or why not?
10. What are the advantages and disadvantages of low fertility rates (below replacement) as are now occurring in Europe? What are the disadvantages and advantages of high fertility rates such as are now occurring in Latin America?
11. Should anything be done by governments to influence the level of fertility in various regions and countries? What?
12. What are the major cultural influences on fertility? What are some major interpersonal factors that influence the decision to have a child?
13. How does period (cohort) influence fertility?
14. How does female employment affect fertility, and how does female fertility affect employment?
15. What are some dilemmas facing young married women and men in the United States, and how might they resolve those dilemmas? What implications do these resolutions have for marriage and family life?
16. What are the characteristics of childless couples?
17. Do you think the rate of childlessness among young couples in the United States will increase, decrease, or stay the same? Why? How about in other regions of the world?
18. Use exchange theory to explain cultural differences in fertility.
19. Can exchange theory explain why among some people, fertility increases as income increases?
20. The data regarding economic factors and fertility appear contradictory. Can you make sense out of those contradictions? Is there any theory that can explain the different economic influences?

Recommended Reading

GRAUERHOLZ, E., and R. T. SERPE. 1985. Initiation and response: The dynamics of sexual interaction. *Sex Roles* 12:1041–1059.

THOMPSON, A. P. 1984. Emotional and sexual components of extramarital relations. *Journal of Marriage and the Family* 46:35–42.

References

BAGOZZI, R. P., and M. F. VAN LOO. 1980. Decision-making and fertility: A theory of exchange in the family. In *Demographic behavior—interdisciplinary perspectives on decision-making*, ed. T. K. Burch, 91–124. Boulder: CO: Westview.

BAHR, S. J., B. A. CHADWICK, and J. H. STAUSS. 1975. The effect of relative economic status on fertility. *Journal of Marriage and the Family* 37:335–343.

BECKMAN, L. J., R. AIZENBERG, A. B. FORSYTHE, and T. DAY. 1983. A theoretical analysis of antecedents of young couples' fertility decisions and outcomes. *Demography* 20:519–533.

BELL, R., S. TURNER, and L. ROSEN. 1975. A multivariate analysis of female extramarital coitus. *Journal of Marriage and the Family* 37:375–384.

BLAKE, J. 1979. Is zero preferred? American attitudes toward childlessness in the 1970s. *Journal of Marriage and the Family* 41:245–257.

BLOOM, D. E., and J. TRUSSELL. 1984. What are the determinants of delayed childbearing and permanent childlessness in the United States? *Demography* 21:591–611.

BOUVIER, L. F. 1984. Planet Earth 1984–2034: A demographic vision. *Population Bulletin* 39(1):3–41, Washington, DC, Population Reference Bureau, Inc.

BUUNK, B. 1980. Extramarital sex in the Netherlands: Motivation in social and marital context. *Alternative Lifestyles* 3:11–39.

CALLAN, V. J. 1985. Comparisons of mothers of one child by choice with mothers wanting a second birth. *Journal of Marriage and the Family* 47:155–164.

CARLSON, J. 1976. The sexual role. In *Role structure and analysis of the family,* ed. F. I. Nye, 101–110. Beverly Hills, CA: Sage.

DEFRONZO, J. 1976. Cross-sectional area analyses of factors affecting marital fertility: Actual versus relative income. *Journal of Marriage and the Family* 38:669–676.

DENNEY, N. W., J. K. FIELD, and M. QUADAGNO. 1984. Sex differences in sexual needs and desires. *Archives of Sexual behavior* 13:233–245.

DE VOS, S. 1980. Women's role orientations and expected fertility: Evidence from the Detroit area, 1978. *Social Biology* 27:130–137.

EDWARDS, J. N. 1973. Extramarital involvement: Fact and theory. *Journal of Sex Research* 9:210–224.

EDWARDS, J. N., and A. BOOTH. 1976. Sexual behavior in and out of marriage: An assessment of correlates. *Journal of Marriage and the Family* 38:73–81.

ESPENSHADE, T. J. 1984. *Investing in children—new estimates of parental expenditures.* Washington, DC: The Urban Institute Press.

EWER, P. A., and E. CRIMMINS-GARDNER. 1978. Income in the income and fertility relationship. *Journal of Marriage and the Family* 40:291–299.

GRAUERHOLZ, E., and R. T. SERPE. 1985. Initiation and response: The dynamics of sexual interaction. *Sex Roles* 12:1041–1059.

HITE, S. 1981. *The Hite report on male sexuality.* New York: Knopf.

HUNT, M. M. 1974. *Sexual behavior in the 70's.* Chicago: Playboy Press.

JOHNSON, R. E. 1970. Some correlates of extramarital coitus. *Journal of Marriage and the Family* 32:449–456.

KENKEL, W. F. 1985. The desire for voluntary childlessness among low-income youth. *Journal of Marriage and the Family* 47:509–512.

KLEMMACK, D. L., and L. L. ROLF. 1980. Heterosexual alternatives to marriage: Appropriateness for older persons. *Alternative Lifestyles* 3:137–148.

MAYKOVICH, M. K. 1976. Attitudes versus behavior in extramarital sexual relations. *Journal of Marriage and the Family* 38:693–699.

MIALL, C. E. 1985. Perceptions of informal sanctioning and the stigma of involuntary childlessness. *Deviant Behavior* 6:383–403.

MOSHER, W. D., and C. A. BACHRACH. 1982. Childlessness in the United States: Estimates from the National Survey of Family Growth. *Journal of Family Issues* 3:517–543.

MOSHER, W. D., and G. E. HENDERSHOT. 1984. Religious affiliation and the fertility of married couples. *Journal of Marriage and the Family* 46:671–677.

NASSIRPOUR, M. 1985. The effect of oil revenue on the fertility pattern in Iran, 1952–1976. *Journal of Marriage and the Family* 47:785–796.

NATIONAL CENTER FOR HEALTH STATISTICS. 1987. *Advance report of final natality statistics, 1985.* Monthly Vital Statistics Report, vol. 36, no. 4, Supp. DHHS Pub. No. (PHS) 87–1120, July 17. Hyattsville, MD: Public Health Service.

PANKHURST, J. G. 1982. Childless and one-child families in the Soviet Union. *Journal of Family Issues* 3:493–515.

PIETROPINTO, A., and J. SIMENAUER. 1977. *Beyond the male myth.* New York: Times Books.

POPULATION REFERENCE BUREAU, INC. 1986a. *Population in perspective: Regional views.* Washington, DC: Population Reference Bureau.

POPULATION REFERENCE BUREAU, INC. 1986b. 1986—the year in population. *Population Today* 14(12):4, Washington, DC: Population Reference Bureau.

POPULATION REFERENCE BUREAU, INC. 1987. World at the halfway mark. *Population Today* 15(4):3,9.

POSTON, D. L., JR., and K. TRENT. 1982. International variability in childlessness: A descriptive and analytical study. *Journal of Family Issues* 3:473–491.

POWERS, M. G., and J. SALVO. 1982. Fertility and child care arrangements as mechanisms of status articulation *Journal of Marriage and the Family* 44:21–34.

RAMU, G. N. 1985. Voluntarily childless and parental couples: A comparison of their lifestyle characteristics. *Lifestyles: A Journal of Changing Patterns* 7:130–145.

RINDFUSS, R. R., S. P. MORGAN, and C. G. SWICEGOOD. 1984. The transition to motherhood: The intersection of structural and temporal dimensions. *American Sociological Review* 49:359–372.

SCHENK, J., H. PFRANG, and A. RAUSCHE. 1983. Personality traits versus the quality of the marital relationship as the determinant of marital sexuality. *Archives of Sexual Behavior* 12:31–42.

STRAITS, B. C. 1985. Factors influencing college women's responses to fertility decision-making vignettes. *Journal of Marriage and the Family* 47:585–596.

THOMPSON, A. P. 1983. Extramarital sex: A review of the research literature. *The Journal of Sex Research* 19:1–22.

THOMPSON, A. P. 1984a. Emotional and sexual components of extramarital relations. *Journal of Marriage and the Family* 46:35–42.

THOMPSON, A. P. 1984b. Extramarital sexual crisis: Common themes and therapy implications. *Journal of Sex and Marital Therapy* 10:45–58.

TIEN, H. Y. 1988. A talk with China's Wang Wei. *Population Today* 16(1):6–8. Washington, DC: Population Reference Bureau.

U.S. BUREAU OF THE CENSUS. 1985. *Population Profile of the United States: 1983–84.* Current Population Reports, Series P-23, No. 145. Washington, DC: U.S. Government Printing Office.

WILKIE, J. R. 1981. The trend toward delayed parenthood. *Journal of Marriage and the Family* 43:583–591.

YANAGISHITA, M. 1988. Projecting a world of 10.4 billion. *Population Today* 16(12)3–4.

CHAPTER 9

Raising Children

Introduction

Michael and Lorraine decided to have a child two years after they were married. Lorraine had completed her degree in education and was teaching math at a local high school. She stopped taking the pill and became pregnant three months later. She finished her first year of teaching and their child was born in August, three years after their marriage.

Lorraine and Michael were thrilled to have their little girl, who they named Debra. The pregnancy and delivery were normal and Debra was healthy. After they brought little Debra home, there were a number of adjustments they had to make. First, Debra takes much physical care. She must be fed, bathed, and watched and she wakes up once or twice every night for feeding. Both Michael and Lorraine have been somewhat tired because their sleep has been interrupted frequently.

Debra restricts their freedom of movement. Wherever they go they must either get someone to watch the baby or take the baby with them. Even going shopping is difficult and it is not always possible to get a sitter.

Debra also is very expensive. There are clothes, doctor visits, vaccinations, diapers, baby food, and baby-sitters. Michael and Lorraine planned carefully for their child and have some money saved. Nevertheless, they have felt some monetary strain as the expenses of the new baby have been more than they anticipated. There is also the problem of day care. Lorraine will begin teaching again in September and will have a neighbor watch the baby. They need the money and Lorraine enjoys teaching, but she feels somewhat uneasy about leaving Debra with a sitter every day at such a young age.

Lorraine and Michael feel a great responsibility toward Debra and want to train her to become a competent adult. They are somewhat nervous because they know it is not easy to be a good parent. They know that the future of societies depends on how well children are socialized.

There are some indications that as a society we have not done particularly well in socializing our children. Crime rates among adolescents are high and our prison population is burgeoning. Many youth are aggressive, abuse drugs, and cannot get along in school.

This chapter examines parenthood and socialization and is organized into five sections. First, there is a discussion of how couples adjust to being parents and what characteristics are associated with normal adjustment. Second, perceptions of the role of parent are explored. Third, parental and family characteristics associated with social competence in children are reviewed. Fourth, there is an examination of adolescence in our society. Finally, there is a brief discussion of what it costs financially to raise children.

Adjusting to Children

Research has shown that many couples have an experience similar to Michael and Lorraine. Those who are not as well prepared may find it considerably more stressful. Parenthood is a highly valued status with many rewards, but it is demanding and adjustment to being a parent is not easy.

Some of the things couples are least prepared for in parenthood are lack of sleep, the energy, time, and responsibility required to care for a child, and the difficulty in going places (Kach and McGhee 1982). Nevertheless, most couples feel that parenthood is a positive experience. Many did not expect their attachment to and love for the baby to be as strong as it is (Kach and McGhee 1982).

Why Parenthood Is Difficult

An examination of role changes after the birth of a child shows why the transition to parenthood may be difficult. In Chapter 1 we identified eight family roles. The child care and child socialization roles are activated when a child is born, and the increased time and effort required to fulfill these two additional roles may produce strain. Furthermore, adding these two roles may leave less time for the performance of other roles, such as the recreational and therapeutic roles. A division of labor for the new roles needs to be established, and there may be some conflict in deciding who does what and how it is done.

Rossi (1968) suggests that adjusting to the parental role may be difficult because it is irrevocable, abrupt, and is often begun with little preparation. It is irrevocable in that once one becomes a parent one is always a parent. One may quit a job or divorce a spouse, but one does not divorce a child. There are few things more reprehensible in our society than a parent who abandons a child. The transition to parenthood is very abrupt. One day the couple is childless and the next day they have a tiny child that must be cared for. Finally, Rossi notes that many of the skills needed for parenthood are not taught in schools and may not be adequately taught in the family of orientation.

What Makes Adjustment Easier

Some couples adjust to parenthood more easily than others. The most important factor affecting their adjustment is marital satisfaction. The higher the marital satisfaction prior to parenthood, the better the adjustment to the new child (Russell 1974; Worthington 1986). Harriman (1986) observed that couples with high marital adjustment appear less vulnerable than couples with low marital adjustment to stresses following the birth of a child. High marital intimacy appears to enable couples to adjust more easily to the demands of parenthood (Stemp, Turner, and Hon 1986).

Another important factor affecting adjustment to parenthood is support from spouse. Because women tend to be responsible for a large majority of baby care tasks, support from their husbands is particularly important (Power and Parke 1984; Steffensmeier 1982; Tietjen and Bradley 1985). Involvement of the father with the baby is associated with better marital and parental adjustment (Goldberg, Michaels, and Lamb 1985; Russell 1974). If the wife expected the husband to be involved with child care and he helps very little, marital satisfaction decreases significantly (Belsky 1985).

Some of the other variables that have been associated with good adjustment to parenthood are preparation for parenthood, wanting the child, and the significance of the parental role in the lives of the couple. In addition, a difficult pregnancy, health problems for the mother after the birth, a baby that cries a great deal, and health problems in the baby all increase the stresses associated with parenthood (Russell 1974).

Parenthood and Marital Satisfaction

Some researchers have found that parenthood has a negative impact on marital satisfaction. For example, Belsky, Lan, and Rovine (1985) studied how marriages changed over the transition to parenthood. They used interviews, questionnaires, and observation to assess marital quality during the last trimester of pregnancy, three months after the birth, and nine months after the birth. They found that there was a moderate decline in marital satisfaction over this period. The marriages became somewhat less romantic and expressive and somewhat more instrumental.

Other researchers have found similar declines in marital satisfaction following the birth of a child, and that the decreases are greater for women than men (Cowan et al. 1985; Waldron and Routh 1981). Using six national surveys, Glenn and McLanahan (1982) found that marital satisfaction was higher among the childless, even after controlling for sex, race, education, religion, employment status, and desired number of children. Similarly, Houseknecht (1979), Polonko, Scanzoni, and Teachman (1982), and Feldman (1981) all observed higher marital quality among the childless.

White, Booth, and Edwards (1986) interviewed a national sample of individuals and found that the presence of children was associated modestly with reduced marital interaction, increased dissatisfaction with finances, and increased dissatisfaction with household division of labor. These three changes tended to reduce the level of marital satisfaction, as shown in Figure 9·1.

However, according to some recent research the effect of children on marital quality may be small. Although Abbott and Brody (1985) found that childless wives reported higher marital satisfaction than mothers with children, planned comparisons revealed that the differences were due primarily to mothers with two children and mothers with male children. The marital quality of mothers with female children was no different than the marital quality of childless wives. Furthermore, childless women in Nigeria have less marital satisfaction than women with children (Denga 1982).

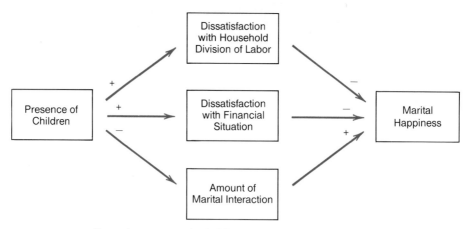

FIGURE 9·1   Effect of Presence of Children on Marital Happiness

SOURCE: Adapted from White, L. K., A. Booth, and J. N. Edwards, "Children and Marital Happiness—Why the Negative Correlation?" *Journal of Family Issues,* 7, 1986, p. 140. Copyright © 1986 by Sage Publications, Inc. Reprinted by permission of Sage Publications, Inc.

McHale and Huston (1985) suggest that declines in marital satisfaction commonly attributed to parenthood may not be due to parenthood. They found that nonparents married for comparable periods of time had decreases in marital satisfaction similar to decreases observed among parents. Because many of the changes attributed to parenthood also occur among nonparents, they concluded that parenthood does not produce a decline in love and marital satisfaction.

White and Booth (1985) found that the negative association between parenthood and marital quality is partially spurious and overstates the negative effects of children on marital quality. Unhappy couples with children are less likely to separate and divorce than unhappy childless couples. Thus, couples without children appear to be happier simply because the unhappy ones have already divorced. White and Booth (1985) maintained that this selectivity in divorce rather than children per se is the major reason childless couples appear to be more satisfied in their marriages. Research by Wait, Haggstrom, and Kanouse (1985) supports the conclusions of White and Booth. Using a national longitudinal sample of young adults, Waite et al. (1985) found that having a child significantly reduces the probability of separation and divorce. In longitudinal or time-series studies, measurements are made at more than one point in time. Waite et al. (1985) examined married couples over time to see if those with children were more or less likely than those without children to divorce at a latter time. They estimated "that by the time the first child reaches his second birthday more than 20 percent of parents would have been divorced or separated if the child had not been born, compared to actual disruption rates of 5–8 percent." (Waite et al. 1985:850).

In summary, the transition to parenthood is often stressful and may have an adverse effect on marital quality. However, longitudinal data and appropriate controls suggest that the adverse effect of children on marital satisfaction has been overstated. The apparent effect of children is due partly to the propensity of childless couples to divorce and to decreased satisfaction that tends to occur among all couples throughout the life course. We turn now to men's and women's perceptions of and involvement in parenting.

Parenting

Satisfaction with parenting is generally high even though there is a considerable amount of stress associated with it (Goetting 1986). Compared to men, women are more involved in parenting and experience greater fulfillment, but they feel more burdened and are less confident about being a parent (Frank et al. 1986; Goetting 1986).

The early stages of parenting are the most intense, in that parents experience the greatest satisfaction and dissatisfaction when their children are young. The greatest dissatisfactions associated with parenthood are related to dis-

One of the most important concerns of mothers and fathers is teaching and disciplining their children. Child socialization is often a joint activity, as shown by these parents playing with their child. *Julie O'Neil/The Picture Cube.*

cipline, financial cost, the child's adjustment outside the family, and the parents' loss of freedom (Goetting 1986).

Perhaps the greatest reward of parenthood is the love that parents feel for their children and the sense of meaningfulness and belonging they experience. Umberson and Gove (1986) noted that parents feel more constraints and obligations than nonparents, but have a greater sense of purpose and meaningfulness to their lives.

Gecas (1976) and Nye (1976) examined parents' perceptions of **child socialization.** Three major conclusions from their research are as follows. First, parents felt the child socialization role was the most important of the eight family roles. Three fourths of the respondents said child socialization was extremely important, and one fourth said it was high on importance. Second, child socialization was fairly stressful for the parents. Wives worried more about child socialization than any other role. Men had considerable worries about the issue too, although they tended to worry more about the provider and therapeutic roles. Third, parents had more conflict about child socialization than any other role.

The norms in the child socialization role are egalitarian. For example, more than 90 percent of the husbands and wives studied by Gecas (1976) said that teaching children right from wrong should be equally shared by parents. Over three fourths said that disciplining children should be equally shared.

The actual enactment of the child socialization role was also fairly egalitarian. For example, three fourths of the husbands and wives reported that they both were equally involved in teaching right and wrong. About half said they were equally involved in disciplining their children.

However, actual behavior was not as egalitarian as the norms. For example, although more than 90 percent of the husbands and wives said that teaching right and wrong should be shared equally, only 75 percent of the couples actually shared equally in this area. Similarly, although about three fourths said discipline should be shared equally, only half of the couples actually did so. A comparison of these differences between expectations and behavior reported by Gecas (1976) is given in Table 9·1.

In recent years there does not appear to have been a major shift in the involvement of fathers in child care. Coverman and Sheley (1986) found that men's time in child care did not change significantly between 1965 and 1975.

The popular and professional media in the United States often portray fathers as unavailable and incompetent. Mackey (1985) examined paternal behavior toward young children in eighteen different cultures. He found that in all of them, men were less involved with children than women. However, when men did interact with their children, their behavior was similar to women's. The American fathers were not derelict as is often portrayed in the media, but were fairly typical compared to the fathers in the other cultures studied.

Recent research has shown that fathers are more nurturant than many professionals previously believed (Walters and Walters 1980). Men can provide quality care and socialization of children, and a growing number of men want to increase their involvement in child care (Sagi and Sharon 1984). Having a nurturant father tends to be associated with cognitive growth and internal self-confidence in children, although sexual identity appears unaffected (Radin 1981; Radin and Sagi 1982).

TABLE 9-1 Husband-Wife Reports of Socialization Norms and Role Enactment (in percentages)

NORM: Who Should Teach the Following Tasks?	TOTAL		Husband Always		Husband More Than Wife		Husband and Wife the Same		Wife More Than Husband		Wife Always		MEAN*	
	H	W	H	W	H	W	H	W	H	W	H	W	H	W
To Eat and Dress Properly	100	100	0	0	2	0	47	23	50	73	1	4	3.51	3.80
To Get Along with Others	100	100	0	0	4	0	87	90	9	10	0	0	3.06	3.10
What Is Right and Wrong	100	100	0	0	5	1	92	94	3	5	0	0	2.98	3.03
To Learn to Take Responsibility	100	100	0	0	15	7	80	88	5	5	0	0	2.89	2.97
To Help in Schoolwork	100	100	0	0	5	8	67	63	27	28	1	1	3.25	3.21
Discipline Children	100	100	0	0	17	13	76	78	7	9	0	0	2.89	2.97
ENACTMENT: Who Teaches Children?														
To Eat and Dress Properly	100	100	0	0	2	0	26	20	68	71	4	9	3.73	3.90
To Get Along with Others	100	100	0	0	7	2	63	59	30	37	0	1	3.23	3.38
What Is Right and Wrong	100	100	0	0	7	2	75	73	17	25	1	0	3.12	3.24
To Learn to Take Responsibility	100	100	0	0	20	14	58	60	21	25	1	1	3.02	3.13
To Help in Schoolwork	100	100	0	0	10	20	24	25	58	49	8	6	3.60	3.37
Discipline Children	100	100	0	0	25	15	50	46	24	38	1	1	3.00	3.24

* Mean scores are based on the following weights: Husband Always = 1, Husband More = 2, Husband-Wife Same = 3, Wife More = 4, Wife Always = 5. Scores above 3.0 indicate the wife should or does enact the role more than the husband.

SOURCE: Gecas, V. 1976. The socialization and child care roles. In *Role structure and analysis of the family*, ed. F. I. Nye, 38, Table 3.1. Beverly Hills, CA: Sage. Reprinted by permission.

Social Competence in Children

All parents want their children to grow up to become well-adjusted adults who enjoy a healthy level of self-esteem and contribute to society. In this section we identify several parental and structural characteristics that have been found to be associated with social competence in children. First, however, the limits of parental influences are discussed.

Limits of Parental Influences

Although parents influence their children in many ways, it should be remembered that there are limits to that influence. There is not a simple cause-and-effect relationship between parental actions and child outcomes. There is no guarantee that a child will become a socially competent adult even under the best of conditions. Conversely, many children from deprived environments do become well-adjusted adults. In fact, given some of the wretched conditions children live in, it is surprising that so many children turn out so well. It appears that many children grow up in spite of their parents and not because of them.

The limits of environmental influences on children have been shown by recent research on twins. Plomin, Loehlin, and DeFries (1985) studied infant development by comparing adopted and nonadopted children. They found that approximately 50 percent of major domains of infant development could be explained by **genetic** influences. In a study of twins, Wilson and Matheny (1983) concluded that the principal link between parental intelligence and child's IQ scores was genetic. Finally, Bouchard (1984) compared twins reared together and apart. He estimated that genetic factors had a strong influence on intelligence and personality. Bouchard (1984:175) maintained that both twin and adoption studies indicate that "common family environmental influences play only a minor role in the determination of personality."

Taken together, these studies do not show that home environment is unimportant in child socialization. Rather, they demonstrate that the influence of the environment is limited by intrinsic biological characteristics. Each child has a unique potential and parents may influence the development of that potential. The question for parents is how they can accomplish this goal.

It should also be recognized that there is a reciprocal influence between parent and child. Children influence parental behavior as well as being influenced by it (Walters and Walters 1980).

What Is Social Competence?

Although many different characteristics may be included in a definition of social competence, Rollins and Thomas (1979) have identified seven child behaviors that are valued in Western society: (1) cognitive development, (2) conformity, (3) creativity, (4) instrumental social competence, (5) internal locus of control, (6) moral behavior, and (7) self-esteem. They also identified five maladaptive behaviors: (1) antisocial aggression, (2) delinquency, (3) drug abuse, (4) learning disabilities, and (5) schizophrenia. To become productive and competent one needs to develop a reasonable number of the seven valued behaviors and to not exhibit the five maladaptive behaviors. Rollins and Thomas (1979) called the seven valued behaviors **social competence** and the five devalued behaviors social incompetence. Although there may be genetic influences on the various components of social competence, particularly on learning disabilities and schizophrenia, there is also evidence that socialization has a significant influence.

Control

How does a parent teach a child to become socially competent? Perhaps the most frequently discussed parental characteristic is **control.** To what degree and in what way should parents attempt to control their children? Folk wisdom says, "spare the rod and spoil the child." The implication is that children will become spoiled (undisciplined, disobedient, incompetent) if they do not receive physical punishment.

Physical punishment of children is very common. Straus and Gelles (1986) reported that over half of all children ages 3 through 17 were slapped or spanked by their parents during the past year. Gecas (1976) asked parents with at least one school-aged child the following question: "If your child intentionally disobeys after you have told her to do something what would you do?" About two thirds of the parents said they would spank or slap the child.

Rollins and Thomas (1979) have completed an extensive review of research on the relationship between parental control and social competence in children. Although the research was not entirely consistent, it appeared that control had a curvilinear relationship with child competence. That is, very low and very high levels of parental control were associated with higher levels of child aggression, drug abuse, and other antisocial behaviors than moderate levels of parental control.

Many other researchers have found that either an extremely permissive or a restrictive environment may be harmful to children. Garbarino, Sebes, and Schellenbach (1984) found that adolescent adjustment problems were more common among families that had no rules or among those that were punishing and overinvolved. Police contacts and self-reported delinquency have been found to be associated with a lack of parental **monitoring** (Patterson and Stouthamer-Loeber 1984), which was defined as parental awareness of where their children are, who they are with, and what they are doing. Olweus (1980) observed that adolescent boys were more aggressive if their parents were coercive (used physical punishment, threats, violent outbursts) or were permissive about aggressive behavior. Initiation to marijuana use was more common when parents were permissive (Kandel and Adler 1982). Barnes, Farrell, and Cairns (1986) found that adolescent drinking was somewhat more likely when control was either very permissive or extremely rigid. Miller et al. (1986) reported that sexual permissiveness was highest among adolescents whose parents had no rules at all, lowest when their parents were moderately strict, and intermediate among adolescents whose parents were very strict. When parents monitored their children's activities, their children were less likely to bear a child out of wedlock (Hanson, Myers, and Ginsburg 1987). A variety of delinquent behaviors have been found to be more frequent when parental supervision is lax

(Newcomer and Udry 1987). Many delinquents themselves perceive that their parents are too permissive (Streit 1981). In summary, antisocial behavior appears to be higher when parental monitoring has been very permissive or extremely strict.

Not only is the amount of parental control important, but how parents attempt to control their children is also instrumental. Inductive control attempts tend to increase social competence in children whereas coercive control attempts tend to decrease it (Rollins and Thomas 1979). For example, children whose parents used primarily coercive methods did not do as well in school, were less likely to internalize their parents' values, had lower self-esteem, and were more likely to be antisocially aggressive and abuse drugs. On the other hand, parents who tended to be inductive in their control attempts were more likely to have children who did well in school, internalized their values, and had high self-esteem.

As mentioned in Chapter 7, inductive control attempt (**induction**) is persuasive. The parents explain what they want and try to persuade their child to comply, but the control attempt is qualified and allows the child a choice. **Coercion,** on the other hand, is an unqualified power assertion that is punitive. It does not grant autonomy to the child but is stated in terms of "You do this or else!"

Other recent research has shown that inductive control is beneficial whereas coercion is detrimental for children. Steinmetz (1979) reported that the conscience development was less and aggressiveness was higher when parents used physical punishment and coercive discipline techniques. Garbarino et al. (1984) found that adolescent adjustment problems were more common when parents tended to be coercive and punishing in their discipline. Adolescent self-esteem and internalization of values tend to be higher when induction rather than coercion is used (Manscill and Rollins 1985; Peterson, Rollins, and Thomas 1985). Abelman (1986) found that when parents used induction rather than coercion their children demonstrated greater ability for prosocial solutions to conflict and were more influenced by prosocial television content. On the other hand, children whose parents were more coercive seemed to be more affected by the antisocial content of television.

Coercion may produce outward compliance for a time, but the adolescents will cease complying with parental expectations if there is little chance of being caught or if they want to assert their autonomy. Induction, on the other hand, is associated with outward compliance as well as internalization of parental expectations.

Support

There is no doubt that the most important parental influence on child socialization is support. A large amount of research has shown that the level of parental support is positively associated with social competence in children.

Support is warmth, acceptance, and nurturance. Praising, approving, encouraging, helping, cooperating, and expressing affection are all supportive behaviors (Rollins and Thomas 1979).

Research has consistently demonstrated that the greater the parental support,

Parental support is one of the most important characteristics in raising a child. Help, warmth, and comfort may be particularly important during stressful situations. *Ulrike Welsch.*

the greater the social competence in children (Rollins and Thomas 1979). This proposition has been supported under a variety of conditions and situations and at different developmental stages of children. Thomas, Weigert, and Winston (1984) studied adolescent identification with mother and father in the United States, Germany, Spain, Puerto Rico, and Mexico. They found in all five countries that adolescents are more likely to identify with supportive parents. Cheung and Lau (1985) observed that Chinese adolescents have higher self-esteem when their parents are supportive. In Sweden, Olweus (1980) noted that aggressiveness in boys was less when maternal support was high. Steinmetz (1979) reviewed a large amount of research on child development and found that supportive behaviors such as acceptance, praise, and love-oriented discipline are positively associated with conscience development, whereas rejection is associated with dependence and aggressiveness. Overall, the research shows that a variety of socially competent behaviors are related to level of parental support, and the effects of support are evident regardless of sex of child, sex of parent, stage of development, or cultural context (Thomas et al. 1984).

Self-esteem is considered to be an important element in the development of social competence. A goal of most parents is to have their child develop a positive self-concept. A number of scholars have found parental support to have an important influence on a child's self-esteem (Amato and Ochiltree 1986; Barber and Thomas 1986; Cheung and Lau 1985; Cooper, Holmen, and Braithwaite 1983; Gecas and Schwalbe 1986; Manscill and Rollins 1985). On the other hand, frequent criticism of children has been shown to lower their self-esteem. Harris and Howard (1984) found that the more criticism teenagers received for a specific behavior or attitude, the more likely they perceived themselves as being that way. Being called "hard to get along with" and "mean" were particularly associated with a negative self-image.

Barber and Thomas (1986) identified four different dimensions of parental support: (1) general support, (2) physical affection, (3) companionship, and (4) sustained contact. Physical contact that covered a longer period of time than a hug or kiss was considered to be sustained contact, such as sitting with the child in one's lap or picking up the child for fun. All four types of support were positively related to self-esteem. Companionship from the mother and sustained contact from the father were the strongest predictors of son's self-esteem, and general support from the mother and physical affection from the father were the strongest predictors of daughter's self-esteem.

Teenage drug use appears to be less when parents are supportive. Barnes et al. (1986) found that adolescent problem drinking was lowest when parental support was high and parental control was moderate. According to Hundleby and Mercer (1987) parental affection, concern, and involvement were associated with less alcohol, tobacco, and marijuana use by adolescents.

Deviant behavior in general tends to be less frequent when parental behavior is supportive. Among blacks and whites, and middle and lower classes, families with delinquent boys tend to be less warm than families with nondelinquent boys (Borduin, Pruitt, and Henggeler 1986). Juvenile offenders perceive that their parents do not take an interest in what they do and don't praise and encourage them (Streit 1981). Aggressiveness in adolescent boys tends to be higher when the mother is more hostile and rejecting, and less warm and positive (Olweus 1980). Youth are less likely to run away if they feel approval and affection from their parents (Nye 1980). Adolescents with severe adjustment problems tend to have parents who exhibit low support (Garbarino et al. 1984). In a review of research in deviant behavior, Bahr (1979) observed that the higher the parental support, the higher the self-esteem, moral commitment, and attachment to parents, which were all negatively associated with deviant behavior.

When the research on control and support is integrated, it is clear that children are more likely to become socially competent if (1) their parents exercise moderate control, (2) the control attempts tend to be inductive rather than coercive, and (3) parental support is high. Too little control may be just as damaging as too much control, but the way control attempts are made is critical. No matter what the level or nature of parental control, it will make little difference if parents are not supportive. Perhaps too many parents and child psychologists have focused on control techniques while neglecting the importance of parental support. A large amount of research has shown that the critical factor in child rearing is for the parents to be supportive—approving, affectionate, accepting, interested, praising, and understanding.

When children have problems, too often the response of parents is to attempt to assert control to straighten the child out. The child often needs direction, but needs love and support much more. A friend of mine was counseling some families with delinquent boys recently. One of his major goals was to get the parents to give their boy one or two sincere compliments each day. The interaction between the boys and their parents had deteriorated to the point that there were never compliments, praises, or positive interactions. The boys felt unloved and criticized. Any good things they did were not recognized. Before any control or direction would be accepted, the boys had to perceive some support from their parents. When my friend was able to get the parents to exhibit some supportive behaviors toward the boys, they would sometimes reciprocate. Over time, mutually supportive behaviors increased and some of the boys felt that their parents did care. When this occurred some of them were able to decrease their antisocial behavior and increase their social competence.

One of the ways parents may develop a more supportive environment for the children is to spend time with them in leisure and recreational activities.

Time spent in family leisure activities tends to increase feelings of support and well-being in children. Bonds are often developed in leisure activities that cannot be built in other ways.   *Ulrike Welsch.*

Parents and children may be able to relax and enjoy each other if they participate in some mutually satisfying activity. Research by McMillan and Hiltonsmith (1982) illustrates the value of spending leisure time with children. They found adolescents' sense of well-being was strongly related to time spent with adults in leisure and recreational activities in the home.

Modeling

Popular folk wisdom suggests that example has a strong influence on children and their development of social competence. Some have suggested that children tend to do what parents do **(modeling)** rather than what parents tell them to do.

Research supports the belief that children model their parents' behavior in many ways. For example, when parents break the law and participate in antisocial behavior, it increases the chance that their children will become delinquent (Geismar and Wood 1986). A number of scholars have found a correlation between criminal behavior in the parents and children. Barnes et al. (1986) found that adolescent drinking can be explained partly by parental models of drinking behavior. Parents who drank heavily were more likely than any other parents to have adolescents who were also heavy drinkers. Hundleby and Mercer (1987) also have observed a modeling effect from parental to adolescent drug use. According to Cohen (1987), children model their parents in educational aspirations and attainments. Overall, the research suggests that parental modeling occurs even during adolescence and that children model antisocial as well as social behaviors.

Marital Conflict

Contrary to what many parents may think, the quality of the husband-wife relationship appears to affect the social competence of children. This effect is evident when children are infants and when they are adolescents.

Isabella and Belsky (1985) studied the quality of the infant-mother attachment during the first year of life. They found a positive correlation between marital quality and infant security. It appeared that the stress of an unsatisfying marriage affected the ability of the child to bond securely with the mother.

Among preschool and school-aged children, parental agreement on child-rearing values and attitudes is positively related to psychological functioning of the children, but more so for boys than for girls (Block, Block, and Morrison 1981). Emery and O'Leary (1982) studied children between the ages of 8 and 17 and found that marital discord was related to behavior problems in boys but not girls. Among adolescents, perceived conflict in the family is related to their psychological adjustment and satisfaction with social life (Dancy and Handal 1984; Enos and Handal 1986). Overall, it appears that severe marital and family conflict may be detrimental to the development of social competence in young children as well as adolescents.

Family Structure

Up to this point we have focused on how interaction within the family affects the development of social competence in children—how control, support, example, and conflict impact on children. The structure of the family may also influence child competence. **Family structure** is the physical composition of the family and refers to such things as family size, child spacing, birth order, number of parents, and parental occupations. In this section we will identify how family structure is related to the development of competence in children.

FAMILY SIZE, SPACING, AND BIRTH ORDER.   Growing up as an only child is not the same as growing up with one or more siblings. A child with five siblings lives in a very different environment than a child with only one sibling. Birth order and the length of time between births may also affect a child. Having a sibling five years older is dissimilar to having a sibling a year older, and being the youngest of three children is not like being the oldest of three. How much effect does family size, spacing, and birth order have on the development of children?

First, let us examine what we know about only children. Although, there is a popular stereotype that the only child is alone, unhappy, and maladjusted, there is no evidence to support it. Glenn and Hoppe (1984) estimated the effect of being an only child on eight dimensions of psychological well-being. They found that only children scored higher than others on all eight dimensions, although the differences were relatively small. Mott and Haurin (1982) found no advantage to being an only child in terms of intelligence, educational progression, career, family, or social-psychological outcomes. Their data did suggest that being an only child was preferable to coming from a large family. According to Kidwell (1978) only children perceive greater parental affect than firstborns, and Blake (1981) maintained that only children do not suffer from lack of siblings. On the other hand, Bell and Avery (1985) noted that only children regard parents as more intrusive than do children with siblings. Overall, there appear to be some advantages and disadvantages to being an only child, but the overall effect on children is very small (Bell and Avery 1985).

Popular wisdom in the press and among professionals is that large families are bad for children. Many assume that the more children there are, the less parents are able to provide personal and economic resources to help each child develop. Parental resources are finite and the greater the number of children, the fewer interpersonal and material resources there are for each child. This has been termed the **dilution model** by Blake (1981, 1985). She noted that children from large families tend to have less ability, lower grades, and lower levels of educational achievement. In a review of existing research, Heer (1985) concluded that family size is related to educational attainment, although it has relatively small effects on occupational status and earnings. In a provocative article titled "Dumber by the Dozen," Zajonc (1975) maintained that intelligence declines with family size. To have smart children, Zajonc suggested that parents have few children and space them far apart. According to Rahav (1982) delinquents tend to come from larger families because parental involvement and control are less as family size increases.

Economic well-being is negatively associated with family size. As the number of children in a family increases, the family standard of living tends to decrease (Espenshade, Kamenske, and Turchi 1983). Delayed childbearing along with small family size may have long-term economic benefits, according to Hofferth (1984).

Kidwell (1981) observed that adolescents perceived their parents to be more punitive and less supportive as families grew in size. As space between siblings increased, perceptions of punitiveness decreased and perceptions of supportiveness increased. Kidwell (1981, 1982) also reported that middleborns, compared to firstborns or laterborns, had lower self-esteem and perceived their parents to be more punitive and less reasonable and supportive.

Other research suggests that the apparent effects of family size, spacing, and birth order may be artifacts of other variables. Heer (1985) identified methodological limitations that may have affected results of many studies. Price, Walsh, and Vilberg (1984) have shown that the formulas used by Zajonc (1975) are logically invalid and that his model's ability to predict intelligence is a mathematical artifact. Mare and Chen (1986) maintained that some of Blake's (1981, 1985) results may be artifactual. Mednick, Baker, and Hocevar (1985) investigated the relationship of family size and birth order with seventeen measures of children's intellectual, psychosocial, and physical growth. The effects of family size and birth order were weak. Family size was related to only one measure of intellectual performance and to none of the psychosocial variables. Galbraith (1982, 1983) demonstrated that individual differences in intelligence were not related significantly to family size, birth order, or spacing. In a comprehensive review of existing research on birth order, Ernst and Angst (1983) concluded that birth order has little or no influence on personality. Finally, Bell and Avery (1985) found that the effects of family size, birth order, and spacing on parent-adolescent relationships were small.

In summary, the research on family size, spacing, and birth order is contradictory. When problems of method are taken into account, many differences assumed to be due to family size, spacing, or birth order appear to be negligible. A number of recent studies with sophisticated controls suggest that the effects of family size, spacing, and birth order on the intellectual and social competence of children are relatively small.

DUAL-EARNER FAMILIES.   One of the major social changes during the past fifty years has been the increase in labor force participation among married women. In 1940 only 9 percent of mothers were employed compared to 57 percent in 1980 (Hoffman 1984). As the proportion of mothers who are employed has increased, some have expressed concern for its possible effects on children. How does the employment of the mother impact on children? In this section we will review briefly what is known about this question.

From World War II to the present there have been numerous studies exploring the possible effects of the employment of mothers on their children. Most of the studies have found that the employment of the mother, by itself, has little effect on children. It depends on the mother, the child, and the situation.

This is illustrated by the experiences of three adolescents. Jane said that when her mother went to work her family situation improved. Her mother liked working and always had interesting things to talk about. Jane's mother seemed to be happier and have higher self-esteem when she worked. She became more confident and informed. And her working enabled the family to do better economically. Jane was able to get clothes and do other things she wanted to do (like take piano lessons) that she had not been able to do before her mother became employed. Jane said her mother spent just as much time with the children after she began working and that the quality of the time was better.

Linda said that she hated it when her mother went to work. Her mother always came home from work both emotionally and physically drained. Linda's mother no longer felt like doing things with the children. She not only spent less time with them but the time she did spend was lower in quality. Linda felt somewhat neglected and hurt when her relationship with her mother deteriorated because of her mother's employment.

Ken said that he resented it when his mother became a leader in their church. His mother was not employed, but she might as well have been. She was seldom there after school and Ken felt that his mother put everything into her church responsibilities and did not have time or attention for him.

These three examples show how employment of the mother may have positive or negative consequences, depending on the situation. Whether a mother is employed or not, the critical factor is the quality of the parent-child interaction. Employment may help, hinder, or have no effect on that interaction. Also, community involvements may have negative effects on children in some circumstances. Just because a woman is not employed does not make her a better mother.

Most of the research on employed mothers has failed to identify differences between the children of employed and nonemployed women. Children of em-

The majority of mothers with young children are employed outside the home. Here a young mother enjoys a conversation with her daughter before she leaves for work. *MacDonald/The Picture Cube.*

ployed mothers do just as well in school as children whose mothers stay at home. In fact, in the lower class, there is some evidence that children do better in school if the mother is employed (Moore and Sawhill 1984). Several studies have found that when the mother is employed the children, particularly daughters, tend to develop less traditional sex role attitudes and to value female achievement (Hoffman 1974, 1984; Lamb 1984; Moore and Sawhill 1984). Children of employed women may become somewhat more responsible and independent, and fathers sometimes do more child care and housekeeping if the mother is employed (Hoffman 1984; Moore and Sawhill 1984).

Over the years one of the concerns has been whether very young children can develop adequate attachment to their employed mothers. Although some scholars have found no significant effects of maternal employment on infant-mother attachment, several recent studies suggest that the likelihood of insecure attachment increases when the mother is employed (Lamb 1984). However, Lamb (1984) and Sroufe and Ward (1984) maintain that maternal employment does not necessarily have an adverse impact on infant-mother attachment, and that the quality of the infant-mother interaction is the critical variable.

In summary, the mother's employment may increase independence and responsibility in children and make their sex role attitudes less traditional. In some cases fathers may become more involved in child care and housekeeping. Among infants maternal employment may in some cases interfere with infant-mother attachment. Nevertheless, the major conclusion from research is that the effects of maternal employment on children depend on a variety of factors, including motives for employment, salary, satisfaction with job, flexibility of hours, attitudes of husband, adequacy of child care, age of children, help with housework, and socioeconomic status (Moore and Sawhill 1984).

It is the situation and meaning of employment that makes the difference, not employment per se. Women who are dissatisfied with staying home and stay home only out of "duty" tend to do poorly as mothers (Sroufe and Ward 1984). On the other hand, if a woman's job leaves her tired and unresponsive to her children, her employment may be harmful to the children. The research is conclusive in showing that the quality of parent-child interaction is the critical factor, not whether or not a mother is employed.

SINGLE-PARENT HOMES.   The proportion of children living in one-parent homes has risen dramatically in recent years. In 1970 85 percent of children were living in a two-parent home, compared to only 74 percent of children in 1985 (U.S. Bureau of the Census, 1980, 1986). More than half of all children will live in a single-parent home at some point before they reach age 18 (Bumpass 1984; Furstenberg and Nord 1982; Hofferth 1985). Hofferth (1985) estimates that white children born in 1980 will spend 25 percent of their childhood in a single-parent home, and black children will spend 44 percent of their childhood in a single-parent home. A large majority of children in single-parent homes are the result of divorce and most of them live with their mother.

What effect does living in a single-parent home have on children? Some maintain that it has negative consequences, and others say it is not the single parenthood that hurts children, but inadequate parenting. Let's look at the evidence.

When children from single-parent homes are compared with children from two-parent homes, it appears that the former are not as well adjusted. Adolescents from single-parent homes take more health risks, such as intemperate drinking and not fastening seat belts (Saucier and Ambert 1983). They tend to start dating earlier and are more likely to have premarital sex, which is related to pregnancy and out-of-wedlock childbearing (Coleman, Gianong, and Ellis 1985; Newcomer and Udry 1987). And they are more susceptible to pressure from friends to engage in deviant behavior (Steinberg 1987).

Children from single-parent homes have poorer social adjustment and do not perform as well academically as children from intact homes, particularly boys (Guidubaldi, Perry, and Nastasi 1986; Hodges et al. 1983). Differences in social and academic adjustment are evident even after six years (Guidubaldi et al. 1986).

Kellam, Ensminger, and Turner (1977) found that children's social and psychological adjustment was related to family structure. They examined the adjustment of school-aged children who lived in four different types of families: (1) two natural parents, (2) mother-grandmother, (3) mother-stepfather, and (4) mother alone. Children in mother-alone homes were at greatest risk for maladjustment whereas children who lived with both natural parents had the best adjustment. However, children in mother-grandmother homes did almost as well as children from intact homes, whereas children in stepparent homes did almost as poorly as children in mother-alone homes. Kellam et al. (1977) concluded that remarriage may not help adjustment, and that mother aloneness was more important than father absence.

Children from single-parent homes evaluate their parents more negatively than do children from two-parent homes (Parish and Kappes 1980). Fathers, who usually are the noncustodial parent in divorce, are rated particularly poorly by their children. Amato (1987) reported that children rated their mothers similarly in support and punishment regardless of family type. However, children in one-parent homes rated their fathers as less supportive and controlling than did children from intact homes.

Glenn and Kramer (1985) suggest that the negative effects of divorce may be long lasting. They found that adults whose parents had divorced consistently rated their happiness and life satisfaction as lower than adults whose parents had not divorced.

Although the research suggests that single-parent homes may place children at risk, there is considerable evidence that it is the quality of parent-child interaction rather than number of parents that is important for children. When viewed cross-culturally, the one-parent family is not necessarily pathological or inferior (Bilge and Kaufman 1983). Lamb (1978) maintains that divorce is not necessarily harmful to children's personality development if the parents are willing and able to care for a child.

Recent research suggests that some of the reported differences between children from single-parent and two-parent homes may represent a **spurious relationship** because relevant variables have not been controlled (Blechman 1982; Kanoy and Cunningham 1984). For example, differences between children from divorced and intact families were reduced substantially when income was controlled (Guidubaldi et al. 1986). Goldstein (1982) found that when parental education and income were controlled, father absence was not related to academic performance. A review of the literature by Wells and Rankin (1985) revealed that the relationship between broken homes and delinquency was weak.

Several scholars have found that it is the amount of parental conflict rather than disruption per se that affects child adjustment. Emery (1982) concluded that much of the association between divorce and child behavior problems may be explained by parental conflict. Luepnitz (1978) maintained that the stress of divorce on children was due more to turmoil involved in parental conflict than living in a one-parent home. Long (1986) found that self-esteem of daughters was related to parental discord but not to family structure. Parental discord appeared to lower self-esteem although parental separation did not. Other research is consistent with their conclusions (Hess and Camara 1979; Nye 1957).

What may be concluded about the effects of living in a one-parent home on children? It appears that the situation is not, by itself, detrimental to children. However, these children may be at risk for several reasons. First, parental conflict is often associated with divorce, and severe parental conflict has been shown to be detrimental to children.

Second, raising children is not easy and having two parents may decrease parental stress and increase the quality of parental monitoring. Role overload is a common complaint of single parents (Bahr 1982).

Third, economic problems are associated with marital disruption. Women usually get custody of the children and a high proportion have only marginal incomes. As noted earlier, when income is controlled the negative effects of single parenthood diminish, but the fact is that a large majority of single parents and their children have very low incomes (Weitzman 1985). Divorce itself may not hurt children, but divorce reduces women's income and a low income impacts negatively on children.

Finally, marital disruption may decrease on adult's capacity to parent. Wallerstein (1985) suggests that marital disruption is often followed by less sensitivity, talk, play, supportiveness, and overall parent-child interaction. This may not be a necessary result of divorce, but Wallerstein found that it is fairly common.

Living in a single-parent home may increase the risk of maladjustment in children because parental conflict, role overload, diminished parenting, and economic problems often accompany single parenthood. Therefore, it is important that single parents receive social and economic support to decrease role overload and economic stress. Separated and divorced parents should be encouraged to keep their children out of their conflicts. Emery (1982) and Wallerstein (1985) have shown that parental conflict is one of the major risks of divorce for children. Finally, single parents need to be sensitive to and supportive of their children. Diminished parenting is the chief hazard for children of divorce but it is not inevitable (Wallerstein 1985). When single parents are warm, sensitive, and available, their children tend to have normal social and cognitive development (Crouter, Belsky, and Spanier, 1984).

SOCIAL CLASS.   The nuclear family is an important unit of social class, transmitting values, attitudes, and behaviors that are associated with social status.

Individuals have the same social status as their nuclear family. How much effect does social class have on child rearing?

There are various conceptions of social class, depending on the purpose at hand. **Social Class** is usually divided into three major divisions: (1) upper class, (2) middle class, and (3) lower class. Class is a ranking that is based on prestige, power, and wealth. Individuals in a given social class are assumed to have some common attitudes and values. Education, occupation, and income are often used as indicators of social class.

Kohn (1969) studied how class is related to child-rearing values. He compared working- and middle-class parents. The working class is sometimes called the upper-lower class or described as blue collar workers. Working-class people usually have stable employment in skilled and semiskilled blue collar occupations.

Kohn found that middle-class parents tend to emphasize self-direction whereas working-class parents emphasize conformity to external authority. The education and occupational positions of middle-class individuals foster flexibility, tolerance, and self-direction. Inner direction is also important. On the other hand, working-class conditions and occupations are less flexible and more authoritarian. Following the dictates of external authority is important. People in working-class occupations do not have much opportunity for self-direction and conformity to authority is often a necessity for their work (Kohn 1969).

Kohn hypothesized that these differences in orientations among working- and middle-class individuals would affect their attitudes and behaviors toward children. Middle-class parents were expected to discipline more using the child's internal motivations whereas working-class parents were expected to discipline more on external consequences than on the motives of the child.

Kohn's research supported his hypotheses. Middle-class parents tended to stress self-direction and autonomy, and working-class parents emphasized neatness, obedience, and conformity to externally imposed rules.

Gecas and Nye (1974) found modest support for Kohn's hypothesis. Middle-class parents were more responsive to the child's motives than working-class parents. However, the differences between the two groups were not very great, and working-class parents were not insensitive to their children's intentions when disciplining them. Gecas and Nye also found that lower-class parents were more likely to use physical punishment compared to middle-class parents who used more verbal reprimands.

In a similar study in Germany, Williamson (1984) also observed that the middle class was somewhat more internal in their discipline of children than the working class. Similarly, German working-class parents were more oriented toward physical punishment than German middle-class parents.

Research in Ireland, Peru, and Italy has found similar class differences in child rearing (Hynes 1985; Kohn 1984). Over the years numerous investigators have observed that lower-class parents are more likely than middle-class parents to use coercive, power-assertive discipline techniques. Lower-class parents are less likely to explain, use induction, or take extenuating circumstances into account (Hoffman 1984).

In Indiana, Caplow et al. (1982) found that middle-class adolescents spend somewhat more time with their parents than do working-class adolescents. The differences were not large, however, and there were more similarities than differences among the two classes.

In summary, social class appears to have a modest but consistent effect on child-rearing attitudes and behavior. Working-class parents compared to middle-class parents tend to use more coercion and physical punishment and be somewhat more oriented to external conformity than self-direction.

When all the evidence is evaluated, it appears that family interaction has a greater influence on social competence in children than family structure. Family size, spacing, birth order, and the mother's employment status have very small effects, and social class has only modest effects. Number of parents in the household appears to be the most important structural variable, because single parenthood is often associated with diminished parenting. However, the critical variable is the quality of parent-child interaction and not the number of parents in the home.

Adolescence

Adolescence, a critical period in the socialization of children, is a transitional stage between childhood and adulthood when one learns to play adult roles and become independent. This stage of development may be difficult because one is no longer a child, yet not quite an adult. It is often portrayed as a difficult period that is fraught with parent-youth conflict.

Research shows that there are substantial differences between adolescents and their parents in perceptions of family communication and cohesion. Parents tend to judge the family as more cohesive than adolescents do (Noller and Callan 1986; Tims and Masland 1985). Nevertheless, adolescents perceive that cohesiveness is fairly high in their families (Noller and Callan 1986). There also is evidence that the conflict between parents and adolescents is less than popularly believed (Willits 1986).

Sebald (1986) examined adolescent orientations toward parents and peers and how they have changed in recent decades. He noted that the extent of peer influence may be less than usually assumed. Although social activities are peer oriented, financial, education, and career concerns tend to be parent oriented. Sebald also observed a decline in parent orientation during the sixties and seventies, but an increase in parental orientation during the eighties.

There is often an intermediate step between leaving one's family of orientation and beginning a family of procreation. Adolescents may leave home for school, work, or military service but not yet marry or establish an independent residence. Many return home for periods after completing school or military service (Goldscheider and Davanzo 1986).

This period of semiautonomy in late adolescence may influence the attitudes and behaviors of young adults. Waite, Goldscheider, and Witsberger (1986) found that young women who lived independently became less traditional in family sex role attitudes, more accepting of employment of mothers, more likely to plan for employment themselves, and lowered their expected family size. Thus, nonfamily living in young adulthood may have an important influence on the attitudes and plans of young adults. This phenomenon has become more common in recent decades as adolescents have been leaving their parental homes earlier and marrying later (Waite et al. 1986).

One of the major tasks of parents is to support their children financially. This may become particularly problematic during adolescence as educational expenses are incurred. We turn now to a discussion of what it costs to raise children.

Costs of Children

As our society grew more industrialized, children became economic liabilities rather than assets. In an agricultural economy children are able to contribute to family income by working on the family farm. In developed countries it requires a considerable economic investment to raise and educate a child, and they contribute little or nothing to the family income. In this section we will review recent estimates by Espenshade (1984) of what it actually costs to raise a child in the United States.

Espenshade (1984) found that the cost of raising a child to age 18 depends on three main factors: (1) number of children, (2) parents' socioeconomic status, and (3) mother's employment status. The amount spent per child decreases as number of children increases. Lower-class families spend less on each child than upper-class families. Mothers who are employed spend more per child than mothers who are not employed. Espenshade (1984) estimates that a high socioeconomic status couple with one child and the mother working full-time will spend about $160,000 to raise a child to age 18 (in 1985 prices). A low socioeconomic status family with three children and a nonemployed mother will spend about $69,000 per child. A middle-class family with two children and a mother who works part-time will spend about $97,000 to raise a child to age 18.

Of the three factors, family size is the most important. As number of children increases from one to three, the amount spent on each child decreases by about 35 percent. Moving from upper to lower class reduces per child expenditures by 24 percent, and mothers who are not employed spend about 19 percent less per child than mothers who are employed (Espenshade 1984).

What proportion of total family income is spent on children? A family with one child spends about one third of its income on the child, a family with two children spends about 43 percent, and a family with three children spends about 50 percent (Espenshade 1984). These figures do not include the cost of a college education, which many families contribute to.

In agricultural settings the economic value of children increases with age. As they get older they contribute significantly to earning the family income. In developed societies the reverse occurs. Children get more expensive as they get older (Espenshade 1984).

A number of years ago an American movie about a large family was titled *Cheaper by the Dozen*. The figures of Espenshade confirm the idea that the costs per child are less as family size increases. However, the economies of scale of additional children are not large. An additional child will cost only 5 to 10 percent less than a previous child (Espenshade 1984). The spacing of children also makes little difference in expenditures per child.

Whites tend to spend more per child than blacks, although the differences are relatively small. And families in metropolitan areas tend to spend more per child than families in rural areas.

The three major expenditures for children are transportation, housing, and food. These three items comprise about three fourths of all expenditures (Espenshade 1984).

Summary

1. The transition to parenthood is often stressful because parents must adjust to loss of sleep and the energy, time, and constraints required by a new baby. Nevertheless, most view parenthood as a positive experience.

2. The difficulties in becoming a parent are due to the addition of the child care and child socialization roles, the required modification of other roles, and the fact that the transition to parenthood is irrevocable, abrupt, and often begins with little relevant training.

3. The adjustment to parenthood is more difficult for women than for men.

4. The adjustment to parenthood is affected by the quality of the marriage as well as by the amount of spousal support, the degree of preparation, and how important the parental role is to one's identity.

5. The stress of parenthood is greater if marital satisfaction is low, the pregnancy was difficult, one has health problems after the birth, and the baby has health problems.

6. Parenthood tends to decrease the quality of the marriage by decreasing the amount of marital interaction, increasing financial dissatisfaction, and increasing dissatisfaction with the division of labor.

7. Childless couples tend to have higher marital satisfaction than couples with children. However, recent research suggests that this difference is due partly to the fact that unhappy childless couples divorce more frequently than unhappy couples with children.

8. Child socialization is considered to be the most important and most stressful family role, and husbands and wives have more conflict over child socialization than any other family role.

9. The norms regarding child socialization are very egalitarian. Although behavior is fairly egalitarian, husbands are much less involved in child socialization than wives.

10. The major disadvantages of parenthood are loss of freedom, difficulties in disciplining children, costs of raising children, and difficulties of children adjusting outside the home.

11. The major satisfactions of parenthood are the love for one's children and a sense of meaning and purpose.

12. Women are less confident than men about parenthood but receive more fulfillment than men from parenthood.

13. The effects of parental training and the family environment are limited by the biological potential of each child. Research suggests that genetic influences may be greater than previously believed.

14. There is a reciprocal influence between parent and child. Children influence parental behavior as well as the reverse.

15. Social competence includes the development of conformity to social rules, creativity, morals, self-esteem, and mental skills. Antisocial aggression, delinquency, drug abuse, learning disabilities, and mental illness are types of social incompetence.

16. The development of social competence in children is associated with parental monitoring and a moderate amount of parental control. Social incompetence is more common when parents are very permissive or excessively controlling.

17. Social competence is more likely when parents use induction rather than coercive control attempts.

18. Support is the most important parental characteristic in the development of social competence. All during childhood and adolescence, parental warmth, nurturance, and support are positively related to the development of social competence in children.

19. There is a tendency for children to model parents in antisocial behaviors such as aggression, drug abuse, and criminal conduct, as well as in prosocial behaviors.

20. High levels of marital conflict are associated with insecure attachment and poor adjustment in children.

21. Family size, spacing, and birth order have small effects on the mental and social development of children.

22. The effect of the employment of mothers on children depends on the meaning of work and the family situation. By itself there is no evidence that the employment of mothers is detrimental to children. If the mother is employed children tend to be somewhat more independent and to have less traditional sex role attitudes than if the mother is not employed.

23. Living in a single-parent home is not necessarily detrimental to children. Parental conflict is more detrimental to children than parental absence per se. However, living in a single-parent home often places children at risk because parental conflict, role overload, economic strain, and diminished parenting are often associated with single parenthood.

24. Social class has relatively small effects on child rearing, although middle-class parents emphasize self-direction and autonomy more and obedience and conformity less than working-class parents.

25. Parent and adolescent perceptions of family conflict and cohesion are often quite different.

26. Parental-youth conflict is less than is often assumed, and parents have greater influence than peers on adolescent decisions regarding money, education, and career. Peers have greater influence than parents on adolescent decisions about social activities.

27. Many young adults have a transitional period of semiautonomous living after they leave the family of orientation but before they marry and establish an adult residence. This period has become somewhat more common and longer in duration in recent decades because youth have been leaving home earlier and marrying later.

28. Children have become economic liabilities in developed societies. The per child costs of raising children depend on number of children, social class, and the employment of the mother.

29. A family with one child spends about one third of its income on the child,

and a two-child family spends about 43 percent. Three children require about half of the family income.

Important Terms

- adolescence
- ✗ child socialization
- coercion
- ✗ control
- dilution model
- family structure
- genetic influences
- induction

- modeling *(implications of)*
- ✗ monitoring
- self-esteem
- ✗ social class
- social competence
- spurious relationship
- support

Questions for Discussion

1. What are the major adjustments that men and women have to make when they have a child?
2. What characteristics help couples adjust to the birth of a child?
3. What could be done in our society to make adjustment to parenthood easier?
4. What are the major rewards of parenthood? What are the major costs of parenthood?
5. Why do couples with children have lower marital satisfaction than couples without children?
6. Why are norms regarding child socialization more egalitarian than behavior? What do you think are the consequences of this gap between ideals and behavior? What could be done to decrease this gap?
7. Are mothers naturally more nurturant than fathers? Are nurturant fathers good for children?
8. Describe the nature versus nurture controversy. How does genetic makeup limit the effects of environment, and how does the environment shape genetic potential? Can this controversy ever be resolved?
9. Describe some ways children influence parents as well as some ways parents influence children.
10. What is social competence?
11. What would you recommend that parents do to increase the chance that their children will develop social competence?
12. Identify conditions under which you would recommend that a mother become employed. Under what conditions would you recommend that a mother not become employed?
13. What could be done to minimize the risks of living in a single-parent home?
14. What are the effects of social class on child socialization?
15. How costly is it to raise a child today? Do you think the costs of children have affected the employment of mothers and the size of families?

16. What is a spurious relationship? Identify some relationships discussed in this chapter that appear to be spurious.
17. In what ways has socialization improved during the past several decades? In what ways has socialization become more difficult during recent decades? What risks do children encounter today that they did not in years past? What benefits do children have today that they did not have in previous years?
18. What could be done to improve socialization for children in our society?

Recommended Reading

GOETTING, A. 1986. Parental satisfaction: A review of research. *Journal of Family Issues* 7:83–109.

PATTERSON, G. R., and M. STOUTHAMER-LOEBER. 1984. The correlation of family management practices and delinquency. *Child Development* 55:1299–1307.

WALLERSTEIN, J. S. 1985. The overburdened child: Some long-term consequences of divorce. *Social Work* 30:116–123.

References

ABBOTT, D. A., and G. H. BRODY. 1985. The relation of child age, gender, and number of children to the marital adjustment of wives. *Journal of Marriage and the Family* 47:77–84.

ABELMAN, R. 1986. Children's awareness of television prosocial fare: Parental discipline as an antecedent. *Journal of Family Issues* 7:51–66.

AMATO, P. R. 1987. Family processes in one-parent, stepparent, and intact families: The child's point of view. *Journal of Marriage and the Family* 49:327–337.

AMATO, P. R., and G. OCHILTREE. 1986. Family resources on the development of child competence. *Journal of Marriage and the Family* 48:47–56.

BAHR, S. J. 1979. Family determinants and effects of divorce. In *Contemporary theories about the family,* vol. 1, ed. W. R. Burr, R. Hill, F. I. Nye, and I. L. Reiss, 615–643. New York: Free Press.

BAHR, S. J. 1982. The pains and joys of divorce: A survey of Mormons. *Family Perspective* 16 (14):191–200.

BARBER, B. K., and D. L. THOMAS. 1986. Dimensions of fathers' and mothers' supportive behavior: The case of physical affection. *Journal of Marriage and the Family* 48:783–794.

BARNES, G. M., M. P. FARRELL, and A. CAIRNS. 1986. Parental socialization factors in adolescent drinking behavior. *Journal of Marriage and the Family* 48:27–36.

BELL, N. J., and A. W. AVERY. 1985. Family structure and parent-adolescent relationships: Does family structure really make a difference? *Journal of Marriage and the Family* 47:503–508.

BELSKY, J. 1985. Exploring individual differences in marital change across the transition to parenthood: The role of violated expectations. *Journal of Marriage and the Family* 47:1037–1044.

BELSKY, J., M. E. LAN, and M. ROVINE. 1985. Stability and change in marriage across the transition to parenthood: A second study. *Journal of Marriage and the Family* 47:855–865.

BILGE, B., and G. KAUFMAN. 1983. Children of divorce and one-parent families: Cross-cultural perspectives. *Family Relations* 32:59–71.

BLAKE, J. 1981. Family size and the quality of children. *Demography* 18 (4):421–442.

BLAKE, J. 1985. Number of siblings and educational mobility. *American Sociological Review* 50:84–94.

BLECHMAN, E. A. 1982. Are children with one parent at psychological risk? A methodological review. *Journal of Marriage and the Family* 44:179–195.

BLOCK, J. H., J. BLOCK, and A. MORRISON. 1981. Parental agreement-disagreement on child-rearing orientations and gender-related personality correlates in children. *Child Development* 52:965–974.

BORDUIN, C. M., J. A. PRUITT, and S. W. HENGGELER. 1986. Family interactions in black, lower-class families with delinquent and nondelinquent adolescent boys. *The Journal of Genetic Psychology* 147 (3):333–342.

BOUCHARD, T. J., JR. 1984. Twins reared together and apart: What they tell us about human diversity. In *Individuality and determinism*, ed. S. W. Fox, 147–184. New York: Plenum.

BUMPASS, L. L. 1984. Children and marital disruption. A replication and update. *Demography* 21 (1):71–82.

CAPLOW, T., H. M. BAHR, B. A. CHADWICK, R. HILL, and M. H. WILLIAMSON. 1982. *Middletown families. Fifty years of change and continuity.* Minneapolis: University of Minnesota Press.

CHEUNG, P. C., and S. LAU. 1985. Self-esteem—its relationship to the family and school social environments among Chinese adolescents. *Youth & Society* 16 (4):438–456.

COHEN, J. 1987. Parents as educational models and definers. *Journal of Marriage and the Family* 49:339–351.

COLEMAN, M., L. H. GANONG, and P. ELLIS. 1985. Family structure and dating behavior of adolescents. *Adolescence* 20:537–543.

COOPER, J. E., J. HOLMEN, and V. A. BRAITHWAITE. 1983. Self-esteem and family cohesion: The child's perspective and adjustment. *Journal of Marriage and the Family* 45:153–159.

COVERMAN, S., and J. F. SHELEY. 1986. Change in men's housework and child-care time, 1965–1975. *Journal of Marriage and the Family* 48:413–422.

COWAN, C. P., P. A. COWAN, G. HEMMING, E. GARRETT, W. S. COYSH, H. CURTIS-BOLES, and A. J. BOLES. 1985. Transitions to parenthood: His, hers, and theirs. *Journal of Family Issues* 6:451–481.

CROUTER, A. C., J. BELSKY, and G. B. SPANIER. 1984. The family context of child development: Divorce and maternal employment. *Annals of Child Development* 1:201–238.

DANCY, B. L., and P. J. HANDAL. 1984. Perceived family climate, psychological adjustment, and peer relationship of black adolescents: A function of parental marital status or perceived family conflict? *Journal of Community Psychology* 12:222–229.

DENGA, D. C. 1982. Childlessness and marital adjustment in Northern Nigeria. *Journal of Marriage and the Family* 44:799–802.

EMERY, R. E. 1982. Interparental conflict and the children of discord and divorce. *Psychological Bulletin* 92 (2):310–330.

EMERY, R. E., and K. D. O'LEARY. 1982. Children's perceptions of marital discord and behavior problems of boys and girls. *Journal of Abnormal Child Psychology* 10 (1):11–24.

ENOS, D. M., and P. J. HANDAL. 1986. The relation of parental marital status and perceived family conflict to adjustment in white adolescents. *Journal of Consulting and Clinical Psychology* 54 (6):820–824.

ERNST, C., and J. ANGST. 1983. *Birth order. Its influence on personality.* New York: Springer-Verlag.

ESPENSHADE, T. J. 1984. *Investing in children: New estimates of parental expenditures.* Washington, DC: The Urban Institute Press.

ESPENSHADE, T. J., G. KAMENSKE, and B. A. TURCHI. 1983. Family size and economic welfare. *Family Planning Perspectives* 15 (6):289-294.

FELDMAN, H. 1981. A comparison of intentional parents and intentionally childless couples. *Journal of Marriage and the Family* 43:593–600.

FRANK, S., C. B. HOLE, S. JACOBSON, R. JUSTKOWSKI, and M. HUYCK. 1986. Psychological predictors of parents' sense of confidence and control and self- versus child-focused gratifications. *Developmental Psychology* 22 (3):348–355.

FURSTENBERG, F. F., JR., and C. W. NORD. 1982. The life course of children of divorce: Marital disruption and parental contact. *Family Planning Perspectives* 14:211–212.

GALBRAITH, R. C. 1982. Sibling spacing and intellectual development: A closer look at the confluence models. *Developmental Psychology* 18 (2):151–173.

GALBRAITH, R. C. 1983. Individual differences in intelligence: A reappraisal of the confluence model. *Intelligence* 7:185–194.

GARBARINO, J., J. SEBES, and C. SCHELLENBACH. 1984. Families at risk for destructive parent-child relations in adolescence. *Child Development* 55:174–183.

GECAS, V. 1976. The socialization and child care roles. In *Role structure and analysis of the family,* ed. F. I. Nye, 33–59. Beverly Hills, CA: Sage.

GECAS, V., and F. I. NYE. 1974. Sex and class differences in parent-child interaction: A test of Kohn's hypothesis. *Journal of Marriage and the Family* 36:742–749.

GECAS, V., and M. L. SCHWALBE. 1986. Parental behavior and adolescent self-esteem. *Journal of Marriage and the Family* 48:37–46.

GEISMAR, L. L. and K. WOOD. 1986. *Family and delinquency.* New York: Human Sciences Press.

GLENN, N. D., and S. K. HOPPE. 1984. Only children as adults: Psychological well-being. *Journal of Family Issues* 5:363–382.

GLENN, N. D., and K. B. KRAMER. 1985. The psychological well-being of adult children of divorce. *Journal of Marriage and the Family* 47:905–912.

GLENN, N. D., and S. McLANAHAN. 1982. Children and marital happiness: A further specification of the relationship. *Journal of Marriage and the Family* 44:63–72.

GOETTING, A. 1986. Parental satisfaction: A review of research. *Journal of Family Issues* 7:83–109.

GOLDBERG, W. A., G. Y. MICHAELS, and M. E. LAMB. 1985. Husbands' and wives' adjustment to pregnancy and first parenthood. *Journal of Family Issues* 6:483–503.

GOLDSCHEIDER, F. K., and J. DAVANZO. 1986. Semiautonomy and leaving home in early adulthood. *Social Forces* 65:187–201.

GOLDSTEIN, H. S. 1982. Fathers' absence and cognitive development of 12- to 17-year-olds. *Psychological Reports* 51:843–848.

GUIDAUBALDI, J., J. D. PERRY, and B. K. NASTASI. 1986. *Long-term impact of divorce on children: A report of a two- and three-year follow-up of a national sample.* Paper presented at the 63rd annual meeting of the American Orthopsychiatric Association, Chicago, April.

HANSON, S. L., D. E. MYERS, and A. L. GINSBURG. 1987. The role of responsibility and knowledge in reducing teenage out-of-wedlock childbearing. *Journal of Marriage and the Family* 49:241–256.

HARRIMAN, L. C. 1986. Marital adjustment as related to personal and marital changes accompanying parenthood. *Family Relations* 34:233–239.

HARRIS, I. D., and K. I. HOWARD. 1984. Parental criticism and the adolescent experience. *Journal of Youth and Adolescence* 13:113–121.

HEER, D. M. 1985. Effects of sibling number on child outcome. *Annual Review of Sociology* 11:27–47.

HESS, R. D., and K. A. CAMARA. 1979. Post-divorce family relationships as mediating factors in the consequences of divorce for children. *Journal of Social Issues* 35:79–96.

HODGES, W. F., H. K. BUCHSBAUM, and C. W. TIERNEY. 1983. Parent-child relationships and adjustment in preschool children in divorced and intact families. *Journal of Divorce* 7:43–58.

HOFFERTH, S. L. 1984. Long-term economic consequences for women of delayed childbearing and reduced family size. *Demography* 21 (2):141–155.

HOFFERTH, S. L. 1985. Updating children's life course. *Journal of Marriage and the Family* 47:93–115.

HOFFMAN, L. W. 1974. Effects on child. In *Working mothers*, ed. L. W. Hoffman and F. I. Nye, 126–166. San Francisco: Jossey-Bass.

HOFFMAN, L. W. 1984. Work, family, and the socialization of the child. In *Review of child development research: Vol. 7: The family*, ed. R. D. Parke, R. N. Emde, H. P. McAdoo, and G. P. Sackett, 223–282. Chicago: University of Chicago Press.

HOUSEKNECHT, S. J. 1979. Childlessness and marital adjustment. *Journal of Marriage and the Family* 41:259–265.

HUNDLEBY, J. D., and G. W. MERCER. 1987. Family and friends as social environments and their relationship to young adolescents' use of alcohol, tobacco, and marijuana. *Journal of Marriage and the Family* 49:151–164.

HYNES, E. 1985. Socialization values and punishment behavior. *Sociological Perspectives* 28(2):217–239.

ISABELLA, R. A., and J. BELSKY. 1985. Marital change during the transition to parenthood and security of infant-parent attachment. *Journal of Family Issues* 6:505–522.

KACH, J. A., and P. E. McGHEE. 1982. Adjustment of early parenthood: The role of accuracy of pre-parenthood experiences. *Journal of Family Issues* 3:375–388.

KANDEL, D. B., and I. ADLER. 1982. Socialization into marijuana use among French adolescents: A cross-cultural comparison with the United States. *Journal of Health and Social Behavior* 23:295–309.

KANOY, K. W., and J. L. CUNNINGHAM. 1984. Consensus or confusion in research on children and divorce: Conceptual and methodological issues. *Journal of Divorce* 7 (4):45–71.

KELLAM, S., M. E. ENSMINGER, and R. J. TURNER. 1977. Family structure and the mental health of children. *Archieves of General Psychiatry* 34:1012–1022.

KIDWELL, J.S. 1978. Adolescents' perceptions of parental affect: An investigation of only children vs. firstborns and the effect of spacing. *Journal of Population* 1:148–166.

KIDWELL, J. S. 1981. Number of siblings, sibling spacing, sex, and birth order: Their effects on perceived parent-adolescent relationships. *Journal of Marriage and the Family* 43:315–332.

KIDWELL, J. S. 1982. The neglected birth order: Middleborns. *Journal of Marriage and the Family* 44:225–235.

KOHN, M. L. 1969. *Class and conformity. A study in values*. Homewood, IL: Dorsey.

KOHN, M. L. 1984. The effects of social class on parental values and practices. In *Work & family*, ed. P. Voydanoff, 119–132. Palo Alto, CA: Mayfield.

LAMB, M. E. 1978. The effects of divorce on children's personality development. *Journal of Divorce* 1 (2):163–174.

LAMB, M. E. 1984. Fathers, mothers, and child care in the 1980s: Family influences on child development. In *Women in the workplace: Effects on families,* ed. K. M. Borman, D. Quarm, and S. Gideonse, 61–88. Norwood, NJ: Ablex.

LONG, B. H. 1986. Parental discord vs. family structure: Effects of divorce on the self-esteem of daughters. *Journal of Youth & Adolescence* 15:19–27.

LUEPNITZ, D. A. 1978. Children of divorce: A Review of the psychological literature. *Law and Human Behavior* 2:167–179.

MCHALE, S. M., and T. L. HUSTON. 1985. The effective of the transition to parenthood on the marriage relationship. *Journal of Family Issues* 6:409–433.

MACKEY, W. C. 1985. A cross-cultural perspective on perceptions of paternalistic deficiencies in the United States: The myth of the derelict daddy. *Sex Roles* 12(5/6):509–533.

MCMILLAN, D. W., and R. W. HILTONSMITH. 1982. Adolescents at home: An exploratory study of the relationship between perception of family social climate, general well-being, and actual behavior in the home setting. *Journal of Youth and Adolescence* 11 (4):301–315.

MANSCILL, C. K., and B. C. ROLLINS. 1985. Family correlates of self-esteem and academic achievement in adolescent youth. *Family Perspective* 19:161–169.

MARE, R. D., and M. D. CHEN. 1986. Further evidence on sibship size and educational stratification. *American Sociological Review* 51:403–412.

MEDNICK, B. R., R. L. BAKER, and D. HOCEVAR. 1985. Family size and birth order correlates of intellectual, psychosocial, and physical growth. *Merrill-Palmer Quarterly* 31(1):67–84.

MILLER, B. C., J. K. MCCOY, T. B. OLSON, and C. M. WALLACE. 1986. Parental discipline and control attempts in relation to adolescent sexual attitudes and behavior. *Journal of Marriage and the Family* 48:503–512.

MOORE, K. A., and I. V. SAWHILL. 1984. Implication of women's employment for home and family life. In *Work & family,* ed. P. Voydanoff, 153–171. Palo Alto, CA: Mayfield.

MOTT, F. L., and R. J. HAURIN. 1982. Being an only child: Effects on educational progression and career orientation. *Journal of Family Issues* 3:575–593.

NEWCOMER, S., and J. R. UDRY. 1987. Parental marital status effects on adolescent sexual behavior. *Journal of Marriage and the Family* 49:235–240.

NOLLER, P., and V. J. CALLAN. 1986. Adolescent and parent perceptions of family cohesion and adaptability. *Journal of Adolescence* 9:97–106.

NYE, F. I. 1957. Child adjustment in broken and in unhappy unbroken homes. *Marriage and Family Living* 19:356–361.

NYE, F. I. 1976. Family roles in comparative perspective. In *Role structure and analysis of the family,* ed. F. I. Nye, 149–174. Beverly Hills, CA: Sage.

NYE, F. I. 1980. A theoretical perspective on running away. *Journal of Family Issues* 1:274–399.

OLWEUS, D. 1980. Familial and temperamental determinants of aggressive behavior in adolescent boys: A causal analysis. *Developmental Psychology* 16 (6):644–660.

PARISH, T. S., and B. M. KAPPES. 1980. Impact of father loss on the family. *Social Behavior and Personality* 8 (1):107–112.

PATTERSON, G. R., and M. STOUTHAMER-LOEBER. 1984. The correlation of family management practices and delinquency. *Child Development* 55:1299–1307.

PETERSON, G. W., B. C. ROLLINS, and D. L. THOMAS. 1985. Parental influence and adolescent conformity: Compliance and internalization. *Youth & Society* 16 (4):397–420.

PLOMIN, R., J. C. LOEHLIN, and J. C. DEFRIES. 1985. Genetic and environmental components of "environmental" influences. *Developmental Psychology* 21 (3):391–402.

POLONKO, K. A., J. SCANZONI, and J. D. TEACHMAN. 1982. Childlessness and marital satisfaction: A further assessment. *Journal of Family Issues* 3:545–573.

POWER, T. G., and R. D. PARKE. 1984. Social network factors and the transition to parenthood. *Sex Roles* 10:949–971.

PRICE, G. G., D. J. WALSH, and W. R. VILBERG. 1984. The confluence model's good predictions of mental age beg the question. *Psychological Bulletin* 96 (1):195–200.

RADIN, N. 1981. Child-rearing fathers in intact families: An exploration of some antecedents and consequences. *Merrill Palmer Quarterly* 27:489–514.

RADIN, N., and A. SAGI. 1982. Child rearing in intact families in Israel and the U.S.A. *Merrill Palmer Quarterly* 28(1):111–136.

RAHAV, G. 1982. Family size and delinquency. *Sociology and Social Research* 66 (1):42–51.

ROLLINS, B. C., and D. L. THOMAS. 1979. Parental support, power, and control techniques in the socialization of children. In *Contemporary theories about the family*, vol. 1, ed. W. R. Burr, R. Hill, F. I. Nye, and I. L. Reiss, 317–364. New York: Free Press.

ROSSI, A. S. 1968. Transition to parenthood. *Journal of Marriage and the Family* 30:26–39.

RUSSELL, C. S. 1974. Transition to parenthood: Problems and gratifications. *Journal of Marriage and the Family* 36:294–301.

SAGI, A., and N. SHARON. 1984. The role of the father in the family: Toward a gender-neutral family policy. *Child and Youth Services Review* 6:83–99.

SAUCIER, J., and A. AMBERT. 1983. Parental marital status and adolescents' health-risk behavior. *Adolescence* 18:403–411.

SEBALD, H. 1986. Adolescence shifting orientation toward parents and peers: A curvilinear trend over recent decades. *Journal of Marriage and the Family* 48:5–13.

SROUFE, L. A., and M. J. WARD. 1984. The importance of early care. In *Women in the workplace: Effects on families*, ed. K. M. Borman, D. Quarm, and S. Gideonse, 35–60. Norwood, NJ: Ablex.

STEFFENSMEIER, R. H. 1982. A role model of the transition to parenthood. *Journal of Marriage and the Family* 44:319–334.

STEINBERG, L. 1987. Single parents, stepparents, and the susceptibility of adolescents to antisocial peer pressure. *Child Development* 58:269–275.

STEINMETZ, S. K. 1979. Disciplinary techniques and their relationship to aggressiveness, dependency, and conscience. In *Contemporary theories about the family*, vol. 1, ed. W. R. Burr, R. Hill, F. I. Nye, and I. L. Reiss, 405–438. New York: Free Press.

STEMP, P. S., R. J. TURNER, and S. HON. 1986. Psychological distress in the postpartum period: The significance of social support. *Journal of Marriage and the Family* 48:271–277.

STRAUS, M. A., R. J. GELLES. 1986. Societal change and change in family violence from 1975 to 1985 as revealed by two national surveys. *Journal of Marriage and the Family* 48:465–479.

STREIT, F. 1981. Differences among youthful criminal offenders based on their perceptions of parental behavior. *Adolescence* 16:409–413.

THOMAS, D. L., A. J. WEIGERT, and N. WINSTON. 1984. Adolescents' identification with father and mother: A multi-national study. *ACTA PAEDOLOGICA* 1:47–68.

TIETJEN, A. M., and C. F. BRADLEY. 1985. Social support and maternal psychosocial adjustment during the transition to parenthood. *Canadian Journal of Behavioral Science* 17:109–121.

TIMS, A. R., and J. L. MASLAND. 1985. Measurement of family communication patterns. *Communication Research* 12(1):35–37.

UMBERSON, D., and W. R. GOVE. 1986. *Family status and social integration: Costs and benefits for psychological well-being.* Paper presented at the annual meeting of the American Sociological Association, New York, August.

U.S. BUREAU OF THE CENSUS. 1980. *Statistical abstract of the United States: 1980.* Washington, DC: U.S. Government Printing Office.

U.S. BUREAU OF THE CENSUS. 1986. *Statistical abstract of the United States: 1987.* Washington, DC: U.S. Government Printing Office.

WAITE, L. J., F. K. GOLDSCHEIDER, and C. WITSBERGER. 1986. Nonfamily living and the erosion of traditional family orientations among young adults. *American Sociological Review* 51:541–554.

WAITE, L. J., G. W. HAGGSTROM, and D. E. KANOUSE. 1985. The consequences of parenthood for the marital stability of young adults. *American Sociological Review* 50:850–857.

WALDRON, H., and D. K. ROUTH. 1981. The effect of the first child on the marital relationship. *Journal of Marriage and the Family* 43:785–788.

WALLERSTEIN, J. S. 1985. The overburdened child: Some long-term consequences of divorce. *Social Work* 30 (2):116–123.

WALTERS, J., and L. H. WALTERS. 1980. Parent-child relationships: A review, 1970–1979. *Journal of Marriage and the Family* 42:807–822.

WEITZMAN, L. J. 1985. *The divorce revolution.* New York: Free Press.

WELLS, L. E., and J. H. RANKIN. 1985. Broken homes and juvenile delinquency: An empirical review. *Criminal Justice Abstracts* 17 (2):249–272.

WHITE, L. K., and A. BOOTH. 1985. The transition to parenthood and marital quality. *Journal of Family Issues* 6:435–449.

WHITE, L. K., A. BOOTH, and J. N. EDWARDS. 1986. Children and marital happiness—why the negative correlation? *Journal of Family Issues* 7:131–147.

WILLIAMSON, R. C. 1984. A partial replication of the Kohn-Gecas-Nye thesis in a German sample. *Journal of Marriage and the Family* 46:971–979.

WILLITS, W. L. 1986. Pluralistic ignorance in the perception of parent-youth conflict. *Youth & Society* 18(2):150–161.

WILSON, R. S., and A. P. MATHENY, JR. 1983. Mental development: Family environment and genetic influences. *Intelligence* 7:195–215.

WORTHINGTON, E. L., JR., and B. G. BUSTON. 1986. The marriage relationship during the transition to parenthood: A review and a model. *Journal of Family Issues* 7:443–473.

ZAJONC, R. B. 1975. Dumber by the dozen. *Psychology Today* (January):37–43.

PART III

Family and Societal Exchanges

CHAPTER 10

Work and the Family

Introduction

Michael is a computer programmer for a firm in Chicago, and Lorraine teaches math in a Chicago high school. Debra is now a year old and is cared for by a neighbor while they are at work. Both enjoy their work and feel their neighbor gives Debra good care at a reasonable price. If an emergency arises either Michael or Lorraine can be called at work, and Lorraine is able to be home by about 4:00 P.M. each day. She and Michael share the household chores.

Frank was a purchasing agent for a steel mill in Ohio until it recently closed down. His wife, Mary, was a special education teacher in the local school and they have three children, ages 16, 12, and 5. They liked the community but were forced to move because the plant closed. The steel company transferred Frank to a plant in Gary, Indiana, and he had to take the job even though he and his family would have preferred to stay in Ohio. The steel company purchased their home and they were able to buy a comparable home in Indiana. The children did not like moving, particularly the oldest daughter who is in high school. Now Mary must try to find a teaching job in Gary. The move has been stressful, but they are thankful that Frank has a good job.

Fred and Ann were not as lucky as Frank and Mary. Fred was a laborer at the steel mill in Ohio that closed. There was no transfer for him after the loss of his job. He could not move because he had no job to go to and his wife, Ann, worked as a seamstress at a local department store. For a while her income was all the family had to live on. After he lost his job they were not able to make the payments on their new home, which they had lived in for only two years. They had to sell their home and rent a small house.

The strain of Fred's unemployment has been hard on the entire family, but they are gradually adjusting. Ann is doing well at her job and it is secure although not high paying. She recently became head of the alterations department of the store.

Fred was able to get a job as a manager trainee at a local drugstore and now has steady employment. He only earns half of what he was earning as a steel worker because new manager trainees do not get paid well. He is hopeful that he will be able to advance and increase his earnings in the near future. Their two children are in high school and are glad both of their parents are now working. Their monetary situation is tight but they are making it at the moment.

These examples illustrate some of the ways work and family life influence each other. Michael and Lorraine are a typical dual-earner, middle-class family. Job loss and unwanted family moves were thrust upon Frank and Mary and on Fred and Ann. It was much easier for Frank and Mary because he was in management and was merely transferred to another company. Fred and Ann faced a period of unemployment and severe income loss.

In this chapter the reciprocal influences of family and work are explored. First, we review different types of family work, how work is divided, how the division of family work has changed in recent years, and factors that influence the allocation of family work. Second, we discuss how market work influences family life, including the impacts of unemployment and two earners. The final section is an examination of how family life influences market work.

Family Work

Types of Family Work

There are two major types of family work. First, there is unpaid work necessary to maintain the home and physical surroundings, called **domestic work.** Common maintenance tasks are shopping for food, cooking, cleaning, washing clothes, lawn care, and child care. The two family roles that are responsible for these tasks are the **housekeeper role** and the **child care role.**

Second, there is work in the labor force to earn money for the family, called **market work.** Family members generally are employed by a firm or person to perform a job. Nye (1976) has termed the role that does this type of work as the **provider role.**

Both types of work are necessary for the family to function. Housework and child care tasks are real production and contribute to the economic well-being of a family, even though performance of these tasks brings no money into the family. For example, Gronau (1977) has estimated that unpaid work at home could be valued at about two thirds of the family's money income.

Division of Family Work

Every family must establish a **division of labor.** How do family members divide up the work that needs to be done? Gender has always been an important factor. Traditionally, men took the role of hunter and soldier because they were physically stronger than women and did not have the burden of bearing and nursing children (Mackey 1985). Women tended to do work closer to home, including household chores and child care.

A family division of labor based on gender continues to exist in many so-

Maintenance tasks such as shopping, cooking, cleaning, and washing clothes are important parts of family work.   *Frank Siteman/The Picture Cube.*

cieties. Men are viewed as the primary providers, and women are assigned housekeeping and child care. Even when women are employed outside the home, they tend to do most of the household chores and child care.

Using a national sample of households, Kooreman and Kapteyn (1987) computed the average amount of time husbands and wives spent in various types of family work. The data were obtained from detailed diary information on time use. As shown in Table 10·1, husbands concentrate on market work while wives concentrate on housework. Men spend about forty-seven hours per week in employment and about thirteen hours in various household chores. Women average seventeen hours in market work and thirty-seven hours in household chores and child care. The total hours spent in family work (employment and various household work) are about equal for husbands and wives.

When a woman is employed the number of hours spent in housework and child care decreases. Wives tend to be employed only part-time (their average weekly hours on the job is only thirty-one). Men's housework time is only slightly higher in two-earner compared to single-earner couples (Kooreman

TABLE 10·1   Husbands' and Wives' Weekly Hours in Family Work in the United States

	Husbands			Wives		
	Two-earner Households	One-earner Households	Total Sample	Two-earner Households	One-earner Households	Total Sample
Employment	49.0	44.8	46.8	31.2	4.6	17.1
Household work	7.9	6.6	7.2	18.8	26.9	23.1
Child care	1.5	2.4	2.0	4.4	8.7	6.7
Obtaining goods and services	3.8	3.6	3.7	5.8	8.9	6.9
	62.2	57.4	59.7	60.2	49.1	53.8

SOURCE: Figures taken from Kooreman and Kapteyn 1987:234, Table 2. © 1987 by The University of Chicago. Reprinted by permission of University of Chicago Press.

and Kapteyn 1987). Other studies of time in market and household work have produced similar results (Nickols and Metzen 1982).

Changes in Family Division of Work

How has the allocation of family work changed in recent years? One of the significant social changes during the past century has been increased involvement of women in the provider role. The proportion of married women in paid employment has increased dramatically in almost every industrialized country (Davis 1984).

In the United States less than 5 percent of married women were in the labor force in 1890. This had increased to almost 25 percent in 1950 and to 50 percent in 1980. In 1986 about 55 percent of married women were employed (see Table 10·2).

Even more dramatic are the changes that have occurred among women with small children, as shown in Table 10·3. In 1986 more than 60 percent of married women with children under age 18 were employed. Fifty-four percent of women

TABLE 10·2   Percentage of Married Women in the Labor Force, United States (1890–1986)

Year	Percentage
1890	4.5
1900	5.2
1920	9.0
1930	11.7
1940	13.8
1950	21.6
1960	30.5
1970	40.8
1980	50.1
1986	54.6

SOURCES: Smith and Ward 1984:10; U.S. Bureau of the Census 1986:383.

TABLE 10·3 Percentage of Married Women in the Labor Force by Age of Youngest Child, United States (1975–1986)

Years	Total	No Children Under 18	With Children Under 18	Children Under 6	Children Under 1
1975	44.5	44.0	44.9	36.8	30.8
1980	50.2	46.0	54.3	45.3	39.0
1986	54.6	48.2	61.4	53.9	49.8

SOURCE: U.S. Bureau of the Census 1986:383.

with preschool children were employed, and 50 percent of women with infants under a year old were employed (U.S. Bureau of the Census 1986).

Recent increases in the employment of married women have occurred primarily among middle-class women. Chadwick and Chappell (1980) compared female labor force participation in the 1920s and 1970s. They found that 44 percent of working-class wives were employed in the twenties and this increased only slightly to 48 percent by the middle seventies. Among middle-class wives, however, the rate of employment was only 3 percent in the twenties and it increased to 42 percent by the 1970s (see Table 10·4).

TABLE 10·4 Percentage of Married Women in Labor Force by Social Class, Middletown (1920–1924 and 1973–1977)

Period	Percentage Employed	
	Working Class	Middle Class
1920–1924	44	3
1973–1977	48	42

SOURCE: Chadwick and Chappell 1980:33. Reprinted by permission.

Only small increases in the amount of housework done by husbands has been observed when their wives have entered the labor force (Coverman and Sheley 1986; Kooreman and Kapteyn 1987; Nickols and Metzen 1982; Pleck 1984). For example, Pleck (1984) found that husbands with employed wives spent 1.8 more hours per week in housework with 2.7 more hours per week in child care than did husbands with nonemployed wives. Very few families hire paid help to do the housework.

Although women's participation in the labor force has increased dramatically in recent decades, women have always contributed in various ways to help their families economically. In preindustrial periods they worked on farms doing whatever was necessary to help raise and market agricultural products. Black women have always been part of America's work force (Smith, E. 1985). Even in highly traditional third-world countries such as Egypt and Mexico, women have participated and continue to participate in the labor force on a formal and informal basis (Taplin 1985; Tiano 1985).

Influences on Allocation of Family Work

A variety of individual and cultural characteristics influence the way family labor is allocated. In addition to gender, economic need has a major influence on work allocation (Gould and Werbel 1983). One of the primary reasons why women have entered the labor force is to help their families achieve desired standards of living (Oppenheimer 1982). For example, during the seventies, increasing housing prices and lagging earnings of young men made it difficult for young married couples to purchase homes. The need for additional income for a home and other necessities drew women into the labor force. The earnings of wives have made it possible for many young couples to purchase a home (Myers 1985).

Need also affects the allocation of housework and child care. Coverman (1985) found that the demand for husbands' domestic labor influences their participation in housework and child care. When men have children and/or employed wives their help is needed at home, and they respond by increasing their involvement.

Family division of labor also depends on economic opportunities. In an analysis of sixty-one societies, Semyonov (1980) found that women's labor force participation increased as economic development increased. More women become employed as job opportunities expand (Ho 1984). When a family needs additional income, the labor market opportunities of the husband and wife influence whether the wife enters the labor force or the husband takes an extra job (Alper and Morlock 1982).

A final determinant of family work allocation is the rewards of various tasks. For example, we would expect that more women would enter the market as female wage rates increase. Devaney (1983) found that over the past two decades female wage rates were major factors in explaining female labor force participation and fertility. Ho (1984) observed that rewards of working have a significant influence on the decision of women to enter the labor force.

Influence of Market Work on the Family

Market work is a necessity for families. Income is needed to purchase food, clothing, and housing, and at least one family member must get a job. Many hours are spent on the job and its influence is pervasive. The ever-present influence of jobs on family life has been referred to as "the long arm of the job" (Komarovsky 1962). In this section we explore ways in which labor force participation of family members affects family life.

Inadequate Income and Unemployment

A large majority of total family income is earnings received from market work (Sawhill 1983). When family income is not adequate, family members often feel stress, which may damage their relationships. In a national survey of families, one third reported that financial pressures had hurt their marriages (Caplovitz 1981). It is common for families to struggle to earn enough to meet basic needs and desires.

The most dramatic impact of market work on family life is when a family member becomes unemployed. Making ends meet is not easy even when one has a job. If one becomes unemployed, the loss can be devastating, as was the case with Fred and Ann. Fred was shocked when he got the notice that the steel plant he had worked at for eighteen years was closing. He was out of a job! He had worked at the plant since he was 22 and now he was unemployed at age 40 with two children and a wife to support. How would he find another job? Why did this have to happen to him? How would he pay his house payments and get his family food and clothing? What about medical bills now that he was no longer covered by company insurance?

How common is **unemployment** in the United States? In 1985 the unemployment rate was 7.2 percent. The rates were much higher for the young, minorities, and women heading families, as shown in Table 10·5. Unemployment was higher among operators, construction workers, and laborers than among other occupations.

The median income of a family is 21 percent less among families with one unemployed member compared to those with no unemployed adults. Fifteen percent of families with one unemployed member have incomes less than the poverty level, compared to only 6 percent among families in which no one is unemployed (Terry 1982).

COPING WITH UNEMPLOYMENT. How do families cope with unemployment? There are five common **coping resources.** First, families try to reduce expenses, particularly for entertainment, food, and gasoline (Larson 1984; Root 1984). Some families cut down on the number of meals, and they may limit their clothes shopping to thrift stores (Caplovitz 1981).

Fred and Ann almost eliminated money for entertainment and cut down drastically on food and transportation expenses. Ann started sewing most of the family's clothes. They could no longer meet their house payments, so they

TABLE 10·5 Percentage Unemployed by Age, Gender, Race, and Marital Status, United States (1985)

Total		7.2
Age:	16–19	18.6
	20–24	11.1
	25–44	6.2
	45–64	4.5
	65 and over	3.2
Gender:	Male	7.0
	Female	7.4
Race:	White	6.2
	Black	15.1
	Hispanic	10.5
Women Maintaining Families		10.4
Married Men, Wife Present		4.3

SOURCE: U.S. Bureau of the Census 1986:390.

Adjusting to the demands of employment is often a challenging family task, but coping with unemployment is extremely stressful. One coping response is to look for another job, as shown by a husband looking for work in the want-ads. *Dave Schaefer/The Picture Cube.*

were forced to sell their home and rent a small house. It was hard moving out of their new home. Their children did not want to leave the neighborhood and the house they now rent is too small. But they had no choice.

A second way families try to cope with unemployment is for other family members to become employed. If the wife is not already employed, she tries to find work. However, for a majority of families in the United States this is not a coping option, for the wives are already employed. For example, Ann became employed two years ago and her income enabled them to purchase their home. The family depending on Ann's income long before Fred became unemployed. Parents with teenage children will encourage them to get a job. Ann and Fred's daughter who was 17 was able to find work at a fast-food restaurant and has been able to purchase her clothes, provide her own spending money, and help purchase gasoline. Their son could not get regular work because he was only 15, but he got a paper route and does lawn jobs in the summer. This has provided him with spending money and enabled him to purchase most of his clothes.

Ann and Fred had the advantage of having two employed adults in the family, and when Fred became unemployed they still had Ann's income. About 20 percent of families in the United States have only one parent in the household, and there is no second adult to help cope with the crisis of unemployment.

A third method of coping with unemployment is to use other available resources. Some families have savings they can use, and some may be able to obtain financial help from relatives. However, most families have no other monetary resources on which to draw. Fred and Ann are typical in that regard. They had been using both of the incomes to support their two children and purchase their home, and they had no savings. Their relatives were sympathetic to their plight but did not have extra money to give or loan to them.

Extended family living is one way family members may receive help from relatives. Tienda and Angel (1982) have shown that extended family structure among blacks and Hispanics is related to economic hardships as well as to cultural circumstances. The extended family may be a resource when earnings are temporarily or chronically low (Angel and Tienda 1982).

A fourth way to cope with unemployment is to seek assistance from the government. In the United States, unemployment compensation provides modest supplements to help individuals who are unemployed. In addition, a family with an income below a certain level can receive public assistance for food and some other necessities. Fred was able to receive an unemployment compensation check during the year he was unemployed, but with Ann's job their total family income was too large to qualify for other public assistance.

A final method of coping with unemployment is to look for new employment. Most unemployed persons do this, but it is usually a difficult and discouraging task. Fred had worked at the steel plant for eighteen years and was not trained to do anything else. There were a few unskilled jobs available but the wages were too low for a man trying to support a family. After a year of looking, Fred was able to get the manager trainee job.

A family's ability to cope with unemployment depends on its resources. Although unemployment was extremely stressful for Fred, Ann, and their children, it was not as devastating as it might have been because Ann had a job. At least they had her income for basic necessities. She also had medical insurance through her work that enabled the family to meet medical expenses. And the two teenage children were able to find jobs to buy their clothes and help buy gasoline. Many families, particularly young, minority, and female-headed families, do not have the resources Fred and Ann had. (Moen 1979, 1980).

 EFFECTS OF UNEMPLOYMENT.   Unemployment is an extremely stressful experience for family members. In addition to the sudden loss of income, how does it affect families? Research indicates that there are four major impacts of unemployment on family interaction.

First, unemployment has negative effects and can cause **psychological dis-**

tress. Anxiety, hostility, and depression tend to increase while self-esteem and life satisfaction tend to decrease (Atkinson, Liem, and Liem 1986; Linn, Sandifer, and Stein 1985; Voydanoff 1987). There is also evidence that unemployment is associated with reduced motivation and less ability to concentrate (Baum, Fleming, and Readdy 1986). The spouse of an unemployed worker feels this strain and in some cases becomes anxious and depressed (Voydanoff 1987).

Second, unemployment tends to be followed by a decrease in the quality of marital communication, a decrease in marital satisfaction, and an increase in marital conflict (Atkinson et al. 1986; Larson 1984; Voydanoff 1987). Unemployment has been found to be one of the best predictors of divorce and separation (Bahr and Galligan 1984; Cherlin 1979; Ross and Sawhill 1975). Liker and Elder (1983) found that a heavy income loss increased financial disputes, which tended to decrease marital satisfaction.

The negative effects of unemployment may be less when family support is high. Linn et al. (1985) suggest that support from family and friends helps bolster the self-esteem of the person who is unemployed. Liker and Elder (1983) observed that the effects of job loss were greatest among those with minimal coping resources. Those with strong marriages before job loss were able to provide greater support and made remarkable marital adaptations to the stress of unemployment.

The third effect of unemployment is on children and parent-child relations. The strain of unemployment may interfere with a parent's ability to support and socialize children. When fathers are unemployed there is a higher risk of rejection and child abuse (Elder, Van Nguwen, and Caspi 1985; Voydanoff 1987).

Children are also affected by pressure on them to work. Fred and Ann's children were required to get jobs to help with family expenses. This may increase the autonomy of teenagers (Voydanoff 1987).

A fourth effect of unemployment is on the division of labor within the home. If teenagers get jobs they will be less available to help with domestic chores. A father who becomes unemployed may spend more time at home and will be more available for household chores. Warr and Payne (1983) examined the behavior of men following job loss. Most of the men spent considerably more time doing household chores and child care as a result of their unemployment.

Effects of Job Satisfaction and Stress

A large majority of families do not have an unemployed member. For better or for worse, they have the privilege of holding a job. Some people enjoy their work, but for others it is drudgery. How much effect do job satisfaction and working conditions have on family life?

There are two different models about how work affects family life. First is the **spillover model** which asserts that satisfactions and stress experienced at work affect family interaction. The second model is termed *segmented* because occupation and family are viewed as independent. According to the **segmented model,** family and occupational roles are two separate worlds and what happens at work does not necessarily influence the family (Yogev and Brett 1983).

There is considerable support for the spillover model. For example, Barling (1984) found that the husband's job satisfaction was positively related to the wife's marital satisfaction. When the work environment was stressful and unsatisfying, marital satisfaction suffered. On the other hand, when the work environment was positive and job satisfaction was high, marital satisfaction tended to be higher. Several other researchers also have observed that work stress can disrupt marital relationships and create psychological stress (Bromet et al. 1988; Jackson and Maslach 1982; Kessler and McRae 1982; Pavett 1986; Pearlin and McCall 1987).

Although severe job stress may have a negative impact on families, effect on the average family may not be large. Pond and Green (1983) found only small correlations between job satisfaction and marital satisfaction, and Yogev and Brett (1983) observed that work and family roles are often segmented.

The effect of occupational conditions on family life may depend on the extent to which it disrupts family roles. Extensive work involvement by men or women may decrease time with the family and produce **inter-role conflict** or **role overload.** Similarly, extensive family demands may make it difficult to fulfill work expectations, resulting in inter-role conflict.

Among both men and women, inter-role conflict and role overload have been found to be associated with low marital satisfaction (Barling 1986a; Nicola and Hawkes 1985). Houseknecht, Vaughan, and Macke (1984) concluded that the relatively high rate of marital disruption among highly educated women is due to the strain caused by efforts to fulfill both occupational and family roles.

The effect of occupational stress on a family depends on **family support.** Suchet and Barling (1986) found that spouse support moderates the negative effects of inter-role conflict on marital satisfaction. In a study of police officers, the stress from their work had less effect on the marital quality when the couples could talk and the men felt supported by their wives (Jackson and Maslach 1982). Similarly, Houseknecht and Macke (1981) found that having a supportive husband was the major factor in the marital adjustment of professional women.

Effects of Employment of Wives

One of the significant changes in family life during the past century has been a large increase in the numbers of married women who are employed outside the home. How has this change affected family life?

EFFECTS ON FAMILY INCOME AND SPENDING PATTERNS.   A major consequence of women's employment is to improve the family's standard of living and increase net worth accumulation and financial security (Foster and Metzen 1981). The average family income is 40 percent higher when both husband and wife are employed compared to families in which only the husband is employed (Foster 1981). White women earn about one fourth of the total family income, and black women earn about one third. Without the earnings of the wives, the number of husband-wife families living in poverty would be more than 50 percent higher than it is now (Shaw and Sproat 1980). In the United States the earnings of wives have become increasingly important for the purchase of homes among young couples (Myers 1985).

The overall family spending patterns do not change, however, when a wife works. Her employment increases family income level but does not alter the basic pattern of expenditures. The percentages of the family income spent on different goods and services are similar for single-earner and dual-earner families (Chadwick and Chappell 1980; Foster, Abdel-Ghay, and Ferguson 1981).

EFFECTS ON DIVISION OF LABOR.   The employment of the wife not only improves family income, but also alters the division of labor. Men tend to do somewhat more child care and housework when their wives are employed (Coverman 1985; Pleck 1984; Ybarra 1982).

EFFECTS ON SEX ROLE ATTITUDES.   The employment of women tends to be associated with egalitarian attitudes. Women who are employed outside the home have more profeminist attitudes on women's rights and sex roles than housewives. And husbands of employed wives are more supportive of feminist positions than husbands of housewives (Smith, T. 1985). Homemakers tend to hold a more traditional view of women's roles than employed women (Stokes and Peyton 1986).

There appears to be a **reciprocal** influence between women's employment and sex role attitudes. Women with egalitarian sex role attitudes are more likely to choose to work outside the home than women with traditional sex role attitudes (Van Loo and Bagozzi 1984). When women are employed in the marketplace, they tend to become more egalitarian in their sex role expectations and their husbands tend to be socialized into a more egalitarian ethic (Petersen and Maynard 1981; Rank 1982).

EFFECTS ON MARITAL SATISFACTION.   Does having two earners have any impact on marital satisfaction? When both partners are employed three major spheres must be integrated: (1) the household, (2) the wife's employment, and (3) the husband's employment. It may be more difficult to integrate three spheres than two, resulting in more strain and inter-role conflict among dual-earner couples than single-earner couples. Gray (1983) found that a majority of professional women experience strain between family and career roles.

Kingston and Nock (1987) analyzed time together among dual-earner and single-earner couples using time diaries. They found that dual-earner couples spent less time together than single-earner couples particularly time eating meals, watching TV, and enjoying recreation together. Time together was related positively to marital quality. They concluded that the time lost because of two earners may hurt marital satisfaction and make it more difficult for partners to sustain each other emotionally. However, Kingston and Nock (1987) noted that dual-earning couples were only a little less companionable than single-earner couples, and that the correlations between time together and marital satisfaction were relatively small.

Overall, the data suggest that under some conditions having two earners may hurt marital quality *if* work time crowds out couple time. The direct effect of the wife's employment on marital quality appears to be relatively small and depends on a variety of situation variables.

Several studies have found that divorce is more common among employed women than among housewives (Cherlin 1979; Mott and Moore 1979). Some have speculated that the strains of having two earners causes marital discord and divorce. However, this relationship appears to be the result of low marital satisfaction rather than employment. That is, the wife's employment, by itself, is not related to marital disruption. The wife's employment *in combination* with low marital satisfaction is associated with divorce (Booth et al. 1984). A woman who is satisfied in her marriage is not going to divorce whether she is employed or not. Women who are unhappy and employed are more likely to divorce than women who are unhappy and not employed. The employment does not cause divorce but provides an economic alternative for women who are in unsatisfying marriages.

EFFECTS ON MENTAL AND PHYSICAL HEALTH.   Some researchers have suggested that the employment of women improves the mental health of women and causes psychological distress among men. The role of homemaker has been portrayed as a stressful and frustrating role that is harmful for the psychological and physical health of women (Bernard 1972; Ferree 1976; Friedan 1963).

Most of the research indicates that being employed or not employed has little effect on the physical and psychological health of married women (Krause and Markides 1985; Shehan 1984; Warr and Parry 1982). It is the fit between actual and desired roles that is related to physical and mental health, rather than employment status per se. Women whose labor force status is compatible with their attitudes tend to have better health than women who have a discrepancy between attitude and employment status (Waldron and Herold 1986). Townsend and Gurin (1981) examined the fit between actual and desired roles among homemakers and employed women. Homemakers who desired a career were more dissatisfied than those who had never wanted a career. The homemakers who did not desire a career were slightly more satisfied than the employed women.

Among men there is no consistent effect of their wife's employment on their psychological well-being (Fendrich 1984). Observable effects appear to be related to expectations rather than the wife's employment per se. A man may feel increased distress if his wife's employment violates expectations of himself and/or his wife. This seems to be more likely among men with traditional sex role attitudes (Hiller and Philliber 1982; Kessler and McRae 1982).

In summary, the research is consistent in showing that the employment status of married women does not by itself affect the physical or mental health of married women or men, but their health is influenced by the degree to which desired roles fit actual roles. It will be stressful physically and psychologically for a woman who wants a career to stay home, and for a woman who wants to stay home to take a job.

EFFECTS ON CHILDREN.   For years, people have been concerned about the effects of the employment of mothers on children. As noted in Chapter 9, most researchers have found few differences between the children of employed and unemployed women (Colangelo, Rosenthal, and Dettmann 1984; Crouter, Belsky, and Spanier 1984; Wise and Joy 1982).

There is some evidence that daughters of employed women are more **androgynous** and independent, admire their mother more, and have a more positive conception of the female role (Crouter et al. 1984). Androgyny refers to having masculine as well as feminine characteristics, such as achievement orientation and social aggressiveness. Boys, on the other hand, tend to have more conflict with their employed mothers, and in the middle class, maternal employment is associated with lower male achievement (Crouter et al. 1984; Montemayor 1984; Montemayor and Clayton 1983).

Until recently most research on the effects of the mother's employment has been done on school-aged children and adolescents. A major concern is how maternal employment may affect infants. Some have feared that normal attachment of child to mother may not occur if the mother leaves infants and toddlers for long hours while she is at work. This issue is particularly relevant today because employment rates have increased more among women with small children than among other women. In 1986 half of all women with children under a year of age were employed (U.S. Bureau of the Census 1986).

In several recent studies of infants and toddlers, security of attachment, emotional adjustment, language development, and problem-solving behavior were not related to maternal employment (Easterbrooks and Goldberg 1985; Owen et al. 1984; Schachter 1981). However, several minor differences have been observed between children of employed and nonemployed mothers. Toddlers with employed mothers tended to be more peer oriented and self-sufficient, whereas children of nonemployed mothers were somewhat more jealous and scored higher on an intelligence test (Schachter 1981). Employed mothers also spent less time with their children than nonemployed mothers, but this time difference was not related to child adjustment. Employed mothers spent an average of two hours less per day alone with their child than nonemployed mothers (Easterbrooks and Goldberg 1985).

Who watches children when their mothers and fathers are at work? A summary of child care arrangements of employed women with children under a year old is shown in Table 10·6. In about one third of the families the child is cared for at home, usually by a relative. In 43 percent of the families the child is cared for in another home, slightly more often by a nonrelative than relative.

TABLE 10·6   Child Care Arrangements of Employed Women with Children Under 1 Year Old, United States (1982) (in percentages)

Care in Child's Home	34.3
Father	13.9
Grandparents	8.9
Other Relations	5.1
Nonrelative	6.4
Care in Another Home	42.7
Grandparents	13.5
Other Relative	6.2
Nonrelative	23.0
Care in Center	5.2
Mother Cares for Child	9.2
Other	8.6

SOURCE: Figures taken from Klein 1985: 405, Table 2.

Only 5 percent of the women use a day care center, and 9 percent watch the child themselves. They may take the child with them to their place of employment and work and watch the child at the same time; some may work at home.

The father is the more likely to watch the child if the women works less than thirty-five hours per week. Women who work more than this are more likely to use a day care center or a nonrelative to watch their child. Black women are more likely than white women to have grandparents or other relatives watch their child, and are more likely to use a day care center (Klein 1985). Child care is a dynamic process and most mothers change child care arrangements frequently (Floge 1985).

If the quality of care is good and if children are able to spend quality time with their parents, they seem to develop normally when both parents are employed. The important question is the quality of the child care, and not whether or not both parents work.

This is well illustrated by Jennifer, age 3, who is watched each day by her grandfather. Her grandmother died a few years ago and her grandfather lives only three blocks away from her home. Her father is a mechanical engineer and her mother is a legal secretary. Both parents like their work and her grandfather likes watching Jennifer. He usually comes to Jennifer's house to take care of her, although sometimes he takes Jennifer to his house. Jennifer has developed a wonderful relationship with her grandfather and is a well-adjusted little girl. And she loves her parents and enjoys spending time with them after work and on weekends. If her grandfather ever needs to call Jennifer's mother, he is able to contact her at work.

Decisions about work and day care should take into account the personality of the child and parent, the degree of stress already in the home, and the quality of the child care (Gamble and Zigler 1985).

Recent research by Gamble and Zigler (1985) shows that the amount of stress in the home influences the effects of out-of-home care on a child. Infants from stable homes who were in quality centers showed no effects of out-of-home care on parent-infant attachment. However, secure parent-infant attachments were much less common among infants from highly stressed families. Gamble and Zigler concluded that short-term separation would not affect a child's development if care is high quality and if parents are emotionally available on a consistent basis. On the other hand, a child who is already in a stressful home environment may be hurt by placement in day care, particularly if the care is not of high quality. Gamble and Zigler noted that insecure attachment is related to pathology later in life.

Another concern when both parents work is the care of school-aged children after school and in the summer. Children who care for themselves are often referred to as **latchkey children.** How many children are in **self-care** and how does this affect them? Coolsen, Seligson, and Garbarino (1985) estimate that about 20 percent of school-aged children (ages 6–12) are in self-care.

There has been little research on the effects of self-care, and the available evidence is not entirely consistent. Research by Gold and Andres (1978) and Rodman, Pratto, and Nelson (1985) suggests that self-care has no detrimental effects on children. They found no significant differences between self-care and adult-care children in academic achievement, social adjustment, or psy-

One of the challenges of family life is managing work and child care roles. Having good quality child care is important for the adjustment of child and parent. Here a mother leaves her child at the day care center on her way to work.   *Martha Stewart/The Picture Cube.*

chological adjustment. Similarly, Steinberg (1986) compared children in grades 5 to 9 in susceptibility to peer pressure. He observed no differences between chidren who were and were not supervised by their parents after school. However, latchkey children whose parents knew where they were and had definite rules for self-care were less susceptible to peer influence to engage in antisocial activity.

On the other hand, Woods (1972) studied black fifth-grade chidren in an inner-city ghetto. Self-care children did not do as well in school and were not as well adjusted socially as children who were cared for by adults. Coolsen et al. (1985) suggest that self-care children may be more fearful than other children.

What conclusions can be drawn from the research cited here? Recent studies with adequate controls suggests that self-care is not detrimental for the average child. Children who can call one of their parents or who have a neighbor they could turn to if needed, may adjust better than children without such support.

The effect of parental employment on the child also depends on parental satisfaction with the job. Children tend to do better socially and psychologically when their parents enjoy their work. On the other hand, low job satisfaction of mother or father is associated with more behavior problems in children (Barling 1986b; Barling and Van Bart 1984). Children tend to do better if their parents have higher job satisfaction, feel good about themselves, and have low role conflict (Alvarez 1985).

Influence of Family Life on Market Work

Not only do job conditions affect family life, but family life influences occupational choice and performance. What transpires in the family may help or hinder one's ability to deal with the job and its problems. In this section we explore some of the ways family structure and interaction affect one's occupation.

A supportive spouse may make it easier to adapt to extra work demands such as overtime or travel. The experiences of family life may help one better understand people at work and their problems. Some turn down promotions and special assignments requiring travel because of family responsibilities. An illness or accident to a family member may create stress that reduces one's ability to concentrate and perform on the job. Conflict at home or a behavior problem with a child may create tension that influences job performance. When divorce occurs women usually obtain custody of the children and must meet the difficult demands of parenthood and a job.

Parenthood

Spillover from family life to work depends on the extent of parental responsibilities. It tends to be less for men than women because women usually have primary responsibility for child care. Women with young children tend to have high levels of spillover and to feel pressure because of the shortage of time (Cooke and Rousseau 1984; Crouter 1984; Kandel, Davies, and Raveis 1985; Voydanoff and Kelly 1984). As children become adolescents the spillover for mothers decreases significantly and becomes similar to the spillover experienced by fathers (Crouter 1984).

There are several family factors that affect whether or not women will sustain employment. The more children a woman has and the higher her husband's income, the less likely it is that she will stay employed (Gordon and Kammeyer 1980; Perrucci and Targ 1982). A woman with a young child is much more likely to terminate employment than a woman without a young child (Felmlee 1984). To accommodate the demands of child rearing, women often take on shift work, part-time work, or temporarily leave a job (Bielby and Bielby 1984; Presser 1987). Women also tend to work closer to home than men and are more likely to limit occupational promotions because of their greater involvement in household chores and child care (Madden 1981). The cost and availability of day care, and the location of the job influence a young mother's decision to become employed (Stolzenberg and Waite 1984).

Waite, Haggstrom, and Kanouse (1986) have shown that the effect of parenthood on a woman's labor force activity is relatively short-lived. Women do not alter their career aspirations during pregnancy and childbirth. They limit employment during the childbearing period but reenter the labor force as they complete their families and child-rearing responsibilities lessen (Shaw 1985; Waite 1980). As noted earlier, more than 50 percent of women with preschool children are now employed outside the home (U.S. Bureau of the Census 1986).

The research of Waite et al. (1986) shows that parenthood also alters men's occupational expectations and behaviors. Using longitudinal data, they found that men's work involvement, wages, and occupational status decreased somewhat after having their first child. Waite et al. suggest that having a child may draw men toward home and increase their involvement with their families. The research of Coverman (1983) is consistent with this interpretation. She observed that among both men and women the amount of time spent in domestic labor had a negative effect on wages.

Employment of Spouse

It is well known that women often compromise career opportunities in favor of their husbands' careers. Recent research by Sharda and Nangle (1981) shows that men also make career sacrifices for their wives' careers. Husbands frequently restrict their mobility to accommodate their wives, especially when their wives are in high-status occupations. Sharda and Nangle (1981) concluded that both wives and husbands tend to accommodate each other by restricting their own **occupational mobility.** Lichter (1982) also observed that family migration is inhibited when the wife is employed.

If a family does move because of the husband's occupation, it disrupts the wife's career. Her employment status, weeks worked, and earnings decrease because of the family relocation. However, Spitze (1984) found that these effects are temporary and do not last beyond the second year after the move. That is, most women are able to find jobs with earnings comparable to the jobs before the move.

Benefits of Family Life on Occupational Success

Up to this point we have discussed how children and family demands may hinder occupational involvement and advancement, particularly among women. Family life also may be beneficial to one's career in a variety of ways. First, the experiences in family life may teach skills that enhance job performance. Maslach and Jackson (1985) studied burnout in several service-oriented occupations. **Burnout** was defined as a depletion of emotional and psychological resources as a result of job stress. They found that both men and women with children scored lower on burnout than childless employees. Maslach and Jackson suggested that being a parent may provide experience and teach skills that help one deal with job stress. For example, being a parent provides experience in dealing with personal problems and may enhance problem-solving and communication skills.

A second benefit of family life on career success may be the emotional support received. The love and support received at home may help individuals cope with job stress (Maslach and Jackson 1985). Pearlin and Johnson (1977) suggested that marital status enabled people to cope more effectively with economic stress, and Cooper et al. (1986) observed that a nurturant husband helped a wife cope with the dual stress of employment and preschool children. Similarly, Rudd and McKenry (1986) found that family support was associated with the job satisfaction of women, and that emotional support was more important than physical assistance.

Some sociologists have suggested that the emotional support one receives in marriage is a major resource that may help one advance occupationally (Mortimer and Lorence 1982; Pfeffer and Ross 1982). However, if one's spouse is employed, they may be less available as a support and this may make occupational advancement more difficult (Pfeffer and Ross 1982).

In a broader sense, families may be very beneficial for economic growth of a country. Families that socialize members to be competent, productive citizens are essential for a healthy market economy (Reynolds 1985; Thompson 1984).

Summary

1. The two types of family work are domestic work to maintain the physical surroundings of the home and market work to earn money for the family.
2. In most societies family work is assigned according to gender. Men are assigned primary responsibility for the provider role, and women are assigned primary responsibility for housework and child care.
3. One of the major social changes during the past century has been the increase in married women's employment. In 1890 less than 5 percent of married women were employed, compared to 55 percent of married women in 1985. Over half of women with preschool children were employed in 1985.
4. Changes in the employment of married women have been much greater in the middle class than the working class.
5. The primary reason married women enter the marketplace is economic need. Other factors that influence women's employment are the availability of jobs and wage rates. Having two earners keeps many families out of poverty and enables some to purchase homes.
6. In 1985 the unemployment rate in the United States was 7.2 percent. The young, minorities, and single women with children have higher rates of unemployment than others.
7. Families cope with financial hardship and unemployment by reducing expenses, having other family members seek employment, using other available resources such as savings, obtaining government assistance, and having the unemployed member seek other employment. Young, minority, and single-parent families have fewer resources and more difficulty in coping with unemployment than other families.
8. Unemployment is associated with increased anxiety, depression, hostility, child abuse, and marital conflict. The stress from unemployment is less if support from family members is high.
9. Job satisfaction and stress affect marital quality and parent-child relationships. The effect of job stress is less when there is emotional support from family members.
10. Dual-earner couples tend to have more egalitarian sex role attitudes and to spend somewhat less time together than single-earner couples.

11. If women are satisfied with their marriages, their employment is not related to marital disruption. Among women in unhappy marriages, their employment is positively related to marital dissolution.

12. The employment of women, by itself, is not related to the physical or mental health of married women or men. The fit between actual and desired roles is related to the physical and mental health of married women and men.

13. There are few significant differences between children whose mothers are and are not employed outside the home. Girls of employed mothers tend to be more androgynous and independent.

14. Among infants, the mother's employment is not related to security attachment, emotional adjustment, or language development.

15. About one third of the children of employed mothers are cared for in their own home, and 43 percent are cared for in another home. Only 5 percent of children of employed mothers use day care centers.

16. Children who are cared for out of the home tend to develop normally if the care is good and if they are able to spend quality time with their parents. However, if there is stress in the home, leaving a child in a day care center may interfere with security attachment.

17. Estimates are that about 20 percent of school-aged children are in self-care after school and during the summers. There is no evidence that self-care affects children negatively in terms of social, psychological, or academic adjustment.

18. The family environment affects work in a variety of ways. One of the major family influences on work is the presence of small children. Women with small children tend to have more inter-role conflict than other women. Women adjust their careers to accommodate their family demands by taking shift work, decreasing working hours, or leaving employment for a period.

19. The effect of parenthood on the employment of women is short term. Women tend not to alter their career aspirations because of parenthood and most who leave the labor force reenter within a few years.

20. Parenthood alters men's careers as well as women's. Men tend to decrease job time and increase family time when parenthood occurs. The greater the time spent in domestic child care and housework, the lower one's wages.

21. Both men and women tend to restrict mobility and make occupational sacrifices for their spouse's career.

22. Family life benefits job performance in a variety of ways. People with children tend to have less "burnout" than individuals who are childless. The support of a spouse may help one cope with job stress and help one advance occupationally.

Important Terms

- androgynous
- burnout
- child care role
- coping resources
- division of labor
- domestic work

- goods of society
- spill over model
- segmented model
- central life interests

- family support
- housekeeper role
- inter-role conflict
- latchkey children
- market work
- occupational mobility
- provider role

- psychological distress
- reciprocal
- role overload
- segmented model
- self-care
- spillover model
- unemployment

Questions for Discussion

1. What are major influences on a family's division of work?
2. How has the division of family work changed during the past century? Why have these changes occurred?
3. How does the division of family work change over the life cycle?
4. What do you feel would be the ideal division of family work and why?
5. Why has there been such a large increase in women's labor force participation during the past century? What class differences exist in this change?
6. What are the major reasons why women become employed?
7. How do families try to cope with inadequate incomes and unemployment? What types of families are least able to cope with unemployment?
8. How does unemployment affect psychological well-being, marital quality, and parenting?
9. How does job satisfaction and stress affect family life?
10. How do single-earner couples and dual-earner couples differ in their spending patterns, division of labor, and sex role attitudes?
11. Compare couples with no earners, one earner, and two earners in the areas of physical health, mental health, and marital quality. What are the benefits and risks of each type of situation?
12. What are the benefits and risks of a mother with an infant becoming employed? What are the benefits and risks if she does not become employed?
13. Suppose that a young married woman with a six-month-old infant is thinking about going to work and asks for your advice. What would you tell her? What factors are relevant to her decision?
14. What are the benefits and risks of a mother with school-aged children becoming employed? What are the benefits and risks if she does not become employed?
15. Suppose a mother with a first grader is thinking about going to work and asks for your advice. What would you tell her? What factors are relevant to her decision?
16. What are the benefits and risks of a father of infants and school-aged children becoming employed? What are the benefits and risks if he does not become employed?
17. How does gender affect employment decisions of parents? How does being married or single affect such decisions?
18. What are some of the ways family life impacts on occupational choice and performance? In what ways does family life hinder occupational success and in what ways does family life support occupational success?

Recommended Reading

CROUTER, A. C. 1984. Spillover from family to work: The neglected side of the work-family interface. *Human Relations* 37:425–442.

KINGSTON, P. W. and S. L. NOCK. 1987. Time together among dual-earner couples. *American Sociological Review* 52:391–400.

VOYDANOFF, P. 1987. *Work and family life.* Newbury Park, CA: Sage.

References

ANGEL, R., and M. TIENDA. 1982. Determinants of extended household structure: Cultural pattern or economic need? *American Journal of Sociology* 87(6):1360–1383.

ALPER, N. O., and M. J. MORLOCK. 1982. Moonlighting husbands or working wives. An economic analysis. *Journal of Family Issues* 3(2):181–198.

ALVAREZ, W. F. 1985. The meaning of maternal employment for mothers and their perceptions of their three-year-old children. *Child Development* 56:350–360.

ATKINSON, T., R. LIEM, and J. H. LIEM. 1986. The social costs of unemployment: Implications for social support. *Journal of Health and Social Behavior* 27:317–331.

BAHR. S. J., and R. J. GALLIGAN. 1984. Teenage marriage and marital stability. *Youth & Society* 15(4):387–400.

BARLING, J. 1984. Effects of husband's work experiences on wives' marital satisfaction. *The Journal of Social Psychology* 124:219–225.

BARLING, J. 1986a. Interrole conflict and marital functioning amongst employed fathers. *Journal of Occupational Behaviour* 7(1–8):1–8.

BARLING, J. 1986b. Fathers' work experiences, the father-child relationship and children's behaviour. *Journal of Occupational Behaviour* 7:61–66.

BARLING, J., and D. VAN BART. 1984. Mothers' subjective employment experiences and the behaviour of their nursery school children. *Journal of Occupational Psychology* 57:49–56.

BAUM, A., R. FLEMING, and D. M. REDDY. 1986. Unemployment stress: Loss of control, reluctance and learned helplessness. *Social Science Medicine* 22(5):509–516.

BERNARD, J. 1972. *The future of marriage.* New York: Bantam.

BIELBY, D. D., and W. T. BIELBY. 1984. Work commitment, sex-role attitudes, and women's employment. *American Sociological Review* 49:234–247.

BOOTH, A., D. R. JOHNSON, L. WHITE, and J. N. EDWARDS. 1984. Women, outside employment, and marital instability. *American Journal of Sociology* 90(3):567–582.

BROMET, E. J., M. A. DEW, D. K. PARKINSON, and H. C. SCHULBERG. 1988. Predictive effects of occupational and marital stress on the mental health of a male workforce. *Journal of Organizational Behavior* 9:1–13.

CAPLOVITZ, D. 1981. Making ends meet: How families cope with inflation and recession. *The Annals of the American Academy for Political and Social Science* 456:88–98.

CHADWICK, B. A., and C. B. CHAPPELL. 1980. The two-income family in Middletown, 1924–1978. In *Economics and the family,* ed. S. J. Bahr, 27–41. Lexington, MA: Lexington Books.

CHERLIN, A. 1979. Work life and marital dissolution. In *Divorce and separation,* ed. G. Levingen and O. C. Moles, 161—166. New York: Basic.

COLANGELO, N., D. M. ROSENTHAL, and D. F. DETTMANN. 1984. Maternal employment and job satisfaction and their relationship to children's perceptions and
behaviors. *Sex Roles* 10(9/10):693–702.

COOKE, R. A., and D. M. ROUSSEAU. 1984. Stress and strain from family roles and
work-role expectations. *Journal of Applied Psychology* 69(2):252–260.

COOLSEN, P., M. SELIGSON, and J. GARBARINO. 1985. *When school's out and no-
body's home.* Chicago: National Committee for Prevention of Child Abuse.

COOPER, K., L. CHASSIN, S. BRAVER, A. ZEISS, and K. A. KHAVARI. 1986. Correlates
of mood and marital satisfaction among dual-worker and single-worker couples. *Social Psychology Quarterly* 49(4):322–329.

COVERMAN, S. 1983. Gender, domestic labor time, and wage inequality. *American
Sociological Review* 48:623–637.

COVERMAN, S. 1985. Explaining husband's participation in domestic labor. *The Sociological Quarterly* 26(1):81–97.

COVERMAN, S., and J. F. SHELEY. 1986. Change in men's housework and child-care
time, 1965–1975. *Journal of Marriage and the Family* 48:413–422.

CROUTER, A. C. 1984. Spillover from family to work: The neglected side of the
work-family interface. *Human Relations* 37(6):425–442.

CROUTER, A. C., J. BELSKY, and G. B. SPANIER. 1984. The family context of child
development: Divorce and maternal employment. *Annals of Child Development* 1:201–238.

DAVIS, K. 1984. Wives and work: The sex role revolution and its consequences. *Population and Development Review* 10(3):397–417.

DEVANEY, B. 1983. An analysis of variations in U.S. fertility and female labor force
participation trends. *Demography* 20(2):147–161.

EASTERBROOKS, M. A., and W. A. GOLDBERG. 1985. Effects of early maternal employment of toddlers, mothers, and fathers. *Developmental Psychology* 21(5):774–
783.

ELDER, G. H., JR., T. VAN NGUYEN, and A. CASPI. 1985. Linking family hardship to
children's lives. *Child Development* 56:361–375.

FELMLEE, D. H. 1984. A dynamic analysis of women's employment exits. *Demography* 21(2):171–336.

FENDRICH, M. 1984. Wives' employment and husbands' distress: A meta-analysis
and a replication. *Journal of Marriage and the Family* 46:871–879.

FERREE, M. 1976. Working-class jobs: Housework and paid work as sources of satisfaction. *Social Problems* 23:431–441.

FLOGE, L. 1985. The dynamics of child-care use and some implications for women's
employment. *Journal of Marriage and the Family* 47(1):143–154.

FOSTER, A. C. 1981. Wives' earnings as a factor in family net worth accumulation.
Monthly Labor Review (January): 53–57.

FOSTER, A. C., M. ABDEL-GHAY, and C. E. FERGUSON. 1981. Wife's employment—its
influence on major family expenditures. *Journal of Consumer Studies and
Home Economics* 5:115–124.

FOSTER, A. C., and E. J. METZEN. 1981. The impact of wife's employment and earnings on family net worth accumulation. *Journal of Consumer Studies and
Home Economics* 5:23–36.

FRIEDAN, B. 1963. *The feminine mystique.* New York: Norton.

GAMBLE, T., and E. ZIGLER. 1985. The effects of infant day care. *The Networker*
(Newsletter of the Bush Programs in Child Development and Social Policy)
6(4):4,7.

GOLD, D., and D. ANDRES. 1978. Developmental comparison between ten-year-old
children with employed and nonemployed mothers. *Child Development* 49:75–
84.

GORDON, H. A., and K. C. W. KAMMEYER. 1980. The gainful employment of women with small children. *Journal of Marriage and the Family* 42:327–336.

GOULD, S., and J. D. WERBEL. 1983. Work involvement: A comparison of dual wage earner and single wage earner families. *Journal of Applied Psychology* 68(2):312–319.

GRAY, J. D. 1983. The married professional woman: An examination of her role conflicts and coping strategies. *Psychology of Women Quarterly* 7(3):235–241.

GRONAU, R. 1977. *Home production—A forgotten industry.* Working Paper No. 148, Chicago: National Bureau of Economic Research.

HILLER, D. V., and W. W. PHILLIBER. 1982. Predicting marital and career success among dual-worker couples. *Journal of Marriage and the Family* 44:53–61.

HO, S. 1984. Women's labor-force participation in Hong Kong, 1971–1981. *Journal of Marriage and the Family* 46:947–953.

HOUSEKNECHT, S. K., and A. S. MACKE. 1981. Combining marriage and career: The marital adjustment of professional women. *Journal of Marriage and the Family* 43:651–661.

HOUSEKNECHT, S. K., S. VAUGHAN, and A. S. MACKE. 1984. Marital disruption among professional women: The timing of career and family events. *Social Problems* 31(3):273–295.

JACKSON, S. E., and C. MASLACH. 1982. After-effects of job-related stress: Families as victims. *Journal of Occupational Behaviour* 3:63–77.

KANDEL, D. B., M. DAVIES, V. H. RAVEIS. 1985. The stressfulness of daily social roles for women: Marital, occupational and household roles. *Journal of Health and Social Behavior* 26:64–78.

KESSLER, R. C., and J. A. MCRAE, JR. 1982. The effect of wives' employment on the mental health of married men and women. *American Sociological Review* 47:216–217.

KINGSTON, P. W., and S. L. NOCK. 1987. Time together among dual-earner couples. *American Sociological Review* 52:391–400.

KLEIN, R. P. 1985. Caregiving arrangements by employed women with children under 1 year of age. *Developmental Psychology* 21(3):403–406.

KOMAROVSKY, M. 1962. *Blue-collar marriage.* New York: Vintage.

KOOREMAN, P., and A. KAPTEYN. 1987. A disaggregated analysis of the allocation of time within the household. *Journal of Political Economy* 95(21):223–249.

KRAUSE, N., and K. S. MARKIDES. 1985. Employment and psychological well-being in Mexican-American women. *Journal of Health and Social Behavior* 26:15–26.

LARSON, J. H. 1984. The effect of husband's unemployment on marital and family relations in blue-collar families. *Family Relations* 33:503–511.

LICHTER, D. T. 1982. The migration of dual-worker families: Does the wife's job matter? *Social Science Quarterly* 63(1):48–57.

LIKER, J. K., and G. H. ELDER, JR. 1983. Economic hardship and marital relations in the 1930s. *American Sociological Review* 48:343–359.

LINN, M. W., R. SANDIFER, and S. STEIN. 1985. Effects of unemployment on mental and physical health. *American Journal of Public Health* 75(5):502–506.

MACKEY, W. C. 1985. A cross-cultural perspective on perceptions of paternalistic deficiencies in the United States: The myth of the derelict daddy. *Sex Roles* 12(5/6):509–533.

MADDEN, J. F. 1981. Why women work closer to home. *Urban Studies* 18:181–194.

MASLACH, C., and S. E. JACKSON. 1985. The role of sex and family variables in burnout. *Sex Roles* 12(7/8):837–851.

MOEN, P. 1979. Family impacts of the 1975 recession: Duration of unemployment. *Journal of Marriage and the Family* 41:561–572.

MOEN, P. 1980. Developing family indicators: Financial hardship, a case in point. *Journal of Family Issues* 1:5–30.

MONTEMAYOR, R. 1984. Maternal employment and adolescents' relations with parents, siblings, and peers. *Journal of Youth and Adolescence* 13(6):543–557.

MONTEMAYOR, R., and M. D. CLAYTON. 1983. Maternal employment and adolescent development. *Theory Into Practice* 22:112–118.

MORTIMER, J. T., and J. LORENCE. 1982. Work and family linkages in the transition to adulthood: A panel study of highly educated men. *Western Sociological Review* 13(1):50–68.

MOTT, F. L., and S. F. MOORE. 1979. The causes of marital disruption among young American women: An interdisciplinary perspective. *Journal of Marriage and the Family* 41:355–365.

MYERS, D. 1985. Wives' earnings and rising costs of homeownership. *Social Science Quarterly* 66(2):319–329.

NICKOLS, S. Y., and E. J. METZEN. 1982. Impact of wife's employment upon husband's housework. *Journal of Family Issues* 3(2):199–216.

NICOLA, J. S., and G. R. HAWKES. 1985. Marital satisfaction of dual-career couples: Does sharing increase happiness? *Journal of Social Behavior and Personality* 1(1):47–60.

NYE, F. I. 1976. *Role structure and analysis of the family.* Beverly Hills, CA: Sage.

OPPENHEIMER, V. K. 1982. *Work and the family.* New York: Academic.

OWEN, M. T., M. A. EASTERBROOKS, L. CHASE-LANSDALE, and W. A. GOLDBERG. 1984. The relation between maternal employment status and the stability of attachments to mother and to father. *Child Development* 55:1894–1901.

PEARLIN, L. I., and J. S. JOHNSON. 1977. Marital status, life-strains and depression. *American Sociological Review* 42:704–715.

PAVETT, C. M. 1986. High stress professions: Satisfaction, stress, and well-being of spouses of professionals. *Human Relations* 39:1141–1154.

PEARLIN, L. I., and M. E. McCALL. 1987. *Occupational stress and marital support: A description of microprosses.* Paper presented at the annual meeting of the Pacific Sociological Association, Eugene, OR, April.

PERRUCCI, C. C., and D. B. TARG. 1982. The influence of family and work characteristics on the sustained employment of college-educated wives. *Sociological Focus* 15(3):191–201.

PETERSEN, L. R., and J. L. MAYNARD. 1981. Income, equity, and wives' housekeeping role expectations. Bringing home the bacon doesn't mean I have to cook it, too. *Pacific Sociological Review* 24(1):87–105.

PFEFFER, J., and J. ROSS. 1982. The effects of marriage and a working wife on occupational wage attainment. *Administrative Science Quarterly* 27:66–80.

PLECK, J. H. 1984. Men's family work: Three perspectives and some new data. In *Work and family: Changing roles of men and women,* ed. P. Voydanoff, 232–241. Palo Alto, CA: Mayfield.

POND, S. B., and S. B. GREEN. 1983. The relationship between job and marriage satisfaction within and between spouses. *Journal of Occupational Behavior* 4:145–155.

PRESSER, H. B. 1987. Work shifts of full-time dual-earner couples: Patterns and contrasts by sex of spouse. *Demography* 24(1):99–112.

RANK, M. R. 1982. Determinants of conjugal influence in wives' employment decision making. *Journal of Marriage and the Family* 44:591–604.

REYNOLDS, N. B. 1985. Families and market: Allies or enemies? *Family Perspective* 19:91–102.

RODMAN, H., D. J. PRATTO, and R. S. NELSON. 1985. Child care arrangements and children's functioning: A comparison of self-care and adult-care children. *Developmental Psychology* 21(3):413–418.

ROOT, K. 1984. The human response to plant closures. *The Annals of the American Academy of Political and Social Sciences* 475:52–65.

Ross, H. L., and I. V. Sawhill. 1975. *Time of transaction. The growth of families headed by women.* Washington, DC: The Urban Institute.

Rudd, N. M., and P. C. McKenry. 1986. Family influences on the job satisfaction of employed mothers. *Psychology of Women Quarterly* 10:363–372.

Sawhill, I. V. 1983. *Employment and family income.* Testimony before the Select Committee on Children, Youth, and Families, July 18.

Schachter, F. F. 1981. Toddlers with employed mothers. *Child Development* 52:958–964.

Semyonov, M. 1980. The social context of women's labor force participation: A comparative analysis. *American Journal of Sociology* 86(3):534–550.

Sharda, B. D., and B. E. Nangle. 1981. Marital effects on occupational attainment. *Journal of Family Issues* 2(2):148–163.

Shaw, L. B. 1985. Determinants of the increasing work attachment of married women. *Work and Occupations* 12(1):41–57.

Shaw, L. B., and K. Sproat. 1980. *Mature women in the work force: Research findings and policy recommendations from the national longitudinal surveys.* Paper prepared for the Office of Research and Development, Employment and Training Administration, U.S. Department of Labor. Ohio State University Center for Human Resource Research.

Shehan, C. L. 1984. Wives' work and psychological well-being: An extension of Gove's social role theory of depression. *Sex Roles* 11(9/10):881–899.

Smith, E. 1985. Black American women and work: A historical review—1619–1920. *Women's Studies Int. Forum* 8(4):343–349.

Smith, J. P., and M. P. Ward. 1984. *Women's wages and work in the twentieth century.* Santa Monica, CA: Rand Corporation.

Smith, T. W. 1985. Working wives and women's rights: The connection between the employment status of wives and the feminist attitudes of husbands. *Sex Roles,* 12(5/6):501–508.

Spitze, G. 1984. The effect of family migration on wives' employment: How long does it last? *Social Science Quarterly* 65(1):21–36.

Steinberg, L. 1986. Latchkey children and susceptibility to peer pressure: An ecological analysis. *Developmental Psychology* 22:1–8.

Stokes, J. P., and J. S. Peyton. 1986. Attitudinal differences between full-time homemakers and women who work outside the home. *Sex Roles* 15(5/6):309–320.

Stolzenberg, R. M., and L. J. Waite. 1984. Local labor markets, children and labor force participation of wives. *Demography* 21(2):157–171.

Suchet, M., and J. Barling. 1986. Employed mothers: Interrole conflict, spouse support and marital functioning. *Journal of Occupational Behavior* 7:167–178.

Taplin, R. 1985. *Women and work in Egypt: A historical perspective.* Paper presented to the Pacific Sociological Association, Albuquerque, NM, April 17–20.

Terry, S. L. 1982. Unemployment and its effect on family income in 1980. *Monthly Labor Review* (April): 35–43.

Thompson, P. 1984. The family and child-rearing as forces for economic change: Towards fresh research approaches. *Sociology* 18(4):515–530.

Tiano, S. 1985. *Women's participation in the Maquiladora workforce: The case of Mexicali.* Paper presented at annual meeting of Pacific Sociological Association, Albuquerque, NM, April.

Tienda, M., and R. Angel. 1982. Headship and household composition among blacks, hispanics, and other whites. *Social Forces* 61(2):508–531.

Townsend, A., and P. Gurin. 1981. Re-examining the frustrated homemaker hypothesis. Role fit, personal dissatisfaction, and collective discontent. *Sociology of Work and Occupations* 8(4):464–488.

U.S. BUREAU OF THE CENSUS. 1986. *Statistical abstract of the United States: 1987.* Washington, DC: U.S. Government Printing Office.

VAN LOO, M. F., and R. P. BAGOZZI. 1984. Labor force participation and fertility: A social analysis of their antecedents and simultaneity. *Human Relations* 37(11):941–967.

VOYDANOFF, P. 1987. *Work and family life.* Beverly Hills, CA: Sage.

VOYDANOFF, P., and R. F. KELLY. 1984. Determinants of work-related family problems among employed parents. *Journal of Marriage and the Family* 46:881–892.

WAITE, L. J. 1980. Working wives and the family life cycle. *American Journal of Sociology* 86(2):272–294.

WAITE, L. J., G. HAGGSTROM, and D. E. KANOUSE. 1986. The effects of parenthood on the career orientation and job characteristics of young adults. *Social Forces* 65(1):28–43.

WALDRON, I., and J. HEROLD. 1986. Employment, attitudes toward employment, and women's health. *Women & Health*, 11(1):79–98.

WARR, P., and G. PARRY. 1982. Paid employment and women's psychological well-being. *Psychological Bulletin* 90(3):498–516.

WARR, P., and R. PAYNE. 1983. Social class and reported changes in behavior after job loss. *Journal of Applied Social Psychology* 13(3):206–222.

WISE, P. S., and S. S. JOY. 1982. Working mothers, sex differences, and self-esteem in college students' self-descriptions. *Sex Roles* 8(7):785–790.

WOODS, M. B. 1972. The unsupervised child of the working mother. *Developmental Psychology* 6:14–25.

YBARRA, L. 1982. When wives work: The impact on the Chicano family. *Journal of Marriage and the Family* 44:169–177.

YOGEV, S., and J. BRETT. 1983. *Patterns of work and family involvement among single and dual earner couples: Two competing analytical approaches.* Paper prepared for Center for Urban Affairs & Policy Research, Northwestern University, Evanston, IL.

CHAPTER 11

Education and the Family

Introduction

Time passes quickly and before long Lorraine and Michael's daughter Debra is five years old. It is time for Debra to start kindergarten and begin her formal education. Michael and Lorraine have looked forward to the time when Debra would begin school. Before they purchased their house they carefully checked out the school district. One of the reasons they bought in the area was because the school district had a very good reputation.

The school year begins and Lorraine and Michael adjust their lives to the school schedule. They start attending the PTA and become involved in several of its activities. They adjust their work and recreation activities to accommodate the school. School is important to Michael and Lorraine because Debra will learn to read and write and gain other necessary skills. Both Lorraine and Michael have college degrees, and they feel that a good education is essential. They also know that Debra will learn other important values in school, including how to get along with others and how to follow rules and take directions.

The school not only teaches needed skills, it provides day care. Now that Debra has started school, Lorraine and Michael no longer need to have the neighbor watch her while they are at work.

Lorraine, Michael, and Debra illustrate how schools affect family life. Sending Debra to school was an important transition in their lives.

They also have had an impact on the school system. They are tax-paying citizens in the district and vote in school elections and in the PTA. Debra is one of the school's pupils and how well she learns depends partly on their efforts and encouragement.

Education is an important part of our society. The amount of education one receives is an important determinant of occupational status and level of earnings. As our society has become more technical, education has become increasingly important.

In this chapter we explore the interface between families and the educational system. We begin by examining how a number of family characteristics affect academic success of children. Then there is a discussion of how marriage and parenthood influence education achievement. Gender differences in education are reviewed next, followed by an analysis of conflict between home and school and what can be done about it.

The Family and Academic Achievement

In this section we examine how several parental, family structural, and child characteristics are related to academic achievement. Then we discuss what family interaction variables are related to achievement.

Social Class

In several studies a positive correlation between **parental education** and **academic achievement** has been found (Bahr and Leigh 1978; Baker 1981; Cohen 1986; Dornbusch, Fraleigh, and Ritter 1986; Hess and Holloway 1984; McBroom 1985; Murnane, Maynard, and Olds 1981; Rumberger 1983; Smith and Cheung 1986). The mother's educational level seems particularly important (Bahr and Leigh 1978; Mercy and Steelman 1982).

Lareau (1987) has demonstrated that parental involvement in education depends on the class position of the parents. Both middle-class and working-class parents wanted their children to do well and supported them in school. However, the two types of parents were different in how they showed support. The working class viewed family life and school as independent spheres, and felt that education of children was the school's responsibility. They did not initiate contact with schools or perceive that they should or could intervene in the education of their children. Teachers were experts and they depended on the schools to educate their children.

In contrast, middle-class parents viewed education of their children as a shared responsibility between parents and schools. They scrutinized the school system, monitored their children's activities, and tried to supplement teacher inputs. It was perceived as their right and duty to read to their children, initiate contact with teachers, and attend school events.

Lareau (1987) maintained that middle-class parents have social and cultural resources that enable them to become more highly involved in the education of their children. Middle-class parents felt that they had some control over the educational environment of their children and were comfortable in approaching and criticizing teachers as well as in helping their children. They also had more time to meet with teachers and become intensely involved with school activities. Working-class parents, on the other hand, did not feel adequate in helping their children with schoolwork, or comfortable about approaching or criticizing teachers. The educational system was perceived to be important but was not something they had the expertise to become involved in. According to Lareau (1987), differences between middle-class and working-class children in educational achievement are due partly to these class differences in parental involvement.

Employment of Mother

Murnane et al. (1981) and Farel (1980) found that the mother's employment status had no effect on the child's educational success, whereas Mercy and Steelman (1982) found a modest negative effect. The bulk of the evidence suggests that the employment of the mother does not affect academic achievement in children. Farel (1980) observed that children did poorer in school when there was an incongruence between the attitudes and behaviors of nonemployed mothers. Apparently, the cognitive dissonance caused by the gap between desired and actual roles had a negative effect on the children.

Ethnic Group

Ethnic group has been found to be related to school success, even after controlling for other relevant variables. Asians tend to do better than other groups, and blacks and Hispanics tend to have lower-than-average grades (Dornbusch et al. 1986).

Family Structure

Family structure refers to characteristics such as number of parents, marital status of parents, and family size. Children from **single-parent** and **blended families** tend not to do as well in school as children who live with two natural parents, and this finding holds when other variables are controlled (Dornbusch et al. 1986). Shaw (1982) found the effects of living in a single-parent home may depend on ethnic group. Among white females, living in a single-parent home was not related to high school completion, whereas black females living in single-parent homes were less likely than black girls from two-parent homes to complete high school.

The data on family size are not consistent. According to Hauser and Sewell (1985) and Mercy and Steelman (1982), family size is negatively related to academic success, although Bahr and Leigh (1978) found that family size was not related to achievement when other variables were taken into account. Bahr and Leigh controlled for educational encouragement, an important variable not included by the others.

Birth Order and Gender

Birth order does not appear to be related to academic success (Hauser and Sewell 1985). Although many have discovered gender differences in abilities and grades, recent work suggests that gender differences are negligible when other variables are taken into account (Dornbusch et al. 1986).

Summary

Parental **social class** has an important influence on the educational achievement of children, and ethnic group and marital status have modest effects. Family size, birth order, the mother's employment status, and gender appear to have little impact on the educational achievement of children.

Family Interaction

What parents and educators are most concerned about is how family interaction may affect educational success. What can parents do to increase the chances that their children will do well in school?

The most important thing parents can do is establish a warm, nurturant relationship with their child. As discussed in Chapter 9, **parental support** is strongly related to social competence in children, which includes cognitive development.

Another essential factor of the home environment is **verbal communication.** Parent-child time in talking together is associated with higher academic achievement (Hess and Holloway 1984). When parents read with their children, they have a greater interest in school and perform better (Hess and Holloway 1984). Discussing issues and exposing children to diverse points of view are also related to school success (Dornbusch et al. 1986).

The nature of parental control is important. In Chapter 9 we noted that children are less socially competent when control is either overly permissive or too strict. **Inductive control** techniques are associated with higher competence whereas **coercive control** attempts are associated with lower competence. School success is related to control in the same way. Parents who exercise a moderate amount of control and emphasize induction tend to have children who perform better in school (Rollins and Thomas 1979).

Dornbusch et al. (1986) found that **joint** (parent-child) **decision making** is

Involvement in sports activities as spectators, cheerleaders, and players has become an important part of the educational experience, and students who participate in sports tend to earn higher grades than students who do not. *Ulrike Welsch.*

associated with higher grades. Children who were left to make decisions without parental input had poorer grades, as did children who had parents who attempted to make decisions without the children's input.

Much has been said about television and its possible effect on grades. Recent research confirms that grades tend to go down as amount of television time increases. When parents and children set some rules for television viewing, grades tend to be somewhat higher (Dornbusch et al. 1986).

How is athletic participation or part-time work related to grades? Participation in sports is positively associated with grades, if participation time does not exceed thirty hours per week. Similarly, students who work part-time tend to have higher grades than those that do not work. When more than twenty hours per week is spent working, however, grades tend to decline (Dornbusch et al. 1986).

Parental interest in school and encouragement are critical factors. When parents are concerned about and interested in school and learning, children tend to be more interested (Lareau 1987; Majoribanks 1979). Encouragement, praise, and availability of parents to help children with their schoolwork tend to induce better performance (Dornbusch et al. 1986; Yao 1985). One of the distinguishing features of parents of high-achieving children is their deep interest and concerned support (Yao 1985).

How should parents react to good or poor grades? Dornbusch et al. (1986)

Students who are employed part-time tend to have higher grades than those who are not employed part-time. *Steve Takatsuno/The Picture Cube.*

maintain that strong negative reactions to poor grades are likely to hurt rather than help students. Restricting the use of the car or imposing a strict curfew also tend to decrease internal motivation for schoolwork, according to Dornbusch et al. (1986). Praise, encouragement, and offers to help seem to be more effective.

Having high expectations are associated with high grades. When parents emphasize studying hard and stress the importance of doing well, children tend to respond. High parental expectations were evident in a recent study of high achievers (Yao 1985), and others have found a correlation between parental expectations and grades (Cohen 1986; Hess and Holloway 1984).

Finally, involvement of parents in the school is associated with higher grades. When parents attend open school nights and PTA and become involved in other ways, their children tend to have higher grades (Dornbusch et al. 1986; Hess and Holloway 1984; Leichter 1979; Stevenson 1986).

Summary

Children's achievement in school tends to be higher when parents talk to them, show interest in their school activities and assignments, take the time to know what they are doing, encourage and help them, expect them to do well, make decisions jointly, and are warm and supportive. Material resources in the home, such a food, housing quality, and family income are not related to academic success (Murnane et al. 1981). It is the human resources of time, encouragement, and interest that make the difference.

The influence of family factors obviously depends on the genetic potential of each person. A child with a low IQ may not be able to complete college no matter how perfect the family educational environment. Genetic factors have a strong influence on educational achievement and should not be discounted. On the other hand, the power of the family environment should not be underestimated either. Research has demonstrated that the family factors identified earlier are important even after controlling for the mother's IQ and the child's IQ measured at an earlier period (Hess and Holloway 1984).

Childbearing, Marriage, and Education

Academic achievement is influenced by experiences and decisions of children as they mature. Adolescence is an important period of socialization and decision making. Decisions of adolescents about marriage and parenthood appear to have a significant influence on their educational outcomes.

Adolescents who get good grades and plan to go college are less likely to have a premarital pregnancy or birth (Miller et al. 1981; Tanfer and Horn 1985). Their educational aspirations influence sexual activity and decisions regarding contraceptive use and parenthood. The causal influence appears to operate in both directions. Women with educational aspirations tend to have lower fertility rates, whereas having a child tends to make it more difficult to continue going to school (Jain 1981).

Marriage is another important decision that may affect educational achievement. Alexander and Reilly (1981) studied how the timing of marriage is related to educational achievement among young men and women. They found that early marriage is detrimental to the educational attainment of women but has no effect on that of men. Deferring marriage enables women to complete more education.

A model summarizing how family characteristics, early childbirth, and early marriage affect educational level is shown in Figure 11·1. The parental characteristics identified earlier (support, communication, joint decision making, induction, interest, encouragement, high expectations, and involvement) tend to increase the educational aspirations of children. The higher those aspirations are, the less likely they are to marry early or experience early childbirth. Thus, high educational aspirations are positively associated with completed education.

Marriage is a crucial transition in the life cycle and has important implications for education. In years past, educational advancement often ended with marriage because the man had to work to support his family while the woman had to take care of the home and the children. However, as advanced education has become increasingly important in our technical society, many people now attend school after they marry. Effective contraception and declining fertility rates have lessened the burdens of child care and enabled many women to continue their education after marriage.

How many married women go to school, and what factors influence the probability that they will continue their education? Davis and Bumpass (1974) found that about 20 percent of women in the United States have attended high school or college after being married. Another 23 percent expect to attend school in the future. Thus, education is becoming common among married women.

What types of women tend to continue their schooling after marriage? Davis and Bumpass (1974) noted that continued schooling was related to five variables.

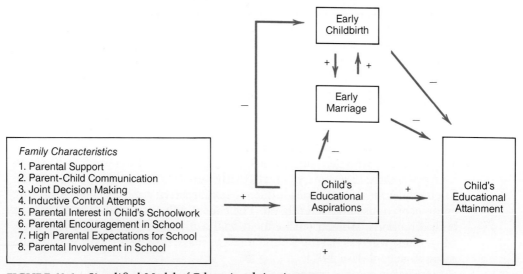

FIGURE 11·1   Simplified Model of Educational Attainment

First, the higher a woman's education at marriage, the more likely she will get additional schooling after marriage. Level of education at first marriage was the strongest predictor of **postmarriage education.** Those who have attended college are likely to continue schooling after marriage.

Second, age at marriage was related to education after marriage. Women who married in their teens were more likely to return to school after marriage. Perhaps this is because they were more likely to have disrupted their education for marriage and therefore had a greater motivation to return to school.

The third variable affecting postmarriage education was current religion. Protestant and Catholic women were least likely to continue their education, followed by Jewish and Mormon women, and then by those with no religious preference. Postmarriage education was almost as high among Jewish and Mormon women as it was among women with no religious preference.

Fourth, women who were divorced or separated were much more likely to return to school than women who were currently married or widowed. The economic plight of divorced and separated women is well known, and undoubtedly this is a powerful force motivating them to get more education.

Finally, sex role attitudes were related to education after marriage. Women with egalitarian sex role attitudes were more likely to seek postnuptial education.

Gender and Education

Gender influences educational opportunities. Both males and females are encouraged to complete high school, but support for a college education has tended to be much stronger for men than women. Because men are seen as the primary providers of the family, a college education has been viewed as more important for men than women.

In the early grades females tend to earn higher grades than males. Dornbusch et al. (1986) suggest that this is because parents treat girls differently than boys. Gender expectations of teachers also may have some effect.

Through high school there are few **gender differences** in achievement. Slightly more females than males complete elementary school, and slightly more males than females complete high school (see Table 11·1). However, the greater educational encouragement of males is reflected in the larger percentage of males that graduate from college. For example, in 1985 only 16 percent of American women over 25 had completed college compared to 23 percent of American men over age 25 (see Table 11·1).

TABLE 11·1 Years of School Completed by Gender, United States (1985)

Cumulative Percentage Completing	Female	Male
Elementary School (8 years)	93.0	92.1
High School	73.6	74.3
College	16.0	23.1

SOURCE: U.S. Bureau of the Census 1986: 122.

TABLE 11·2   Scores on Scholastic Aptitude Test (SAT) and American College Test (ACT) of College-Bound Seniors by Gender, United States (1970–1985)

	1970	1975	1980	1985
SAT				
Verbal				
Male	459	437	428	437
Female	461	431	420	425
Math				
Male	509	495	491	499
Female	465	449	443	452
ACT				
Composite				
Male	20.3	19.5	19.3	19.4
Female	19.4	17.8	17.9	17.9
English				
Male	17.6	17.1	17.3	17.6
Female	19.4	18.3	18.3	18.6
Math				
Male	21.1	19.3	18.9	18.6
Female	18.8	16.2	16.2	16.0

SOURCE: U.S. Bureau of the Census 1986:135.

A comparison of verbal and mathematical aptitudes of college-bound men and women is shown in Table 11·2. **SAT** and **ACT** aptitude scores declined among both men and women between 1970 and 1980, and since then they have risen somewhat. Women tend to score higher than men on language and verbal ability, and men tend to score higher on mathematical aptitude. In recent years the male-female difference in verbal aptitude has decreased, and according to the SAT test men now score higher than women on verbal aptitude. These differences could be due partly to differential encouragement and opportunity given to males in the later years of high school.

In recent years, however, encouragement and opportunity for female education has increased substantially. This is reflected in the greater proportion of female college graduates (see Table 11·3). In 1950 less than one fourth of college graduates were women but in 1985 there were more women college graduates than men.

TABLE 11·3 Percentage of College Graduates That Were Women, United States (1950–1985)

1950	23.8
1960	35.2
1970	43.0
1980	49.1
1985	50.8

SOURCE: U.S. Bureau of the Census 1987: 140.

TABLE 11·4   Percentage of Graduates That Were Women
in Selected Professions, United States (1960–1985)

	1960	1970	1980	1985
Medicine (M.D.)	5.5	8.4	23.4	30.4
Dentistry (D.D.S. or D.M.D.)	0.8	0.9	13.3	20.7
Law (L.L.B. or J.D.)	2.5	5.4	30.2	38.5
Engineering	0.4	0.8	8.7	12.5

SOURCE: U.S. Bureau of the Census 1987:151.

It is well known that women have been encouraged much more in traditionally female courses such as home economics, education, and nursing than
in traditionally male fields such as engineering, math, or medicine. Recent
figures show that opportunities for women in nontraditional fields have been
increasing.

Table 11·4 shows the increasing proportion of female graduates in medicine,
dentistry, law, and engineering for the period 1960 to 1985. For example, in
1960 only 6 percent of medical degrees were awarded to women, compared to
30 percent in 1985. In 1960 less than 3 percent of the law degrees were earned
by women compared to 39 percent in 1985.

These statistics reflect much improvement in the status of women in education; however large disparities continue to exist. For example, more than
87 percent of engineeering graduates are men, and more than 79 percent of
dentistry degrees are earned by men. Law is the least segregated of the four
professions listed in Table 11·4, and yet almost two thirds of law graduates
are men. As opportunities expand and social change continues, perhaps the
ratio of women to men graduates will continue to increase.

Gender differences in education are the result of subtle and complex socialization influences that occur over time. Baker and Entwisle (1987) have
shown that gender differences in academic expectations are affected by sub-
tleties of daily interaction between mother and child in the context of school
experience. Children acquire an academic self-image as they progress in school
that is shaped by expectations and sanctions received from parents, friends,
and the school environment. Parents may not even be aware of the influence
of their daily interactions with their children about school issues.

Family and School Conflict

The family and the school are two distinct institutions whose interests sometimes conflict. Parents may not like some values taught in schools or may feel
that the quality of instruction is poor. In other cases the school instruction
may be adequate, but the environment may be unsafe or unhealthy. Some
parents complain that their children are harassed and abused by other students.
Others feel the school is a place where their children acquire bad habits and
are exposed to illicit drugs. The opportunity for free public education turns
into a negative experience for them.

What options do parents have in these types of situations? They may send their child to a private school, if there is one available that has a better environment and if they can afford it. Most of the time private school is not a viable alternative.

Another possibility is for parents to remove their children from the school and teach them at home. Most states have **compulsory education** laws, but in some locations parents are allowed to teach their children at home if they meet certain conditions. A Wisconsin case has clarified under what circumstances parents might be allowed to teach their children at home.

Members of the Amish religion refuse to send their children to formal schooling beyond the eighth grade because of the so-called worldly influence that they feel such additional education would impose. The Amish provide continuing informal vocational training to their children that is designed to prepare them for life in the rural Amish community. They sincerely believe that high school attendance will corrupt their children and endanger both their own and their children's salvation.

Wisconsin law requires that children attend school until age 16, and the state of Wisconsin filed a suit against the Amish to force them to comply. At the initial hearing the Wisconsin court ruled against the Amish parents. If they did not send their children to school, the state could declare them neglectful and legally take custody of their children.

The Amish appealed the decision to the U.S. Supreme Court, which reversed the lower court decision and ruled in favor of the Amish (*Wisconsin v. Yoder et al.*, 406 U.S. 205, 1972). The court said that the state's interest in universal education is not totally free from a balancing process when it impinges on other fundamental rights, such as the freedom of religion and the interest of parents with respect to the upbringing of their children.

The Amish showed that their method of informal education was appropriate for their lifestyle. Crime rates in their communities are low, they are productive citizens, and they do not accept public welfare from the state. There was no evidence that forgoing additional formal schooling would either impair the children's physical or mental health or prevent them from becoming self-supporting. The Amish demonstrated the sincerity of their religious beliefs, the interrelationship of those beliefs with their mode of life, and the hazards of compulsory education for the survival of their communities.

The state supplied no evidence that granting an exemption to the Amish would adversely affect the state's interest in compulsory education or be a burden on the state. Therefore, the Supreme Court ruled in favor of the Amish. **Wisconsin v. Yoder** showed that there is a balance between the state's interest in compulsory education and parental rights.

Although the Amish situation is very different than that of most families, the case suggests that parents are not necessarily compelled to send their children to school if they can demonstrate that they are receiving adequate instruction at home. This usually means that the school district reviews the curriculum the children are taught at home and tests them periodically to verify that they are making educational progress.

There is evidence that children in **home schools** can learn needed skills (Reynolds and Williams 1986). However, it takes a great deal of time, commitment, and organization by the parents, and it becomes less viable as children

Children tend to receive higher grades when their parents are involved in school activities such as plays, social functions, and sporting events. Here parents enjoy a school-sponsored baseball game.   *Eric Roth/The Picture Cube.*

get older. Parents may be able to teach their children adequately in the elementary grades, but it seems impractical at the high school level. Parents usually do not have the skills or equipment to competently teach secondary-level mathematics, chemistry, or biology. Home schools may also hinder the social development of some children.

Many parents are dissatisfied with aspects of their children's school environment, but do not want or are unable to remove their children from public school. They may not have the time or skill to teach their children at home and may feel the school environment is best for normal social development. What are their alternatives?

Most teachers and schools are responsive, to some degree, to parental involvement and suggestions. Communicating concerns to teachers, administrators, and school boards may bring about change. Parents may also participate in PTA and school board meetings. In most school districts, meetings of the school board are open to the public. School board members are usually elected persons and therefore are generally responsive to citizen input. In this way parents may express their concerns and become involved in school decision making. Furthermore, most schools allow parents to visit school occasionally and encourage parental involvement as tutors, teacher aides, and in other ways. Participation of this kind enables a parent to observe the school environment personally. And as noted earlier, when parents are involved in various school activities, their children tend to earn higher grades.

Summary

1. Parental education, particularly the mother's, is positively related to the educational achievement in children.

2. Asian children tend to do better than average in school whereas black and Hispanic children tend to earn below average grades.

3. Children in single-parent or blended families tend to earn lower grades and are less likely to graduate from high school than other children.

4. Family size, birth order, and the employment status of the mother are not consistently related to academic achievement.

5. Children tend to receive higher grades when their parents are warm and supportive, talk to their children about problems and issues, read to their children, show an interest in their children's schoolwork and activities, encourage their children in school, offer to help their children when needed, expect their children to get good grades, exercise a moderate amount of control, use inductive control attempts, and use joint decision making.

6. Being either extremely permissive or overly strict is associated with low grades. When a child receives low grades, help and encouragement rather than positive or negative sanctions appear to produce improvement.

7. The amount of TV watching has a negative association with grades. Working after school and participation in sports are associated with higher grades, if involvement is not excessive.

8. Material resources such as type of home and amount of family income are not related to academic achievement.

9. Adolescents with good grades and who desire a college education are less likely than other adolescents to experience an early childbirth or marriage. Early marriage and parenthood are detrimental to the educational achievement of women.

10. The proportion of women who receive schooling after marriage has increased in recent years. Almost one half of all married women have gone to school since marriage or expect to go to school in the future.

11. The higher the level of education and the lower the age at marriage, the more likely a married woman will attend school. Being divorced or separated, having egalitarian sex role attitudes, and being nonreligious are associated with educational attendance after marriage.

12. The proportion of college graduates that are women has increased from less than one fourth in 1950 to more than one half in 1983.

13. There have been significant increases in the proportion of women graduates in high status professions such as medicine, law, and engineering. However, a large majority of graduates in these fields continues to be men.

14. *Wisconsin v. Yoder* established that the state may not force parents to send their children to school if the parents provide a viable alternative.

Important Terms

- academic achievement
- ACT
- blended family
- coercive control
- compulsory education
- gender differences

- genetic influences
- home school
- inductive control
- joint decision making
- parental education
- parental support

- post-marriage education
- SAT
- single-parent family
- social class
- verbal communication
- *Wisconsin v. Yoder*

Questions for Discussion

1. How do parental education, ethnic group, and parental marital status affect the academic success of children? Why?
2. Explain why you think Asian children tend to do so well academically. What is it about their family environment that stimulates academic achievement?
3. Explain why you think children in single-parent and blended families do not do as well academically as children who live with two natural parents.
4. Suppose your child comes to you with a poor report card. What could you do that is likely to result in an improved report card next term?
5. What are the key aspects of the family environment that influence academic achievement in children?
6. What is the role of natural ability (genetics) in academic achievement? Which is more important for academic success, natural ability or family environment?
7. How does marriage affect academic attainment? Has this changed in recent years? Why or why not?
8. What types of women tend to go to school after they are married? Why? Is this changing?
9. Why did the SAT and ACT scores decline during the sixties and seventies? Do you think family environment had anything to do with this decline? Explain why or why not. Why did the decline stop about 1980?
10. Why has there been a decrease in the male-female difference in verbal scores on the ACT and SAT tests?
11. Do men have more natural ability at math than women? Do you have any evidence to support your conclusion?
12. Why has the proportion of female college graduates increased so much during the past twenty-five years?
13. What are the major barriers to women's educational achievement? What can be done to eliminate these barriers and continue to expand the educational opportunities of women?
14. Do you agree with the decision of the U.S. Supreme Court in *Wisconsin v. Yoder*? Why or why not?
15. The court said in *Wisconsin v. Yoder* that there is a balancing of interests between parents and the state. What are the major interests of parents and what are the major interests of the states? Under what types of situations would the states' interests supercede the parents' interests, and when should the parents' interests override the states' interests?

Recommended Reading

MURNANE, R. J., R. A. MAYNARD, and J. C. OHLS. 1981. Home resources and children's achievement. *Review of Economics and Statistics* 63:369–377.

YAO, E. L. 1985. A comparison of family characteristics of Asian-American and Anglo-American high achievers. *International Journal of Comparative Sociology* 26:198–208.

References

ALEXANDER, K. J., and T. W. REILLY. 1981. Estimating the effects of marriage timing on educational attainment: Some procedural issues and substantive clarifications. *The American Journal of Sociology* 87(1):143–156.

BAHR, S. J., and G. K. LEIGH. 1978. Family size, intelligence, and expected education. *Journal of Marriage and the Family* 40:331–335.

BAKER, D. P., and D. R. ENTWISLE. 1987. The influence of mothers on the academic expectations of young children: A longitudinal study of how gender differences arise. *Social Forces* 65(3):670–694.

BAKER, M. H. 1981. Mother's occupation and children's attainments. *Pacific Sociological Review* 24(2):237–254.

COHEN, J. 1986. *Parents as educational models and definers.* Paper presented at the American Sociological Meeting, New York, August.

DAVIS, N. J., and L. L. BUMPASS. 1974. *The continuation of education after marriage among women in the U.S.: 1970.* Working Paper 74–5 for National Institutes of Health, Public Health Service, Department of Health, Education, and Welfare.

DORNBUSCH, S. M., M. J. FRALEIGH, and P. L. RITTER. 1986. *Families and schools.* A report to the National Advisory Board of the Study of Stanford and the Schools, Palo Alto, CA.

FAREL, A. M. 1980. Effects of preferred maternal roles, maternal employment, and sociodemographic status on school adjustment and competence. *Child Development* 51:1179–1186.

HAUSER, R. M., and W. H. SEWELL. 1985. Birth order and educational attainment in full sibships. *American Educational Research Journal* 22(1):1–23.

HESS, R. D., and S. D. HOLLOWAY. 1984. Family and school as educational institutions. In *Review of child development research, vol. 7: The family,* ed. R. D. Parke, R. N. Emde, H. P. McAdoo, and G. P. Sackett, 179–222. Chicago: University of Chicago Press.

JAIN, A. K. 1981. The effect of female education on fertility: A simple explanation. *Demography* 18(4):577–595.

LAREAU, A. 1987. Social class differences in family-school relationships: The importance of cultural capital. *Sociology of Education* 60:73–85.

LEICHTER, H. J. 1979. Families and communities as educators: Some concepts of relationships. In *Families and communities as educators,* ed. H. J. Leichter, 3–94. New York: Teachers College Press.

McBROOM, W. H. 1985. The influence of parental status variables on the status aspirations of youths. *Adolescence* 20(77):115–127.

MARJORIBANKS, K. 1979. *Families and their learning environments: An empirical analysis.* London: Routledge and Kegan Paul.

MERCY, J. A., and L. CARR STEELMAN. 1982. Familial influence on the intellectual attainment of children. *American Sociological Review* 47:532–542.

MILLER, B. C., G. O. JENSON, M. N. KRUEGER, T. C. PETERSON, and A. M. WEINER. 1981. *Teenage pregnancy.* A research report prepared for the Utah State Office of Education. Departments of Family & Human Development and Home Economics and Consumer Education, Utah State University.

MURNANE, R. J., R. A. MAYNARD, and J. C. OHLS. 1981. Home resources and children's achievement. *The Review of Economics and Statistics* 63(3):369–377.

REYNOLDS, P. L., and D. D. WILLIAMS. 1986. *Understanding family schools as alternatives to public education.* Paper presented at the Education and the Family conference at Brigham Young University, Provo, UT.

ROLLIINS, B. C., and D. L. THOMAS. 1979. Parental support, power, and control techniques in the socialization of children: In *Contemporary theories about the family,* vol. 1, 317–364. New York: Free Press.

RUMBERGER, R. W. 1983. The influence of family background on education, earnings, and wealth. *Social Forces* 61:755–773.

SHAW, L. B. 1982. High school completion for young women: Effects of low income and living with a single parent. *Journal of Family Issues* 3:147–163.

SMITH, H. L., and P. P. L. CHEUNG. 1986. Trends in the effects of family background on educational attainment in the Philippines. *The American Journal of Sociology* 91(6):1387–1408.

STEVENSON, D. L. 1986. *Parental involvement in schooling and the child's school performance: Influences of age, gender, and mother's education.* Paper presented at annual meeting of American Sociological Association, New York, August.

TANFER, K., and M. C. HORN. 1985. Contraceptive use, pregnancy and fertility patterns among single American women in their 20s. *Family Planning Perspectives* 17(1):10–19.

U.S. BUREAU OF THE CENSUS. 1986. *Statistical abstract of the United States: 1987.* Washington, DC: U.S. Government Printing Office.

U.S. BUREAU OF THE CENSUS. 1987. *Statistical abstract of the United States: 1988.* Washington, DC: U.S. Government Printing Office.

YAO, E. L. 1985. A comparison of family characteristics of Asian-American and Anglo-American high achievers *International Journal of Comparative Sociology* 26(3–4):198–208.

CHAPTER 12

Government and the Family

Introduction

One June afternoon (June 8) fifteen-year-old Gerald Gault and his friend decided to liven things up by calling Gerald's neighbor, Mrs. Cook. When she answered the phone they made some lewd comments. Mrs. Cook complained to the police who came and arrested Gerald and took him to the children's detention home. At the time Gerald's mother and father were both at work. No notice that Gerald was being taken into custody was left at the Gault home, and no other steps were taken to advise his parents that Gerald had been arrested.

When Gerald's mother arrived home about 6 o'clock she sent Gerald's older brother to look for him at a friend's house. He learned that Gerald had been taken into custody by the police. Gerald's mother and brother went to the detention home and the probation officer, Mr. Flagg, explained why Gerald had been arrested and said a hearing would be held the next day, June 9, at 3 o'clock.

On June 9, Gerald, his mother, his older brother, and probation officers Flagg and Henderson appeared before Juvenile Judge McGhee. The complainant, Mrs. Cook, was not there and no one was sworn in. No transcript or recording was made of the hearing, and no record of the substance of the proceeding was prepared. The judge questioned Gerald about the phone call and there was disagreement about what had happened. Mrs. Gault recalled that Gerald said he only dialed Mrs. Cook's number and handed the telephone to his friend, Ronald Lewis. Officer Flagg and Judge McGhee claimed that Gerald had admitted making some lewd remarks. At the conclusion of the hearing the judge said he would think about the matter and sent Gerald back to the detention home.

On June 11 or 12 Gerald was released and driven home. There was no explanation in the record as to why he was kept in the detention home or why he was released. On that day Mrs. Gault received a note signed from Officer Flagg stating that another hearing on Gerald's delinquency would be held on June 15 at 11:00 A.M.

At the June 15 hearing, Gerald, his father and mother, Ronald Lewis and his father, and Officers Flagg and Henderson were present along with Judge McGhee. Again there was disagreement as to what Gerald had actually said, and Judge McGhee recalled some admission by Gerald of a lewd statement. Mrs. Cook was not present. Mrs. Gault requested that Mrs. Cook be present, but Judge McGhee said she did not have to attend the hearing. The judge did not speak to or communicate with Mrs. Cook at any time, although Officer Flagg talked to her by telephone on June 9. A report made by the probation officers was filed with the court but not disclosed to Gerald or his parents. It listed the charge as "lewd phone calls." At the conclusion of the hearing Judge McGhee committed Gerald to the state industrial school until he was 21.

In juvenile cases no appeal is permitted by Arizona law. Gerald's parents appealed the decision to the Arizona State Supreme Court, which referred it to the Superior Court for a hearing. On August 17 there was a hearing in Superior Court in which Judge McGhee was cross-examined regarding the reasons for his decision. He said Gerald violated a section of the Arizona Criminal Code that states that any person who uses vulgar, abusive, or obscene language in the presence of a woman or child is guilty of a misdemeanor. The adult penalty for this act is $50 or imprisonment for not more than two months. The judge also testified that there is an Arizona statute that defines a delinquent child as one who is habitually involved in immoral matters. Judge McGhee gave three reasons for concluding that Gerald Gault was such a child. First, at the time of his arrest Gerald was still on six months probation for having been with another boy who had stolen a wallet from a lady's purse. Second, he said Gerald had admitted making other nuisance phone calls in the past. Third, he reported that two years earlier Gerald had stolen a baseball glove and lied about it. Regarding the last charge, there had been no hearing and no accusation because of lack of material evidence. After hearing Judge McGhee's testimony, the Superior Court dismissed the appeal of Mr. and Mrs. Gault. The Gaults made a second appeal to the Arizona Supreme Court that was also dismissed. In summary, a fifteen-year-old boy was arrested and sentenced to six years in a juvenile prison for making an obscene phone call. This conviction was upheld by three courts—a juvenile court, a superior court, and the Arizona Supreme Court. An adult who committed the same offense could only have been jailed for a maximum of two months.

The Gaults then appealed the decision to the U.S. Supreme Court, which reversed the decision because Gerald's constitutional rights were violated (**in re Gault,** 387 U.S. 1, 1967). The high court said that Gerald was denied due process rights guaranteed by the **Fourteenth Amendment,** namely the right to notice of charges, the right to counsel, the right to confront and cross-examine his accusers, the right to a transcript of the proceedings, the privilege against self-incrimination, and the right to appellate review.

The *Gault* case illustrates how different governmental agencies can intervene in family life. Some governmental action regulates individual behavior and is intrusive, whereas other policies limit the nature and extent of intervention by governmental agenices. When Gerald Gault violated the law, the police and juvenile court intervened and jailed him. The Supreme Court overturned the decision and said states could remove a juvenile from his family only under certain specified conditions.

The purpose of this chapter is to examine how government policies impact on families. The first section is a discussion of how government policy is made, followed by an analysis of the major policies that impact on family life.

The Formulation of Law

Governmental policies are made in three major ways. First, rules that establish specific appropriate and inappropriate behavior are written down as formal laws called **statutes.** In American society a special elected body called the **legislature** has the task of making the statutes.

Second, the actions of executive agencies help formulate law. Once laws are passed, various agencies are assigned the task of carrying out or executing them. A given agency formulates many specific regulations that are not part of the legislation but which are needed to administer a law. For example, there are many regulations of the Internal Revenue Service that are not in the tax statutes passed by the U.S. Congress. The regulations are made to deal with many specific situations that are not spelled out in the legislation. In this way agencies in the executive branch of government "make" law administratively, which may be called **executive regulation.**

Court decisions are the third way governmental policy is made. When there is a law violation or a conflict concerning how to interpret a law, the courts resolve the conflict. Most statutes are fairly general and the courts must apply them to specific cases. This requires the interpretation of broad and ambiguous phrases. The court rulings become **case law** and set **precedents** for future decisions. The different branches of government often seem to contradict each other, but this provides a system of checks and balances that is deliberate.

The *Gault* case is a good example of how the process of government policy-making works. The Arizona legislature established by statute a set of laws pertaining to juveniles. Some of the procedures were not specified in the statutes but were established administratively by the police, the detention home, and the juvenile court workers. When there was a conflict between the Gaults and the state of Arizona regarding the interpretation of the law, the courts were used to resolve the dispute. The decision of the U.S. Supreme Court in *Gault* set a precedent that became case law. Juvenile courts all over the United States were required to change their statutes and procedures to be consistent with the *Gault* decision. In this way law was made by court decision.

Governmental policy is made at many different levels. Most laws that affect families are state laws. According to the **Tenth Amendment** of the U.S. Constitution, anything not specifically given to the federal government is left to the states. Thus, all laws regulating marriage, reproduction, child rearing and divorce are state laws and each of the fifty states makes its own. Although the federal government may not legislate family matters, federal influence is exercised through the Constitution and decisions of the Supreme Court. The *Gault* case is a good example. The federal government did not and could not dictate what Arizona's juvenile law should be but the Supreme Court invalidated the Arizona law on the grounds that it violated basic rights guaranteed by the Constitution. In this way the federal government constrains state law.

Family policy in the United States is a combination of two opposing forces.

On the one hand, laws are passed that regulate individual and family behavior. On the other hand, the Constitution and courts limit the nature and extent of governmental regulation of family behavior. There is a strong norm of **family autonomy** in the United States. According to this principle, families should be left alone and do best without interference, unless there is clear evidence that an important regulation or right is being violated.

Marriage Laws

Because of the state's interest in the family, governments regulate the formation and functioning of marriages. In the United States there are two basic steps to forming a legally recognized marriage. First, a marriage license must be obtained. Second, a marriage ceremony must be performed by an official who is approved by the state.

Regulation comes through specifying the conditions for obtaining a license, and there are several restrictions. First, individuals may not obtain a license if they are currently married to another person. Second, people may not marry someone in their immediate family of orientation (father, mother, brother, sister, son, or daughter), and some states prohibit marriages among first cousins. Third, homosexual marriages are banned. Bigamy, incest, and homosexual relationships are criminal offenses that can result in prison terms in most states. A final restriction on marriage is age. In many jurisdictions one must be at least age 14 to marry with parental consent and age 18 to marry without it.

A marriage license is issued only if the parties are mentally competent and willingly choose to marry. The key to mental competence is a person's capacity to consciously consent to the marriage contract. A person with severe mental retardation may be denied a marriage license on the grounds that he or she is not capable of understanding or fulfilling normal marital expectations. Most states also have some regulations for health purposes, such as requiring a physical exam and a blood test before a license is issued.

What happens if the law is violated? The consequences depend on the nature and extent of the infraction. Minor violations usually have little or no effect. For example, if a clerk issued a license without the required blood test, the couple would be considered to be legally married even though there was a technical violation of the law. When major violations occur the marriage may be voided but it is usually considered to be valid until it is formally annulled by a court. To illustrate, suppose a boy and girl who are both age 16 obtain a marriage license with a forged parental consent form. If they marry and no one challenges the marriage, their marriage is valid even if the parents and everyone else becomes aware of their fraud. However, upon discovering the forgery, the parents could go to court and have the marriage voided.

Some of the common grounds for annulment are impotency, fraud, mental incapacity, duress, and a prior existing marriage. A New Jersey case illustrates an annulment that was granted because of fraud. A man maintained he was a practicing Orthodox Jew in order to marry a Jewish woman he loved. When she discovered after the marriage that he did not, in fact, adhere to the tenets of orthodox Judaism and had misrepresented his religious beliefs in order to marry her, she filed for an annulment. The court agreed that her religious beliefs were essential to her marriage and that she could not properly perform the duties of a wife and mother, as outlined in her faith, without support of a husband holding the same beliefs. He had knowingly deceived her and the court granted her the annulment (*Bilowit v. Dolitsky*, 124 N.J. Super. 101, 1973).

In the United States, marriage is considered to be a fundamental right that is protected by the Constitution. In **Zablocki v. Redhail** (434 U.S. 374, 1978) the Supreme Court affirmed that right once again. Mr. Redhail was a high school student in 1972 and a paternity action was instituted against him. He appeared in court and admitted that he was the father of a girl born out of wedlock in July 1971. The court ordered him to pay $109 monthly child support until the child reached age 18. From May 1972 until August 1974 Mr. Redhail was unemployed and indigent and made no support payments.

In September of 1974 he filed for a marriage license and the application was denied. Wisconsin law states that anyone with child support obligations cannot be given a marriage license unless he proves he has paid his support obligations and demonstrates that the child is not and is not likely to become a public charge. Mr. Redhail had not paid his support obligations and was $3,700 in arrears. His child had been a public charge since birth, through the Aid to Families with Dependent Children (AFDC) program.

Mr. Redhail then filed a complaint in district court on behalf of himself and the class of Wisconsin residents in a similar situation. The complaint stated that he was planning to marry a woman who was expecting a child in March of 1975 and that he wanted the marriage to be lawful. The suit said the Wisconsin statute violated the **due process** and **equal protection clauses** of the Fourteenth Amendment.

A three-judge panel reviewed the law and said that the Wisconsin law was unconstitutional. On appeal, the Supreme Court affirmed the decision (*Zablock v. Redhail*, 434 U.S. 374, 1978). A woman who is pregnant has a right, based on previous court decisions, to seek an abortion of her expected child. Surely, the court reasoned, a decision to marry and raise a child in a traditional family setting must receive equivalent protection. If the appellee's right to procreate means anything at all, it must imply some right to enter the only relationship in which the state of Wisconsin allows sexual relations to legally take place. Because the Wisconsin law interfered with the right to marry, the court said it cannot be upheld unless it serves a legitimate and important state interest. The state of Wisconsin argued that the law served two purposes. First, it furnishes an opportunity to counsel the applicant as to the necessity of fulfilling prior support obligations. Second, it protects the welfare of children born out of wedlock.

The Supreme Court said these are legitimate and important objectives but the means for reaching them are questionable and infringe upon the right to marry. The statute merely prevented Mr. Redhail from getting married but did not deliver any money into the hands of his child. It did not limit in any way new financial commitments other than those arising out of the contemplated marriage. There was no evidence that counseling took place, that this type of restriction was needed to bring about the counseling, or that it really helped the financial status of the children. Therefore, the court said the law could

What should government do to help collect child support from fathers? Here young children seek government assistance to obtain child support from their fathers. *Carolyn Hine/The Picture Cube.*

not be justified by the interests of the state and declared it unconstitutional. Although states have the right to regulate marriage, those regulations must be directly related to important state objectives or they will be declared invalid.

Although marriage is the legal and preferred way to form a family, there are two other ways that marriage relationships are formed, as discussed in Chapter 1. Couples that live together without benefit of marriage have a relationship with legal rights and obligations. Second, when a child is born, a familylike relationship is formed with legal rights and responsibility. These relationships are regulated by the state whether or not a formal marriage ceremony has taken place. For example in **Marvin v. Marvin** (18 Cal. 3d 660, 1976) the California Supreme Court ruled that claims for alimony, child support, and maintenance could appropriately be granted to nonmarried persons.

A related case occurred recently in Hawaii. A couple had lived together for twenty-four years without benefit of marriage. The court ruled that because the couple lived together for an extended period of time, they should be treated as if they were married. The wife was awarded one half the value of their residence and half of their properties (*Artiss v. Artiss,* 8 Family Law Reporter 2313, 1982).

These two cases illustrate that when two people live together, a legal obligation is created just as if they were married. If they disagree as to how property and money should be divided, they may go to the courts to resolve that conflict. However, as mentioned in Chapter 1, intervention by the state is stronger in marriages than in cohabitation. For example, Michelle Marvin was awarded nothing after living with Lee Marvin for seven years. In some states no compensation has been awarded even after lengthy periods of cohabitation. For example, in 1979 the Illinois Supreme Court allowed no compensation to Victoria Hewitt when she separated from Robert Hewitt after fifteen years of nonmarital cohabitation (*Hewitt v. Hewitt,* 77 Ill. 2d 49, 1979).

In marriage there is also a legal duty for husband and wife to support each other, although it comes to no one's attention unless there is a conflict that is taken to court. What that means practically is that any couple married or unmarried can develop any kind of sexual or monetary relationship, as long as they both agree. If there is a conflict as to how money should be distributed, then they may go to the court and certain types of agreements may be enforced.

Marriage is entered into as a contractual agreement, but the contract may not be changed or released upon consent like other contracts, and its exact nature is not spelled out. In that sense, marriage may be the ultimate in consumer fraud (Krause 1977).

Sexual Behavior

Another important area in which the state may intervene is sexual behavior. Based on the principle of privacy and family autonomy, individuals are again free to do what they want. However, if there is disagreement between them or certain behaviors come to the knowledge of others, their behavior may be restricted. One area where the state has intervened is the selling of contraceptive devices. In 1965 Connecticut had a law that forbid the sale of contraceptives. That law was challenged, and the Supreme Court ruled that married couples have the right to decide whether or not to have children and that the state law restricting the sale of contraceptives to them was unconstitutional (*Griswold v. Connecticut,* 381 U.S. 479, 1965).

In a later decision it was argued that the right to privacy extends to unmarried individuals. The court said that if the **right of privacy** means anything it is the right of an individual, married or single, to be free of unwanted governmental intrusion into matters so fundamentally affecting a person as to the decision whether to bear or beget a child (*Eisentadt v. Baird,* 405 U.S. 938,

1972). These decisions used the U.S. Constitution as a defense for individual privacy and freedom and limited the authority of states to pass laws in certain areas.

Perhaps one of the most controversial areas of state intervention is in the decision to have an abortion. Many states have had laws that limit abortions, and until the 1970s it was a crime in many states to abort an unborn child, unless it was necessary to preserve the health of the mother. Texas had such a law, and in 1970 Jane Roe, an unmarried pregnant woman, filed a suit challenging the constitutionality of the Texas criminal abortion laws. She claimed that the abortion laws were unconstitutional because they abridged her right of personal privacy and allowed abortion only when necessary to save the life of the mother. She wanted an abortion but her life was not in danger from the pregnancy. In a classic decision, the U.S. Supreme Court declared the Texas abortion law unconstitutional (**Roe v. Wade,** 410 U.S. 110, 1973). The court said that although a woman's right to terminate her pregnancy is not absolute, the right to privacy does include her decision as to whether or not to terminate a pregnancy. They argued that an unborn fetus is not a person and therefore is not entitled to the protection of the Fourteenth Amendment. *Roe v. Wade* invalidated most of the abortion laws in the United States. In 1976, laws requiring parental or spousal approval for an abortion were struck down by the Supreme Court in **Planned Parenthood v. Danforth** (428 U.S. 52, 1976). The court ruled that it was unconstitutional to require written consent from a spouse before an abortion could be performed. They also ruled that states could not require parental consent for abortions for females under age 18.

In a 1980 Utah case (*H.L. v. Matheson*, 101 S. Ct. 1164, 1981), the Supreme Court ruled that states may require doctors to notify the parents of minors before they perform an abortion. It was argued that this type of state intrusion is acceptable because it does not give parents the veto power over the abortion decision but does allow them to be informed of their child's abortion. Several court cases have also ruled that although women have a right to obtain an abortion, state and federal governments are not required to pay for the procedures (*Harris v. McRae*, 448 U.S. 297, 1980).

Sexual relations are a social and legal expectation of marriage. If a marriage is not consummated it is grounds for annulment in most states. If one spouse permanently refuses sexual activity, it is also grounds for divorce.

One of the primary functions of marriage is to bear and rear children. This is a social and legal expectation. If one spouse refuses to have children, the other has grounds for divorce.

Surnames

Another social expectation is that a wife will take the name of her husband. However, this is a custom rather than a legal requirement. There is no formal law in any state requiring a wife to change her surname to that of her husband. If she continues to use her birth name *exclusively, consistently,* and *nonfraudulently* after marriage, her legal name need not be changed as a result of her marriage. Although it is a widespread custom for a woman to take her husband's surname upon marriage, this custom has not become law. The number of women who retain their birth names is probably increasing.

However, even when a woman continues to use her birth name after marriage, regulatory statutes and practices may require her to use her husband's surname. For example, Alabama has an unwritten regulation requiring each married female driver's license applicant to use her husband's surname. This regulation was challenged on the grounds that it violated the equal protection clause of the Fourteenth Amendment. The Alabama law was upheld in court because of long-standing custom, administrative convenience for the state, and because a woman could change her name easily by applying to a probate court (*Forbush v. Wallace*, 341 U.S. 970, 1972). This means that agencies may continue to require a married woman to use her husband's name. However, a woman may avoid such a requirement by formally applying in court to keep her birth name.

Support

In most societies the task of providing food, clothing, and shelter for a family is assigned to men. Mackey (1985) indicates that tasks which systematically interfere with child care are generally precluded from women and fall into the lot of men, such as hunting. In American society the task of supporting a family has been primarily the husband's (Hill, Rossen, and Sogg 1981). In recent years there has been a trend toward equality in family support obligations. Some statutes place the duty to support the husband on the wife if he is unable to support himself. There is a recent trend toward equalizing the duty of support.

If a husband does not provide adequate financial support for his wife or child, what are their alternatives? They may buy the necessities for which the father or husband will be held liable, or bring suit against the father or husband for support. For example, a merchant may sell goods to a wife or child and charge them to the husband. However, this is not a very effective tool for imposition of support. Merchants do not like to have a wife or child buy things in the name of the husband because they are required to make a decision on whether or not an item is necessary. In addition, persons who need such laws generally do not have credit extended to them.

Although the husband is required by law to support his wife and children, courts tend not to get involved in financial disputes except in matters of divorce and child support. They are not equipped to settle the countless number of family financial disputes that could be brought into court. Furthermore, there is no assurance that the courts could settle family budget disputes justly or better than the parties themselves.

On the other hand, statutes in almost every state make it a crime for a husband to fail to support his wife. To be guilty of nonsupport a husband must willfully fail to provide for his wife. The basic criteria in determining support are the needs of the woman and children and the ability of the man to pay. If the wife deserts her husband, he is still obligated to support her. For example, in *Campas v. Campas* (304 N.Y.S. 2d 876, 1969) the wife left her husband without explanation. She received public assistance to help support herself and filed a suit against her husband for support. He contended that he was not liable for support because his wife abandoned him. The court ruled that her abandonment was not sufficient reason to relieve him of his duty to support.

Both parents are obligated to provide support for their children. In return for that support, children must submit to reasonable demands from their parents. *Roe v. Doe* (272 N.E. 2d 567, 1971) illustrates this principle. A twenty-year-old woman was supported by her father while she attended college out of state. The daughter moved out of the college dormitory even though her father had told her she must live there. When her fathered discovered that she had moved out of the dorm, he directed her to return home and attend school in their hometown. She refused and he stopped all further support. She filed suit in court contending that he had a duty to support her. He maintained that he had no obligation to support her because she had abandoned her home for the purpose of avoiding reasonable parental control. The court ruled in favor of the father, stating that parents may impose reasonable regulations on their children in return for maintenance and support. If children voluntarily leave home to avoid parental discipline and restraint, they forfeit their legal claim to support.

Children

In American society families are given much autonomy in child socialization, but the state will intervene under certain conditions. The state reserves the right to assume the role of the parent under a legal doctrine called **parens patriae.** In addition, parents may request governmental intervention to help solve certain problems. In this section we review some of the specific ways in which the state intervenes on behalf of children.

Neglect and Abuse

The most common reason for government intervention is child neglect. If parents do not properly feed, clothe, and protect their children they can be charged with **neglect.** Similarly, when children do not receive needed medical care or do not attend school, the parents are considered neglectful.

One of the key issues is deciding under what conditions the state should intervene on behalf of children. Two cases illustrate this dilemma.

Ricky Green was sixteen years old and suffered from paralytic scoliosis. He was unable to stand or walk and without undergoing a surgical procedure called spinal fusion he would be bedridden for the rest of his life. Ricky's mother was a Jehovah's Witness and although she consented to the surgery, she refused to give her permission for Ricky to have blood transfusions. The surgery could not be done safely without blood transfusions and therefore the director of the state hospital for crippled children in Elizabethtown, Pennsylvania, filed a petition to declare Ricky an abused child and appoint an alternative guardian. The purpose was to appoint a guardian who would allow Ricky to have the blood transfusions and undergo the surgery.

The court felt that the state did not have an interest of sufficient magnitude to outweigh the parent's religious beliefs when the child's life was not immediately imperiled by his physical condition (*In re Green*, 448 Pa. 338, 1972).

However, the court felt that it was necessary to determine Ricky's own wishes because he was intelligent and of sufficient maturity to make such a decision. At a later hearing Ricky stated that he did not want the operation. His decision was not based on religious beliefs alone. He had already been hospitalized for a long period, and there was no assurance that the operation would be successful.

If Ricky had stated that he wanted the operation, the court probably would have ordered the surgery. This would be consistent with the Supreme Court's view that a minor female has a right to an abortion and that parental consent is not required before the procedure.

The Green decision was based on the principle that the state cannot necessarily intervene on behalf of a child if the condition is not life threatening. On the other hand, it was evident from the ruling that the child's own wishes were an important part of the decision.

In another case, Phillip Becker, age 11, had Down's Syndrome. He was mentally retarded and had a large hole between the ventricles of his heart. As a result, abnormally high pressures were being exerted on the blood vessels in his lungs. The vessels could tolerate this pressure for an uncertain period of time, but if the hole was not patched surgically irreversible lung damage would eventually occur. This lung damage would probably cause persistent and severe shortness of breath, heart failure, and even death. Unless this condition were corrected, Phillip would probably not live beyond the age of 30. Corrective surgery, if performed properly, might prevent the lung damage and give Phillip a normal life expectancy. Phillip's parents had refused to permit the operation. A petition to legally override the parent's wishes and to allow the surgery was denied and in an appeal the denial was affirmed. This case again shows that although parental authority over the child is limited in medical decisions, their wishes are usually complied with if the medical problem is not life threatening (*In re Becker*, 92 Cal. App. 3d 796, 1979; 445 U.S. 949, 1980).

A recent Colorado case shows a more life-threatening condition in which the courts did intervene. A young twelve-year-old boy had seizures (*In re V.L.E.*, Colorado Supreme Court 5–10–82, 8 Family Law Reporter 2437, 1982). The county Department of Social Services filed a petition alleging that he was dependent and neglected because his mother refused to provide medical care necessary for his health and well-being. The district court declared him a neglected child and directed the department to arrange for his medical treatment. He was prescribed the medication Dilantin to control his seizures. His mother appealed, and the Colorado Supreme Court reversed the lower court's decision. The court found no proof that the boy's life was in danger through lack of medical care. During the course of the appeal, he had stopped taking his medication and consequently experienced continuous seizures, resulting in serious dysfunctioning. After the appeal, the department filed a new dependency and neglect petition alleging that the boy's life was endangered by his mother's refusal to provide medical care. This time the court held that the condition was life threatening. The court reasoned that there was justification for medical treatment because of the danger to the boy's life.

These cases illustrate the uncertainty regarding the right and circumstances under which courts can intervene on behalf of children when the parents are unwilling to get medical treatment. Parental autonomy is a strong norm in our society and is constitutionally protected. On the other hand, the state has an interest in the health and welfare of the children. These interests often conflict, and the courts attempt to balance them. Parents have a large say in the welfare of their children, particularly if conditions are not life threatening. The state has the authority to intervene, however, if the condition is life threatening (Sokolosky 1981).

There are other types of neglect besides absence of medical care. Parents may fail to properly feed and clothe their children. As long as children are functioning and are reasonably normal, the state is not able to intervene. When cleanliness and health conditions become a severe problem, however, the state has the obligation and the right to intervene. However, the state's first duty is to attempt to help the parents correct the deficiency. The general procedure is to have the state's Department of Social Services or Division of Family Services try to improve the conditions by helping the parents provide better physical care of their children.

Removing Children from Their Parents

Only in extreme cases of neglect or abuse does the state have the right to permanently remove children from their parents. There must be clear and convincing evidence that the interests of the children would be best served by terminating parental rights, as shown by **Santosky v. Kramer** (455 U.S. 71, 1982). The three children of John and Annie Santosky were removed from their custody and placed in foster homes in 1973 after episodes of physical abuse and neglect. The youngest child was only three days old when he was taken from his parents to avoid eminent danger to his life and health. Five years later there was a hearing held to permanently remove or terminate the rights of the Santoskys. A family court judge acknowledged that the Santoskys had maintained contact with their children but found that the visits were "superficial and devoid of any real emotional content." He ruled that the best interests of the children required permanent termination of the parents' custody. The Santoskys appealed the ruling, contesting the constitutionality of the **preponderance of evidence** standard used in the decision.

The Supreme Court overturned the decision. They ruled that the rights of natural parents are constitutionally protected and said there must be **clear and convincing evidence** before any state may permanently terminate the rights of parents. This case shows that the court believes strongly in family autonomy and that children cannot be removed from their parents unless there is strong, convincing evidence.

Education

One of the important societal functions assigned to parents is to see that their children are trained so that they can be productive citizens. In industrialized societies education has become an important aspect of child socialization. In the United States the law requires that children attend school. What happens if parents refuse to send their children to school? In some circumstances the state can declare that the children are neglected and force the parents to send them to school or legally remove the children from the parents' custody if the parents will not comply. Again the government may only intervene in certain specified circumstances. In recent years parents have been given the freedom to educate their children in alternative ways.

The case of *Wisconsin v. Yoder*, which was discussed in Chapter 11, helped establish the rights of parents to educate their children outside the formal educational system. The case showed that there is a balance between the state's interest of compulsory education and parents' rights. If the parents have an alternative means of education and can demonstrate this, they are not compelled to send their children to public schools.

Institutionalizing Children Against Their Will

Up to this point we have reviewed some decisions in which the state and the parents have had conflicts over whether their children should receive medical care or formal education. What happens when the parents want to institutionalize a child against the wishes of that child? Some maintain that a formal adversary hearing is necessary to protect the child. This would insure that normal constitutional safeguards such as the ability to have a written notice of the charges, and the opportunity to cross-examine the witnesses would be present. Others feel that such a decision should be made jointly by expert medical opinion and the parents, and that an adversary proceeding is unnecessary.

This issue faced the Supreme Court in *Parham v. J. R.* (442 U.S. 584, 1979). This was a class action suit brought by minor children alleging that they had been deprived of their liberty without procedural due process. Mental health laws in Georgia permitted parents to have their children admitted involuntarily to a mental facility with an administrative hearing but without a court hearing.

The court ruled that Georgia's procedures are reasonable and consistent with the constitutional guarantees. They said that the risk of error of a parental decision is great enough that some type of inquiry should be made by a neutral fact-finder to determine whether requirements for admission are satisfied. This neutral fact-finder should inquire carefully about the child's background and the decision maker must have the authority to refuse to admit the child who doesn't satisfy medical standards for admission. The child's need for commitment must be reviewed periodically by an independent procedure. However, they said that a formal adversary hearing is not required and need not be conducted by a lawyer or judicial officer.

The court emphasized that unless the parents are found to be neglectful or abusive, they must retain a substantial role in the decision. The presumption is that parents will act in the best interests of the child most of the time. The court noted that scarce funds and psychiatric time should not be diverted to adversary hearings that might harm the parent-child relationship. They said priority should be given to diagnosis and treatment rather than to time-consuming preadmission hearings.

A related case occurred in Texas in 1979 (**Addington v. Texas,** 441 U.S. 418, 1979). Frank O'Neil Addington was committed in 1975 to the Austin State Hospital for an indefinite period of time following a civil trial. His mother had filed the appropriate petition following his arrest on the misdemeanor charge of "assault by threat" against her. Addington had been committed seven times between 1969 and 1975 for brief periods to various state mental hospitals and three times for indefinite periods. He appealed on the basis that the standard of proof used in the case should have been "beyond a reasonable doubt" rather than "clear and convincing evidence."

The **beyond reasonable doubt** standard is an extremely high standard that is used in criminal cases. On the other end of the continuum is a standard called **preponderance of evidence,** which is used in civil cases. In between these two extremes is a standard called **clear and convincing evidence.**

Mr. Addington argued that he should have the same standard applied to him that criminals have—that to deprive him of his liberty the evidence should be beyond a reasonable doubt. The state of Texas, on the other hand, felt that in mental cases confinement could occur if there is clear and convincing evidence. The Supreme Court ruled that the standard of clear and convincing evidence was sufficient to meet the requirements of due process guaranteed by the Fourteenth Amendment and that "beyond a reasonable doubt" would place an unreasonable burden on the state. However, they noted that mentally ill patients have the right to treatment, periodic review of their condition, and immediate release when no longer deemed to be dangerous to themselves or others.

These two decisions show that depriving children of their liberty by being admitted to a mental hospital is not the same as being sent to jail. The evidence must be convincing that the child needs hospitalization, and this must be ascertained by a neutral fact-finding body in addition to the parents. However, if the parents request treatment and the authorities agree that treatment is needed, the child may be admitted against the child's will, even though no formal court hearing has been held.

Overall, there appears to be a balancing of the rights of the child and the rights of the parents. The stringent requirements of the criminal law are not imposed on the parents because it is assumed that they generally have the best interests of the child at heart. On the other hand, the decision is not left completely up to the parents, but must be affirmed by clear and convincing evidence from a neutral fact-finder.

Inappropriate Governmental Intervention

There is often a conflict about under what conditions the state should be allowed to intervene on behalf of children. We have reviewed situations where the state intervened for medical and educational reasons to protect children. Occasionally statutes allow interventions for other purposes. Two recent cases illustrate how the state may intervene inappropriately.

Margaret Wambles was a white woman who had never married but had a son who had lived with her continuously from his birth until he was almost four years old. At that time he was forcefully taken from her by Officer L. Cocktee Conn under the orders of Judge Thetford of the Montgomery Family Court. Judge Thetford did so without prior notice or hearing, which was lawful under Alabama law. The investigation that led to the termination of Miss Wambles' parental rights was prompted by Mr. Coppage. He had previously lived intermittently with Margaret Wambles and claimed to have fathered her son. Mr. Coppage claimed that Miss Wambles was neglecting the child and that she was living with and entertaining several black men. Officer Conn was commissioned by the county Youth Facility to enter Miss Wambles' home and determine the conditions there. He found conditions to be quite normal with the exception that there was a black man living there. After delivering his report, he was then commissioned to obtain a pick-up order by the same agency, which he did from Judge Thetford. The child was taken from the home crying in protest.

The court ruled in favor of Miss Wambles and said no parental conduct that was harmful to her son had been identified. The definition of neglect in the Alabama statute was declared unconstitutional because it was vague and allowed infringement on the fundamental right of **family autonomy** (*Roe v. Conn*, 417 F.Supp. 769, 1976)

The important aspect of this ruling was that parents are protected by the Constitution in terms of due process. The fact that a judge and/or social workers feel that the conditions may be harmful is not sufficient to remove a child from the home. Specific behavior that is harmful to the child must be identified. Otherwise, any unusual or unconventional behavior could be labeled as neglect.

This principle is illustrated by **Stanley v. Illinois** (405 U.S. 645, 1972), which was discussed in Chapter 1. When Joan Stanley died, Peter Stanley lost custody of their children because Joan and Peter had not been married. On appeal, the Supreme Court said that the state of Illinois could not presume that unmarried fathers were unsuitable or neglectful parents without individualized proof. The court emphasized that the law has recognized family relationships unlegitimized by a marriage ceremony. Children of married parents, divorced parents, and unmarried mothers can be removed only after proof of neglect. If unmarried fathers could have their children removed without proof of neglect, that would constitute a denial of their right to equal protection of the law. Therefore, the Illinois statute was unconstitutional.

Together these cases show that parental rights extend beyond marriage. Furthermore, they show that conditions that may not meet local standards of propriety such as cohabitation, interracial marriage, and the like cannot be used to deprive parents and children of their relationship, which is fundamental. The severing of that relationship should occur only in extreme situations.

Poverty

The family is responsible for providing adequate food, clothing, and shelter for its members, particularly children. During the past fifty years a wide variety of income-maintenance programs have been established in the United States to help support individuals and families in difficult economic situations. These programs are a way in which the government intervenes on behalf of families with economic problems.

Danziger and Plotnick (1981) have analyzed the types and effects of **income-maintenance** programs in the United States. In this section we will review some of the major results of their study.

They found that public social welfare expenditures grew from about 35 percent of all government spending in 1950 to about 55 percent in 1980. After adjusting for inflation, expenditures were over three times as large as they

A major impact of government on families is providing financial assistance for
families with low incomes, as shown here by a mother and her child applying for
welfare.   *Ulrike Welsch.*

were in 1965. During that period the government increased social security
and instituted medicare and medicaid.

Large numbers of families receive social welfare benefits. Danziger and
Plotnick showed that payments are received on a scale far larger than is usually
perceived. In 1965, 37 percent of all households received a cash transfer from
the government, compared to over 42 percent in 1980.

Although these programs help families in need, they also discourage work.
As labor income increases in a family, welfare benefits fall and this diminishes
the rewards of working. Because some families participate in several welfare
programs at the same time, the total loss in benefits caused by increased
earnings may be larger than the earnings themselves.

There is also concern that welfare payments encourage marital instability. In about half of the states, a family with two parents but no earnings becomes eligible for cash benefits only if the father deserts the family. If he stays, the family will be eligible only for food stamps. Although the program has been widely criticized for encouraging marital instability, there is no evidence that fathers actually leave families in order for them to obtain welfare.

Income-maintenance transfers are received by more than 40 percent of all households and account for more than 10 percent of all household income. This reduces the incidence of poverty substantially. For example, Danziger and Plotnick estimated that over 12 percent of American families were removed from poverty in this way.

Income-maintenance transfers improve the living standards of the poor and provide access to essential goods and services. Their major drawback is that they reduce the number of hours worked. According to Danziger and Plotnick (1981), hours worked declined by 7 percent from what they would have been if we had not had an expansion of social welfare expenditures between 1950 and 1976. Social welfare programs not only reduce work efforts in households but also increase tax burdens among those who are employed.

One way governments impact on families is through educational programs, such as this Headstart classroom in Detroit. Evidence suggests that Headstart programs have been effective in helping disadvantaged pre-school children prepare for elementary school.   *Robert Eckert/The Picture Cube.*

There are a variety of other educational, nutritional, and medical programs that are available for individuals and families. One of the most well known is Headstart, which funds about 1,200 local programs that are intended to bridge the gap in early childhood development. There is some evidence that Headstart programs help disadvantaged children learn so that they may begin their formal education on a more equal basis with their peers.

Marital Dissolution

The government not only regulates family formation, it also regulates family dissolution (see Chapter 16). Here we briefly review how the government regulates the dissolution of marriages.

A marriage is a contract between a man, a woman, and the state. The state has an interest in the stability of marriages and the obligations created by marriage. An individual may not dissolve a **marriage contract** without the official approval of the state.

The state's regulation of marital dissolution is designed to protect the weak and the innocent. Children are a primary concern, and the state has the power to determine child custody and protect the economic interests of children. The state also resolves disputes and protects the economic interests of both adults.

The U.S. Supreme Court has ruled that all individuals have a right to obtain a divorce. In a Connecticut case a couple's divorce petition was denied because they could not pay the required court fees. The couple filed a suit and the court ruled in their favor, saying that they could not be denied access to a divorce merely because of their inability to pay the court fees (**Boddie v. Connecticut,** 401 U.S. 371, 1971).

The initial step in the divorce process is for one party to file a legal document with the court stating the reasons for divorce. This is called the **divorce complaint** and often includes a request for a certain type of monetary and child custody settlement. It is possible for individuals to file the divorce complaint themselves but most people hire an attorney.

After the divorce complaint is filed it is formally served on the other spouse. If the other spouse does not contest the terms of the complaint, one spouse appears before a judge who reviews the terms of the settlement and formally decrees that the couple is divorced.

In most divorces there is some disagreement over the money, property, or children. In some cases the parties negotiate directly with each other, and in other situations the attorneys negotiate for the parties and the two seldom communicate directly. Usually an acceptable compromise is reached, although this is often a slow and painful process because of the emotion and bitterness involved. After a compromise is achieved, the attorneys draft it into a formal settlement agreement that becomes part of the divorce decree. Occasionally the parties are unable to reach an agreement, and a court trial is used to settle their differences. The judge weighs the evidence presented by each attorney and resolves the disputes by court order.

The attorneys play a key role in the divorce process. One of the initial steps in the divorce process is the hiring of an attorney by one party. Lawyers inform their clients of their legal rights, provide legal advice, and file necessary legal documents with the court. They also provide personal counseling, assess the facts, and handle negotiations for their clients (Cavanagh and Rhode 1976). Attorneys are biased advocates who speak for the client's best interest.

Adding no-fault laws has had little effect on the adversarial way in which divorce cases are processed. With or without no-fault laws, an attorney who is hired to represent one spouse cannot ethically give legal advice to the other. Attorneys are advocates for their clients and usually attempt to achieve the optimal settlement possible. Legal ethics require that attorneys represent their clients zealously. This encourages attorneys to take extreme positions that are sometimes unnecessarily divisive and aggravate relations between spouses (Cavanagh and Rhode, 1976; Coogler 1977; Spanier and Casto 1979; Weiss 1975).

Current divorce policy in the United States may be summarized as follows:

1. A civil judge must review every divorce case to insure that the rights of the weak and innocent are protected. Judges may overrule agreements made between divorcing parties if they regard the decisions as unconscionable, though they rarely do.
2. If disputes are not resolved by the parties themselves, an adversary proceeding is used to settle the differences. A judge hears evidence presented by an advocate for each party and then resolves the disputes by court order. This **adversary system** extends far beyond the courtroom and affects bargaining all during the divorce process (Mnookin and Kornhauser 1979).

There are two major assumptions underlying this policy. First, divorcing couples cannot be trusted to make decisions regarding their money and children by themselves. Hence, a judge must review *all* divorce agreements to insure that they are legal and fair. Second, it is assumed that in a "contest between two opponents justice will somehow emerge" (Eisler 1977:39).

Two major changes that have occurred in divorce policy are the removal of misconduct as a grounds for divorce and the removal of gender as a criterion for settlements. Traditionally one spouse had to formally charge the other with misconduct to obtain a divorce. During the late 1960s and 1970s many states changed the divorce law, and by 1985, all fifty states had passed some type of no-fault divorce statute (Freed and Walker 1986).

No-fault laws removed misconduct as a legal reason for divorce but did not necessarily eliminate it from consideration in awarding alimony and child support. Nevertheless, there is also a trend toward minimizing fault in awarding alimony and child support. The two primary criteria in determining economic payments have become the need of the recipient and the ability of the spouse to pay.

Summary

1. The government affects family life in a wide variety of ways. It regulates formation, functioning, and dissolution of families, yet protects families by limiting the nature and extent of governmental intervention in family life.

2. Governmental policies that affect families are made in three ways. Legislation is passed, executive agencies formulate regulations, and courts make rulings that become precedents. There are two major levels of governmental regulation: federal and state. The *Gault* case illustrates the nature of governmental involvement in family life and the interplay among legislation, executive agencies, and courts, and between state and federal governments.

3. According to the Tenth Amendment of the U.S. Constitution, anything not specifically given to the federal government is left to the states. All laws regulating marriage, reproduction, child rearing, and marital dissolution are state laws and each of the fifty states makes its own.

4. Although the federal government may not legislate family matters, federal influence is exercised through the U.S. Constitution and decisions of the U.S. Supreme Court. In recent years federal influence has been increased by broader interpretation of the equal protection clause of the Fourteenth Amendment in support of family autonomy and individual privacy.

5. Marriage is regulated by licensing but the licensing requirements may not infringe on the fundamental right to marriage. A marriage contract must be voluntarily made by a person who is able to understand the nature of the commitment. Certain types of relationships are prohibited in marriage, specifically bigamous, incestuous, and homosexual relationships.

6. Although marriage is the legally preferred way to begin a family, there are two other ways that legal family relationships are formed. First, couples who live together without being married create a marital like relationship that has legal rights and responsibilities similar to marriage. Second, when a child is born the parent-child unit becomes a family with rights and responsibilities similar to other families.

7. Marriage is entered as a contract but it may not be changed or released upon the consent of the parties as with other contracts. The exact nature of the contract is not specified as in other contracts.

8. State regulation of sexual behavior has become less restrictive in recent years because of new interpretations of the right of privacy.

9. In *Roe v. Wade* the U.S. Supreme Court ruled that the right to privacy includes the right of a woman to decide whether or not to terminate a pregnancy. The court also ruled that the fetus is not a person and therefore is not entitled to constitutional rights. A female can obtain an abortion without the consent of her parents or her husband. Although a woman has the right to obtain an abortion, the government is not obligated to pay for it.

10. Although it is a custom that a woman take the name of her husband at marriage, there is no formal requirement that a wife change her name at marriage as long as she is consistent and nonfraudulent.

11. The husband and wife have a duty to support each other, and both have a legal obligation to support their children. Nevertheless, in practice the responsibility is greater for the husband than the wife. The major criteria for determining support are need and ability to pay.

12. Under the doctrine of *parens patriae*, the government may intervene on the behalf of children if parents are not fulfilling their legal obligations. However, parents have a right to liberty, privacy, and family autonomy as guaranteed by the Ninth and Fourteenth Amendments of the Constitution.

There must be clear and convincing evidence of parental neglect or abuse before the state can intervene and make decisions against the parents' wishes or remove the children from the home.

13. The fact that a judge or social worker feels that conditions may be harmful is not sufficient to remove a child from the home. Parents are not required to send their children to school if they can provide an adequate alternative. The state cannot administer medical treatment against the parents' wishes unless parental refusal creates a life-threatening condition for the child.

14. The right to conceive and raise one's children is one of the basic civil rights according to the U.S. Supreme Court. Law has recognized family relationships not legitimized by a marriage ceremony. Fathers have rights equal to mothers and the parent-child relationship is constitutionally protected.

15. Forty-two percent of households in the United States receive some type of cash transfer from the government. Income-maintenance payments account for more than 10 percent of household income in the United States. These transfers reduce the incidence of poverty substantially; over 12 percent of American families are removed from poverty by income transfers. The major limitation of income transfers is that they create a disincentive to work.

16. The state regulates marital dissolution through the court system. A couple must formally file for a divorce with the court, and a judge must review the case and approve of it before a divorce is granted. The functions of the court are to legally dissolve the marriage, resolve disputes between the divorcing parties, and protect the weak and innocent, particularly the children. Divorce is a legal process that uses the adversary system. Two major changes in divorce policy in recent years have been adding no-fault grounds for divorce and making the statutes more gender neutral.

Important Terms

- *Addington v. Texas*
- adversary system
- beyond a reasonable doubt
- *Boddie v. Connecticut*
- case law
- clear and convincing evidence
- divorce complaint
- due process
- equal protection clause
- executive regulation
- family autonomy
- Fourteenth Amendment
- income maintenance
- *In re Gault*
- legislation
- marriage contract
- *Marvin v. Marvin*
- neglect
- *parens patriae*
- *Parham v. J. R.*
- *Planned Parenthood v. Danforth*
- precedents
- preponderance of evidence
- right of privacy
- *Roe v. Wade*
- *Santosky v. Kramer*
- *Stanley v. Illinois*
- statute
- Tenth Amendment
- *Wisconsin v. Yoder*
- *Zablocki v. Redhail*

Questions for Discussion

1. What are the due process rights guaranteed by the Fourteenth Amendment?
2. What are the three ways laws are formulated? Give an example of each way.
3. Why are most laws that affect families state laws?
4. How does the federal government influence family laws when it cannot legislate in that area?
5. What constitutes a valid marriage? Under what conditions is a marriage considered to be void?
6. In addition to legal marriage, how are family relationships formed?
7. How is marriage a contract? In what ways is marriage a status?
8. A contract lawyer once said, "Marriage is the ultimate in consumer fraud." What do you think was the basis for his statement?
9. What is the constitutional basis for the abortion decisions of the U.S. Supreme Court?
10. Is the fetus a legal person?
11. Must a minor obtain parental approval to obtain an abortion?
12. Must a wife who wants a abortion obtain the approval of her husband?
13. Are state governments obligated to pay for abortions?
14. Must a woman assume the name of her husband at marriage?
15. What are the major criteria used to determine child and spousal support?
16. Does a woman have a legal obligation to support her husband? Does she have a legal obligation to support her children?
17. What is the legal standard used to make decisions in criminal trials?
18. What is the legal standard used to make decisions in civil actions? Is there more than one standard used? If so, what is each standard and under what conditions is each used?
19. Under what conditions can a child be removed from the custody of its parents?
20. Under what conditions can parents be compelled to provide medical care for their child?
21. Are parents required to send a child to school? What obligations do parents have regarding the education of their children?
22. Under what conditions can parents institutionalize their children against their children's will?
23. How have custody laws discriminated against fathers?
24. How common is income maintenance?
25. Review the benefits and costs of income maintenance.
26. Why do states regulate the dissolution of marriages?
27. What are the purposes of divorce courts?
28. Describe the legal process of marital dissolution.

Recommended Reading

BRIELAND, D., and J. A LEMON. 1985. *Social work and the law* 2d ed. St. Paul: West Publishing.

WALLACH, H. C. 1981. Approaches to child and family policy. Boulder, CO: Westview.

References

CAVANAGH, R. C., and D. L. RHODE. 1976. The unauthorized practice of law and pro se divorce: An empirical analysis. *Yale Law Journal* 86:103–184.

COOGLER, O. J. 1977. Changing the lawyer's role in matrimonial practice. *Conciliation Courts Review* 15(September): 1–12.

DANZIGER, S., and R. PLOTNICK. 1981. Income maintenance programs and the pursuit of income security. *Annals of the American Academy of Political and Social Sciences* 453:130–152.

EISLER, R. T. 1977. *Dissolution: No-fault divorce, marriage, and the future of women.* New York: McGraw Hill.

FREED, D. J., and T. B. WALKER. 1986. Family law in the fifty states: An overview. *Family Law Quarterly* 19:331–441.

HILL, M. G., JR., H. M. ROSSEN, and W. S. SOGG. 1981. *Family law.* 2d ed. St. Paul: West Publishing.

KRAUSE, H. D. 1977. *Family law in a nutshell.* St. Paul: West Publishing.

MACKEY, W. C. 1985. A cross-cultural perspective on perceptions of paternalistic deficiencies in the United States: The myth of the derelict daddy. *Sex Roles* 12:509–533.

MNOOKIN, R. H., and L. KORNHAUSER. 1979. Bargaining in the shadow of the law: The case of divorce. *Yale Law Review* 88:950–997.

SOKOLOSKY, W. 1981. The sick child and the reluctant parent—a framework of judicial intervention. *Journal of Family Law* 20:69–104.

SPANIER, G. B., and R. F. CASTO. 1979. Adjustment to separation and divorce: An analysis of 50 case studies. *Journal of Divorce* 2:241–253.

WEISS, R. S. 1975. *Marital separation.* New York: Basic.

Cases

- Addington v. Texas, 441 U.S. 418, 1979
- Artiss v. Artiss, 8 Family Law Reporter 2313, 1982
- Becker, in re, 92 Cal. App. 3d 796, 156 Cal.Rptr. 48, 1979, Cert. denied, 445 U.S. 949, 1980
- Bilowit v. Dolitsky, 124 N.J. Super. 101, 1973
- Boddie v. Connecticut, 401 U.S. 371, 1971
- Campas v. Campas, 61 misc. 2d 49, 304 N.Y.S. 2d 876, 1969
- Eisentadt v. Baird, 405 U.S. 938, 1972
- Forbush v. Wallace, 341 U.S. 970, 1972
- Gault, in re, 387 U.S. 1, 1967
- Green, in re, 448 Pa. 338, 1972
- Griswold v. Connecticut, 381 U.S. 479, 1965
- H. L. v. Matheson, 101 S.Ct. 1164, 1981
- Harris v. McRae, 448 U.S. 297, 1980
- Hewitt v. Hewitt, 77 Ill. 2d 49, 1979
- Marvin v. Marvin 18 Cal. 3d 660, 1976
- Parham v. J. R., 442 U.S. 584, 1979
- Planned Parenthood v. Danforth, 428 U.S. 52, 1976
- Roe v. Conn, 417 F.Supp. 769, 1976

- Roe v. Doe, 29 N.Y. 2d 188, 324 N.Y.S. 2d 71, 272 N.E. 2d 567, 1971
- Roe v. Wade, 410 U.S. 110, 1973
- Santosky v. Kramer, 455 U.S. 71, 1982
- Stanley v. Illinois, 405 U.S. 645, 1972
- V. L. E., in re, Colorado Supreme Court 5–10–82, 8 Family Law Reporter 2437, 1982
- Wisconsin vs. Yoder, 406 U.S. 205, 1972
- Zablocki v. Redhail, 434 U.S. 374, 1978

CHAPTER 13

Health and the Family

Introduction

Lorraine and Michael decided to have another child. They anxiously awaited the new arrival and the doctor said everything seemed normal. The baby's heartbeat was strong and they expected the child to be healthy, as Debra had been. Their second child was a boy, as they had hoped, but he was not normal physically. His arms and legs were deformed. The child's internal organs were healthy and there was no mental abnormality but their doctor said he might never walk. Several doctors examined their child and they did not know what had caused the problem. One doctor speculated that the baby might have had polio while in the womb.

Michael and Lorraine were stunned, and could hardly believe this was happening to them. It seemed like a bad dream. Lorraine said, "Why me! What have I done to deserve this?"

Their initial shock turned to depression as they contemplated raising a crippled child. How would they pay for medical care? Would Lorraine be able to continue working? How would they face the burden of raising him? They were anxious and uncertain as they began their new role as parents of a handicapped child.

Jerry was a barber and made enough for his family to live comfortably. As an independent business man, he had to work long hours to build his clientele. His efforts paid off, gradually he was able to save a modest amount of money, and he and his wife hoped to purchase a home in the future.

Then his wife Tammy sudddenly took ill. Her joints swelled badly and became so painful that she had to stay in bed most of the time. After seeing several doctors, Tammy was diagnosed as having rheumatoid arthritis. She and Jerry were told there was no known cure, and treatment consisted of giving her drugs to help reduce the pain and swelling.

The drugs helped and she was able to walk around, do her household chores, and watch their two children. However, the disease gradually progressed, her hands and feet became twisted, and she was not able to move around normally. She walked with a limp and was embarrassed because of the deformities in her hands and feet. The medicine thinned her blood and she bruised very easily.

Her husband helped her as much as he could with the household chores, but he had to be gone from 8 A.M. until 6 P.M. at work.

Financially the disease was devastating. They quickly used up their savings for medical bills and medicine. The medical insurance Jerry had purchased would not cover a long-term, chronic illness like rheumatoid arthritis. He had to pay about half of his weekly paycheck for Tammy's medicine.

Stan and Donna had one child. He was doing well as a real estate agent, and she worked as a nurse at a local hospital. One summer Stan became severely depressed. He had difficulty getting up in the morning and just could not pull himself out of it. He finally went to see a psychiatrist who counseled him and gave him some antidepressant drugs. Stan still felt like life was not worth living and was extremely depressed. He was immobilized.

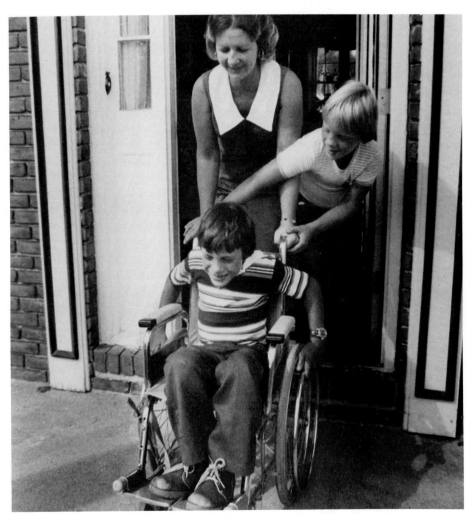

A family with a handicapped child has many adjustments to make, such as helping the child move from one place to another.   *David S. Strickler/The Picture Cube.*

Donna had never faced such a thing and didn't know what to do. She continued to work and was able to support them, but it was difficult financially without Stan's income. Because he was a salesman, if he didn't work he didn't get paid. With the help of drugs and counseling, Stan was able to improve after about a month and was able to start working part-time. He gradually got better and was able to lead a relatively normal life, with the help of medication and counseling.

Six months later, however, he went into another serious depression. The doctor told Donna that even with medication and counseling Stan's depression would probably reoccur periodically for the rest of his life. During the serious episodes Stan would have to quit work for a period, and the doctor would increase the dosage of medication.

It was very hard on Donna and their daughter, Jenny. Sometimes Donna felt strained and overburdened, as she had to care for Jenny and Stan and earn the family income. Occasionally she would resent the fact that Stan was depressed and feel anger toward him. Then she would feel guilty. Many times she would say to herself, "Why me?" She sometimes wondered if his depression was related to their marital relations and how she reacted to Stan.

These three families illustrate some of the ways health affects family life. Lorraine and Michael were never the same after their handicapped son was born. Tammy was physically handicapped by her arthritis, and she and Jerry struggled throughout the remainder of her life because of her illness. Stan's depression made Donna feel deprived and guilty.

In this chapter the interrelationships between family and health are explored. After defining health, there is a discussion of how family structure and interaction affect physical and mental health. In the next two sections we explore drug abuse and sexually transmitted diseases. Then we examine how families cope with illness and conclude by analyzing how medical institutions impact on families.

What Is Health?

It is difficult to define health, although healthy persons are able to function normally both physically and mentally. Normality depends on one's reference group with regard to age and sex. If a sixty-year-old man loses his hair, it is not considered a sign of ill health. Receding hair is a normal part of the aging process for males and a medical doctor will not be consulted. On the other hand, if a woman of any age or a child starts losing hair, people will ask what disease has caused it, and a doctor will be consulted immediately. Various mental and physical traits may be considered healthy for one sex or age group and unhealthy for another.

Health is generally divided into two types: physical and mental. **Physical health** includes the ability of all limbs and organs to perform their proper functions. **Mental health** is the ability to think, be alert, and relate normally to other people.

Diseases that are habitual are called **chronic;** and **acute** disease is very severe. Some types of disease are chronic and not acute, such as mild arthritis.

Other may be acute but not chronic, such as a severe injury that later heals. The rheumatoid arthritis of Tammy was both acute and chronic, because it was severe and lasted over the remainder of her life.

Family Influences on Health

Family structure and interaction influence health in a variety of ways. Eating habits acquired in one's family may contribute to health. Safety practices may minimize accidents in the home, and cleanliness may decrease the chance of members contracting certain communicable diseases. Communication patterns and level of stress may contribute to mental illness among family members. In this section we begin by exploring the relationship between family environment and physical health.

Physical Health

Heart disease is the leading cause of death and disability in the United States (National Center for Health Statistics 1987; Venters 1986). The family environment influences patterns of eating, smoking, and physical activity, which are related to the development of heart disease (Venters 1986).

Many of these patterns are learned in early childhood. For example, parents who eat large quantities of food and who lack interest in physical activity tend to have children who eat excessively and are sedentary. Similarly, individuals are influenced by the eating and leisure patterns of their spouses (Venters 1986).

Being married has been found to be related to lower rates of heart disease. When a heart attack occurs, married people have better survival rates than nonmarried people. This is probably because of the **support** and assistance a spouse provides during the emergency and rehabilitation periods.

Family patterns also affect the susceptibility to other types of diseases. For example, smoking is strongly related to the development of lung cancer and emphysema (Mattson, Pollack, and Cullen 1987). Lack of exercise and excessive eating are related to obesity and high blood pressure (Venters 1986). Consumption of beverages containing caffeine has been found to be associated with the presence and severity of premenstrual syndrome (Rossignol 1985).

Verbrugge (1986) studied how social roles are related to physical health. She looked at a variety of health indicators, including self-rated health status, number of chronic conditions in the past year, number of restricted activity days due to illness, job limitations due to health, and number of health problems.

The best predictor of poor health was having too few roles. Dissatisfaction with one's roles and having very many time constraints were also related to poor health. Contrary to popular opinion, having numerous roles was associated with good health, if time pressures were not excessive. These relationships were similar for men and women, although women tended to have poorer health than men because they were liable to have fewer roles and were more dissatisfied with their main role in life (Verbrugge 1986).

A more complete examination of how women's family roles are related to physical health was recently conducted by Verbrugge and Madans (1985). They

TABLE 13·1   Ranking of Women's Physical Health by
Employment, Marital, and Parental Status

Best	1. Employed, Married, Children
	1. Employed, Married, No Children
	3. Employed, Nonmarried, No Children
	4. Employed, Nonmarried, Children
	5. Nonemployed, Married, Children
	6. Nonemployed, Married, No Children
	7. Nonemployed, Nonmarried, Children
Worst	8. Nonemployed, Nonmarried, No Children

SOURCE: Verbrugge and Madans 1985: 704. Reprinted by
permission of Milbank Memorial Fund © 1985.
NOTE: Top 2 groups tied on health ranking.

found that employed women had better health than nonemployed women, and
that married women were healthier than nonmarried women. No consistent
differences were found between the health of mothers and nonmothers.

When Verbrugge and Madans (1985) looked at the roles of employment, marriage, and parenthood in combination, they found that the best physical health
was among women who had the triple roles of job, spouse, and mother, whereas
women without a job, spouse, or child had the worst health. Nonmarried women
who combined children with a job had more health problems than married
women who combined children and job. Raising children and working without
the help of a husband appeared to aggravate physical health, as shown in Table
13·1.

Verbrugge and Madans (1985) also found that choice of roles was important.
Women who entered roles by choice had better physical health than women
who were forced by circumstance to take on certain roles. Others have found
that the ability to choose roles is related to good physical health (Waldron and
Herold 1986). Unwelcome roles such as marital dissolution, single parenthood,
child disability, and having a sick spouse were associated with poorer physical
health (Hibbard and Pope 1987; Muller 1986). Furthermore, unhappy marriages
and marital disruption tend to be associated with lower functioning of the
immune system, which suggests that they may increase the risk of morbidity
and mortality (Kiecolt-Glazer et al. 1987).

Mental Health

In recent years there has been increased interest in mental health and how
family life influences psychological well-being. In this section we review how
family life is related to mental health, particularly depresssion, which is a
prevalent disorder (Weissman 1987).

As with physical health, mental health may be affected by social and genetic
factors. Although **depression** and other mental disorders may be transmitted
genetically, there is no specific evidence of genetic transmission (Baron et al.
1983; Klerman et al. 1985). It appears that there must be genetic **vulnerability**
plus certain environmental conditions to produce a mental disorder such as
depression (Klerman et al. 1985).

What family factors are related to depression and other mental disorders?
There is evidence that people who feel love and support from their family tend

to suffer less depression and psychopathology (Procidano and Heller 1983). Family support may not lessen the stress, but it acts as a buffer or cushion that decreases the impact of stress (Clark 1983; Holahan and Moos, 1985, 1986; Levitt, Weber, and Clark 1986; Mitchell, Cronkite, and Moos 1983; Wethington and Kessler 1986).

As noted in Chapter 6, individuals in intimate, satisfying marriages tend to experience less depression than individuals who are not married, or who are divorced or in unhappy marriages (Haring-Hidore et al. 1985; Kessler and Essex 1982; Kiecolt-Glazer et al. 1987; Markides and Farrell 1985; Pearlin and Johnson 1977; Weissman 1987). On the other hand, high disagreement, perceptions of inequity, and poor communication in marriage tend to be positively associated with depression and neuroticism (D'Arcy and Siddique 1985; Keith and Schafer 1987; Moffit, Eisen, and Goldney 1985; Schafer 1985). Women who have separated or divorced also tend to have higher rates of problem drinking than other women (Wilsnack and Cheloha 1987).

Similar to research on physical health, research on mental health shows that the psychological benefits of occupying multiple roles outweigh the strains, if the demands are not excessive (Aneshensel, Ferrichs, and Clark 1981; Froberg, Gjerdingen, and Preston 1986). Having few role demands also is related to problem drinking among women (Wilsnack and Cheloha 1987). However, the benefits of carrying both family and work roles appear to be more beneficial for men than women because women carry a much heavier load than men at home. Cleary and Mechanic (1983) found that the demands of having small children in the household were psychologically stressful for employed women and counteracted the advantage of employment.

What are some of the family situations that may be related to poor mental health? Stephens (1985) identified four types of relationships that seemed to contribute to depression and suicide attempts among the fifty women she studied. All of the women had feelings of low self-worth and depression, and the suicide attempt was a desperate effort to escape or change the situation.

The first type of relationship was termed **smothering love** by Stephens. The women had unrealistic expectations of the love relationship and were constantly disappointed. If they did not receive constant love and admiration, they felt unloved. Any decrease in time or attention was interpreted as emotional abandonment and the women would demand more attention or become depressed.

Sexual infidelity of their partner was another common theme among these women. The infidelity along with the strained relationship seemed to contribute to their depression.

Physical abuse was frequent among several of the women. They faced frequent **battering** from their spouses and their fear and hopelessness seemed to precipitate their suicide attempt.

The final family pattern was called **denial of affection** by Stephens. These women described their partners as uncaring, unemotional, and unwilling to compliment or express affection to them. Their lives seemed lonely and meaningless.

There are many types of family situations that are stressful and may contribute to depression and poor mental health. The findings of Stephens are consistent with the research cited earlier which showed that satisfying, intimate relationships contribute to mental health and help shield individuals from the negative effects of life stresses (Gove, Hughes, and Style 1983; Kessler and Essex 1982).

Up to this point our discussion has focused on husbands and wives. Marital and family relationships also appear to affect the mental health of children. Holahan and Moos (1987) found that the quality of the family environment was related to psychological and physical health problems in children. Kelso et al. (1984) suggested that marital dissatisfaction of parents is related to psychiatric problems in children. The research of Bassuk, Rubin, and Lauriat (1986) indicates that children in disrupted, unstable families tend to develop anxiety, depression, and learning difficulties.

Family therapists have long recognized that poor family communication may be harmful to children's mental health. In particular, they maintain that inconsistent communication is a major factor in the development of schizophrenia because it places children in a double bind in which they cannot comply with two contradictory requests (Bateson et al. 1956). Clark and Cullen (1974) found a positive association between exposure to conflicting communications and the presence of schizophrenia. However, they observed that this association was weak under conditions of strong social support and concluded that social support counters the noxious effects of conflicting communication.

Lopez (1986) has identified four family situations that appear to be related to depression among college students. First, **parent-child overinvolvement** may interfere with the transition to adulthood. When parent and child are enmeshed, adolescents are not able to lessen their emotional dependence on their parents, which makes it difficult for them to become independent and interferes with their transition to adulthood.

A second problematic situation is **parent-child role reversal.** The adolescent becomes a nurturant and supportive caretaker for the parent, while the parent takes on a dependent, childlike role, acts helpless, and seeks reassurance. In this situation the dependency needs of adolescents are not met, and they tend not to express frustration or hostility directly to parents because of their parents' helplessness.

A third situation that may contribute to adolescent depression is an abnormal **parent-child coalition** in which the child sides with one parent against the other. The alliance with one parent becomes stronger than the marital dyad. The child becomes torn between the two parents and sex role and gender-identity conflicts may result.

The final family situation identified by Lopez (1986) was marital conflict and instability. The adjustment of adolescents tends to be lower when their parents have high levels of conflict.

Family Relationships and Drug Abuse

Drug abuse has become an important health issue in our society. Physical and mental health may be impaired by excessive drug use. Adolescent drug use has become a particular concern because many alcoholics and drug addicts begin their use during adolescence (Macdonald 1984).

During the past twenty-five years there have been large increases in the use of illicit drugs such as marijuana and cocaine. During the past five years, however, there have been decreases in the use of several illicit drugs, although cocaine use has increased. A summary of drug use among high school seniors, college students, and young adults in the United States is shown in Table 13·2. The study reported on the percentage of students and young adults who had used various drugs during the previous month. About one fourth of high school seniors had taken marijuana and 6 percent had used cocaine. Almost one in five had experimented with cocaine at one time (Johnston, O'Malley, and Bachman 1987).

College students had usage rates similar to high school seniors. During the previous month 22 percent had taken marijuana and 7 percent had used cocaine (Johnston et al. 1987).

Young adults in their twenties had rates similar to high school seniors. Twenty-two percent had used marijuana and 8 percent had taken cocaine. Forty percent of young adults age 27 reported that they had taken cocaine at least once in their lives (Johnston et al. 1987).

Studies of adolescent drug use have shown that the influence of peers and siblings is more important than the influence of parents. The strongest predictor of adolescent drug use is association with peers who use drugs (Hundleby and Mercer 1987; Kandel and Adler 1982; Needle et al. 1986). However, the family environment has important direct and indirect influences on adolescent drug use.

Parents and siblings influence drug use directly by acting as models. When parents smoke tobacco and drink alcohol their children are more likely to use alcohol, marijuana, and other drugs (Byram and Fly 1984; Fawzy, Coombs, and Gerber 1983; Hundleby and Mercer 1987; Kandel and Adler 1982; Needle et al. 1986; Tec 1970).

Parents influence drug use indirectly through their behavior and attitudes. When parents drink alcohol, their children are likely to choose friends who drink alcohol, and having friends who drink alcohol is related to marijuana experimentation and use (Kandel and Adler 1982). Parental influence is also indirect through educational and religious influences. The religious values and educational aspirations of adolescents are influenced by their parent's attitudes

TABLE 13·2 Percentage of High School Students, College Students, and Young Adults Who Reported Use of Various Drugs During Past Month, United States (1986)

	High School Seniors	College Students	Young Adults
Alcohol	65	80	75
Cigarettes	30	22	31
Marijuana	23	22	22
Amphetamines	6	4	4
Barbiturates	2	0	1
Tranquilizers	2	1	2
Cocaine	6	7	8
Heroin	0	0	0
LSD	2	1	1

SOURCE: Johnston et al. 1987: 29, 180, 207.
NOTE: Rounded to nearest whole percentage.

and values. Adolescent values and educational aspirations affect the choice of friends (Marcos, Bahr, and Johnson 1986).

One of the most important family influences on drug use is parental support. In Chapter 9 parental support was found to be strongly related to social competence in children. The research on drug abuse shows that when parents are warm and supportive, adolescents are much less likely to use illicit drugs (Barnes, Farrell, and Cairns, 1986; Byram and Fly 1984; Dembo et al. 1986; Fawzy et al. 1983; Harbin and Maziar 1975; Hundleby and Mercer 1987; Marcos et al. 1986; Streit and Oliver 1972; Tec 1970). Conversely, when there is hostile conflict and alienation between adolescents and their parents, substance abuse tends to be more common (Thompson and Wilsnack 1987).

In Chapter 9 it was noted that **monitoring** the child's whereabouts played a central role in delinquency (Hirschi 1983; Patterson and Stouthamer-Loeber 1984). When parents monitor their children's behavior and are aware of their activities, their children are much less likely to use illicit drugs such as marijuana and cocaine (Bahr 1988).

In summary, existing research shows that to decrease the probability of adolescent drug use, parents need to be warm and supportive, monitor their children's behavior, have enjoyable activities as a family, and not drink alcohol or take drugs themselves. Peer influences are powerful, but choice of peers are influenced by one's family. Furthermore, the effect of peers may be less when parental support and monitoring are high.

Sexually Transmitted Diseases

There is growing concern about sexually transmitted diseases, particularly **AIDS** (Acquired Immune Deficiency Syndrome). They have become important health and family issues, and therefore are discussed briefly here.

In prior decades syphilis and gonorrhea assumed major importance among venereal diseases. Recently a new generation of sexually transmitted diseases has surfaced as treatment of gonorrhea and syphilis has improved. For a review of the nature, incidence, and treatment of various sexually transmitted diseases, see DeFries, Friedman, and Corn (1985) and Rinear (1986).

AIDS has become the most feared of the sexually transmitted diseases because of its extremely high death rate and increasing prevalence. It is estimated that 1.5 million persons in the United States are infected with the AIDS virus (Hopkins 1987). Initial research indicates that 40 percent of those infected with the virus will develop the disease (Rinear 1986). Near the end of 1987 more than 40,000 people in the United States had actually been diagnosed as having AIDS (Hopkins 1987; Koblinsky, Preston, and Vaughn 1987). Individuals who carry the virus but have no symptoms of the disease are able to transmit the disease to others (Hopkins 1987). Predictions are that 270,000 Americans will develop AIDS by 1991 (Koblinsky et al. 1987). In 1986 the World Health Organization estimated that between 5 and 10 million people in the world carried the AIDS virus, and they projected that by 1990 at least fifty million people would be infected (Heise 1988).

Many health authorities consider AIDS to be the number one health problem in America. The number of reported cases doubles every seven to nine months, there is no vaccine or cure, and virtually all who acquire the disease die within three years (Rinear 1986). It was first thought to be a gay disease because more than 70 percent of the cases were among homosexual or bisexual men (Laurence 1985). However, in Africa there are equal numbers of women and men with AIDS and heterosexual transmission of AIDS is increasing rapidly in the United States (Koblinsky et al. 1987; Rinear 1986).

The primary way AIDS is transmitted is through sexual contact or sharing intravenous drug needles and syringes. An infected woman may also pass the virus to her child, before birth or through her breast milk, and it may be passed in blood transfusions. There is no evidence that the AIDS virus may be transferred by casual contact with people carrying the virus (Koblinsky et al. 1987).

Because there is no cure or effective treatment, prevention is the only way to combat the disease. The three known ways to prevent AIDS, herpes, and other sexually transmitted diseases are sexually monogamy with an uninfected person, use of condoms, or sexual abstinence (Hopkins, 1987; Koblinsky 1987).

About half of all sexually transmitted diseases are contracted by people under age 25. Many sexually active young persons use no form of contraception. Therefore, transmission of AIDS among teenagers and young adults is likely to increase substantially. The only way to prevent this is through appropriate education by parents, schools, and the medical establishment.

Testing of high risk individuals or of people in high risk areas is a strategy that may also be helpful in controlling AIDS. For example, in one New York hospital 2.4 percent of women seen in a prenatal clinic tested positively for

Since there is no cure or effective treatment for AIDS, prevention is the only known way to combat the disease. Here children are taught how to prevent AIDS and other sexually-transmitted diseases.   *Doug Menuez/Picture Group.*

the AIDS virus. Appropriate testing and counseling would benefit the women, their husbands, and their unborn children (Hopkins 1987).

Coping with Illness

An illness is a **stressor** that families attempt to cope with. There has been a large amount of research on different types of stressors and how families react to them (Boss 1987; Hansen and Johnson 1979; Hill and Hansen 1964). An illness is an unexpected event that families did not choose. The amount of stress a family faces depends on the type of stressor, how families define the stressor, and the resources available to respond to the stressor.

There are numerous types of illnesses that families face and have to react to. Some are chronic but relatively minor and families adjust to them easily. Others are acute and strain families to the limit, but pass with time. And some illnesses are acute and chronic, such as AIDS and cancer. In this section we will discuss four major health stressors and how families react to them: (1) heart attack, (2) cancer, (3) birth of handicapped child, (4) mental illness.

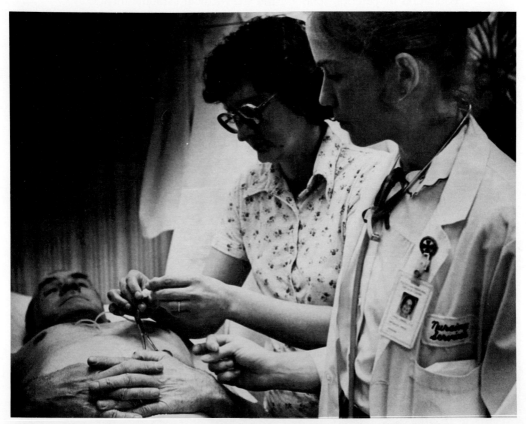

Family members play an important role in health care. This husband is receiving a blood thinner through a catheter in his chest, while his wife gets instruction from the nurse in how to clean the tube and care for the skin at home. *Tom Kelly.*

Heart Attack

Ben is fifty years old and is a foreman at a steel mill. He has worked there for 25 years. He is married to Kelli and they have three children, ages 15, 18, and 20. He is not overweight and has been in excellent health all of his life.

While at work he suddenly feels severe chest pains and is rushed to the hospital. He has suffered a severe heart attack. He stays in the hospital for two weeks and gradually improves. After coming home the doctor starts him on a walking program and he gradually works his way up to three miles a day. Ben is also put on a strict low cholesterol diet. After six weeks he feels much better and is able to start work again. The experience has been difficult for the entire family but things have gradually improved and are near normal now that Ben is back to work.

When the heart attack occurred, Kelli and the children did not know if Ben was going to live or die. When he lived they wondered if he would be able to recover and live a normal life again. His wife had to take over many of the responsibilities that he had assumed. She worried about finances, although they did have a good insurance plan through the steel company. Luckily, Ben was able to recover and they are now leading a normal life.

As noted earlier in this chapter, heart disease is the leading cause of death and disability in the United States. It accounts for almost 40 percent of all deaths. About 1.3 million persons suffer heart attacks each year and half survive the attacks (Dhooper 1983).

Dhooper (1983) studied forty families of patients who had had their first heart attack. The sample was restricted to patients under sixty years of age who had no history of previous major illness. Data were collected at three points in time, during the hospitalization, a month after discharge from the hospital, and three months later. Four major areas of family functioning were examined: (1) emotional health, (2) children, (3) household management, and (4) finances.

The immediate reaction to the heart attack was shock, disbelief, and fear that the spouse would die. The stress of the heart attack produced sleeplessness, loss of appetite, and headaches among the spouses. The children responded by feeling anxious, crying, and missing the sick parent. Children between the ages of 6 and 12 were the most adversely affected by the heart attack. After the spouse returned home the stress and anxiety decreased for both spouses and children. After the patient had been home three months most families reported that things were back to normal. Some anxiety remained over the realization that the heart had been permanently damaged by the attack (Dhooper 1983).

The heart attack disrupted the management of the household in a variety of ways. Regular mealtimes were suspended and many household chores were postponed. Sleeping hours changed for some and social activities and church attendance were often suspended. However, the disruption of the household tended to be temporary. Most of the families said their household was back to normal by three months after the patient came home.

Preschoolers were too young to understand the seriousness of the heart attack. Teenagers were upset but most continued going to school and participating in social activities. By the third month, most families reported that their children's lives were back to normal. Methods of coping consisted of taking the child to see the sick parent, explaining the condition and treatment, and encouraging the children to continue in their activities.

There was no financial strain when the heart attack occurred, although some worried about later financial stress. Less than one half of the families studied by Dhooper (1983) had comprehensive medical insurance. When the patient came home from the hospital many families started feeling financial pressure. Prescribed medicines for the patient were a new expense, and in half of the families the patient's income had stopped or been drastically reduced. By the three-month interview over a third of the families still felt financial strain. Even when the patient had returned to work, debts created by the illness were a serious problem for some. To cope with the financial stress, families used savings, reduced everyday expenses, sought help from relatives, and delayed paying bills.

In summary, the heart attack was emotionally stressful for family members, but the stress tended to decrease with time. By three months emotional strain had decreased and the household was back to normal for most families. Many families experienced financial strain, and unlike the other stresses, financial problems increased with time. The families with inadequate medical insurance were most vulnerable financially. There was little financial help received from relatives or friends and government agencies were unresponsive. Most families did not meet government eligibility criteria and when they did, government procedures were too slow to be helpful (Dhooper 1983).

Cancer

Cancer is the second leading cause of death in the United States, and rates have been increasing in recent years (National Center of Health Statistics 1987). There are many different types of cancer, and the impact on the family depends on the nature of the disease. The following example illustrates how cancer affected a family from the perspective of a young boy.

Tim was 12 when it was discovered that his brother Tom, age 10, had cancer. As the disease progressed, the family situation changed dramatically. Tim and his older sister Jane had to take on much more responsibility for the running of the household. They started doing wash, cooking, and cleaning. Tim missed being able to play with his brother Tom, who was in the hospital. Tim also missed his mother and wished he would be able to see her more. She spent long hours at the hospital with Tom.

Tim loved his brother and felt bad that he could no longer play with him. At the same time, Tim felt jealous because Tom got all of his mother's attention while Tim got to see so little of her. Tim longed to have his mother give him some personal attention. Yet, he felt guilty for feeling jealous of his sick brother. Although it was very hard having his brother get sick, it did seem to increase family unity in some ways.

The research of Barbarin, Hughes, and Chesler (1985) and Fife, Norton, and Groom (1987) supports the experience reported by Tim. In a study of thirty-two couples that had a child with cancer, Barbarin et al. (1985) reported that family cohesiveness was strengthened by the experience. The spouse was the most important source of support for adults. Husbands felt more support if their wives were available at home rather than always being at the hospital. Wives felt more support if their husbands were involved in the care of the sick child. Although family cohesion increased after the onset of cancer, the continual struggle to cope with the disease had a negative impact on family cohesion. As the number of hospitalizations increased, perceptions of spousal support and marital satisfaction decreased.

Fife et al. (1987) studied thirty-four families for a year after leukemia was diagnosed in a child. Families with high cohesion and support before diagnosis of leukemia were able to maintain that cohesion over time. However, families that had problems before the diagnosis had difficulty coping with the stress of the disease and experienced a decrease in cohesion and support. Family cohesion appeared to be a resource that enabled families to cope with the stress of cancer.

Fife et al. (1987) also observed that the four to six months after diagnosis appeared to be a critical period. As the reality of the disease set in along with the fatigue of treatment, marital satisfaction began to decline. By the end of a year, there was a decline in marital satisfaction of both mothers and fathers as well as an increase in the incidence of depression.

Lewis (1986) has observed that the onset of cancer results in considerable emotional strain among family members. They have feelings of fear, helplessness, uncertainty, anger, and injustice. Sleep is often disrupted and many people express a need for emotional support.

Household roles usually must be altered. Lewis (1986) reported that about one third of families affirmed that their roles had changed because of the illness. Parenting time for well children may diminish, companionate time with spouse may decrease, and household chores are often reallocated. Fife et al. (1987) found that families with school-aged children were particularly vulnerable to stresses related to changing family roles.

Many families experience financial stress, although this depends on insurance benefits. Patients as well as other family members express concern over money.

Lewis (1986) identified three other issues that surface as a result of the illness. First, many families become concerned with the meaning of life, what happens after death, and the personal vulnerability of each family member. Second, physical intimacy becomes a concern. Feelings of love and affection among patients may tend to increase. In one study almost half of the patients reported an increased desire for physical closeness since the illness, whereas about one third said they had a decreased desire for sexual activity (Lewis 1986). Third, support services for families with cancer often were seen as inadequate. Many families expressed a need for personal counseling but were unaware of such a service.

The stress associated with cancer is similar in many ways to the stress associated with a heart attack. Emotional reactions of fear, helplessness, and uncertainty occur. Household roles must be reallocated, and financial strain is often present. However, a heart attack is often sudden, followed by death or gradual recovery and return to normalcy. Cancer diagnosis is often followed by a progressive deterioration over months or years, and a return to normalcy may not occur. The length of the stress created by cancer appears to cause a decrease in marital satisfaction and family cohesiveness (Barbarin et al. 1985; Fife et al. 1987).

Handicapped Child

Earlier in this chapter we gave an example of how the birth of a handicapped child affected a family. The effect depends, of course, on the nature of the handicap. Leifson (1979) studied forty-seven families with handicapped children. She interviewed them within two weeks after the birth of the child and again six months later. She found that the couples' initial reactions were shock, grief, guilt, and depression. Some could not believe it and said, "What did I do wrong?" Others expressed anger and resentment.

Leifson (1979) examined what family characteristics were related to the functioning of the couples. First, she found that family cohesion was important. Couples who had affectionate, satisfying marriages were able to adjust to the crisis and could function better as a couple. A second variable related to couple functioning was adaptability. Couples that were flexible and able to adjust their roles were doing better six months after the birth than couples who were fairly rigid.

Age, education, and insurance also were found to be related to functioning (Leifson 1979). Couples who were older had a harder time adjusting to the handicapped child. Individuals with more education were able to adjust more easily than individuals with less education. Finally, having adequate insurance eased the financial and emotional stress associated with the birth of a handicapped child.

Mental Illness

There has been little research on how various types of mental illness affect family interaction. The material for this section is taken from the work of Gubman and Tessler (1987) on how mental illness impacts on families.

In recent years there has been a trend away from institutionalizing patients with mental problems. Legally there has been a move toward placing people in the least restrictive alternative, which is usually living with the family rather than in an institution. About two thirds of psychiatric patients who are discharged from hospitals return to family residences (Gubman and Tessler 1987).

How does a mentally ill family member impact on other family members? Often family members feel helpless and guilty. They feel helpless because they don't know what to do to cope with the situation. They feel guilty for resenting the mentally ill member and the burden, and they may wonder if they contributed to the illness in some way.

One half to three fourths of families perceive the care of a mentally ill member to be burdensome. There is added financial responsibility for care and medicine. The responsibility may require some family members to miss work and may constrain social and leisure activities. Family roles may have to be reallocated. Ill parents may not be able to support their families materially or do household chores. Companionship and attention among well family members may be reduced. The presence of the patient may increase family conflict and disturb existing patterns (Gubman and Tessler 1987).

The strain of a mentally ill family member may be emotionally stressful on other family members, particularly the primary caretaker. For example, Gubman and Tessler (1987) reported that mothers with a mentally disturbed child had more depression and anxiety than a comparable group of mothers without a mentally disturbed child. As contact with the mentally ill family member increases, the amount of stress experienced by family members also tends to increase.

Family bonds are remarkably stable in the face of mental illness. However, if the illness becomes perceived as chronic with little hope of improvement, family bonds may tend to break down (Gubman and Tessler 1987).

Conclusion

General reactions appear to be similar across different illnesses. Family members react to heart disease, cancer, a handicapped child, and mental illness with shock, guilt, depression, and helplessness. The effect of a particular illness depends on its severity, how family members define it, and the family resources. Key **coping resources** are **family cohesiveness, adaptibility,** money, and kin support. Long-term illnesses such as cancer and mental illness may strain families to the limit and decrease cohesiveness and marital quality of even the most well-adjusted families.

McCubbin et al. (1980) have suggested that a family's ability to respond to a crisis such as illness depends on three types of resources. The first type are **personal resources** such as money, education, physical health, problem-solving skills, and self-esteem. Second, there are **family system resources** such as adaptability, cohesiveness, shared power, and group problem-solving ability. Finally, there is **social support,** which is emotional and physical support from the nuclear family, kin, neighbors, friends, and institutions such as hospitals.

Families and Health Care Institutions

Families interact with and respond to doctors, nurses, social workers, hospital administrators, and insurance companies. For health care to be optimum, families and the medical establishment must work together. Too often the medical institutions do not take into account the needs of families in their treatment.

Among families in which a member had a heart attack, a great majority did not receive any help from social service agencies, even though most of the hospitals have social service departments. Most families are unaware of the services available to them (Dhooper 1983). Lewis (1986) observed that cancer treatment is not synchronized with the needs of families, which creates additional stress for families in an already stressful situation. Family members often express a need for emotional support, counseling, and home care equipment, yet are unaware of available services. Apparently, the different aspects of the medical establishment are not coordinated, and doctors and nurses do not refer families to appropriate support services.

Leifson (1979) asked parents of handicapped children what doctors and nurses could have done to help. The parents wished the doctors and nurses would have talked to them plainly and directly. They wanted to know what their child's condition was and what future prospects were. Doctors tended not to take the time to even minimally inform the parents of their child's medical condition. When they did talk to the parents, they were vague or used medical jargon rather than explaining the situation clearly. The parents also wanted the nurses and doctors to listen to their questions and be more sensitive to their feelings. Finally, they wished the nurses could have set up a program to help them or at least referred them to appropriate agencies.

Gubman and Tessler (1987) reported that families can be a great aid in the treatment of mental illness if they are taken into account. They reported on two studies in which family members took classes that explained the possible causes of schizophrenia and what family members could do to help the ill member. Group sessions were held weekly to help the family members. The mental problems among a control group of individuals whose families had not participated in the classes were much higher than among individuals whose families had taken the classes.

The research suggests that the medical establishment needs to take a family perspective when treating illness. If they do, their treatments would be much more effective. Families need to be seen as partners in health care rather than being ignored. Existing counseling services need to be upgraded to help families with various options during the course of long-term illnesses such as cancer, AIDS, and mental illness.

Summary

1. Family patterns of eating, exercise, and lifestyle are related to the physical health or family members.
2. Having numerous roles is associated with good physical health, whereas having too few roles is associated with poor physical health. Having undesirable, dissatisfying roles is also associated with poor physical health.
3. Employment and marriage are associated with good physical health.
4. Employed persons who are parents have better physical health if they are married rather than unmarried.
5. Married persons suffer less depression and psychopathology than unmarried persons.
6. The intimacy of a satisfying marriage is the factor that insulates married persons against stress. Unhappily married persons have levels of depression comparable to unmarried persons, whereas happily married persons have much less depression.
7. Individuals who play multiple roles have less depression than persons with few roles. However, being employed and raising small children is stressful for women.
8. Smothering love, infidelity, physical abuse, and denial of affection are family patterns related to depression.
9. When children regularly receive contradictory messages, they have a greater-than-average susceptibility to schizophrenia. However, strong support can counteract some of the harmful effects of contradictory messages.

10. Depression among adolescents is more likely if in their family of orientation they are exposed to (a) parental overinvolvement, (b) parent-child role reversal, (c) abnormal parent-child coalition, or (d) serious marital conflict.

11. Drug abuse is common among adolescents and young adults in the United States. About one fourth of adolescents and young adults had taken marijuana during the previous month in one study. One in five high school seniors has tried cocaine, and 40 percent of young adults have taken cocaine.

12. Peers have the strongest influence on adolescent drug use.

13. Adolescents whose parents are highly supportive and monitor their activities are less likely to take illicit drugs. Parents who drink alcohol are somewhat more likely than nondrinkers to have adolescents who take illicit drugs.

14. Family members tend to react to diseases such as heart disease, cancer, a handicapped child, and mental illness with shock, disbelief, guilt, depression, and helplessness. Illness often disrupts household routines and creates emotional and financial stress.

15. The effect of a given illness depends on its severity, how family members define it, and family resources. Key coping resources are family cohesiveness, flexibility, marital satisfaction, and support from kin and community.

16. The continued stress of long-term illnesses such as cancer and mental illness tends to decrease family cohesiveness and marital satisfaction.

17. In the United States the health care system has not treated diseases from a family perspective or coordinated support services for families. Treatment appears to be more effective if it is administered from a family system perspective.

Important Terms

- acute
- adaptability
- AIDS
- battering
- chronic
- coping resources
- denial of affection
- depression
- drug abuse
- family cohesiveness
- family system resources
- mental health
- monitoring
- parent-child coalition
- parent-child overinvolvement
- parent-child role reversal
- personal resources
- physical health
- smothering love
- social support
- stressor
- support
- vulnerability

Questions for Discussion

1. Give some examples of acute and chronic illnesses.
2. What is mental health? What is mental illness? How is mental illness related to the norms of a group or society?

3. How is family structure related to physical health? How is family inter-action related to physical health?
4. How are number and desirability of roles related to physical health?
5. How and why are employment, marital status, and parenthood associated with physical health?
6. Explain how genetics may affect mental health. How might the social environment influence mental health?
7. How and why is marital status related to mental health? Do married people experience less stress than unmarried people?
8. How are number and desirability of roles related to mental health?
9. What types of family environments are related to poor mental health?
10. How is family communication related to mental health?
11. In what ways do parents influence the probability that their children will take illicit drugs?
12. How is the spread of AIDS affecting family relationships?
13. How may families help in the prevention and treatment of AIDS?
14. Compare the effects of heart disease, cancer, a handicapped child, and mental illness on families. In what ways do families react to them similarly? What are some unique stresses of each situation?
15. What are major coping resources of families for illness? What types of families have most difficulty coping with illness?
16. What would you suggest that families do to prepare for the possibility of a major illness such as cancer or heart attack?
17. In what ways do health care institutions interfere with the abilities of families to cope with illness? What could be done to improve the ability of health care institutions to support families?

Recommended Reading

BARBARIN, O. A., D. HUGHES, and M. A. CHESLER. 1985. Stress, coping, and marital functioning among parents of children with cancer. *Journal of Marriage and the Family* 47:473–480.

DHOOPER, S. S. 1983. Family coping with the crisis of heart attack. *Social Work in Health Care* 9:15–31.

GUBMAN, G. D., and R. C. TESSLER. 1987. The impact of mental illness on families: Concepts and priorities. *Journal of Family Issues* 8:226–245.

KOBLINSKY, S. A., J. E. PETERSON, and G. G. VAUGHN. 1987. Educating adolescents about AIDS. *Journal of Home Economics* 79 (No. 4):33–38.

References

ANESHENSEL, C. S., R. R. FRERICHS, and V. A. CLARK. 1981. Family roles and sex differences in depression. *Journal of Health and Social Behavior* 22:379–393.

BAHR, S. J. 1988. *Family relationships and adolescent drug use.* Paper presented at Pacific Sociological Association meeting, Las Vegas, NV, April 8.

BARBARIN, O. A., D. HUGHES, and M. A. CHESLER. 1985. Stress, coping, and marital functioning among parents of children with cancer. *Journal of Marriage and the Family* 47:473–480.

BARNES, G. M., M. P. FARRELL, and A. CAIRNS. 1986. Parental socialization factors and adolescent drinking behaviors. *Journal of Marriage and the Family* 48:27–36.

BARON, M., R. GRUEN, L. ASNIS, and J. KANE. 1983. Familial relatedness of schizophrenia and schizotypal states. *American Journal of Psychiatry* 140(11):1437–1442.

BASSUK, E. L., L. RUBIN, and A. S. LAURIAT. 1986. Characteristics of sheltered homeless families. *American Journal of Public Health* 76(9):1097–1101.

BATESON, G., D. JACKSON, J. HALEY, and J. WEAKLAND. 1956. Toward a theory of schizophrenia. *Behavioral Science* 1:251–264.

BOSS, P. 1987. Family stress. In *Handbook of marriage and the family,* ed. M. B. Sussman and S. K. Steinmetz, 695–723. New York: Plenum.

BYRAM, O. W., and J. W. FLY. 1984. Family structure, race and adolescents' alcohol use: A research note. *American Journal of Drug Alcohol Abuse* 10(3):467–478.

CLARK, A. W. 1983. The relationship between family participation and health. *Journal of Occupational Behaviour* 4:237–239.

CLARK, A. W., and W. S. CULLEN. 1974. Social support. A counter to pathogenic communication. *Interpersonal Development* 5:50–59.

CLEARY, P. D., and D. MECHANIC. 1983. Sex differences in psychological distress among married people. *Journal of Health and Social Behavior* 24:111–121.

D'ARCY, C., and C. M. SIDDIQUE. 1985. Marital status and psychological well-being: A cross-national comparative analysis. *International Journal of Comparative Sociology* 26(3–4):149–166.

DEFRIES, Z., R. C. FRIEDMAN, and R. CORN, eds. 1985. *Sexuality: New perspectives.* Westport, CT: Greenwood Press.

DEMBO, R., G. GRANDON, L. LA VOIE, J. SCHMEIDLER, and W. BURGOS. 1986. Parents and drugs revisited: Some further evidence in support of social learning theory. *Criminology* 24(1):85–104.

DHOOPER, S. S. 1983. Family coping with the crisis of heart attack. *Social Work in Health Care* 9(1):15–31.

FAWZY, F. I., R. H. COOMBS, and G. GERBER. 1983. Generational continuity in the use of substances: The impact of parental substance use on adolescent substance use. *Addictive Behaviors* 8:109–114.

FIFE, B., J. NORTON, and G. GROOM. 1987. The family's adaption to childhood leukemia. *Social Science Medicine* 24(2):149–168.

FROBERG, D., D. GJERDINGEN, and M. PRESTON. 1986. Multiple roles and women's mental and physical health: What have we learned? *Women & Health* 11(2):79–95.

GOVE, W. R., M. HUGHES, and C. B. STYLE. 1983. Does marriage have positive effects on the psychological well-being of the individual? *Journal of Health and Social Behavior* 24:122–131.

GUBMAN, G. D., and R. C. TESSLER. 1987. The impact of mental illness on families. *Journal of Family Issues* 8(2):226–245.

HANSEN, D. A., and V. A. JOHNSON. 1979. Rethinking family stress theory: Definitional aspects. In *Contemporary theories about the family,* ed. W. R. Burr, R. Hill, F. I. Nye, and I. L. Reiss, vol. 1, 582–603. New York: Free Press.

HARBIN, H. T., and H. M. MAZIAR. 1975. The families of drug abusers: A literature review. *Family Process* 14:411–431.

HARING-HIDORE, M., W. A. STOCK, M. A. OKUN, and R. A. WITTER. 1985. Marital status and subjective well-being: A research synthesis. *Journal of Marriage and the Family* 47:947–953.

HEISE, L. 1988. AIDS: New threat to the third world. *World Watch* 1 (No. 1):19–27.

HIBBARD, J. H., and C. R. POPE. 1987. Employment characteristics and health status among men and women. *Women and Health* 12:85–101.

HILL, R., and D. A. HANSEN. 1964. Families under stress. In *Handbook of marriage and the family,* ed. H. T. Christensen, 782–819. Chicago: Rand McNally.

HIRSCHI, T. 1983. Crime and the family. In *Crime and public policy,* ed. J. Q. Wilson, 53–68. San Francisco: Institute for Contemporary Studies.

HOLAHAN, C. J., and R. H. MOOS. 1985. Life stress and health: Personality, coping, and family support in stress resistance. *Journal of Personality and Social Psychology* 49(3):739–747.

HOLAHAN, C. J., and R. H. MOOS. 1986. Personality, coping, and family resources in stress resistance: A longitudinal analysis. *Journal of Personality and Social Psychology* 51(2):389–395.

HOLAHAN, C. J., and R. H. MOOS. 1987. Risk, resistance, and psychological distress: A longitudinal analysis with adults and children. *Journal of Abnormal Psychology* 96(1):3–13.

HOPKINS, D. R. 1987. Public health measures for prevention and control of AIDS. *Public Health Reports* 102:463–467.

HUNDLEBY, J. D., and G. W. MERCER. 1987. Family and friends as social environments and their relationship to young adolescents' use of alcohol, tobacco, and marijuana. *Journal of Marriage and the Family* 49:151–164.

JOHNSTON, L. D., P. M. O'MALLEY, and J. G. BACHMAN. 1987. *National trends in drug use and related factors among American high school students and young adults, 1975–1986.* National Institute on Drug Abuse, DHHS Publication No. (ADM) 87–1535. Washington, DC: U.S. Government Printing Office.

KANDEL, D. B., and I. ADLER. 1982. Socialization into marijuana use among French adolescents: A cross-cultural comparison with the United States. *Journal of Health and Social Behavior.* 23:295–309.

KEITH, P. M., and R. B. SCHAFER. 1987. Relative deprivation, equity/inequity and psychological well-being. *Journal of Family Issues* 8:199–211.

KELSO, J., M. A. STEWART, L. BULLERS, and R. EGINTON. 1984. The measure of marital satisfaction: A questionnaire to screen parents for marital problems. *Child Psychiatry and Human Development* 15(2):86–103.

KESSLER, R. C., and M. ESSEX. 1982. Marital status and depression: The importance of coping resources. *Social Forces* 6:484–507.

KIECOLT-GLASER, J. K., L. D. FISHER, P. OGROCKI, J. C. STOUT, C. E. SPEICHER, and R. GLASER. 1987. Marital quality, marital disruption, and immune function. *Psychosomatic Medicine* 49:13–34.

KLERMAN, G. L., P. W. LAVORI, J. RICE, T. REICH, J. ENDICOTT, N. C. ANDREASEN, M. B. KELLER, and R. M. A. HIRSCHFIELD. 1985. Birth-cohort trends in rates of major depressive disorder among relatives of patients with affective disorder. *Archives of General Psychiatry* 42:689–693.

KOBLINSKY, S. A., J. E. PRESTON, and G. G. VAUGHN. 1987. Educating adolescents about AIDS. *Journal of Home Economics* 79:33–38.

LAURENCE, J. 1985. Acquired immune deficiency syndrome: Interaction of viral, genetic, environmental, and sociological factors. In *Sexuality: New perspectives,* ed. Z. DeFries, R. C. Friedman, and R. Corn, 189–218. Westport, CT: Greenwood.

LEIFSON, J. 1979. *Family crisis: The handicapped child.* Ph.D. diss., Family Studies Program, Brigham Young University, Provo, UT.

LEVITT, M. J., R. A. WEBER, and M. C. CLARK. 1986. Social network relationships as sources of maternal support and well-being. *Developmental Psychology* 22(3):310–316.

LEWIS, F. M. 1986. The impact of cancer on the family: A critical analysis of the research literature. *Patient Education and Counseling* 8:269–289.

LOPEZ, F. G. 1986. Family structure and depression: Implications for the counseling of depressed college students. *Journal of Counseling and Development* 64:508–511.

McCubbin, H. I., C. B. Joy, A. E. Cauble, J. K. Comeau, J. M. Patterson, and R. H. Needle. 1980. Family stress and coping: A decade review. *Journal of Marriage and the Family* 42(4):855–871.

Macdonald, D. I. 1984. *Drugs, drinking, and adolescents.* Chicago: Year Book Medical Publishers.

Marcos, A. C., S. J. Bahr, and R. E. Johnson. 1986. Test of a bonding/association theory of adolescent drug use. *Social Forces* 65(1):135–161.

Markides, K. S., and J. Farrell. 1985. Marital status and depression among Mexican Americans. *Social Psychiatry* 20:86–91.

Mattson, M. E., E. S. Pollack, and J. W. Cullen. 1987. What are the odds that smoking will kill you? *American Journal of Public Health* 77(4):425–431.

Mitchell, R. E., R. C. Cronkite, and R. H. Moos. 1983. Stress, coping, and depression among married couples. *Journal of Abnormal Psychology* 92(4):433–448.

Moffit, P. F., P. Eisen, and R. D. Goldney. 1985. Wives' higher neuroticism scores: Some more relevant factors. *Personality and Individual Differences* 6(1):97–106.

Muller, C. 1986. Health and health care of employed women and homemakers: Family factors. *Women & Health* 11(1):7–26.

National Center for Health Statistics. 1987. *Advance report of final mortality statistics, 1985.* Monthly Vital Statistics Report, Vol. 36, No. 5, Supp. DHHS Pub. No. (PHS) 87–1120. Hyattsville, MD: Public Health Service.

Needle, R., H. McCubbin, M. Wilson, R. Reineck, A. Lazar, and H. Mederer. 1986. Interpersonal influences in adolescent drug use—The role of older siblings, parents, and peers. *The International Journal of the Addictions* 21(7):739–766.

Patterson, G. R. and M. Stouthamer-Loeber. 1984. The correlation of family management practices and delinquency. *Child Development* 55:1299–1307.

Pearlin, L. I., and J. S. Johnson. 1977. Marital status, life-strains and depression. *American Sociological Review* 42(5):704–715.

Procidano, M. E., and K. Heller. 1983. Measures of perceived social support from friends and from family: Three validation studies. *American Journal of Community Psychology* 11(1):111–121.

Rinear, C. E. 1986. *The sexually transmitted diseases.* Jefferson, NC: McFarland & Co.

Rossignol, A. M. 1985. Caffeine-containing beverages and premenstrual syndrome in young women. *American Journal of Public Health* 75(11):1335–1337.

Schafer, R. B. 1985. Effects of marital role problems and the self-concept on wives' depressed mood. *Journal of Consulting and Clinical Psychology* 53(4):541–543.

Stephens, B. J. 1985. Suicidal women and their relationships with husbands, boyfriends, and lovers. *Suicide and Life Threatening Behavior* 15(2):75–87.

Streit, F., and H. G. Oliver. 1972. The child's perception of his family and its relationship to drug use. *Drug Forum* 1(3):283–289.

Tec, N. 1970. Family and differential involvement with marihuana: A study of suburban teenagers. *Journal of Marriage and the Family* 32:656–664.

Thompson, K. M., and R. W. Wilsnack. 1987. Parental influence on adolescent drinking: Modeling, attitudes, or conflict? *Youth and Society* 19:22–43.

Venters, M. H. 1986. Family life and cardiovascular risk: Implications for the prevention of chronic disease. *Social Science Medicine* 22(10):1067–1074.

Verbrugge, L. M. 1986. Role burdens and physical health of women and men. *Women & Health* 11(1):47–77.

VERBRUGGE, L. M., and J. H. MADANS. 1985. Social roles and health trends of
American women. *Milbank Memorial Fund Quarterly/Health and Society*
63(4):691–735.

WALDRON, I., and J. HEROLD. 1986. Employment, attitudes toward employment, and
women's health. *Women & Health* 11(1):79–98.

WEISSMAN, M. M. 1987. Advances in psychiatric epidemiology: Rates and risks for
major depression. *American Journal of Public Health* 77(4):445–451.

WETHINGTON, E., and R. C. KESSLER. 1986. Perceived support, received support, and
adjustment to stressful life events. *Journal of Health and Social Behavior*
27:78–89.

WILSNACK, R. W., and R. CHELOHA. 1987. Women's roles and problem drinking
across the lifespan. *Social Problems* 34:231–248.

CHAPTER 14

Religion and the Family

Introduction

As children, Lorraine and Michael were taken to church by their parents. They continued to attend church occasionally as teenagers and young adults. They were married in a Protestant church and always felt that the principles they learned in church were important.

Michael and Lorraine are not fanatical about religion, but they believe in God and feel that religious training is important for their children. Since Debra was born, they have gone to church regularly and each of their two children were christened in church shortly after birth. They prayed and turned to their minister for support and advice after their handicapped child was born. Several of their friends are couples who go to the same church. Religious participation has become an important part of their family life.

Many religious rituals, such as marriage and christening, are important family events and religious attendance is often done as a family. Religion offers explanations, comfort, and support in times of need, such as when Michael and Lorraine's handicapped child was born. Religious leaders often provide counseling and other assistance for members of their congregation.

In this chapter we review the interface between family and religion. There are five major sections. We begin by discussing the reciprocal influences of family and religion in social change. Second, we review recent trends in religious participation in America. Third, we explore the relationship between religiosity and satisfaction. Fourth, we identify the relationship between religiosity and several family characteristics. Finally, we discuss the family characteristics of several major religious groups.

Religion, Family, and Change

Family life has changed dramatically during the past century. Many of these changes have been discussed in previous chapters, so only brief mention is made here. Increasing life expectancy has extended the life cycle. Family size has decreased dramatically as birth control has become widely available. Our economy has become a family wage economy in which family members work outside the home. There has been a large increase in the proportion of women employed outside the home. Division of labor and sex role attitudes have become more egalitarian. The incidence of premarital sex has increased along with the incidence of divorce and remarriage.

As these changes have occurred, it appears that the power of religion over individual thought and behavior has declined. Nevertheless, religion does reflect these changes, although to a more moderate extent. For example, Fundamentalist Protestants are less egalitarian in sex role attitudes than other groups, but they have become more egalitarian along with the rest of American society. It's just that the extent of change has been less for them than other groups (Thornton 1985). Similarly, fertility has decreased considerably among Catholics as it has among American society as a whole, but the decrease has been smaller (Heaton and Goodman 1985). Family patterns also influence organized religion. In the early 1900s religious institutions were almost unanimously opposed to divorce. As the divorce rate increased and public acceptance of it grew, many religions became much more accepting of divorce (Halem 1980). Most religions no longer view divorce as a sin, sanctions against divorce have weakened, and some religions have established support services for the divorced (Ripple 1978; Thornton 1985).

Birth control is another example of how family changes have influenced the positions of religious organizations. Churches were overwhelmingly against birth control well into the twentieth century. However, as birth control became available and used more frequently, most churches modified their positions (Thornton 1985). Similarly, as sex role attitudes have become more egalitarian, many religions have changed their practices, and women clergy are not uncommon today. Traditional religious positions on sex roles, premarital sex, cohabitation, birth control, abortion, and homosexuality have been modified in response to social change (Thornton 1985).

Religious Beliefs and Trends

Religion is an important aspect of American life. Ninety percent of Americans have a religious preference, and 80 percent say that religion is important in their lives (Gallup 1985). Even those with no religious affiliation tend to pray and feel that religious training is important. Three fourths of those with no religious affiliation would like their children to have religious training (Gallup 1985). However, 39 percent of those who go to church feel that organized religion is not effective in helping people find meaning in life. About 33 percent of Americans have had a religious experience that they describe as dramatic and life changing (Gallup 1985).

There is a common belief that **secularization** has occured in America, that religious belief and participation are waning. Recent research shows that this is a myth. Analyzing national data over a period of almost fifty years, Hout and Greeley (1987) did not observe a downward trend in church attendance. Using data from the twenties and seventies, Bahr and Chadwick (1985) compared residents of Middletown on religious belief and practice and found no evidence that religiosity had declined. To the contrary, it seemed that religious devoutness had increased over the fifty-year period. Religious attendance has risen from 20 percent to 50 percent; the number of church buildings per capita

Fifty percent of Americans say religion is important in their lives, and religious belief and participation has increased in recent years. For some families, attending religious services together is an important family activity. *McCoy/The Picture Cube.*

had increased, and the proportion of families that made financial contributions to churches rose. Gallup (1985) reported that Americans are more interested in religious and spiritual matters today than they were five years ago. There has also been an increase in religiosity among college students (Gallup 1985; Hastings and Hoge 1986).

Affiliation with organized religion in the United States may be grouped into six major categories: (1) **Catholic;** (2) **Fundamentalist Protestant** (such as Pentecostal, Jehovah Witness, Southern Baptist, and Baptist); (3) **Protestant** (such as Lutheran, Methodist, Congregational, Episcopalian, Presbyterian, and Unitarian); (4) **Jew;** (5) Other; and (6) No Religion. About 80 percent of Americans say they are Christians.

The six groups differ markedly in their beliefs about family life and other matters. About 90 percent of the Fundamentalist Protestants believe in a life after death, compared to 75 percent of the Catholics, 25 percent of the Jews, and 46 percent of those with no religion (Smith 1984). The Fundamentalists are more likely than the other religious groups to oppose birth control information for teenagers, abortion, premarital sex, extramarital sex, divorce, and egalitarian roles. Jews and those with no religious affiliation are most accepting of these behaviors, and Protestants are in the middle. Catholics are closer to the Fundamentalists on these issues (Hertel and Hughes 1987; Smith 1984).

There is considerable variation in the concentration of religious groups by region of the country. Fundamentalist Protestants tend to be concentrated in the South and parts of the northern plains. Protestants are more common in the Midwest and West, and Catholics are concentrated in the Northeast, upper Midwest, and Southwest. The West (Washington, Oregon, and California) has residents of many different religions and none dominates (Hill 1985). Regional differences in religion have not diminished in recent years, and may have increased. There is a tendency to belong to a congregation rather than a denomination, especially among Protestants (Hill 1985).

Religiosity and Happiness

A number of scholars have found that happiness and satisfaction with life are higher among the religious than nonreligious (Witter et al. 1985). For example, Gallup (1985) reported that 68 percent of the "highly spiritually committed" are "very happy," compared to 46 percent of the "moderately spiritually committed," and only 30 percent of the "highly uncommitted." Mackie and Brinkerhoff (1986) found that individuals with no religious affiliation had lower self-esteem and less satisfaction with life than religious persons. In a study by Smith (1984), about 45 percent of those involved in religion said they get a "very great deal" of satisfaction from their families, compared to only 29 percent of those with no religion. Religion appears to be a stronger predictor of satisfaction than gender or socioeconomic status (Mackie and Brinkerhoff 1986). Finally, some religious and family indicators are negatively associated with suicide rates (Stack 1985).

Religiosity and Family Life

What are some of the family characteristics that are associated with **religiosity?** In this section we review available research relevant to this question.

Marriage

Belonging to a church is associated with being married. For example, among persons with no religion, 19 percent of men and 13 percent of the women over age 30 have never married. Among those with a religious preference, comparable percentages are 7 percent for men and 6 percent for women (Heaton and Goodman 1985).

Individuals who attend church regularly are somewhat more likely to be married than infrequent attenders. Bahr and Chadwick (1985) reported that

TABLE 14·1   Religion in Which Spouse Was Raised (Percentage) by Religion in Which Respondent Was Raised. Pooled Data from Six U.S. National Surveys (1973—1978)

Religion in Which Respondent Was Raised	*Religion in Which Respondent's Spouse Was Raised*						
	Protestant	*Catholic*	*Jewish*	*No Religion*	*Other*	*Total*	*(N)*
Protestant	83.7	13.4	0.3	2.4	0.2	100.0	(4,050)
Catholic	34.9	62.0	0.5	2.1	0.5	100.0	(1,568)
Jewish	10.3	7.5	80.1	1.4	0.7	100.0	(146)
No Religion	59.7	17.5	1.3	18.8	2.6	100.0	(154)
Other	31.3	25.0	0.0	1.6	42.2	100.0	(64)
Total	68.0	26.2	2.3	2.7	0.8	100.0	(5,982)

SOURCE: Glenn, N. D. 1982. Interreligious marriage in the United States: Patterns and recent trends. *Journal of Marriage and the Family* 44:559, Table 3. Copyrighted 1982 by the National Council on Family Relations, 1910 West County Road B, Suite 147, St. Paul, Minnesota 55113. Reprinted by permission.

90 percent of those who attended church at least monthly had married at least once, compared to 86 percent of those who attended less often. Heaton and Goodman (1985) also found that rates of marriage were higher among those who attend church regularly.

How common is **religious homogamy** in marriage? Glenn (1982) found that a large majority of persons marry within their own religion (see Table 14·1). For example, more than 80 percent of Jews and Protestants and 60 percent of Catholics marry someone of their own faith.

TABLE 14·2   Homogamous and Heterogamous Marriages of Protestants, Catholics, and Jews in the United States (1957 and 1973–1978)

	1957	*1973–1978*	*(N)*
Percentage of married Protestants[a]			
Married to Protestants	95.5	92.6	
Married to Catholics and Jews	4.5	7.4	
	100.0	100.0	(3,846)
Percentage of married Catholics[a]			
Married to Catholics	87.9	82.0	
Married to Protestants and Jews	12.1	18.0	
	100.0	100.0	(1,451)
Percentage of married Jews[a]			
Married to Jews	96.3	88.2	
Married to Protestants and Catholics	3.7	11.8	
	100.0	100.0	(136)
Percentage of Protestants, Catholics, and Jews[a]			
Married to persons of the same religion	93.6	89.7	
Married to persons of a different religion	6.4	10.3	
	100.0	100.0	(5,433)

[a] Persons married to persons who were not Protestant, Catholic, or Jewish are excluded from the base for the percentages.

SOURCE: Glenn, N. D. 1982. Interreligious marriage in the United States: Patterns and recent trends. *Journal of Marriage and the Family* 44:557, Table 1. Copyright 1982 by the National Council on Family Relations, 1910 West County Road B, Suite 147, St. Paul Minnesota 55113. Reprinted by permission

In the United States interreligious marriage has been increasing, and Glenn (1982) maintains that there are few strong barriers against it. However, there is still a widespread belief that the religious preferences of husband and wife should agree. Many persons change religious preference after marriage to reach this ideal, as shown in Table 14·2. About 90 percent of married persons have the same religion as their spouse (Glenn 1982).

People who are active in a religion are less likely than inactive persons to marry outside their religion. The number of potential marriage partners within one's religion also affects the rate of interreligious marriage (Barlow 1977).

Contraception and Fertility

Some religions encourage childbearing and discourage the use of contraception, most notably Catholics. Recent studies show that contraceptive patterns are converging among different religious groups. However, Catholic couples are still somewhat less likely to use contraception than members of other religious groups (Mosher and Goldsheider 1984).

Fertility rates are also converging, but Catholics continue to have fertility rates moderately higher than persons in other religions (Compton, Coward, and Wilson-Davis 1985). Heaton and Goodman (1985) reported that Catholic women average about 2.4 children, compared to 2.3 for Fundamentalist Protestants and 2.0 for Protestants and nonreligious women (see Table 14·3). Catholic women who take communion frequently tend to have slightly more children than Catholic women who do not (Mosher and Hendershot 1984).

The study of Middletown by Bahr and Chadwick (1985) illustrates how religion may affect childbearing. Those low on religiosity were more likely to have no children or one child than those high on religiosity (see Table 14·4). Those who attended church regularly were much more likely to have three or four children than those who did not attend regularly

Marital Satisfaction, Divorce, and Remarriage

There is a growing body of evidence that religion is associated with happier and more stable marriages. For example, in Middletown 60 percent of those who attended church regularly reported being very satisfied with their marriages, compared to only 43 percent of those who attended less often (Bahr and Chadwick 1985). Individuals with no religious affiliation were much more likely to be dissatisfied in their marriages, as shown in Table 14·5. A number of other researchers have found that religiosity is positively related with marital

TABLE 14·3   Children Ever Born to Women by Religious Affiliation, United States (1978–1983)

Catholics	Liberal Protestants	Conservative Protestants	Mormon	No Religion
2.38	2.03	2.27	3.31	2.02

Note: Standardized for marital duration. Included only women with first marriage intact
SOURCE: Heaton, T. B., and K. L. Goodman. 1985. Religion and family formation. *Review of Religious Research* 26(4):349, Table 1. Reprinted by permission.

TABLE 14·4   Religiosity and Fertility Among Married Adults, Middletown
(1977–1978)

| Number of Children | Indicators of Religiosity | | | | |
| | Religious Preference | | | Church Attendance | |
	Catholics (n = 107)	Protestants (n = 621)	None (n = 117)	At Least Monthly (n = 397)	Less Often (n = 472)
0	41%	31%	43%	27%	38%
1	4	15	15	10	16
2	19	21	23	22	19
3	14	17	10	18	14
4 or more	22	17	9	22	13
Total	100%	101%	100%	99%	100%

SOURCE: Bahr, H. M., and B. A. Chadwick. 1985. Religion and family in Middletown,
U.S.A. *Journal of Marriage and the Family* 47:412, Table 3. Copyrighted 1985 by the
National Council on Family Relations, 1910 West County Road B, Suite 147, St. Paul,
Minnesota 55113. Reprinted by permission.

satisfaction (Filsinger and Wilson 1984; Glenn and Weaver 1978; Hendershott
1986; Smith 1984; Wilson and Filsinger 1986).

Some researchers have suggested that the relationship between religiosity
and marital satisfaction is due to other variables, such as socioeconomic status
or social desirability. Perhaps because of the emphasis on marriage taught in
churches, religious persons are less likely to admit to marital problems. The
work of Filsinger and Wilson (1984) suggests that this is *not* the case. Even
after controlling for social desirability, socioeconomic status, income, number
of children, and length of marriage, they found that religiosity was related to
marital satisfaction. In fact, the most consistent and strongest predictor of
marital satisfaction was religiosity.

Not unexpectedly, divorce also is related to religious preference and religiosity. Bumpass and Sweet (1972) reported that divorce rates of Catholics and
Jews were below average whereas among persons with no religion they were

TABLE 14·5   Religiosity and Marital Satisfaction Among the Currently Married,
Middletown (1977–1978)

| Marital Satisfaction | Indicators of Religiosity | | | | |
| | Religious Preference | | | Church Attendance | |
	Catholics (n = 88)	Protestants (n = 540)	None (n = 70)	At Least Monthly (n = 319)	Less Often (n = 320)
Very satisfied	56%	60%	50%	60%	43%
Satisfied	34	36	34	31	44
Neutral	6	3	9	8	11
Dissatisfied or very dissatisfied	3	2	7	2	3
Total	99%	101%	100%	101%	101%

SOURCE: Bahr, H. M., and B. A. Chadwick. 1985. Religion and family in Middletown,
U.S.A. *Journal of Marriage and the Family* 47:412, Table 2. Copyrighted 1985 by the
National Council on Family Relations, 1910 West County Road B, Suite 147, St. Paul,
Minnesota 55113. Reprinted by permission.

TABLE 14·6   Divorce and Remarriage by Religion

	Gender	Catholics	Liberal Protestants	Conservative Protestants	Mormons	No Religion
Percentage of Ever Married	Male	19	24	28	14	39
Who Have Divorced	Female	23	31	31	19	45
Percentage of Ever Divorced						
Who Are Currently Remarried	Male	50	63	62	67	48
	Female	35	50	55	53	37

SOURCE: Heaton, T. B., and K. L. Goodman. 1985. Religion and family formation. *Review of Religious Research* 26(4):349, Table 1. Reprinted by permission.

above average. Heaton and Goodman (1985) documented that divorce is more frequent among the nonreligious, and a summary of their findings is shown in Table 14·6. Among those with no religion, about 42 percent of the ever-married couples have divorced, compared to less than 30 percent of the Protestants and about 21 percent of the Catholics. Bahr and Chadwick (1985) have shown that church attendance is also related to divorce (see Table 14·7).

As mentioned earlier, some religious organizations encourage marriages to be religiously homogamous. Is marital homogamy associated with marital satisfaction? Both Heaton (1984) and Hendershott (1986) found that there is a positive association between the two factors. As for divorce, Bumpass and Sweet (1972) found that religiously homogamous marriages had lower-than-average divorce rates, particularly among Jews, whereas interfaith marriages tended to have higher-than-average divorce rates.

Among those who divorce, the religious are much more likely to remarry than the nonreligious (Heaton and Goodman 1985). Among men who divorce, less than half of the nonreligious remarry, compared to about 58 percent among the religious. Comparable percentages for women are 37 percent among the nonreligious and about 47 percent among the religious. Table 14·6 shows re-

TABLE 14·7   Religiosity and Marital Status, Middletown (1977–1978)

	Indicators of Religiosity				
	Religious Preference			Church Attendance[a]	
Marital Status	Catholics (n = 130)	Protestants (n = 760)	None (n = 154)	At Least Monthly (n = 398)	Less Often (n = 473)
Single/never married	16%	10%	18%	10%	14%
First marriage	68	68	59	77	60
Remarried	2	6	8	3	8
Divorced or separated	6	9	12	4	12
Widowed	7	6	2	7	6
Total	99%	99%	99%	101%	100%

[a] Figures on attendance do not include no-preference respondents.

NOTE: Differences between Catholics and Protestants are not statistically significant; differences between the affiliated (Catholics and Protestants) and no-preference respondents and between high and low attenders are significant at the .01 level.

SOURCE: Bahr, H. M., and B. A. Chadwick. 1985. Religion and family in Middletown, U.S.A. *Journal of Marriage and the Family* 47:411, Table 1. Copyrighted 1985 by the National Council on Family Relations, 1910 West County Road B, Suite 147, St. Paul, Minnesota 55113. Reprinted by permission.

Many couples began their marriage with a religious ceremony. Marital satisfaction and stability tend to be higher among the religious than the non-religious. *Tom Kelly.*

marriage rates of five major religious groups. Catholics remarry at rates similar to those with no religion compared to Protestants who remarry at much higher rates.

Child Socialization

As mentioned earlier, even parents who are not affiliated with a church want their children to receive religious training (Gallup 1985). Does religious involvement of children have much effect on their behavior? Sloan and Potvin (1986) found that a variety of types of delinquent acts were less common among those who were involved in a religion. Others have observed that religiosity tends to deter delinquent activity (Albrecht, Chadwick, and Alcorn 1977; Peek, Curry, and Chalfant 1985), and Amoateng and Bahr (1986) reported that adolescents who attend church regularly use less alcohol and marijuana than adolescents not involved in religious activities.

As noted in Chapter 4, religiosity is related to adolescent sexual activity and pregnancy. Studer and Thornton (1987) found that religious commitment decreases the propensity of adolescents to engage in sexual intercourse. However, they also found that among those that do become sexually active, religiosity is associated with less effective use of contraceptives. This may be due to a lack of communication about contraceptives and fear of social disapproval.

Gender Roles

As women have entered the labor force in increasing numbers and attitudes have become more egalitarian, religions have responded in various ways. Some have adapted by allowing women to become ministers and fill leadership positions. Others have opposed egalitarian roles and women clergy (Hargrove, Schmidt, and Davaney 1985). In this section we discuss what is known about the relationship between sex roles and religion.

In recent years most religious groups have become more egalitarian in gender role attitudes. Fundamentalist Protestants appear to have changed the least. They strongly oppose abortion, birth control for teenagers, divorce, and new roles for women. Protestants, on the other hand, tend to favor availability of birth control and abortion and nontraditional roles for women (Smith 1984).

Brinkerhoff and Mackie (1985) studied how religion is related to gender role attitudes among college students, and found a positive association between them. People who were more religious tended to have more traditional attitudes, and religiosity had a stronger association with gender role attitudes than demographic variables, including gender and socioeconomic status.

Gender role attitudes varied significantly among the various religious denominations. Those with no religion were most egalitarian, followed by Catholics, regular Protestants, Fundamentalist Protestants, and **Mormons.** Current religion was more strongly related to gender role attitudes than childhood religion.

In a study of the general adult population, McCandless (1986) also found that religiosity is related to gender role attitudes. Belief, church attendance, and church experience were associated with traditional views regarding segregation of roles and employment of women.

Family Life Cycle

There is not much data on how religiosity changes over the family life cycle. Because of the strong desire of most parents to have their children receive religious training, we would expect that religiosity may be higher during the child-rearing years. In a study of Mormon families, Johnson and Duke (1982) found this to be the case. Religiosity increased at marriage and increased further during the child-rearing years. After children left home there was a decrease in religiosity among women, but not among men. Religiosity increased somewhat during the retirement years

Summary

Compared to those with no religion, individuals who are involved in a religion are more likely to marry. Among those who marry, the religious tend to have more children and higher marital satisfaction, and are less likely to divorce. Among those who divorce, the religious are more likely to remarry. Children of those involved in religion have lower rates of delinquency and drug use, and gender role attitudes tend to be more traditional among the highly religious. There is considerable variance among different religious denominations, and some of these differences are discussed in the next section. Of course, the findings are based on statistical associations, and direction of causality is not clear. For example, does religious involvement encourage people to stay married, or do people who get divorced tend to decrease their church attendance? Undoubtedly, there are some of both types of influences involved.

Family Life in Different Denominations

Family values and behavior vary considerably among different denominations. In this section we describe and compare family characteristics of six different religious groups as follows: (1) Protestants, (2) Catholics, (3) Jews, (4) Fundamentalist Protestants, (5) Mormons, and (6) No Religion. We separate Fundamentalist Protestants from regular Protestants because of the large differences that have been identified between the two groups (Heaton and Goodman 1985; Hill 1985; Smith 1984). Although Mormons are a small religious group, they are included because data are available and they provide an interesting contrast to the other religious denominations.

Recent Gallup polls reveal that about 64 percent of Americans are Protestants, 25 percent are Catholics, and 2 percent are Jews. About 7 percent claim no religious affiliation, and the remaining 2 percent belong to a variety of other denominations. Protestants are 34 percent of the population, and Fundamentalist Protestants comprise 30 percent of the population (Hout and Greeley 1987; Smith 1984).

Protestants

Protestants are "middle of the road" with regard to many family patterns. They tend to favor egalitarian roles and accessibility to birth control and abortion (Smith 1984). About 94 percent marry at least once, and they average about two children per couple (Heaton and Goodman 1985). Their rates of marriage, divorce, and remarriage are about average for American society. Protestants are the largest religious group in America, and about 40 percent attend church weekly (Hout and Greeley 1987).

Catholics

The American Catholic family has felt a tension between the personal autonomy that is highly valued in American society and obedience to hierarchical authority (D'Antonio 1985). The Catholic Church teaches that (1) bearing and raising children is the main purpose of marriage, (2) abstinence is the only legitimate means of birth control, (3) there should be sexual abstinence outside of marriage, and (4) marriage is sacred and cannot be dissolved except by annulment (D'Antonio 1985). According to Catholic dogma, abortion and artificial birth control are wrong and divorce is not recognized. In the eyes of the Church it is a sin to remarry because divorce is not recognized.

Many Catholics have not accepted these teachings and there is evidence that contraceptives are widely used (Heaton and Calkins 1983). Between 1968 and 1975 Catholic church attendance fell, apparently because of the Church's teachings on sexuality, but very few have left the Church (Hout and Greeley 1987). Since that time church attendance has increased somewhat.

The family life of Catholics reflects this tension between social changes in the United States and the official teachings of the Church (McNamara 1985). About 90 percent of Catholics marry, which is lower than all other religious groups, except those with no religion. Catholic birthrates have declined but are still somewhat higher than those of Protestants. They average about 2.4 births per couple (Heaton and Goodman 1985). Catholics have relatively low rates of divorce and low rates of remarriage among the divorced.

Jews

Jews place a strong emphasis on family unity and nurturance, yet are progressive with regard to gender roles (Brodbar-Nemzer 1986a). They tend to have small families, accept birth control and abortion, discourage divorce, and emphasize education.

In American society, groups with egalitarian attitudes and low fertility rates tend to have relatively high divorce rates. Jews, however, have low divorce rates even though they tend to have egalitarian attitudes and low fertility (Brodbar-Nemzer 1986b, 1988; Friedman and Rogers 1983; Linzer 1984; Smith 1984).

Members of this Jewish family feel a sense of purpose and togetherness as they experience a religious ritual together.   *Janice Fullman/The Picture Cube.*

Jews who have greater commitment to Jewish rituals have lower divorce rates than Jews with less religious commitment (Brodbar-Nemzer 1986b, 1988).

Fundamentalist Protestants

Fundamentalist Protestants have conservative views of marriage and family life. They oppose abortion and teenagers using birth control, and large families are encouraged. Divorce is discouraged and gender role attitudes tend to be traditional (Smith 1984).

About 96 percent marry at least once, which is a high marriage rate. They do not have as many children as Catholics but tend to have more children than Protestants, Jews, or those with no religion. They average about 2.3 children per couple (Heaton and Goodman 1985). Although they frown on divorce, they have higher divorce rates than any other religious group except those with no religion. After divorce they have higher-than-average remarriage rates, especially among women (Heaton and Goodman 1985).

Mormons

Mormons encourage childbearing, oppose abortion, and discourage divorce. Gender role attitudes tend to be traditional, although they are egalitarian in many behaviors (Brinkerhoff and Mackie 1985).

Marriage and fertility rates among Mormons are very high and divorce is low. More than 97 percent marry at least once, which is higher than any other religious group. Women in intact marriages average about 3.3 children, which is about one child more than any other religious group (Heaton and Goodman 1985; Toney, Golesorkhi, and Stinner 1985). Divorce rates are lower than any other group and when divorce does occur, Mormons remarry more often than people of other religious groups.

No Religion

Compared to other religious groups, people with no religion have the lowest rates of marriage, fertility, and remarriage, and the highest rates of divorce (Heaton and Goodman 1985). They are more accepting of pornography, premarital sex, extramarital sex, and homosexuality than any other group (Hertel and Hughes 1987; Smith 1984). In their attitudes they are very egalitarian, show a high level of support for abortion, and do not favor stricter divorce laws (Hertel and Hughes 1987). Those with no religious affiliation are lower than religious affiliates on life satisfaction (Smith 1984).

Summary

A comparison of marriage, divorce, remarriage, and fertility rates by religion is shown in Table 14·8. Protestants are in the middle in terms of marriage, divorce, and remarriage. Catholic families tend to have more children, less divorce, and less remarriage than most other religious groups. Fundamentalist Protestants are more likely to marry but also more likely to divorce and remarry, and their family size is in the middle. Our data on Jews are not as complete

TABLE 14·8   Rank Order of Marriage, Divorce, Remarriage, and Fertility by Religion

	Rank				
	1	2	3	4	5
Percentage of those over 30 who have *ever married*	Mormon	Fundamentalist Protestant	Liberal Protestant	Catholic	None
Percentage of ever-married persons who have *divorced*	None	Fundamentalist Protestant	Liberal Protestant	Catholic	Mormon
Percent of ever-divorced persons who are currently remarried	Mormon	Fundamentalist Protestant	Liberal Protestant	Catholic and None	
Children ever born	Mormon	Catholic	Fundamentalist Protestant	Liberal Protestant	None

SOURCE: Heaton, T. B., and K. L. Goodman. 1985. Religion and family formation. *Review of Religious Research* 26(4):350, Table 2. Reprinted by permission.

as for the other religious groups, but Jews have low fertility and divorce rates. Mormons have more marriage, less divorce, and more remarriage after divorce than the other religions examined here. The most distinguishing feature of Mormon families is their high fertility rate. They average one more child than Catholics, who have the second highest fertility rate. At the other extreme are those with no religious affiliation. They are the least likely to marry, have the fewest number of children, have the highest divorce rate, and are the least likely to remarry after divorce (Heaton and Goodman 1985).

Summary

1. There is a reciprocal influence between religious institutions and family life. As family patterns have changed, most religious organizations have modified their positions and become more accepting of birth control, abortion, and divorce. At the same time, family life is influenced by the teachings of religious institutions.

2. A large majority of Americans have a religious preference and feel that religion is important. Even most without a religious preference would like their children to have religious training.

3. Religious attendance and belief have not waned during the past fifty years, and in recent years religiosity in America appears to have increased.

4. Happiness and satisfaction with life tend to be higher among the religious than the nonreligious.

5. Persons affiliated with a religion are more likely to marry than persons with no religious affiliation.

6. Religious homogamy in marriage is very common but has decreased somewhat in recent years. Some people change religious preference after marriage in order to have the same religion as their spouse. About 90 percent of married persons have the same religion as their spouse.

7. With the widespread availability and use of contraception, differences among religious groups in fertility have been decreasing. Nevertheless, religious persons tend to have more children than the nonreligious, and Catholics tend to have more children than Protestants or Jews.

8. The religious have higher marital satisfaction and less divorce than the nonreligious. There is higher marital satisfaction and less divorce among those who marry within their religion compared to those who marry outside their religion. Among those who divorce, the religious are more likely to remarry than the nonreligious.

9. Adolescents who attend church regularly are involved in less delinquent behavior and drug abuse than adolescents who are not involved in religious activity. Teenage sexual activity is less frequent among the religious. However, among those who do engage in sexual activity, religious commitment is associated with less effective contraceptive use.

10. Those with no religious affiliation tend to have more egalitarian gender role attitudes than those involved in a religion. Catholics and Protestants are more egalitarian than Fundamentalist Protestants.

11. Religiosity tends to increase at marriage and during the child-rearing years, and tends to decrease after children have left home.

12. Protestants are middle of the road with regard to marriage, fertility, divorce, and remarriage. Catholics have higher-than-average fertility and low divorce and remarriage rates. Jews have low fertility and divorce rates. Fundamentalist Protestants have high marriage and divorce rates, along with above-average fertility. Mormons have the highest rates of marriage, fertility, and remarriage, and the lowest rate of divorce. Those with no religion have the lowest rates of marriage, fertility, and remarriage, and the highest rate of divorce.

Important Terms

- Catholic
- Fundamentalist Protestant
- Jew
- Mormon
- Protestant
- religiosity
- religious homogamy
- secularization

Questions for Discussion

1. How have (a) family life and (b) religious organizations changed during the past century?
2. List some concrete examples of how families have influenced religious organizations.
3. What are some ways religious dogma has influenced family life?
4. Why do a large majority of those with no religious affiliation want their children to receive religious training?
5. What evidence is there that Americans are becoming less religious? What evidence is there that Americans are becoming more religious?
6. Do you think secularization is a myth? Why or why not?
7. Identify the major religious groups in America, what proportion each is of the population, and some of the differences among the groups in beliefs and practice.
8. What is the relationship between religion and quality of life? Why?

9. How is religion related to marriage?
10. Why do religious people tend to have more children than nonreligious people?
11. What is the relationship between marital satisfaction and religion? Why?
12. Why do religious people tend to have less egalitarian attitudes than the nonreligious?
13. How does religiosity change over the life cycle and why?
14. Describe some of the family characteristics of the major religious groups within the United States.
15. Some have argued that religious participation tends to reduce the quality of family life. In what ways do you think it does?
16. Some have argued that religious participation tends to improve the quality of family life. In what ways do you think it does?
17. Religious groups with egalitarian attitudes tend to have above-average divorce rates. However, Jews tend to have egalitarian attitudes and yet have a low divorce rate. Why?

Recommended Reading

BAHR, H. M., and B. A. CHADWICK. 1985. Religion and family in Middletown, USA. *Journal of Marriage and the Family* 47:407–414.

THOMAS, D. L., ed. 1988. *The religion and family connection: Social science perspectives*. Salt Lake City: Bookcraft.

References

ALBRECHT, S. L., B. A. CHADWICK, and D. S. ALCORN. 1977. Religiosity and deviance: Application of an attitude behavior contingent consistency model. *Journal for the Scientific Study of Religion* 16(3):263–274.

AMOATENG, A. Y., and S. J. BAHR. 1986. Religion, family, and adolescent drug use. *Sociological Perspectives* 29(1):53–76.

BAHR, H. M., and B. A. CHADWICK. 1985. Religion and family in Middletown, U.S.A. *Journal of Marriage and the Family* 47:407–414.

BARLOW, B. A. 1977. Notes on Mormon interfaith marriages. *The Family Coordinator* 26:143–151.

BRINKERHOFF, M. B., and M. MACKIE. 1985. Religion and gender: A comparison of Canadian and American student attitudes. *Journal of Marriage and the Family* 47:415–429.

BRODBAR-NEMZER, J. Y. 1986a. Marital relationships and self-esteem: How Jewish families are different. *Journal of Marriage and the Family* 48:89–98.

BRODBAR-NEMZER, J. Y. 1986b. Divorce and group commitment: The case of the Jews. *Journal of Marriage and the Family* 48:329–340.

BRODBAR-NEMZER, J. Y. 1988. The contemporary American Jewish family. In *The religion and family connection: Social science perspectives*, ed. D. L. Thomas, 66–87. Salt Lake City: Bookcraft.

BUMPASS, L. L., and J. A. SWEET. 1972. Differentials in marital instability: 1970. *American Sociological Review* 37:754–766.

COMPTON, P. A., J. COWARD, and K. WILSON-DAVIS. 1985. Family size and religious denomination in Northern Ireland. *Journal of Biosocial Science* 17:137–145.

D'ANTONIO, W. V. 1985. The American Catholic family: Signs of cohesion and polarization. *Journal of Marriage and the Family* 47:395–405.

FILSINGER, E. E., and M. R. WILSON. 1984. Religiosity, socioeconomic rewards, and family development: Predictors of marital adjustment. *Journal of Marriage and the Family* 46:663–670.

FRIEDMAN, N., and T. F. ROGERS. 1983. *The Jewish community and children of divorce.* New York: National Jewish Family Center, American Jewish Committee.

GALLUP, G. 1985. Religion in America. *The Annals of the American Academy of Political and Social Sciences* 480:167–174.

GLENN, N. D. 1982. Interreligious marriage in the United States: Patterns and recent trends. *Journal of Marriage and the Family* 44:555–566.

GLENN, N. D., and C. N. WEAVER. 1978. A multivariate, multisurvey study of marital happiness. *Journal of Marriage and the Family* 40(2):269–282.

HALEM, L. C. 1980. *Divorce reform. Changing legal and social perspectives.* New York: Free Press.

HARGROVE, B., J. M. SCHMIDT, and S. G. DAVANEY. 1985. Religion and the changing role of women. *The Annals of the American Academy of Political and Social Sciences* 480:117–131.

HASTINGS, P. K., and D. R. HOGE. 1986. Religious and moral attitude trends among college students, 1948–84. *Social Forces* 65(3):370–377.

HEATON, T. B. 1984. Religious homogamy and marital satisfaction reconsidered. *Journal of Marriage and the Family* 46:729–733.

HEATON, T. B., and S. CALKINS. 1983. Family size and contraceptive use among Mormons: 1965–75. *Review of Religious Research* 25(2):103–114.

HEATON, T. B., and K. L. GOODMAN. 1985. Religion and family formation. *Review of Religious Research* 26(4):343–360.

HENDERSHOTT, A. 1986. *Religiosity and marital satisfaction: An exploration of the relationship.* Paper presented at the American Sociological Association meeting, New York, August.

HERTEL, B. R., and M. HUGHES. 1987. Religious affiliation, attendance, and support for "pro-family" issues in the United States. *Social Forces* 65(3):858–882.

HILL, S. S. 1985. Religion and region in America. *The Annals of the American Academy of Political and Social Sciences* 480:132–142.

HOUT, M., and A. M. GREELEY. 1987. The center doesn't hold: Church attendance in the United States, 1940–1984. *American Sociological Review* 52:324–345.

JOHNSON, B. L., and JAMES T. DUKE. 1982. *Religiosity through the family life cycle: A study of Mormon families.* Paper presented at Tenth World Congress of Sociology, International Sociological Association, Mexico City, Mexico, August 15–21.

LINZER, N. 1984. *The Jewish family.* New York: Human Sciences Press.

MCCANDLESS, N. J. 1986. *The influence of religious factors on sex role attitudes.* Paper presentated at American Sociological Association meetings, New York, August.

MACKIE, M. M., and M. B. BRINKERHOFF. 1986. Blessings and burdens: The reward-cost calculus of religious denominations. *Canadian Journal of Sociology* 11(2):157–181.

MCNAMARA, P. H. 1985. American Catholicism in the mid-eighties: Pluralism and conflict in a changing church. *The Annals of the American Academy of Political and Social Sciences* 480:63–74.

MOSHER, W. D., and C. GOLDSCHEIDER. 1984. Contraceptive patterns of religious and racial groups in the United States, 1955–76: Convergence and distinctiveness. *Studies in Family Planning* 15(3):101–111.

MOSHER, W. D., and G. E. HENDERSHOT. 1984. Religion and fertility: A replication. *Demography* 21(2):185–191.

PEEK, C. W., E. W. CURRY, and H. P. CHALFANT. 1985. Religiosity and delinquency over time: Deviance deterrence and deviance amplification. *Social Science Quarterly* 66(1):120–131.

RIPPLE, P. 1978. *The pain and the possibility.* Notre Dame, IN: Ave Maria Press.

SLOAN, D. M., and R. H. POTVIN. 1986. Religion and delinquency: Cutting through the maze. *Social Forces* 65(1):87–105.

SMITH, T. W. 1984. America's religious mosaic. *American Demographics* 6:19–23.

STACK, S. 1985. The effect of domestic/religious individualism on suicide, 1954–1978. *Journal of Marriage and the Family* 7(2):431–447.

STUDER, M., and A. THORNTON. 1987. Adolescent religiosity and contraceptive usage. *Journal of Marriage and the Family* 49:117–128.

THORNTON, A. 1985. Reciprocal influences of family and religion in a changing world. *Journal of Marriage and the Family* 47:381–394.

TONEY, M. B., B. GOLESORKHI, and W. F. STINNER. 1985. Residence exposure and fertility expectations of young Mormon and non-Mormon women in Utah. *Journal of Marriage and the Family* 7(2):459–465.

WILSON, M. R., and E. E. FILSINGER. 1986. Religiosity and marital adjustment: Multidimensional interrelationships. *Journal of Marriage and the Family* 48:147–151.

WITTER, R. A., W. A. STOCK, M. A. OKUN, and M. J. HARING. 1985. Religion and subjective well-being in adulthood: A quantitative synthesis. *Review of Religious Research* 26(4):332–342.

PART IV

Contemporary Issues

CHAPTER 15

Family Violence

Introduction

In western society we marry for love. The family, above all, is an affectional unit. It is begun in romance and is a place where we expect love, warmth, respect, and kindness to abound. When children come, they are to be reared with warmth and affection.

However, reality is often different from this ideal. In many families physical violence is common. The intimacy and intensity of family life sometimes lead to hurt, frustration, and physical violence. In fact, the family is one of our most violent institutions (Gelles and Straus 1985).

How can family members who love each other actually be violent with one another? To see how this happens, let us take a brief look at a violent episode in two different families.

Don came home somewhat late one evening tired and frustrated. His foreman had criticized him all day long and he was tired of people being "on his case." If someone else criticized him he felt he would explode. He also felt uneasy because he wondered if he might lose his job. The steel industry was not doing well, and because his foreman disliked him, he might be one of the first ones to go if layoffs were necessary. On the way home he stopped at a bar to have a drink and relax a little.

By the time he walked in the door it was 6:30 P.M. and his wife, Mary, had been expecting him at 5:30. Mary had been with their six-month-old baby all day and was tired. She was looking forward to relaxing together over a nice dinner. When Don did not make it home on time she felt frustrated and unappreciated. She thought, "I have been home all day with the baby and have fixed a nice dinner, and he doesn't even care enough to make it home on time."

When Don walked in the door, Mary let out her frustrations on Don. "Where have you been! I had a nice dinner fixed and now it is ruined. You should have at least called and told me you would be late."

For Don that was the straw that broke the camel's back. He just couldn't

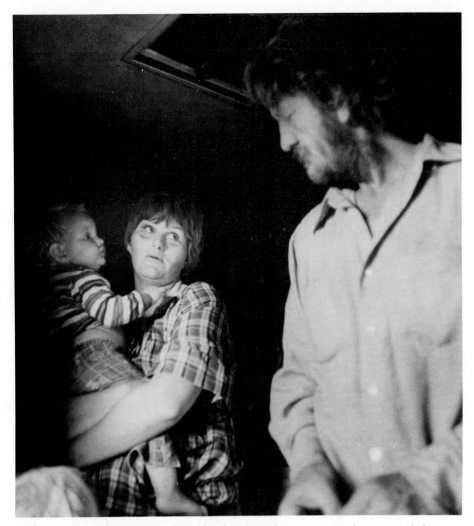

Each year more than 10 percent of husbands and wives are violent toward their spouses and 60 percent of children are victims of violence from their parents. Here a woman looks fearfully toward her husband, who earlier had blackened her eyes during an argument.   *Stephen Shames/Visions.*

take it anymore. Don yelled, "Oh, be quiet! I have had it up to here with your mouth."

Mary was upset with Don's response and yelled back "Be quiet yourself. Let's see you try to stay home all day and watch this baby. I am tired of being your slave."

Don was furious and screamed, "Shut up, you mouthy bitch," and swung and slapped Mary across the face. She said, "Don't you dare hit me!" In a rage he hit Mary several more times and knocked her to the floor.

In anger and guilt, he walked out of the room and left the house. Mary was left there crying on the floor with several bruises and a cut on her face.

Now let us look at the Patterson family. Joan's husband is a truck driver and he is gone a lot. They have a little boy named Ben who is a year old. Ben is very active and is into everything. Joan gets frustrated with Ben and sometimes feels overrun. Ben doesn't mind very well and sometimes she just can't take his messes and crying. She spanks him regularly and occasionally hits him hard.

The other day she was in watching TV and Ben got up to the sink, turned the water on, and got water all over the kitchen floor. Joan just couldn't take another mess and screamed at Ben and knocked him off the chair he was on. She then picked him up, spanked him, and put him in his crib. When he wouldn't stop crying she pulled down his diaper and spanked him with a belt until welts appeared. The reason he wouldn't stop crying was that he had sustained a severe bump on his head when he had been knocked off the chair.

Anyone who has been married or been a parent knows that occasionally we all get very frustrated and angry. Many people resort to physical violence when faced with these frustrations, just like Don and Joan did. In this chapter we explore the extent and nature of family violence in the United States. We begin by defining violence and identifying the different types. Then violence against children is discussed, followed by an examination of spouse violence. The last section is a review of other types of family violence, including sibling violence and elder abuse.

What is Violence?

The terms abuse and violence are often used loosely to refer to a variety of different types of behaviors. In this chapter we follow Straus and Gelles (1986) and define **violence** as an act carried out with the intent of causing physical pain or injury to another person.

There are two key elements to this definition. First, it must be a physical act. *Thinking* about hitting or killing someone is not violent. Only when thoughts are put into action do they become violent. Second, there must be an intent to hurt. If a baseball pitcher accidentally loses control of a pitch and it hits the batter in the head, that is not a violent act. However, if the pitcher purposely throws for the batter's head, it is.

To understand the nature of violence there are four other dimensions that need to be considered. First is the **seriousness of violence.** Many acts of violence are relatively mild such as a slap or shove, whereas a shooting is extremely serious.

Another important characteristic is the **legitimacy of violence.** For example, in American society it is legitimate to spank a child on the buttocks but not on the head. Slapping a child may be considered all right but slapping a spouse is normally not considered appropriate.

A third dimension is the **extent of injury caused by violence.** This may range from none to death. An act might be very serious yet cause no injury, such as when one fires a gun at another and misses.

Finally, the **motivation for violence** is an important consideration. A parent who spanks a child for playing in the street may be motivated out of love and concern for the child's safety. When Don hit Mary he was simply frustrated and wanted Mary to stop criticizing him. In some cases there is a desire to kill because of intense hatred.

The four dimensions we have described may be used to analyze different violent acts. For example, a spanking of a child may (1) not be serious, (2) produce no injury, (3) be motivated by love, and (40 be legitimate. Using the same criteria, Don's assault on Mary was (1) relatively serious, (2) produced bruises and cuts, (3) was motivated out of frustration, and (4) was not legitimate.

Violence Against Children

Violence against children is not new. Throughout history children have been beaten and even killed (Amedeo-Eineker 1985; Lenoir-Degoumois 1983). In some cultures children were sacrificed, in others unwanted children were killed. Children who were illegitimate or had severe handicaps were particularly at risk. From ancient times to the present, violence against children has been accepted or even encouraged in order to train children properly (Gelles and Cornell 1985). In this section we review rates and trends in violence against children and identify characteristics associated with it.

Rates

How much violence is there against children in American society? Two national surveys conducted by Straus and Gelles (1986) have enabled us, for the first time, to move beyond speculation to reliable estimates of family violence.

Straus and Gelles (1986) divided violent acts into three categories, based on seriousness. First, **minor violence** was any of the following three types of acts: (1) threw something, (2) pushed, grabbed, or shoved, (3) slapped or spanked. Second, **severe violence** included the following: (4) kick, bit, or hit with fist, (5) hit or tried to hit with something, (6) beat up, (7) threatened with knife or gun, and (8) used knife or gun. The third category was called **very severe violence.** It was a subset of severe violence, and included being kicked, bitten, or hit with a fist, being beaten up, or having a gun or knife used. Straus and Gelles (1986) also combined these eight violent acts into an index of overall violence.

Table 15·1 shows the parent-to-child violence reported by Straus and Gelles (1986). The figures are rates of abuse per thousand children ages 3 to 17 per year. About six of every ten children in the United States suffered at least one violent act from their parents in 1985. More than one in ten children suffered severe violence, and about 2 percent were victims of very severe violent acts from their parents.

These data may be interpreted in different ways. On the one hand, it is deplorable that more than half of America's children suffer violent acts from their parents each year, and 10 percent experience severe violence. This appears to be an extremely high rate of violence inflicted upon children from their parents. On the other hand, about 90 percent of children receive no severe violence during a year. Many of the violent acts are minor, such as a spank or shove, and many of the children may suffer only a small number of minor violent acts during a year.

Homicide is the fifth leading cause of death among children. Among infants under a year old, 6 per 100,000 are murdered each year. Among children between

TABLE 15·1   Parent-to-Child Violence: Comparison of Rates in 1975 and 1985

Type of Violence	Rate per 1,000 Children Aged 3 through 17[a]		t for 1975–1985 Difference
	1975 n = 1,146	1985 n = 1,428	
A. Minor Violence Acts			
1. Threw something	54	27	3.52**
2. Pushed/grabbed/shoved	318	307	0.54
3. Slapped or spanked	582	549	1.68
B. Severe Violence Acts			
4. Kicked/bit/hit with fist	32	13	3.31*
5. Hit, tried to hit with something	134	97	2.91*
6. Beat up	13	6	1.86
7. Threatened with gun or knife	1	2	0.69
8. Used gun or knife	1	2	0.69
C. Violence Indexes			
Overall violence (1–8)	630	620	0.52
Severe violence (4–8)	140	107	2.55*
Very severe violence (4, 6, 8)	36	19	2.67**

[a] For two-caretaker households with at least one child 3 to 17 years of age at home.
* $p < .01$; ** $p < .001$ (two-tailed tests)
SOURCE: Straus, M. A., and R. J. Gelles. 1986. Societal change and change in family violence from 1975 to 1985 as revealed by two national surveys. *Journal of Marriage and the Family* 48:469, Table 1. Copyrighted 1986 by the National Council on Family Relations, 1910 West County Road B, Suite 147, St. Paul, Minnesota 55113. Reprinted by permission.

the ages of 1 and 4, about 2.4 per 100,000 are killed each year by homicide, compared to 1.3 among children ages 5 to 14 (National Center for Health Statistics 1986). About two thirds of infant homicide victims are killed by a parent. Among children over a year old who become homicide victims, about one fourth are killed by a parent (Gelles and Cornell 1985). An infant who is an only child of young parents has the greatest risk of being killed, and boys are killed more often than girls (Anderson et al. 1983).

Are there differences between mothers and fathers in violence toward children? Gelles and Straus (1985) reported that mothers were slightly more likely than fathers to be violent and to be severely violent toward their children. Boys were more likely than girls to receive violence from their parents (Gelles and Cornell 1985).

Trends

There have been many reports in the media about the increasing rates of violence in our society. The data of Straus and Gelles (1986) show that parent-to-child violence has decreased during the past ten years. The rate of very severe violence decreased from 36 per 1,000 in 1975 to 19 per 1,000 in 1985, a decrease of 47 percent. There was little change in overall violence, but severe and very severe violence decreased rather dramatically.

A study in England also found a recent decrease in severe violence toward children. In a study of over 6,000 children from 1977 to 1982, overall rates of physical injury increased but the percentage of serious and fatal injuries decreased (Creighton 1985).

Reasons for Parent-Child Violence

Why are parents violent toward their children? Raising children is difficult and all parents become frustrated and extremely angry with their children occasionally. But why do some become violent while others do not? In this section we will identify some of the characteristics that are associated with violence toward chidren and integrate them into a model.

ECONOMIC STRESS.   Economic problems tend to be associated with higher rates of violence against children. Krugman et al. (1986) and Steinberg, Catalano, and Dooley (1981) observed that physical abuse of children is more common when unemployment is higher. Steinberg et al. (1981) used longitudinal data and observed that in areas where unemployment increased, rates of child abuse subsequently increased. Others have documented that families with low incomes and economic stress are more likely to abuse their children (Gelles and Cornell 1985; Hawkins and Duncan 1985a; Smith 1984).

LOW PARENTING SKILLS.   Parents who are violent toward their children tend to lack parenting skills and knowledge about normal child development, and they may expect unrealistic things of their children (Azar and Rohrbeck 1986; Azar et al. 1984; Garbarino 1983; Vasta 1982; Vesterdal 1983). For example, parents have been known to injure six-month-old children because they were not toilet trained (Gelles and Cornell 1985).

   Abusive parents tend to use fewer facilitating behaviors and show less positive affect than nonabusive parents (Wolfe 1985). Lahey et al. (1984) found that abusive mothers engaged in more negative physical behaviors and fewer positive behaviors toward their children than did a control group of nonabusive mothers, even though there was no difference between abused and nonabused children in behavior. In general, abusive parents use less effective child management techniques (Wolfe 1985).

STRESS AND DEFICIENT COPING SKILLS.   There is considerable evidence that abusive parents face excessive stress (Vasta 1982). As mentioned earlier, abusive parents tend to suffer more economic stress than nonabusive parents. Abusers are also more likely to report emotional distress, depression, and health problems, which may impair parental competence (Lahey et al. 1984; Wolfe 1985). Passman and Mulhern (1977) and others (Smith 1984) have shown that parents are more punitive when under stressful situations. Furthermore, there is evidence that abusive parents have poor problem-solving skills, which makes them less able to cope effectively with stress (Azar et al. 1984; Garbarino 1983).

SOCIAL ISOLATION.   Parents who physically abuse their children tend to be socially isolated. Compared to abusive parents, nonabusive parents tend to have more support from family and friends and are better at seeking out support (Smith 1984). Both formal and informal networks are deficient, which leaves abusive parents without adequate social support in times of stress (Gelles and Cornell 1985).

CHILD ILLNESS.   There is evidence that illness of the child is associated with physical abuse. Hawkins and Duncan (1985b) observed that children with chronic illness, emotional disturbance, hyperactivity, mental retardation, and physical handicaps were at higher risk of abuse than normal children. Excessive crying was also associated with higher rates of abuse. Sherrod et al. (1984) have shown that childhood illness is a stress that often precedes and may trigger abuse. In general, children who are harder to care for are at greater risk for physical abuse (Garbarino 1983; Gelles and Cornell 1985; Lenington 1981; Smith 1984; Vasta 1982).

VIOLENCE IN FAMILY OF ORIENTATION.   A number of studies have shown that individuals who were victims of or observed violence as children are more likely to be abusers as adults (Gelles 1982b; Gelles and Cornell 1985; Steinmetz 1987; Straus, Gelles, and Steinmetz 1980; Vasta 1982; Vesterdal 1983). Growing up in a family where hitting is observed or experienced may teach acceptance of violence as a way of dealing with problems. One learns through experience that violence is a way to cope with problems and get one's wishes.

SUBCULTURE OF VIOLENCE.   Cultural or subcultural values that tolerate or accept violence seem to contribute to family violence (Vasta 1982). Wolfgang and Ferracuti (1967) have suggested that in some areas there is a **subculture of violence** that is a part of lifestyles, socialization, and interpersonal relationships. In such groups violence becomes a part of life, a way of dealing with difficult problems and situations. Hitting children and other family members may be an accepted way of coping with frustrations, protecting oneself, and teaching children (Smith 1984). People who live in such subcultures learn to be violent and accept it as a way of life.

HIGH MARITAL CONFLICT.   Parents who have extensive conflict with their partners tend to use more violence on children (Smith, 1984; Wolfe 1985). High rates of conflict tend to create stress and may make parents less sensitive to their children's needs.

SINGLE PARENT OR REMARRIED.   Children who live with two natural parents suffer less abuse than children living with a single parent or with a stepparent (Daly and Wilson 1985; Gelles 1982b; Lenington 1981; Martin and Walters 1982). Presumably this is because of the greater stress associated with single parenthood and remarriage.

OTHER FACTORS.   Research has not found that mental illness of the parents is related to physical abuse of children. Most abusive parents are relatively normal psychologically, although Wolfe (1985) found evidence that they may tend to be immature and self-centered.

The research on alcoholism is not consistent. Krugman et al. (1986) suggest that alcoholism may contribute to child abuse, but Orme and Rimmer (1981) found no support for an association between alcoholism and child abuse. Gelles and Cornell (1985) found that alcohol was not directly related to abuse and suggest that drunkenness may be used as an excuse for child abuse.

Race does not appear to be related to violence toward children. In their national survey of family violence, Straus et al. (1980) found the rates of violence toward children were similar for blacks and whites.

Family size does not appear to be related to child abuse either. Gelles and Straus (1985) reported that parents with two children tended to physically abuse their children more often than parents with one child. However, as family size increased further, the rate of violence toward children did not increase.

SUMMARY.   A model integrating how these variables influence violence toward children is shown in Figure 15·1. Parents are likely to inflict at least one act of mild violence on their children if they lived in a family and subculture where violence was used. Subculture and family experiences provide an environment where violence is learned and becomes an accepted way of life. Deficient coping skills and low parenting skills also contribute to the use of violence. Parents may not know how to react to certain situations other than with violence.

Deficient coping skills, low parenting skills, economic stress, child illness, social isolation, high marital conflict, and being a single parent or remarried tend to be associated with increased levels of stress. The propensity to use violence and the level of stress interact to increase the risk of severe violence. High levels of stress will tend to increase the likelihood that mild violence will turn into severe violence.

The model in Figure 15·1 explains parent-to-child violence as a function of situational stress and social learning. People learn to use violence as a coping mechanism in their culture and home. Structural stress in combination with social learning leads to violence (Gelles and Cornell 1985).

Abuse of Adolescents

As noted earlier, physical abuse tends to decrease as children get older. However, abuse of adolescents is fairly common, and psychological and sexual abuse tend to increase with age (Garbarino, Schellenbach, and Sebes 1986). There is evidence that adolescents who are abused are overrepresented among runaways and other delinquent offenders (McCormack, Janua, and Burgess 1986; Paperny and Deisher 1983).

In a review of adolescent maltreatment, Garbarino et al. (1986) found that the risk of adolescent abuse is greater if there is a stepparent in the home or if the adolescent has developmental problems. There is also evidence that families high in conflict and low on support and cohesion have higher rates of adolescent abuse (Garbarino et al. 1986). This is consistent with the research cited earlier on younger children that showed that violence was more common when there is high marital conflict, low parenting skills, and remarriage.

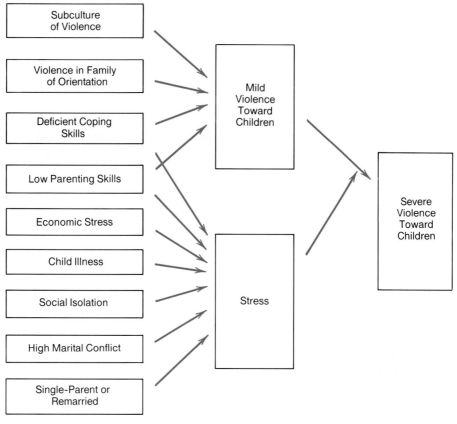

FIGURE 15·1   A Model for Violence Toward Children

Sexual Abuse

Sexual abuse may not be considered violent according to the definition used by Straus and Gelles (1986). It does not necessarily result in physical harm to a child. However, sexual abuse, particularly incest, is regarded with abhorrence in our society. Sexual abuse is a felony in most states and the penalty includes a prison term. The legal and social sanctions against it are generally more severe than the sanctions against physical violence, unless the violence is very severe.

There is little valid research on sexual abuse within the family. Available evidence suggests that it may be more common than popularly believed. In a Los Angeles survey, Wyatt (1985) found that almost 50 percent of young women between the ages of 18 and 36 had been sexually abused prior to age 18, although most abusers were not family members. Baker and Duncan (1985) estimated sexual abuse rates at about 10 percent. Sexual abuse is not limited to girls. In a survey by Baker and Duncan (1985) 8 percent of the males reported they had suffered sexual abuse before the age of 16.

In the study by Wyatt (1985), 16 percent of the perpetrators were uncles, cousins, brothers, stepbrothers, or grandfathers; most were cousins or uncles. Another 6 percent of the offenders were stepfathers, foster fathers, or the mother's boyfriend. About 2 percent of the acts were committed by fathers.

Over half of the sexual abuse was limited to fondling. About one fourth was sexual intercourse or attempted sexual intercourse. The most common location was the home, and three fourths of the incidents involved a single occurrence by a given perpetrator (Wyatt 1985).

The harm of sexual abuse is well documented. Sexually abused adolescents are more likely than nonabused adolescents to feel anxious and suicidal. Many adolescents who run away from home have been sexually abused. Male victims tend to fear adult men, and females report being confused about sex (McCormack et al. 1986).

Initial reactions to sexual abuse include fear, anxiety, depression, anger, and hostility. Long-term effects include depression, low self-esteem, self-destructive behavior, substance abuse, and sexual maladjustment. Sexual abuse involving father figures, force, and genital contact appear to be the most damaging (Browne and Finkelhor 1986; Brunngraber 1986).

Preventing Abuse

Given the high rate of physical violence against children, what can and should be done about it? One possibility is to use screening devices to identify high risk parents prior to abuse. This suggestion is not feasible because we are not able to predict future abuse accurately. The characteristics identified earlier are associated with abuse, but are ineffective in predicting abuse precisely. For example, Milner et al. (1984) reported tht a majority of parents with elevated scores on their Child Abuse Potential Inventory did not abuse. Similarly, only 6 percent of high risk mothers subsequently abused their children in a study done by Altemeier et al. (1984). The 6 percent is much higher than the 1 percent of abuse found among mothers predicted not to be at risk. However, they were wrong in 94 percent of the cases in which they predicted that abuse would occur.

Various legal remedies have been proposed, but the effectiveness of most legal interventions is questionable (Herman 1985; Stein 1984). The current system of police, social workers, and criminal sanctions does not appear to be particularly effective (Shireman, Miller, and Brown 1981).

Myers (1985) suggests a therapeutic rather than an adversarial approach to help reduce child abuse. He contends that our criminal justice system is punitive, accusatory, and stigmatizing and does not help the victim or offender in family violence cases. A more fruitful approach may be to spend time and resources on therapy for the child, family, and abuser rather than for the rigors of the legal process.

Some recent efforts to help child abuse offenders appear promising. Wolfe, Sandler, and Kaufman (1981) developed a program to train abusive parents in parenting skills and self-control. Observations of parents in their homes and parental reports revealed improvements in parental effectiveness. A follow-up after one year revealed no suspected or reported incidents of child abuse among those who participated in the program. Others have shown that a cognitive-behavioral treatment program for child abusers appears encouraging (Azar and

Twentyman 1986; Koverola, Elliot-Faust, and Wolfe 1984; Wolfe and Sandler 1981).

Marital Violence

Rates

Table 15·2 shows rates of husband-to-wife and wife-to-husband violence found in the national survey done by Straus and Gelles (1986). The data show that in 1985 about 11 percent of the husbands were violent toward their wives and 3 percent were severely violent. Women's rates were similar; about 12 percent were violent toward their husbands and more than 4 percent were severely violent. There was violence by at least one spouse in 16 percent of the couples and almost 6 percent experienced severe violence.

A breakdown by specific violent acts is shown in Table 15·3. Wives were more likely than husbands to throw something or slap. Husbands were slightly more likely to push or shove. Wives were also more likely than husbands to kick, bite, hit, or threaten with a gun or knife. There was no difference between wives and husbands in actual use of a gun or knife, whereas men were much more likely than women to beat up their spouse.

The data show relatively high rates of violence between husbands and wives, and that wife-to-husband violence is somewhat higher than husband-to-wive violence. However, a substantial amount of wife-to-husband violence appears to be retaliation or self-defense (Goetting 1987; Straus and Gelles 1986).

A more complete description of family violence was provided by the National Crime Survey (Klaus and Rand 1984). It included only severe family violence that would be considered a crime legally. Eighty-eight percent of all crimes by

TABLE 15·2 Marital Violence: Comparison of Rates in 1975 and 1985

	Rate per 1,000 Couples		t for 1975–1985
Violence Index	*1975*	*1985*	*Differences*
A. Husband-to-Wife			
Overall violence (1–6)	121	113	0.91
Severe violence (4–8)	38	30	1.60
("wife beating")			
B. Wife-to-Husband			
Overall violence (1–6)	116	121	0.57
Severe violence (4–8)	46	44	0.35
C. Couple			
Overall violence (1–6)	160	158	0.20
Severe violence (4–8)	61	58	0.46
Number of Cases	2,143	3,520	

SOURCE: Straus, M. A., and R. J. Gelles. 1986. Societal change and change in family violence from 1975 to 1985 as revealed by two national surveys. *Journal of Marriage and the Family* 48:470, Table 2. Copyrighted 1986 by the National Council on Family Relations, 1910 West County Road B, Suite 147, St. Paul, Minnesota 55113. Reprinted by permission.

TABLE 15·3 Marital Violence: Comparison of Specific Acts (1975–1985)

Type of Violence	Husband-to-Wife		Wife-to-Husband	
	1975	1985	1975	1985
A. Minor Violence Acts				
1. Threw something	28	28	52	43
2. Pushed/grabbed/shoved	107	93	83	89
3. Slapped	51	29**	46	41
B. Severe Violence Acts				
4. Kicked/bit/hit with fist	24	15*	31	24
5. Hit, tried to hit with something	22	17	30	30
6. Beat up	11	8	6	4
7. Threatened with gun or knife	4	4	6	6
8. Used gun or knife	3	2	2	2
Number of cases	2,143	3,520	2,143	3,520

$* p < .05; ** p < .01$ (two-tailed t tests for 1975–85 differences).

SOURCE: Straus, M. A., and R. J. Gelles. 1986. Societal change and change in family violence from 1975 to 1985 as revealed by two national surveys. *Journal of Marriage and the Family* 48:471, Table 3. Copyrighted 1986 by the National Council on Family Relations, 1910 West County Road B, Suite 147, St. Paul, Minnesota 55113. Reprinted by permission.

relatives were assaults, 10 percent were robberies, and 2 percent were rapes. About one third of the assaults were classified as aggravated assaults, indicating the use of a weapon or serious injury. Half of the victims were actually injured by the assault, although 80 percent suffered only cuts and bruises. About 60 percent of the violent crimes were committed by spouses.

The survey illustrates the repetitive nature of spouse abuse. About one fourth of those who had been attacked by their spouses said similar assaults had occurred at least three times during the previous six months. Women were victims of criminal assaults three times more often than men (Klaus and Rand 1984).

One of the acts of violence not included in most studies is **marital rape,** which is forcing a spouse to have sex against her will. There have been two recent studies of marital rape. First, in a survey of 930 ever-married women by Russell (1982), 14 percent reported being raped by a husband or ex-husband. Second, Finkelhor and Yllo (1983, 1985) found that 10 percent of a sample of 326 New England women said they had been forced to have sex in marriage. Given the reluctance of women to define sexual assaults of their husbands as rape, it seems safe to conclude that *at least* 10 percent of women have been raped within marriage (Steinmetz 1987).

Men who rape their wives usually also abuse their wives in other ways (Pagelow 1986). Furthermore, marital rape is usually not a single incident; research suggests that about three fourths of women who have been raped in marriage have been raped more than once (Pagelow 1986).

Homicide is the most violent act of all. Statistics from the FBI indicate that about one fourth of all homicide victims are killed by another family member, and about 11 percent are killed by their spouse (Federal Bureau of Investigation 1985).

Husband-wife homicides tend to be extremely violent in terms of the number of stabbings or shots that occur. They are more violent than nonfamily homicides. In about two thirds of the cases a gun is the weapon. Knives are the second most commonly used weapon, and wives are more likely than husbands to use them (Howard 1986). About 85 percent of husband-wife homicides occur at home. The bedroom is the most lethal room followed by the kitchen (Wolfgang 1956). Wives are much more likely to be killed than husbands. Recent FBI data indicate that in about 64 percent of husband-wive homicides the wife is the victim (Federal Bureau of Investigation 1985). When wives kill their husbands it is usually in response to serious physical and verbal abuse (Goetting 1987; Howard 1986).

Trends

Has marital violence changed during the past decade? The data from Straus and Gelles (see Tables 15·2 and 15·3) show that marital violence decreased somewhat from 1975 to 1985. The decreases were generally small, although severe husband-to-wife violence decreased from 38 to 30 percent. The data in Table 15·3 show that husbands were significantly less likely to slap, kick, or bite their wives in 1985 than 1975.

No trend data are available for marital rape. Data on marital homicide show two trends in recent years. First, there has been a large increase in the proportion of wives who are victims of homicide. In 1967 husband and wives killed each other in about equal proportions. By 1985 husbands killed wives almost twice as often as wives killed husbands. In 1985 wives represented 64 percent of all husband-wife homicide victims (Federal Bureau of Investigation 1985; Howard 1986).

A second trend is the increasing use of guns as the homicide weapon. In the fifties about one third of the time a gun was the murder weapon. This increased to 50 percent in the sixties. In the eighties the gun was the weapon in almost two thirds of husband-wife homicides (Goetting 1987; Howard 1986).

Reactions to Marital Violence

When faced with violent attacks from a spouse, one may retaliate, endure, try to stop the violence, or attempt to leave. We noted earlier that women who kill their husbands often are responding to repeated incidents of physical abuse. But killing a spouse is a terrifying thought, even if it occurs in self-defense. Perhaps the most rational responses to battering are to seek help to try to stop the violence or to leave the relationship.

One of the surprising findings is that so many battered women choose to remain in their relationships. One half to two thirds of battered women tend to remain with their abusive partners (Strube and Barbour 1983). Why do some women remain in an abusive relationship while others leave?

Research suggests that there are two major factors that influence the decision to leave a relationship. First, economic dependency is the major determinant. Women who are employed are much more likely to leave than women who depend entirely on their husband for support. Second, commitment to the relationship is important. Women who have lived with their husbands for a number of years or say they love them, are less likely to leave (Gelles and Cornell 1985; Strube and Barbour 1983, 1984).

Two other factors also have some influence on the decision to stay or leave. First, if the husband promises to change, many women are willing to give him a chance. Second, women who feel they have nowhere else to go are more likely to stay (Strube and Barbour 1984).

Many women seek outside help and some abusive husbands are then able to stop their battering. Bowker (1983) studied 136 women who had been successful in getting their husbands to stop abusing them. Some used personal strategies such as talking, threatening, avoidance, and passive defense (using arms, hands, and feet to protect the body). Police, lawyers, and social service agencies were formal sources of help. Informal help was sought from friends, neighbors, and relatives. Passive defense was the most frequently used personal strategy, friends were the most common informal source of help, and social services were the most often used formal source of help. All of the different strategies were effective at some times. The personal determination of the victim was the critical factor in eliminating violence rather than the type of help that was received (Bowker 1983).

Reasons for Marital Violence

There are many reasons why marital violence occurs. In this section we identify some of the major characteristics that have been found to be associated with marital violence. Several of the characteristics were identified earlier because they also are associated with child abuse.

ECONOMIC STRESS.   A number of studies have shown that marital violence is more likely to occur in low income families. Men who are unemployed are especially likely to batter their wives (Steinmetz 1987). Gelles and Cornell (1985) reported that violence against wives is almost twice as high among the unemployed. Generally, lower-class couples tend to experience more marital violence than middle- or upper-class couples (Lockhart 1987).

STRESS AND SOCIAL ISOLATION.   Stress may come from a variety of sources, including financial problems and marital difficulties. A number of studies and theories have established a link between stress and marital violence (Gelles and Cornell, 1985; Steinmetz 1987).

Individuals who assault often feel isolated and alone. As noted earlier, they tend to have fewer contacts with friends, neighbors, and relatives, and engage in fewer social activities. They lack social support during stress (Gelles and Cornell 1985).

VIOLENCE IN FAMILY OF ORIENTATION.   One of the most consistent findings in violence research is that children learn violent behavior in their family of orientation. A number of researchers have found that individuals who have observed and experienced violence in their families as children are likely to approve of violence and use it as adults (Gelles and Cornell 1985; Kruttschnitt, Heath, and Ward 1986; Steinmetz 1987). Rosenbaum and O'Leary (1981) reported that abusive husbands compared to nonabusive husbands were more likely to have been abused as children and more likely to have witnessed parental spouse abuse. Using a national probability sample, Ulbrich and Huber (1981) found that men who had observed their fathers hitting their mothers were more likely to approve of violence against women than men who had not had the experience. However, it is important to realize that growing up in a violent home is only one factor among many that influences spouse abuse. Many people who come from violent backgrounds are not violent as adults, and many persons who grew up in nonviolent homes are violent toward others as adults (Gelles and Cornell 1985; Stark and Flitcraft 1985).

SUBCULTURE OF VIOLENCE.   As with child abuse, spouse abuse is undoubtedly influenced by cultural and subcultural forces. Violence is often accepted and even glorified in the media, sports, and military. A variety of scholars have suggested that cultural and subcultural norms accept and even encourage marital violence (Carlson 1984; Pagelow 1986; Steinmetz 1987).

STATUS INCONSISTENCY AND STATUS INCOMPATIBILITY.   **Status inconsistency** is defined as a situation where one's occupation and education are not consistent. For example, if a man with a college education is a construction laborer, his job is not consistent with his education.

  Status incompatibility is a situation where marital partners have very different occupational or educational levels. For example, if a man has less education and a lower status occupation than his wife, they would be described as having status incompatibility.

  Hornung, McCullough, and Sugimoto (1981) found that marital violence is associated with both status inconsistency and status incompatibility. When the husband's occupation is below his educational level, the risk of violence is particularly high. Similarly, women who have a high occupational status relative to their husbands are more likely to be abused than women whose occupational status is equal to or lower than their husbands' status. Women whose education is low relative to their husbands also experience a high incidence of violence. Men high in occupational status tended to have low rates of wife abuse.

ALCOHOL.   A number of studies have shown that alcohol use is associated with marital violence. A high percentage of men who assault their wives have been drinking (Gelles and Cornell 1985; Rosenbaum and O'Leary 1981; Van Hasselt, Morrison, and Bellack 1985; Steinmetz, 1987). To illustrate, Corenblum (1983) found that among individuals who had never struck their spouse while sober, 45 percent had done so when intoxicated. However, it is unclear how alcohol use influences marital violence. Perhaps men drink, lose control, and then abuse their wives. Or do angry men drink in order to get courage to vent their anger? Does alcohol provide men with an excuse for their violent behavior? Whatever the mechanism, it is well established that men who drink heavily are more likely to physically assault their wives. Drinking may facilitate battering but does not appear to be the cause of violence (Waits 1985).

AUTOCRATIC DECISION MAKING.   Egalitarian decision making is associated with nonviolence. Straus et al. (1980) observed that wife-dominant and husband-dominant couples were more violent than democratic couples. Husband-dominant couples had the highest levels of wife beating and husband beating. Apparently, the discussion involved in democratic decision making helps resolve conflicts and reduces the risk of violence.

AGE.   Marital violence tends to occur much more frequently among young couples. The rate of marital violence is twice as high among couples under age 30 as among those over 30 (Gelles and Cornell 1985).

LOW SELF-ESTEEM.   There is some evidence that men who assault their wives tend to be low in self-esteem. They may feel inadequate and violence may be an effort to assert themselves. Because of their low self-esteem, they may feel more threatened by certain situations than a man with higher self-esteem (Gelles and Cornell 1985).

Related to self-esteem is the finding of Rosenbaum and O'Leary (1981) that abusers are less assertive with their wives than nonabusers. Perhaps men who feel inadequate are not able to assert themselves in nonviolent ways, and violence is an attempt to be assertive.

SUMMARY.   The variables we have described have been found to be some of the most important correlates of marital violence and to be similar to the correlates of parent-to-child violence. Research has shown that there is a substantial correlation between spouse abuse and child abuse (Gelles and Cornell 1985; Stark and Flitcraft 1985). Individuals tend to acquire cultural values that accept and encourage violence. If one experiences violence while growing up, one will learn that violence is one method of coping with problems. Economic problems, status inconsistency, and status incompatibility are all situations that are likely to increase stress and may lower feelings of esteem and adequacy. Social isolation produces loneliness and leaves couples deficient in the supports needed to cope with various stresses. Autocratic decision making and alcoholism may negatively affect marital satisfaction and decrease problem-solving effectiveness, which will increase stress.

These variables have been integrated into a model in Figure 15·2. As with any model, it does not capture the complexity of marital violence or all relevant variables. However, it does integrate several of the major correlates

There have been many different theories used to explain why marital violence occurs (Carlson 1984; Gelles and Cornell 1985; Long, Witte, and Karr 1983; Steinmetz 1987). The models presented in Figures 15·1 and 15·2 are based primarily on social learning theory and social situation theory. According to **social learning theory,** violence is learned the way one learns anything else. People learn to be violent through socialization in homes and through influences from friends, media, and schools.

Social situation theory assumes that family violence arises out of structural stress such as unemployment, social isolation, and status inconsistency. The social situation creates stress and opportunities for violence. Learning may also play a part in social situation theory, for how one reacts to different social situations is influenced by socialization.

The models in Figures 15·1 and 15·2 are also compatible with exchange theory. According to exchange theory, much of human behavior can be explained

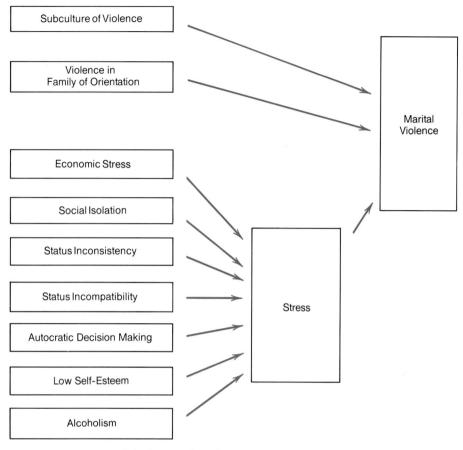

FIGURE 15·2   A Model of Marital Violence

by examining rewards and costs involved in family interactions. People often use violence to achieve desired ends and to minimize costs in a painful situation.

These theories have implications for ways to reduce marital violence. According to social situation theory, increases in formal and informal supports are needed to reduce the structural stress. Learning theory suggests that there needs to be educational efforts and media campaigns to interfere with the cycle of violence. The reductions in violence during the past decade reported by Straus and Gelles (1986) suggest that existing educational campaigns may have had some impact. Exchange theory suggests that violence can be reduced by making it less rewarding and more costly (Gelles 1982a). In the next section we will review and evaluate attempts to reduce marital violence.

Reducing Marital Violence

Cultural attitudes are tolerant of marital violence, and our laws and justice system reflect that tolerance. The legal system in the United States tends to be unresponsive to the problem (Buda and Butler 1984). Police are reluctant to arrest unless a serious injury has occurred (Zoomer 1983). The normal police practice is to talk to the assailant, and rarely is a referral made to a social agency (Brown 1984). Prosecutors practice a great deal of discretion and treat marital assaults differently than other assaults. Men who assault their wives are seldom charged, and when they are they are treated more leniently than individuals who commit nonfamily assaults (Ellis 1984; Wasoff 1982). In short, a battered woman who turns to the criminal justice system for help finds it unresponsive, slow, and unpredictable (Ford 1983).

Social service agencies in the executive branch of government are not much better. Some states have passed laws to provide **shelters** for women, giving the impression that they are doing something, yet have provided no funding for those shelters (Schechter 1981). Many existing services are underfunded and not coordinated.

What can be done to reduce marital violence in our society? Waits (1985) suggests four strategies. First, police should be required to arrest persons who assault their spouses. This would be a clear message that marital violence is not acceptable in our society. It would provide the victim with immediate protection from further assaults and might deter the perpetrator from committing similar offenses in the future.

Recent research in Minneapolis showed that Waits' suggestion has merit. An experiment was set up in which police randomly responded in three dif-

Police are sometimes called to intervene in violent family fights. In some areas police receive training on the nature of family violence and how to intervene.
Donna Ferrato/Visions.

ferent ways to cases of simple domestic assault. Cases involving serious injury were excluded from the study for ethical reasons. The three different responses were (1) arrest, (2) talk, and (3) an order to leave for eight hours. The behavior of the suspect was then monitored for six months to determine the extent of future marital violence. Both police records and victim reports revealed that suspects who were arrested showed less subsequent violence than suspects who were just talked to or ordered to leave home (Sherman and Berk 1984). This occurred even though most were jailed for only a short period. Almost half were released within twenty-four hours, and 86 percent were released within a week.

The data suggest that even if no further legal action is taken, arrest is not a waste of time in cases of domestic violence. There seems to be something about the process of arresting a person and locking him or her up for a day that deters future violence. It should be added that Sherman and Berk (1984) do not recommend that police be *required* to make an arrest in all cases of marital assault. They prefer a *presumption* of arrest, which means that an arrest must be made unless there are clear, justifiable reasons why an arrest should not be made.

The second suggestion of Waits (1985) is to train police about the nature of marital violence and how to handle domestic calls. This would help overcome bias and ignorance of police about marital violence.

Third, Waits (1985) recommends that prosecutors take the lead in handling cases of marital violence. The victim should be the witness, not the leader. As was noted earlier, prosecutors treat marital assaults differently than other assaults, and Waits is recommending that they be treated in the same way. Some states require a judicial hearing before a case is dropped. This is designed to protect a woman from succumbing to pressure from her husband to drop a case prematurely. Victims are subject to complex pressures, and consistency among prosecutors appears to be important (McLeod 1983).

Waits' final suggestion is to develop better coordination among social services and the legal system. Pretrial diversion to counseling is an effective response in many cases, but it should be backed by commitment to reinstate charges if the batterer commits additional violent acts. Communicating this to the abuser may be an important deterrent to future violence.

One of the recent responses to the problem of marital violence has been the establishment of shelters for battered women. Berk, Newton, and Berk (1986) have studied how use of a shelter may impact on future violence. They found that the effects depend on the attitudes of the victim. Women who have started taking control of their lives seem to benefit from shelter use. Going to the shelter may be an important step toward establishing a new, independent lifestyle. On the other hand, for some women going to the shelter may encourage retaliation. Berk et al. (1986) suggest that the solution to this problem may be better support from the legal system, as suggested by Waits.

Community services have an important role in reducing marital violence. Star (1982) has identified four major types of services and their problems. *Counseling* services provide individual and marital therapy for individuals involved in family violence. These are essential to help victims and perpetrators understand their situations and help resolve their problems. The second type of service is *education*. It includes such things as assertiveness training, parenting classes, and anger management. *Support services* are needed to help reduce stress. These include involvement in support groups such as Parents Anonymous where individuals can meet and talk to others who have experienced similar problems. Paraprofessionals who may help with transportation or provide homemaking services are also support services. Finally, *mediation* is crisis intervention designed to defuse a volatile situation and refer people to other services.

Services to reduce family violence face several obstacles. First, funding is always a problem. As noted earlier, some legislatures have passed statutes authorizing shelters but have not appropriated funds.

Second, evaluation of programs is needed. Many programs are begun but not systematically monitored and evaluated for effectiveness. For example, the research of Sherman and Berk (1984) demonstrated the effectiveness of arrests in reducing marital violence. Before their research the conventional wisdom was that arrests did not help and might encourage retaliation. Without valid evaluation, research decisions are based on conventional wisdom which, as Sherman and Berk (1984) showed, may be incorrect. The result will be that ineffective programs are perpetuated, and effective ones are not developed and maintained.

A third issue is **burnout.** Working in social services with members of violent families can be stressful. Activities and training to maintain morale and decrease burnout are needed.

Finally, Star (1982) notes that community support is often a problem. Some people may not want a shelter in their neighborhood and may not be aware of its value.

Learning successful conflict resolution techniques may be an important aspect of efforts to reduce marital violence. People sometimes use violence when they feel they have no other resources to resolve a conflict (Gelles and Cornell 1985). Teaching people techniques of conflict resolution may provide them with alternative resources for dealing with stressful situations. Martin et al. (1987) have shown that successful conflict resolution is much more likely in nonviolent families.

Other Types of Family Violence

There are a variety of other types of family violence that we review here. The data are incomplete because these other forms of violence have not been as well researched as parent-to-child and marital violence.

Child-to-Parent Violence

Data from a national sample of families with children between the ages of 10 and 17 shows that 9 percent of parents said their children had been violent toward them at least once during the past year. In 3 percent of the families the parents had suffered severe violence from their child—being kicked, punched, bitten, or having a knife or gun used (Cornell and Gelles 1982).

Sons commit more parental violence than daughters. Among sons, violence increases with age, whereas it decreases with age among daughters. Mothers

TABLE 15·4   Percentage of Families with Child-to-Parent
Violence by Gender and Severity

Gender of Child	Gender of Parent	Overall Violence	Severe Violence
Son	Mother	11	4
	Father	8	2
Daughter	Mother	9	5
	Father	4	0

SOURCE: Cornell and Gelles 1982:11, Table 1. Reprinted by
permission.

are abused more than fathers and daughters are as severely violent toward
mothers as sons are. For a summary of child-to-parent violence by sex of child
and parent, see Table 15·4.

Three factors seem common in child-to-parent violence. First, there is evidence of a learning component within the family. Sons and daughters are more
likely to be violent toward their mothers if their mothers have been abused
by their fathers (Cornell and Gelles 1982). Second, there is evidence that abusive
children have poor self-concepts. Finally, children who attack parents may have
been given too much control for their maturity level, and may attack parents
out of a sense of frustration (Gelles and Cornell 1985).

Sibling Violence

Nothing seems more common than siblings who fight. Steinmetz (1987) reports
that about 75 percent of children with siblings have at least one violent episode
during a year. There is an average of twenty-one violent acts between siblings
per year. Almost 50 percent of siblings are kicked, punched, and bitten annually.
Sixteen percent beat each other up. Less than 1 percent threaten to use or
actually use a gun or knife on a sibling (Steinmetz 1987). Figures from the
Federal Bureau of Investigation (1985) indicate that about 2 percent of all
homicides are one sibling killing another.

Boys appear to be slightly more violent than girls, but the difference is small
(Gelles and Cornell 1985). Felson (1983) found that outside the family, boys
were much more violent than girls, but that inside the family there were no
gender differences. Sibling violence tends to decrease with age, and children
are more violent with siblings who are close to the same age (Felson 1983;
Gelles and Cornell 1985).

Felson (1983) suggests that sibling rivalry has little to do with sibling violence. Most violence is what he calls **instrumental violence**—a child fights
to gain use of tangible goods or avoid unpleasant tasks.

Parental intervention seems to increase sibling violence rather than reduce
it. Perhaps younger siblings are more cautious about fighting if they know
their parents will not intervene (Felson 1983).

In egalitarian households, sibling violence is also higher than in a more
autocratic situation. The equality enables the younger sibling to complete
more favorably for rewards than in a more autocratic situation where the older
child gets more rewards by virtue of age (Felson 1983).

What can parents do to decrease the probability of sibling and child-to-parent violence? Research cited earlier provides several clues. First, they must not be violent themselves. A variety of studies show that children are more likely to use violence if their parents do (Ulbrich and Huber 1981). Second, parents need to be supportive and nurturant. Feelings of nonsupport and parental rejection are related to fighting (Loeber and Dishion 1984). Third, parents need to keep their marital conflicts within reasonable bounds. High rates of marital conflict are associated with violence in children (Loeber and Dishion 1984). Fourth, parents need to give children a strong message that violence is not acceptable. Permissiveness of aggression by parents is associated with increased violence by children (Olweus 1980). Fifth, parents need to be monitor their children's behavior but *not* use coercive discipline techniques. Poor parental monitoring is associated with higher rates of fighting, and parental coerciveness increases the level of aggression in children (Loeber and Dishion 1984; Olweus 1980).

Some people believe that exposure to television violence may increase violence in children, but that hypothesis has not been supported by research (Freedman 1984, 1986; Kruttschnitt, Heath, and Ward 1986). With regard to violence, children tend to model their *parents* rather than the television.

Elder Abuse

In recent years **elder abuse** has become an important issue. Research has just begun to be generated on this problem. Estimates are that between 4 and 10 percent of the dependent elderly suffer physically abusive acts from their children who care for them (Pillemer and Sinkelhor 1988; Steinmetz 1987; White 1989). About 4 percent of abuse may be considered moderate or severe (White 1989). It is difficult to obtain accurate estimates of elder abuse because the elderly are unwilling to report it. A consequence of their reporting it may be that they will be placed in an institution (Gelles and Cornell 1985).

Abused elderly persons tend to be females who are frail and mentally or physically impaired. They are usually between the ages of 75 and 85 and depend on the abuser to meet daily necessities (White 1989).

The typical abuser is the spouse or daughter of the abused. Pillemer and Sinkelhor (1988) found that the rate of abuse was 41 per 1,000 among elders who lived with their spouse, and 44 per 1,000 among those who lived with their children. The abusing child is usually a middle-aged daughter who has the primary caregiving responsibilities for her frail parent.

Two main factors seem to be associated with elder abuse. First, violence toward the elderly is associated with level of family stress. Steinmetz (1987) reported that families with high stress (such as financial problems or having small children) had elder abuse scores five times higher than families with low stress. A second factor is dependency. The more dependent elders are, the more likely they will be abused. Of course, stress and dependency go together, for a higher level of dependency will increase the level of stress (Gelles and Cornell 1985; Hickey and Douglass 1981; Steinmetz 1987).

Two theories that help explain elder abuse are the same ones that explain marital violence, namely social learning theory and social situation theory. Children and spouses who abuse the elderly have learned abusive behavior from the broader culture as well as in their family of orientation. They may feel burdened and isolated with the caregiving required. The situation may cause financial hardship and there may be a feeling of being trapped (White 1989).

Summary

1. Violence is an act carried out with the intent of causing physical pain or injury to another person. Violence may be classified according to seriousness, legitimacy, extent of injury, and motivation.

2. About 60 percent of children are the recipients of at least one violent act from their parents per year. More than 10 percent of children suffer severe violence each year.

3. Homicide is the fifth leading cause of death among children. Infants are at greater risk than older children, and more boys than girls are killed. Among children over a year of age that are killed, abut one fourth are killed by a parent.

4. Mothers are more likely than fathers to be violent and severely violent toward their children. Boys are more likely than girls to be treated violently.

5. From 1975 to 1985 there was a substantial decrease in severe and very severe parent-to-child violence.

6. Some of the major variables associated with parent-to-child violence are economic stress, low parenting skills, deficient coping skills, social isolation, child illness, high marital conflict, single parenthood, remarriage, stress, violence in family of orientation, and subcultural violence.

7. Abuse of children tends to decrease as they get older.

8. Valid data on rates of sexual abuse are not available, but available information indicates that sexual abuse of children is common. Children who are sexually abused often have a variety of psychological problems.

9. Programs to help child abusers develop parenting skills and self-control appear promising for reducing violence toward children.

10. More than 10 percent of husbands and wives are violent toward their spouses each year and more than 3 percent are severely violent. Women are slightly more violent than men. However, women are victims of criminal assaults three times more often than men.

11. Data suggest that at least one in ten married women have been raped by their husbands.

12. About one fourth of all homicide victims are killed by a family member and about 11 percent of victims are killed by their spouse. The gun is the usual weapon and most homicides occur at home. Wives are considerably more likely to be killed by a husband than to kill a husband.

13. There has been a modest decrease in the total amount of marital violence during the past decade. There has been an increase in the proportion of marital homicides in which the gun is the murder weapon. Among all husband-wife homicides, the percentage in which the wife is the victim has increased substantially during the past two decades.

14. Women who stay with an abusive husband tend to be economically dependent and have a commitment to the relationship.

15. Some of the characteristics associatd with marital violence are economic stress, social isolation, violence in family of orientation, living in a violent

subculture, status inconsistency, status incompatibility, use of alcohol, autocratic decision making, low self-esteem, age, and stress.

16. The legal system tends to be tolerant of marital violence by being unresponsive, slow, and unpredictable.

17. There is evidence that if police would arrest husbands who are violent toward their wives, rather than simply talk to them, marital violence would decrease.

18. Use of a shelter may help some women escape a violent relationship, although it may encourage retaliatory violence among dependent women who return to their husbands.

19. Each year about one in ten parents has suffered violent acts at the hands of their children. In 3 percent of families, children have been severely violent toward their parents. Sons are more violent than daughters, and mothers are attacked more than fathers.

20. Children who are violent toward their parents tend to have observed violence in their family, have poor self-concepts, and may have been given too much control.

21. About three fourths of children with siblings have at least one violent episode with a sibling each year. Boys appear slightly more violent than girls and sibling violence decreases with age.

22. Sibling violence is more common in egalitarian households and if the parents intervene in sibling fights.

23. To decrease violence among children, parents should be nonviolent themselves, keep marital conflict within reasonable limits, monitor their children's behavior, not be permissive toward aggression, not be coercive, and be supportive.

24. Estimates are that from 4 to 10 percent of the dependent elderly suffer abuse at the hands of their spouse or children. Family stress and the dependency of the elderly person are the two major factors associated with elder abuse.

Important Terms

- burnout
- elder abuse
- extent of injury caused by violence
- instrumental violence
- legitimacy of violence
- marital rape
- minor violence
- motivation for violence
- seriousness of violence
- severe violence
- shelter
- social learning theory
- social situation theory
- status incompatibility
- status inconsistency
- subculture of violence
- very severe violence
- violence

Questions for Discussion

1. What is violent behavior? Give several concrete examples.
2. How violent is American society? Give examples of violence in movies, television, sports, schools, and homes. Is violence glorified?

3. What types of violent acts are legitimate in our society and what types are not legitimate?
4. Can a violent act be serious and not produce an injury? Can an act low in seriousness produce extensive injury?
5. Is motivation important in evaluating violent acts? Explain.
6. Why do you think parental violence against children has decreased in recent years? What should we do to reduce parent-to-child violence even more?
7. Are mothers more violent than fathers? How? Why?
8. What are some of the factors that contribute to violence against children?
9. How does sexual abuse harm children?
10. In what ways are women more violent than men? In what ways are men more violent than women? Why?
11. Why are marital homicides more violent than other homicides?
12. Among marital homicides, why has the ratio of women's to men's deaths increased in recent years?
13. Why do so many women stay with their husbands even after suffering repeated physical abuse? What could be done to change this?
14. What are the major variables that are associated with marital violence?
15. What could be done to reduce the amount of marital violence?
16. Why do you think arresting a batterer reduces subsequent marital violence even if there is not further legal action?
17. Why do children abuse their parents? What could be done to reduce child-to-parent violence?
18. Outside the family boys are much more violent than girls, but within the family girls are about as violent as boys. Why?
19. Why is parental intervention in sibling quarrels associated with higher levels of sibling violence? Under what conditions do you think parents should intervene in sibling fights, and why?
20. Why is there more sibling violence in egalitarian families?
21. What could parents do to decrease the amount of sibling violence among their children?
22. What could be done to protect the dependent elderly from abuse?
23. Is our society a violent society? Why?
24. Is violence ever justified in families? Why or why not? Under what conditions?
25. Why is the American family so violent?
26. Is violent behavior ever a positive force?
27. If someone attacked you, would you fight back or run? Why? Would your response be different if your attacker was bigger or smaller than you, a man or a woman, a family member, or not?
28. How would you want your son to react if he were pushed around by some classmates at school? Would you want your daughter to react any differently? Would it make any difference if the aggressors were boys or girls?
29. Under what conditions do your think someone should endure abuse without retaliating? Under what conditions do you think someone should try to withdraw from the abusive situation without retaliating? Under what conditions do you think someone should retaliate abuse with violence?

Recommended Reading

LOEBER, R., and T. J. DISHION. 1984. Boys who fight at home and school: Family conditions influencing cross-setting consistency. *Journal of Consulting and Clinical Psychology* 52:759–768.

ROSENBAUM, A., and K. DANIEL O'LEARY. 1981. Marital violence: Characteristics of abusive couples. *Journal of Consulting and Clinical Psychology* 49:63–71.

WOLFE, D. A. Child-abusive parents: An empirical review and analysis: *Psychological Bulletin* 97:462–482.

WOLFE, D. A., J. SANDLER, and K. KAUFMAN. 1981. A competency-based parent training program for child abusers. *Journal of Consulting and Clinical Psychology* 49:633–640.

References

ALTEMEIER, W. A., S. O'CONNOR, P. VIETZE, H. SANDLER, and K. SHERROD. 1984. Prediction of child abuse: A prospective study of feasibility. *Child Abuse & Neglect* 8:383–400.

AMEDEO-EINEKER, S. 1985. *Socio-cultural determinants of child abuse.* Paper presented at annual meeting of Pacific Sociological Association, Albuquerque, NM, April 17–20.

ANDERSON, R., R. AMBROSINO, D. VALENTINE, and M. LAUDERDALE. 1983. Child deaths attributed to abuse and neglect: An empirical study. *Children and Youth Services Review* 5:75–89.

AZAR, S. T., D. R. ROBINSON, E. HEKIMIAN, and C. T. TWENTYMAN. 1984. Unrealistic expectations and problem-solving ability in maltreating and comparison mothers. *Journal of Consulting and Clinical Psychology* 52(4):687–691.

AZAR, S. T., and C. A. ROHRBECK. 1986. Child abuse and unrealistic expectations: Further validation of the parent opinion questionnaire. *Journal of Consulting and Clinical Psychology* 54(6):867–868.

AZAR, S. T., and C. T. TWENTYMAN. 1986. Cognitive-behavioral perspectives on the assessment and treatment of child abuse. *Advances in Cognitive-Behavioral Research and Therapy* 5:237–267.

BAKER, A. W., and S. P. DUNCAN. 1985. Child sexual abuse. A study of prevalence in Great Britain. *Child Abuse & Neglect* 9:457–467.

BERK, R. A., P. J. NEWTON, and S. F. BERK. 1986. What a difference a day makes: An empirical study of the impact of shelters for battered women. *Journal of Marriage and the Family* 48:481–490.

BOWKER, L. H. 1983. *Beating wife-beating.* Lexington, MA: Lexington Books.

BROWN, S. E. 1984. Police responses to wife beating: Neglect of a crime of violence. *Journal of Criminal Justice* 12:277–288.

BROWNE, A., and D. FINKELHOR. 1986. Impact of child sexual abuse: A review of the research. *Psychological Bulletin* 99(1):66–77.

BRUNNGRABER, L. S. 1986. Father-daughter incest: Immediate and long-term effects of sexual abuse. *Advances in Nursing Science* 8(4):15–35.

BUDA, M. A., and T. L. BUTLER. 1984. The battered wife syndrome: A backdoor assault on domestic violence. *Journal of Family Law* 23(3):359–390.

CARLSON, B. E. 1984. Causes and maintenance of domestic violence: An ecological analysis. *Social Service Review* 58(4):569–587.

CATE, R. M., J. M. HENTON, J. KOVAL, F. S. CHRISTOPHER, and S. LLOYD. 1982. Premarital abuse. *Journal of Family Issues* 3(1):79–90.

CORENBLUM, B. 1983. Reactions to alcohol-related marital violence. *Journal of Studies on Alcohol* 44(4):665–674.

CORNELL, C. P., and R. J. GELLES. 1982. Adolescent to parent violence. *Urban and Social Change Review* 15:8–14.

CREIGHTON, S. J. 1985. An epidemiological study of abused children and their families in the United Kingdom between 1977 and 1982. *Child Abuse & Neglect* 9:441–448.

DALY, M., and M. WILSON. 1985. Child abuse and other risks of not living with both parents. *Ethology and Sociobiology* 6:197–210.

ELLIS, J. W. 1984. Prosecutorial discretion to charge in cases of spousal assault: A dialogue. *Journal of Criminology Law & Criminology* 75(1):56–102.

Federal Bureau of Investigation. 1985. *Uniform crime reports.* Washington, DC: U.S. Government Printing Office.

FELSON, R. B. 1983. Aggression and violence between siblings. *Social Psychology Quarterly* 46(4):271–285.

FINKELHOR, D., and K. YLLO. 1983. Rape in marriage: A sociological view. In *The dark side of families*, ed. D. Finkelhor, R. J. Gelles, G. T. Hotaling, and M. A. Straus, 119–130. Beverly Hills, CA: Sage.

FINKELHOR, D., and K. YLLO. 1985. *License to rape.* New York: Holt.

FORD, D. A. 1983. Wife battery and criminal justice: A study of victim decision-making. *Family Relations* 32:463–475.

FREEDMAN, J. L. 1984. Effect of television violence on aggressiveness. *Psychological Bulletin* 96(2):227–246.

FREEDMAN, J. L. 1986. Television violence and aggression: A rejoinder. *Psychological Bulletin* 100:372–378.

GARBARINO, J. 1983. Children and youth service review. *Children and Youth Services Review* 5(5–6):3–6.

GARBARINO, J., C. SCHELLENBACH, and J. SEBES. 1986. *Understanding families at risk: Adolescent maltreatment.* New York: Aldine.

GELLES, R. J. 1982a. Applying research on family violence to clinical practice. *Journal of Marriage and the Family* 44:9–19.

GELLES, R. J. 1982b. Domestic criminal violence. In *Criminal violence*, ed. M. E. Wolfgang and N. A. Weiner, 201–235. Beverly Hills, CA: Sage.

GELLES, R. J., and C. P. CORNELL. 1985. *Intimate violence in families.* Beverly Hills, CA: Sage.

GELLES, R. J., and M. A. STRAUS. 1985. Violence in the American family. In *Crime and the family*, ed. A. J. Lincoln and M. A. Straus, 88–110. Springfield, IL: Chas. C Thomas.

GOETTING, A. 1987. Homicidal wives: A profile. *Journal of Family Issues* 8:332–340.

HAWKINS, W. E., and D. F. DUNCAN. 1985a. Perpetrator and family characteristics related to child abuse and neglect: Comparison of substantiated and unsubstantiated reports. *Psychological Reports* 56:407–410.

HAWKINS, W. E., and D. F. DUNCAN. 1985b. Children's illnesses as risk factors for child abuse. *Psychological Reports* 56:638.

HERMAN, D. M. 1985. A statutory proposal to prohibit the infliction of violence upon children. *Family Law Quarterly* 14(1):1–52.

HICKEY, T., and R. L. DOUGLASS. 1981. Neglect and abuse of older family members: Professionals' perspectives and case experiences. *Gerontologist* 21(2):171–176.

HORNUNG, C. A., B. C. MCCULLOUGH, and T. SUGIMOTO. 1981. Status relationships in marriage: Risk factors in spouse abuse. *Journal of Marriage and the Family* 43:675–692.

HOWARD, M. 1986. Husband-wife homicide: An essay from a family law perspective. *Law and Contemporary Problems* 49(1):63–88.

KLAUS, P., and M. RAND. 1984. *Family violence.* Washington, DC: U.S. Department of Justice, Bureau of Justice Statistics.

KOVEROLA, C., D. ELLIOT-FAUST, and D. A. WOLFE. 1984. Clinical issues in the behavioral treatment of a child abusive mother experiencing multiple life stresses. *Journal of Clinical Child Psychology* 13(2):187–191.

KRUGMAN, R. D., M. LENHERR, L. BETZ, and G. E. FRYER. 1986. The relationship between unemployment and physical abuse of children. *Child Abuse & Neglect* 10:415–418.

KRUTTSCHNITT, C., L. HEATH, and D. A. WARD. 1986. Family violence, television view habits, and other adolescent experiences related to violent criminal behavior. *Criminology* 24(2):235–267.

LAHEY, B. B., R. D. CONGER, B. M. ATKENSON, and F. A. TREIBER. 1984. Parenting behavior and emotional status of physically abusive mothers. *Journal of Consulting and Clinical Psychology* 52(6):1062–1071.

LENINGTON, S. 1981. Child abuse: The limits of sociobiology. *Ethology and Sociobiology* 2:17–19.

LENOIR-DEGOUMOIS, V. 1983. The manifestations of ill-treatment of children: Historical background. *International Journal of Offender Therapy and Comparative Criminology* 27(1):55–60.

LOCKHART, L. L. 1987. A reexamination of the effects of race and social class on the incidence of marital violence: A search for reliable differences. *Journal of Marriage and the Family* 49:603–610.

LOEBER, R., and T. J. DISHION. 1984. Boys who fight at home and school: Family conditions influencing cross-setting consistency. *Journal of Consulting and Clinical Psychology* 52(5):759–768.

LONG, S. K., A. D. WITTE, and P. KARR. 1983. Family violence: A microeconomic approach. *Social Science Research* 12:363–392.

McCORMACK, A., M. JANUA, and A. W. BURGESS. 1986. Runaway youths and sexual victimization: Gender differences in an adolescent runaway population. *Child Abuse & Neglect* 10:387–395.

McLEOD, M. 1983. Victim noncooperation in the prosecution of domestic assault. *Criminology* 21(3):395–416.

MARTIN, M. J., W. R. SCHUMM, M. A. BUGAIGHIS, A. P. JURICH, and S. R. BOLLMAN. 1987. Family violence and adolescents' perceptions of outcomes of family conflict. *Journal of Marriage and the Family* 49:165–171.

MARTIN, M. J., and J. WALTERS. 1982. Familial correlates of selected types of child abuse and neglect. *Journal of Marriage and the Family* 44:267–276.

MILNER, J. S., R. G. GOLD, C. AYOUB, and M. M. JACEWITZ. 1984. Predictive validity of the child abuse potential inventory. *Journal of Consulting and Clinical Psychology* 52(5):879–884.

MYERS, J. E. B. 1985. The legal response to child abuse: In the best interest of children? *Journal of Family Law* 24(2):149–269.

National Center for Health Statistics. 1986. Advance report of final mortality statistics, 1984. *Monthly Vital Statistics Report,* vol. 35, no. 6, Supp.(2). DHHS Pub. No. (PHS) 86–1120. Hyattsville, MD: Public Health Service.

OLWEUS, D. 1980. Familial and temperamental determinants of aggressive behavior in adolescent boys: A causal analysis. *Developmental Psychology* 16(6):644–660.

ORME, T. C., and J. RIMMER. 1981. Alcoholism and child abuse. *Journal of Studies on Alcohol* 42(3):273–287.

PAGELOW, M. D. 1986. *Marital rape: But if you can't rape your wife, who can you rape?* Paper prepared for presentation at the annual meeting of the Pacific Sociological Association, Denver, CO, April.

PAPERNY, D. M., and R. W. DEISHER. 1983. Maltreatment of adolescents: The relationship to a predisposition toward violent behavior and delinquency. *Adolescence* 18(71):499–506.

PASSMAN, R. H., and R. K. MULHERN. 1977. Maternal punitiveness as affected by situational stress: An experimental analogue of child abuse. *Journal of Abnormal Psychology* 86(5):565–569.

PILLEMER, K., and D. SINKELHOR. 1988. The prevalence of elder abuse: A random sample survey. *Gerontologist* 28:51–57.

ROSENBAUM, A., and K. DANIEL O'LEARY. 1981. Marital violence: Characteristics of abusive couples. *Journal of Consulting and Clinical Psychology* 49(1):63–71.

RUSSELL, D. E. N. 1982. *Rape in marriage.* New York: Macmillan.

SCHECHTER, L. F. 1981. The violent family and the ambivalent state: Developing a coherent policy for state aid to victims of family violence. *Journal of Family Law* 20(1):1–42.

SHERMAN, L. W., and R. A. BERK. 1984. The specific deterrent effects of arrest for domestic assault. *American Sociological Review* 49:261–272.

SHERROD, K. B., S. O'CONNOR, P. M. VIETZE, W. A. ALTEMEIER. 1984. Child health and maltreatment. *Child Development* 55:1174–1183.

SHIREMAN, J., B. MILLER, and H. F. BROWN. 1981. Child welfare workers, police, and child placement. *Child Welfare League of America* 30(6):413–422.

SMITH, S. L. 1984. Significant research findings in the etiology of child abuse. *Social Casework* 65(6):337–346.

STAR, B. 1982. Reducing family violence. *Urban and Social Change Review* 15(1):15–20.

STARK, E., and A. FLITCRAFT. 1985. Woman-battering, child abuse and social heredity: What is the relationship? *Sociological Review Monograph* 31:147–171.

STEIN, T. J. 1984. The child abuse prevention and treatment act. *Social Service Review* (June):302–314.

STEINBERG, L. D., R. CATALANO, and D. DOOLEY. 1981. Economic antecedents of child abuse and neglect. *Child Development* 52:975–985.

STEINMETZ, S. K. 1987. Family violence. In *Handbook of marriage and the family,* ed. M. B. Sussman and S. K. Steinmetz, 725–765. New York: Plenum.

STRAUS, M. A., and R. J. GELLES. 1986. Societal change and change in family violence from 1975 to 1985 as revealed by two national surveys. *Journal of Marriage and the Family* 48:465–479.

STRAUS, M. A., R. J. GELLES, and S. K. STEINMETZ. 1980. *Behind closed doors: Violence in the American family.* Garden City, NY: Doubleday, Anchor Press.

STRUBE, M. J., and L. S. BARBOUR. 1983. The decision to leave an abusive relationship: Economic dependence and psychological commitment. *Journal of Marriage and the Family* 45:785–793.

STRUBE, M. J., and L. S. BARBOUR. 1984. Factors related to the decision to leave an abusive relationship. *Journal of Marriage and the Family* 46:837–844.

ULBRICH, P., and J. HUBER. 1981. Observing parental violence: Distribution and effects. *Journal of Marriage and the Family* 43:623–631.

VAN HASSELT, V. B., R. L. MORRISON, and A. S. BELLACK. 1985. Alcohol use in wife abusers and their spouses. *Addictive Behaviors* 10:127–135.

VASTA, R. 1982. Physical child abuse: A dual-component analysis. *Developmental Review* 2:125–149.

VESTERDAL, J. 1983. Etiological factors and long term consequences of child abuse. *International Journal of Offender Therapy and Comparative Criminology* 27(1):21–54.

WAITS, K. 1985. The criminal justice system's response to battering: Understanding the problem, forging the solutions. *Washington Law Review* 60:267–329.

WASOFF, F. 1982. Legal protection from wife beating: The processing of domestic assaults by Scottish prosecutors and criminal courts. *International Journal of the Sociology of Law* 10:187–204.

WHITE, M. 1989. Elder abuse. In *Aging and the family*, ed. S. J. Bahr and E. T. Peterson. Lexington, MA: Lexington Books.

WOLFE, D. A. 1985. Child-abuse parents: An empirical review and analysis. *Psychological Bulletin* 97(3):462–482.

WOLFE, D. A., and J. SANDLER. 1981. Training abusive parents in effective child management. *Behavior Modification* 5(3):320–335.

WOLFE, D. A., J. SANDLER, and K. KAUFMAN. 1981. A competency-based parent training program for child abusers. *Journal of Consulting and Clinical Psychology* 49(5):633–640.

WOLFGANG, M. E. 1956. Husband-wife homicides. *Corrective Psychiatry and Journal of Social Therapy* 2:263–271.

WOLFGANG, M., and F. FERRACUTI. 1967. *The subculture of violence*. London: Tavistock.

WYATT, G. E. 1985. The sexual abuse of Afro-American and white-American women in Childhood. *Child Abuse & Neglect* 9:507–519.

ZOOMER, O. J. 1983. On the social causes and function of violence against women. *International Journal of Offender Therapy and Cooperative Criminology* 27(2):173–183.

CHAPTER *16*

Separation and Divorce

Introduction

Edward is obviously nervous as he takes the stand. He testifies that his es-
tranged wife, Emily, has a violent temper and has frequently abused their
children and on one occasion attacked him. His testimony suggests that Emily
is unstable and unfit as a parent. Edward seeks a judgment giving him custody
of their three children. After Edward's testimony, Emily takes the stand. Her
testimony contradicts Edward's and portrays him as a cold, hostile man who
cares little for her or the children. She feels strongly that all three children
should be placed in her custody.

A psychologist then provides the court with an evaluation of the fitness of
Edward and Emily as custodians of the children. Each is portrayed as being
an adequate parent in most respects, although each has some psychological
problems. The psychologist favors placing all three children with the father,
but he reports that the boy prefers to live with the father and the two girls
with their mother.

After hearing the final arguments of the two lawyers, the judge signs the
official divorce decree. The two girls, ages 10 and 6, are awarded to the mother,
and the boy, who is 13, to the father. Edward is ordered to pay $400 a month
to Emily for child support and alimony. He must also pay the fees of both
attorneys, a total of $10,000.

As they leave the courtroom, Edward is emotionally exhausted. He feels that
Emily and her attorney have lied and taken advantage of him, and that the
judge has allowed this fraud to occur. Edward wonders how he will manage
financially and fears that he will seldom be able to see his daughters. He is a
bitter and defeated man.

Emily is equally bitter and feels that Edward made exaggerated and distorted
statements about her competence as a person, wife, and mother. In her mind,
he has driven her son away from her. She tried to be a good wife and mother

for fourteen years and her reward is the loss of her son, no training, no job, and minimal financial support.

Fourteen years earlier Edward and Emily were married in a church and vowed to stand by each other in sickness and in health, for better or worse. They loved each other and were looking forward to raising a family together. As time passed, many problems arose and love turned to dislike and disgust. Finally, the burden of living together became too great and they parted, disillusioned and bitter.

They both wanted custody of all three children and felt that the other was not a fit parent. After separating, each hired an attorney and a bitter struggle over custody and money ensued. The legal process took over a year and ended with the formal trial. The courtroom was the final battleground in which each tried to expose the other and emerge as the victor. In the end both felt defeated.

After the formal court trial their conflict will continue. Edward will have difficulty meeting all the expenses simply because two residences are more expensive than one and he must pay the attorneys' fees. Therefore, he will occasionally miss a payment and will sometimes be late or send only part of the amount ordered by the judge. After all, he feels it is unjust anyway. Emily will not be anxious to allow him to visit their two girls and will be less cooperative when the support payments are tardy or incomplete. This will anger Edward and he will feel even less of an obligation to make support payments or to allow Emily to see their son. And so the conflict goes.

Edward and Emily are an example of many couples who formally dissolve their relationships each year. In this chapter we examine the process of marital dissolution. Six major questions are addressed: (1) What is the history of divorce in the United States? (2) What is current divorce policy? (3) What are the trends in divorce rates and how much divorce currently exists? (4) Why does divorce and separation occur? (5) What is the divorce process like? (6) What are common reactions and adjustments to divorce for adults and children?

History of American Divorce Law

In the United States, divorce law was influenced significantly by English law and values. The southern colonies followed the position of the Church of England and did not allow divorce. The New England colonies, on the other hand, permitted divorce for serious marital misconduct such as adultery, desertion, and extreme physical cruelty. Divorce became an **adversary system** that was placed under the jurisdiction of civil courts.

Marriage was seen as the cornerstone of society and was considered to be a lifelong union between one man and one woman. Divorce was an evil to be avoided and was granted only for a serious moral transgression by one party against the other. The purpose of the divorce was to punish the guilty party and provide relief for the innocent person.

Gradually divorce became more common and its grounds were expanded. Marriage evolved from a sacred bond to a civil **contract** that could be dissolved if necessary. Rather than being an evil, divorce was viewed increasingly as an unfortunate but necessary solution to marital failure.

This emerging view of divorce was not consistent with the law on the books,

This woman watches as her husband walks out, a common occurrence in American families. It is estimated that about one-half of all current marriages will end in separation or divorce. *Nancy Batas/The Picture Cube.*

and during the twentieth century a large gap developed between statute and practice. In statute, divorce was denied unless there was marital misconduct, and it was illegal for a husband and wife to mutually agree to divorce. In practice, perjury and collusion were used to circumvent the statutes. Individuals exaggerated and lied about marital offenses and some couples even worked together to present false evidence. The law was frequently used as a negotiating tool by the spouse who was less eager for divorce. She or he would agree not to contest the divorce action in return for concessions regarding money and children. Lawyers and judges knowingly allowed and participated in this perjury and collusion (Krause 1977). "Dressed up as divorce for misconduct, consent divorce, abhorred in the official law of all states, [became] an established institution of American law" (Rheinstein 1972:63).

With changing attitudes and increasing demand for divorce, laws based on fault (i.e., marital misconduct) came under increasing criticism. The major arguments against fault laws may be summarized as follows: First, because they are not consistent with prevailing attitudes, fault requirements encourage dishonesty and undermine the integrity of the legal process (Krause 1977; Rheinstein 1972; Spanier and Anderson 1979). Second, fault laws tend to increase hostility and conflict between spouses. This is not necessary and tends to make an unhappy, stressful situation worse. Finally, it is unrealistic to identify one spouse as the guilty party, because rarely is one spouse solely responsible for the marital problems.

Rising divorce rates focused attention on these criticisms and stimulated a movement toward **no-fault divorce.** New York and California were the first states to enact no-fault legislation. In 1967 New York added the no-fault grounds "living separate and apart" to several traditional grounds of marital misconduct. The separation period was shortened from two years to one year in 1972. California broke more completely with tradition and eliminated all types of marital misconduct as grounds for divorce. The California Family Law Act, which became effective in 1970, established "irreconcilable differences" as the sole grounds for divorce. By 1985 all fifty states had passed some type of no-fault divorce statute. In 15 states irreconcilable differences or **irretrievable breakdown** was the sole grounds, and in the other states no-fault grounds were added to traditional fault grounds of divorce (Freed and Walker 1986).

Marriage and divorce laws are legislated by each state, and divorces are granted by state civil courts. This power was given to each state by the Tenth Amendment of the U.S. Constitution. An amendment to the Constitution would be required before the Congress could legislate on marriage and divorce. As America grew and became more mobile, many felt a need for uniform federal legislation and lobbied for a constitutional amendment in this area. These efforts failed:

> . . . the Congress could not be moved to propose an amendment to extend federal legislative power to the field of family life. Between 1884 and 1947 motions were introduced in every new Congress, variously striving to achieve uniform federal legislation on marriage and divorce, or on divorce alone, or at least to inhibit migratory divorce. None of these proposals ever came to a vote. Only a single one reached the stage of committee discussion (Rheinstein 1972:46).

Although the Congress cannot legislate marriage and divorce laws, considerable federal influence has been exerted in this area by the U.S. Supreme Court. Their rulings on sex discrimination have prompted a number of states to modify their statutes. For example, in March of 1979 the court ruled that an Alabama statute allowing **alimony** only for wives is unconstitutional (**Orr v. Orr,** 440 U.S. 268). They held that unless a sex classification serves some important and specific governmental objective, it violates the equal protection principles of the Fourteenth Amendment. The ten states that permitted only wives to receive alimony were forced to change their statutes to allow either spouse to receive it (Freed and Foster 1981). The net effect of federal influence has been to create greater uniformity among the various state divorce laws.

Current Divorce Policy

Although federal influence has increased in recent years, marriage continues to be a state-regulated status that requires action by a state court for dissolution. Adding no-fault laws has had little effect on the adversarial way in which divorce cases are processed. With or without no-fault laws, an attorney who is hired to represent one spouse cannot ethically give legal advice to the other. Attorneys are advocates for their clients and usually attempt to achieve the optimal settlement possible. Legal ethics require that attorneys represent their clients zealously, which encourages attorneys to take extreme positions that are unnecessarily divisive (Cavanaugh and Rhode, 1976; Coogler 1977; Weiss 1975). It is not uncommon for attorneys to advise their clients to engage in conflict-escalating behavior (McKenry, Herrman, and Weber 1978). Thus, the divorce process continues to be structured as a contest between two opponents (Eisler 1977; Elkin 1977).

Current divorce policy can be summarized as follows:

1. A civil judge must review every divorce case to insure that the rights of the weak and innocent are protected. He may overrule agreements made between a divorcing husband and wife if he regards their decisions as unconscionable, although he rarely does.
2. If disputes are not resolved by the parties themselves, an adversary proceeding is used to settle the differences. A judge hears evidence presented by an advocate for each party and then resolves the dispute by court order. This adversary system extends far beyond the courtroom and affects bargaining all during the divorce process (Mnookin and Kornhauser 1979).

There are two major assumptions underlying this policy. First, divorcing couples cannot be trusted to make decisions regarding their money and children by themselves. Hence a judge must review *all* divorce agreements to insure that they are legal and fair. Second, it is assumed that in a "contest between two opponents justice will somehow emerge" (Eisler 1977:39).

Trends in Divorce Rates

During the past century there has been a gradual increase in the U.S. divorce rate. There are substantial increases following each major war, after World War I there was a modest increase, and then the divorce rate decreased during the early years of the Depression. The divorce rate started increasing again during the late thirties and increased dramatically during and after world War II. It decreased substantially in the late forties and then remained relatively stable for about twenty years. The divorce rate began increasing again in 1962 and rose sharply in the late sixties and early seventies and the divorce rate was relatively stable from 1980 to 1988 (National Center for Health Statistics 1986, 1987, 1988). Figure 16·1 shows the divorce rates in the United States since 1925. The highest divorce rate was in 1979 and there were slight decreases during the early 1980s.

The total yearly number of United States divorces surpassed 1 million 1975 and in the 1980s stabilized at a little below 1.2 million. There are two adults involved in every divorce and, on the average, one child. Thus, about 3.5 million individuals in the United States are affected directly by divorce each year. With current divorce rates, about half of all first marriages will eventually end in divorce (Norton and Moorman 1987; Schoen et al. 1985).

An examination of divorce by age cohort was recently completed by Norton and Moorman (1987). They obtained a projected lifetime divorce rate for each cohort by adding the total number of divorces that have occurred to the total that will occur if current age-specific divorce rates continue. The projected

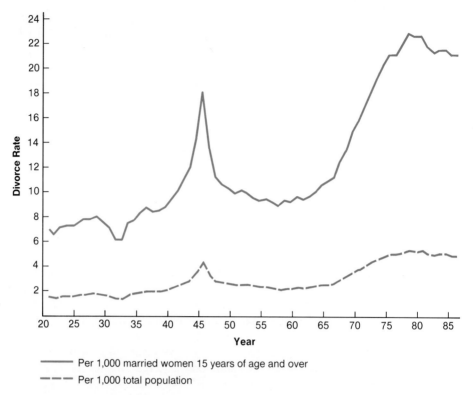

FIGURE 16·1   United States Divorce Rates (1920–1987)
SOURCES: National Center for Health Statistics 1986, 1987, 1988.

lifetime divorce rate for women between the ages of 55 and 59 (in 1985) was
24 percent. The comparable rates were 36 percent for women ages 45 to 49
and 56 percent for women ages 35 to 39. Thus, in the span of twenty years
the lifetime divorce rate more than doubled, from 24 percent to 56 percent.
They projected that the lifetime divorce rate for women between the ages of
25 and 29 (in 1985) will be 54 percent.

There are several major reasons why the divorce rate increased during the
sixties and seventies. First, there were more economic alternatives available
than in the past, particularly for females. Because of these greater educational
and employment opportunities as well as increased financial support from the
government, wives did not feel as constrained to stay in an unsatisfying marriage. Similarly, husbands did not feel as obligated to stay in a bad marriage
as they had in earlier periods. Thus, economic alternatives made it easier than
previously for people to divorce if their marriage was not satisfactory. This
suggests that American marriage has not necessarily deteriorated but that
more unsatisfactory marriages are ending in divorce today than in previous
decades.

A second reason for the rising divorce rates was that the purposes of marriage
had changed somewhat over time. In days gone by, marriage was considered
an important economic institution and was vital for educating individuals in
religious and occupational realms. Today, the primary function of the family

is affection. People marry for love and expect it to be a happy, pleasurable state. Love is a fragile thing and if love diminishes or changes, there are few other bonds to keep the marriage together. If the purpose of marriage is affection, and affection is gone, why should it continue?

Third, people's expectations for marriage are high in our society. Unrealistically high expectations about marriage may be another reason why the divorce rate increased.

Fourth, a trend toward individualism and away from group sacrifice undoubtedly was one of the reasons why the divorce rate increased. People in American society seek individual rights and self-fulfillment and don't want to be fettered by group obligations. Marriage is a group obligation that limits personal autonomy. Sociologist William Goode notes that we want "more personal freedom, more self-seeking, more room for developing our own interest and personalities, and less responsibility toward others. Most of us are not willing to accept the deep, real restrictions on choices that a strengthened family life would require" (1976:17).

Finally, it is worth noting that the three periods in which the U.S. divorce rate rose sharply followed major wars. These were periods of rapid social change in which traditional patterns and values were questioned and modified. Increases in rates of divorce and suicide typically are associated with periods of social upheaval and change (Durkheim 1951).

Along with these social trends, the laws of divorce have changed. The empirical evidence suggests, however, that the laws have not affected the divorce rate. Divorce rates began increasing about eight years before no-fault laws were passed, and increases in divorce rates were similar for states with and without no-fault statutes (Dixon and Weitzman 1980; Mazur-Hart and Berman 1977; Michael 1977; Schoen, Greenblatt, and Mielke 1975; Sell 1979; Wright and Stetson 1978).

Why Divorce Occurs

Now let us turn to the question of why an individual couple decides to get a divorce. What characteristics differentiate couples who get a divorce from those that stay together? Let's look at two couples who illustrate this difference.

Elaine and Allen have been married nineteen years, have four children, and are not particularly satisfied with their marriage. There are many things that they do not like about each other, but somehow they have managed to stay together. Many times during their marriage Elaine has thought about divorcing Allen, but for various reasons she has never actually filed for divorce. Allen is a traveling salesman who is frequently away from home. This makes it easier for them to maintain a stable marriage and keep the amount of conflict between them within tolerable limits. Allen's income is about average, and Elaine is an independent person who manages the home and children efficiently. They do not communicate well but they have done their best to be good parents. They have had some good times together with their children. Neither is very happy with the marriage, but each has decided not to seek a divorce. What is it that keeps Elaine and Allen together even though their marriage is unsatisfactory?

In contrast, Jim and Nola recently divorced after twelve years of marriage and the births of two children. Their personalities are very different, and they did not communicate very well while they were married. Jim is somewhat passive and does not take much initiative whereas Nola is known for her initiative and achievement orientation. She feels that while she was married she had to do almost everything with regard to bills, the children, and maintenance of the home. Nola is a professor at a local university and is able to support herself and her children.

An Exchange Theory of Divorce

— Explains why people do of a get out of relationship.

Why have Elaine and Allen stayed together whereas Jim and Nola have divorced? Levinger (1979) has set forth an exchange framework that helps explain why divorce occurs. He maintains that marital cohesiveness depends on the **attractions** (rewards) of the marriage, and **barriers** (costs) to leaving the marriage, and the **alternative attractions** outside the marital relationship. In exchange terminology, the marriage stays together because of the **rewards** of the marriage, the **costs** of leaving the marriage, and the rewards of an alternative to the existing marriage. This model suggests that divorce depends on much more than marital satisfaction. Some people will stay in a marriage because the costs of leaving the marriage are too great, even though they are very unsatisfied. Others may stay in a marriage because they perceive no viable alternative. Or, the alternative may be even less satisfactory than the current situation.

Levinger categorized attractions into three types: **material rewards, symbolic rewards, and affectional rewards.** Material rewards would be such things as family income and home ownership. Some people are attracted to a marriage because of the material benefits. Symbolic rewards may be such things as prestige from educational or occupational status. Affectional rewards would be physical attraction and companionship.

Barriers can also be classified according to material, symbolic, and affectional nature. The expense of divorce and the loss of economies of scale (savings obtained by purchasing larger quantities) are **material barriers.** For example, a large residence is generally less expensive than two small residences. Similarly, it is usually cheaper for a couple to buy food than for two individuals to purchase food separately. A **symbolic barrier** would be a religious commitment to marriage or the fact that being married is part of one's identity. One may stay married not because it is attractive, but because one attaches much importance to marriage and its continuance. An **affectional barrier** would be children. Some may decide not to get a divorce because they fear not being able to see their children frequently and associate with them.

Levinger also categorized alternative attractions into material, symbolic, and affectional. The ability of one's spouse to earn income independently of the other would be a **material alternative.** The opportunity to be independent and develop one's self would be a **symbolic alternative** to marriage. If one is attracted to someone other than one's spouse, there is an **affectional alternative** to the current marriage.

Research on Reasons for Divorce

We will review available research to determine what variables are most important in predicting marital dissolution. One interesting study on this topic was recently done by Booth and White (1980). They interviewed 1,364 married persons about whether they had thought of divorce or not. They found that thinking about divorce was common during the first ten years of marriage and then gradually declined. Almost one in five admitted to thinking about divorce during this period.

To measure thinking about divorce Booth and White used the following question: "Sometimes people become so upset and dissatisfied with their marriage that they think about getting a divorce. Has this happened to you within the last two years?" They found that individuals with preschoolers were about twice as likely to have considered divorce within the last two years than those with no children or older children. Those who married earlier, particularly in the teenage years, were more likely to think about getting a divorce. Those who belong to a religious denomination were less likely to think about divorce, and strong affiliates with a religion were much less likely to think about divorce than those who were not. They found that income level was not strongly associated with thinking about divorce but being employed full-time was. Those who were considering divorce had fewer barriers to leaving the marriage. They had jobs, perceived the family income as below average, were not religious, married young, and had not been married very long.

Bumpass and Sweet (1972) studied separations and divorces among a national sample of females. They found that the most important and consistent predictor of marital separation was age at marriage. Women who married in their teens were much more likely than others to experience marital disruption. A number of researchers have found that teenage marriages carry a high risk of divorce (Bahr and Galligan 1984; Booth and Edwards 1985; Kiernan 1986; Moore and Waite 1981; Thornton 1978).

Why do early marriers have higher divorce rates? Booth and Edwards (1985) found that inadequate role performance is the major factor. It appears that individuals who marry in their teens may not have the skills needed to sustain a relationship. Booth and Edwards (1985) found that lack of sexual faithfulness, inadequate understanding, disagreement, and a lack of companionship were the major sources of dissatisfaction associated with early marriage.

Bumpass and Sweet (1972) also found that women who were premaritally pregnant were slightly more likely to dissolve their marriage, but women whose first births were illegitimate had substantially higher levels of disruption. Women whose parents had experienced a divorce or separation were more likely to be involved in a divorce themselves, and individuals who had been previously married had higher rates of marital disruption than those who were in their first marriage. There also was evidence that interfaith marriages had higher rates of marital instability.

Furstenberg (1979) has done additional research on the relationship between premarital pregnancy and marital disruption. His data indicate that the courtship process is disrupted by premarital pregnancy and this decreases the time needed to prepare for the marriage. This finding is consistent with the ex-

Teenage marriages have a much higher rate of divorce than marriages that begin after age 20.   *Stephen Shames/Visions.*

planation from role theory that *anticipatory socialization* is related to the ease of transition into a role. Anticipatory socialization is the training and preparation one receives before actually carrying out a given role or task, for example, if an engaged couple baby-sat for an infant together or participated in other joint activities before they married. Furstenberg found that the marriages tended to be unstable unless the couple had known each other for a considerable length of time and had had an exclusive relationship prior to the pregnancy.

Furstenberg discovered that economics was the most important reason for the high rates of disruption among marriages preceded by a pregnancy. Marriages frequently floundered because the husband was not able to support the family. His research suggests the importance of material attractions and barriers in keeping marriages together.

One of the intriguing findings of Bumpass and Sweet was that divorce may be transmitted across generations. Research by Pope and Mueller (1976) also shows that individuals whose parents have divorced are more likely to divorce. They found, however, that the effects were small.

In a study of five hundred divorced persons by Albrecht and Kunz (1980), four major reasons were given by the respondents for their divorces: 1) infidelity, 2) loss of love for each other, 3) emotional problems, and 4) financial problems. In their marriages the affectional and material rewards were gone and it simply became too costly to stay in the relationship. Some of the perceived barriers to obtaining a divorce were concern over financial support, particularly for females. Albrecht and Kunz suggested that many wives put up with unsatisfactory marriages because of their inability to provide for themselves and their children. Two other important barriers for divorce were children and personal religious beliefs. The concern about the children was particularly a barrier for the men. The data also suggest that people choose divorce because of individual unhappiness and the desire to get out of a bad situation.

Experience and research suggests that money is an important factor in the decision to divorce. However, the actual amount of income earned appears to have little effect on the decision to divorce. Ross and Sawhill (1976) found, for example, that family income was not related to marital stability. They did find, however, that an unstable income and a lack of assets were related to higher separation rates. Galligan and Bahr (1978) found that income level was not related to marital breakup but level of debt was. They suggested that learning how to manage money is critical for marital success and that debt places a significant strain on couples. Similarly, Booth et al. (1986) found that the accumulation of assets reduces the propensity to divorce.

Kitson, Holmes, and Sussman (1977) studied couples who had filed for divorce and tried to determine which factors induced them to reconcile and which induced them to go through with the divorce. They observed that those with a relatively high expected income for the coming year were more likely to reconcile. For such couples, the divorce would have been a material cost and this acted as a barrier against going through with it. Another important factor was the employment status of the wife. Employed wives were more likely to go through with the divorce than nonemployed wives. Again this is evidence for an alternative material reward to the marriage. Those who frequently attended church and those who had major health problems were also more likely to reconcile than other individuals. These might all be interpreted as symbolic costs of the divorce.

The most important factor in predicting whether a couple would reconcile or divorce was how well one spouse lived up to the other's expectations as a parent. Some who were unhappy in their marriage and had filed for divorce subsequently reconciled because their spouse was a good parent to the children. The data of Kitson et al. (1977) suggest that it is the costs of divorce and not the rewards of marriage that tend to keep many couples together.

Waite, Haggstrom, and Kanouse (1985) suggest that children are a strong

A bad marriage is better than a good divorce. No one wants to change divorce laws.

barrier to divorce. They studied the marital disruption of a national sample of young persons over a period of three years. Twenty percent of the childless couples separated or divorced within two years compared to 7 percent of the couples with a child.

Married couples on welfare appear more likely to get a divorce than low-income couples who are not on welfare (Bahr 1979). Similarly, Hannan, Tuma, and Groeneveld (1977) and Bishop (1980) have shown that couples who receive an income supplement are more likely to divorce than those who do not. These data can again be interpreted in terms of an alternative material attraction outside the marriage.

Bennett, Blanc, and Bloom (1988) examined how premarital cohabitation was related to subsequent marital dissolution, using data from the Women in Sweden survey. They found that woman who cohabited had significantly higher dissolution rates and a weaker commitment to marriage than those who had not cohabited.

A study by Hayes, Stinnett, and DeFrain (1980) provides some insights regarding the process of marital dissolution. They interviewed 138 individuals who had divorced after at least fifteen years of marriage. First, three fourths felt that their partner had not been easy to talk to. The inability or unwillingness to share feelings and being too judgmental were commonly perceived communication problems. The typical pattern was a lack of communication, as almost half said they seldom had quarreled. Another factor was that the relationship damaged self-esteem. A majority of the respondents said that their spouse had "seldom" or "never" contributed to their self-esteem. The burden of facing criticism and derogatory remarks became too great and the decision to divorce followed. A third problem was lack of companionship. Shared activities decreased with time and many could not think of anything they did together that gave them pleasure. Fourth, a majority expressed dissatisfaction with the amount of affection they had received in the marriage. Finally, the attempt by one to control the other was listed as a problem by many of the respondents.

Summary of Divorce Risk Factors

From available research it is possible to identify a number of characteristics that are associated with divorce. Although none of them can predict divorce with high accuracy, they may be considered risk factors because couples in these situations are somewhat more likely to terminate their marriages than couples without these characteristics. We conclude this section with a summary of the major risk factors discovered in divorce research.

1. *Teenage marriage.* One of the most consistent predictors of marital breakup is early marriage. Many couples that marry in their teens frequently have difficulties supporting families and have not had time to really get to know each other and prepare for marital roles. Avoiding teenage marriages is good advice for couples.
2. *Short courtships.* A number of studies have shown that short acquaintances have higher divorce rates. It takes time to adjust to a person and

prepare for marriage. Choosing properly, learning to adjust to each other, and role preparation all ease the transition into actual marriage.

3. *Premarital pregnancy.*   Several studies indicate that pregnancies and births before marriage increase the risk of divorce.

4. *Financial debt.*   Studies suggest that avoiding debt is particularly important for marriage. Having a high income is not important but having a stable well-managed income is. Even under the best conditions, adjustments in marriage will be difficult. There are always conflicts between individuals because of unique differences. Mismanagement and debt can strain even the best marriages.

5. *Education.*   Schooling increases employability and future income and may also improve communication skills and other competencies necessary for adequate performance of various marital roles.

6. *Unemployment.*   Financial security is important and unstable employment is unsettling and increases the risk of divorce.

7. *Religious activity.*   Those who attend religious services regularly are less likely to get a divorce than those who do not.

8. *Premarital cohabitation.*   Cohabiting premaritally increases the risk of marital dissolution, apparently because cohabitors have a weaker commitment to marriage than noncohabitors.

The Dissolution Process

Alientation Process

Divorce does not just suddenly happen. Couples usually go through a process of alienation in which the two gradually drift apart. Waller and Hill (1951) studied the process of alienation and identified seven stages that people often pass through on the road to divorce. First they discovered that there was some disturbance of the affectional and sexual life of the pair. As things got difficult in the marriage, feelings of affection would decrease and there would be a loss of rapport and some withholding of affectional and sexual responses. A second transitional point in this process is the moment in which the possibility of divorce is mentioned. Waller and Hill felt that this is equivalent to the declaration of love in the courtship process. Each person has probably thought of divorce but when it is first mentioned it is then out in the open.

A third point in this process occurs when the appearance of solidarity is broken. People tend to keep their troubles to themselves, and when significant friends and others learn that a couple is having trouble, the marriage is on a different basis. Waller and Hill referred to this as the master symptom of alienation, when the world around the couple becomes aware that their marriage is no longer viable. The fourth stage is the actual decision to divorce, which has usually taken a long time.

The fifth stage is the crisis of separation, and the sixth stage is the actual divorce. The final stage in this process, according to Waller and Hill, is the period of mental conflict, which is the period of rebuilding after the breakup of the marriage.

During courtship two people meet, gain rapport, and gradually develop into a functioning unit as a couple. Alientation may be conceived as a reversal of this process. A couple will stop functioning as a dyad and have less commitment to each other. They may notice personality differences and ways they do not complement each other. This will lead to less accurate role taking and less self-disclosure. Communication often becomes more difficult and eventually ends in the dissolution of the relationship.

The decision to divorce, the act of physically separating, and the filing of the divorce petition are three important steps in the process of divorce. Some move through these steps quickly, and others take a great deal of time. Melichar and Chiriboga (1985) found that women who spent more time between the decision to divorce and the actual separation tended to adjust more easily to the divorce. Perhaps this was a period of psychological adjustment and preparation. Women who went slowly from separation to legal action, however, tended to feel more stymied than women who moved more quickly.

The Legal Progress of Divorce

Whenever a divorce occurs there are three parties involved: ths husband, the wife, and the state. Divorce is a legal process and individuals must comply with state regulations to obtain it. As the alienation process proceeds and divorce is contemplated, one of the first steps for most people is to contact a lawyer to help them through the legal process.

The legal system affects the dissolution process in different ways, depending on the couple. Sometimes one party simply withdraws from the marriage and disappears, and the other party hires an attorney and files for a simple, **uncontested divorce.** The deserted party is left with any children and the judge awards custody to him or her. No monetary settlement is made, either because the whereabouts of the departed spouse is unknown or there is no money to divide. One spouse simply departs and does not ask for or offer anything. The two spouses make their own way as best they can. In this type of situation, lawyers do nothing regarding property settlement and custody. The simply ask a few questions, fill out the required legal forms, and file them with the court.

More commonly, the husband and wife know they're getting a divorce and negotiate in some way over the money and the property. There's alienation and bitterness between husband and wife, but they resign themselves to the situation and work out mutually acceptable settlement terms. They decide that one or the other should have the children, and they divide up the property. Then one spouse hires an attorney who drafts a formal settlement agreement and files the divorce papers. The judge then reviews the agreement and awards the divorce. In this situation the attorney is not highly involved in any bargaining, as the two individuals resolve most of the differences by themselves. Typically the amount of property and money involved is not large. Most divorces fit into this type of situation. An attorney is brought in merely to put the document in legal form and file the appropriate papers with the court.

A third type of situation is where one or more attorneys are heavily involved in the divorce process. Prolonged conflict over child custody, child support, and property division usually occur in this type of situation. In the beginning one spouse may hire an attorney and file a legal complaint requesting divorce, custody of the children, and a certain amount in money and property. The other spouse becomes angered by these "unreasonable demands" and hires an attorney, who files a countersuit. The two attorneys bargain with each other on behalf of their clients and attempt to win the best settlement possible. Usually after many charges, countercharges, threats and legal maneuverings, the parties reach a compromise. This is drafted into a formal settlement agreement and becomes part of the order set forth by the judge in the divorce decree. Occasionally an agreement is not reached and a court trial results. Then the judge weighs the evidence presented by each attorney and resolves the disputes by court order.

Consequences of Divorce for Adults

Marital dissolution is a major life transition that is often stressful, and Holmes and Rahe (1967) rated it as more stressful than all other transitions except death of a spouse. Bloom, White, and Asher (1979) examined the empirical literature on this topic and found that separated and divorced persons have higher-than-average rates on a number of physical and emotional disorders. Alcoholism, psychiatric problems, disability, and illness were more common among the separated and divorced. Automobile accident rates were higher among divorced than married persons. Finally, deaths from suicide, homicide, and disease were found more frequently among the maritally disrupted. Kiecolt-Glaser et al. (1987) observed that marital disruption increased depression and immune system dysfunctioning, leading to increased morbidity (disease rates) and mortality (death rates).

Why Divorced Persons Have Poorer Health

There are three explanations for the overrepresentation of separated and divorced persons among people with various physical and mental problems. First, the stress of uncoupling may produce higher rates of physical and emotional disorders (**stress hypothesis**). According to this idea, it is the transition from being married to unmarried that produces the problems. A second explanation is that being married insulates or cushions one from a variety of stresses (**cushion hypothesis**). Married people may face just as many stresses as the divorced, but having a spouse with which to share burdens may make it easy to tolerate a variety of stresses. Finally, people who already are prone to certain types of physical and mental problems may be poorer marital risks. For example, a person who is an alcoholic may be a poor marital risk and thus, the alcoholism may produce the divorce rather than the divorce being the cause of alcoholism. According to this hypothesis, certain disabilities that exist before marriage select people out as poor marital risks (**selectivity hypothesis**).

Existing research provides some support for all three of these hypotheses. Bloom et al. (1979) found that some physical and emotional illnesses precede and help precipitate marital disruption. Similarly, Erbes and Hedderson (1984) reported that separation and divorce is more likely to occur among men with low psychological well-being.

The work of Bloom et al. (1979) provides some support for the stress hypothesis. As noted earlier, marital disruption was associated with increased risk of physical and mental difficulties. Similarly, Kiecolt-Glaser et al. (1987) found that marital disruption increased depression and decreased the functioning of the immune system.

The cushion hypothesis is supported by the work of Pearlin and Johnson (1977), which was discussed in Chapter 6. Married people under severe economic strain suffered much less depression than unmarried persons with a similar amount of strain. Pearlin and Johnson suggested that marriage can act as a protective barrier against various stress: "Marriage does not prevent economic and social problems from invading life, but it apparently can help people fend off the psychological assaults that such problems otherwise create" (p. 714).

How Stressful Is Divorce?

In a study of eight-nine divorced persons, Bahr (1982) asked the following question: "How stressful was the experience of obtaining the divorce?" One woman reported that the divorce process was a relief and that the stress she had experienced was in trying to make the marriage work. Another said the actual divorce was "relieving, exciting, wonderful!" Some people said that although the divorce process was very stressful, the most difficult time was before the separation. Most described the divorce experience as difficult and painful. A man age 36 said, "I went through hell. I couldn't believe it was happening." Sixty-nine percent reported that it was very stressful whereas only 5 percent said it was not stressful at all. Clearly, divorce is a major transition in life and produces a substantial amount of stress.

Albrecht's (1980) survey of five hundred divorced persons produced similar results. Almost one fourth characterized the experience as a traumatic nightmare, and 40 percent said it was stressful but bearable. Altogether a total of 63 percent said divorce was either stressful or traumatic. More females than males described their divorce as traumatic (27 percent compared to 16 percent). When asked what was the most difficult period, slightly over 50 percent said "before the decision to divorce." Only 3 percent indicated that "now" was the most difficult time. When asked to compare their present situation with the predivorce period, 93 percent said their present situation was better, and only 2 percent said it was worse. These figures demonstrate that although divorce is stressful for most people, it is preferable to staying in a difficult marriage.

The most traumatic change in lifestyle following divorce was a decrease in income among females (Albrecht 1980). Forty-eight percent reported that their post divorce income was much lower than the income of close friends and associates. The comparable percentage for males was only 7 percent. The females were also more likely than the males to increase their contact with relatives after divorce.

Espenshade (1979) found that the median income for families headed by males was over twice as great as the median income for families headed by females. A review of time series data on the ratio of income to family needs revealed that over a six-year period divorced women had a 7 percent reduction in living standards whereas divorced men experienced a 17 percent increase. Married couples had an increase of 21 percent over the same period.

A major consequence of divorce for women and children is a substantially reduced income, which decreases below the poverty line for one in five women who divorce. This poor, divorced woman is making a purchase with food stamps. *Kevin Horan/Picture Group.*

An analysis of poverty data yielded equally dramatic differences between males and females. The proportion of males who were below the poverty line was altered little by divorce. For females, there was a net increase of 17 percent who became poor since experiencing divorce. Four percent who had been poor climbed out of poverty while 21 percent of the nonpoor had become poor over the six-year study period (Espenshade 1979).

Over the short term, divorce is particularly devastating for women. Weitzman (1981, 1985) found that one year after the divorce, men had a 42 percent increase in their standard of living compared to a 73 percent decrease for women. Others also have observed large decreases in the economic well-being of women after divorce (Day and Bahr 1986; McLindon 1987; Weiss 1984).

To determine the specific problems associated with being divorced, Bahr (1982) asked respondents the following question: "What are some of the difficulties you have encountered since being divorced?" The purpose was to let people identify and describe their difficulties without any suggestions from the interviewer. The most common problem following divorce was lack of money. Almost one fourth of the males had financial problems compared to

43 percent of the females. The males complained about being left with the bills after divorce and the difficulty in trying to keep up with support payments. The females talked of the constant financial strain resulting from divorce, and some said it was difficult to find adequate work with limited job skills. The costs of two residences make divorce an expensive undertaking that produces financial stress for a substantial number of divorced persons. The females had financial difficultly almost twice as often as the males did.

A second difficulty was the increased responsibility following divorce. Over 40 percent of the females said the dual responsibilities of being a parent and provider were stressful. Some typical comments were:

"I am overwhelmed with the responsibility."
"It is difficult being the only disciplinarian of the children."
"Everything must be done by yourself."
"I am overwhelmed with the children."
"Working and trying to take care of the children is difficult."
"The balance between home and work is hard."

Providing and caring for children is often difficult for two parents. It can be particularly stressful when one has to do it alone. Because females almost always obtain custody, men seldom feel the same pressure of increased responsibility.

In Bahr's sample, about one person in five said they had difficulty in dealing with emotions resulting from the divorce experience. Men were much more likely than females to report such problems, 39 percent compared to 12 percent. The major emotional problems were being hurt, loss of trust, feelings of failure, depression, guilt, and loss of self-esteem. The following are a sample of comments:"

"I was a devoted wife and mother and was just abandoned. I can't understand why. It hurt and was devastating."
"I have a fear of women and will have difficulty trusting in another relationship."
"I am now distrustful of men."
"For a year I have felt guilty for having left."
"It is difficult having to deal with what has happened in the marriage."
"Emotional adjustment is difficult."
"It was hard on my self-esteem. I asked myself, 'Am I still acceptable?' "
"I don't trust a single soul from this experience."

People invest much in marriage, and when it dissolves a substantial number have a sense of failure and loss that is difficult to adjust to.

Loneliness is another major adjustment. This is again primarily a male problem. Almost one third of the men but only 14 percent of the women said loneliness was a problem. Females usually have the children and appear to have stronger social supports and kinship bonds than men. One third of the men said a major problem was that they missed their children. After divorce the man may be carefree and single, but the detachment produces loneliness and alienation.

A number of respondents (16 percent) reported prejudice and social stigma against divorced persons. The social adjustment to singlehood and dating was also mentioned by 16 percent. A few claimed that harassment from their ex-spouse created stress. One female in ten said she had encountered no difficulties since being divorced, compared to only 3 percent of men who made such a claim.

Overall, the two major difficulties for divorced females were financial problems and the increased responsibility of supporting and caring for children. For males, emotional problems and loneliness were the two most difficult things to adjust to, although one fourth also said finances were a problem. The stress of divorce does not appear greater for females than males, but the type of strains are different. Divorced females need more money and help with their children. Divorced males need more social interaction, particularly with their children. Children and time complicate divorce. Those who were married for short periods of time and had no children did not appear to have as many difficulties.

How Does Divorce Improve Life?

As mentioned earlier, many choose divorce because they feel it will improve their life situation. Albrecht (1980) found that almost all divorced persons report their current circumstances to be better than their predivorce situation. In what specific ways does divorce improve people's situations? To help answer these questions Bahr (1982) asked the following: "What aspects of your life have improved since you became divorced?"

One third of the females and one fourth of the males mentioned that their self-esteem had improved since the divorce. Typical comments were as follows:

- "My self-esteem has increased. I am no longer belittled by my former spouse."
- "I can face reality and like myself again."
- "I feel I have some self-worth."
- "You discover you have the ability to survive on your own."

The criticism and verbal attacks some people face in marriage are difficult to handle. Many men and women experience a new sense of worth and self-confidence when divorce ends these verbal attacks.

One third of the women but only 6 percent of the men mentioned that divorce had relieved tension and helped bring peace of mind for them. They described their life since the divorce as "more relaxed and less tense." A number mentioned that they now have a new peace of mind and calmness. For example, one woman said, "I was on the brink of a nervous breakdown with him. Now I have more peace of mind."

About one fifth of the respondents also said they had learned new skills as a result of the divorce. These included assertiveness, listening skills, and greater sensitivity to others. One man said he now looks for different qualities in others. Another said he gained a knowledge of things to do and not to do in his next marriage. There was no male-female difference in this category.

A number of people said the absence of conflict was an improvement and some simply said they were happier now. Nineteen percent of the females and

3 percent of the males reported that everything or almost everything had improved. Only a small minority (4 percent) said nothing had improved.

Two things that few people mentioned were finances and children. Only 6 percent said the situation was better for the children, and 6 percent said their finances had improved.

In summary, many divorced persons reported an improved self-image and more peace of mind. They felt stifled in the marriage, and divorce brought a sense of freedom and independence. However, very few said that divorce had improved their finances or the life situation of their children. The need for self-esteem, peace, and independence are great and apparently override considerations of money and children.

Long-term Responses to Divorce

Wallerstein (1986) has provided us with one of the few longitudinal studies of divorced persons. She interviewed all members of sixty families that had recently gone through a divorce and then reinterviewed them again eighteen months, five years, and ten years later.

Few of the couples studied by Wallerstein recognized their own contribution to the marital breakup. After 10 years more than half of the women and 40 percent of the men said they had absolutely *no responsibility* for the divorce. Only 2 percent of the women and 30 percent of the men admitted considerable liability in the demise of their marriages.

One of the striking features of the couples studied by Wallerstein was that for many their anger and bitterness had not faded even after remarrying and ten years. Forty percent of the women and 30 percent of the men still felt bitter over being exploited and rejected.

Wallerstein made an assessment of overall *quality of life* based on the quality of interpersonal relationships, general contentment with life, freedom from severe loneliness, and socioeconomic status and stability. She also measured *psychological functioning* using five dimensions: (1) self-concept, (2) quality and emotional depth of relationships, (3) capacity for sustained commitment to tasks and goals, (4) adequate resolution of divorce-engendered psychological disequilibria, and (5) reality judgments.

She found that after ten years the quality of life had improved for both partners in only 10 percent of the cases. In 20 percent of the divorced couples the quality of life of both partners had significantly worsened.

A summary of Wallerstein's (1986) data on psychological functioning and quality of life is shown in Table 16·1. The data suggest that divorce may be harder psychologically on men than women. Sixty-four percent of the women had improved their psychological funtioning since divorce, compared to only 16 percent of the men. However, more women than men had deteriorated psychologically (20 percent compared to only 12 percent). In overall quality of life 55 percent of the women had improved over the ten years compared to only 32 percent of the men.

Wallerstein observed that women over age 40 at the time of the divorce were particularly disadvantages psychologically and economically. Even after ten years many felt lonely and rejected and were psychologically and economically below what they had been in marriage. None of the twelve women who were

TABLE 16·1   Change in Psychological Functioning and
Quality of Life Ten Years After Divorce by Gender (Percentages)

	Psychological Functioning		Quality of Life	
	Men	Women	Men	Women
Improved	16	64	32	55
No Change	72	16	22	6
Deteriorated	12	20	46	40

SOURCE: Percentages taken from Wallerstein 1986:68–69.

over age 40 at the time of the divorce had remarried. In contrast, many women
in their twenties and thirties at the divorce had made significant psychological
and economic improvements over the decade since the divorce.

Factors Related to Divorce Adjustment

A critical question is what factors seem to affect adjustment to divorce. Spanier
and Casto (1979) conducted lengthy interviews with fifty divorced persons and
found that postseparation adjustment is related to three major factors: (1)
economic success, (2) social interaction, and (3) heterosexual dating. Those
with better financial situations had superior adjustment. Those who had more
social contact with relatives, friends, and community persons had fewer adjustment problems. Very few (7 percent) of those who dated regularly or lived
with someone of the opposite sex had serious problems, whereas almost half
of those with few or no heterosexual relationships were having major adjustment difficulties.

Several other studies have found postdivorce adjustment to be more difficult
for those with financial problems (Bahr 1982; Bloom et al. 1979; Kitson and
Raschke 1981; Spanier and Casto 1979). In the survey by Bahr, 75 percent of
those who earned less than $15,000 per year reported their divorce experience
as very stressful, compared to only 59 percent of those with incomes above
$15,000. The respondents were also asked whether their financial situation
was worse, about the same, or better than before the separation. Over 80 percent
of those with a worse financial situation said the divorce was very stressful,
compared to about 60 percent of those whose financial situation was the same
or better. Money may not bring happiness but it decreases the stress of divorce.

Most researchers have found that educational level is not strongly related
to amount of stress following divorce (Kitson and Raschke 1981), although
Everly (1978) recently observed that those with more education had an easier
transition from being married to being divorced. In Bahr's (1982) study those
with college degrees were somewhat less likely to report the divorce process
as very stressful. Only half of the college-educated said divorce was very stressful compared to almost three fourths (73 percent) of those without college
degrees. Similarly, those with high-status occupations reported slightly less
stress than those in lower-status occupations.

Divorce adjustment has also been found to be affected by age and duration
of marriage. Those who are older and have been married longer tend to have

more stress at divorce than younger people who have not been married as long (Bahr 1982; Chiriboga, Roberts, and Stein 1978; Goode 1956; Kitson and Raschke 1981; Wallerstein 1986). This may be due to the greater opportunity costs of divorce for older persons. **Opportunity costs** are opportunities that are lost by a particular decision. Older persons have invested more time in the marriage than younger persons and will have more difficulty finding another spouse. Remarriage rates are much greater for those under age 30 (Koo and Suchindran 1980)

In summary, these data indicate that four major factors affect postdivorce adjustment: (1) age, (2) friendship networks, (3) financial resources, and (4) heterosexual dating. If a person decides to divorce, it will be easier if he or she is young and has friends, heterosexual dating opportunities, and an adequate income.

Consequences of Divorce for Children

Proportion of Children Who Experience Divorce

In recent years the proportion of children affected by divorce has increased substantially. According to estimates, at least half of all children will live in a one-parent family before they reach age 18 (Bumpass 1984; Furstenberg and Nord 1982; Glick 1979). Hofferth (1985) estimates that white children born in 1980 will spend 25 percent of their childhood in a single-parent home, and comparable black children will spend about 44 percent of their childhood in a single-parent home.

Adjusting to Divorce

For many children divorce is a difficult transition and living in a single-parent family creates certain risks (Hetherington 1979). However, many of the risks appear to be due to conditions associated with divorce rather than separation itself. A brief review of this research follows.

Nye (1957) studied adolescents from "unhappy unbroken" and "broken" homes. He found that adolescents in broken homes had less psychosomatic illness, less delinquent behavior, and better adjustment to parents than do children in unhappy unbroken homes (p. 358). The two groups did not differ on adjustment in school or church. These data suggest that parental conflict is more stressful than marital disruption.

Hess and Camara (1979) observed that the relationships among family members were more potent influences on child behavior than marital status. Furthermore, they reported that any negative effects of divorce were greatly mitigated when positive relationships with both parents were maintained. The child's relationship with the noncustodial parent was as important as the relationship with the custodial parent.

A review of Leupnitz (1978) indicated that the major stress of divorce is the turmoil resulting from parental conflict and the one-parent home. Raschke and Raschke (1979) reported that the self-concepts of children were lower when there were high levels of family conflict but that self-concept was not related to whether the family was intact, single parent, or reconstituted. Emery (1982) concluded that the long-term pathogenic effects of divorce are due to conflict and not separation per se. Conflict that is openly hostile and of longer duration has a greater impact. He also observed that a warm relationship with at least one parent can partially buffer the negative effects associated with separation. Emery suggested that parents should attempt to keep their children out of their angry disagreements and maintain an individual relationship with each child.

Bilge and Kaufman (1983) maintained that the one-parent family is common in other cultures and that problems result from the lack of supportive social networks rather than marital disruptions per se. The importance of adequate social networks was demonstrated by Kellam, Ensminger, and Turner (1977). They studied a poor urban community on the south side of Chicago. Two major dimensions of mental health were used, psychological well-being and social adjustment.

These two dimensions of mental health were assessed at two time periods, during first grade and again during third grade for 1,300 children. They found that children in mother-alone families had lower social adaptation and psychological well-being compared to children in mother/father and mother/grandmother families. This suggests that the presence of two adults is important for the psychological well-being and social adaptation of children. However, children in mother/stepfather families were similar to those in mother-alone families, probably because of the difficulties in adjusting to a stepfather. They concluded from these findings that it was mother aloneness and not father absence that increases the risk of social and psychological maladaptation.

Wallerstein and Kelly (1980) claimed that the most important influence on good childhood adjustment was a stable, loving relationship with both parents. Children who received erratic visits from the noncustodial parent were anguished by the inconsistency, even after five years. They reported that some contact was better than none and that the disinterested father left behind a legacy of depression and damaged self-esteem.

In the ten-year follow-up, Wallerstein (1985) noted three types of children that were particularly burdened by divorce. First were children who were responsible for their own care. The custodial parent was simply not around very much, and the children came home to an empty house and were left to themselves. The parent was not available at critical times for comfort, consultation, and monitoring.

The second situation was when children were burdened by responsibility for a depressed or troubled parent. These children were placed in an adultlike therapeutic role for their parent, which they were not be to handle

Third, children were burdened if they were always caught between the ongoing conflicts of their parents. Such children often faced continual parental bickering over custody and visitation, sometimes leading to long-term legal disputes.

The primary cause of the burden for children was what Wallerstein (1985) referred to as diminished parenting. The divorce led to less talk, play, attentiveness, and emotional support. Others have found that effective parenting is critical in the adjustment of children to divorce (Stolberg and Bush 1985; Woody et al. 1984).

Wallerstein (1986) found that the importance of the relationship with the noncustodial parent did not diminish over the ten-year period of her study. Some children yearned for visits from their fathers and others expressed intense anger toward fathers who did not provide economic support when they could. During adolescence there was a heightened need to establish a relationship with the father, especially among girls.

The effects of divorce on children may be long lasting. Wallerstein (1984, 1985) found that even after ten years many children were overburdened by the divorce. In a study by Guidubaldi, Perry, and Nastasi (1986) negative impacts of divorce on children were evident after six years. Glenn and Kramer (1985) reported that young adults whose parents had divorced tended to have poorer psychological well-being.

Four major conclusions may be drawn from this research:

1. By itself, the intactness of marriage does not appear to have a significant impact on the self-concept, psychological well-being, or social adjustment of children. However, many of the family changes that tend to occur with divorce do harm children, namely diminished parenting, economic stress, parental conflict, and loss of contact with one parent.
2. The higher the level of conflict between parents and the longer its duration, the lower the social and psychological adjustment of children.
3. Children's adjustment to divorce is substantially better if they are able to have regular contact with the noncustodial parent.
4. A positive relationship with at least one parent decreases the risk of problems following divorce.

Implications of Research

These findings on children of divorce have several implications. First, neither an unhappy marriage nor a divorce is congenial for children. Remaining in a relationship with high levels of conflict may be just as detrimental to children as a divorce. The level and duration of conflict between the parents appears to be more important than their marital status.

Second, divorce does not necessarily decrease parental conflict. Some children of divorce are burdened by continual parental conflict.

Third, children of divorce do significantly better if their family has adequate income (Guidubaldi et al., 1986). The economic impact of divorce on children needs to be taken into account as decisions are made.

Fourth, divorcing parents who are concerned about their children would do well to (1) come to some type of cooperative arrangement so their children are not caught continually between acrimonious exchanges, and (2) maintain regular contact between the noncustodial parent and the children. The marriage may dissolve but parenthood does not, and children have a right to and need a relationship with both parents. The involvement of fathers with their children is influenced significantly by the ease with which they are able to see their children (Tepp 1983).

Summary

1. Marriage gradually evolved from a sacred status to a civil contract and the demand for divorce increased dramatically. A large gap developed between the law on the books and the law in actual practice. In law, divorce was granted for only a serious wrong by one partner against the other. In practice, divorce was easily obtained for incompatibility and marital conflict.

2. No-fault laws were passed as a result of the increasing demand for divorce, the realization that rarely is only one party to blame, and a desire to make the law consistent with actual practice. No-fault laws have had little effect on divorce rates, the adversary system, or basic court procedure.

3. The two major functions of divorce courts are to protect the weak and innocent and resolve disputes. A judge must review every divorce agreement and resolve any disputes the parties cannot work out themselves.

4. During the past century there has been a gradual increase in U.S. divorce rates, with large increases after major wars and decreases during economic depressions.

5. Some of the social characteristics associated with an increase risk of divorce are early age at marriage, a short acquaintance, premarital pregnancy, debt, unemployment, and religious inactivity.

6. Some of the major reasons individuals give for seeking a divorce are infidelity, lack of love, emotional problems, and financial problems. Two major barriers to divorce are a lack of financial resources and children. Some of the major factors that influence the decision to actually divorce are personal unhappiness and opportunities for alternative financial support.

7. Separated and divorced persons have higher-than-average rates of mental and physical pathology. Three explanations for this are that (a) people with problems are more likely to divorce, (b) marriage makes it easier to face certain stresses, and (c) the process of uncoupling is stressful.

8. The two major adjustments for females following divorce are decreased financial resources and role overload from rearing children alone and working. The two major adjustments of males are loneliness because they lose contact with the children and emotional problems. Some males also face financial problems.

9. The major benefits of divorce are improved self-esteem, more peace of mind, and independence and freedom.

10. Adjustment to divorce is easier if one is young and has adequate financial resources, frequent contact with friends and relatives, and heterosexual relationships.

11. The major risks of divorce for children are the conflict between their parents and the lack of contact with the noncustodial parent. Children who adjust well to divorce tend to (a) have parents who put their marital conflicts behind them and (b) maintain frequent contact with both parents.

Important Terms

- adversary system
- affectional alternative
- affectional barrier
- affectional rewards
- alimony
- alternative attractions
- attractions
- barriers
- contract
- costs
- cushion hypothesis
- irretrievable breakdown

- material alternative
- material attractions
- material barriers
- no-fault divorce
- *Orr v. Orr*
- rewards
- selectivity hypothesis
- stress hypothesis
- symbolic alternative
- symbolic barriers
- symbolic rewards
- uncontested divorce

Questions for Discussion

1. How is marriage a status and how is it a contract?
2. How has the view of divorce in American society changed during the past two hundred years?
3. Describe the gap that developed between the divorce law on the books and the divorce law in actual practice.
4. What are some of the reasons that no-fault laws were passed?
5. How did no-fault laws affect the divorce process?
6. What are the functions of courts in the divorce process?
7. Describe how U.S. divorce rates have changed during the past seventy-five years.
8. What are some of the reasons for changes in U.S. divorce rates during the past twenty-five years?
9. Give specific examples of the different types of attractions, barriers, and alternative attractions.
10. What are some of the major variables that are related to the probability of divorce?
11. What are some of the major reasons that individuals give for obtaining a divorce?
12. What are common adjustment problems that males and females face when they divorce?
13. What are some of the ways divorce improves the life situation for individuals?
14. What characteristics seem to make the adjustment to divorce easier for adults?
15. What are the major risks of divorce for children?
16. What are some of the social characteristics that are related to a positive adjustment of children to divorce?

Recommended Reading

NORTON, A. J., and J. E. MOORMAN. 1987. Current trends in marriage and divorce among American women. *Journal of Marriage and the Family* 49:3–14.

WALLERSTEIN, J. S. 1985. The overburdened child: Some long-term consequences of divorce. *Social Work* 30:116–123.

WALLERSTEIN, J. S. 1986. Women after divorce: Preliminary report from a ten-year follow-up. *American Journal of Orthopsychiatry* 56:65–77.

WEITZMAN, L. J. 1985. *The divorce revolution.* New York: Free Press.

References

ALBRECHT, S. L. 1980. Reactions and adjustments to divorce: Differences in the experiences of males and females. *Family Relations* 29 (January):59–68.

ALBRECHT, S. L., and P. R. KUNZ. 1980. The decision to divorce: A social exchange perspective. *Journal of Divorce* 3 (Summer):319–337.

BAHR, S. J. 1979. The effects of welfare on marital stability and remarriage. *Journal of Marriage and the Family* 4:553–560.

BAHR, S. J. 1982. The pains and joys of divorce: A survey of Mormons. *Family Perspective* 16 (Fall):191–200.

BAHR, S. J., and R. J. GALLIGAN. 1984. Teenage marriage and marital stability. *Youth & Society* 15(4):387–400.

BENNETT, N. G., A. K. BLANC, and D. E. BLOOM. 1988. Commitment and the modern union: Assessing the link between premarital cohabitation and subsequent marital stability. *American Sociological Review* 53:997–1008.

BILGE, B., and G. KAUFMAN. 1983. Children of divorce and one-parent families: Cross-cultural perspectives. *Family Relations* 32 (January):59–71.

BISHOP, J. 1980. The negative income-tax experiments: Some reflections on their implications for a theory of the family. In *Economics and the family,* ed. S. J. Bahr, 95–121. Lexington, MA: Lexington Books.

BLOOM, B. L., S. W. WHITE, and S. J. ASHER. 1979. Marital disruption as a stressful life event. In *Divorce and separation,* ed. G. Levinger and O. C. Moles, 184–200. New York: Basic.

BOOTH, A., and J. N. EDWARDS. 1985. Age at marriage and marital instability. *Journal of Marriage and the Family* 47(1):67–75.

BOOTH, A., D. R. JOHNSON, L. K. WHITE, and J. N. EDWARDS. 1986. Divorce and marital instability over the life course. *Journal of Family Issues* 7(4):421–441.

BOOTH, A. and L. WHITE. 1980. Thinking about divorce. *Journal of Marriage and the Family* 42 (August):605–616.

BUMPASS, L. L. 1984. Children and marital disruption: A replication and update. *Demography* 21(1):71–82.

BUMPASS, L. L., and J. A. SWEET. 1972. Differentials in marital stability: 1970. *American Sociological Review* 37 (December):754–766.

CAVANAUGH, R. C., and D. L. RHODE. 1976. The unauthorized practice of law and pro se divorce: An empirical analysis. *Yale Law Journal* 86:103–184.

CHIRIBOGA, D. A., J. ROBERTS, and J. A. STEIN. 1978. Psychological well-being during marital separation. *Journal of Divorce* 2:21–36.

COOGLER, O. J. 1977. Changing the lawyer's role in matrimonial practice. *Conciliation Courts Review* 15 (September):1–12.

DAY, R. D., and S. J. BAHR. 1986. Income changes following divorce and remarriage. *Journal of Marriage and the Family* 9(3):75–88.

DIXON, R. B., and L. J. WEITZMAN. 1980. Evaluating the impact of no-fault divorce in California. *Family Relations* 29:297–307.

DURKHEIM, E. 1951. *Suicide: Study in sociology.* New York: Free Press.

EISLER, R. T. 1977. *Dissolution: No-fault divorce, marriage, and the future of women.* New York: McGraw-Hill.

ELKIN, M. 1977. Post-divorce counseling in a conciliation court. *Journal of Divorce* 1:55–65.

EMERY, R. E. 1982. Interparental conflict and the children of discord and divorce. *Psychological Bulletin* 91 (September):310–330.

ERBES, J. T., and J. J. C. HEDDERSON. 1984. A longitudinal examination of the separation/divorce process. *Journal of Marriage and the Family* 46(4):937–941.

ESPENSHADE, T. J. 1979. The economic consequences of divorce. *Journal of Marriage and the Family* 41:615–625.

EVERLY, K. 1978. *Leisure networks and role strain: A study of divorced women with custody.* Ph.D. diss. Syracuse University.

FREED, D. J., and H. H. FOSTER, JR. 1981. Divorce in the fifty states: An overview. *Family Law Quarterly* 14 (Winter):229–283.

FREED, D. J., and T. B. WALKER. 1986. Family law in the fifty states: An overview. *Family Law Quarterly* 19(4):331–442.

FURSTENBERG, F. F. 1979. Premarital pregnancy and marital instability. In *Divorce and separation,* ed. G. Levinger and O. C. Moles, 83–98. New York: Basic.

FURSTENBERG, F. F., and C. W. NORD. 1982. The life course of children of divorce: Marital disruption and parental contact. *Family Planning Perspectives* 14 (July/August):211–212.

GALLIGAN, R. J., and S. J. BAHR. 1978. Economic well-being and marital stability: Implications for income maintenance programs. *Journal of Marriage and the Family* (401):283–290.

GLENN, N. D., and K. B. KRAMER. 1985. The psychological well-being of adult children of divorce. *Journal of Marriage and the Family* 47:905–912.

GLICK, P. C. 1979. Children of divorced parents in demographic perspective. *Journal of Social Issues* 4:170–182.

GOODE, W. J. 1956. *After divorce.* New York: Free Press.

GOODE, W. J. 1976. State intervention and the family: Problems of policy. *Brigham Young University Law Review* 1976:715–721.

GUIDUBALDI, J., J. D. PERRY, and B. K. NASTASI. 1986. *Long-term impact of divorce on children: A report of a two- and three-year follow-up of a national sample.* Paper presented at the 63rd annual meeting of the American Orthopsychiatric Association, Chicago, April.

HANNAN, M. T., N. B. TUMA, and L. P. GROENEVELD. 1977. Income and marital events. *American Journal of Sociology* 82 (May):1186–1211.

HAYES, M. P., N. STINNETT, AND J. DEFRAIN. 1980. Learning about marriage from the divorced. *Journal of Divorce* 4 (Fall):23–29.

HESS, R. D., and K. A. CAMARA. 1979. Post-divorce family relationships as mediating factors in the consequences of divorce for children. *Journal of Social Issues* 4:79–96.

HETHERINGTON, E. M. 1979. Divorce: A child's perspective. *American Psychologist* 34:851–858.

HOFFERTH, S. L. 1985. Updating children's life course. *Journal of Marriage and the Family* 47(1):93–115.

HOLMES, T. H., and R. H. RAHE. 1967. The social readjustment rating scale. *Journal of Psychomatic Research* 2:213–218.

KELLAM, S. G., M. E. ENSMINGER, and R. J. TURNER. 1877. Family structure and the mental health of children. *Archives of General Psychiatry* 34 (September):1012–1022.

KIECOLT-GLASER, J. K., L. D. FISHER, P. OGROCKI, J. C. STOUT, C. E. SPEICHER, and R. GLASER. 1987. Marital quality, marital disruption, and immune function. *Psychosomatic Medicine* 49:13–34.

KIERNAN, K. E. 1986. Teenage marriage and marital breakdown: A longitudinal study. *Population Studies* 40:35–54.

KITSON, G. C., W. M. HOLMES, and M. B. SUSSMAN. 1977. *Predicting reconciliation: A test of the exchange model of divorce.* Paper read at the meeting of the American Sociological Association, Chicago, September.

KITSON, G. C., and H. J. RASCHKE. 1981. Divorce research: What we know, what we need to know. *Journal of Divorce* 4 (Spring): 1–37.

KOO, H. P., and C. M. SUCHINDRAN. 1980. Effects of children on women's remarriage prospects. *Journal of Family Issues* 1:497–515.

KRAUSE, H. D. 1977. *Family law in a nutshell.* St. Paul, MN: West Publishing.

LEUPNITZ, D. A. 1978. Children of divorce: A review of the psychological literature. *Law and Human Behavior* 2:167–179.

LEVINGER, G. 1979. A social psychological perspective on marital dissolution. In *Divorce and separation,* ed. G. Levinger and O. C. Moles, 37–60. New York: Basic.

MCKENRY, P. C., M. S. HERRMAN, and R. E. WEBER. 1978. Attitudes of attorneys toward divorce issues. *Conciliation Courts Review* 16 (September):11–17.

MCLINDON, J. B. 1987. Separate but unequal: The economic disaster of divorce for women and children. *Family Law Quarterly* 21:351–409.

MAZUR-HART, S. F., and J. J. BERMAN. 1977. Changing from fault to no-fault divorce: An interrupted time series analysis. *Journal of Applied Social Psychology* 7:300–312.

MELICHAR, J., and D. A. CHIRIBOGA. 1985. Timetables in the divorce process. *Journal of Marriage and the Family* 47:701–708.

MICHAEL, R. T. 1977. *Why has the U.S. divorce rate doubled within the decade?* Working paper N 202, Stanford, CA: National Bureau of Economic Research.

MNOOKIN, R. H., and L. KORNHAUSER. 1979. Bargaining in the shadow of the law: The case of divorce. *Yale Law Review* 88:950–997.

MOORE, K. A., and L. J. WAITE. 1981. Marital dissolution, early motherhood and early marriage. *Social Forces* 60(1):20–40.

NATIONAL CENTER FOR HEALTH STATISTICS. 1986. *Advance report of final divorce statistics, 1984.* Monthly Vital Statistics Report vol. 35, no. 6, Supp. DHHS Pub. No. (PHS) 86–1120. Hyattsville, MD: Public Health Service.

NATIONAL CENTER FOR HEALTH STATISTICS. 1987. *Annual summary of births, divorces, and deaths: United States, 1986.* Monthly Vital Statistics Report, vol. 35, no. 13. DHHS Pub. No. (PHS) 87–1120. Hyattsville, MD: Public Health Service.

NATIONAL CENTER FOR HEALTH STATISTICS. 1988. *Births, marriages, divorces, and deaths for 1987.* Monthly Vital Statistics Report, vol. 36, no. 12. DHHS Pub. No. (PHS) 88–1120. Hyattsville, MD: Public Health Service.

NORTON, A. J., and J. E. MOORMAN. 1987. Current trends in marriage and divorce among American women. *Journal of Marriage and the Family* 49:3–14.

NYE, F. I. 1957. Child adjustment in broken and unhappy unbroken homes. *Marriage and Family Living* 19 (November):356–361.

PEARLIN, L. I., and J. S. JOHNSON. 1977. Marital status, life-strains and depression. *American Sociological Review* 42 (October):704–715.

POPE, H., and C. W. MUELLER. 1976. The intergenerational transmission of marital instability: Comparisons by race and sex. *Journal of Social Issues* 32:49–66.

RASCHKE, H. J., and V. J. RASCHKE. 1979. Family conflict and children's self-concepts: A comparison of intact and single-parent families. *Journal of Marriage and the Family* 41:367–374.

RHEINSTEIN, M. 1972. *Marriage stability, divorce, and the law.* Chicago: University of Chicago Press.

ROSS, H. L., and I. V. SAWHILL. 1975. *Time of transition: The growth of families headed by women.* Washington, DC: The Urban Institute.

SCHOEN, R. H., N. GREENBLATT, and R. B. MIELKE. 1975. California's experience with nonadversary divorce. *Demography* 12:223–243.

SCHOEN, R., W. URTON, K. WOODROW, and J. BAJ. 1985. Marriage and divorce in twentieth century cohorts. *Demography* 22(1):101–114.

SELL, K. D. 1979. Divorce law reform and increasing divorce rates. In *Current issues in marriage and the family,* ed. J. G. Wells, 290–308. New York: Macmillan.

SPANIER, G. B., and E. A. ANDERSON. 1979. The impact of the legal system on adjustment to marital separation. *Journal of Marriage and the Family* 41:605–613.

SPANIER, G. B., and R. F. CASTO. 1979. Adjustment of separation and divorce: A qualitative analysis. In *Divorce and separation,* ed. G. Levinger and O. C. Moles, 211–227. New York: Basic.

STOLBERG, A. L., and J. P. BUSH. 1985. A path analysis of factors predicting children's divorce adjustment. *Journal of Clinical Child Psychology* 14(1):49–54.

TEPP, A. V. 1983. Divorced fathers: Predictors of continued paternal involvement. *American Journal of Psychiatry* 140(11):1465–1469.

THORNTON, A. 1978. Marital instability differentials and interactions: Insights from multivariate contingency table analysis. *Sociology and Social Research* 62(4):572–595.

WAITE, L. J., G. W. HAGGSTROM, and D. E. KANOUSE. 1985. The consequences of parenthood for the marital stability of young adults. *American Sociological Review* 50:850–857.

WALLER, W., and R. HILL. 1951. *The family: A dynamic interpretation.* Rev. ed. New York: Holt.

WALLERSTEIN, J. S. 1984. Children of divorce: Preliminary report of a ten-year follow-up of young children. *American Journal of Orthopsychiatry* 54(3):444–452.

WALLERSTEIN, J. S. 1985. The overburdened child: Some long-term consequences of divorce. *Social Work* 30(2):116–123.

WALLERSTEIN, J. S. 1986. Women after divorce: Preliminary report from a ten-year follow-up. *American Journal of Orthopsychiatry* 56(1):65–77.

WALLERSTEIN, J. S., and J. B. KELLY. 1980. *Surviving the breakup: How children cope with divorce.* New York: Basic.

WEISS, R. S. 1975. *Marital separation.* New York: Basic.

WEISS, R. S. 1984. The impact of marital dissolution on income and consumption in single-parent households. *Journal of Marriage and the Family* 46:(1):115–128.

WEITZMAN, L. 1981. The economics of divorce: Social and economic consequences of property, alimony, and child support awards. *UCLA Law Review* 28:1181–1268.

WEITZMAN, L. 1985. *The divorce revolution.* New York: Free Press.

WOODY, J. D., P. E. COLLEY, J. SCHLEGELMILCH, P. MAGINN, and J. BALSANEK. 1984. Child adjustment to parental stress following divorce. *Social Casework: The Journal of Contemporary Social Work* 65(7):405–412.

WRIGHT, G. C., JR., and D. M. STETSON. 1978. The impact of no-fault divorce law reform on divorce in American states. *Journal of Marriage and the Family* 40:575–580.

CHAPTER 17

Alternative Family Forms

Introduction

The traditional concept of a family is that of a man and woman who marry and have children, who raise and nurture those children, and who remain together until one partner dies. However, an increasing number of familes do not conform to this pattern. Many couples cohabit without formal marriage. Among couples who marry, there appears to be an increase in childlessness. During the past twenty-five years separation and divorce have increased dramatically, creating a large increase in the number of single-parent families. Most who divorce subsequently remarry, creating many remarried or "blended" families. In addition, there appears to be an increase in the number of persons who never marry and a growing acceptance of same-sex relationships. In short, there is great diversity in the nature of family life.

In this chapter we review the incidence and nature of unmarried couples, childless couples, single-parent families, blended families, plural and group marriage, same-sex relationships, and singlehood. For some of these alternative family forms the available information is limited, because there has been little empirical research.

Unmarried Couples

An **unmarried couple** is a man and woman who live together in the same household without being formally married. As discussed in earlier chapters, unmarried couples are families legally and socially. They have a marriagelike relationship with legal rights and obligations. Many cohabiting couples have children, and they may turn to the courts to resolve disputes just like couples who have been formally married.

During the past twenty years there has been a significant increase in the number of unmarried couples in the United States. There were almost four times as many in 1985 as in 1970. There were half a million unmarried couples in 1970 compared to 1.5 million in 1980 and almost 2 million in 1985. Between 1984 and 1985 there was little change in the number of unmarried couples

TABLE 17·1   Trends in Cohabitation by Age and Parental Status

	1970	1980	1985
Percentage with Children Under Age 15	37	27	30
Percentage Within Different Age Groups			
Less than 25	11	26	21
25–44	20	53	61
45–64	36	14	12
65 or more	34	7	6

SOURCE: U.S. Bureau of the Census 1986a: 42.

(U.S. Bureau of the Census 1986a). Spanier (1983) estimated that unmarried couples represent about 4 percent of all couples.

Census figures provide only the number of couples who are currently cohabiting. Many other couples have cohabited prior to marriage, as **cohabitation** or trial marriage has become a stage in the courtship process, as explained in Chapter 5. In the United States and in most other countries, legal marriage is preferred to cohabitation and most cohabitors intend to marry eventually (Goldman and Pebley 1981; Lewin 1982; Skolnick 1981). It is estimated that in the United States between 20 and 50 percent of young married couples have cohabited prior to marriage (Gwartney-Gibbs 1986; Mika and Bloom 1981; Skolnick 1981).

Cohabitation occurs among all different age groups, although it has increased primarily among young adults. The proportion of unmarried couples under the age of 25 doubled between 1970 and 1985. During the same period the proportion between ages 25 and 44 tripled (see Table 17·1). In 1985 more than eight out of ten cohabitors were under age 45.

Almost one third of unmarried couples have at least one child under the age of 15. The proportion of unmarried couples with dependent children has decreased somewhat during the past fifteen years, as shown in Table 17·1.

About half of all cohabitors have never been married, and one third are divorced. A relatively small percentage are separated or widowed. Women are more likely than men to cohabit after being widowed, as shown in Table 17·2.

As the amount of cohabitation has increased it has become more accepted socially and legally (Blanc 1984). However, marriage continues to be more preferred than cohabitation and has a higher legal status. If Michelle Marvin

TABLE 17·2   Marital Status of Cohabitators by Gender (1985)

Marital Status	Females	Males
Never Married	51	54
Separated	8	8
Divorced	33	34
Widowed	8	4

SOURCE: U.S. Bureau of the Census 1986a: 42.

had been legally married to Lee Marvin she would have received one half of the money he had earned during the seven years they lived together. Some courts have awarded economic settlements when unmarried couples dissolve their relationships, but others have not (Crutchfield 1981). At best, the economic status of a cohabiting partner is uncertain.

Furthermore, many economic benefits of marriage are not available to co-habitors. For example, a surviving spouse has specific inheritance rights and is entitled to a social security death benefit. If a cohabitor's partner dies there is no social security death benefit, and inheritance is uncertain without a will (Blumberg 1981).

One benefit of cohabitation is that alimony terminates automatically upon remarriage. If one cohabits rather than remarries, one may be able to continue receiving alimony, at least for a period (Oldham 1981).

Newcomb (1986) studied cohabitation, marriage, and divorce among more than seven hundred adolescents over a period of nine years. He found that prior to cohabitation, future cohabitors were more sexually active than those who did not cohabit. Cohabitors also had more drug use, lower life satisfaction, less traditional personality traits, and poorer relationships with family and friends.

Although cohabitation is similar to marriage in many ways, it is often viewed as a transitory period or trial marriage. Consequently, it may not have the commitment and stability that marriage has. Recent research suggests that this is the case. Kurdek and Schmitt (1986) found that married couples experience less tension than cohabiting couples. Couples who lived together prior to marriage had slightly less marital satisfaction and significantly higher divorce rates than couples who did not cohabit prior to marriage (Bennett, Blanc, and Bloom, 1988; DeMaris and Leslie 1984; Newcomb 1986).

In summary, cohabitation has increased substantially during the past twenty years. Although many people live with someone of the opposite sex for a period, cohabitation tends to be transitory. At any given time the proportion of families that are unmarried couples is relatively small. About 3 percent of all families in the United States are unmarried couples (U.S. Bureau of the Census 1986a).

Childless Couples

In American society, married couples ideally have children. Indeed, one of the traditional purposes of marriage has been to bear and raise children, and couples who do not do so, for whatever reason, deviate from a strong social norm. Such marriages are nontraditional, particularly if they are childless by choice (Veevers 1980).

Even though fertility rates have declined substantially in recent decades, there is still a strong norm against childlessness. Miall (1985, 1986) has demonstrated the stigma that **childless couples** feel and how they cope with it.

As shown in Table 17·3, between 1970 and 1985 there was an increase in childlessness among ever-married women. Because improved nutrition and medical procedures probably reduced the amount of involuntary childlessness, there appears to have been an increase in voluntary childlessness.

An analysis of childlessness by race is shown in Table 17·4. Whites have

There has been an increase in childlessness among American couples. Voluntarily
childless couples tend to be highly educated, earn high incomes, and be nonreligious. *Ken Robert Buck/The Picture Cube.*

considerably more childlessness than blacks, and blacks have more childlessness than Hispanics. Non-Catholics have more childlessness than Catholics
(Bloom and Trussell 1984; Poston and Kramer 1986).

Although childlessness has increased in recent years, voluntary childlessness
is still rare. Mosher and Bachrach (1982) estimated that only about 2 percent
of ever-married women between the ages of 15 and 44 are voluntarily childless.
Voluntary childless couples tend to be highly educated, earn high incomes,
and be nonreligious (Mosher and Bachrach 1982; Ramu 1985).

TABLE 17·3 Percentage of Ever-Married Women Who Are Childless, United
States (1970–1985)

	1970	1980	1985
All Women	16.4	18.8	20.3
Women Age 40–44	8.6	6.6	8.0

SOURCE: U.S. Bureau of the Census 1986a:
64.

TABLE 17·4   Percentage of Ever-Married Women Who Are
Childless By Race, United States (1985)

	White	*Black*	*Spanish Origin*	*Total*
All Women	21.3	11.9	14.6	20.3
Women Age 40–44	8.4	6.1	5.0	8.0

SOURCE: U.S. Bureau of the Census 1986a: 64.

Single-Parent Families

The number of **single-parent families** has increased dramatically in recent
decades, due primarily to the increase in the divorce rate. As noted in Chapter
16, more than half of all children will spend some time in a single-parent home
by the time they reach age 18 (Bumpass 1984b; Hofferth 1985).

The growth of single-parent families in the United States is shown in Table
17·5. In 1970 about 11 percent of all families with minor children were single-
parent families. By 1985 single-parent families comprised more than one of
every five families with minor children. According to projections of Glick
(1984), by 1990 one fourth of all families with children under age 18 will be
single-parent families. Although there has been a modest increase in the number of men who head single-parent homes, almost 90 percent of single-parent
homes with minor children are headed by women (U.S. Bureau of the Census
1986a).

Single-parent homes are particularly prevalent among minorities. For example, 44 percent of black families are headed by women compared to 16 percent
among white families (U.S. Bureau of the Census 1986a).

An examination of single parenthood from the perspective of the child is
shown in Table 17·6. Eighty percent of white children under age 18 live with
both parents compared to 68 percent of Hispanic children and 40 percent of
black children. Almost 16 percent of white children live with their mother
only, compared to 27 percent of those from Spanish origin and 51 percent of
blacks. Fewer than 3 percent of minor children live with only their father, and

TABLE 17·5   Married Couples, Single Parents, and Unmarried Couples with Children Under Age 18, United
States (1970–1990) (in percentages)

	1970	*1980*	*1985*	*1990[a]*
Married Couples	88.3	79.4	76.3	73.1
Single-Parent Families	11.1	19.3	21.7	24.8
Female-Headed	9.9	17.3	18.9	22.3
Male-Headed	1.2	2.0	2.8	2.5
Unmarried Couples	0.7	1.4	1.9	2.0

SOURCE: U.S. Bureau of the Census 1986a:42,48; Glick
1984:23.

[a] The 1990 figures are based on projections of Glick (1984), modified to include unmarried couples.

TABLE 17·6   Living Arrangements of Children Under Age
18, United States (1985) (in percentages)

	Black	Spanish Origin	White	Total
Both Parents	39.5	67.8	80.0	73.9
Mother only	51.0	26.6	15.6	20.9
Divorced	11.3	7.3	8.1	8.5
Married, spouse absent	12.4	11.1	4.1	5.4
Never married	24.8	6.5	2.1	5.6
Widowed	2.5	1.7	1.3	1.5
Father Only	2.9	2.2	2.4	2.5
Neither Parent	6.6	3.3	2.0	2.7

SOURCE: U.S. Bureau of the Census 1986a: 48.

the rates are similar among the different ethnic groups. The high proportion of black mothers who have never married is striking.

Single parenthood is a disadvantaged status both economically and socially. Single parents are less satisfied with life and less well adjusted than comparable persons in their first marriages (Fine, Donnelly, and Voydanoff 1986). They tend to move more often than other families and often live in low socioeconomic areas (Cook and Rudd 1984; Norton and Glick 1986). The striking feature of single-parent households is the low level of income, as noted in Chapter 16. For example, only 9 percent of two-parent families have incomes less than $10,000, compared to 25 percent of male-headed families and 53 percent of female-headed families. On the other side of the scale, 26 percent of two-parent households with minor children earn more than $40,000 per year, compared to 11 percent of male-headed households and only 2 percent of female-headed households (Norton and Glick 1986).

The economic problems of female-headed families result from three factors. First, single mothers have low earnings. They are not highly educated and do not have the ability to obtain well-paying jobs. Second, fathers usually do not pay child support. Only about 40 percent of white fathers and 19 percent of black fathers pay any child support (Garfinkel and McLanahan 1986). Among fathers that do pay, the amount tends to be small. Support payments from noncustodial fathers make up only 10 percent of the income of white mothers and 3.5 percent of the income of black mothers (Garfinkel and McLanahan 1986). A third reason for low income of single mothers is the small amount of public assistance received from the government.

Parenting also is more difficult in single-parent than in two-parent families. In Chapter 16 we mentioned that trying simultaneously to support their children and care for them was stressful for most divorced women. Dornbusch et al. (1985) reported that youth in mother-only households are more likely to make decisions without parental input and more apt to participate in deviant activities than youth living with two natural parents. This finding held even after controlling for family income and parental education. They found that the presence of another adult in the household was associated with more parental involvement in adolescent decision making and less deviant behavior, particularly among males.

McLanahan, Wedemeyer, and Adelberg (1981) have studied how support networks help single parents adjust. They identified three different types of support networks: (1) the **family of origin network** made up of relatives, (2) the **extended network** composed of new friendships, and (3) the conjugal network made up of a male along with some relatives and friends. McLanahan et al. suggested that the family network appears to be especially useful in providing security, reassurance, and emotional support but may not provide interpersonal intimacy. The extended network tends to provide reassurance and intimacy but not security. The conjugal network may provide intimacy and reassurance but is less secure.

McLanahan et al. (1981) indicated that the helpfulness of the different types of networks depends on a woman's role orientation and how close knit the networks are. Loose-knit networks may be best for women who are attempting to establish a new identity, whereas close-knit networks may be more advantageous for women attempting to maintain their existing identities (McLanahan et al. 1981).

Men usually do not obtain custody of their children following divorce, and there is a popular belief that men are not competent to raise children alone. However, Orthner and Lewis (1979) concluded that men's competence in child rearing is much greater than is usually assumed.

Greif (1985) studied more than one thousand men who had custody of their children following divorce. Why did the fathers obtain custody? In 60 percent of the cases the ex-wife did not want custody for personal, emotional, or financial reasons. In about one third of the cases the children chose the father because they were close to him emotionally or because of his financial capability. In about one third of the cases the father felt he was more competent than his ex-wife to parent. Finally, in 20 percent of the cases the father vigorously sought custody (these categories are not mutually exclusive; in some cases two categories applied to one situation; see Greif 1985).

Blended Families

Another very common family type is the **blended family** or **stepfamily,** which is created by remarriage. As divorce rates have risen in the United States, blended families have become more common.

Rates and Characteristics of Remarriages

About three fourths of all divorced persons eventually remarry (Glick 1984). In 20 percent of currently married couples at least one spouse has been previously divorced. Given that half of current marriages will end in divorce and three fourths of divorced persons will remarry, we can expect that more than one third ($.5 \times .75 = .375$) of all persons who marry will experience a remarriage.

The interval between divorce and remarriage decreased between 1975 and 1980. In 1975 the average time between first divorce and remarriage was 3.2

Because of high rates of divorce and remarriage, blended families have become increasingly common in the United States. In this family, both husband and wife have children from a previous marriage, and they have two children from their present marriage.   *Ellis Herwig/The Picture Cube.*

years, and this decreased to 2.2 years in 1980. In 1985 it was 2.3 years (Norton and Moorman 1987).

Men are somewhat more likely to remarry than women. According to Glick (1980) about 84 percent of divorced men and 74 percent of divorced women eventually remarry. In recent years, remarriage rates among women have been decreasing and Norton and Moorman (1987) estimate that the proportion of divorced women who remarry will decrease to at least 70 percent. However, remarriage rates of women under age 30 with children have increased in recent years (Glick and Lin 1986).

Age is one of the best predictors of remarriage. The older one is at the time of divorce, the less likely one will remarry, particularly for women. For example, Glick and Lin (1986) found that 72 percent of women who had divorced before age 30 had remarried, compared to 21 percent of those divorced during their thirties, and only 7 percent of those divorced after age 40.

The greater the number of children, the less likely women will remarry. However, in recent years more women with one child have remarried than women with no children (Glick and Lin 1986). Mothers under age 30 are remarrying in greater numbers and sooner after divorce than in previous years, while more of the divorced, childless women are remaining divorced. Men who have custody of children tend to remarry relatively soon after divorce (Glick 1984).

Among divorced men, the higher the education and earnings, the more likely they will remarry. The opposite is true for divorced women; the higher the education and earnings, the less likely remarriage will occur (Glick and Lin 1986). Women who have not completed high school have the highest rates of remarriage, and those with a college education have the lowest rates.

The Remarriage Process

Remarriage is a complex process that involves at least six developmental tasks (Goetting 1982). First, there is **emotional remarriage,** which is the process of establishing a bond of attraction, commitment, and trust. Because of the failure and rejection usually experienced during the divorce, establishing a new emotional relationship is often difficult. A second aspect of remarriage is **psychic remarriage.** This is changing one's identity from a single person to a married person. The **community remarriage** involves adjusting one's friendship networks. Some unmarried friends may be replaced by married friends. The fourth task is the **parental remarriage.** This is adjusting to the children of both partners. As a stepparent, one becomes involved in the raising of a spouse's children. As a parent, one must adjust parent-child relationships to include a new spouse. The **economic remarriage** is the fifth developmental task. This is complicated by the fact that men often have financial obligations from their first marriages. Finally, **legal remarriage** must be dealt with. Marriage is a legal institution and it is influenced by a variety of legal regulations (Goetting 1982).

People in their first marriage usually begin as a couple. When children arrive the parental role is added. In remarriages there are often three different subsystems existing at the start of the marriage (Keshet 1980). First, there is the **new couple subsystem.** Second, there is the **ex-spouse subsystem.** This existed before the new couple subsystem, and there are continuing relationships with the ex-spouse. Third, there is the **parent-child subsystem.** This system also existed before the new couple subsystem, and may require adjustment. Because women usually have custody of any children, a man must enter the lives of his wife's children when remarriage occurs. Children may have difficulty accepting the stepparent. And there is the noncustodial parent to deal with. If a man has children who are in the custody of his ex-wife, he must adjust his new family to previously established visiting and support schedules.

Remarriage and Well-Being

Are remarried people as happy as people in first marriages? Does the stress associated with divorce make it difficult for individuals to succeed in a second marriage? Available evidence suggests that remarried persons tend to be as happy and well adjusted as persons in first marriages. Fine et al. (1986) compared individuals in first marriages and remarriages on several measures of well-being, including anxiety, depression, marital satisfaction, and child problems. They found no differences between individuals in first marriages and remarriages on any of the dimensions.

Buehler et al. (1986) made comparisons among four remarriage groups: (1) neither former spouse had remarried; (2) only husband had remarried; (3) only wife had remarried; (4) both former spouses had remarried. They compared the four groups on self-esteem, parental satisfaction, divorce-related stress, and economic well-being. There were no differences among the four groups on any of the variables exept economic well-being. Women who had remarried had higher economic well-being than women who had not remarried. Furthermore, women who had remarried but whose former husband had not remarried tended to have higher economic well-being than women in the group in which both spouses had remarried. This suggests that remarrying improves the economic situation for women. On the other hand, when the husband remarries, it tends to hurt the economic status of the former wife.

Longitudinal research by Day and Bahr (1986) is consistent with the findings of Buehler et al. (1986). Per capital income of women increased substantially upon remarriage, whereas the per capita income of men decreased substantially.

Weingarten (1980) found that the individuals in remarriages were similar to individuals in first marriages with regard to marital adjustment, parental adjustment, and overall well-being. Albrecht (1979) observed high levels of marital satisfaction among his sample of remarried persons. Using three national surveys, Glenn and Weaver (1977) found no differences in the marital satisfaction of men in first marriages and remarriages. Women in first marriages had somewhat higher marital satisfaction than women in remarriages, although the differences were not large.

The major problems encountered by remarried couples concern children and money (Ihinger-Tallman and Pasley 1987). In that sense the couples are no different from their counterparts in first marriages. Stepparenting and visitation may make child rearing stressful, and distributing resources to one's former and current marriage is bound to create conflicts.

There is also some evidence that *boundary maintenance* may be a problem, that is, clear definitions of what your family is and who it includes. Among remarried couples there may be some ambiguity regarding who is the family, because there is a blending of individuals from previous marriages (Ihinger-Tallman and Pasley 1987).

Another problem of remarried families is loyalty conflicts. Children may feel disloyal to one parent if they side with the other during a conflict. There may also be feelings of loyalty involved in interactions between stepparent and stepchild.

What can be concluded from these studies? Taken together, the research is remarkably consistent in showing few differences between first marriages and remarriages in marital satisfaction and overall well-being. However, the blending of individuals from previous marriages may create some stress.

Divorce Among Remarriages

There is some evidence that remarriages are slightly more prone to divorce than first marriages. Using data from the National Survey of Family Growth, McCarthy (1978) observed that divorce among second marriages was slightly higher than among first marriages. However, second marriages among blacks were more stable than first marriages. Glick (1984) also found that whites are more likely than blacks to become redivorced.

Using census data, Glick (1984) estimated that about 60 percent of men and 54 percent of women in remarriages will divorce, which is slightly higher than the rates for first marriages. However, Norton and Moorman (1987) have observed a recent decline in the rates of divorce among remarriages. They suggested that future rates of redivorce will be similar to the rates of first divorce.

Several scholars have tried to ascertain why remarriages are more prone to divorce than first marriages. White and Booth (1985) studied a national sample of 1,673 marriages over a period of three years. Consistent with other research, they found that remarriages were as satisfying as first marriages, but that remarriages did have a higher divorce rate, particularly marriages in which both spouses had been married before. Double remarriages were twice as likely as first marriages to end in divorce during the three-year period.

White and Booth (1985) suggested that the presence of stepchildren is a major reason why remarriages have a higher probability of divorce than first marriages. Compared to parents without stepchildren, parents with stepchildren were more likely (1) to perceive that their children caused them problems, (2) to be dissatisfied with their spouse's relationship with their children, (3) to think their marriage has a negative effect on their relationship with their own children, and (4) to wish they had never remarried. Because of this stress, stepfamilies tend to move teenagers out of the home faster than biological families. White and Booth's data suggest that the presence of stepchildren creates stress in remarriages and is the major reason they have a higher rate of divorce.

Children and Remarriage

About one sixth of all children in the United States live in a blended family (Cherlin and McCarthy 1985). About half of all children whose mother divorces will experience the remarriage of their mother within five years (Bumpass 1984b).

Stepparents are often viewed in a negative light in children's literature, such as the stepmother who mistreated Cinderella. How do children feel about stepparents and how do they adjust to remarriages? Fine (1986) compared the views of college students from intact, single-parent, and stepparent homes. He found that stepparents, particularly stepmothers, were viewed less positively among all three groups. However, students from single-parent and remarried families did not view stepmothers as negatively as students from intact families. Fine's research suggests that exposure to stepparents may decrease negative stereotypes and increase appreciation for them.

In a study of remarriages, Giles-Sims (1984) examined the roles of stepparents in child care and socialization. The respondents felt that stepparents should be involved in child rearing but did not expect them to be as involved as biological parents. Equal sharing of child-rearing tasks occurred in less than one third of the families, even though half said that natural parents and stepparents should share equally in child rearing.

Children in remarried families tend to have somewhat poorer adjustment than children in first marriages, and the relationship between stepparent and stepchild is often somewhat strained (Ihinger-Tallman and Pasley 1987). Kellam, Ensminger, and Turner (1977) found that children in mother-stepfather families had significantly lower social and psychological adjustment than children in mother-grandmother or mother-father families. The research by White and Booth (1985) showed that children are a significant stress among remarried couples. Because of the stress, teenagers living in stepfamilies tend to leave the home somewhat earlier than teenagers living with two natural parents. There is also evidence that rates of child abuse are substantially higher in remarried families than in two-natural-parent homes (Wilson and Daly 1987; Wilson, Daly, and Weghorst 1980).

Summary

About three fourths of divorced persons eventually remarry. Men remarry somewhat more often than women, and the chance of remarriage is much higher for those who are under age 30. Remarriage is often stressful because of the blending of individuals from different families. Nevertheless, individuals who remarry are similar to individuals in first marriages with regard to marital satisfaction and overall well-being. Remarriages have a somewhat higher divorce rate than first marriages, primarily because of the stress of stepparenting. Children in remarriages are more likely to be abused than children in first marriages and tend to leave the home earlier than children living with two natural parents.

Plural and Group Marriage

Plural marriage and **group marriage** are rare alternative family forms. Murdock (1949) did not find a single society in which group marriage was practiced, although some religious groups have had group marriage. For example, group marriage existed for a time in the Oneida Community during the nineteenth century (Foster 1981).

Polyandry (having more than one husband) has been practiced in a few societies but is extremely rare (Nye and Berardo 1973). **Polygyny** (having more than one wife) has been a feature of many societies, and Murdock (1949) found that 75 percent of societies had a normative preference for it. However, even in those societies the vast majority of marriages were monogamous.

Two demographic factors constrain the widespread practice of plural marriage. First, there are about equal numbers of men and women in most societies. For every man who takes a second wife there will be another man denied the opportunity to marry. Second, most men do not have the economic resources to support more than one wife (Nye and Berardo 1973).

Polygyny was practiced in the nineteenth century among Mormons (Foster 1981). There are occasional reports in the media of groups that still practice plural marriage in Utah and Arizona. There are no reliable data on the actual prevalence of plural marriage in the United States, but it is against the law and those that practice it must do so covertly.

Same-Sex Relationships

Same-sex (homosexual) relationships have attracted increasing attention in recent years. The term **gay** is used to describe a male homosexual and **lesbian** to a female homosexual. In a legal sense a same-sex relationship is not a family. There has been some attempt to gain legal recognition for homosexual marriage. However, homosexual relationships to date have not been legally accepted as valid marriages (*Baker* v. *Nelson*, 191 N.W.2d 185, 1971; Brieland and Lemmon 1985).

It is not illegal to be a homosexual but it is illegal to perform homosexual acts. There is also a strong social stigma against gay and lesbian relationships and many persons consider homosexuality to be unnatural and immoral (Siegel 1986). Nevertheless, there appears to be increasing tolerance for this lifestyle.

No one knows how much homosexuality exists. Hunt (1974) estimated that 3 percent of males and between 1 and 3 percent of females were exclusively homosexual. Some estimate that one third of males and 13 percent of females have had a homosexual experience (Siegel 1986). Gays and lesbians can be found among all professions.

Research on homosexuals suggests that managing the stigma is an important issue. Gays often keep their homosexuality a secret except among certain close friends. They may become involved in homosexual bars, organizations, and friendship networks that provide support and friendship (Elliot 1986).

Same-sex relationships tend to be less stable and exclusive than heterosexual relationships. Homosexuals have a need for intimacy and a desire for permanence, just like heterosexuals, yet many question whether sex and love should be linked and some do not want their relationships to resemble nuclear marriages (Elliot 1986). Lesbians have a stronger desire for exclusivity than gays. However, Macklin (1987) suggests that a majority of gay men are also interested in long-term relationships.

Research on lesbians suggests that many have long-term, exclusive relationships. The greater the equality, the more satisfying the relationships. Many described their relationships as close and satisfying, and said they value both autonomy and intimacy (Macklin 1987).

Most homosexuals who become parents do so through a previous marriage. In one recent study, 16 percent of the gay men and 26 percent of the lesbian women had been previously married. Fourteen percent of the lesbians had children while they were married (Macklin 1987).

Satisfaction among same-sex couples appears to be related to some of the same variables that affect heterosexual relationships. Kurdek (1988) studied the relationship quality of sixty-five gay couples and forty-seven lesbian couples. Thirty-four of the gay couples permitted sex outside the relationship, and thirty-one did not. All of the lesbian couples were sexually exclusive. The lesbian couples as a group had higher satisfaction than the gay couples. High trust, high social support, and frequently shared decision making were associated with high relationship satisfaction among both the gay and lesbian couples.

Singlehood

There has been an increase in **singlehood** in the United States. Being single is defined as not being currently married and includes never-married, divorced, and widowed individuals. Although over 90 percent of all persons marry at least once during their lives, many persons spend considerable portions of their adult lives as unmarrieds. In this section we will review the trends in singlehood in the United States.

Life is dynamic, and each year many people who are single become married and many married people become single. On any given day about 37 percent of the adult population is single (U.S. Bureau of the Census 1986a). More women than men are single largely because women live longer, leaving a much larger proportion of women as widows. Women are also somewhat more likely to be currently divorced than men because more men than women remarry. Men are more likely than women to never marry. In 1985 25 percent of the

The proportion of the adult population that is single has been increasing during the past 15 years. In some areas clubs have been organized by single adults.   *Enrico Ferorelli/DOT.*

TABLE 17·7   Marital Status of Adult Population, by Gender (1970–1985) (in percentages)

	1970	1975	1980	1985
Never Married				
Females	13.7	14.6	17.1	18.2
Males	18.9	20.8	23.8	25.2
Total	16.2	17.5	20.3	21.5
Married				
Females	68.5	66.7	63.0	60.4
Males	75.3	72.8	68.4	65.7
Total	71.7	69.6	65.5	63.0
Widowed				
Females	13.9	13.4	12.8	12.6
Males	3.3	2.7	2.6	2.6
Total	8.9	8.3	8.0	7.9
Divorced				
Females	3.9	5.3	7.1	8.7
Males	2.5	3.7	5.2	6.5
Total	3.2	4.6	6.2	7.6

SOURCE: U.S. Bureau of the Census 1986a: 38–39.

men had never married compared to only 18 percent of the women (see Table 17·7).

Census data show that the proportion of the adult population that is single has been increasing during the past fifteen years, as shown in Table 17·7. In 1970 16 percent of the adult population had never married compared to more than 21 percent in 1985. The proportion of the population that is widowed has decreased slightly, and the percentage that is divorced has increased from 3 percent to almost 8 percent.

Table 17·8 shows the proportion of all households that are nonfamily households. A family household, according to the U.S. Census, includes all married couples and all parents living with children regardless of marital status. In 1985 almost 28 percent of all households in the United States were nonfamily households. Twenty-four percent were individuals living alone. Women were more likely than men to live alone.

The proportion of persons in various single statuses varies according to age and gender, as shown in Table 17·9. For example, at ages 18 and 19 over 97 percent of men have never married. This decreases with time and only 5 percent of men never marry during their lives. Widowhood is similar except that it increases with age. At age 20 virtually no men or women are widows. Among persons over age 75, 23 percent of the men and 68 percent of the women are widows. Being divorced peaks in the middle years. Ten percent of men and 14 percent of women between the ages of 35 and 44 are divorced.

Why has there been an increase in singlehood in recent years? The major reasons appear to be an increase in the divorce rate and an increase in age at marriage.

Cargon and Melko (1982) have studied some of the myths and realities

TABLE 17·8 Nonfamily and Family Households in United States (1980–1990) (in percentages)

	1980	1985	1990[a]
Female Householder	15.4	16.1	16.5
Living alone	14.0	14.6	—
Male Householder	10.9	11.7	12.7
Living alone	8.6	9.1	—
Total Nonfamily Households	26.3	27.7	29.2
Living alone	22.7	23.7	—
Total Family Households	73.7	72.3	70.8
Married couple	60.8	58.0	56.3
Male householder	2.1	2.6	2.7
Female householder	10.8	11.7	11.8
Total Households	100.0	100.0	100.0

[a] Projected Figures. No projections on proportion living alone were available.

SOURCE: U.S. Bureau of the Census 1986a:42; 1986b.

regarding single persons. Singles value success, growth, and friends more than marrieds, whereas marrieds tend to value love and community service more than singles. Married persons are somewhat better off economically than unmarried persons. Single persons are more likely than married persons to be lonely and feel that they have no one with whom they can really share. In

TABLE 17·9   Marital Status of Adult Population by Gender and Age (1985)

	Percentage Distribution				
	Never Married	Married	Widowed	Divorced	Total
Male	**25.2**	**65.7**	**2.6**	**6.5**	**100.0**
18–19 years	97.1	2.9	0.0	0.0	100.0
20–24 years	75.6	23.0	0.0	1.4	100.0
25–29 years	38.7	55.2	0.0	6.0	100.0
30–34 years	20.8	69.7	0.1	9.5	100.0
35–44 years	9.4	79.9	0.4	10.3	100.0
45–54 years	6.3	83.8	1.2	8.7	100.0
55–64 years	6.1	83.9	3.7	6.2	100.0
65–74 years	5.2	81.3	9.3	4.2	100.0
75 years and older	5.3	69.3	22.7	2.7	100.0
Female	**18.2**	**60.4**	**12.6**	**8.7**	**100.0**
18–19 years	86.7	12.5	0.1	0.7	100.0
20–24 years	58.5	38.0	0.2	3.3	100.0
25–29 years	26.4	65.2	0.5	7.9	100.0
30–34 years	13.5	73.1	1.0	12.4	100.0
35–44 years	6.8	77.1	2.0	14.0	100.0
45–54 years	4.6	76.3	7.0	12.1	100.0
55–64 years	3.7	70.0	17.4	8.9	100.0
65–74 years	4.4	51.1	38.9	5.6	100.0
75 years and older	6.2	23.8	67.7	2.4	100.0

SOURCE: U.S. Bureau of the Census 1986a: 39.

contemplated and attempted suicides, there are substantially greater numbers of singles than marrieds. Singles have more sexual partners than marrieds but do not have sexual experiences as frequently.

Summary

1. During the past two decades there has been a large increase in the number of unmarried couples in the United States. Unmarried couples comprise about 4 percent of all couples and about 3 percent of all families.

2. Childlessness has increased somewhat in recent years but is still relatively rare. About 2 percent of ever-married women between ages 15 and 45 are voluntarily childless. Couples who are voluntarily childless tend to be highly educated, earn high incomes, and be nonreligious. There is more childlessness among whites than blacks.

3. The number of single-parent families has increased dramatically in recent decades. More than half of all children will spend some time in a single-parent home before they reach age 18. In 1985 more than 20 percent of all families with minor children were single-parent families. About 90 percent of single-parent homes are headed by women.

4. Single parenthood is more prevalent among blacks than among Hispanics and more prevalent among Hispanics than whites.

5. Single-parent families tend to have very low incomes because of the low earning capacity of single mothers, the low amount of child support paid by fathers, and the low level of public assistance.

6. Parenthood is more difficult for single parents than married parents. The task of simultaneously trying to work and care for children is stressful for them.

7. Children in single-parent homes are more likely than children in two-parent homes to make decisions without parental input and more likely to participate in deviant activities.

8. Blended families have become very common as divorce rates have risen. About three fourths of all divorced persons eventually remarry. More men than women remarry, and the chance of remarriage is less among those who are older and those with more than one child. Among women the higher the education and earnings, the less likely remarriage will occur; among men, the higher the education and earnings, the more likely remarriage will occur.

9. Remarriage is a complex process that involves emotional, psychological, parental, economic, and legal changes. Remarriage requires a blending of existing roles as parent and ex-spouse with the role of spouse.

10. Remarried couples tend to be as happy and well adjusted as couples in their first marriage.

11. Remarriages tend to have a slightly higher divorce rate than first marriages. The presence of stepchildren creates stress and is the major reason for the higher divorce rate among remarriages.

12. About 17 percent of all children in the United States live in a blended family. Children who live in blended families tend to have poorer social and psychological adjustment than children in first marriages. Children

in blended families are more likely to be abused and tend to leave home earlier than children in first marriages.

13. There appears to be increasing tolerance for same-sex relationships, although they are still illegal and stigmatized socially. Same-sex relationships tend to be less stable and less exclusive than heterosexual relationships. The characteristics associated with satisfying same-sex relationships appear to be similar to those associated with satisfaction in opposite-sex relationships.

14. Singlehood has increased in recent years because of increases in divorce and delay in first marriages. About 37 percent of the adult population are single.

15. Women are more likely than men to be single because they live longer and remarry less often. Men are more likely than women to never marry.

16. The four most common types of nontraditional families are unmarried couples, childless couples, single-parent families, and remarried families. All have increased substantially in numbers in recent years.

17. Life in nontraditional family types is often transitory, probably because of social pressure to move toward more traditional family types. Many unmarried couples marry, most childless couples have a child, a large majority of single parents remarry, and most never-married persons eventually marry. Thus, more people experience nontraditional family status at some time in their lives than may be reflected by the data.

Important Terms

- blended family
- childless couples
- cohabitation
- community remarriage
- conjugal network
- economic remarriage
- emotional remarriage
- ex-spouse subsystem
- extended network
- family of origin network
- gay
- group marriage
- homosexual
- legal remarriage

- lesbian
- new couple subsystem
- parental remarriage
- parent-child subsystem
- plural marriage
- polyandry
- polygyny
- psychic remarriage
- same-sex relationships
- singlehood
- single-parent family
- stepfamily
- unmarried couple

Questions for Discussion

1. How are unmarried couples like married couples? How are they different?
2. What are the benefits of cohabiting without marriage? What are the risks?
3. Why do you think there has been an increase in cohabitation?

4. Among what types of people is cohabitation more likely?
5. Why has childlessness increased? Why is there less childlessness among blacks than whites?
6. What characteristics are related to childlessness and why?
7. Why has the number of single-parent families increased so dramatically?
8. What are the advantages of being a single parent? What are the disadvantages of being a single parent?
9. Why do single-parent families have such low incomes?
10. What do your think should be done to improve the economic situations of single-parent families in the United States? How feasible are your suggestions?
11. Is living in a single-parent home harmful for children? How?
12. What advice would you give single parents about raising socially competent children?
13. Why do women obtain custody of children 90 percent of the time in divorce? Do you think that should change? Why or why not?
14. Why do more men than women remarry?
15. Why is education positively associated with remarriage for men and negatively associated with remarriage for women?
16. Are remarried persons as happy and adjusted as persons in first marriages?
17. What are some of the unique stresses associated with remarriage?
18. What are some of the unique advantages associated with remarriage?
19. Why do remarriages have a higher divorce rate than first marriages?
20. What are some of the stresses children in remarriages face?
21. What advice would you give a mother who is remarrying? What advice would you give a man who is about to become a stepfather?
22. Why is plural marriage so uncommon, even in cultures where it is normatively accepted?
23. How has the public view of homosexuality changed in recent years?
24. Do you think homosexual relationships should be made legal? Why or why not?
25. Why has singlehood increased in recent years?
26. How do men and women differ in their types of singlehood? Why?
27. What are some types of alternative family forms that are not discussed in this chapter?
28. How strong is the social pressure against cohabitation, childlessness, and singlehood? Is this changing?
29. Is there a stigma against remarriage and stepparenthood? How strong is it? Has this stigma changed in recent years?

Recommended Reading

GARFINKEL, I., and S. S. McLANAHAN. 1986. *Single mothers and their children.* Washington, DC: The Urban Institute Press.
IHINGER-TALLMAN, M., and K. PASLEY. 1987. *Remarriage.* Newbury Park, CA: Sage.
WHITE, L. K., and A. BOOTH. 1985. The quality and stability of remarriages: The role of stepchildren. *American Sociological Review* 50:689–698.

References

ALBRECHT, S. L. 1979. Correlates of marital happiness among the remarried. *Journal of Marriage and the Family* 41:857–867.

BENNETT, N. G., A. K. BLANC, and D. E. BLOOM. 1988. Commitment and the modern union: Assessing the link between premarital cohabitation and subsequent marital stability. *American Sociological Review* 53:997–1008.

BLANC, A. K. 1984. Nonmarital cohabitation and fertility in the United States and Western Europe. *Population Research and Policy Review* 3:181–193.

BLOOM, D. E., and J. TRUSSELL. 1984. What are the determinants of delayed childbearing and permanent childlessness in the United States? *Demography* 21(4):591–611.

BLUMBERG, G. G. 1981. Cohabitation without marriage: A different perspective. *UCLA Law Review* 28:1125–1181.

BRIELAND, D., and J. A. LEMMON. 1985. *Social work and the law* 2d ed. St. Paul: West Publishing Co.

BUEHLER, C., M. J. HOGAN, B. ROBINSON, and R. J. LEVY. 1986. Remarriage following divorce. Stressors and well-being of custodial and noncustodial parents. *Journal of Family Issues* 7:405–420.

BUMPASS, L. 1984a. Some characteristics of children's second families. *The American Journal of Sociology* 90(3):608–623.

BUMPASS, L. 1984b. Children and marital disruption: A replication and update. *Demography* 21(1):71–82.

CARGAN, L., and M. MELKO. 1982. *Singles. Myths and realities.* Beverly Hills, CA: Sage.

CHERLIN, A., and J. McCARTHY. 1985. Remarried couple households: Data from the June 1980 current population survey. *Journal of Marriage and the Family* 47:23–30.

COOK, C. C., and N. M. RUDD. 1984. Factors influencing the residential location of female householders. *Urban Affairs Quarterly* 20(1):78–96.

CRUTCHFIELD, C. F. 1981. Nonmarital relationships and their impact on the institution of marriage and the traditional family structure. *Journal of Family Law* 19(2):247–261.

DAY, R. D., and S. J. BAHR. 1986. Income changes following divorce and remarriage. *Journal of Divorce* 9(3):75–88.

DeMARIS, A., and G. R. LESLIE. 1984. Cohabitation with the future spouse: Its influence upon satisfaction and communication. *Journal of Marriage and the Family* 46(1):77–84.

DORNBUSCH, S. M., J. M. CARLSMITH, S. J. BUSHWALL, P. L. RITTER, H. LEIDERMAN, A. H. HASTORF, and R. T. GROSS. 1985. Single parents, extended households, and the control of adolescents. *Child Development* 56:326–341.

ELLIOT, F. R. 1986. *The family: Change or continuity?* Atlantic Highlands, NJ: Humanities Press International.

FINE, M. A. 1986. Perceptions of stepparents: Variation in stereotypes as a function of current family structure. *Journal of Marriage and the Family* 48:537–543.

FINE, M. A., B. W. DONNELLY, and P. VOYDANOFF. 1986. Adjustment and satisfaction of parents. A comparison of intact, single-parent, and stepparent families. *Journal of Family Issues* 7(4):391–404.

FOSTER, L. 1981. *Religion and sexuality. The Shakers, the Mormons, and the Oneida Community.* Urbana and Chicago: University of Illinois Press.

GARFINKEL, I., and S. S. McLANAHAN. 1986. Single mothers and their children. A new American dilemma. Washington, DC: The Urban Institute Press.

GILES-SIMS, J. 1984. The stepparent role. Expectations, behavior, and sanctions. *Journal of Family Issues* 5(1):116–130.

GLENN, N. D., and C. N. WEAVER. 1977. The marital happiness of remarried divorced persons. *Journal of Marriage and the Family* 39:331–337.

GLICK, P. C. 1980. Remarriage. Some recent changes in variations. *Journal of Family Issues* 1(4):455–478.

GLICK, P. C. 1984. Marriage, divorce, and living arrangements. *Journal of Family Issues* 5(1):7–26.

GLICK, P. C., and S. LIN. 1986. Recent changes in divorce and remarriage. *Journal of Marriage and the Family* 48:737–747.

GOETTING, A. 1982. The six stations of remarriage: Developmental tasks of remarriage after divorce. *Family Relations* 31:213–222.

GOLDMAN, N., and A. R. PEBLEY. 1981. Legalization of consensual unions in Latin America. *Social Biology* 28(1–2):49–61.

GREIF, G. L. 1985. Single fathers rearing children. *Journal of Marriage and the Family* 47(1):185–191.

GWARTNEY-GIBBS, P. A. 1986. The institutionalization of premarital cohabitation: Estimates from marriage license applications, 1970 and 1980. *Journal of Marriage and the Family* 48:423–434.

HOFFERTH, S. L. 1985. Updating children's life course. *Journal of Marriage and the Family* 47:93–115.

HUNT, M. 1974. *Sexual Behavior in the 1970's.* New York: Dell.

IHINGER-TALLMAN, M., and K. PASLEY. 1987. *Remarriage.* Beverly Hills, CA: Sage.

KELLAM, S. G., M. E. ENSMINGER, and J. TURNER. 1977. Family structure and the mental health of children. *Archives of General Psychiatry* 34:1012–1022.

KESHET, J. K. 1980. From separation to stepfamily. A subsystem analysis. *Journal of Family Issues* 1(4):517–532.

KURDEK, L. A. 1988. Relationship quality of gay and lesbian cohabiting couples. *Journal of Homosexuality* 16:91–115.

KURDEK, L. A., and J. P. SCHMITT. 1986. Early development of relationship quality in heterosexual married, heterosexual cohabiting, gay, and lesbian couples. *Developmental Psychology* 22(3):305–309.

LEWIN, B. 1982. Unmarried cohabitation: A marriage form in a changing society. *Journal of Marriage and the Family* 44:763–773.

McCARTHY, J. 1978. A comparison of the probability of the dissolution of first and second marriages. *Demography* 15(3):345–359.

MACKLIN, E. D. 1987. Nontraditional family forms. In *Handbook of marriage and the family,* ed. M. B. Sussman and S. K. Steinmetz, 317–353. New York: Plenum.

McLANAHAN, S. S., N. V. WEDEMEYER, and T. ADELBERG. 1981. Network structure, social support, and psychological well-being in the single-parent family. *Journal of Marriage and the Family* 43:601–612.

MIALL, C. E. 1985. Perceptions of informal sanctioning and the stigma of involuntary childlessness. *Deviant Behavior.* 6:383–403.

MIALL, C. E. 1986. The stigma of involuntary childlessness. *Social Problems* 33(4):268–282.

MIKA, K., and B. L. BLOOM. 1981. Adjustment to separation among former cohabitators. *Journal of Divorce* 4(2):45–66.

MOSHER, W. D., and C. A. BACHRACH. 1982. Childlessness in the United States: Estimates from national survey of family growth. *Journal of Family Issues* 3:517–543.

MURDOCK, G. I. 1949. *Social structure.* New York: Macmillan.

NEWCOMB, M. D. 1986. Cohabitation, marriage and divorce among adolescents and young adults. *Journal of Social and Personal Relationships* 3:473–494.

NORTON, A. J., and P. C. GLICK. 1986. One-parent families: A social and economic profile. *Family Relations* 35:9–17.

NORTON, A. J., and J. E. MOORMAN. 1987. Current trends in marriage and divorce among American women. *Journal of Marriage and the Family* 49:3–14.

NYE, F. I., and F. M. BERARDO. 1973. *The family. Its structure and interaction.* New York: Macmillan.

OLDHAM, J. T. 1981. Cohabitation by an alimony recipient revisited. *Journal of Family Law* 20(4):615–655.

ORTHNER, D. K., and K. LEWIS. 1979. Evidence of single-father competence in child rearing. *Family Law Quarterly* 13(1):27–47.

POSTON, D. L., JR., and K. B. KRAMER. 1986. Patterns of childlessness among Catholic and non-Catholic women in the U.S.: A log-linear analysis. *Sociological Inquiry* 56:506–522.

RAMU, G. N. 1985. Voluntarily childless and parental couples: A comparison of their lifestyle characteristics. *Journal of Changing Patterns* 7(3):130–145.

SIEGEL, L. J. 1986. *Criminology.* 2d ed. New York: West Publishing.

SKOLNICK, A. 1981. The social contexts of cohabitation. *American Journal of Comparative Law* 29:339–358.

SPANIER, G. B. 1983. Married and unmarried cohabitation in the United States: 1980. *Journal of Marriage and the Family* 45:277–289.

U.S. BUREAU OF THE CENSUS. 1986a. *Statistical abstract of the United States: 1987.* Washington, DC: U.S. Government Printing Office.

U.S. BUREAU OF THE CENSUS. 1986b. *Projections of the number of households and families: 1986 to 2000.* Current Population Reports, Series P-25, no. 986. Washington, DC: U.S. Government Printing Office.

VEEVERS, J. E. 1980. *Childless by choice.* Toronto: Butterworths.

WEINGARTEN, H. 1980. Remarriage and well-being. *Journal of Family Issues* 1(4):533–559.

WHITE, L. K., and A. BOOTH. 1985. The quality and stability of remarriages: The role of stepchildren. *American Sociological Review* 50:689–698.

WILSON, M., and M. DALY. 1987. Risk of maltreatment of children living with stepparents. In *Child abuse and neglect: Biosocial dimensions,* ed. R. Gelles and J. Lancaster, 215–232. New York: Aldine.

WILSON, M., M. DALY, and S. J. WEGHORST. 1980. Household composition and the risk of child abuse and neglect. *Journal of Biosocial Science* 12:333–340.

CHAPTER 18

Gender Roles

Introduction

Perhaps no characteristic is more important in family life than gender. Males and females have some distinct biological and social differences, and family roles are usually assigned according to gender. Throughout this book we have identified gender differences in many facets of family life. Men are more involved in the provider role, and women tend to do more of the child care and housekeeping. Even when both partners are employed full-time and have egalitarian attitudes, women tend to have primary responsibility for child care.

Lorraine and Michael illustrate well a typical pattern of gender differences in families. They both have college degrees, his in computer science and hers in secondary education. She has worked all during their marriage except for a month of leave after the birth of each of their two children. They have a modern, egalitarian marriage and believe in sharing in the provider, housekeeper, and child care roles. They put that belief into action, as Lorraine has always worked and Michael has always been extensively involved in child care and household chores.

However, Lorraine takes more of the responsibility for child care than Michael because of their different work schedules. She is able to come home each day by 4:00 P.M., whereas it is 5:30 before he is able to make it home. She also is off during the summers and cares for the children then.

Michael earns $35,000 per year compared to only $20,000 for Lorraine. Computer programmers earn considerably more than high school teachers and she only works nine months each year. Because the family has become more dependent on his income than hers, his work takes priority. Although they are egalitarian in many ways, they still have somewhat of a traditional division of labor.

In this chapter we examine men's and women's attitudes and behavior regarding gender roles. The chapter is divided into six major sections. First, we review the history of the movement toward gender equality in order to understand how gender roles have changed. Second, we identify major gender differences that continue to exist and discuss recent attempts to reduce those differences. Third, the ambivalence of our society toward gender equality is discussed. Fourth, we explore the question of nature versus nurture in the formation of gender roles. Fifth, gender differences in health are examined. Finally, we discuss the large gender difference in violence, drug abuse, and incest.

The Movement Toward Gender Equality

In colonial America women could neither vote nor serve on juries. When a woman married she could not own property or make contracts herself. Any property she owned before marriage came under the control of her husband. Wives were to perform the housekeeper, child care, and child socialization roles and the husbands' role was to provide the physical essentials of life and protect their wife and children.

In the nineteenth century the **Married Women's Property Acts** were passed in all the states. They gave married women the right to (1) be employed without their husband's permission, (2) control their own earnings, (3) control property they brought to the marriage, and (4) make contracts (Lee 1980).

In 1848 the first national women's rights convention was held in Seneca Falls, New York. The **Declaration of Sentiments** was produced during this convention. It was patterned after the Declaration of Independence and stated that men and women are created equal, that women have inalienable rights and have been oppressed, and it insisted that women be granted all the rights and privileges of male citizens (Lee 1980).

The next important step was adding the Thirteenth, Fourteenth, and Fifteenth Amendments to the U.S. Constitution in 1866. The **Thirteenth Amendment** freed the slaves, the **Fourteenth Amendment** gave them equal rights, and the **Fifteenth Amendment** gave blacks the right to vote. Women fighting for the vote opposed the Fourteenth Amendment because section two refers to the right of *male* citizens to vote but says nothing about women's rights.

Probably the most important aspect of the Fourteenth Amendment is the **equal protection clause,** which states that "no State shall . . . deny to any person within its jurisdiction the equal protection of the laws." This amendment introduced the word *equal* to the Constitution. The purpose of the equal protection clause was to insure equal treatment of black males, but the language refers to persons and not just to males (Lee 1980).

The first gender discrimination case under the Fourteenth Amendment was *Bradwell v. Illinois* (83 U.S. 130) in 1873. Myra Bradwell challenged an Illinois statute that would not allow women to practice law. Ms. Bradwell lost her case and was not allowed to become an attorney.

In the late nineteenth century the women's suffrage movement gained momentum. Women finally gained the right to vote when the Nineteenth Amendment was passed in 1920.

In 1923 the **Equal Rights Amendment** (ERA) was first introduced in Congress. It was reintroduced in every succeeding Congress until it finally passed both houses in March of 1972. It then had to be ratified by three fourths of the states. The time for ratification was seven years, but was extended three more years to June 30, 1982. Only thirty-five states ratified the ERA, and it died in 1982 after a bitter struggle. The ERA has been reintroduced in succeeding congresses but has not yet passed both houses. However, sixteen states have provisions in their constitutions that prohibit gender discrimination (Lee 1980).

Perhaps one of the most important events in the movement toward gender equality was a change in the interpretation of the Fourteenth Amendment by the Supreme Court. After the death of their adopted son, Sally and Cecil Reed, who were separated, both filed a petition to become the administrator of their son's estate. Although both were qualified, the probate court ruled in favor of the father because of an Idaho statute which stated that males are preferred over females as executors of estates. Eventually the case was appealed to the Supreme Court. They ruled that because it favored males over females, the Idaho statute violated the equal protection clause of the Fourteenth Amendment.

Reed v. Reed (404 U.S. 71, 1971) was important because it was the first time that the Supreme Court applied the equal protection clause of the Fourteenth Amendment to gender discrimination. That was over one hundred years after the amendment was passed. Of course, it is no coincidence that the ruling came at the time it did. Gender discrimination had become an important social issue during the early seventies and congressional hearings on the ERA were held before the *Reed v. Reed* decision was handed down.

After *Reed* a series of Supreme Court decisions outlawed many existing laws that treated men and women differently. As noted in Chapter 12, in **Stanley v. Illinois** (405 U.S. 645, 1972) the court said a law that treated unmarried fathers differently than unmarried mothers violated the equal protection clause. Unmarried men could no longer be denied custody rights without a hearing showing that they were unfit.

Frontiero v. Richardson (411 U.S. 677, 1973) established that the military may not have a different standard for women than it does for men officers who claim dependents. Up to that time a man could obtain increased housing and medical benefits by claiming his wife as a dependent. He did not have to prove that she actually depended on him for support, but only that she was his wife. Sharon Frontiero was a lieutenant in the U.S. Air Force who was married to Joseph Frontiero, a full-time college student. The Air Force would not allow her to claim Joseph as a dependent unless she proved that she provided more than one half of his support. The court ruled that the law violated the equal protection clause of the Fourteenth Amendment.

Another important case was **Weinberger v. Wiesenfeld** (420 U.S. 636, 1975), which rejected gender discrimination between widows and widowers in Social Security death benefits. Paula Wiesenfeld had been the principal support for herself and her husband for two years. Each year the maximum Social Security amount was deducted from her salary. After she died in childbirth, her husband applied for Social Security survivors' benefits for himself and his son. He was denied benefits because the law said they were available only to women. The court said such gender-based distinctions violated the equal protection clause.

Other cases established that the age of majority cannot be different for males and females (*Stanton v. Stanton,* 421 U.S. 7, 1976; *Craig v. Boren,* 429 U.S. 190, 1976). A law requiring widowers but not widows to prove dependency status in order to receive Social Security survivors' benefits was declared unconstitutional (*Califano v. Goldfarb,* 430 U.S. 199, 1977). It became illegal for states to require only males to pay alimony (*Orr v. Orr*, 440 U.S. 268, 1979). Alimony was to be based on need and ability to pay rather than gender. Child custody laws became gender neutral in many states. In short, many laws that treated men and women differently were eliminated.

However, many laws that treat men and women differently have still been allowed to stand. For example, because of differences in male and female roles in the military, the Supreme Court has ruled that different promotion standards for women are permissable (*Schlesinger v. Ballard*, 419 U.S. 498, 1975). Because widows are usually poorer than widowers, the Supreme Court upheld a Florida law that granted a property tax exemption to widows but not to widowers (*Kahn v. Shevin*, 416 U.S. 351, 1974).

Because some laws that differentiate between men and women have been struck down and others have been upheld, there is some confusion regarding what the standard of the Supreme Court is on gender discrimination. The current standard applied to gender discrimination is called **judicial scrutiny.** To pass judicial scrutiny, a law must serve an *important governmental objective* and must be *substantially related* to the achievement of that objective (Lee 1980).

Judicial scrutiny is a strong standard but is not as strong as **strict judicial scrutiny,** the standard applied to race. If a law treats blacks differently than whites, it automatically comes under strict judicial scrutiny because it involves race, a suspect classification. The court will declare such a law unconstitutional unless it can be established that the law serves a *compelling governmental objective* and is *necessary* for the accomplishment of that objective. This almost never happens, and laws of this type invariably are declared unconstitutional. However, in some cases the court has been convinced that laws that treat men and women differently are substantially related to an important governmental objective (Lee 1980).

During the period in which the Supreme Court gave the Fourteenth Amendment a new interpretation, the Congress passed a number of statutes whose purpose was to eliminate gender discrimination. Perhaps the most important was **Title VII of the Civil Rights Act** of 1964, which outlawed sex discrimination in hiring. In 1971 the **Equal Employment Opportunities Commission** was given the power to litigate to give the Civil Rights Act some force. The Equal Credit Opportunity Act was passed in 1975 to stop credit discrimination against women. Sex and marital status are no longer required for a credit application in which no collateral is pledged. Discrimination against pregnant women was the target of the 1978 Pregnancy Discrimination Act. **Title IX of the Education Amendments** of 1972 was passed to eliminate gender discrimination in education.

The executive branch of government added to this trend with Executive Order 11246 in 1965 and Executive Order 11375 in 1974, which mandated **affirmative action.** The purpose was to increase the employment opportunities of females and minorities.

In summary, during the past two centuries there has been a gradual movement toward gender equality. Key milestones were the Married Women's Property Acts, the Nineteenth Amendment which gave women the right to vote, the new interpretation given the Fourteenth Amendment by the U.S. Supreme Court, and federal statutes outlawing gender discrimination.

Before 1900 women could not vote, serve on juries, or practice law. Fewer than one in twenty married women was employed outside the home. Most women received little formal education. Today more than half of all college graduates are women, and over 50 percent of women with minor children are employed outside the home. There have been large increases in the number of women in prestigious professions, such as doctors and lawyers. Compared to the nineteenth century, there have been marked changes in gender roles. Legally and socially men and women are equals in many ways.

Gender Equality Today

Although there has been a movement toward gender equality, large differences in gender roles remain. Roles within the home and in the marketplace continue to be allocated according to gender. Men tend to specialize in the provider role while women tend to become heavily involved in the child care, child socialization, and housekeeping roles. The structure and norms of the marketplace seem to reinforce these gender differences. In this section we review how this traditional gender division of labor tends to give men superior economic power and women superior relationship power.

Economic Power

One of the major differences between men and women is in **economic power.** Women generally do not receive as much encouragement during their education as men do. They face more barriers to educational and occupational advancement because they bear the children and usually do most child care, child socialization, and housekeeping. When women enter the marketplace they are paid much less than men. The law may state that men and women are equal, but economically they are far from it.

In 1985 women earned 69 cents for every dollar men earned (Bureau of Labor Statistics 1985). This was an increase from 64 cents in 1980, although change during the past thirty years has been relatively small (Shaw and Sproat 1980). In 1984 the median annual earnings of men and women were $19,438 and $9,584, respectively (U.S. Bureau of the Census 1986).

Why do women earn only 69 percent of what men earn? There are several possible explanations. First, women's low wages may simply reflect the fact that few women are employed in high-status occupations (Rytina 1982). However, even within a given occupational category there are large differences between the wages of men and women.

Rytina (1982) has examined the earnings of men and women within specific occupations. A summary of the median earnings of the ten highest paid occupations for men and women in 1981 is shown in Table 18·1. Among both lawyers and physicians women earned only 71 percent of what men earned. Women in the highest paid occupational group earned only 83 percent of the earnings of men employed in the occupation that ranked twentieth in median earnings (Rytina 1982).

A second reason why women earn less than men is experience in the marketplace. Women are more likely to drop out of the labor force for a period to

TABLE 18·1 Occupations with Highest Media Weekly
Earnings for Men and Women Employed Full-Time in Wage
and Salary Work

	Median Earnings ($)
Men	
Aerospace and Astronautical Engineers	619
Stock and Bond Sales Agents	589
Chemical Engineers	583
Economists	580
Lawyers	574
Sales Managers, except retail trade	566
Physicians	561
Electrical and Electronics Engineers	555
School Administrators, College and University	552
Industrial Engineers	549
Women	
Operations and Systems Researcher Analysts	422
Computer Systems Analysts	420
Lawyers	407
Physicians	401
Social Scientists	391
Teachers, College and University	389
Postal Clerks	382
Engineers	371
Ticket, Station, and Express Agents	370
School Administrations, Elementary and Secondary	363

SOURCE: Rytina 1982:30, Tables 1 and 2.

have a child, and this decreases the time in the labor force to develop skills.
Exiting from employment for a period may decrease experience and advancement opportunities and may make it more difficult to keep one's skills current.
Leigh (1982) and Ragan and Smith (1981) have shown that this is a significant
factor in gender wage differentials. Both reported that about half of the gender
wage gap can be accounted for by differences in labor force experience. Put
another way, their research suggests that when we compare men and women
who are in similar occupations and have comparable experience, women will
earn about 85 percent of what men earn.

In a similar way, Duncan et al. (1984) estimated how much education, work
experience, work continuity, and patterns of absenteeism contributed to differences between the wages of women and men. They found that these skill
factors accounted for one third of the difference in the gender wage gap. When
men and women in their sample with similar occupational skills were compared, the women earned about 80 percent of what the men earned. Taken
together, the existing research demonstrates that work experience and work
continuity explain between one third to one half of the gender differences in
wage rates.

A third explanation for the gender wage gap is time spent in domestic labor.
Coverman (1983) found that the amount of time spent in housework and child

care was negatively related to wage rates. That is, the more time one spends in domestic labor, the lower one's wages. This relationship held for both men and women in the working and middle class. Because women usually do a majority of the housework and child care, this may be an important factor in explaining gender wage differentials. Coverman (1983) suggests that housework and child care need to be distributed more equally before gender wage differences can be eliminated.

A fourth and final reason for the gender wage gap is simply gender discrimination. Women may be paid less than men not because they are less skilled or experienced, but simply because they are women.

There is considerable evidence to support this last explanation. The research cited earlier on experience accounted for only half of the gender wage gap. Comparisons of men and women with the same education and employed full-time in identical occupations still show substantial differences in wage rates (Rytina 1982). Reward structures are different for men and women even when they have similar characteristics and are in similar jobs (Ferber, Green, and Spaeth 1986). When women discontinue work for a period it hurts their wages more than it does for men (Ragan and Smith 1981).

Having a college education appears to lessen the problem of gender discrimination in employment. Filer (1983) reported that gender discrimination was substantially less among women with college degrees than for those who stopped their education after high school. There also appears to be no gender differences in unemployment rates (Johnson 1983; U.S. Bureau of the Census 1986).

There is evidence that occupational segregation of men and women has declined rapidly during the past decade. Beller (1985) reported that the rate of decline in occupational segregation doubled during the seventies. Women's entry into managerial occupations was dramatic, although craft occupations (skilled jobs such as electrician and plumber) remain heavily male and clerical occupations heavily female.

The difference between men and women in economic power is particularly evident when gender differences in economic well-being following divorce are examined. Women's economic well-being decreases dramatically following divorce while men's *real* income tends to increase, as reviewed in Chapter 16 (Day and Bahr 1986; Weitzman 1985). In recent decades the situation has gotten worse for women rather than better. One reason for the deterioration has been the legal trend toward gender equality.

In the name of equality, alimony and child support are being awarded less frequently, and when they are awarded, the amounts in real dollars are smaller than in the past (Dixon and Weitzman 1980; Seal 1979; Weitzman 1985). The length of the awards has also decreased.

Rather than being viewed as a long-term entitlement for contributions to a marriage, alimony increasingly is seen as short-term compensation to help wives rehabilitate themselves economically (Freed and Foster 1984; Weitzman 1985). Today, family assets are less likely than in the past to be granted exclusively to the wife. The primary asset of many marriages is the home, and in the past it usually became the wife's. The new equality has changed this and in some cases has forced the sale of the home to divide the property equally. The net result of the movement toward gender equality has been a substantial

decrease in money and property received by women who divorce (Dixon and
Weitzman 1980; Seal 1979; Weitzman 1985).

Why has this occurred? Legally it has been assumed that men and women
are equal economically, even though this is not usually the case. Even in so-
called egalitarian marriages, like Lorraine and Michael's, there is often a fairly
traditional division of labor. The husband is the primary wage earner and has
invested heavily in his job. The wife has chosen an occupation that does not
pay as well and allows her to attend to the child care and housekeeping. Often
she leaves the labor force for a period during childbearing years.

When such a marriage dissolves these differences do not automatically van-
ish. In most cases women obtain custody of the children, and men maintain
superior economic ability. Equity would require that monetary transfers be
made from husband to wife. However, the recent movement toward gender
equality has resulted in fewer economic transfers from husbands to wives. It
is assumed that men and women are equally situated and that monetary
transfers are needed only temporarily, if at all. It also is assumed that existing
marital assets should be divided equally.

However, a fairer standard would be **vertical equity**—treating men and
women differently because they are in different economic situations. Because
the wife usually has custody of the children, child-rearing responsibilities are
not equal. Usually women's occupational skills are less valuable than men's
because they have forgone opportunities to build skills. Those women who
work often have deliberately chosen low-paying jobs, such as teaching, because
that allows them flexibility to care for their children. Many women lose tenure
because they leave the labor force for periods during childbearing years. In
short, vertical equity would demand that divorced women and men be treated
differently. However, under current divorce law men and women are treated
as if they were economic equals, when in fact there are large differences between
them.

Reducing Economic Inequities

AFFIRMATIVE ACTION.   In the long run, improving educational and employment opportunities for women is probably the single best solution to the economic problems they face. In recent years there have been several attempts
to decrease discrimination and increase employment opportunities for women.
One such attempt has been affirmative action.

It became apparent that more was needed than laws which state that discrimination is illegal. An absence of overt discrimination was not enough,
and positive actions by employers to encourage employment of women were
needed. Affirmative action was an attempt to encourage employers to look for
and make opportunities to hire minorities and women. Executive Order 11246
was issued in 1974 and stipulated that federal contractors develop and implement affirmative action plans to correct deficiencies in minority and female
employment (Leonard 1986).

Has affirmative action been effective? Although there has been much debate,
affirmative action appears to have been beneficial for both women and minorities. Leonard (1986) found that the growth of female employment was

Occupational segregation of men and women has declined rapidly during the last decade. There are increasing numbers of females working with males in professional occupations, as shown by these architects working together. *Ellis Herwig/ The Picture Cube.*

significantly greater among contractor than noncontractor establishments. He concluded that affirmative action and Title VII have been significant tools in improving the economic situation of women and minorities.

Eberts and Stone (1985) assessed the influence of affirmative action on promotions to administrative positions in elementary and secondary education. Using longitudinal data they compared New York and Oregon in the early and late 1970s. They found that discrimination present during the early 1970s declined by more than half by the latter part of the decade. They concluded that this was due to affirmative action and the enforcement of laws relating to equal opportunity in employment.

COMPARABLE WORTH.   Because the wage gap between men and women is still rather large, many have proposed that we implement **comparable worth.** For example, for a library to function, both a librarian and a truck driver are needed. The work of the librarian is essential in cataloging the books and managing the library. The truck driver is needed to transport the books to the library and unload them. Both are essential roles that are of comparable worth. Yet truck drivers, who are usually men, tend to earn considerably more than librarians, who tend to be women.

Advocates of comparable worth say that women's work has been inadvertently undervalued (Becker 1986). Long-standing traditions and institutional forces have crowded women into certain occupations and set their wages lower than men's wages. Proponents maintain that supply and demand and wage flexibility play only a small role in wage differentials and that intervention in the market is needed to change the situation. They propose that we consciously evaluate the worth of different occupations and adjust their wages accordingly. Because the work of librarians is worth as much as the work of truck drivers, the wage of librarians would be adjusted upward.

Advocates suggest that comparable worth would significantly change relative wages but would have only a small effect on overall wage costs. Furthermore, decreasing gender discrimination would lead to more efficient use of the talents of millions of women, thereby increasing economic efficiency (Aaron and Lougy 1986).

Opponents of comparable worth maintain that wages are determined largely by supply and demand. They maintain that job evaluation is inherently subjective and that interfering with the market would be inefficient. It would result in large wage increases for millions of jobs, resulting in price increases and economic inefficiency. According to them, the goal of maximizing profits will eliminate discrimination in the long run. They also maintain that the half of the gender wage gap that is unexplainable may be due to factors other than discrimination (Aaron and Lougy 1986).

Aaron and Lougy (1986) have analyzed gender differences in wages and the possible effect of comparable worth. They maintain that women would continue to earn considerably less than men even if comparable worth was aggressively applied by the courts. According to them, much of the wage gap is due to the fact that companies with mostly male employees tend to pay higher wages than companies with mostly women employees.

To date, courts have been reluctant to apply comparable worth (Gaston 1986) and its merits will continue to be debated and studied (Becker 1986; Fischel and Lazear 1986).

REDUCING GENDER DISCRIMINATION IN DIVORCE.   To help bring equity to divorced women and their children, Congress passed the **Child Support Amendments of 1984** (Public Law 98–378). Initial evaluations suggest that collections of support have increased since passage of the new law (*American Family* 1987). The courts have also begun to recognize the economic value of women's nonmonetary contributions as homemaker, parent, and contributor to economic well-being (Freed and Foster 1984). However, these changes will not alter the situation dramatically. To significantly reduce the gender inequities in divorce will require systematic changes in divorce legislation. An increase in the number and amount of support awards along with innovative and aggressive enforcement of awards will also be needed (McLindon 1987).

In summary, perhaps the greatest difference in the roles of men and women is economic power. Although there has been a social and legal movement toward gender equality in the marketplace, women tend to be economically disadvantaged. They usually do not receive the same encouragement and opportunities for educational and occupational advancement that men do. Women tend to do most child care and housekeeping, even when they are employed. Because women bear the children and usually care for them, they often have discontinuous labor force participation, which decreases their wages. Women tend to be employed in lower paying jobs, and even in comparable occupations women earn considerably less than men. When a divorce occurs, women receive little compensation for their child care and housekeeping efforts and tend to have very low incomes.

Affirmative action and comparable worth have been efforts to reduce gender discrimination in employment. Several laws have been passed to produce greater economic equity in divorce settlements. However, the movement toward equality has hurt many women economically because it has treated men and women as equals when family and employment opportunities and responsibilities are far from equal.

Relationship Power

We now turn to a discussion of gender differences in **relationship power.** We described many times in earlier chapters how family roles are allocated according to gender. The roles women play are more oriented toward nurturance, care, and emotional support than men's roles.

Socially and legally there has been movement toward equality in family roles. A number of scholars have found that gender role attitudes have become less traditional, more liberal, and more egalitarian (Adamek and Miller 1984; Cherlin and Walters 1981; Dambrott, Papp, and Whitemore 1984; McBroom 1984; Tallichet and Willits 1986; Werner and LaRussa 1985). Nye (1976) suggested that major changes have occurred in attitudes about family roles. A majority of husbands and wives he surveyed felt that child socialization and child care should be shared equally. Over half of his respondents felt that housekeeping is a shared responsibility and almost half felt similarly about the provider role.

Legal changes have coincided with changes in gender role attitudes. Many states have modified their laws so that both men and women now have a duty to support each other and their children. Upon divorce, alimony and child support are supposed to be awarded based on need and ability to pay, not on gender. Women may be required to pay alimony just like men.

Laws regarding child custody have also become gender neutral. It is no longer assumed that the mother should have custody of the children. Most states have rejected the presumption that women should be the custodian during the so-called tender years. Over 60 percent of the states have passed laws that equalized parental rights to child custody, and at least thirty-one states have passed laws permitting custody to be shared jointly between divorcing parents (Freed and Foster 1984). The law increasingly recognizes that fathers can nurture children and that they have the right to obtain custody.

Although attitudes and laws have become more gender neutral, many traditional gender role attitudes persist. Werner and LaRussa (1985) observed that many particular sex role stereotypes have changed little over the past two decades. Both women and men tend to view men as more forceful, independent, and stubborn than women. Both sexes continue to see women as more emotional, giving, and submissive than men. Magazines continue to portray women as dependent on men (Davis 1985).

Furthermore, there are still large gender differences in the performance of family roles, as we have noted in previous chapters. Nye (1976) found that women tend to be more skilled at performing the therapeutic role than men.

Women continue to be much more involved and competent than men in child care and socialization, even though the norms are fairly egalitarian. As women have increased their involvement in the provider role there has not been a comparable increase of men in the child care, socialization, and housekeeper roles (Losh-Hesselbart 1987).

Although the child custody laws have become sex neutral, there has been little change in actual custody awards following divorce. Women obtain custody in about nine of every ten divorce cases, and there have been only slight increases in the number of husbands who receive custody or in the number of joint custody awards (Dixon and Weitzman 1980; McGraw, Sterin, and Davis 1982).

A woman who wants to leave an unhappy marriage is able to maintain daily contact with her children, for she almost always obtains custody. A man who wants to leave an unhappy marriage almost always loses daily contact with his children. He must choose between an unhappy marriage and his children or a divorce and loss of children. Even if he is a competent, involved father, he almost never obtains custody, and a divorce will result in the loss of much interaction with his children and of many parental privileges.

The severance of those relationships may be one reason why divorce is harder psychologically on men than women. Whereas the primary stresses for women who divorce are money and trying to balance work and child care, men's primary stresses are emotional problems and loneliness (Bahr 1982). Following divorce men tend to have poorer adjustment, more suicidal feelings, less stability, and more tension than women (Zeiss, Zeiss, and Johnson 1981). Coping with these relationship stresses may also be related to the higher rates of alcoholism and suicide among men. Just as women suffer economically after divorce, men appear particularly vulnerable psychologically after divorce. In short, the differences in gender roles appear to place men at a disadvantage socially and emotionally.

Kranichfeld (1987) recently reviewed the literature on family power and suggested that women have more power than is often assumed. She noted that women are at the very center of the family affectively and structurally, whereas men are often isolated from the family. This involvement in family relationships gives women a kind of power that men do not have, and neither men's superior economic power nor physical strength can substitute for this type of power.

In summary, despite a movement toward gender equality in attitudes and law, large gender differences in gender roles remain. Even in so-called egalitarian marriages, roles tend to be allocated in a fairly traditional way. As a result, men have much more economic power than women, and women tend to have more relationship power. These differences become particularly evident when marriages are dissolved.

How Equal Should Women and Men Be?

Equality is an important American value. The Fourteenth Amendment states that all persons are equal under the law. But how equal should men and women be? Most individuals favor equality as a value but are somewhat ambivalent regarding absolute equality between the sexes. This ambivalence is evident in decisions of the Supreme Court and in attitudes of feminists as well as the general public.

The Supreme Court has applied the Fourteenth Amendment to gender differences and has outlawed many laws that treat women and men differently. However, the court has allowed many laws that discriminate between men and women to stand. The court is not entirely clear what types of gender distinctions are permissable and what types are not permissable under the law (Freedman 1984).

Attitudes among the general public have become much more egalitarian, but many traditional attitudes persist. There seems to be uncertainty about what the roles of men and women should be, particularly within marriage.

General ambivalence regarding gender roles was evident in the defeat of the Equal Rights Amendment. Most persons agree with the general value of equality between the sexes, but what does that mean on a practical level? Would it require that women be drafted, even mothers of small children? Would statutory rape laws be invalidated? Would lesbian and gay marriages become legal? Would organizations such as boy scouts or single-sex colleges become illegal? Would it further hurt women and children of divorce? Apparently, many people do not want absolute gender equality. Uncertainty about how far the ERA would take us in that direction led to its defeat. Inequities produced by "equality" in divorce laws showed that the label equality does not necessarily result in equitable treatment (D'Souza 1986; Lee 1980; Wardle 1984; Weitzman 1985).

The ambivalence regarding gender roles has become particularly evident within the feminist movement, where there has been a massive erosion of support for its causes among American women (D'Souza 1986). Some have seen so-called equality hurt women economically, particularly when divorce occurs (Weitzman 1985). Others think that feminist ideas regarding sexual freedom have led to the degradation of women. Betty Friedan worries because of the denial of the importance of the family and thinks that women should reconsider their need to love and be loved (D'Souza 1986).

During the past century there have been large changes in gender role attitudes, laws, and behaviors. Most people favor the movement toward gender equality and would not want to go back to previous times. Attitudes tend to be more egalitarian than behaviors, indicating that additional change is desired and may occur. However, many are ambivalent about how equal male and female roles should become, particularly within the family.

Nature Versus Nurture

A perennial question is the degree to which gender differences are influenced by biology and by socialization (**nature versus nurture**). At one extreme is the belief that virtually all gender differences are learned through socialization. On the other hand, some believe that many male and female behaviors are due to innate differences that we are born with.

It is relatively easy to identify major physical differences between men and women that appear to be due to biology and not to learning. Males tend to be larger and stronger than females, particularly after puberty (Clarke 1986; Eaton and Enns 1986; Heyward, Johannes-Ellis, and Robert 1986; Thomas and French 1985). Men grow facial hair, have lower voices, and lose their hair as they age. Women are able to bear and nurse children, have higher voices, and tend not to go bald or have extensive facial hair.

The question is to what extent identifiable physical and biological differences affect behaviors of men and women. Those of the nature school of thought believe that the assignment of gender roles is based on innate differences between the sexes. For example, some maintain that it is in the nature of women to be more nurturant and caring than men. Mother love is viewed as an innate female characteristic that makes women uniquely qualified to care for and nurture children. This is the rationale used for the assignment of women to the child care and socialization roles.

The other side of the argument is that men can learn to nurture children just as well as women can. Proponents maintain that the greater skill of women in nurturing is due to the fact that women are assigned and taught to nurture.

Men can learn to care for children just like women can, and being warm and nurturant is an important part of a father's role.   *Ulrike Welsch.*

They believe that traditional gender roles are based on cultural norms rather than on innate gender characteristics.

There is no way to determine definitively how much of gender role behavior is due to biology and how much is due to social learning. However, there is considerable evidence that many things that have been assumed in the past to be innately male or female have little to do with innate male-female characteristics. For example, in **Bradwell v. Illinois** (83 U.S. 130, 1873) it was assumed that practicing law would take women out of their "natural" role. Today more than one third of law graduates are women, and many women function admirably both as mothers and attorneys. There are undoubtedly many gender differences between men and women that are assumed to be innate when in fact they are based on cultural beliefs and have little or nothing to do with the innate characteristics of men and women.

However, there are gender differences that have been assumed to be learned which may have a genetic base. Quantitative ability is one possibility, where research has repeatedly shown that males score higher than females. It is commonly assumed that this is due to cultural encouragement of males and discouragement of females in this area. Recent research indicates that there

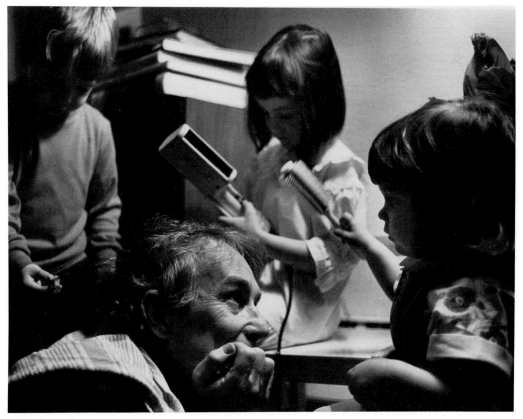

We do not know how much gender-role differentiation is due to genetics and how much is due to social learning. It is clear, however, that the attitudes and behaviors of parents and other adults influence the gender roles of their children.
Donna Ferrato/Visions.

may be a genetic basis to these gender differences. Based on research on the differentiation, structure, and function of the brain, Velle (1984) suggests that there is a high probability that genetic factors are important determinants of gender differences in quantitative ability. Whether future research confirms this hypothesis remains to be seen.

One common gender difference that appears to be due to genetics is longevity. Women live on the average about seven years longer than men (National Center for Health Statistics 1986). Some researchers have said that this difference is merely a reflection of the contrasting social roles of men and women and has nothing to do with biology. Current evidence, however, clearly indicates that gender differences in longevity are biological. For example, the death rate for male infants under one year old is 30 percent larger than for females (National Center for Health Statistics 1986). It seems improbable that social roles can explain this large gender difference at such a young age. Women appear to be biologically superior to men as far as longevity is concerned.

The debate regarding gender roles will continue. There is no way at present to demonstrate how much of gender role differentiation is due to genetics and how much is due to social learning. It is clear that men can nurture children and that women can fulfill the provider role. The traditional division of labor in the home may be influenced more by the demands of procreation than on innate psychological characteristics of men and women. Lorraine and Michael's division of labor was based partly on the fact that Lorraine was the one who carried and bore the children. Research into family division of labor confirms that reproductive constraints have influenced the gender division of labor (Losh-Hesselbart 1987; Mackey 1985).

Gender and Health

As noted earlier, there are some dramatic gender differences in health. In this section we review how men and women differ in physical and mental health.

Death and Physical Health

One of the pervasive differences between men and women is longevity. Men have higher death rates than women for each of the fifteen leading causes of death (see Table 18·2). More than three times as many men than women kill themselves, and men are over three times as likely as women to be murdered. Accidental deaths occur almost three times more frequently among men than women. Heart disease, the leading killer in the United States, kills men almost twice as frequently as women.

Researchers have speculated that the contrasting social roles of men and women undoubtedly make a difference, but death rates among infants show that **genetics** also plays a part. As far as longevity goes, females appear superior to males genetically.

Although women live longer than men, they appear to have more physical health problems. Table 18·3 is a summary of selected health conditions by gender. For most acute and chronic diseases, women have higher rates than men. Men suffer more injuries and have more visual and hearing impairments

TABLE 18·2   Ratio of Age-Adjusted Male-to-Female Death Rates for Fifteen Leading
Causes of Death; United States (1984)

Rank	Causes of Death	Ratio of Male to Female
	All Causes	1.75
1	Disease of Heart	1.94
2	Malignant Neoplasms	1.47
3	Cerebrovascular Diseases	1.17
4	Accidents	2.78
	Motor Vehicle Accidents	2.60
5	Chronic Obstructive Pulmonary Diseases and Allied Conditions	2.23
6	Pneumonia and Influenza	1.80
7	Diabetes Mellitus	1.05
8	Suicide	3.83
9	Chronic Liver Disease and Cirrhosis	2.22
10	Atherosclerosis	1.31
11	Nephritis, Nephrotic Syndrome, and Nephrosis	1.52
12	Homicide	3.28
13	Certain Conditions Originating in Perinata Period	1.29
14	Septicemia	1.40
15	Congenital Anomalies	1.16

SOURCE: National Center for Health Statistics 1987:6.

TABLE 18·3   Selected Health Indicators in United States by Gender (1986)

	Females	Males
1. *Acute Conditions (rates per 1,000)*[a]		
Infective and Parasitic	232	172
Upper Respiratory	425	385
Disgestive System	76	76
Injuries	244	308
2. *New Cases of Cancer (Rates per 1,000)*	455	455
3. *Selected Chronic Conditions (Rate per 1,000)*		
Heart Conditions	86.0	79.3
High Blood Pressure	137.5	104.1
Arthritis	165.3	94.9
Diabetes	27.5	21.3
Visual Impairments	28.2	42.7
Hearing Impairments	74.5	107.1
Migraine	46.5	15.8
4. *Percentage of Persons with No Activity Limitations*	85.4	86.1
5. *Drug Use*		
Percentage of Adults Who Currently Smoke	29	35
Percentage of Adults Using Alcohol in Past Month	46	69
Percentage of Adults Using Marijuana in Past Month	3	10

[a] Acute conditions which were medically attended or caused at least 1 day of restricted activity.
SOURCE: U.S. Bureau of the Census 1986:103,104,106,107.

than women. New occurrences of cancer are about equally distributed among men and women. Most other ailments are more common among women than men, including heart disease. Of course, this also may be an indication of the genetic superiority of women—more women than men survive when they contract certain diseases. Many more men than women smoke cigarettes, drink alcohol, and use marijuana.

Mental Health

There is considerable evidence that women have poorer mental health than men (Aneshensel, Frerichs, and Clark 1981; Weissman 1987). As discussed earlier, this may be related to differences in gender roles (Cleary and Mechanic 1983; D'Arcy and Siddique 1985; Muller 1986; Verbrugge 1986; Waldron and Herold 1986). However, other research suggests that men's mental health may be as poor or worse than women's. Suicide, homicide, and drug use may be ways of coping with mental distress. Men are more likely than women to commit suicide, be killed violently, and abuse alcohol and drugs. Women, on the other hand, are more likely to be depressed and to misuse pain relievers and other prescription drugs. Perhaps men do not have better mental health than women, but they react to stress and depression in a different way.

Gender Roles and Social Problems

Although gender roles are frequently discussed and studied, seldom do people relate the large gender differences in our society to many of the major social problems. In this section we review some of these gender differences.

Violent crime in our society is primarily a male problem. In 87 percent of all cases of violent personal crime, the offender is a male (Siegel 1986). The arrest ratio for violent crimes is nine males for every female. Within the family, women are the victims of criminal violence three times more often than men (Klaus and Rand 1984).

Men are not only the primary perpetrators of violence, they are the usual victims of violence. Men are almost four times more likely than women to be a homicide victim (National Center for Health Statistics 1986).

Violence toward oneself is also much more of a male than female problem. The suicide rate is almost four times greater among men than women (National Center for Health Statistics 1986).

The lifestyle of men is much more hazardous. Men are more than twice as likely as women to die in an accident and 2.6 times more likely to die in an automobile accident (National Center for Health Statistics 1987)

As noted earlier, men have higher mortality than women for each of the fifteen leading causes of death. Men are 22 percent more likely than women to die of cancer and 14 percent more likely to die of heart disease. Of course, this makes widowhood more of a problem for women than men.

Drug abuse has become a serious social problem and a lot of money is being spent to try to cope with it. This too is more of a problem among males than females. Alcoholism is six times more prevalent among men than women

(Albrecht 1986). Among young adults, more than twice as many men than women use marijuana daily. Men have higher prevalence rates of most other illicit drugs including cocaine, heroin, and LSD (Johnston, O'Malley, and Bachman 1986). Males use stimulants slightly more than females. The one drug that females abuse more than males is tranquilizers, but male-female differences are small (Johnston et al. 1986).

One of the most socially abhorred acts is incest. As noted in Chapter 15, incest appears to be more common than popularly believed. In a large majority of cases the father is the perpetrator. Herman (1981) found that 81 percent of incest cases were father-child and 3 percent were mother-child. The remaining 16 percent of the cases were nonparental incest.

As noted earlier, one of the serious problems in our society is the poverty of single-parent homes, often caused by the refusal or inability of men to support their children. Whether they have fathered a child out of wedlock or left children because of divorce, they usually do not support their children economically.

Taken together, this does not paint a very positive picture of men in our society. Men compared to women are much more violent and careless and more likely to abuse alcohol and other drugs. Serious family violence is usually instigated by fathers and they are almost always the perpetrators of incest. Many men father children and then do not support them, creating poverty for many women and children.

Summary

1. During the past two centuries there has been a gradual movement toward gender equality. Key milestones were the Married Women's Property Acts, the Nineteenth Amendment, applying the Fourteenth Amendment to gender, Title VII of the Civil Rights Act of 1964, and affirmative action.

2. The new interpretation of the Fourteenth Amendment required that a law which treats men and women differently will be constitutional only if it serves an important governmental objective and is substantially related to the achievement of that objective. This standard is called judicial scrutiny.

3. Roles within the family continue to be allocated according to gender. Even in egalitarian families the husband tends to be the primary provider and the wife usually does most of the child care, child socialization, and housekeeping.

4. Men have considerably more economic power than women. On the average, women earn 69 percent of what men earn. Women earn less than men because they are in lower status occupations, have less continuous employment, spend more time in domestic labor, and face gender discrimination.

5. Even when compared to men with similar jobs and the same amount of education, experience, and job tenure, women earn considerably less than men. Discrimination is less among college educated women than those who have not attended college.

6. The economic plight of women is particularly evident following divorce.

Women are treated by the law as economic equals when their economic abilities and responsibilities are not equal.

7. Affirmative action has been implemented to decrease the economic inequity between men and women. Comparable worth has been advocated but not implemented to any large degree. Efforts to increase child support enforcement have been moderately successful in increasing child support payments.

8. Women have considerably more relationship power then men. This is particularly evident after divorce, as women obtain child custody in 90 percent of the cases.

9. Although gender equality is a widely held value in the United States, there is considerable uncertainty regarding how equal men and women should be. The persistence of some traditional stereotypes, the defeat of the ERA, recent Supreme Court rulings, and even attitudes among feminists are evidence of the uncertainty.

10. There is debate about the gentic and social bases of gender roles. A correspondence between biological characteristics and specific behaviors has not been established, although reproductive constraints have influenced the gender division of labor. It is clear that men can nurture children and women can fulfill the provider role.

11. Women live an average of seven years longer than men. Men have higher death rates than woman for each of the fifteen leading causes of death. These gender differences are due to genetics as well as the different social roles of men and women.

12. Women have more chronic and acute health problems than men, as well as more depression and psychopathology. However, men have higher rates of suicide, homicide, and alcoholism. This suggests that men's mental problems may be as serious as women's, but that men react to them differently.

13. Many of the serious crimes in our society are perpetrated by men. Men compared to women are much more violent and careless and more likely to abuse alcohol and other drugs. Serious violence within the family is usually committed by men, and fathers are almost always the offenders in incest cases. Many men father children and then do not contribute to the economic support, creating poverty among women and children.

Important Terms

- affirmative action
- *Bradwell v. Illinois*
- Child Support Amendments of 1984
- comparable worth
- Declaration of Sentiments
- economic power
- Equal Employment Opportunities Commission
- equal protection clause
- Equal Rights Amendment
- Fifteenth Amendment

- Fourteenth Amendment
- *Frontiero v. Richardson*
- genetics
- judicial scrutiny
- Married Women's Property Acts
- nature versus nurture
- *Reed v. Reed*
- relationship power
- *Stanley v. Illinois*
- strict judicial scrutiny
- Thirteenth Amendment
- Title VII of the Civil Rights Act
- Title IX of the Education Amendments
- vertical equity
- *Weinberger v. Wiesenfeld*

Questions for Discussion

1. Why do you think it took over one hundred years for the Supreme Court to apply the Fourteenth Amendment to gender discrimination? Why did the new interpretation of the amendment come when it did?
2. Why did the ERA not pass Congress until 1972?
3. Summarize some of the key Supreme Court cases on gender equality.
4. How is judicial scrutiny different from strict judicial scrutiny?
5. Why are women paid so much less than men even though the gender discrimination in employment has been against the law for over twenty-five years?
6. What is affirmative action? In what ways has it been effective? In what ways has it not been effective?
7. In what ways are women discriminated against?
8. In what ways are men discriminated against?
9. What do you think could be done to reduce gender discrimination?
10. How has the trend toward equality helped men and women? In what ways has the trend toward equality hurt men and women?
11. What is the difference between equality and equity?
12. What is comparable worth? What are its pros and cons? To what extent do you think comparable worth should be implemented?
13. Do women really have more relationship power than men? In what ways? Are there ways in which men have more relationship power than women? How?
14. Why was the ERA defeated?
15. What are some of the advantages of the ERA? What are some possible risks of the ERA?
16. Why has there been an erosion of support within the feminist movement? What are some positive outcomes of the feminist movement? What are some negative consequences of the feminist movement?
17. How equal do you think men and women should be?
18. What differences between men and women seem to be due to social

learning, in your opinion? What part does genetics play in gender differences?

19. Do you think gender differences in quantitative ability and verbal ability are due to learning or genetics? Why?
20. Why are men so much more violent than women? Is this due to biology or learning?
21. Why do men take drugs and kill themselves so much more than women do?
22. Many men have abdicated their parental responsibilities. Why? What could be done to improve the situation?
23. Why do women earn less than men?
24. Why do gender differences in wages persist even though it is illegal under current law in the United States?
25. What can be done to decrease gender differences in wages? Answer this question from the perspective of a spouse, parent, and policymaker. That is, what could you do within your own marriage to help improve women's wages? And what could you do as a parent to help your daughters get fair occupational treatment? Finally, if you had political power what would you do to help decrease the gender wage gap?
26. What are the major gender differences in mortality and morbidity? Why do they exist? Do you expect that those differences will change in the next decade?
27. What evidence is there that men have poorer physical and mental health than women? What evidence is there that women have poorer physical and mental health than men? Who is really healthier, men or women?
28. What evidence is there that genetics contributes to gender differences in health? What evidence is there that social roles contribute to gender differences in health? What is more important, genetics or environment in contributing to gender differences in health?

Recommended Reading

AARON, H. J., and C. M. LOUGY. 1986. *The comparable worth controversy.* Washington, DC: The Brookings Institution.

D'SOUZA, D. 1986. The new feminist revolt. *Policy Review* 35:46–52.

EAGLY, A. H. 1987. *Sex differences in social behavior: A social-role interpretation.* Hillsdale, NJ: Erlbaum.

References

Aaron, H. J., and LOUGY, C. M. 1986. *The comparable worth controversy.* Washington, DC: The Brookings Institution.

ADAMEK, R. J. and M. MILLER. 1984. Changes in coed's sex role concepts: 1969 and 1980. *Sociological Spectrum* 4:71–87.

ALBRECHT, S. L. 1986. Alcohol consumption and abuse. In *Utah in demographic perspective,* ed. T. K. Martin, T. Heaton, and S. J. Bahr, 245–258. Salt Lake City: Signature.

AMERICAN FAMILY. 1987. Support enforcement increases. *American Family 10* (January–February).

ANESHENSEL, C. S., R. R. FRERICHS, and V. A. CLARK. 1981. Family roles and sex differences in depression. *Journal of Health and Social Behavior* 22:379–393.

BAHR, S. J. 1982. The pains and joys of divorce: A survey of Mormons. *Family Perspective* 16 (4):191–200.

BECKER, M. E. 1986. Barriers facing women in the wage-labor market and the need for additional remedies: A reply to Fischel and Lazear. *The University of Chicago Law Review* 53 (3):934–949.

BELLER, A. H. 1985. Changes in the sex composition of U.S. occupations, 1960–1981. *Journal of Human Resources* 20:235–250.

BUREAU OF LABOR STATISTICS. 1985. Employment in perspective: Women in the labor force. Report 726, Fourth Quarter 1985. Division of Employment and Unemployment Analysis, Bureau of Labor Statistics, Washington, DC.

CHERLIN, A., and P. B. WALTERS. 1981. Trends in United States men's and women's sex-role attitudes: 1972 to 1978. *American Sociological Review* 46:453–460.

CLARKE, D. H. 1986. Sex differences in strength and fatigability. *Research Quarterly for Exercise and Sport* 57 (2):144–149.

CLEARY, P. D., and D. MECHANIC. 1983. Sex differences in psychological distress among married people. *Journal of Health and Social Behavior* 24:111–121.

COVERMAN, S. 1983. Gender, domestic labor time, and wage inequality. *American Sociological Review* 48:623–637.

D'ARCY, C., and C. M. SIDDIQUE. 1985. Marital status and psychological well-being: A cross-national comparative analysis. *International Journal of Comparative Sociology* 26:149–166

D'SOUZA, D. 1986. The new feminist revolt—this time it's against feminism. *Policy Review* 35:46–52.

DAMBROT, F. H., M. E. PAPP, and C. WHITMORE. 1984. The sex-role attitudes of three generations of women. *Personality and Social Psychology Bulletin* 10 (3):469–473.

DAVIS, P. A. 1985. *Women in advertisements: A 1983 follow-up analysis of the portrayal of women in magazine ads.* Paper presented at the Pacific Sociological Association Conference in Albuquerque, NM, April.

DAY, R. D., and S. J. BAHR. 1986. Income changes following divorce and remarriage. *Journal of Divorce* 9 (3):75–88.

DIXON, R. B., and L. J. WEITZMAN. 1980. Evaluating the impact of no-fault divorce in California. *Family Relations* 29:297–307

DUNCAN, G. J., R. D. COE, M. E. CORCORAN, M. S HILL, S. D. HOFFMAN, and J. N. MORGAN. 1984. *Years of poverty, years of plenty.* Ann Arbor, MI: Survey Research Center, Institute for Social Research, University of Michigan.

EATON, W. O., and L. R. ENNS. 1986. Sex differences in human motor activity level. *Psychological Bulletin* 100 (1):19–28.

EBERTS, R. W., and J. A. STONE. 1985. Male-female differences in promotions: EEO in public education. *The Journal of Human Resources* 4:504–521.

FERBER, M. A., C. A. GREEN, and J. L. SPAETH. 1986. Work power and earnings of women and men. *American Economic Review* 76:53–58.

FILER, R. K. 1983. Sexual differences in earnings: The role of individual personalities and tastes. *Journal of Human Resources* 18:83–99.

FISCHEL, D. R., and E. P. LAZEAR. 1986. Comparable worth and discrimination in labor markets. *The University of Chicago Law Review* 53 (3):891–918.

FREED, D. J., and H. H. FOSTER. 1984. Family law in the fifty states: An overview. *Family Law Quarterly* 17:365–447.

FREEDMAN, A. E. 1984. Sex equality, sex differences, and the Supreme Court. *The Yale Law Journal* 92 (6):913–968.

GASTON, C. L. 1986. An idea whose time has not come: Comparable worth and the market salary problem. *Population Research and Policy Review* 5:15–29.

HERMAN, J. L. 1981. *Father-daughter incest.* Cambridge, MA: Harvard University Press.

HEYWARD, V. H., S. M. JOHANNES-ELLIS, and J. F. ROMER. 1986. Gender differences in strength. *Quarterly for Exercise and Sport* 57 (2):154–159.

JOHNSON, J. L. 1983. Sex differentials in unemployment rates: A case for no concern. *Journal of Political Economy* 90:293–303.

JOHNSTON, L. D., P. M. O'MALLEY, and J. G. BACHMAN. 1986. *Drug use among American high school students, college students, and other young adults—national trends through 1985.* Rockville, MD: National Institute on Drug Abuse.

KLAUS, P., and M. RAND. 1984. *Family violence.* Washington, DC: U.S. Department of Justice, Bureau of Justice Statistics.

KRANICHFELD, M. L. 1987. Rethinking family power. *Journal of Family Issues* 8:42–56.

LEE, R. E. 1980. *A lawyer looks at the equal rights amendment.* Provo, UT: Brigham Young University Press.

LEIGH, D. E. 1982. The national longitudinal surveys: A selective survey of recent evidence. *Review of Public Data Use* 10:185–201.

LEONARD, J. S. 1986. What was affirmative action? *American Finance Review* 76 (2):359–382.

LOSH-HESSELBART, S. 1987. Development of gender roles. In *Handbook of marriage and the family,* ed. M. B. Sussman and S. K. Steinmetz, 535–564. New York: Plenum.

McBROOM, W. H. 1984. Changes in sex-role orientations: A five-year longitudinal comparison. *Changes in Sex-Role Orientations* 2 (7/8):583–592.

McGRAW, R. E., G. J. STERIN, and J. M. DAVIS. 1982. A case study in divorce law reform and its aftermath. *Journal of Family Law* 20:443–487.

MACKEY, W. C. 1985. A cross-cultural perspective on perceptions of paternalistic deficiences in the United States: The myth of the derelict daddy. *Sex Roles* 12:509–533.

McLINDON, J. B. 1987. Separate but unequal: The economic disaster of divorce for women and children. *Family Law Quarterly* 21:351–409.

MULLER, C. 1986. Health and health care of employed women and homemakers: Family factors. *Women and Health* 11:7–26.

NATIONAL CENTER FOR HEALTH STATISTICS. 1986. Advance report of final mortality statistics, 1984. *Monthly Vital Statistics Report* vol. 35, no. 6, Supp. (2). DHHS Pub. No. (PHS) 86–1120. Hyattsville, MD: Public Health Service.

NATIONAL CENTER FOR HEALTH STATISTICS. 1987. Advance report of final mortality statistics, *1985. Monthly Vital Statistics Report,* vol. 36, no. 5, Supp. DHHS Pub. No. (PHS) 87–1120. Hyattsville, MD: Public Health Service.

NYE, F. I. 1976. *Role structure and analysis of the family.* Beverly Hills, CA: Sage.

RAGAN J. F., JR., and S. P. SMITH. 1981. The impact of differences in turnover rates on male/female pay differentials. *Journal of Human Resources* 16:343–365.

RYTINA, N. F. 1982. Earnings of men and women: A look at specific occupations. *Monthly Labor Review* (April):25–31.

SEAL, K. 1979. A decade of no-fault divorce: What it has meant financially for women in California. *Family Advocate* 1 (4):10–15.

SHAW, L. B., and K. SPROAT. 1980. *Mature women in the work force: Research findings and policy recommendations from the National Longitudinal Surveys.* Paper prepared for the Office of Research and Development, Employment and Training Administration, U.S. Department of Labor. Columbus, OH: Ohio State University Center for Human Resources Research.

SIEGEL, L. J. 1986. *Criminology.* 2d ed. St. Paul, MN: West Publishing.

TALLICHET, S. E., and F. K. WILLITS. 1986. Gender-role attitude change of young women: Influential factors from a panel study. *Social Psychology Quarterly* 49 (3):219–227.

THOMAS, J. R., and K. E. FRENCH. 1985. Gender differences across age in motor performance: A meta-analysis. *Psychological Bulletin* 98 (2):260–282.

U.S. BUREAU OF THE CENSUS. 1986. *Statistical abstract of the United States: 1987.* Washington, DC: U.S. Government Printing Office.

VELLE, W. 1984. Sex differences in intelligence: Implications for educational policy. *Journal of Human Evolution* 13:109–115.

VERBRUGGE, L. M. 1986. Role burdens and physical health of women and men. *Women and Health* 11:47–77.

WALDRON, I., and J. HEROLD. 1986. Employment, attitudes toward employment, and women's health. *Women and Health* 11:79–98.

WARDLE, L. D. 1984. The impact of the proposed Equal Rights Amendment upon family law. *Journal of Family Law* 23 (4):477–517.

WEISSMAN, M. M. 1987. Advances in psychiatric epidemiology: Rates and risks for major depression. *American Journal of Public Health* 77:445–451.

WEITZMAN, L. J. 1985. *The divorce revolution—the unexpected social and economic consequences for women and children in America.* New York: Free Press.

WERNER, P. D., and G. W. LaRussa. 1985. Persistence and change in sex-role stereotypes. *Sex Roles* 12 (9/10):1089–1100.

ZEISS, A. M., R. A. ZEISS, and S. M. JOHNSON. 1981. Sex differences in initiation of and adjustment to divorce. *Journal of Divorce* 4 (2):21–33.

PART *V*

Completing the Life Course

CHAPTER 19

The Aging Family

Introduction

The last three stages of the family life cycle are launching families, middle-aged families, and retired families (see Chapter 2). The **launching stage** is the period between the time the first and last child leaves home. Today launching usually begins when the parents are in their middle forties and lasts about ten years. **Middle age** is the period between the launching of the last child and retirement and typically lasts nine years. The final stage of the life cycle lasts from retirement until one spouse dies. Given current mortality rates this stage lasts about six years. Widowhood comes next, and the average woman will spend nine years as a widow.

To illustrate the later stages of the life cycle, let us briefly describe the experiences of Michael and Lorraine as they go through these periods in their lives.

Years pass quickly and before long Debra has graduated from high school and leaves home to attend college. Lorraine and Michael have started the launching stage of the family life cycle. They miss having Debra around on a daily basis but they still see her during vacations and summertime.

Don, their crippled son, has adjusted amazingly well. He had numerous operations on his hands and legs between the ages of 2 and 14. He cannot run or throw a ball, but the operations have enabled him to walk somewhat normally. He has gone to a regular school and lives a relatively normal life.

Three years later Don starts college, but decides to go to a local college and live at home. Debra is beginning her last year of college and announces her engagement to be married the following summer.

Debra completes her education, marries, and moves with her husband to a city four hundred miles east of her hometown. Don finishes college and decides to attend law school. He leaves home and Lorraine and Michael are completely alone for the first time since early in their marriage.

Don meets a woman at law school and they decide to get married. He finishes his degree, marries, and takes a job with a law firm in Washington, D.C.

Michael and Lorraine have officially completed the launching stage, which has taken them ten years. Michael is 53 and Lorraine is 51. Having their children leave is hard in many ways. They love them and miss having daily contact with them. Yet, it is good to see their children grow up and become competent adults. There is more time now for them to do things together, including some traveling.

Financially, Lorraine and Michael are better off than they ever have been. It was a strain supporting two children in college but now both are married and have jobs. Michael and Lorraine are in good health and enjoy their work. Middle age is a pleasurable time for them.

Before long Debra announces that she is going to have a child. It is hard for Lorraine and Michael to think of themselves as grandparents, but they take the news in stride and enjoy their little granddaughter very much. They do not get to see her as much as they would like, but usually manage to visit her about once a month.

Now that the children are gone, Michael and Lorraine think more about **retirement** and doing some of the things they have always wanted to do. Health and the possibility of death are concerns that they talk about. Michael is established in his career and now spends less time working than when he was younger. His relationships with Lorraine and with his children and grandchild have become more important for him than before.

Michael's parents are still alive and in relatively good health. Lorraine's father died of a massive heart attack four years ago at age 70. Her mother is not in good health but still lives alone. Lorraine has been thinking of having her come and live with them.

Within a few years Lorraine's mother becomes depressed and physically unable to do many things herself. Lorraine and Michael decide to have her come and live with them. It is quite a burden for Lorraine to teach school and care for her elderly mother. Her mother's condition deteriorates over the next two years and they have to put her in a nursing home. They continue to visit her several times a week.

Before long it is time for Michael to retire. Lorraine is 63 and also decides to retire. They enjoy their retirement for five years until they learn that Michael has cancer. He gradually deteriorates and dies a year later at age 71. The final six months are stressful for Lorraine as she has to care for Michael and watch him deteriorate.

Lorraine was married to Michael for forty-eight years and now has to face life alone. Being a widow is frightening and lonely, but she manages to adjust moderately well. Her health is still relatively good and she has some neighborhood friends. Debra and Don both visit two or three times a year and she calls them regularly. But it is hard to live alone.

Lorraine and Michael illustrate many of the transitions that couples go through from the launching of their children until the death of one spouse. Of course, the specific timing and nature of the transitions vary among couples. Widowhood sometimes occurs well before retirement. Some couples are child-

As couples approach retirement, they often put more emphasis on their family relationships and spend more time together in leisure activities. *Ulrike Welsch.*

less, and others experience a divorce in the middle years. In short, each family
has a unique career that often does not fit neatly into the typical life cycle
stages.

In this chapter we review the aging process as families pass through the
later stages of the life cycle. We begin by discussing some major changes that
have occurred in the family life cycle during the past fifty years. Then we
examine three major transitions in the family life cycle: launching, middle
age, and retirement. The chapter concludes with reviews of widowhood and
gender differences in aging.

Life Cycle Changes

Perhaps the most significant change in family life during the past century has
been the expansion of the later stages of the life cycle, as noted in Chapter 2.
Two major demographic changes have caused this extension. First, there has

been a dramatic increase in longevity. Since 1900 life expectancy in the United States has increased by more than twenty-five years. In 1900 it was less than fifty years compared to seventy-five years in 1985 (Bengtson 1986). Second, there has been a decrease in fertility rates. In 1957 the total fertility rate was 3.7 children per woman, whereas in 1984 it was 1.8 children per woman (Bengtson 1986).

These changes have compressed the childbearing and child-rearing years, and extended the middle and latter stages of the family life cycle. In 1984 men married on the average at age 26 and women at age 24 (National Center for Health Statistics 1987a). The average woman will currently have two children, at ages 26 and 29. The retirement age is 65, and life expectancy for men and women is 71 and 78, respectively (National Center for Health Statistics 1987b). Using these statistics, a profile of the family life cycle of the average couple has been constructed. They spend two years as a married couple without children, eighteen years in the child-rearing stages, ten years launching their two children, nine years in middle age between launching and retirement, and six years as a retired couple. The wife spends nine years as a widow following her husband's death.

The average woman will spend almost as much time retired and widowed as she did raising children at home. She will spend twenty-five years in the last three stages of the life cycle plus nine more years as a widow, compared to only twenty-one years in the first five stages of the family life cycle.

The increase in longevity along with the decline in fertility has produced what has been termed the **graying of America.** The proportion of the population that is over age 65 has increased substantially and will continue to increase during the next two decades.

The **aged dependency ratio** shows this trend well. It is the number of people age 65 and over for every one hundred persons between the ages of 20 and 64. In 1950 the aged dependency ratio was 14 and it increased to 19 by 1980. In 1990 it will be 21, and it is projected to increase to 22 by the year 2000 (Chen 1986).

Three other important social trends have had a significant impact on later-life families. First, as noted in Chapter 10, there has been a large increase in the labor force participation of women. Second, there has been a substantial increase in divorce, as discussed in Chapter 16. Although much of this increase has been among young couples, there also has been an increase in divorce among older couples. Finally, gender differences in longevity have produced large gender differences in the marital status and living arrangements of persons over age 65.

The Launching Stage

The launching stage is a period in which children begin to leave home. This is often not an abrupt transition. College-aged children may leave to attend school but may return regularly on weekends and vacation periods. Many will return home to live during the summer months. Some may leave home and

TABLE 19·1 Percentage of Young Adults Living with Their Parents by Gender and Age, United States (1940, 1970, and 1984)

	1940	1970	1984
Women			
18–19	68	72	75
20–24	40	31	37
25–29	19	7	11
Men			
18–19	83	83	85
20–24	58	44	53
25–29	27	12	17

SOURCE: Glick, P. C., and S. Lin. 1986. More young adults are living with their parents: Who are they? *Journal of Marriage and the Family* 48:108, Table 1. Copyrighted 1986 by the National Council on Family Relations, 1910 West County Road B, Suite 147, St. Paul, Minnesota 55113. Reprinted by permission.

then return after completion of school or military service. Marriage is often seen as the official launching, because after that most couples establish their own permanent residence.

Several scholars have noted that the proportion of young adults living with their parents increased moderately between 1970 and 1985 (Clemens and Axelson 1985; Glick and Lin 1986; Schnaiberg and Goldenberg 1986). For example, as shown in Table 19·1, the proportion of young men between the ages of 20 and 24 that were living with their parents increased from 44 percent in 1970 to 53 percent in 1984. The comparable increase for young women was from 31 percent to 37 percent (Glick and Lin 1986).

This change occurred for several reasons. First, many young persons may have had difficulty finding employment. It also may be related to the decreasing size of American families. Smaller families may make it easier for young adults to stay, or for those who leave to return. Finally, the age at first marriage has been increasing in the United States, which delays the age at which young adults tend to establish their own residences.

Children who are being launched may require substantial financial assistance for college expenses, even though they are independent in other ways. This may create financial strain for many families in this stage. Maintaining morale continues to be an important family task as individuals leave and roles are adjusted. Social control usually becomes less important as children become autonomous young adults.

Middle Age

Middle age is the period between the launching of the last child and retirement. During this stage the maintenance of morale is critical as couples make adjustments. Socialization of children is no longer a major concern, but that of grandchildren often emerges as an important issue. Socialization of the husband and wife to new roles, however, is the most important.

Mid-life crisis

The period after all the children are gone is often a period of turmoil and adjustment. Couples without children may also go through a period of adjustment as retirement approaches. This period of crisis or adjustment is often termed the **mid-life crisis** for men and the **empty nest syndrome** for women. For both it is a period of assessment in which there is some disillusionment and a need to adjust to the realities of life.

Ciernia (1985a) surveyed 227 businessmen between the ages of 35 and 60, and 69 percent acknowledged having a mid-life crisis. However, it was not a severe crisis for most men but rather a period of assessment and adjustment.

For both women and men, middle age is a time to assess where one is and where one wants to go. There is often a tension between stagnation and generation. The latter includes not only increased interest in future generations but also interest in generating oneself. There is often a shift in time perspective from "time lived" to "time left" (Hagestad and Burton 1986; Tamir 1982).

At this period in their lives many men realize that they are not going to reach the occupational goals they had set for themselves earlier. They must accept their failures and learn to live with them. Among men who have been successful occupationally, some feel dissatisfied and do not think that their sacrifices have been worth it. In either case, men at this stage in life often feel a need for more personal fulfillment. They may disengage from work somewhat and put more emphasis on family life or other personal relationships (Tamir 1982).

Women also evaluate their accomplishments and desires at mid-life. Some regret not having had the opportunity for career development that most men have had. Others feel lost when the children leave and wonder what their role is now. Many embark on professional careers during this period (Poloma, Pendleton, and Garland 1981). Some enter college to obtain a degree as well as to achieve independence and a sense of identity (Hildreth, Dilworth-Anderson, and Rabe 1983). Others move in and out of the labor force (Moen 1986).

During this stage in life many men become more sensitive and nurturant as they place more emphasis on relationships. At the same time women tend to become more assertive, independent, and interested in mastery of the outside world (Hagestad and Burton 1986). Rossi (1986) noted that men and women do not lose their existing traits, but add new traits to their existing repertoire. As a result gender roles within the family tend to become more **androgynous** as aging occurs (Rossi 1986; Tamir 1982).

Middle age is also a time when individuals become more concerned with their health and mortality. Wrinkles, balding, fat deposits, and general physical decline become evident.

Some have suggested that divorce, drinking, and suicide become more common during middle age because of the mid-life crisis. Although some people may react to middle age in this way, there is no evidence that this is a general tendency. Divorce and heavy drinking tend to go down at mid-life, and suicide rates vary little between young adulthood and middle age (Ciernia 1985b).

Marital Satisfaction and Stability

How does marital satisfaction change as couples move through the life cycle? Although the data are not entirely consistent, recent research indicates that marital satisfaction tends to increase somewhat after children leave home (Brubaker 1985; Treas and Bengtson 1987). The usual explanation for this is that rearing children may be stressful and that companionship and shared activities may increase after the children are launched.

Several recent scholars have studied long-term marriages and their characteristics. Lauer and Lauer (1986) studied 351 couples who had been married for fifteen years or more. They divided the couples into three types: (1) happy, (2) unhappy, and (3) mixed (one partner happy and one unhappy). In 85 percent of the couples both spouses said they were happily married. Other researchers also have found high marital satisfaction among enduring marraiges (Treas and Bengtson 1987). Of course, many of the couples with unhappy relationships divorced earlier in their lives.

Among the happily married couples, the most frequently mentioned reason for staying together was that the husband and wife liked each other and enjoyed being with each other. The second most frequently mentioned reason was commitment (Lauer and Lauer 1986).

Swensen and Trahaug (1985) also found that commitment was an important ingredient in long-term marriages. In fact, in their study those whose commitment increased over time tended to express more love and had fewer marital problems than couples with less commitment (Swensen and Trahaug 1985).

Among the mixed and unhappy couples the most frequently named reason for staying together was the belief that marriage is a long-term commitment. Almost half of those in unhappy marriages also mentioned that they had stayed together for the children (Lauer and Lauer 1986).

Both the happy and unhappy long-term marriages were characterized by strong commitment to the marriage. The distinguishing feature was that individuals in the happy marriages said that they liked their spouse and viewed him or her as a best friend.

The happily married couples tended to have three additional characteristics. First, they agreed on life's aims and goals. Second, they laughed together and tried to maintain humor. None of the unhappy couples listed humor as a reason for staying together. Finally, the happy couples usually developed skills to handle conflict effectively, such as calmness, flexibility, and attacking the issue rather than one's spouse (Lauer and Lauer 1986).

In a similar study, Mudd and Taubin (1982) found that affection, altruism, commitment, and democracy were important ingredients of stable long-term marriages. Planning and economic opportunity were also found to be important (Mudd and Taubin 1982).

Divorce and Remarriage

The divorce rate is not large among middle-aged couples, although it has been increasing in recent years. Smyer and Hofland (1982) estimated that divorcees to couples in middle age comprise about 17 percent of all divorces. Among all

TABLE 19·2   Remarriage Rates by Age and Gender, United States (1984[a])

	Age	Women	Men
All Remarriages	45–49	45.1	118.2
	50–54	26.5	83.4
	55–59	13.4	61.7
	60–64	8.7	44.8
	65 and over	2.2	18.1
Previously Widowed	45–64	11.3	55.7
	65 and over	1.9	16.4
Previously Divorced	45–49	49.5	117.8
	50–54	33.0	78.2
	55–59	17.6	58.8
	60–64	12.3	45.8
	65 and over	4.8	23.9

[a] Rates per 1,000 population in specified age group.

SOURCE: National Center for Health Statistics 1987a:12–13.

women between the ages of 45 and 64, about 11 percent are currently divorced. Among men in the same age group the proportion of currently divorced is 7.5 percent (U.S. Bureau of the Census 1986). Because of remarriage, many more have been divorced than are currently divorced.

Because of age, divorce after a long-term marriage is particularly stressful (Berardo 1982). In Chapter 16 we noted that difficulty in adjusting to divorce increases as age increases.

Remarriage is fairly common among divorced and widowed persons between the ages of 45 and 64, as shown in Table 19·2. Remarriage rates decline dramatically as age increases and are much higher among men than among women. Each year about 5 percent of the women between ages 45 and 49 remarry, compared to 12 percent of the men. Among divorced persons between the ages of 60 and 64, about 1 percent of the women and 5 percent of the men remarry each year. Among middle-aged persons (ages 45 to 64) who are widowed, approximately 1 percent of the women and 6 percent of the men remarry in a year (National Center for Health Statistics 1987a).

Grandparenting

Most people become grandparents during their middle years although there is considerable variation in the age at which this happens. About three fourths of all individuals over age 65 have living grandchildren (Brubaker 1985).

Most people enjoy being grandparents and feel it is an important role. About 80 percent of grandparents are happy with the relationship they have with their grandchildren, and a majority say it is easier than parenthood and that they enjoy it more (Brubaker 1985). Grandfathers are somewhat less satisfied with grandparenthood than grandmothers, although they talk more about responsibility toward grandparenting than do grandmothers (Thomas 1986).

Grandparents differ widely in how they interact with grandchildren. Some

About three-fourths of all persons over age 65 have living grandchildren. Most enjoy their relationship with their grandchildren and see them regularly. *Tom Kelly.*

are most concerned about developing a warm, personal relationship whereas others are more distant and impersonal. Some play the role of indulger, and others emphasize setting a good example and are concerned about their grandchildren's moral development (Brubaker 1985). Middle-aged grandparents (ages 45 to 60) tend to be more willing to give advice and take responsibility for watching and disciplining a grandchild than grandparents who are older than age 60 (Thomas 1986).

About three fourths of grandparents see a grandchild at least once a week (Troll 1983). A good grandparent is described as one who shows love, sets a good example, helps if asked, and does not spoil the grandchild or interfere with parental upbringing (Brubaker 1985).

Too much grandparenting may be as bad as too little. Grandparents want to be involved but generally do not want to be surrogate parents. When grandparenting comes too early it is sometimes stressful and may be rejected, especially if too much responsibility is placed on a grandparent (Hagestad and Burton 1986).

Caregiving

There is a strong norm that care of elderly parents **(caregiving)** is the responsibility of their children. In a three-generation study, Campbell and Brody (1985) found that Americans hold this value even more strongly than the Japanese, and that the youngest generation affirms it most strongly. Children expect to provide more help than their parents often expect from them (Martin, Ko, and Bengtson 1987). The better the parent-child relationship, the greater the responsibility felt by adult children. Daughters feel more responsibility for the care of elderly parents than sons (Brubaker 1985; Martin et al. 1987).

Adult children are the most frequent caretakers of homebound elderly, followed by spouse and other relatives (Treas and Bengtson 1987). The child who does the caregiving is usually a daughter. Sons tend to become the caregiver only if there is no female sibling available (Horowitz 1985).

The women who provide the caretaking tend to be middle-aged women who often have many other demands placed on them. They may have adolescents at home or young adult children who require attention and financial support. The middle-aged generation often provides substantial amounts of economic support, child care, and emotional support to their children while at the same time offering emotional support and care to their parents (Troll 1982).

The well-being of middle-aged caretakers depends on several factors. First, if they have good health themselves they are able to withstand the burden much more easily. Second, having adequate social contacts with other people decreases the amount of stress associated with care for an elderly parent. Third, affection for the parent tends to be associated with less burden. Finally, financial stress tends to be associated with greater burden (Stull, Kosloski, and Montgomery 1986).

Retirement

The retirement stage of the family career typically begins at age 65 when the husband stops working, although there is considerable variability in the timing. In some cases husband and wife will both retire together. Married women tend to retire earlier than unmarried women, primarily to synchronize their retirement with their husbands'. Because the wife tends to be younger than the husband, in some cases he will retire before her.

There is a reciprocal relationship between marriage and retirement, and each may influence the other in a variety of ways.

Adjusting to Retirement

The actual effect of retirement on the marriage depends on the pre-retirement relationship. Brubaker (1985) suggests that retirement will amplify both the positive and negative qualities within marriages. On the one hand, retirement provides opportunities for companionship that did not exist when one or both spouses were employed. On the other hand, the additional time together may increase tension and conflict among couples who do not enjoy being together.

Retirement tends to have little effect on the division of labor in the family (Brubaker 1985). The pre-retirement division of labor tends to stay the same after retirement, and women continue to do more household work than men. If the health of the wife deteriorates, however, the husband's involvement in household chores increases significantly (Szinovacs 1989).

There is usually a reduction in income following retirement, and expenditure patterns change considerably. Chen and Chu (1982) found that couples over age 65 tend to spend higher proportions of their income on food, utilities, medical care, gifts, and contributions than couples under age 65. Nonretired couples spend relatively more on clothing, household furnishings, transportation, education, and recreation. The reason for these changes is that older couples tend not to be as mobile as previously and have less of a desire for outdoor activities as their health declines. They have also already accumulated many durable goods such as a house, car, and furniture and do not need to spend as much on these after retirement.

Satisfaction with retirement is influenced by health, marital status, and income. Health and financial problems decrease satisfaction, and the unmarried are less satisfied than the married. The retirement experience appears similar for both men and women, although women tend to have somewhat lower satisfaction because they may have lower incomes and are less likely to be married (Maxwell 1985; Seccombe and Lee 1986).

Hill and Dorfman (1982) studied a sample of wives whose husbands had recently retired. The wives reported that increased companionship, flexibility of schedule, and time available for desired activities were some of the positive aspects of retirement. Some of the negative aspects were financial problems and too much togetherness. Health of husband, adequate income, husband's participation in household tasks, and joint decision making were all correlated with the satisfaction of the wife with retirement (Hill and Dorfman 1982).

There is a popular conception that loneliness is a serious problem among the aged. Almost two thirds of American adults think that loneliness is a very serious problem for most people over age 65 (Harris 1981). Recent research suggests that this may not be the case. Revenson and Johnson (1984) found that loneliness decreased as age increased, and that people over age 65 experienced less loneliness than any other age group (see Table 19·3). They also found that retired persons were more satisfied with their relationships than their younger counterparts. Neither gender nor living alone was related to loneliness. They found, however, that the loss of an intimate attachment through divorce or widowhood was related to loneliness.

Sexual Activity After Retirement

Sexual activity tends to decline in frequency as people age, however a sizable portion of couples continue to be sexually active into old age. A study of couples who had been married fifty years showed that 50 percent were still active sexually (Brubaker 1985). Very few older couples have no sexual activity. Sex is not limited to intercourse but includes variations of holding, touching, and caressing. Interest in sex tends to be higher than actual sexual activity (Brubaker 1985; Garza and Dressel 1983).

TABLE 19·3 Loneliness by Age

Age	Loneliness* Score	N
18–24	15.2	276
25–34	14.6	651
35–44	13.8	445
45–54	14.0	289
55–64	12.8	216
65–74	11.4	105
75+	6.7	13

SOURCE: Revenson, T. A., and J. L. Johnson. 1984. Social and demographic correlates of loneliness in later life. *American Journal of Community Psychology* 12(1):78, Table 2.

* Loneliness scores ranged from 0 (not lonely at all) to 20 (extremely lonely).

Golden Wedding Anniversary Couples

Either divorce or death dissolves most marriages before couples reach their golden wedding anniversary. Glick and Norton (1977) estimated that only about 20 percent of first marriages will survive to the golden wedding anniversary. Couples who have been married that long tend to be very satisfied with their relationships. Two important characteristics of these couples are companionship and accommodation, and they tend to share household and leisure activities. Retirement enabled them to spend time together and share many activities (Brubaker 1985).

Couples married for fifty years reported that the most satisfying periods of their lives were childbearing, the preschool years, and the period after retirement. The least satisfying years were described as childbearing (again), launching, and middle age (Brubaker 1985). The fact that childbearing was rated among the most and least satisfying periods attests to the joys and stresses associated with becoming parents. Earlier in this chapter we noted some of the stresses associated with the launching and middle-aged periods of the life cycle.

Divorce and Remarriage

The divorce rate among elderly couples is small, less than 3 percent according to estimates of Uhlenberg and Myers (1981). Of all women over age 65, about 4.3 percent are currently divorced. Among comparable men, 3.7 are currently divorced (U.S. Bureau of the Census 1986). Of course, some of those may have divorced in earlier years, and other divorced persons may have remarried.

Remarriage rates among persons over age 65 are relatively low. About five of every thousand divorced women over age 65 remarry each year. By comparison about twenty-four of every thousand divorced men over age 65 remarry each year. Comparable rates per thousand among widowed persons are two for women and sixteen for men, respectively (see Table 19·2).

Physical Health

Earlier we mentioned that satisfaction with retirement was affected by health. The illness of a spouse may have a major impact on older couples. A spouse usually takes on the role of caregiver as the health of one partner declines.

Johnson (1985) studied seventy-six late-life marriages in which either the wife or husband was recuperating from a hospital stay. She found that most of the couples had high marital satisfaction and that the healthy spouse provided much support. Marital satisfaction did not vary by socioeconomic status, gender of caregiver, or level of impairment. However, social isolation was stressful for the caregiver.

Caring for an ill spouse over a long period of time is physically and emotionally draining, and the caregiver is likely to feel overwhelmed and inadequate. Social support from others and good health of the caregiver are important in adjusting to the caregiver role (Brubaker 1986).

Mental Health

As noted in Chapter 13, mental health tends to be associated with number of social roles, and retired people are in the process of role disengagement. Their children are raised and they are no longer employed. Health often restricts their activities. Consequently, they may become depressed and feel that they no longer have a purpose in life. In this section we discuss some of the characteristics associated with mental well-being of the elderly.

Being married has a significant influence on subjective well-being. A variety of indicators of psychological adjustment and subjective well-being have been found to be higher among the elderly who are married compared to those who are not married (Ferraro and Wan 1986; Lawton, Moss, and Kleban 1984; Leonard 1982; Revenson and Johnson 1984).

Not only is marital status important, but the quality of the marriage affects well-being. Older couples with substantial marital conflict tend to have higher levels of depression than couples with lower levels of conflict (Keith and Schafer 1986). Income and physical health are other factors that have been found to be associated with well-being of the aged (Ferraro and Wan 1986; Leonard 1982). In a study of 504 elderly persons, Raymond, Michals, and Steer (1980) found that being restricted in physical activity was positively associated with depression.

Having friends to associate with is critical for the well-being of elderly persons (Ward, LaGory, and Sherman 1985). Baldassare, Rosenfield, and Rook (1984) observed that perceived companionship was the best predictor of happiness among the elderly. Being involved in a social network tends to buffer the effects of stress (Cohen, Teresi, and Holmes 1985).

In some cultures there is a belief that couples with few or no children will not be taken care of in old age. For example, in China a major stumbling block to the acceptance of the one-child family policy has been fear about security in old age (Goldstein and Goldstein 1986). Are elderly childless couples deprived because they do not have children to care for and support them?

Rempel (1985) compared elderly with and without children on a variety of subjective and objective variables, and she found that the two groups were similar in many ways. The childless were more financially secure and had better health, whereas elderly parents had more friends, were more integrated into the neighborhood, were less lonely, and were more generally satisfied with life. Rempel's data confirm that the elderly's adult children do provide emotional and financial support that is beneficial for their well-being. However, the childless did have social networks that provided needed support and had comparable well-being on a number of variables.

How important are siblings to the well-being of the elderly? McGhee (1985) found that the availability of a sister had a positive influence on the life satisfaction of elderly women. Among men the availability of a brother had a positive but small association with life satisfaction. Having cross-sex siblings was not related to life satisfaction for men or women.

At the retirement stage people often look back at their lives and what they have accomplished. They have regrets over some decisions, and they set priorities for the future. Kinnier and Metha (1986) recently surveyed 316 adults at three stages of the life cycle to compare their regrets and priorities in life. The responses of the eighty persons over age 65 were revealing.

The most frequently cited regret among all three groups was that they did not take their education seriously enough. Among the persons over age 65, the second most common regret was that they had not spent enough quality time with their families (more men than women listed this as a regret). The top priority among the middle aged and the retired was their family, and its importance increased with age (Kinnier and Metha 1986).

Widowhood

Sooner or later we all will die. When one partner dies, the other must face life alone. It is usually the woman who is faced with widowhood, as 70 percent of women outlive their husbands (Treas and Bengston 1987).

In only a small percentage of cases does widowhood occur suddenly, without warning. For the majority there is a struggle with health before the death and usually the surviving wife cares for her ill husband before he dies (Brubaker 1985).

The adjustment to widowhood usually follows three stages (Brubaker 1985). First, there is **bereavement,** the loss or crisis stage. During this period there is usually grief, disbelief, and a sense of loss and abandonment. Mourning over the loss of a loved one and heavy involvement of family and friends take place. During this period bereaved individuals tend to have significantly more depression and psychopathology than nonbereaved persons (Farberow et al. 1987).

The second stage is a transitional period, where one must try to go on and establish a life without one's spouse. During this period one begins to form a new identity as an unmarried person. Support from friends and family tends to decrease somewhat.

The final stage is the establishment of a new lifestyle. This is the reorganization of one's life as a single person. For some a remarriage will occur (Brubaker 1985).

Feinson (1986) and Lund, Caserta, Dimond, and Gray (1986) compared men

Half of all women over age 65 are widowed, compared to only 14 percent of men over age 65. The loss of a spouse through death is a major reason for loneliness in late life and is often a difficult adjustment. *Ulrike Welsch.*

and women in their adjustment to widowhood. They found that the adjustment process was similar for both men and women in terms of emotional problems, depression, and life satisfaction.

During the first year after widowhood, loneliness is the primary problem area. The sudden loss of an intimate attachment is a major reason for loneliness in later life (Revenson and Johnson 1984). The absence of one's companion in doing various things is difficult to get used to (Clark, Siviski, and Weiner 1986; Singh and Gill 1986). Loneliness tends to decrease with time as one increases involvement with family and friends (Revenson and Johnson 1984; Roberto and Scott 1986).

What characteristics are related to successful adjustment to widowhood? Several studies have found that people with low self-esteem have greater difficulty coping with bereavement. These individuals tend to experience higher levels of stress and depression (Johnson, Lund, and Dimond 1986; Lund et al. 1985). Preparation for the loss of spouse and the development of friendship networks also appear to be related to adjustment to bereavement (Ferraro, Mutrin, and Barresi 1984; Haas-Hawkings et al. 1985). Having a network of friends one feels close to and which enable the widowed to express their feelings is particularly important (Dimond, Lund, and Caserta 1987).

A large number of widowed persons live alone, particularly women. Forty-one percent of women over age 65 live alone and the proportion of older men and women living with their children has declined by 50 percent during the past thirty-five years (Brubaker 1985; U.S. Bureau of the Census 1986). However, living alone does not mean widowed persons are isolated. They tend to have more involvement with children, siblings, other relatives, and friends than married individuals (Brubaker 1985).

Remarriage rates among widowed persons are small, particularly those over age 65, as shown in Table 19·2.

Gender and Aging

One of the striking features of the aging population is the decreasing **sex ratio.** Among persons over age 65 there are about sixty-eight males for one hundred females (U.S. Bureau of the Census 1986).

Table 19·4 shows differences among men and women in widowhood. Among persons between ages 55 and 64, 17 percent of the women are widowed compared to less than 4 percent of the men. Forty percent of the women between the ages of 65 and 74 are widowed compared to less than 10 percent of the men. More than two thirds of women over age 75 are widowed compared to only 23 percent of the men.

Table 19·5 shows living arrangements by age and gender. Three fourths of men over age 65 live with their spouse, compared to only 38 percent of comparable women. Only 15 percent of men over age 65 live alone, compared to 41 percent of women.

What is the quality of life for women and men in their older years? Haug and Folmar (1986) studied the quality of life of 647 persons ages 65 to 74, 75 to 84, and 85 or over. Two thirds of the respondents were female. They examined physical health, functional ability, income adequacy, social contact, psychological distress, and cognitive ability.

The women had lower quality of life on all of the indicators, particularly those women over age 85. The women were more likely than the men to not have a spouse, to live alone, and to suffer emotional, cognitive, and health losses. This is consistent with Verbrugge's (1984) finding that older women have more acute and chronic health problems than men, although women's problems tend to be less life threatening.

TABLE 19·4   Marital Status of Population by Age and Gender, United States (1985)

Marital Status	Age								
	18–19	20–24	25–29	30–34	35–44	45–54	55–64	65–74	75+
Women									
Single	86.7	58.5	26.4	13.5	6.8	4.6	3.7	4.4	6.2
Married	12.5	38.0	65.2	73.1	77.1	76.3	70.0	51.1	23.8
Widowed	0.1	0.2	0.5	1.0	2.0	7.0	17.4	38.9	67.7
Divorced	0.7	3.3	7.9	12.4	14.0	12.1	8.9	5.6	2.4
Men									
Single	97.1	75.6	38.7	20.8	9.4	6.3	6.1	5.2	5.3
Married	2.9	23.0	55.2	69.7	79.9	83.8	83.9	81.3	69.3
Widowed	0.0	0.0	0.0	0.1	0.4	1.2	3.7	9.3	22.7
Divorced	0.0	1.4	6.0	9.5	10.3	8.7	6.2	4.2	2.7

SOURCE: U.S. Bureau of the Census 1986:39.

TABLE 19·5   Living Arrangements by Age and Gender: United States (1985) (in percentages)

Living Arrangements	15–19	20–24	25–44	45–64	65+
Total					
Live Alone	0.7	5.8	8.6	11.1	30.2
Live With Spouse	3.2	28.0	66.9	74.8	53.4
Live With Other Relatives	93.3	53.2	18.0	11.5	13.9
Live With Nonrelatives	2.8	12.9	6.4	2.7	2.4
Females					
Live Alone	0.7	4.9	8.9	13.3	41.1
Live With Spouse	5.3	34.9	67.5	69.6	38.3
Live With Other Relatives	90.8	49.0	21.3	15.2	18.4
Live With Nonrelatives	3.2	11.5	4.3	2.0	2.1
Males					
Live Alone	0.7	6.8	10.5	8.7	14.7
Live With Spouse	1.1	21.2	66.3	80.4	75.0
Live With Other Relatives	95.7	57.6	14.5	7.4	7.5
Live With Nonrelatives	2.5	14.4	8.7	3.5	2.9

SOURCE: U.S. Bureau of the Census 1986:46.

Summary

1. During the past century, longevity has increased dramatically while fertility has decreased. This has compressed the childbearing and child-rearing years and extended the middle and later stages of the family life cycle.

2. The launching stage is the period when children begin to leave home. At current fertility levels and marriage rates it will extend about ten years for the average family. In recent years the proportion of young adults living at home has increased, which may delay the completion of the launching stage for many families.

3. Middle age is the period between launching of the last child and retirement and will typically last about nine years.

4. The mid-life crisis is a period of personal assessment for women and men. During this period men tend to become more sensitive and nurturant while women become more assertive and independent.

5. Marital satisfaction usually increases somewhat during the middle years.

6. Important characteristics of happy, long-term marriages are liking one's spouse, commitment, common goals, humor, altruism, and democracy. \

7. Most parents become grandparents during middle age. Grandparenting is enjoyable for most persons. A good grandparent is viewed as one who shows love, sets a good example, helps if asked, does not spoil the grandchild, and does not interfere with the parents.

8. Couples in middle age are often caught in the middle between launching adolescents and caring for aged parents. Female children usually do most of the caretaking. The extent of burden in caring for an aging parent depends

on the health of the caretaker, adequate social contacts, affection for the parent, and the amount of financial stress.

9. The retirement typically lasts about six years for couples. Satisfaction with retirement depends on health, financial stress, and marital status. It provides opportunities for increased marital companionship if that is desired.

10. The frequency of sexual activity declines with age although very few couples discontinue sexual relations entirely.

11. Golden anniversary couples tend to be very satisfied with their marriages. Companionship and accommodation are two common features of couples who make it to their golden wedding anniversary.

12. Maintaining physical and mental health are important tasks of aging couples. Being married, high marital satisfaction, adequate income, good physical health, and having friends are all positively associated with good mental health among elderly couples.

13. Two common regrets of elder persons are that they did not take advantage of their educational opportunities and that they did not spend enough quality time with their families.

14. About seven out of ten women outlive their husbands. The average married woman will be a widow for nine years.

15. The adjustment of widows and widowers appears to be similar. Loneliness is one of the major adjustments.

16. Good self-esteem, friendship networks, and preparation are all related to successful adjustment to widowhood.

17. Among persons over age 65 there are sixty-eight men for every one hundred women. Elderly women are much more likely than elderly men to be widowed, to live alone, and to have chronic health problems.

Important Terms

- aged dependency ratio
- androgynous
- bereavement
- caregiving
- empty nest syndrome
- graying of America

- launching stage
- middle age
- mid-life crisis
- retirement
- sex ratio

Questions for Discussion

1. What are the major changes that have occurred in the life cycle during the past century? Why did these changes occur?
2. How have the changes in the family life cycle affected gender roles?
3. One of the social concerns today is the increase in the aged dependency ratio. Why is that a problem and what should we do about it?
4. Why is the launching stage stressful for parents?
5. Why are more young adults staying at home in recent years?

6. What is the mid-life crisis? Do both men and women tend to experience it?
7. How do men and women change during the middle-aged years?
8. What are the major characteristics of happy long-term marriages? What can you personally learn from those couples?
9. Why are remarriage rates so much higher for men than for women?
10. What are the characteristics of a good grandparent? What are the stresses of being a grandparent? What are the advantages?
11. Why do women usually have the major care of aging parents? How can we change this?
12. The problem of the frail elderly appears to be increasing in our society. What should we do to solve it?
13. What are some of the opportunities that retirement presents to married couples? What are some of the problems associated with retirement?
14. Does loneliness increase with age? Why? What are some of the major reasons for loneliness among aging persons?
15. What are some of the key characteristics of couples whose marriages last fifty years?
16. What are some characteristics associated with good mental health in old age?
17. What are the major adjustments one usually faces when a spouse dies? What types of individuals tend to adjust more adequately to widowhood?
18. Is the quality of life better for elderly men or women? Why?
19. How has the aged sex ratio changed during the past century? Why? What, if anything, should be done about it?

Recommended Reading

BRUBAKER, T. H. 1985. *Later life families.* Beverly Hills, CA: Sage.
LAUER, R. H., and J. C. LAUER. 1986. Factors in long-term marriages. *Journal of Family Issues* 7:382–390.
ROSSI, A. S. 1986. Sex and gender in an aging society. *Daedalus* 115:141–169.

References

BALDASSARE, M., S. ROSENFIELD, and K. ROOK. 1984. The types of social relations predicting elderly well-being. *Research on Aging* 6(4):549–559.
BENGTSON, V. L. 1986. Sociological perspectives on aging, families and the future. In *Dimensions in aging: The 1986 Sandoz Lectures in Gerontology,* ed. M. Bergener, 237–262. London: Academic.
BERARDO, D. H. 1982. Divorce and remarriage at middle age and beyond. *Annals of the American Academy of Political and Social Science* 464:132–139.
BRUBAKER, E. B. 1986. Caring for a dependent spouse. *American Behavioral Scientist* 29(4):485–496.
BRUBAKER, T. H. 1985. *Later life families.* Beverly Hills, CA: Sage.
CAMPBELL, R., and E. M. BRODY. 1985. Women's changing roles and help to the elderly: Attitudes of women in the United States and Japan. *The Gerontological Society of America* 25(6):584–592.

CHEN, Y. 1986. Utah's unique population structure. In *Utah in demographic perspective*, ed. T. K. Martin, T. B. Heaton, and S. J. Bahr, 289–295. Salt Lake City: Signature Books.

CHEN, Y., and K. CHU. 1982. Household expenditure patterns. The effect of age of family head. *Journal of Family Issues* 3(2):233–250.

CIERNIA, J. R. 1985a. Death concern and businessmen's midlife crisis. *Psychological Reports* 56:83–87.

CIERNIA, J. R. 1985b. Myths about male midlife crises. *Psychological Reports* 56:1003–1007.

CLARK, P. G., R. W. SIVISKI, and R. WEINER. 1986. Coping strategies of widowers in the first year. *Family Relations* 35(3):425–430.

CLEMENS, A. W., and L. J. AXELSON. 1985. The not-so-empty-nest. The return of the fledgling adult. *Family Relations* 34:259–264.

COHEN, C. I., J. TERESI, and D. HOLMES. 1985. Social networks, stress, and physical health: A longitudinal study of an inner-city elderly population. *Journal of Gerontology* 40(4):478–486.

DIMOND, M., D. A. LUND, and M. S. CASERTA. 1987. The role of social support in the first two years of bereavement in an elderly sample. *The Gerontologist* 27:599–604.

FARBEROW, N. L., D. E. GALLAGHER, M. J. GILEWSKI, and L. W. THOMPSON. 1987. An examination of the early impact of bereavement on psychological distress in survivors of suicide. *The Gerontologist* 27:592–598.

FEINSON, M. C. 1986. Aging widows and widowers: Are there mental health differences? *International Journal of Aging and Human Development* 23(4):241–255.

FERRARO, K. F., E. MUTRAN, and C. M. BARRESI. 1984. Widowhood, health, and friendship support in later life. *Journal of Health and Social Behavior* 25:245–259.

FERRARO, K. F., and T. T. H. WAN. 1986. Marital contributions to well-being in later life. *American Behavioral Scientist* 29(4):423–437.

GARZA, J. M., and P. L. DRESSEL. 1983. Sexuality and later-life marriages. In *Family relationships in older life*, ed. T. H. Brubaker, 91–108. Beverly Hills, CA: Sage.

GLICK, P. C., and S. LIN. 1986. More young adults are living with their parents: Who are they? *Journal of Marriage and the Family* 48:107–112.

GLICK, P. C., and A. J. NORTON. 1977. Marrying, divorcing, and living together in the U.S. today. *Population Bulletin*, vol. 32, no. 5, pp. 1–39. Washington, DC: Population Reference Bureau.

GOLDSTEIN, A., and S. GOLDSTEIN. 1986. The challenge of an aging population: The case of the People's Republic of China. *Research on Aging* 8:179–199.

HAAS-HAWKINGS, G., S. SANGSTER, M. ZIEGLER, and D. REID. 1985. A study of relatively immediate adjustment to widowhood in later life. *International Journal of Women's Studies* 8(2):158–167.

HAGESTAD, G. O., and L. M. BURTON. 1986. Grandparenthood, life context, and family development. *American Behavioral Scientist* 29(4):471–484.

HARRIS, L. 1981. *Aging in the eighties: America in transition.* Washington, DC: National Council on Aging.

HAUG, M. R., and S. J. FOLMAR. 1986. Longevity, gender, and life quality. *Journal of Health and Social Behavior* 27:332–345.

HILDRETH, G. J., P. DILWORTH-ANDERSON, and S. M. RABE. 1983. Family and school life of women over age fifty who are in college. *Educational Gerontology* 9:339–350.

HILL, E. A., and L. T. DORFMAN. 1982. Reaction of housewives to the retirement of their husbands. *Family Relations* 31:195–200.

HOROWITZ, A. 1985. Sons and daughters as caregivers to older parents: Differences in role performance and consequences. *The Gerontologist* 25(6):612–617.

JOHNSON, C. L. 1985. The impact of illness on late-life marriages. *Journal of Marriage and the Family* 47(1):165–172.

JOHNSON, R. J., D. A. LUND, and M. F. DIMOND. 1986. Stress, self-esteem and coping during bereavement among the elderly. *Social Psychology Quarterly* 49(3):273–279.

KEITH, P. M., and R. B. SCHAFER. 1986. Housework, disagreement, and depression among younger and older couples. *American Behavioral Scientist* 29(4):405–422.

KINNIER, R. T., and A. T. METHA. 1986. *Regrets and priorities at three stages of life.* Paper presented at the convention of the American Psychological Association, Washington, DC, August.

LAUER, R. H., and J. C. LAUER. 1986. Factors in long-term marriages. *Journal of Family Issues* 7(4):382–390.

LAWTON, M. P., M. MOSS, and M. H. KLEBAN. 1984. Marital status, living arrangements, and the well-being of older people. *Research on Aging* 6(3):323–345.

LEONARD, W. M. 1982. Successful aging: An elaboration of social and psychological factors. *International Journal on Aging and Human Development* 14(3):223–232.

LUND, D. A., M. S. CASERTA, and M. F. DIMOND. 1986. Gender differences through two years of bereavement among the elderly. *The Gerontological Society of America* 26(3):314–320.

LUND, D. A., M. S. CASERTA, M. F. DIMOND, and R. M. GRAY. 1986. Impact of bereavement on the self-conceptions of older surviving spouses. *Symbolic Interaction* 9(2):235–244.

LUND, D. A., M. F. DIMOND, M. S. CASERTA, R. J. JOHNSON, J. L. POULTON, and J. R. CONNELLY. 1985. Identifying elderly with coping difficulties after two years of bereavement. *Omega* 16(3):213–224.

McGHEE, J. L. 1985. The effects of siblings on the life satisfaction of the rural elderly. *Journal of Marriage and the Family* 47(1):85–91.

MARTIN, M. E., C. KO, and V. L. BENGTSON. 1987. *Filial responsibility and patterns of caregiving in three generation families.* Paper presented at Pacific Sociological Association meeting in Eugene, OR, April.

MAXWELL, N. L. 1985. The retirement experience: Psychological and financial linkages to the labor market. *Social Science Quarterly* 65:22–33.

MOEN, P. 1986. *Women's life transitions in the middle years: A longitudinal analysis.* Paper prepared for presentation at the Annual Meetings of the American Sociological Association, New York, August.

MUDD, E. H., and S. TAUBIN. 1982. Success in family living—Does it last? A twenty-year follow-up. *The American Journal of Family Therapy* 10(1):59–67.

NATIONAL CENTER FOR HEALTH STATISTICS. 1987a. Advance report of final marriage statistics, *1984. Monthly Vital Statistics Report*, vol. 36, no. 2, Supp.(2). DHHS Pub. No. (PHS) 87–1120. Hyattsville, MD: Public Health Service.

NATIONAL CENTER FOR HEALTH STATISTICS. 1987b. Advance report of final mortality statistics, *1985. Monthly Vital Statistics Report*, vol. 36, no. 5, Supp., DHHS Pub. No. (PHS) 86–1120. Hyattsville, MD: Public Health Service.

POLOMA, M. M., B. F. PENDLETON, and T. N. GARLAND. 1981. Reconsidering the dual-career marriage. *Journal of Family Issues* 2(2):205–224.

RAYMOND, E. F., T. J. MICHALS, and R. A. STEER. 1980. Prevalence and correlates of depression in elderly persons. *Psychological Reports* 47:1055–1061.

REMPEL, J. 1985. Childless elderly: What are they missing? *Journal of Marriage and the Family* 7(2):343–348.

REVENSON, T. A., and J. L. JOHNSON. 1984. Social and demographic correlates of loneliness in late life. *American Journal of Community Psychology* 12(1):71–85.

ROBERTO, K. A., and J. P. SCOTT. 1986. Confronting widowhood. *American Behavioral Society* 29(4):497–511.

ROSSI, A. S. 1986. Sex and gender in an aging society. *The Aging Society* 115(1):141–169.

SCHNAIBERG, A., and S. GOLDENBERG. 1986. From empty nest to crowded nest: Some contradictions in the returning-young-adult syndrome. Paper prepared for the annual meetings of the American Sociological Association, New York, August 31.

SECCOMBE, K., and G. R. LEE. 1986. Gender differences in retirement satisfaction and its antecedents. *Research on Aging* 8(3):426–440.

SINGH, G. M., and S. GILL. 1986. Problems of widowhood. *The Indian Journal of Social Work* 37(1):67–71.

SMYER, M. A., and B. F. HOFLAND. 1982. Divorce and family support in later life. *Journal of Family Issues* 3(1):61–77.

STULL, D. E., K. D. KOSLOSKI, and R. J. V. MONTGOMERY. 1986. Predictors of well-being among caregivers of the elderly. Paper presented at the 57th annual meeting of the Pacific Sociological Association, Denver, CO, April.

SWENSEN, C. H., and G. TRAHAUG. 1985. Commitment and the long-term marriage relationship. *Journal of Marriage and the Family* 47:939–945.

SZINOVACZ, M. 1989. Retirement, couples, and household work. In *Aging and the family*, ed. S. J. Bahr and E. T. Peterson. Lexington, MA: Lexington Books.

TAMIR, L. M. 1982. Men at middle age: Developmental transitions. *Annals of the American Academy of Political and Social Sciences* 464:47–56.

THOMAS, J. L. 1986. Age and sex differences in perceptions of grandparenting. *Journal of Gerontology* 41(3):417–423.

TREAS, J., and V. L. BENGTSON. 1987. The family in later years. In *Handbook of marriage and the family*, ed. M. B. Sussman and S. K. Steinmetz, 625–628. New York: Plenum.

TROLL, L. E. 1982. Family life in middle and old age: The generation gap. *The Annals of the American Academy of Political and Social Sciences* 464:38–46.

TROLL, L. E. 1983. Grandparents. The family watchdogs. In *Family relationships in older life*, ed. T. H. Brubaker, 63–76. Beverly Hills, CA: Sage.
ships in older life, ed. T. H. Brubaker, 63–76. Beverly Hills, CA: Sage.

UHLENBERG, P., and M. A. P. MYERS. 1981. Divorce and the elderly. *The Gerontologist* 21:276–282.

U.S. BUREAU OF THE CENSUS. 1986. *Statistical abstract of the United States: 1987.* Washington, DC: U.S. Government Printing Office.

VERBRUGGE, L. M. 1984. A health profile of older women with comparisons to older men. *Research on Aging* 6(3):291–322.

WARD, R. A., M. LaGORY, and S. R. SHERMAN. 1985. Social networks and well-being in the older population. *Sociology and Social Research* 70(1):102–111.

Name Index

Aaron, H. J., 398
Abbott, D. A., 163
Abdel-Ghay, M., 208
Abel, R. L., 122
Abelman, R., 170
Adamek, R. J., 399
Adams, G. R., 85
Adelberg, T., 373
Adler, I., 169, 271
Aizenberg, R., 154
Albrecht, S. L., 111, 295, 347, 352, 355, 376, 407
Alcorn, D. S., 295
Aldous, J., 27
Alexander, K. J., 230
Alper, M. O., 202
Altemeier, W. A., 313, 316
Alvarez, W. F., 213
Amato, P. R., 172, 179
Ambert, A., 179
Ambrosino, R., 311
Amedeo-Eineker, S., 310
American Family, 398
Amoateng, A. Y., 295
Anderson, E. A., 339
Anderson, J. G., 47
Anderson, R., 311
Anderson, S. A., 104, 105
Andreasen, N. C., 268
Andres, D., 211
Aneshensel, C. S., 102, 406
Angel, R., 205
Angst, J., 176
Antill, J. K., 112
Asher, S. J., 351, 357
Asnis, L., 268
Atkenson, B. M., 312
Atkinson, T., 206
Avery, A. W., 175, 176
Axelson, L. J., 421
Ayoub, C., 316
Azar, S. T., 312, 316

Bachman, J. G., 271, 407
Bachrach, C. A., 60, 65, 154, 370
Bagozzi, R. P., 154, 208
Bahr, H. M., 181, 288, 290, 292, 294
Bahr, S. J., 47, 78, 85, 106, 109, 130, 132, 136, 139, 153, 172, 180, 206, 225, 226, 272, 295, 345,
347, 348, 352, 353, 354, 355, 357, 358, 376, 395, 400
Baj, J., 341
Baker, A. W., 315
Baker, D. P., 233
Baker, M. H., 225
Baker, R. L., 176
Baldassare, M., 429
Ball, R. E., 43
Balsanek, J., 360
Banister, J., 37, 38
Bankart, B. M., 40
Bankart, C. P., 40
Barbarin, O. A., 276, 278
Barber, B. K., 172
Barbour, L. S., 319, 320
Barling, J., 206, 207, 212
Barlow, B. A., 292
Barnes, G. M., 169, 172, 174, 272
Barnes, H. L., 108
Barnett, L., 107, 109
Baron, M., 268
Barresi, C. M., 431
Bassuk, E. L., 270
Bateson, G., 270
Baum, A., 206
Bauman, K. E., 64
Beavin, J., 17
Becker, M. E., 397, 398
Beckman, L. J., 154
Bell, N. J., 175, 176
Bell, R., 147, 148
Bell, R. A., 107, 108, 109
Bellack, A. S., 321
Beller, A. H., 395
Belsky, J., 163, 174, 180, 209, 210
Bengston, V. L., 420, 423, 426, 430
Bennett, N. G., 348, 369
Berardo, D. H., 424
Berardo, F. M., 378
Berg, J. H., 89, 90
Berk, R. A., 325, 326
Berk, S. F., 325
Berman, J. J., 343
Bernard, J., 101, 209
Betz, L., 312, 314
Bielby, D. D., 213
Bielby, W. T., 213

Bigelow, H. F., 25
Bilge, B., 179, 359
Billy, J. O., 61
Bishop, J., 348
Blake, J., 154, 175, 176
Blanc, A. K., 348, 368, 369
Blechman, E. A., 179
Block, J., 174
Block, J. H., 174
Blood, R. O., Jr., 123
Bloom, B. L., 351, 357, 368
Bloom, D. E., 154, 155, 348, 369, 370
Blumberg, G. G., 369
Bohrnstedt, G., 61
Boles, A. J., 163
Bollman, S. R., 108, 326
Booth, A., 113, 148, 163, 164, 209, 345, 347, 377, 378
Borduin, C. M., 172
Borgatta, E., 61
Boss, P., 274
Bouchard, T. J., Jr., 168
Bouvier, L. F., 150
Bowker, L. H., 320
Bradley, C. F., 163
Braithwaite, V. A., 172
Braver, S., 214
Brett, J., 106, 206, 207
Brinkerhoff, D. B., 109, 110
Brinkerhoff, M. B., 290, 296, 299
Brodbar-Nemzer, J. Y., 47, 48, 298, 299
Broderick, C., 16, 17
Broderick, C. B., 126, 136
Brody, E. M., 39, 40, 426
Brody, G. H., 163
Broman, C. L., 42, 43
Bromet, E. J., 207
Brommel, B. J., 129, 130
Brown, H. F., 316
Brown, S. E., 324
Browne, A., 316
Brubaker, E. B., 431
Brubaker, T. H., 423, 424, 425, 426, 427, 428, 429, 430
Brunngraber, L. S., 316
Buchsbaum, H. K., 179
Buda, M. A., 323
Buehler, C., 376

439

Subject Index